Urban Government

Urban Government

A Reader
in Administration and Politics

Revised Edition

EDITED BY *Edward C. Banfield*
HARVARD UNIVERSITY

The Free Press, New York

Collier-Macmillan Limited, London

Preface to the Revised Edition

IT IS astonishing how much has happened in and to the cities in the eight years since the first edition of this book appeared. There have been fundamental changes in public opinion (in 1961 the first civil rights revolutionaries had just begun to take their seats at segregated lunch counters), in the rules governing the electoral process (the first one-man one-vote bombshell had not yet burst), and in the techniques of management (planners were beginning to talk about benefit-cost ratios but few of them had ever set eyes on a computer). Not until I set about revising the book did I realize how much the situation had changed and how much it needed to be brought up to date.

The changes have not been such as to require changing the general character and plan of the book, however. I have retained the original structure, the intention of which is to place the materials within an analytical framework that will make their larger significance apparent to the student. The approach is also the same in that it is concerned with how urban government works rather than with rules-of-thumb for its improvement. The distribution of emphasis is much as it was except that I have enlarged Part VII, Problems of Management, to give a much fuller account of the various kinds of planning that are making their appearance in response to the growing scale and complexity of urban problems. My hope is that students of city planning will find it useful to have these materials brought together in one place.

I believe that about half the material in the book is new. I have not hesitated to retain articles that I consider classics (Norton Long's two, for example) or to print very long articles which could not be cut without serious injury (for example, the note from the *Harvard Law Review* on City Government in the State Courts). There are readings that are very up-to-date (on Negro politics, riots, and reapportionment of local government, for example) but I have not knowingly sacrificed anything of analytical importance for the sake of being topical.

All of the readings in the last Part are new. They all contribute to a single theme, of course—how policy is formed—but the reader should note that each of them contributes to other parts of the book as well. Harold Kaplan's article on Metro Toronto, for example, adds something to the section on Metropolitan Organization, Richard A. Cloward and Frances Fox Piven's article on welfare adds something to the section on Influence and Leadership, and H. R. Wilde's article on the Milwaukee riot adds something to at least three sections: The Theory of Good Government, The Trend of Urban Politics, and Influence and Leadership. My own article on the public library might be read in connection with the section on Problems of Management.

The bibliography has been brought up to date and an index has been added.

Preface to the First Edition

THIS IS a collection of the readings that I have found most valuable in teaching courses on urban government to both undergraduate and graduate students.

The readings come from so many places that even if each were readily available it would be a tedious task for a librarian to bring them all together on a reserve shelf. But many, like Henry Jones Ford's theory of corruption, would not be available at all in most libraries, and some, like Rexford G. Tugwell's evaluation of the career of Robert Moses, have never before appeared in print.

A book of this kind can be used in at least three ways: as a supplement to a textbook, in place of a textbook as an accompaniment to classroom lectures, or as a basis for a discussion series. It has been my experience that readings of this sort help give analytical depth to a course. The usual textbook provides a descriptive account of the more formal aspects of governmental structure and process, and then leaves it up to the instructor to show the student the larger meaning of what has been described. This book is designed to help him do this. Accordingly, I have selected the readings for the *ideas* that they contain.

Since some instructors will want to use the book without an accompanying text, the essential descriptive materials are supplied here in the form of a Glossary. Because the Glossary contains all of the background information necessary for understanding the readings, many students will find it useful to begin by reading the Glossary from start to finish.

The approach of this book differs from that of most texts in several respects. The most important difference, perhaps, is that this book tries to explain what really happens in urban government and to do so largely in terms of the concepts and theories of social scientists. Most textbooks on state and local government are preoccupied with what "experts" think *ought* to be the case; this one is occupied with what *really is* the case. While the views of reformers and experts are represented, they are not assumed to be authoritative, and they are placed in juxtaposition with those of social scientists. Thus, for example, the student is exposed not only to the usual criticisms of the big city machine but also to the views of the eminent sociologist, Robert K. Merton, on the machine's latent functions.

This emphasis on the social scientist's view of things as they are, as distinguished from what they ought to be, has inevitably led to a much heavier emphasis on politics than is common in most textbooks on urban government. Works on urban government all too often assume that the tasks of city government are almost entirely matters of administration—collecting garbage, repairing streets, putting out fires, and so on. Without belittling the importance of such activities, this book seeks to give politics—the struggle for power and the management of conflict —the attention that it deserves.

Politics would be important even if it had no consequences extending beyond the boundaries of the city. But the fact is that American national politics is to a very large extent local politics, and no one can possibly understand the national political system without first understanding politics in the cities, especially the larger ones. This is another reason for the emphasis here on politics.

This book focuses on the processes rather than on the techniques of government. Most students, for example, do not need to know anything about the technique of designing and filling out the forms of a city budget. Not one in a thousand will ever have use for such information, and the rare one who will can certainly best get it on the job. On the other hand, all students should know the kinds of things that are explained by William H. Brown, Jr. and Charles E. Gilbert in their article on capital programming in Philadelphia: what capital programming is, why it is done, how it is organized, what its connection with city planning is, what its political setting is, and what are the practical and theoretical limitations upon its effectiveness.

Some of the readings provide models for students who would like to go into the local community and do research of their own. The selections from Mark K. Adams, James Q. Wilson, Robert A. Dahl, and Kenneth E. Gray and David Greenstone should all be suggestive to the student who wants to try his hand at this and to the class that is carrying on a joint research project. These examples show how much can be done without a computing machine, providing one has sound legs and a good mind.

Each Section of the book is preceded by an introductory note formulating the central questions around which it is organized, underlining the points that the editor believes are of the greatest analytical interest, and showing the relevance of each reading to the general themes of the book.

The bibliography lists items generally regarded as standard references on each topic. These are annotated for the benefit of the non-specialist.

The author acknowledges with thanks the assistance of Martha Derthick, who prepared the Glossary and the Bibliography.

September, 1961

Contents

An Overview

Analytical Contents

THE THEORY OF "GOOD GOVERNMENT"

V. **The Trend of Urban Politics**

VIII. The Formation of Policy

I

Urban Government as a Subject for Study

GOVERNMENT serves two very different functions. One is that of providing goods and services that cannot be, or at any rate are not, provided under other, private, auspices. With respect to this *service* function, government is in many ways like a private enterprise. Private enterprise provides certain kinds of goods and services to people called "customers"; public enterprise provides other kinds of goods and services to people called "taxpayers." Both types of enterprise are judged by how well and how cheaply they supply the goods and services that are wanted.

The other function of government is to deal with conflict. Wherever there are people, there are bound to be differences of opinion and of interest. Politics is any kind of activity—reasonable discussion, heated argument, bribery, fighting, balloting, and so on—by which conflict in matters of public importance is carried on. Government deals with this conflict by regulating the manner in which it is carried on, by arranging compromises and balancing interests, and by imposing settlements which the parties to the disputes have to accept.

Whereas the service function is of necessity performed consciously and deliberately, the political function is often, but not always, performed as a more or less accidental by-product of a politician's effort to get office or of a bureaucracy's effort to maintain and expand itself.

Perhaps it is for this reason that many people regard "administration," or the carrying out of the service function, as the "real" justification for government, while they look on "politics," or the process by which conflict is handled, as a necessary evil, if not indeed as an irrational aberration.

Because the service function is so conspicuously important in the government of cities, many writers have treated it as if it were, or ought to be, the *only* function of city government. The usual textbook emphasis on the service role of city government relies implicitly, and often explicitly, upon a conceptual scheme appropriate to the normative study of administration. This perspective introduces a bias that hides other, perhaps more significant, dimensions of governmental activity.

In some places, city government is indeed much more a matter of administration than of politics. This is true in Great Britain, and also in many small, middle-class American cities. In these places, matters are usually decided on grounds that are (or at least seem to be) technical rather than political. In large, polyglot American cities, however, the case is different. In such cities, efficiency—the avoidance of waste—is of little or no interest to many voters, and conflict among groups and interests is pervasive and sharp. Despite the pleas of reformers, the people with something at stake have never agreed either to respect the neutrality of administration and to leave certain matters out of politics or to forego advantages that could be had by mixing local issues with state and national ones.

But the political character of government in all of our larger and many of our smaller cities need not necessarily be considered pathological. The successful management of conflict is a social function valuable enough in itself to justify, as a rule, whatever loss of efficiency in the performance of the service functions the injection of politics into administration may cause.

The effective management of conflict is valuable because it permits and encourages the expression of competing interests and opinions while at the same time preventing the eruption of violence and the eventual breakdown of social organization. But even more important, it is valuable as a way of discovering the concrete content of the common good. Political struggle is the means by which society develops the meaning of justice and of good. This is so even when the particular matter in question—say, the location of a housing project—is in itself trivial. Even though a concrete matter may be trivial to start with, it is often transformed and given great significance by ideological or symbolic elements that are introduced to serve someone's purpose. Thus the agitation over what is a trivial matter to begin with may prove useful in the elucidation of moral questions of the deepest interest to all mankind. For Aristotle, whose categories Norton E. Long believes provide the most appropriate framework for the study of local government, the city is above all an ethical association. It comes into existence (to paraphrase Aristotle slightly) for the sake of its service functions, but it exists for the sake of the good life. How to establish empirically the influence of "regime" on the style and content of a city's government is one of the problems discussed by James Q. Wilson in an article which stresses the importance of comparative studies. The final reading in this section, by Edward C. Banfield, represents an effort to apply the advice given here on what to study and how to study it. The article (1) treats "actions which increase conflict" (as opposed to persons) as the relevant unit of analysis, (2) is comparative, and (3) compares two conceptions of "citizen, constitution, and ruling class."

Aristotle and the Study of Local Government

Norton E. Long

THE DISCIPLINE OF POLITICAL SCIENCE is characterized by compartmentalization into special fields of empirical research. These fields are most commonly treated as a species of contemporary institutional history, and scarcely more attempt is made to identify, test, and correlate key hypotheses and their logical consequences than is made by the historian. The preoccupation of political theorists with the monuments of the past, the history of ideas, and moral speculation has led to a neglect of the urgent task of providing theoretical unification for the discipline, a comprehensive theoretical description of our present body of empirical data, and an adequate directing framework for new research. Lack of such theory results in an anarchy of intellectual laissez faire, uncompensated for by an "unseen hand" producing an effective, productive cooperation among us. The net result is that research is not additive in its findings, and that each individual must in a sense go it alone.

The alternative to rugged intellectual individualism is not some theoretical five-year plan to regiment research. Rather it is to recognize the need, and get at the business of working up generalized empirical theory that can guide research in specific areas and meaningfully interrelate all areas. Hopefully there will be many such theories competing in the market place of ideas, subjecting themselves to the test of facts and guiding empirical research into theoretically significant channels. This neglected aspect of political science, so well appreciated by Aristotle, badly needs rehabilitation in the discipline. It does not mean a new plague of methodologists, with large foundation ·grants to work out schemes for working out schemes for manufacturing high-level theory. Methodology will most fruitfully develop out of serious work in important problems. The history of the discipline has pretty well indicated what a number of these are. It seems likely that the dearth of general

Reprinted from Social Research, *24, No. 3 (Autumn, 1957), 287–310, by permission of the publisher and of the author.*

empirical theory is due not to lack of methodology, but to lack of a sustained structured interest in the profession.

We have acted on a sort of hope that if enough facts are collected they will somehow sort and illuminate themselves. A becoming modesty and an overwhelming respect for the ancients have paralyzed our own originality and made historians of us all. It is high time we took courage and renewed the high enterprise that was carried forward not only by careful scientists like Aristotle, but even by inspired dilettantes like Rousseau. We may well hope that if this enterprise is put on a continuing organized basis, empirical theory in political science can have an ongoing career in John Dewey's sense, rather than resembling as it now does the history of the great works of art, with no more interconnection and development than that between Rembrandt and Picasso.

Perhaps as promising a place as any to start the business of building an empirical theory is with the field of local government. The nearer we get to the ultimate face-to-face groups of the family, the clan, the tribe, the village, the town, the city, the county, the closer we come to dealing with phenomena that promise generality and provide useful points of departure for the investigation of the power and opinion structures that characterize differing political systems. The unity of politics for scientific inquiry, if unity there be, lies in the continuum of mutual influence and interaction that links the person, the family, the hamlet, the city, the region, the nation, and the world with one another as interrelated foci of interest and influence in a commonly shared dynamic field.

One of the major weapons of scientific inquiry is comparison, the notation of significant similarities and differences between the objects compared. Certainly the father of the profession, Aristotle, with his detailed comparison of constitutions, was a comparative-government man if ever there was one, and his conception of constitutions was broad and realistic enough to range from the ethos of the ruling class and the techniques of dictatorship and revolution to the statics and dynamics of prevailing economic systems. By itself, however, the commandment to compare is insufficient if we do not insist on the selection of the significant for comparison.

Here indeed is the rub for the crude empiricist: out of the multitude of things that might be compared, how to select the significant? Fortunately, this is no problem *ab ovo*. We are the heirs to a tradition that has wrestled for upwards of two thousand years with the question of what are the significant phenomena of politics; nor is our own contemporary culture barren of value systems to guide us in the selection of "interesting" hypotheses; and lastly, despite its lack of a satisfactory career, political science has empirical theories of politics sufficient to suggest "interesting topics" for comparative analysis. Indeed, were we to utilize some of our most promising empirical theory that has lain dormant in the clutches of metaphysicians, moral philosophers, and the historians of ideas, we might witness a renaissance in the discipline similar to that occasioned by the rediscovery of the classics in other ages.

But for such a rebirth, no servile and uncomprehending imitation will do. Only a creative use of the perennial sources of insight furnished by truly great minds deeply grounded in the realities of political behavior can given a Baconian direction to what in the past has lent itself to a priestly and snobbish ritual of the great books, where in all truth the wisdom of an Aristotle or a Plato is so securely embalmed that no dangerous breath of life can emerge to disturb the complacent and un-comprehending repetition of formulae grown meaningless and empty of contemporary significance.

It will be the contention of this paper that an application of the Aristotelian categories of analysis to the phenomena of local government will make for the development of theory capable of unifying the discipline.

I

The key to Aristotle's political philosophy lies in his identification of politics with ethics—his conception of the state as being most significantly a medium for the realization of some conception of the good life, and indeed as being the master institution for this purpose, to which all others are teleologically subservient. Aristotle's exclusive pre-occupation with the city-state as the chosen vehicle for man's ethical self-realization has given his work a deceptive appearance of irrelevance to later and widely different forms of political life. The ethical and sociological interest central to Greek political thought was replaced by Roman legalism, and the Christian separation of church and state un-dermined the primacy of the state's ethical role.

Rehabilitation of Greek political thought by theorists such as Rousseau and Hegel has seemed, on the one hand, to abandon empirical inquiry for metaphysical speculation and, on the other, to enthrone an ethical theory fraught with the menace of totalitarian absolutism. Em-pirical investigation into the ethical nature of political associations has by and large been treated either as identical with some variant of Hegelian metaphysics or as an attempt to resurrect the natural-law theory slain by Hume. But one may well reject Hegel, and Marx, and natural law, one may even be a good disciple of Hume, and still insist on the reality of ethics as an empirical datum of the first magnitude. Its neglect is little short of an evisceration of the subject matter of politics.

One may well go along with Aristotle in insisting on the prime significance of ethics as a "brute fact" of politics without accepting

Aristotelian metaphysics. Aristotle the political scientist can be severed from Aristotle the metaphysician. The ethical structures of political societies are not merely oughts for the sermons of theologians and the homilies of moral philosophers, but in all scientific seriousness are most significant *is*'s for empirical inquiry. Lest I be misunderstood on this point, I mean no disparagement of rational evaluation of ethical structures. There is no more important function than that of evaluation. It uses, but differs from, science. Value structures, however, are most significant empirical facts for scientific inquiry, if we would understand the groups and societies whose behavior is informed by them.

For Aristotle the structure of politics is a structure of institutions, running from the family through the village and the town to the state, each subordinate institution contributing its appropriate part to the final end embodied in the polis state. The state is characterized by its regime, which exemplifies a particular conception of the good life, be it the wealth of oligarchy, the freedom of democracy, or the martial spirit of a timocracy. The ethical principle embodied in the constitution sets the standard for distributive justice in the state; determines the nature and composition of the politeuma, the ruling class, whose members in one sense are or personify the constitution; and informs the subordinate institutions with their appropriate roles in each particular type of constitution.

The Aristotelian conception of autarchy or self-sufficiency sets the limit to the progression of social institutions. The final unit, the state, is self-sufficient and therefore inclusive of all the others. Self-sufficiency depends in part on military and economic considerations, but most significantly on ethical. It is for this reason that Aristotle, the tutor of Alexander and the friend of Antipater, could retain his allegiance to the city-state in the face of the bitter facts of Greek experience.

But again, Aristotle's predilection for the city-state form by no means limits to the city-state the applicability of the concept of ethical self-sufficiency. As a concept for analyzing the units of government, and the relations of individual and subordinate groups to them, ethical self-sufficiency can play a role similar to that of sovereignty, and more discriminating. The delimitation of ethical communities, and the description of their interrelationships and participants, may be sociologically and politically more meaningful than comparable legal analysis.

The nature of the state, as opposed to its lesser political subdivisions, is that it is ethically "sovereign." Its end is the highest, to which all other associations contribute or should contribute, and are subordinate. Aristotle was well aware that not all actual governments were of such a character. The governments of the barbarians, and indeed many of the Greek governments, exemplified no ethically satisfying end in which citizens as opposed to mere subjects could participate. An ethically satisfying state was for Aristotle a requirement for the fullest development of man. It is not merely a metaphysical requirement, but one that human nature will strive for, however imperfectly, in particular and adverse circumstances. It is thus an empirical fact of human behavior, not just a moral postulate.

The simple scheme of Book I of the *Politics* describes an ethically graded series of associations rising from the household to the polis, with each step in the ascent characterized by an ethically more inclusive and higher end. On the basis of this analysis, local government is differentiated from the higher levels of government as ethically insufficient to stand by itself and as merely ministerial to an end more adequately realized in a higher level. Thus for Aristotle and Plato the village is, if not a "city of pigs," still too uncivilized for the highest human self-realization. It is inadequate to provide the scope necessary to the fullest self-realization of man, and is therefore lacking in self-sufficiency.

If on one end of the ethical scale of associations, the village is inadequate and the household even more so, the polis itself is characterized by ethical self-sufficiency and a degree of economic and military competence. Aristotle is not talking about an isolated state in an international vacuum. There will be treaties and alliances, economic, military, and for other purposes; there may be Pan Hellenic Festivals and Olympic Games—and thus there are more broadly inclusive associations than the polis (the state). But these broader associations are characterized by partial and less inclusive purposes. They do not contemplate "the whole end of man."

If one puts the Aristotelian schema aside for the moment, and considers the ordering of associations and especially governmental associations in accordance with the value—and perhaps one should say the felt value—of their ethical ends, it is clear that the Aristotelian picture of a neatly ascending hierarchy, though logically attractive, may or may not be the case from one situation to another. Just as the Austinean schema would give us a neatly ascending order to the final sovereign, so the Aristotelian would give us a hierarchy mounting to the ethically sovereign association. The polemics on sovereignty have frequently led to metaphysical debates between monists and pluralists. A similar logomachy could develop from any conception of an ethically sovereign state. What is important is to investigate the ethical character of governmental associations as significant empirical data of political life.

As an empirical fact, any given state is a community of communities. Some of the most important of these communities are formally political in character. They serve ends that are variously interrelated, and these ends rate more or less highly as values to the participants in the communities. A well ordered state would be, for Aristotle, one in which the subordinate communities were articulated instrumentally and ethically with the final community, the state. This would mean that a democratic state would ideally call for democratic local government, or that an oligarchical state would call for oligarchical local government.

In practice, to be sure, the ideal may be far from realized. But this is more than a mere matter of the aesthetic disruption of a tidy-minded constitution-maker's organization chart. If Aristotle's theory of revolution is empirically warranted, this contradiction in the ethical constitution of the state is productive of stasis—is in fact a present indication of the disintegration of the ethical constitution of the state. In the more homely terms of Lincoln, "a house divided against itself cannot stand." For Lincoln as for Aristotle, ethical principles embodied in the values of living men struggle for institutional life, for survival and expansion. The very stuff of politics is made up of these conflicts, and the most significant meaning of institutions lies in the ethic that structures the variety of human attitudes toward them, ranging from ardent participation and advocacy through lukewarmness and apathy to violent protest and opposition.

A vast modern nation state, such as the United States, contrasts sharply in territory and population with the city-state of antiquity. It is not, however, the ethically formless mass that Aristotle so despised in Babylon, though Aristotle's strictures of Babylon are not without telling applicability to the megalopolis of our day and to the nation itself. The belief that a despotic rule over slaves is the only possible political organization for a large territory was not clearly Aristotle's final view, since his advice to Alexander urged the latter to rule the Greeks as a leader though the barbarian despotically, as a master. Be this as it may, the empirical fact is that however different the participation and the interaction, the modern nation-state can have citizens rather than subjects, and can and does have a constitution in the Aristotelian sense. This constitution is of great significance for the subordinate associations in the state.

Aristotle's analysis of constitutions is complex. It is nowhere systematically spelled out in the *Politics*, but in general I believe Sabine is right in contending that, for Aristotle, constitutional government ideally requires a government of law over willing subjects in the common interest. Any or all of these qualities might be lacking, however, and there would still be a kind of constitution—if, for Aristotle, a perverted one. Aristotle's empirical analysis led him to identify several interacting aspects of constitutions as going concerns. In one aspect they are a certain ordering of offices; this is the legal constitution, concerned with the formal division of power. In another there is the economic or, more broadly speaking, the sociological constitution, the actual economic and social structure of the society that underlies and informs the legal constitution. And there is finally the ethical constitution, the conception of the good life that rationalizes the whole social and legal structure and provides the principle of distributive justice in

the state. These three aspects of the constitution are in dynamic interaction, though for Aristotle the ethical is clearly the most important.
In shorthand, Aristotle describes the constitution as the ruling class
and the ruling class as the constitution. The ruling class is the ethic of
the constitution made flesh, embodying it. Because it does, it is the
ruling class, and because this ethic is generally accepted it rules over
willing subjects. How important the ethical constitution is, and how
painful deviations from it may beome, are illustrated by Gunnar
Myrdal in *The American Dilemma.*

II

Professor Louis Hartz has argued that American political life
has been characterized by a massive acceptance of a Lockean ethic.
Implicit in this ethic is a justification for a given "ordering of offices":
a certain type of ruling class and its recruitment and a set of supporting
economic and social institutions. The bearers of this ethic are driven
to seek its institutionalization through society. The United States is
certainly no tight little city-state, but a continent with wide variation
in social and economic conditions. Local heresies from the central
conception of the good life are inevitable. And yet, looking at the
formal "ordering of the offices," the legal structure of the subpolities
of the American polity, there is an apparent monotonous uniformity
that makes most texts in state and local government arid in the
extreme. Does this mean that the overriding ethic of the national polity
has indeed informed the political subdivisions, as in Aristotelian theory
it ideally should? Or does it mean that political scientists, despite
Aristotle's example to the contrary, have confined themselves merely to
the legal constitution, and have neglected the social-economic and
the ethical?

In view of the continental sweep of American politics, we can
expect state and local governments to show a wide deviation from the
national norm, to have individual constitutions in the Aristotelian
sense, with significant differences that cannot be adequately described
in the strong-mayor, weak-mayor, city-manager, and commission legal
typology that divides our municipal Gaul into four unequal parts.
V. O. Key has urged, and in his *Southern Politics* has begun to make
respectable, a recognition of the deviant that has hitherto been the
province of the muckraker and the journalist rather than of the
orthodox political scientist. A comparative approach would open a rich
mine of local "constitutions," varying from the narrowest oligarchy to
the freest democracy, and from the most brutal tyranny to a near
philosopher-king. A recent *Saturday Evening Post* headlined a story,
"Tyrant in Texas," the story of George Parr, so-called Duke of Duval
County. This regime lasted for years, under the forms of law. Bell

County, Kentucky, killed its opponents with impunity and dominated the courts, and its tyranny was finally overthrown only from without. The Imperial Valley in California exhibits a brutal oligarchy that tolerates no nonsense from its helots. The investigations of the La Follette Civil Liberties Committee documented the deviant local constitutions. The company towns of the nineteenth century not only illustrate the concentration of economic and political power in a ruling oligarchy or tyranny, but provide a classic example of the transition of oligarchy to a broader based polity.

Thus, under the deceptive uniformity of an apparently similar legal structure, a wide range of actual variance appears in the "constitutions" of our local governments. And it is under these "constitutions" that many, if not most, people have to live the most significant parts of their lives. We have no adequate information as to these "actual constitutions," the degree of their prevalence in their different forms, and the extent to which they cover, for practical purposes, the political life of those subject to them. We are even in the dark as to any cumulative trends.

It may be disquieting to realize that, in respects important for significant groups of the population, the American government that counts is oligarchical or tyrannical rather than democratic. The implications for the superior levels of government of variant constitutions below are serious. As Madison pointed out, an advantage that the expanse of the country gives to federalism is the possibility of restricting political contagion to the infected governmental cell, walling it off, and, after rallying the healthy corpuscles, restoring the normative order. Another advantage lies in the capacity to tolerate, under the cloak of lip service to the respectable national norm, wide deviations in practice dictated by differing social and economic situations.

Yet local government on the firing line must be a major determinant of the realities at the national level. Caciquism, the rule of local chieftains, made a mockery of parliamentary democracy in eastern Europe, parts of Italy, Spain, and South America. Perhaps the *tutelle administrative* of France may indicate the real possibility of centralized national democracy unsupported by extensive local foundations. Or one may see in France's apathetic masses a result that Burke foresaw in a metaphysical constitution that denies the necessity of mediating institutions between individual and nation. Surely the trends of our local constitutions, as they develop toward a more extensive prevalence of oligarchy, democracy, or ochlocracy, and their variants, are highly signifiant for the future of state and national government.

Each local jurisdiction, with important powers of police, justice, and taxation, can resemble a feudatory, with high, middle, and low justice; can constitute a little world for some, if not all, of its inhabitants; and can as truly represent a way of life as ancient Athens. The Aristotelian view sees the relationship between levels of government as most importantly a hierarchy of increasingly more self-sufficient ethical associations, until in the state self-sufficiency is attained. A part of the reason for the more primitive associations entering into the higher is military and economic, but by themselves these motives would not constitute a sufficient bond to produce a new political unity. Thus a NATO, or even an EDC, does not constitute a state, nor will a private or public international coal-and-steel cartel produce one. A community or friendship for business may produce a cartel or an International Rotary, a similar association for defense may produce a military alliance, but by themselves these purposes are insufficient to structure a political union. For this, according to Aristotle, a commonly shared and participated-in conception of a good life is essential.

The significance of this for local government, and its relation to the higher levels of government, lies in the widely felt differences regarding the importance of the various communities' purposes. The sense of the significance of the community's ethical value varies as between communities, and as between inhabitants of the same community. Thus a citizen of Quebec may find his provincial loyalty far more meaningful than his Canadian citizenship. Robert E. Lee, wending his way sadly back to his native Virginia, illustrates a type of conflict that reaches beyond the formal context of legal federalism. The scale of areal and governmental loyalties has a wide range of possibilities. While secession may not be a realistic possibility for Yorkville Nazis, a species of spiritual and even politically effective secession can occur. Nullification is not just a Southern states-rights phenomenon, and the non-enforcement of federal and state law is a significant aspect of political geography.

Not only may citizens of local governments limit or even cut their allegiance to state and national governments, by apathy and neglect, if not outright revolt; also at the local level they may exhibit little or no allegiance. Many an ardent young progressive is condemned to live in the Republican desert of an otherwise charming suburb. The split between the local citizens and the purely national citizens is a common problem of party politics. Thus the question of who are and who are not citizens is more than a mere legalism, although legal right is not without relevance. A most significant question of citizenship is that asking who participates in the ethical conception of the good life, embodied in the constitution of the community, and how the community's institutions, both formal and informal, are designed to effectuate participation.

If Aristotle, Plato, the Catholic church, the American Legion, the totalitarian states, and many others are right in the critical political importance they assign to education, then the educational systems, both formal and informal, that characterize our communities are of central significance. These institutions not only indoctrinate youth in the spirit of the polity; they also serve in part to separate the men of gold from the men of silver and the men of brass. The free and easy Periclean high school of the older small community mixed all social classes, nationalities, races, and religions in a school whose creed was likely to be Locke and Jefferson with a dash of the Napoleonic gospel that every private carries a marshal's baton in his knapsack.

A principal political effect of the motor car and the bedroom suburb has been the one-class school. For certain racial and national minorities, segregation and the peculiar operations of the real-estate trade had already, to some extent, produced this independently in the larger cities. The extent to which a counter-trend at institutions of higher learning may overcome the influence of early education is problematic. In so far as churches, boy scouts, other youth organizations are an important factor in the role training and indoctrination of youth, they well warrant study. Each community has a system of educational institutions to indoctrinate youth in the spirit of the polity and confirm them in the principle of distributive justice by which role allocation is justified.

The political effect of parochialization of the schools is widely recognized. Yet study of the school system as a "brute fact" of American politics, and as much so as the party system, is avoided—and at the cost of losing that refreshing and serene realism that characterizes Greek political thought. We may, and in fact as disciples of Locke we must, reject the Aristotelian identification of politics with pedagogy. The ideal of the state as a glorified Rugby is incompatible with a political philosophy that refuses to see the individual and society as reaching their fulfillment in the state. But while rejecting the meta-physical idea of the ethical ultimacy of the state, and its corollary that the state should be an all-inclusive educational institution, we must acknowledge the important political functions of education.

The struggle for the minds of men is a pervasive and never ending battle. Recently the newpapers of an Ohio city rebuked the local leaders of the AFL for seeking to organize the schoolteachers with the avowed intent of getting across to the students a point of view sympathetic to labor. The union leaders replied to the outraged rebuke that this was the only way they had to break the monopoly of their opponents on the formal educational system. The process of education is central to the indoctrination of the young and the recruitment of the governing class. It complements and sometimes competes with the family, the church, and other social organizations that perform similar functions.

III

For Aristotle the key to the constitution is the governing class. Here is the human embodiment of the constitution. It spells out in clearly legible "big letters" what may be obscure or hidden in the legal constitution. The governing class represents or appears to represent the qualities that exemplify the conception of the good life that informs the constitution. Its members are looked up to and admired, since they most fully reflect the ideal. Their position is felt to be just, to be legitimate, because in terms of the particular constitution it is just that the richest, the most noble, the most learned, should rule.

The institutions of the society, if it is to be stable, must buttress and reinforce the principle of legitimacy. So viewed, ideally, all institutions are shaped to give effect to an ethical norm; viewed in another respect, all institutions are shaped to support the claims of a particular governing class. Thus the Federalist parson and pedagogue justified the government of the wise and the good, who turned out to be the rich and the well born. Art, literature, religion, and manners, and the social structures through which they operate, are pregnant with political consequences. They serve to support or undermine a given political order. As Irving Babbitt once remarked, all great revolutions are preceded by a revolution in the dictionary. The key value terms of a society undergo a change, sapping the symbols of legitimacy of a given order.

Governments, local and state, may range from a tight oligarchy of wealth to a demagogic mass dictatorship. For the most part, pure forms are rare. As Aristotle pointed out, there are many claims to political power: wealth, free birth, numbers, noble birth, military prowess, and the like. All of these have a real but limited justice. A stable constitution requires that no single claim prevail, and that at least wealth be tempered by numbers. In fact, this mixed government or polity is best achieved through the predominance of the middle class. Where the rich confront the poor with little or no middle class between them, the city is divided into irreconcilable armed camps. A sociological and economic substructure is necessary to support a given constitution, and that constitution will be radically altered by economic change, as from a peasant democracy to an urban proletariat. Thus Aristotle recognizes that ruling class, legal constitution, ethical order, and economy are interdependent. Changes in one aspect have significant consequences for all others in the dynamic equilibrium of the constitution.

When we apply Aristotle's conception of constitution to state and local governments, each unit of government may be conceived of as possessed of a ruling class. From the composition and character of this ruling class emerges the real nature of the local government's constitution, as opposed to the formal legal order. The holders of political office represent a small fraction of the ruling class; the offices of the formal political order may be among the less important in the community. The separation of church and state, of politics and economics, veils some of the jagged peaks of the pyramid of power. The princes of the church, the presidents of the banks, the editors of the newspapers, the manufacturers, the labor-union leaders, the leaders of society, of fraternal organizations, of nationality and racial groups are not, as such, officers of the formal government. But if government be regarded as a decision-making process, much of the action of the formal government is mere ratification of decisions made by these holders of social power. For this reason Marx and his followers have maintained that bourgeois democracy is a fraud, in which the pseudo-equality of the ballot box hides the realities of the unequal distribution of power. As John Adams wrote to Jefferson, there are nobles in Boston as well as in Madrid.

Conservatives in the early American state constitutional conventions protested again and again that abolition of the property qualification for office or suffrage would prove pernicious or nugatory. Property was an indestructible part of political power, and failure to recognize it in the constitution would lead either to a demagogic assault on wealth or to the devising of informal means whereby wealth would achieve its inevitable influence in the power structure of the community. To the realists of the eighteenth and early nineteenth centuries the struggle between the rich and the poor, the few and the many, seemed as invariant a problem of politics as it did to Plato and Aristotle. The opponents of the Daniel Shays, while doubtless seeking to provide in the constitution an instrumentality for the solution of common social problems, frequently argued in terms reminiscent of the pages of Thucydides. Their advocacy was couched in the language of frightened oligarchs seeking to band themselves together in a league to furnish mutual aid and comfort against one another's threatening democracies.

The wisdom of the fathers is full of reference to the bloody social politics of the republics of antiquity. In no respect does their political science seem more faulty than in its gloomy prophecies that political democracy means social democracy, and social democracy means class war. On the other hand, the twin inventions of representation and federalism—in which the authors of the *Federalist* set considerable stock as so extending the feasible territorial limits of free government as to diffuse and dilute interests, and so break the force of faction— have appeared to succeed beyond their fondest hopes. Given their dour view of the nature of man, the Federalists could scarcely have dreamed that our cities and local governments would be so free of the mischief of faction as would appear from contemporary textbooks. One would never gather from a text on local government that the prime fact of politics is the struggle of classes, or that the central question of government is the ruling class.

The gulf between Aristotle and the eighteenth-century realists, on the one hand, and contemporary political science on the other is vividly apparent in the preoccupation of the former with stasis and the problems of class rule, and our present attitude of avoidance or indifference toward these issues. In part, this difference of approach results from a belief that the phenomena of class struggle, which are fundamental in Aristotelian analysis, are simply not exemplified in the American scene. In part, it is due to a belief in a fundamental social-harmony theory, similar to that of classical economics. This view results in a conception of a system of political laissez faire in which, as in eonomic laissez faire, no one rules. Free political competition exists in much the same way as free economic competition.

A more realistic view would see our political organization as a system that, while differing in part, is nonetheless comparable to a system of Greek city-states or to the feudal lordships and free cities of the Middle Ages, clusters of power and local government under varying degrees of external control. In Aristotle's sense, each local government may, and often will, have a ruling class of its own, once independent and now subject to or participant in a ruling class of the new more comprehensive political unit. Looked at historically and analytically, there is a continuum between the independent small governments of one period and the local governments embraced in the empires and nation-states of succeeding epochs. The cycle of building larger aggregates may halt and reverse itself, bringing about the renewed independence of lesser communities; or both the process of aggregation and that of disintegration may go forward at the same time, interacting together. Thus the study of state formation and international relations joins hands with the study of local government.

Secession, separatism, colonial nationalism, revolution, and imperialism are pervasive categories of political analysis. The ethical self-sufficiency of the community and the supremacy and independence of its ruling class are two aspects of statehood that local governments approach as limits. If they are attained, local governments become independent states; if lost, they become incorporated in larger units.

Ethical self-sufficiency means in practice that a political community possesses ideal goals whose significance for the politically decisive part of the community transcends the goals of any more or less inclusive community. The supremacy of the ruling class is derived from its commonly accepted relation to those goals from which it derives its legitimatized power. In practice, the community may possess both ethical self-sufficiency and a ruling class of its own and still fail of political independence. The captivity of the Jews under Babylon and Rome is a case in point. Ireland and Poland in recent history were incorporated as foreign bodies into alien sovereignties. But in Hobbes' terms they indeed formed "worms in the body politic." In any event, the material conditions of independent statehood depend in part on the surrounding facts of other powers.

The ethical self-sufficiency or the ideal goals of communities can be regarded as technologies for permitting large-scale cooperation, both by giving a decisive number of inhabitants participating roles and by structuring and legitimatizing a ruling class and its roles—creating an area and a personnel with shared legitimate power. The possibility of creating such goals with an appropriate ruling group is decisive not only for the creation of larger state structures in the international sphere, but equally for the solution of metropolitan problems internally. Of course, in either the international or the domestic sphere, problems may be "solved" by the force of conquest or fiat. Even here, however, the transformation of might into an accepted and acceptable right remains.

IV

The inappropriateness, for the solution of major current problems, of our existing structure of state and local governments is a common lament of citizen, scholar, and public official. The satellite suburb entrenched in its baneful legal autonomy, the rotten-borough state, the under-represented urban population, all exemplify the conflict between the dynamics of change and the statics of a vested interest in the institutional status quo, with its passing ideals and its challenged power structure. Just as internal local government structures are menaced by the sweep of change, so the international state structure itself, in its embodiment of a bygone distribution of power and purpose, is challenged by new and legally unrecognized facts and forces.

The process of adjustment of institutional structure to the emerging new facts of life may proceed more peacefully within states, where there exists a more or less accepted mechanism for the transfer of power, than between states, where commonly accepted instrumentalities for adjustment and the saving of face are lacking. In the extreme case, and always as a real alternative, there remains the possibility of revolution in the one case and war in the other. A major achievement of political institutions is to make possible the non-violent adaptation of the status quo to the necessities of change.

Edward Hallett Carr, in his *Twenty Years Crisis*, has well expressed the problem of politics as the institutionalization of peaceful change. In this sense war and revolution are extreme means necessitated by the failure of institutions to adapt to major new facts of power. One does not have to share in Carr's apparent worship of the "bitch goddess success" to appreciate the force of this position. From it, as from that of Marx and Aristotle, the assumption of the normality of "social harmony," that underlies much economic and political analysis, seems naive, hypocritical, or pollyanna. Thus a study of American politics that focuses on parties and elections is, while important, radically insufficient, open to the same criticism that Marx leveled at the economists. It assumes the permanence of the system and therefore neglects the dynamics of its structure. It neglects the dynamics of political structure.

The evisceration of politics by abstracting from it vital Aristotelian elements, now isolated in sociology and economics, accounts in part for the emptiness and insufficiency of analysis.

For Aristotle the ruling class and revolution were two of the main concepts of political analysis. Investigation guided by these concepts inevitably leads to concern for the realities of social power, its acquisition, distribution, limits, transfer, and loss. Power capabilities, a term we glibly bandy about in the analysis of international relations, has equal meaning in terms of local, state and national government. The process of political change can be fruitfully viewed from the standpoint of changes in the composition and techniques of the ruling class, its relation to the value symbols of the society, and the dynamics of economic and cultural change.

There is certainly room for the important study of the politics and technology of cooperation. In the larger sense, however, this is a subcategory of the greater process of the dynamics of group adjustment. And even in the study of supposedly instrumental politics—as for example the fringe problem of metropolitan cities—the structure of a local ruling class and the possibility of galvanizing it into effective action is a decisive element for success. The differing fortunes of urban redevelopment in Pittsburgh—where the Mellon family and its leading scion, Richard Mellon, exert an effective hegemony—and in those communities with a jealous group of contending notables bear witness to the very everyday and very practical consequences of the structure of the local ruling class.

The emergence of labor leaders as powerholders without social status constitutes a source of instability for local constitutions and local ruling classes. Whether they will be crushed or ignored, or admitted to the country clubs and the honor-laden posts of our society, is on the agenda of history. The nationality leaders, from the Boston Irish to the Slavonians, have fought a long-drawn battle for inclusion into the upper ranks of the status system. When Harvard College conferred an honorary degree on Cardinal O'Connell of Boston the reconciliation of State Street with Lake Street was finally ratified.

The basic adjustment of the ruling class to new facts of power, compelling the admission of new elements and signalizing the decline of old, is not always easy, and sometimes is violent. The La Follette Civil Liberties Committee records the violent objection to the emergence of union power.

Sometimes the problems of intergroup adjustment approximate those with which we are painfully familiar in international life. The Negro population strains at the dikes of segregation with all the pent-up energy of a nation seeking its place in the sun. Quite literally it seeks to conquer living space, space that cannot be purchased. Violence is a technique that lies ready at hand. Despite feelings of guilt, in terms of both the plutocratic principle of justice—they have the money—

and the democratic principle—they are fellow citizens—those next to the problem, feeling menaced, deny Negroes membership in a community controlled by these principles. The prevention of warfare depends on the institutionalized technique of mobilizing the neutrals.

But the solution will require granting the same accolade to the Negro leaders that has been accorded other nationality groups by the ruling class. Failing that, the Negroes would remain a community within a community, struggling for a recognition that can finally be accorded only by the ruling class. In an important sense the Negroes as a group are excluded from becoming fully participating citizens, and thus are fair game for the revolutionary appeal of communists and alien agents. Symbolic participation in community acceptance, through the leaders' attainment of social-status positions, is a major attribute of citizenship in a mass state. Thus the ruling class becomes a medium for the representation of groups and the resolution of their conflicts. It may be a far more significant center of representation than city council or legislature.

The composition, interrelation, and changes of local ruling classes give significance to the local election returns. The president of the Central Labor Union Council and the archbishop do not change with the elections. What difference, then, do the elections make? How does the apparent change in formal political power relate to and affect the real distribution of social power? The political institutions are not only a device for doing the day-by-day work of meeting commonly accepted needs; they are also a mechanism for facilitating the peaceful readjustment of the balance of social power. The legal structure may obstruct or facilitate this. It may be more accessible to some groups, some levels of government, some agencies of government than to others, in their struggle for recognition and change. And the contest will be carried on in private organizations whose decisions may frequently outweigh the public in importance.

The concept of the ruling class provides a corrective for the superficialities of the formal legal order as a true description of the actualities of political power; and the Aristotelian analysis of revolutions provides a more searching analysis of political process than our preoccupation with formal elections. The seeming inapplicability of city-state experience to the macroscopic phenomena of the nation-state has served to limit Aristotelian analysis to the office of a profound but tenuous philosophic inspiration.

That this should have occurred despite the deep appreciation of early American theorists for the classic categories of analysis is in all probability due to the great appeal of both the facts and the myth of classless society. As Professor Hartz has pointed out, American experience has been peculiar in having a democratic revolution without the necessity of overthrowing a feudal order. The absence of class consciousness may well be due, as Professor Hartz contends, not only to the bounty of nature but even more to the fact that the middle class, never made class-conscious by struggle with a nobility, has failed to tutor the workers in their "historic" role.

Surely a part of the reason for the failure of political science to make use of the concept of the ruling class is the disrepute of Marxism and its works, and the crudity of much of vulgar Marxism. The Italian realists, such as Mosca, have remained curiosities from which to quote an occasional line with approval, but despite even the enormous vogue of Pareto they have failed to stimulate systematic study and reorientation. Elite studies there have been, but these have had the appearance of being esoteric when they have not been damned as antidemocratic.

The Aristotelian conceptions of citizen, constitution, and ruling class can be transferred from the city-state to an examination of the phenomena of government at local, state, and national levels, and even of politics, including the international. To raise the question of who are citizens, and in what sense, at each level of government, is to pinpoint crucial political issues that legal categories neglect and obscure. A functional conception of citizenship is as fruitful as a functional conception of party membership.

That a city like New York may best be regarded as made up largely of resident alien merchants and mechanics, gathered for trade and pleasure, and therefore lacking in civic motivation may explain some of the necessities of its government. That the ruling class of town X are branch-plant managers taking their orders from Pittsburgh and hoping to be promoted elsewhere is a more vital political fact than the town's possession of a city-manager form of government, though the two may be related. The suburban residence of large elements of a metropolitan ruling class, and its ethos of irresponsibility may be a more potent cause of central city disintegration than would be revealed by any analysis of the multiplicity of legal jurisdictions. Rural domination of state legislatures and the orientation of urban masses toward Washington and the presidency are deeply related to the current institutional technique for bolstering oligarchic power.

The interrelations between the geographically separated ruling classes, the difference in their composition, the formal legal constitutions through and alongside which they operate, the varying ethics that legitimatize their power, and the revolutionary movements for altering their composition, winning recognition for new elements, or overthrowing them—these are the vital stuff of politics. Their investigation can give real meaning to the shadowy phenomena of legal structures and elections, pointing to the large and cumulative phenomena and escaping the mere flux of the headlines.

We Need to Shift Focus

James Q. Wilson

THE PRINCIPAL PROBLEM in the study of urban politics is less with its means than with its ends. The journals and bookshelves are choked with articles and volumes arguing at white heat and in sometimes strident tones the "methodology" of urban political studies— arguing, in short, the means by which one should seek the answers to questions in this field. At the center of this controversy can be found the bloody but unbowed figure of Floyd Hunter; around him, his sociological defenders trade blows with his political-science attackers. Even to mention the controversy now requires a footnote of staggering length to refer the reader to the endless literature on this subject.[1]

I think this has gone on long enough. The methodological issue— how we study urban politics—is not a trivial issue; but it is not the fundamental one, either. It was a secondary issue when it was first raised, and it is a secondary issue now. The basic issue is not how we answer questions but what questions we want to answer; ultimately, we should be more concerned with where we are going than with how we get there.

We have been in danger for some time, it seems to me, of developing, at least with respect to urban affairs, a kind of "apolitical" political science. This is unfortunate, for I am sufficiently loyal to my own field to believe that political science, to a greater extent than sociology or economics (the disciplines to which we are most in danger of selling out), has had a fundamental preoccupation with the ends of human action. It is because of this preoccupation, indeed, that the study of politics in our universities has always included the study of political philosophy as well as the study of political facts. Although these two wings of the profession are often at war over the claims each makes,

1. I will omit the conventional footnote and refer instead to an anthology: Charles Press, ed., *Main Street Politics* (East Lansing, Mich.: Institute for Community Development, 1962).

Reprinted from Essays in Political Science, *edited by Edward H. Buehrig (Bloomington: Indiana University Press, 1966), pp. 131–150, by permission of the publisher.*

both have (or should have) one concern in common: the ends and outcomes of political action. Just as the political philosopher is properly concerned with systematically inquiring into the moral quality of political action (more than with the history of ideas), so the political empiricist is properly concerned with systematically explaining why political action has one outcome rather than another.

Various analytical concepts can be used to organize (or justify) political inquiry, but almost all of those in common use share this concern for ends. Politics may be the study of power, but a power relationship presupposes a difference in ends that a wielder of influence attempts to overcome. Politics may be the study of conflict; what is in conflict, however, are the goals of the actors. Politics may be the study of political development, modernization, or legitimacy; it is difficult to raise these issues, however, without asking why development, modernization, and legitimacy are important. The answer, it seems to me, is that each implies that government will serve some ends and not others, will distribute goods and services to benefit one group and not another, or will mobilize loyalty for one cause and not for another.

Not every political science study, certainly, need be considered unpublishable if it fails to explain differences in policy outcomes. One can list an imposing number of intellectually interesting questions that have no immediate or obvious connection with ends. Without discounting the value of studying such matters, I would argue that the traditions, the classic literature, and the special competence of our profession have always been, in mood if not in practice, ultimately concerned with the ends of political action. Social science seeks to explain human behavior; political science, whatever else it may do, at the very least seeks to explain why some ends and not others are served by the community and the state. "Who governs?" is an interesting and important question; an even more interesting and more important question, it seems to me, is "What *difference* does it make who governs?"

Norton E. Long called our attention to the importance of such research objectives in his article "Aristotle and the Study of Local Government."[2] Like almost everything else he has written, this essay was widely influential. At least, part of it was, for it now appears that his readers got only half the message. They certainly acted as if they had paid close heed to his suggestions that Aristotle, in addition to being concerned with the formal or legal constitution of the community, was concerned as well with its "economic" or "sociological" constitution—"the actual economic and social structure of the society that underlies and informs the legal constitution."[3] The more important

2. Norton E. Long, "Aristotle and the Study of Local Government," in *The Polity* (Chicago: Rand McNally, 1962), pp. 222–41.
3. *Ibid.*, p. 228.

part of the message, which seems to have been forgotten, was that the reason for this concern with the regime (now called the "power structure") was that the "regime exemplifies a particular conception of the good life, be it the wealth of oligarchy, the freedom of democracy, or the martial spirit of timocracy." How a city is governed, in short, should make a difference in what ends that city serves.

It is entirely possible, of course, that the character of the regime makes no difference at all in what ends are served; this would be a discouraging finding, to be sure, but nonetheless one of the greatest theoretical importance. No greater blow to both hot-blooded advocates of "good government" and cool-eyed defenders of machine politics could be delivered than to establish that, after all, procedures make no difference. (How the political philosophers would react is a matter of conjecture, but they are a hardy lot who may admire Socrates for drinking the hemlock but have no intention of trying any themselves.)

Many problems stand in the way of making meaningful intercity comparisons. Nothing, it seems to me, is clearer than the fact that simple two-by-two tabulations relating easily specified variables will not get us very far. If they could, then performing some rank-order correlations among the tables in the *Municipal Yearbook* (perhaps throwing in material from the *City and County Data Book* for good measure) would answer our questions. Any graduate student could do it. But it is not simply because professors are unlikely to admit that any graduate student could do their work that such procedures are, by and large, blind alleys. Political events are too complex for any single variable (or any two variables) to explain very much, particularly since we are dealing with cities that are all part of one nation and, broadly, one culture. (Cultural uniformity is both a blessing and a curse: on the one hand, it makes it possible to "hold constant" many variables while looking at a few critical ones; on the other hand, it reduces—perhaps eliminates—the variation in those variables we do examine.)

Comparative analyses of urban political systems are hard precisely because it is so difficult to specify outcomes. We have become fairly sophisticated about inputs: we have studied the distribution of influence, forms of government, city ecology, and party organization. But we have only begun to suggest what it is that cities *do* that might be affected by these inputs. James Coleman, Maurice Pinard, and others have begun to analyze the incidence of water-fluoridation among various kinds of cities in a way that suggests that the character of the city's regime may have a considerable influence independently of the distribution of preferences among the citizens.[4] Amos Hawley has offered

4. Maurice Pinard, "Structural Attachments and Political Support in Urban Politics: The Case of Fluoridation Referendums," *American Journal of Sociology*, March, 1963, pp. 513–26.

some data concerning the adoption of urban-renewal programs that have the same implication, although his findings are being questioned by some other sociologists.[5] Oliver P. Williams and Charles R. Adrian, in the most ambitious effort thus far to relate regimes to outcomes, have shown some important policy variations—in four middle-sized cities in Michigan—that depend on community differences.[6]

These efforts have not been completely successful. There are several reasons for this, all of them indicative of the difficulties inherent in comparative analysis. Most importantly, the available data on city "inputs" and "outputs" are not readily comparable without extensive reworking. One might assume, for example, that a city's budget would be the most important and most available source of information about what a city does: the ends it serves and the resources it allocates to attain them. In fact, budgets have so far proved to be a poor source of reliable information. Expenditures are differently classified in different cities; functions performed in one city by the general administration are performed in another by an independent board or commission; state and federal grants-in-aid are a large portion of some cities' expenditures and a small portion of others'; and there are great differences in what money will buy (an old, high-density city may spend much more on school construction or police protection and still buy less education or safety than a newer, low-density city, because the costs of equivalent units of such services are functions of, among other things, land values and land uses). Not only is it difficult to know what the figures in budgets mean, but it is problematical whether the budget allows sufficient freedom of action to the politicians to permit them to make any meaningful decisions about resource allocation.[7] Cities are (or think they are) pinched for revenue, so much of which must go for the maintenance of "essential" services that little, if anything, is left over for new programs. (This fact in itself is important, for in principle many of these services are not "essential" in the sense that government must administer them or, if government does administer them, that it must pay for them out of tax revenue. One might have thought that their high degree of local autonomy would have encouraged at least a few cities in America to experiment more than they have with user charges or private management.)

The systematic data on inputs are in only slightly better form. The *Municipal Yearbook,* for example, conceals more than it reveals by its

5. "Community Power and Urban Renewal Success," *ibid.,* January, 1963, pp. 422–31. Hawley's findings have been challenged in Bruce C. Straits, "Community Adoption and Implementation of Urban Renewal," *ibid.,* July 1965, pp. 77–82.

6. Oliver P. Williams and Charles R. Adrian, *Four Cities* (Philadelphia: University of Pennsylvania Press, 1963).

7. Cf. the account of budget-making in New York City given in Lillian Ross, "$1,031,961,754.73," in Oliver P. Williams and Charles Press (eds.), *Democracy in Urban America* (Chicago: Rand McNally, 1961), pp. 418–35.

classification of some cities as "partisan" and some as "nonpartisan." (Boston and Chicago are "nonpartisan" in an utterly different sense from Los Angeles or Detroit; many writers have explained why this is so, but there seems as yet to be no way of using better categories for the kind of routine but essential fact-gathering service that the International City Managers' Association performs for us). Election data are in even worse shape. Efforts are now under way to put the collection of local election data on a more systematic basis, but the task that confronts the brave scholars who are trying to effect this change makes the job Richard Scammon did for national and state voting statistics simple by comparison. As long as the citizens of Los Angeles, for example, refuse to accommodate scholars by adopting a small-ward system for tabulating votes, the scholars will have to do electoral analysis by using as the basic unit either one city of 2.5 million or several thousand precincts of a few hundred people each. But at least in Los Angeles you know where the precincts are. In some other large cities, precinct lines change frequently between elections, but nobody in the cities seems to have kept track of what these changes have been.

Even if input and output data could be put into usable form, it is not at all clear what they would show. The most obvious indicators of the quality of life in our cities —per capita income, median school years completed, home ownership, morbidity rate, participation in cultural activities—are not much affected by the form or functioning of city government.[8] The American city is not Aristotle's self-sufficient city-state; the life chances of an American city dweller are much more the function of aggregate national and regional factors (economic growth, the structure of the labor market, national security) than of factors over which local officials and "power structures" have much control. It would be hard to sustain the argument that the distribution of those things *most* important to *most* people is greatly affected by the distribution of power in the community. It is not by any means clear that much can be said even about those things that concern the "attentive elite" in our cities—such as the efficiency of municipal services. The measurement of municipal services has made little progress since Herbert Simon and Clarence Ridley first (unsuccessfully) tried it, the reason being that the services supplied by different cities and the tastes of the consumers in different cities are rarely the same.[9]

8. Cf. Edward C. Banfield and James Q. Wilson, *City Politics* (Cambridge, Mass.: Harvard University Press, 1963), pp. 329–46.

9. Clarence Ridley and Herbert Simon, *Measuring Municipal Activities* (Chicago: International City Managers' Association, 1938) and Alice Vandermeulen, "Guideposts for Measuring the Efficiency of Governmental Expenditure," *Public Administration Review*, Winter, 1950, pp. 7–12. Recently, renewed attention has been paid to the problems of criteria, as a result of the effort to apply cost-benefit analysis to municipal services. See the papers in Howard G. Schaller, *Public Expenditure Decisions in the Urban Community* (Washington, D.C.: Resources for the Future, 1963).

In the long run, none of these problems may prove insuperable; and certainly every reasonable effort to develop and refine data sources that are useful in making gross intercity comparisons or helpful as indicators of urban trends ought to be encouraged. Several of my colleagues are energetically pressing the search for gross, "hard data" observables that will make it possible to assert interesting facts about the outcomes of city politics without having, as Norton Long puts it, "to hide under the mayor's bed." It certainly would make for a more efficient and systematic social science of cities if it were possible to answer the important questions by knowing how the data are correlated instead of where the bodies are buried. I am warmly sympathetic to efforts to get the first kind of answers, but I am not optimistic that for the foreseeable future we shall be able to avoid the necessity of disinterring a few political skeletons. A political sociology or even political economy of cities may be the ultimate objective, but a political anthropology is still very much in order.

Input-output analysis in the study of urban politics has made even less progress (if that is possible) than input-output analysis in political science generally. It is still necessary to study the contents of the black box, and not simply to examine what goes in and what comes out. No substitute has yet been found for the intelligent observer who can find the tribal informants and extract from them a rich, complex, and largely subjective account of the lives, values, goals, habits, and methods of the city fathers. We can, however, begin to shift the focus of such research to stress (1) new *objectives* of analysis, (2) new *levels* of analysis, and (3) new *units* of analysis.

The new objectives would emphasize, as I have said before, an effort to explain the outcomes of community politics and government. There are two broad strategies for making this effort. First, one can begin, as Williams and Adrian have done, with a small number of communities that are presumably different in important ways and then seek to understand what differences, if any, in the ends of government action there are among the cities and what aspects of the cities—social, economic, ecological, or political—account for these differences. Finding the differences, though not simple, is of course the easiest part of the investigation. The harder part lies in attributing causation among the enormous number of possible explanations. Solving the problem of identifying the dependent variables (by intensive study of a few communities that one hopes will provide different outcomes) makes it that much harder to solve the problem of specifying the independent variables. The second approach is to find some measure of an outcome (for example, the adoption of an urban-renewal or fluoridation program, the level of welfare or educational expenditures, or the crime rate) and apply that measure to a very large number of cities. The familiar techniques of multivariate and regression analysis would then be used to discover what "input" factors are associated with the variation in the dependent variable. The problem with this approach, as I hope I have made clear by now, is that for most of the interesting outputs we have no reliable measures. We have lots of "measures" (like the FBI Uniform Crime Reports, educational expenditures per pupil in average daily attendance, and net project costs for urban-renewal projects completed or authorized), but nobody knows for sure what any of these "measures" measure. The crime rates are the most notoriously unreliable, but the others are not much better. Solving the problem of specifying the independent variables (by having enough cities in our sample to make statistical techniques useful) makes it that much harder to solve the problem of specifying the content of the dependent variables. The seemingly inevitable gains and losses associated with these two research strategies make me think that there is at work in social science an equivalent of the Heisenberg Uncertainty Principle, such that success in determining the magnitude of one variable precludes the possibility of determining the magnitude of another.

The easy (and conventional) way out of this Hobson's choice is to say that the method one picks depends on the questions one wants to answer, and then to change the subject. This is of course true, but it never really works that way. The method one chooses rarely depends simply on what questions one seeks to answer; it really depends on the personal research style of the investigator, almost regardless of what method is theoretically best.[10] Recognizing this, I am willing to go a bit further than the easy answer and suggest that, at this stage, although much bolder experimentation with aggregate-data analysis is needed, real progress still requires the intensive study of a small number of communities. This is so not simply because it happens to be my research style, but also because intensive "outcome-oriented" research is critically necessary to enable us to learn in detail what the "outcomes" are, how they may be measured (if at all), and what factors *seem* to be causally related to them.

The level, as well as the ends, of analysis should be specified. In principle (and to a considerable extent in practice) there are three possible levels: the individual, the group or organization, and the system. I think it fair to say that almost all the research on urban politics done over the last several years has emphasized the second level.[11] One now can refer to a sizable number of respectable studies on urban party organizations, pressure groups, leadership patterns, "power structures,"

10. A brilliant account of the meaning of theory and research is Michael Polanyi, *Personal Knowledge* (Chicago: University of Chicago Press, 1958), especially chaps. IV, VI, X.

11. The same point I am here making with respect to urban political studies has been made with respect to organizational theory in Peter M. Blau, "The Comparative Study of Organizations" (paper delivered at the annual meeting of the American Political Science Association, Chicago, September, 1964).

and the like. These organizations or groups or cliques, however, operate within a system, constrained not only by the character of the system as a whole but by the preferences of the individuals (voters, members of voluntary associations, newspaper readers, and party workers) whose dispensation (or indifference) is required before action can be concerted toward organizational or community goals. Much more needs to be done at the organizational level; I would be the last to urge anyone to abandon studies of this sort. All kinds of institutions have received only the sketchiest study—newspapers, the more important voluntary and civic associations, and municipal bureaucracies, to name only three obvious examples. Nevertheless, the great void exists at the other two levels: that of the individual and that of the urban political system as a whole.[12]

I do not say this in order to open up a sterile controversy about reductionism in social science. I know there are always a few scholastics around who insist on pointing out for the twentieth time why one cannot (or can) explain collective behavior as the consequence of individual attributes. The point I want to make is somewhat different: analysis entirely at one structural level (a) makes explanations of the outputs of whole systems unlikely and (b) reduces the possibility of comparative study. It has the first deficiency because it does not take into account the constraints (or, from another perspective, opportunities) facing organizations; it has the second because the study of a single institution or organization almost invariably leads the research deeper and deeper into the organization and farther and farther away from those *gross* characteristics of the organization that distinguish it from others in the same community or indicate its similarity to comparable organizations in other communities. There is no inevitable reason why this should be so except for the very real fact that knowledge tends to come in dissertation-sized chunks; trying to force a graduate student who has learned enough about one organization to satisfy his thesis committee to go out and do the same thing on a similar organization in a different city is widely regarded as an unfair labor practice.

Despite the popularity of survey and electoral research during the last fifteen or twenty years, little of this research has been done on cities. This is not surprising; cities have rarely been the arena in which momentous national issues are fought out. The current civil-rights con-

12. There are some conspicuous exceptions. Edward C. Banfield, *Political Influence* (New York: Free Press, 1961) not only analyzes the behavior of some of the principal organizations involved in Chicago politics but discusses the consequences for public policy of the distribution of influence in the community as a whole. Robert A. Dahl, *Who Governs?* (New Haven: Yale University Press, 1961) combines an analysis of organizations and elites with a study of voter attitudes and political participation. The forthcoming study of southern Negroes by Donald Matthews and James Prothro uses survey and local-informant data in combination to show the relationship between the distribution of attitudes and the level of organizational activity in various communities.

troversy may change all this. One continuing difficulty, of course, has been that a principal source of funds—the federal government—has not in the past been anxious to sponsor research that had as its major categories ethnicity and religion, and that was explicitly directed toward political questions in some congressman's district.

There is reason to believe that some of these constraints will be relaxed or got around. The important thing, however, is to decide what questions are worth asking of local voters. It seems to me that the city is the best place to explore the kinds of attachments citizens have to the polity—their sense of obligation or duty, their conception of the public interest, and the extent to which (or the circumstances in which) their preferences in community programs are the product of rational self-interest or of learned cultural norms.[13] These are difficult questions to answer in any circumstances; but they are doubly so when the question at issue is stated in general terms, resolved in a remote place, and experienced only indirectly—in short, when it is a "momentous national issue." It is the very ordinariness of local concerns—garbage collection, police protection, street repair, school programs—that make them valuable as tools to explore the nature of citizenship and civility. These services are directly experienced, their quality is (in principle) calculable in terms of narrow self-interest, and they are paid for by a variety of interesting tax and revenue procedures that have a very uneven incidence.

Furthermore, survey and electoral analyses done intensively in one or a few cities permit heavy sampling of certain groups that are more thinly dispersed in the national population—Negroes, Italians, Poles, and Jews, for example—and about which our knowledge is largely fragmentary and impressionistic. (Our understanding of middle-class Negroes has not kept pace with our interest in them, in part because they are such tiny portions of random national samples.) Survey research can help us to understand the city in a way that, until now, we have not; but the help will be limited unless some professional constraints are eased. The drive for impeccable technique has progressed at the expense of substantive knowledge, precisely because (among other reasons) the most interesting questions are the most difficult to phrase and code. (One valuable source of survey data about urban politics—the Detroit Area Study—has not fully realized its promise, largely, I think, because it has not asked very interesting questions; and it has not done so, I would guess, in part because the answers to such questions are extraordinarily difficult to handle in a routinized and easily replicable manner.) It has been said before but I

13. Edward C. Banfield and I have explored some of these matters, using data from municipal referenda elections, in "Public-Regardingness as a Value Premise in Voting Behavior," *American Political Science Review,* December, 1964, pp. 876–87. We are now testing some of these hypotheses by means of interviewing.

will say it again: we need to exploit more fully the techniques of Samuel Lubell and David Riesman before we can decide to what extent the techniques of the Survey Research Center are applicable.

The urban political system is, like the individual, a level of analysis where the need at present is for less rather than more rigor.[14] (The level of organizational analysis is one where *more* rigor—or at least more effort at being systematic—is required.) By "urban political system" I mean something rather simple—for example, in what politically important respects do the growing cities of the Southwest differ from the stagnant or declining cities of the Northeast? What difference to politics do the facts of affluence, a rapid increase in population and land values, and an in-migration of already acculturated, middle-class families (instead of alien, lower-class families) make?[15] What important differences does city size make in the issues that arise and in the manner in which those issues are resolved (or not resolved)?[16] What have been the secular trends for different kinds of cities over the last half-century? (Several fascinating changes suggest themselves, but they have largely been ignored in contemporary research. Not very long ago, in any strike the police were automatically on the side of business; today the police are either neutral or—in some cases—on the side of the unions. Not long ago, known thieves running on pro-thievery platforms could be elected to high municipal office; today, hardly any *known* thieves stand a chance.)

Analyzing urban political systems as systems cannot be done simply by trying to look at the system "whole," for there are always as many "wholes" as there are observers. Furthermore, it may be that not all of urban politics has the character of a "system"—that is, of a set of interdependent variables. Attention must therefore be given to the appropriate *units* of analysis. Most recently, the unit employed by the political scientist has been the *issue*, and that employed by some (though by no means all) sociologists has been the *elite*. As we all know by now, these differences (among others) have led to different research findings. Looking at issues—i.e., at conflict—one is more likely to find pluralism, contention, and bargaining. Looking for elites, one is more likely to *find* elites (i.e., persons who possess a disproportionate share of some resource, such as income, prestige, or putative power). Having recognized this, I do not feel that truth lies in eclecticism.

14. On the subject of comparative urban studies, see the excellent treatment in H. Douglas Price, "Comparative Analysis in State and Local Politics: Potential and Problems" (paper presented before the annual meeting of the American Political Science Association, New York City, September, 1963).

15. *Ibid.*, pp. 17–20, and H. Douglas Price, review of *Who Governs?* in *Yale Law Journal*, July, 1962, especially pp. 1094–95.

16. The subject has been opened up by James G. Coke, "The Lesser Metropolitan Areas of Illinois," *Illinois Government* (published by the Institute of Government and Public Affairs, University of Illinois), no. 15, November, 1962.

Using both methods simultaneously may only add the errors of one to the shortcomings of the other. I happen to believe that the issue-oriented approach is, in most circumstances, the most fruitful one— in part because American cities, to a greater extent than cities almost anywhere else, are engaged in managing conflict; in part because many of the crucial features of a system are best seen under conditions of strain and conflict; and in part because asking people who they think is "powerful," no matter how carefully the findings are subsequently validated, is at best a waste of time and at worst misleading.

The real difficulty with the issue-oriented approach is not that it is wrong but that it leaves a great deal unsaid. Some communities produce few, if any, obvious issues.[17] In other communities, certain matters do *not* become issues because some group that can influence the civic agenda manages to suppress certain demands; these "non-issues" may be even more interesting than the problems that do find a place on the agenda.[18] Furthermore, in any city, what is of greatest importance to the daily lives of the citizens and most influential in the conduct of American government as a whole may not be issues at all but may instead be certain services and institutions that are largely taken for granted.

I suggest that the most challenging area for new research on cities is to take as the unit of analysis the routine behavior of the city as it provides certain services or as it conducts its political affairs. Three examples of such units are the system of justice, the educational system, and the welfare system.

The system of justice—and my early research suggests that it *is* a system and not simply a collection of institutions such as courts, prosecutors, and police officers—should be examined as a means by which the community exemplifies and enforces its normative codes. The system of justice, I suspect, is best seen not in the highly publicized murder trial but in the routine disposition of drunks, vagrants, shoplifters, auto thieves, and fornicators.

The problem in examining education is not to justify its importance (that, I take it, is obvious) but to find some way of assessing its output. If professional school administrators cannot tell us how to recognize good as opposed to poor education or how to measure how "much" education we are producing, then political scientists concerned with the outome of urban governmental arrangements cannot be blamed

17. Cf. Arthur Vidich and Joseph Bensman, *Small Town in Mass Society* (Princeton, N.J.: Princeton University Press, 1958), chaps. V–VIII, and James S. Coleman, *Community Conflict* (Glencoe, Ill.: Free Press, 1959).

18. See Peter Bachrach and Morton S. Baratz, "Decisions and Nondecisions: An Analytical Framework," *American Political Science Review*, September, 1963, pp. 632–42, especially pp. 641–42, and Banfield, *Political Influence*, pp. 9-10.

for avoiding the field for so long.[19] Nonetheless, interesting issues remain. How, and by what criteria, are educational resources allocated among various groups and neighborhoods within the community? How is the distribution of influence within the school system related to the kinds of subjects and the types of students taught? If taxable income and teachable children continue to abandon the central city, what alternatives exist for the management of America's great experiment with mass education under public auspices?

The politics of welfare programs in our cities ought to be broadly conceived, to include not only the conventional forms of public assistance and relief but all measures by which the city government, implicitly or explicitly, seeks to redistribute income. The larger and older central cities are, in some cases, well on their way to becoming the urban equivalents of Indian reservations in which perpetual wards of the state are subsidized by a system of "welfare colonialism" that creates serious problems (e.g., subsidizing broken homes) while solving others (e.g., preventing starvation). We know little of how (or by whom) the goals of these programs are set, how politics intervenes (if at all) in the administration of these programs, or how the level of welfare expenditures differs from city to city. New programs in the welfare field, such as federally sponsored "community action" organizations in lower-class neighborhoods, raise interesting questions about the sort of incentives necessary to mobilize the impoverished; the implications of these incentives for the goals and tactics of the organizations; and the propriety of using public revenues to support a program that, at least in some cities, consists very largely of organized political and civic action directed *against* the governmental institutions that are paying the bill.

Thinking back over all this, I suspect I may have emphasized more than I meant to the need for goal-oriented comparative research on cities. There are, I should like to repeat, many intellectually interesting questions that, if answered, do not necessarily illuminate the question of outcomes. (No one, by the way, has to my knowledge ever proposed a satisfactory set of criteria for distinguishing intellectually interesting from intellectually uninteresting questions. Maybe that is because devising such criteria does not seem intellectually interesting.) Understanding politics, a very difficult subject to comprehend, is intrinsically satisfying; and it needs no other justification than that. I here emphasize the ends of community action, not because there is no other way to do research, but because I feel political science has, in some degree, a peculiar mission and competence: to think simultaneously about the quality of the ends that are served and the reasons

19. A fruitful beginning was made almost thirty years ago; but, until the Syracuse studies were begun, no one tried to follow it up. See Nelson B. Henry and Jerome G. Kerwin, *Schools and City Government* (Chicago: University of Chicago Press, 1938).

why those ends, and not others, are in fact served.[20] But also I feel that a preoccupation with outcomes is the most meaningful way to do comparative research, that it is a preoccupation closest to the subjective states of the principal actors in politics, and that it directs attention to "high stakes" matters rather than "low stakes" matters. Although we have had a number of studies about community conflict that have told us something about how urban renewal or fluoridation programs are enacted or defeated, in the long run these programs may turn out to be trivial, or very nearly so.[21] For most people, the stakes are low (even for the most involved actors, the stakes may be as much the fun of playing a civic game as a real concern with the outcome). Those matters over which the community has any significant control that have high stakes for most of us are few compared to those found at the national level; but they include how our children are educated, how our taxes are levied, how (and to what end) our poor are supported, how the use of our land is controlled, and how (and in whose behalf) our criminal laws are enforced. To a great extent, they include many of the matters that, taken together, make up some significant part of what we mean when we speak of civility. And that, I feel, is not an unworthy subject.

20. The current functionalist approach to comparative government has recently been criticized, in a similar way, for failing to use policy as an explicit variable: Roy Pierce, "Comparative Politics: Liberty and Policy as Variables," *American Political Science Review*, September, 1963, pp. 655–60.

21. This does not mean that nothing significant can be learned from such issues. Two important "single city" studies have been done on urban-renewal politics: Peter Rossi and Robert Dentler, *The Politics of Urban Renewal: The Chicago Findings* (New York: Free Press, 1961) and Harold Kaplan, *Urban Renewal Politics: Slum Clearance in Newark* (New York: Columbia University Press, 1963).

The Management
of Metropolitan Conflict

Edward C. Banfield

THE RAPID GROWTH of the metropolitan populations will not necessarily have much political effect. To be sure, many new facilities, especially schools, highways, and water supply and sewage disposal systems, will have to be built and much private activity will have to be regulated. But such things do not necessarily have anything to do with politics: the laying of a sewer pipe by a "public" body may involve the same kinds of behavior as the manufacture of the pipe by a "private" one. Difficulties that are "political" arise (and they may arise in "private" as well as in "public" undertakings) only in so far as there is conflict— conflict over what the common good requires or between what it requires and what private interests want. The general political situation is affected, therefore, not by changes in population density or in the number and complexity of the needs that government serves ("persons," the human organisms whose noses are counted by census-takers, are not necessarily "political actors") but rather by actions which increase conflict in matters of public importance or make the management of it more difficult. In what follows, such actions will be called "burdens" upon the political system.

In judging how a political system will work over time, increases and decreases in the burdens upon it are obviously extremely relevant. They are not all that must be considered, however. Changes in the "capability" of a system, that is, in its ability to manage conflict and to impose settlements, are equally relevant. The "effectiveness" of a political system is a ratio between burdens and capability. Even though the burdens upon it increase, the effectiveness of a system will also increase if there is a sufficient accompanying increase in its capability. Similarly, even though there is an inrease in capability, the effectiveness of a system will decrease if there is a more than commensurate increase in burdens.

Reprinted by permission from DAEDALUS, The Journal of the American Academy of Arts and Sciences, *Vol. 90 (Winter 1960), pp. 61–78.*

In this article an impressionistic account will be given with respect to two contrasting political systems, the British and the American, of the burdens metropolitan affairs place upon them and of their changing capabilities. Naturally, the focus of attention will be upon *ratios* of burdens to capabilities and upon the significance of these ratios for metropolitan affairs.

The Tasks of British Local Government

Until recently British local government (meaning not only government that is locally controlled but all government that deals with local affairs) had, by American standards, very little to do. Until three or four years ago there was little traffic regulation in Britain because there were few cars (the first few parking meters, all set for two hours, were installed in London in the summer of 1958). Now all of a sudden there are 5,500,000 cars—more per mile of road than in any other country—and the number is increasing by a net of 1,500 per day; by 1975 there are expected to be 13,500,000. Obviously, the need for roads and parking places will be enormous. But the automobile will create other and graver problems for local government. When there are enough cars and highways, there will doubtless be a "flight to the suburbs." The central business districts will be damaged, and so will mass transit (94 percent of those who now enter London do so by public transportation) and the green belts.[1]

Law enforcement has been relatively easy in Britain up to now. The British have not been culturally disposed toward violence or toward the kinds of vice that lead to major crimes. (There are only 450 dope addicts in all of Britain, whereas in Chicago alone there are from 12,000 to 15,000.) British opinion, moreover, has not demanded that some forms of vice be made illegal, much less that vice in general be suppressed. In England adultery is not illegal, and neither is prostitution, although it is illegal to create a nuisance by soliciting. Physicians in England may prescribe dope to addicts. (In the United States, where this is illegal, black-market prices prevail and the addict must usually resort to crime

1. Dame Evelyn Sharp, Permanent Secretary, Ministry of Housing and Local Government, recently pointed out that the expected population increase in England and Wales in the next 15 years (nearly three million) is almost double the increase on which plans have been based. The number of separate households, moreover, is growing faster than the number of people. Much of the demand for new housing, she said, is demand for better and more spacious housing. All this has increased the pressure on land, especially on the green belt, and particularly around London. The Government policy, she said, was to encourage the building of houses for owner occupation, and how to follow this without wrecking the effort to preserve the green belt was one of the most difficult problems facing the planning authorities. She said there were also increasing demands on land by industry, for great new roads, car parking and garaging and for power. *The Times,* 23 October 1959.

to support his habit. In Chicago a week's supply of heroin costs at least $105; to realize this much, the addict must steal goods worth about $315. According to the estimate of a criminal court judge, about $50 million worth of goods is shoplifted every year in the central business district of Chicago by addicts.[2]) Never having tried to suppress drinking, gambling, or prostitution, the British have no organized crime.

The task of law enforcement is also becoming more difficult, however. Dope addiction, and consequently crimes of violence, will increase with the number of West Indians and others who are not culturally at home in England. In the past year the horde of London prostitutes has been driven underground, where they may prove a powerful force tending toward the corruption of the police.[3] As traffic fines increase in number and amount, the bribery of the police by motorists will also increase. "All Britain's big cities," an *Observer* writer recently said, "now have enclaves of crime where the major masculine trades appear to be pimping and dealing in dubious second-hand cars."[4]

Even if motorists, dope addicts, and prostitutes do not seriously corrupt it, the police force is bound to deteriorate. The British have had extraordinarily fine policemen, partly because their social system has hitherto offered the working class few better opportunities. As it becomes easier to rise out of the working class, the police force will have to get along with less desirable types. It is significant that the Metropolitan Police are now 3,000 men short.

State-supported schooling, one of the heaviest tasks of local government in the United States, has been a comparatively easy one in Britain. Four out of five British children leave school before the age of 16. The British, it is said, are not likely to develop a taste for mass education.[5] They are demanding more and better state-supported schools, however, and no doubt the government will have to do more in this field.

It would be wrong to infer that because of these changes the burden upon the British political system will henceforth be comparable to that upon our own or, indeed, that it will increase at all. Conceivably, the new tasks of local government will have no more political significance than would, say, a doubling of the volume of mail to be carried by the post office. One can imagine, for example, two opposite treatments of the London traffic problem, one of which would solve the problem with-

2. These facts were supplied by Dr. Arnold Abrams of Chicago in a private communication.

3. The Wolfenden Committee considered this possibility and concluded that the measures it proposed (chiefly to make it easier for police officers to establish "annoyance") justified the risk. Its measures, the Committee said, were not "likely to result in markedly increased corruption. There are other fields of crime where the temptation to the police to succumb to bribery is, and will continue to be, much stronger than it is here." *Report of the Committee on Homosexual Offenses and Prostitution,* Cmnd. 247, September 1957, p. 96.

4. "Table Talk," *The Observer,* 15 May 1960.

5. Sir Geoffrey Crowther, "English and American Education," *The Atlantic,* April 1960.

out creating any burden upon the political system and the other of which would leave the problem unsolved while creating a considerable burden.

Possibility 1. The Ministry of Transport takes jurisdiction over London traffic. Acting on the recommendations of a Royal Commission, the Minister declares that the central city will be closed to private automobiles. His decision is acclaimed as wise and fair—"the only thing to do"—by everyone who matters.

Possibility 2. The boroughs retain their control over traffic because the Minister is mindful of organized motorists. People feel that it is an outrageous infringement of the rights of Englishmen to charge for parking on the Queen's highway or to fine a motorist without having first served a summons upon him in the traditional manner. Traffic is unregulated, and everyone complains bitterly.

As this suggests, "governmental tasks" are "political burdens" only if public opinion makes them so. What would be an overwhelming burden in one society may not be any burden at all in another. What would not be a burden upon a particular political system at one time may become one at another. It is essential to inquire, therefore, what changes are occurring in the way such matters are usually viewed in Great Britain and in the United States. The factors that are particularly relevant in this connection include: the intensity with which ends are held and asserted; the willingness of actors to make concessions, to subordinate private to public interests, and to accept arbitration; and, finally, the readiness of the voters to back the government in imposing settlements.

The Relation of Citizen to Government

The British have a very different idea from ours of the proper relation between government and citizens. They believe that it is the business of the government to govern. The voter may control the government by giving or withholding consent, but he may not participate in its affairs. The leader of the majority in the London County Council, for example, has ample power to carry into effect what he and his policy committee decide upon; it is taken for granted that he will make use of his power (no one will call him a boss for doing so) and that he will not take advice or tolerate interference from outsiders.

Locally as well as nationally, British government has been in the hands of the middle and upper classes. Civil servants, drawn of course entirely from the middle class, have played leading and sometimes dominant roles. Most elected representatives have been middle or upper class. The lower class has not demanded, and apparently has not wanted, to be governed by its own kind or to have what in the United States is called "recognition." Although Labour has controlled the London County Council since 1934, there have never been in the

Council any such gaudy representatives of the gutter as, for example, Alderman "Paddy" Bauler of Chicago. The unions have kept people with lower-class attributes, and sometimes people of lower-class origins as well, off the ballot. They would not have done so, of course, if the lower class had had a powerful itch to have its own kind in office. (In that case the unions would themselves have been taken over by the lower class.) As Bagehot said in explaining "deferential democracy," "the numerical majority is ready, is eager to delegate its power of choosing its ruler to a certain select minority."[6]

The ordinary man's contact with government inspires him with awe and respect. (Is government respected because it pertains to the upper classes, or does causality run the other way, the upper classes being respected because of their association with government?) "The English workingman," an Englishman who read an earlier draft of this article said, "seems to think that the assumption of governmental responsibilities calls for the solemnest of blue suits. They tend to be so overawed by their position as to be silenced by it."

The ethos of governing bodies, then, has been middle or upper class, even when most of their members have been lower class. So has that of the ordinary citizen when, literally or figuratively, he has put on his blue suit to discharge his "governmental responsibilities" at the polls.

Consequently the standards of government have been exclusively those of the middle and upper classes. There has been great concern for fair play, great respect for civil rights, and great attention to public amenities—all matters dear to middle- and upper-class hearts. At the same time there has been entire disregard for the convenience and tastes of the working man. London pubs, for example, are required by law to close from two until six in the afternoon, not, presumably, because no one gets thirsty between those hours or because drinking then creates a special social problem, but merely because the convenience of pub keepers (who would have to remain open if competition were allowed to operate) is placed above that of their customers. Similarly, trains and buses do not leave the center of London after eleven at night, not presumably, because no one wants to go home later, but because the people who make the rules deem it best for those who cannot afford taxis to get to bed early.

It is not simply class prejudice that accounts for these things. By common consent of the whole society the tastes of the individual count for little against prescriptive rights. When these rights pertain to the body politic—to the Crown, in the mystique—then the tastes of the individual may be disregarded entirely. Public convenience becomes everything, private convenience nothing.

As heirs of this tradition, the British town planners are in a fortunate position. They do not have to justify their schemes by consumers' preferences. It is enough for them to show that "public values"

6. Walter Bagehot, *The English Constitution,* ch. IX.

are served, for by common consent any gain in a public value, however small, outweighs any loss of consumers' satisfaction, however large. Millions of acres of land outside of London were taken to make a green belt without anyone's pointing out that workingmen are thus prevented from having small places in the country and that rents in the central city are forced up by the reduction in the supply of land. It is enough that a public amenity is being created (an amenity, incidentally, which can be enjoyed only by those having time and money to go out of London). The planning authorities of the London County Council, to cite another example of the general disregard for consumers' tastes, consider the following questions, among others, when they pass upon an application to erect a structure more than 100 feet in height:

> Would it spoil the skyline of architectural groups or landscapes? Would it have a positive visual or civic significance? Would it relate satisfactorily to open spaces and the Thames? Would its illuminations at night detract from London's night scene?

It is safe to say that the planners do not weigh the value of a gain in "visual significance" against the value of a loss in "consumer satisfaction." In all probability they do not try to discover what preferences the consumer actually has in the matter. Certainly they do not make elaborate market analyses such as are customarily used in the United States in planning not only shopping places but even public buildings.

Green belts and the control of the use of land are only part of a plan of development which includes the creation of a dozen satellite towns, "decanting" the population of the metropolis, and much else. Where these sweeping plans have not been realized, it has not been because of political opposition. There has been virtually no opposition to any of these undertakings. The real estate, mercantile, banking, taxpayer, and labor union interests, which in an American city would kill such schemes before they were started, have not even made gestures of protest. The reason is not that none of them is adversely affected. It is that opposition would be futile.[7]

The Direction of Change

Obviously, a political system that can do these things can do much else besides. If the relation between government and citizen in the next half century is as it has been in the past, the "govern-

7. An English friend comments: "I think you underestimate the sensitivity of central government to local or even private pressures. Parliamentary questions and debates, M.P.s' correspondence, lobbying, etc., provide plenty of opportunity for needling Ministers. The difference [between American and British practice] is, I think, that in Britain the government is not necessarily deflected by the pressures although it does its best to placate them. It does *not* ride rough-shod over protests; it lumbers on, writhing under the criticism and dispensing half-baked compromises."

mental tasks" that were spoken of above will not prove to be "political burdens" of much weight. One can hardly doubt, for example, which of the two ways of handling London traffic would, on this assumption, be more probable.

There is reason to think, however, that fundamental changes are occurring in the relations between government and citizen. Ordinary people in Britain are entering more into politics, and public opinion is becoming more ebullient, restive, and assertive. The lower class no longer feels exaggerated respect for its betters,[8] and if, as seems reasonable to assume, respect for public institutions and for political things has been in some way causally connected with respect for the governing classes, the ordinary man's attachment to his society may be changing in a very fundamental way. British democracy is still deferential, but it is less so than a generation ago, and before long it may be very little so.

It would not be surprising if the lower class were soon to begin wanting to have its own kind in office. Lower-class leaders would not necessarily be less mindful of the common good and of the principles of fair play than are the present middle and upper class ones, however. The ethos of the British lower class may not be as different from that of the other classes as we in America, judging others by ourselves, are likely to imagine.

There is in Britain a tendency to bring the citizen closer to the process of government. Witness, for example, a novel experiment (as the *Times* described it) tried recently by an urban district council. At the conclusion of its monthly meeting, the council invited the members of the public present (there were about twenty) to ask questions. According to the *Times:*[9]

> The Council, having decided to cast themselves into the arms of the electorate, had obviously given some thought to how they could extricate themselves if the hug became an uncomfortable squeeze. The chairman, after expressing the hope that the experiment would be successful, suggested a few rules. It was undesirable, he said, that such a meeting should become an ordinary debate with members of the public debating with members of the council and perhaps members of the council debating with each other. He decreed that the public should be restricted to questions on policy or factual information. He finished the preliminaries by saying that if things got out of hand he would rise and would then expect all further discussion to cease.
>
> This last precaution proved to be unnecessary. The public were

8. Such an incident as the following, which is supposed to have occurred about the time of the First World War, would be inconceivable today: Hulme [the poet] was making water in Soho Square in broad daylight when a policeman came up. "You can't do that here." Hulme: "Do you realize you're addressing a member of the middle class?" at which the policeman murmured, "Beg pardon, sir," and went on his beat. Christopher Hassall, *Edward Marsh, Patron of the Arts: A Biography* (London, Longmans, Green and Company, 1959), p. 187.

9. The *Times,* 24 November 1959.

pertinent, probing, and shrewd in their questions, but content to observe the proprieties. The more vexed of domestic questions of Nantwich (the demolition of old property, road repairs, housing, and the like) were thrown down quickly and in every case received reasoned replies. The atmosphere of the chamber continued to be one of high good humor.

Carried far enough, this kind of thing would lead to the radical weakening of government. (There is no use giving people information unless you are going to listen to their opinions. And if you do that, you are in trouble, for their opinions are not likely to be on public grounds, and they are virtually certain to conflict.) The British are not likely to develop a taste for what in American cant is called "grass-roots democracy," however; the habit of leaving things to the government and of holding the government responsible is too deeply ingrained for that. What the public wants is not the privilege of participating in the process of government but, as the Franks Committee said, "openness, fairness, and impartiality" in official proceedings.[10]

The tastes of the ordinary man (consumers' preferences) will be taken more into account in the future than they have been in the past, not because the ordinary man will demand it (he may in time, but he is far from doing so now) but because the ruling elite—an elite that will be more sophisticated in such things than formerly—will think it necessary and desirable. The efforts of the Conservative government to let the market allocate housing are a case in point. These have been motivated, not by desire to deprive the workingman of advantages he has had for half a century (that would be out of the question), but by awareness that people's tastes may be best served in a market. The cherished green belts are now being scrutinized by people who are aware of consumer demand for living space, and some planners are even beginning to wonder if there is not something to be said for the American system of zoning. It is not beyond the bounds of possibility that the British will exchange their system of controls of the use of land, which as it stands allows the planner to impose a positive conception, for something resembling ours, which permits the user of land to do as he pleases so long as he does not violate a rule of law.

The conclusion seems warranted that twenty or thirty years from now, when today's children have become political actors, governmental tasks which would not place much of a burden on the political system may then place a considerable one on it. Governmental tasks like traffic regulation will be more burdensome politically both because there will be insistent pressure to take a wider range of views and interests into account, but also, and perhaps primarily, because the ruling group will have become convinced that the preferences of

10. *Report of the Committee on Administrative Tribunals and Enquiries,* Cmnd. 218, July 1958.

ordinary people ought to count for a great deal even when "public values" are involved. It is not impossible that the elite may come to attach more importance to the preferences of ordinary people than will the ordinary people themselves.

The Contrasting American Tradition

Local government in the United States presents a sharply contrasting picture. It has been required to do a great deal, and the nature of American institutions and culture has made almost all of its tasks into political burdens.

Although there have always been among us believers in strong central government, our governmental system, as compared to the British, has been extraordinarily weak and decentralized. This has been particularly true of state and local government. The general idea seems to have been that no one should govern, or failing that, that everyone should govern together. The principle of checks and balances and the division of power, mitigated in the Federal government by the great powers of the presidency, were carried to extreme lengths in the cities and states. As little as fifty years ago, most cities were governed by large councils, some of them bicameral, and by mayors who could do little but preside over the councils. There was no such thing as a state administration. Governors were ceremonial figures only, and state governments were mere congeries of independent boards and commissions. Before anything could be done, there had to occur a most elaborate process of give and take (often, alas, in the most literal sense) by which bits and pieces of power were gathered up temporarily, almost momentarily.

It was taken for granted that the ordinary citizen had a right—indeed, a sacred duty—to interfere in the day-to-day conduct of public affairs. Whereas in Britain the press and public have been excluded from the deliberations of official bodies, in the United States it has been common practice to require by law that all deliberations take place in meetings open to the public. Whereas in Britain the electorate is never given an opportunity to pass upon particular projects by vote, in the United States it usually is. In Los Angeles, according to James Q. Wilson, "The strategy of political conflict is more often than not based upon the assumption that the crucial decision will be made not by the City Council of Los Angeles, the Board of Supervisors of the county, or the legislature of the state, but by the voters in a referendum election."[11]

11. James Q. Wilson, *A Report on Politics in Los Angeles,* Joint Center for Urban Studies of Massachusetts Institute of Technology and Harvard University, 1959, pp. 1–13.

Los Angeles is an extreme case, but the general practice of American cities, a practice required by law in many of them, is to get the voters' approval of major expenditures. The New York City government, one of the strongest, is now having to choose between building schools and making other necessary capital expenditures; it cannot do both because the voters of the state have refused to lift the constitutional limit on debt. Such a thing could not happen in London; there all such decisions are made by the authorities, *none of whom is elected at large*.

The government of American cities has for a century been almost entirely in the hands of the working class.[12] This class, moreover, has had as its conception of a desirable political system one in which people are "taken care of" with jobs, favors, and protection, and in which class and ethnic attributes get "recognition." The idea that there are values, such as efficiency, which pertain to the community as a whole and to which the private interests of individuals ought to be subordinated has never impressed the working-class voter.

The right of the citizen to have his wishes, whether for favors, "recognition," or something else, served by local government, has been an aspect of the generally privileged position of the consumer. If the British theory has been that any gain in public amenity, however small, is worth any cost in consumer satisfaction, however large, ours has been the opposite: with us, any gain to the consumer is worth any cost to the public. What the consumer is not willing to pay for is not of much value in our eyes. Probably most Americans believe that if the consumer prefers his automobile to public transportation his taste ought to be respected, even if it means the destruction of the cities.

We have, indeed, gone far beyond the ideal of admitting everyone to participation in government and of serving everyone's tastes. We have made public affairs a game which anyone may play by acting "as if" he has something at stake, and these make-believe interests become subjects of political struggle just as if they were real. "The great game of politics" has for many people a significance of the same sort as, say, the game of business or the game of social mobility. All, in fact, are parts of one big game. The local community, as Norton E. Long has maintained in a brilliant article, may be viewed as an ecology of games: the games serve certain social functions (they provide determinate goals and calculable strategies, for example, and this gives an element of coordination to what would otherwise be a

12. A couple of generations ago politics was literally the principal form of mass entertainment. See Mayor Curley's account of the Piano-Smashing Contest, Peg-leg Russell, the greased-pig snatch and other such goings-on at Caledonian Grove. When the working class could pay more than twenty-five cents for its all-day family outing, it went to Fenway Park and baseball pushed politics into second place. James M. Curley, *I'd Do It Again!* (New York, Prentice Hall, 1957), pp. 54–55.

chaotic pull and haul), but the real satisfaction is in "playing the game."[13]

Since the American political arena is more a playground than a forum, it is not surprising that, despite the expenditure of vast amounts of energy, problems often remain unsolved—after all, what is really wanted is not solutions but the fun of the game. Still less is it surprising that those in authority seldom try to make or impose comprehensive solutions. The mayor of an American city does not think it appropriate for him to do much more than ratify agreements reached by competing interest groups. For example, the mayor of Minneapolis does not, according to a recent report, "actively sponsor anything. He waits for private groups to agree on a project. If he likes it, he endorses it. Since he has no formal power with which to pressure the Council himself, he feels that the private groups must take the responsibility for getting their plan accepted."[14]

American cities, accordingly, seldom make and never carry out comprehensive plans. Plan making is with us an idle exercise, for we neither agree upon the content of a "public interest" that ought to override private ones nor permit the centralization of authority needed to carry a plan into effect if one were made. There is much talk of the need for metropolitan-area planning, but the talk can lead to nothing practical because there is no possibility of agreement on what the "general interest" of such an area requires concretely (whether, for example, it requires keeping the Negroes concentrated in the central city or spreading them out in the suburbs) and because, anyway, there does not exist in any area a government that could carry such plans into effect.[15]

Change in the United States

The relation of the citizen to the government is changing in the United States as it is in Britain. But the direction of our development is opposite to that of the British: whereas their government is becoming more responsive to popular opinion and therefore weaker, ours is becoming less responsive and therefore stronger. In state and

13. Norton E. Long, "The Local Community as an Ecology of Games," *American Journal of Sociology*, 1958, 64: 252.

14. Alan Altshuler, *A Report on Politics in Minneapolis* (Cambridge, Joint Center for Urban Studies of Massachusetts Institute of Technology and Harvard University, 1959), pp. 11–14. The writer has described the posture of Mayor Daley of Chicago, the undisputed boss of a powerful machine, in similar terms. This suggests that it is not lack of power so much as a sense of what is seemly that prevents American mayors from taking a strong line. See E. C. Banfield, *Political Influence* (New York, The Free Press, 1961), ch. 9.

15. See E. C. Banfield and M. Grodzins, *Government and Housing in Metropolitan Areas,* (New York, McGraw-Hill, 1958), esp. chs. 3 and 4.

local government this trend has been under way for more than a generation and it has carried far. Two-thirds of our smaller cities are now run by professional managers, who, in routine matters at least, act without much interference. In the large central cities, mayors have wider spheres of authority than they did a generation ago, much more and much better staff assistance (most of them have deputies for administrative management), and greater freedom from the electorate. These gains are in most cases partly offset, and in some perhaps more than partly, by the decay of party machines, which could turn graft, patronage, and other "gravy" into political power, albeit power that was seldom used to public advantage.

Reformers in America have struggled persistently to strengthen government by overcoming the fragmentation of formal authority which has afflicted it from the beginning. The council manager system, the executive budget, metropolitan area organization—these have been intended more to increase the ability of government to get things done (its capability, in the terminology used above) than to make it less costly or less corrupt.[16]

One of the devices by which power has been centralized and the capability of government increased is the special function district or authority. We now commonly use authorities to build and manage turnpikes, airports and ports, redevelopment projects and much else. They generally come into being because the jurisdictions of existing general-purpose governments do not coincide with the areas for which particular functions must be administered. But if this reason for them did not exist, they would have to be created anyway, for they provide a way of escaping to a considerable extent the controls and interferences under which government normally labors. The authority, as a rule, does not go before the electorate or even the legislature; it is exempt from the usual civil-service requirements, budget controls, and auditing, and it is privileged to conduct its affairs out of sight of the public.

The success of all these measures to strengthen government is to be explained by the changing class character of the urban electorate. The lower-class ideal of government, which recognized no community larger than the ward and measured advantages only in favors, "gravy," and nationality "recognition," has almost everywhere gone out of fashion. To be a Protestant and a Yankee is still a political handicap in every large Northern city, but to be thought honest, public-spirited, and in some degree statesmanlike is now essential. (John E. Powers, the candidate expected by everyone to win the 1959 Boston mayoralty election, lost apparently because he fitted too well an image of the Irish politician that the Irish electorate found embarrassing and wanted to repudiate.) Many voters still want "nationality recognition," it has

16. See Don K. Price, "The Promotion of the City Manager Plan," *Public Opinion Quarterly,* Winter 1941, pp. 563–578.

been re
follow
who h
those
Irish,
and
to th
Ang

val
of
at-

ir
a

Puerto ...llbillies creates a crosscurrent of some
importa... n, at least, these newcomers will prefer
the old ...ward boss and his "gravy train." How this
anomaly ...ger pattern of middle-class politics is hard
to imag... er class will simply be denied representation.
And po... crease of per capita income being what it
is, the a... people into the middle class will take place
faster t... imagines.

Conclusions

...gued in this paper that the tasks a government
must p... mber and complexity of goods and services it
must su... ecessary relation to political matters. Tasks may
increas... mpanying increase in the burden placed upon a
politica... important questions for political analysis, therefore, c... ulation density or other indicators of the demand
for goo... s, but rather the amount and intensity of conflict
and th... the government for managing it. Looked at from
this st... ppears that the effectiveness of British government
in mat... concern will probably decrease somewhat over the
long ru... nds that will be made upon it in the next generation
will be... burdensome than those of the recent past (although
also v... urdensome than the same demands would be in
Americ... e capacity of the government will be somewhat less.
The e... s of local government in the United States, on the
other ... probably increase somewhat. Local government has
had m... to perform here than in Britain, and these have imposed
enorm... ater burdens. The tasks of local government will doubtless i... ere too in the next generation, but the burdens they
impos... obably decline. American local government is becoming
strong... readier to assert the paramountcy of the public interest,
real o... d.
A... h each system has moved a considerable distance in the
directi... the other, they remain far apart and each retains its
origin... aracter. The British, although more sensitive to public
opinio... ll believe that the government should govern. And we,
althou... cknowledging that the development of metropolitan areas
shoul... planned, still believe that everyone has a right to "get in on
the a... nd to make his influence felt. Obviously, the differences are
cruci... nd although the trend seems to be toward greater effectiveness
here ... l toward reduced effectiveness in Britain, there can be no
doubt... at in absolute terms the effectiveness of the British system is

and will remain far greater than that of ours. Despite the increase in the tasks it must perform, the burden upon it will remain low by American standards, and its capability will remain high. Matters which would cause great political difficulty here will probably be easily settled there.

The basic dynamic principle in both systems has not been change in population density but rather change in class structure. It is the relaxation of the bonds of status that has caused the British workingman to enter more into politics, that has made his tastes and views count for more, and that has raised questions about the right of an elite to decide matters. In America the assimilation of the lower class to the middle class and the consequent spread of an ideal of government which stresses honesty, impartiality, efficiency, and regard for public as well as private interest have encouraged the general strengthening of government.

The mere absence of dispute, acrimony, unworkable compromise, and stalemate (this, after all, is essentially what the concept "effectiveness" refers to in this connection) ought not, of course, to be taken as constituting a "good" political order. Arrogant officials may ignore the needs and wishes of ordinary citizens, and the ordinary citizens may respectfully acquiesce in their doing so, either because they think (as the British lower class does) that the gentleman knows best or (as the American middle does) that the expert knows best. In such cases there may be great effectiveness—no dispute, no acrimony, no unworkable compromise, no stalemate—but far from signifying that the general welfare is being served, such a state of affairs signifies instead that the needs and wishes with which welfare under ordinary circumstances, especially in matters of local concern, is largely concerned are not being taken into account. To say, then, that our system is becoming somewhat more and the British system somewhat less effective does not by any means imply "improvement" for us and the opposite for them. It is quite conceivable that dispute, acrimony, unworkable compromise, and stalemate may be conspicuous features of any situation that approximates the idea of general welfare.

Such conclusions, resting as they do on rough and, at best, common-sense assessments, amply illustrate the difficulty of prediction, and—since the causal principles lie deep in social structure and in culture—the utter impossibility within a free society of a foresighted control of such matters.

II

Urban Government in the Federal System

In a country as vast as the United States, a central government cannot very well carry on all public affairs. Some functions must be performed on a local basis and some on a more-than-local-but-less-than-national one. But although some such division of labor may be an evident necessity, the principles of it—and still less the concrete application of the principles—have never been easy to decide upon. Where the boundaries of the local and of the more-than-local-but-less-than-national jurisdictions should be drawn and what activities should be carried on within each of them are questions that have had to be agitated, discussed, and settled anew by each generation. The rate of social change, as well as the nature of the change, has made impossible any permanent or generally satisfactory answers.

Everyone agrees that local questions should be decided locally. And everyone agrees that when the two interests conflict, the interest of a local public should be subordinate to that of a larger one. But in their practical application these two principles have continually clashed, and efforts to formulate a workable compromise in abstract terms have again and again come to nothing. Part of the difficulty derives from the fact that it is impossible to define abstractly what is "local" and what is not. Moreover, the accidents of history—above all the great compromises by which the federal system was created in

1787—have had to be taken as fixed features of the situation. The problem has been further aggravated by the fact that party politicians have always been able to make political capital from mixing state and national politics with local ones.

The first two readings of this section show the complexity of local, state, and federal relations at the present time. Wallace S. Sayre and Herbert Kaufman, who describe the government of New York City, and Morton Grodzins, who presents a paradigm of federal and state impacts on the local scene, both use the term "shared functions" and emphasize the unreality of any notion of a strict "division of powers." The early historical developments leading to this complexity are described by Frank J. Goodnow in an excerpt from one of the first (1904) textbooks on city government. He shows how the centralization that characterized local government in Colonial times was replaced by extreme decentralization in the period of Jacksonian democracy; how the sphere of municipal activity grew and how local government changed from an organization for the satisfaction of local needs to one that was also, and primarily, an agent of state government; and how the legislatures interfered with the cities for political reasons, thus engendering a long and largely unavailing struggle by them for "home rule." (For a definition of this term, see the Glossary). The readings that follow bring his account up to date. Home Rule is evaluated in the light of present circumstances by a committee of practical men, the Chicago Home Rule Commission, who conclude that what is a proper distribution of powers between cities and states is at bottom a political question and must therefore remain unsettled. In their discussion of "the problem of the stable majority" (something that would not have seemed a problem at all to Aristotle!) the anonymous authors of the Note from the *Harvard Law Review* show that state courts have not hesitated to interfere in the operation of local government when they thought minority interests needed protection. Recently (1968) the Supreme Court of the United States has also taken a hand in the organization of local government. In Avery v. Midland County, Tex., it says that the principle of "one man, one vote" applies to local as well as to state elections. A city, town, or county, it says, "may no more deny the equal protection of the laws than it may abridge freedom of speech, establish an official religion, arrest without probable cause, or deny due process of the law." How the central cities and the suburbs have been affected by the court's earlier application of the "one man, one vote" rule to the apportionment of state legislatures is analyzed by William J. D. Boyd.

The rapid growth of the suburbs has brought to the fore the question of how to cope with problems that are in some sense metropolitan. In 1965 there were 224 Standard Metropolitan Statistical Areas (see Glossary); in no case do the boundaries of an SMSA, or indeed of a metropolitan area otherwise defined, coincide with those of a general-purpose government. So long as this is the case area-wide needs must be met, if they are to be met at all, by cooperation among general-purpose governments having local jurisdictions and by special-purpose ones having area-wide jurisdictions.

The most common way of dealing with metropolitan problems has been by the creation of special districts. These, as John C. Bollens explains, usually have only one function—for example, water supply, sewage disposal, rapid transit, or air pollution control. If it has only one or two functions, a special district cannot possibly plan comprehensively for metropolitan area development.

Many proposals have been made for a multifunctional approach. But what functions are to be considered "metropolitan" rather than "local"? Oliver P. Williams, Harold Herman, Charles S. Liebman, and Thomas R. Dye analyze this question very acutely. Edward C. Banfield and Morton Grodzins think that the importance, as well as the number, of metropolitan problems has been somewhat exaggerated and that in any case sweeping reforms are politically out of the question. Their proposal for action—a realistic one, they say—is based on the assumption that the formal structure of government will in most places remain essentially unchanged for a long time to come. Luther Gulick, a former city administrator of New York and President of the Institute for Public Administration, believes that metropolitan reorganization is one of the urgent needs of the day. He finds more metropolitan (as opposed to local) problems than do Banfield and Grodzins and he is more sanguine than they about the political possibilities of change; accordingly he is led to propose creation of an altogether new level of local government.

In the final reading of this section Robert H. Connery and Richard H. Leach put forward their view of the proper role of the Federal government in metropolitan affairs and make some observations on the trend of federal-local relations. It is interesting that Goodnow, writing about sixty years before them, remarked that nothing need be said about the federal government, since it had no connection with city affairs.

THE SYSTEM OF
SHARED FUNCTIONS

Intergovernmental Relations in New York City

Wallace S. Sayre and Herbert Kaufman

THE OFFICIALS of the governments of New York State, the United States, and of neighboring states and localities are deeply involved in the government and politics of New York City. This is due to the dependence of all the major components of a modern industrial society upon each other, an interdependence engendered by the economic, transportation, and communication systems. A more specific reason, however, is the division and sharing of powers, functions, and responsibilities among the city, the higher levels of government, and adjacent units of government. For both these reasons officials and employees of other governments are constantly drawn, or inject themselves, into the contest for the stakes of politics in the city. By the same token, officials and employees of the city are constantly engaged in efforts to influence their counterparts in other governments.

The City Is an Agent

All three levels of government operate within the City of New York, serving, regulating, and taxing the inhabitants. But there is an important difference between federal and state officials and employees

Reprinted from Governing New York City *(New York: The Russell Sage Foundation, 1960), pp. 558–62.*

as against city officials and employees. The personnel of the federal agencies (the largest in the area being the Post Office Department, the Department of Defense, the Treasury Department, and the State Department, but with many others also represented) are engaged exclusively in executing the provisions of federal law. Similarly, the personnel of the state agencies in the city (all 20 departments of the state government are represented here) are concerned primarily with the execution of state law. Most city officials and employees, however, are in both theory and practice agents of the state government (or, in a few instances, such as some phases of welfare, arterial highways, and urban renewal and slum clearance, also agents of the federal government). That is to say, the laws they administer are almost entirely laws enacted by the state government (or, in the cases noted, by the federal government), and their activities are supervised in varying measure by state (and/or federal) personnel.

This aspect of the situation of New York City is by no means unique to New York. In American constitutional theory, municipal corporations are traditionally regarded as creatures of the state governments. There is no inherent right of local self-government, and their existence and powers, as well as the designation and powers of their officials, are subject to state control except as the state constitution provides otherwise. They are held to function in a dual capacity, namely, as agents of the state and as organizations for the provision of local service. The attitude engendered by this tradition is particularly evident in the detail and specificity of the state laws administered by the New York City Board of Education, Department of Welfare, Department of Personnel, Board of Elections, finance agencies, as well as the Police, Fire, Buildings, and Correction Departments. (The first three of these are also tightly supervised by state administrative officers.) The Housing, Transit, and Triborough Bridge and Tunnel Authorities, creatures of the state like the city itself, are similarly circumscribed by state law. Indeed, while most of the remaining agencies and officers of the city carry out local law essentially, their programs planned and directed primarily at the municipal level, they, too, derive their authority from broad state legislative authorizations and are limited by a variety of broad statutory restrictions.

The influence of the federal government upon the city government springs not from constitutional theory but from fiscal pre-eminence. Federal financial assistance, it is true, has not only been warmly welcomed but actively sought by city officials. Nevertheless, the purposes for which federal money has been made available have been federal purposes, and the federal government has quite naturally exercised the prerogative of every donor to set conditions for every grant and to check up to make sure that the conditions are fulfilled.

Thus, constitutional theory and financial realities have combined to cast city officials and employees in the role of agents of the higher levels of government. The relationship is firmly established and widely accepted; many federal and state officials deem it their right and duty to influence decisions and actions of city officials and employees, and the latter have had little choice but to accept this as their lot.

The City Is a Claimant

Federal and state officials are furnished with incentives to influence decisions and actions of city officials not only by the general view that the city is an agent of the higher units of government but also by the requests and demands of the city officials themselves. City officials exert these claims upon the other governmental levels for several reasons. First, they are not indifferent to the decisions and actions of federal and state personnel directly serving, regulating, and taxing the people of the city. Second, they are continually in need of financial assistance to maintain (let alone to expand) their own operations. Third, their powers are limited, and they are compelled constantly to seek new authority to meet new conditions.

Thus, for example, city leaders (as well as congressmen from the city and the United States Senators from New York) tend to seek increases in the New York harbor work of the United States Army Corps of Engineers. They labor to get for New York City a substantial share of the contracts for defense and other federal functions and to demand adequate federal services (which bring with them both jobs and pay-rolls) for this area. Mayor La Guardia used all the influence he could muster to try to persuade the Post Office Department to designate Floyd Bennett Field in Brooklyn instead of Newark Airport as the airmail terminus for the metropolitan region. Mayor Wagner urged the federal government to adjust its tax program so as to aid commuter railroad services. In much the same fashion, but on a smaller scale, city officials bring pressure to bear on the state government. If their demands are met, city leaders may regard as solved, at least temporarily, problems with which they would otherwise have to deal. If their requests are rejected, they may find themselves compelled to allocate their own time and energy and some of the fiscal resources of the city to solving or alleviating these problems. If the Corps of Engineers, for instance, were to reduce drastically its dredging of the harbor, it is not unlikely that the city government would have to assume all or part of this burden in order to protect the flow of commerce so important to the economy of the region. Curtailed defense contracts and federal expenditures in the city usually mean a heavier welfare load and perhaps a significant decline in tax revenues. One factor leading to the construction of La Guardia Airport was La Guardia's inability to persuade the

Post Office Department to name Floyd Bennett Field as the regional airmail terminal; New York became the terminal when the new field was completed. It seems unlikely the federal and state tax policies will—or, for that matter, can—relieve fully the acute commuter railroad crisis in the metropolitan area, and this will continue to occupy the attention of city officials for a long time to come and probably to claim an increasing share of the finances of the municipality. In short, what state and federal officials do or fail to do in the way of direct service in the New York area will play an important part in the behavior and policies of city leaders. In this sense, then, the federal and state governments often influence the contest for the stakes of politics within the city, and the influence is frequently a response to a request of the city officials themselves.

City leaders also generate federal and state influence by their success in securing financial aid from those levels of government. State constitutional tax and debt limits circumscribe the ability of the city to raise and borrow money. Even if these were entirely removed, the city would still be restricted by economic considerations—specifically, the danger of driving business and residents out of New York, and of injuring the city government's credit standing in the bond market. Furthermore, many of the more productive forms of taxation—excise, liquor and tobacco and gasoline sales, and income—have been so extensively employed by the state and federal governments that any but the most modest additional city levies would make the totals prohibitive. This confines the city in effect to a relatively inelastic tax base (real property) supplemented by a variety of "nuisance" taxes and a general retail sales tax. To render even its traditional services, let alone the new ones for which a dynamic city constantly creates a demand, such as public health and social welfare, traffic management, air pollution control, and slum clearance, the city has been forced to seek fiscal help from the state legislature and Congress. Whenever such help is forthcoming, it usually brings with it some policy stipulations, some form of supervision and control, and occasionally some inquiry or investigation to assess the urgency of the alleged need. Indeed, Governor Dewey responded in 1953 to one of the city's repeated requests for funds by securing legislation creating a Temporary State Commission to study the government of the city to determine whether the needs could be met by increasing the efficiency of the city's governmental machinery. Governor Rockefeller in 1959 similarly obtained legislation establishing a temporary state-city commission (a "Little Hoover Commission") to examine the city government and propose improvements in its structure and functioning. The search for money often brings the city a measure of relief, but it also results in increased federal and state influence in the municipal governmental decision-making process.

The same is true of the city's quest for additional authority.

Despite a home-rule amendment to the state constitution, and amplifying home-rule legislation, city leaders are not free to regulate or tax citizens within the city's borders in any way they like nor can they provide at will any services they want to. They must always find a constitutional or statutory base for the activities of the city government. In general, new enterprises, new programs and policies, and new forms of taxation cannot be fitted into existing provisions. The city is obliged to apply for grants of additional power. For some purposes—for example, to construct bridges over navigable waters—it needs the approval of federal officials. Consequently, city leaders themselves constantly involve state and federal officers in the local decision-making process. That is not to suggest that city officials are pleased with this state of affairs nor does it imply necessarily that the higher levels of government are displeased with it. On the contrary, it will shortly be seen that the state government in particular insists on preserving it. Nevertheless, things being as they are, the immediate cause of much of the participation of state and federal officials and employees in the government and politics of the city is the initiative taken by city leaders in quest of added powers.

In sum, not necessarily because city officials prefer it but because they often cannot help it, their role as claimants upon the higher levels of government for direct service, financial assistance, and additional authority has provided impetus and justification for the exercise of continual influence upon city decisions by the higher units of government.

Federal and State Impacts

Morton Grodzins

THE VIEW of the federal system as a three-layer cake invariably sees the national and state governments as separate layers stacked neatly above local government. Close under the bottom layer, as the platter on which the cake rests, is the mass of citizens. In less image-laden terms, it is almost universally stated that local governments are "closest" to the people.

The layer-cake view, and the vocabulary that goes with it, are inadequate for understanding the operation of the American system. Utilizing the concept of shared function, rather than that of separated and layered governments, this chapter analyzes the variety of state and federal impacts upon the local scene. It becomes apparent that there is no consistent correspondence between local units of government and "closeness" to the people, however closeness is defined.

I.
A Paradigm of Federal and State Impacts on the Local Scene

Table [1] provides a convenient method of summarizing the variety of ways in which the federal government supplies services at the local level. One route is the direct one. No other government intervenes between agency and citizen when the national government delivers mail, or imposes an income tax, or prohibits use of channels of inter-state commerce to manufacturers who do not comply with nationally defined "fair" labor standards. Similarly, disability payments for veterans and checks for those insured under the Old Age and Survivors program are mailed directly from federal offices. Contracts are negotiated directly between federal administrators and local businessmen. An FBI man may arrest you if you drive a stolen car across a state border. Where such direct federal-citizen contacts exist, it should not be assumed that the central government alone occupies a field of service or regulation.

Reprinted from The American System *by Morton Grodzins, edited by Daniel J. Elazar (Chicago: Rand McNally & Company, 1966), pp. 190–197.*

Significant sharing of functions exists in these endeavors, as in others.

A second federal avenue for local activity is through what we have called "federally engineered local governments." These are special governmental units created by the states to meet specific federal demands in order to participate in certain federal programs, whose structures and responsibilities follow precise patterns established by federal law. The United States Department of Agriculture has been primarily responsible for the proliferation of these little governments. During the 1940's it seemed to some that "the federal government was on the way to establishing its own system of local government to match that of the state."[1] In 1940, according to one estimate, almost 893,000 people were serving in one capacity or another in local governments sponsored by the Department of Agriculture: as directors or advisors of committees, operating personnel, or in other capacities.[2] Some of the enthusiasm disappeared from this program with the end of the New Deal and the retirement of M. L. Wilson, Undersecretary of

TABLE [1] *Channels of Federal Activity on the Local Scene*

Mode of Activity	Examples
1. Federal direct-to-people activities	Old Age and Survivors Insurance Veterans' benefits Mail delivery Taxation Licensing
2. Federally engineered local governments, relatively independent of state or local governments	Soil Conservation Agricultural Stabilization and Conservation Grazing Service Advisory Board
3. Federally engineered local governments, relatively dependent on state or local governments	Selective Service Civil Defense Rationing during World War II Public housing and urban redevelopment (in some states)
4. Federal grants channeled through states	Welfare, highways, employment security, forestry, vocational education, public health, etc.
5. Federal grants and other aid directly to local governments	Airports (in some states) Public housing and urban redevelopment (in some states) Flood control School construction (in some states) Disaster relief (in some cases) Technical assistance in many fields Services by contract

1. Paul N. Ylvisaker, *Intergovernmental Relations at the Grassroots* (Minneapolis: University of Minnesota Press, 1956), p. 42.

2. Carleton R. Ball, "Citizens Help Plan and Operate Action Programs," *Land Policy Review*, Vol. III, No. 2 (March–April, 1940), pp. 19–27.

Agriculture and chief apostle of the new "agricultural democracy." But many aspects of the system still flourish. The country is blanketed by Agricultural Stabilization and Conservation Committees, Soil Conservation Districts, Extension Service sponsoring groups, Rural Electrification Cooperatives, farm-loan associations, advisory boards for the Grazing Service, and similar instrumentalities of local government in agriculture.

Local elections are the customary way of organizing these governments. In Indiana, for example, the local ASC committee is selected by the votes of all eligible farmers in a given township, the nominees being put forward by a county selection board consisting of the County Farm Agent, the Soil Conservation Service Officer, a representative of the Farmers Home Administration, the president of the County Farm Bureau, and the president of the local Farmers Union. Township chairmen, elected by the local committee, serve as delegates to a county ASC convention which in turn elects a county committee. There is a state committee selected through similar mechanisms. Full-time local officers are appointed by both county and state committees. They work closely with the local citizens' groups and with federal employees in programs that provide federal payments under the soil bank, crop price-support, and conservation programs. State laws are of course necessary to establish this elaborate edifice of local governments for the implementation, and partial local control, of federal programs in agriculture. The federally sponsored governments work collaboratively with the regularly constituted local units, as well as with state agencies. But their mission and the scope of their action is essentially defined by federal legislative and administrative action. They are local governments under direct federal supervision.

A third channel of federal activity at the local level may also be characterized as a federally engineered local government. But here the federally engineered units are directly related to, and more immediately under the supervision of, the states or the regularly constituted local governments. These federally engineered local governments, unlike those described above, are not merely permissibly authorized by state law; they are relatively dependent upon state or local administrative offices for their day-to-day operations. The prototype of this sort of federal activity is supplied by the national Selective Service system. This program is, of course, defined by national legislation. But it is administered through the states. State Selective Service directors are appointed by recommendation of the Governors and members of local boards, and are effectively chosen at state headquarters. Within guidelines defined in Washington, the choice of particular individuals for induction into the armed services is made by the local committees, and appeals go initially to state committees. Rationing of scarce commodities was similarly handled during World War II, and the postwar Civil Defense organization follows the same general lines, the latter becoming increasingly a state-local program that receives federal assistance. In other programs of this sort cities and counties, rather than states, play the principal intermediary role. For example, federal legislation encourages the establishment of independent or quasi-independent public housing and urban redevelopment boards.[3] Appointments to a city public housing board are usually made by the mayor, sometimes with council approval and always with state legislative authorization. The board then becomes responsible for the administration of the federally aided programs. Extensive direct local-federal contacts are maintained. The "independence" of the local housing and urban renewal boards still leaves them in most cases financially dependent upon city budgets and politically dependent upon city political leaders.

A fourth type of federal involvement at the local level is widely believed to illustrate the proper federal-local relationship and is often falsely assumed to be the only one. This is the grant-in-aid device of channeling federal funds through state offices for the provision of services at the local level. Grants of land were made by the federal government to both states and localities from the very first days of union and indeed before the Union was established. The modern cash grant began in 1884 with the Hatch Act, providing each state with funds for the establishment of agricultural experiment stations at the land-grant colleges. As with earlier land and later cash grants, regulations accompanied the federal contribution. The federal grant-in-aid to the states, now a characteristic feature of the American system, is the major device for fulfilling national programs for highways, employment security, agricultural extension, forestry, vocational education and rehabilitation, and public health.[4] Some programs by their very nature—employment security, for example—are administered at the local level through state offices. Within broad federal standards, state-by-state variations characterize other grant activities. Public assistance programs, for example, are administered directly from state offices in some states, by counties in others, and by municipalities in still others. And examples can be found of both state and local administration with and without local financial participation.

Most grant programs to states involve local officials in one way or another. Involvement ranges from the city whose main street is a federally aided highway to a county whose federally aided welfare department accounts for the major fraction of the budget. In a number

3. The legislation in fact authorizes federal aid to any public housing agencies: state, county, municipality, or other government entity or public body authorized to engage in low-rent housing or slum clearance or urban renewal. In practice, quasi-independent agencies have been established to operate most of these programs on the local scene.

4. For discussion of the grant system see Chapter Three; for fiscal problems of grants, see Chapter Fifteen.

of federal programs that formally channel funds for local purposes through state agencies, these agencies in fact play a minor and *pro forma* role. This was the case, for example, in the grants to Casa Grande and Benton for sewage disposal systems. But whether the state's role is *pro forma* or not is a matter of state—not federal or local—choice. When states choose to become active participants in any program carried on within their borders that directly affects their citizens, they are invariably able to do so.

This is true even in another group of grant programs that does not involve the states at all, except for passing the necessary enabling legislation. The consequent direct federal grants to local units of government are thus a fifth mode of federal activity on the local scene. Direct federal grants to localities are made for a number of programs, including watershed protection and flood control, disaster relief, school construction in "federally-affected" areas, certain health grants, and, in some states, public housing, urban renewal, and airport construction.[5] New York, however, is actively involved in the public housing programs conducted by its local subdivisions because the state government provides financial and technical assistance alongside similar federal aids and its plans are often superior to those prepared under the aegis of Washington. No new federal-local "starts" in Arkansas were possible without the governor's approval simply because he chose to exercise his prerogatives to assign priorities for political reasons.

This fivefold paradigm of federal impacts on the local scene cannot be taken as anything more than a convenient device for furthering analysis and understanding. Like all such schemes, whatever clarity it may provide is partially offset by what it hides. On the one hand it does not take into account national activities that are not "carried out" on the local scene but that may nevertheless have the greatest "local impact" of all: for example, foreign policy and military programs which may include the "local" consequence of complete destruction. On the other hand some of the distinctions established among the various avenues of federal impact on local affairs may be clearer in statement than they are in actuality. There are important technical differences, for example, between situations in which (a) the federal government channels funds through the states for local sewage disposal systems

---

5. The Federal Airport Act of 1946 authorizes the Federal Aeronautics Administration to deal directly with any airport "sponsor": state, city, county, village, or other governmental entity. The Act, however, gives states the opportunity to require localities to channel applications through state agencies. Roughly half the states allow direct local-federal relationships. In some, state grants may supplement federal money. For fuller discussion of the formulation of this act, see Chapter Ten. Though not involving grants of funds, a very large range of additional federal aids are also made directly available to local governments. These include technical advice in many fields, contractual arrangements for federal services (school curriculum surveys, for example) and contributions of many other sorts, all available on request of local officers (see above, Chapter Six).

and (b) the federal government deals directly with municipalities in the planning and construction of airports. Actual operations may in fact be quite similar. In the sewage disposal program, local officers or their representatives may deal directly with federal officials, keeping the state agency informed but not expecting or receiving from it any active assistance. Thus, the channeling requirement may be practically quite meaningless. From the other direction, the states are not left out of consideration even when the federal government deals directly with local governments. Where state laws allow direct federal aid to localities for airport development, local officers are nevertheless obliged to consult state officials in order to relate their own airport plans to those of other municipalities or of the state itself. Even if this direct local-state contact with respect to airports does not take place, there are inevitable indirect contacts. State legislation is necessary in the first place to enable municipalities to construct and operate an airport. Important airport zoning regulations are dependent upon state legislation, and state police powers are directly involved in airport regulations for health and safety. Finally, localities are dependent upon state action, or lack of action, for their revenue, and no local expenditures, including airport expenditures, are possible without continuous reference to the state executive and legislature.[6]

This discussion of what the paradigm conceals has one incidental by-product: an underscoring of the point previously made that states and local units of government must perforce work together on all activities. No alterations in federal legislation with respect to the channeling of funds alters this absolute, if sometimes antagonistic, union between states and local units. The very indivisibility of state-local activities means that in some degree all local functions are also state functions. It is nevertheless convenient to distinguish for states, as for the federal government, the several ways that states contribute to the bundle of local services.

All local functions must rest upon state authorizations of one sort or another. This purely permissive state role aside, the fivefold table of channels of federal activity on the local scene may be compared with three categories of local action by the states (Table [2]). State governments (1) directly supply services to the local community; and they do so indirectly (2) by providing financial aid to local units for specified programs as well as (3) by making mandatory certain local functions even though no specific financial aid is supplied.

No two states do the same things in the same way. But all states directly do some of their own highway building, providing funds to local units for other aspects of the highway program, and all states, without exception, provide directly for higher education, although funds

6. See Report of the Committee on Federal Grants-in-Aid, *Federal Grants-in-Aid* (Chicago: Council of State Governments, 1949), pp. 239–40.

and forms vary dramatically. Every state also provides some direct-to-citizen health, welfare, and hospital services; all license the major and certain minor professions; all maintain parks and other recreational facilities; all provide correctional institutions; and all have some sort of program for the development and conservation of natural resources. Some states give direct benefits to veterans, and some operate alcoholic beverage distribution systems. A few are responsible for housing programs. And some states have more or less uncommon direct functions, for example, the system of Savings Bank Life Insurance in Massachusetts, New York, and Connecticut. These are only samples of the wide range of direct-to-citizen functions carried on by the states.

A very large fraction of all state expenditures is in the form of fund transfers to local units of government. And the largest part of these sums is for state-specified purposes, notably education, highways, and public welfare. (In 1957, $7.3 billion, or 30 per cent, of state general expenditures were payments to local units, of which $6.2 billion, or 85 per cent, was for the three specified functions.) This method of fulfilling state-defined programs is indirect only in the sense that locally selected officers are in actual supervision although they work, of course, under state, and in many cases federal, standards. Functions

TABLE [2] *Channels of State Activity on the Local Scene*[a]

Mode of Activity	Examples
1. State direct-to-people activities	Highways
	Higher education
	Health and hospitals
	Welfare
	Recreation
	Courts and correctional institutions
2. State aid to local units for specified activities	Education
	Highways
	Welfare
	Safety
	Health and hospitals
3. Local activities made mandatory by state law	Local elections
	School standards
	Fire and police protection
	Courts and jails
	Tax assessment and collection standards
	Health program
	Sewage standards

[a] The table intentionally does not take account of the fact that all local government activities rest upon state law. A notable demonstration of the singleness of state and local governments is the fact that it is difficult to find any direct state activity (category 1) that does not overlap state-aided or state-ordered local activities or both (categories 2 and 3).

that in one state are carried out directly, in other states are carried out indirectly (welfare and health services are particularly diverse in this respect). There are also state-by-state variations in the local government through which state aid is channeled for specific purposes. Educational aid may, for example, be given to municipalities, to counties, or to special school districts; hospital funds are also diversely channeled to local governments with many states in addition operating hospitals directly.

The other indirect channel for fulfilling state functions on the local scene involves no specific cash grants. Here are found virtually endless obligations imposed upon local units by state constitutions, laws, and administrative regulations. They vary widely from state to state and no less widely by area of activity. Minnesota laws, for example, provide a complicated and detailed calendar controlling local authorities with respect to such matters as the timing of tax levies, the holding of elections, the filing of reports and accounts of all sorts, the dates of town meetings, schedules for reviewing tax assessments, *ad infinitum*. The same sort of specifications cover substantive fields. Tax and debt limits and rules for tax assessment and collection are fixed; requirements for various local units to operate courts and jails are detailed; standards for fire and health protection are set forth; police units and their organization are made mandatory; rules for school construction and curricula are established. The state statute books are in large part a record of local obligations.

THE PLACE OF THE CITY
IN THE SYSTEM

The Historical Development
of the City's Position

Frank J. Goodnow

English City Government in the
Eighteenth Century

IN ORDER to understand the beginning of city government in the United States it is necessary to consider briefly the system existing in England in the eighteenth century. For that was the model on which the American system was framed. The English system of city government existing at the time this country was settled was based on certain rather well-defined principles. In the first place, the cities, or boroughs, as they were commonly called, were incorporated through a grant by the crown to each locality of its own special charter. There was, therefore, no uniform system of city government in England, except in so far as all the special charters were governed by certain generally applied principles.

In the second place, what was incorporated by the English charter was not the district, nor the people living in the district, but only the municipal officers, or these officers and a narrow body of freemen or voters. The official name of an English municipal corporation was indicative of this condition of things, being, for example, "The Mayor,

Reprinted from City Government in the United States (*New York: Appleton-Century-Crofts, Inc., 1904*), *pp. 43–68; 73–75, and 77–79.*

Aldermen, and Councillors of ——," or "The Mayor and Jurats of ——,"
or "The Mayor, Aldermen, and Commonalty of ——."

In the third place, and partly as a result of the character of the
incorporation just described, the form of government provided by these
charters was distinctly oligarchical in character. In most instances the
council, which was the governing body of the corporation, was a self-
perpetuating body, although in some cases its members were elected
by the narrow body of freemen or voters already alluded to.

In the fourth place, the sphere of action of the English municipal
corporation of the eighteenth century was a very narrow one. The corporation had control of its property and finances, and had the power to
pass local ordinances, mainly of a police character. Its officers, or certain
of its officers, were further frequently intrusted by royal commission
with important duties relative to the administration of civil and criminal
justice, and the preservation of the peace.

During the latter part of the eighteenth century the population of
cities had greatly increased. This increase of the population made
necessary an enlargement of the sphere of municipal activity. The
corporate organization of the cities was, however, bad. It was bad
because the cities were prostituted in the interest of the national political
parties. Under these conditions the city government could not with
safety be intrusted with the discharge of the new functions of government. The result was the formation, by special acts of Parliament, of
trusts or commissions, not connected with the borough council, for
the discharge of these main functions, such as paving, lighting, and
even watching the streets.

Such was the system of city government existing in England during
the seventeenth and eighteenth centuries, and it is safe to say that
whatever may have been the depths to which any American city has
fallen, it is doubtful whether it ever sank so low as were English
boroughs at the beginning of the nineteenth century.

Early American City Government

But, with all its faults, the English system was made the
model of the system which was established in the North American
colonies.

The first municipal corporation of any importance to be established
in this country was that of New York. New York received its first
charter in 1665. This charter was unsatisfactory, and in 1683 a petition
was made to Governor Dongan to give the city a more satisfactory
frame of municipal government. Governor Dongan, in 1686, issued to the
city of New York a charter which has been since that time the basis of

its municipal government. It has, of course, been subjected to frequent amendment, but the history of New York, as a municipality, may be said to date from the time of its issue. In 1708 another charter, known as the Cornbury charter, was issued to the city, and in 1730 the most important provisions of the Dongan and Cornbury charters were incorporated into a new charter, known as the Montgomerie charter, which was issued to the city by Governor Montgomerie.

Soon after the issue of the charter of 1686 to the city of New York, the city of Philadelphia received a charter, namely, in 1701, from which year may be said to date the history of Philadelphia as a city. During the eighteenth century other charters were issued to various municipal corporations by the governors of the North American colonies. The municipal corporations which were thus established were in the main confined to the central colonies of New York, New Jersey, Pennsylvania, Maryland, and Virginia. We find almost no instances of the formation of municipal corporation in New England.[1]

By 1746 the colonial period of municipal incorporation seems to have closed. The advantages of the system were, however, apparent just as soon as population began to gather in the cities after the Revolutionary War. Beginning with the existence of the states as independent political communities there appeared a large number of new municipal charters; and by the beginning of the nineteenth century the only considerable urban community in the United States which was not incorporated was Boston, which, as late as 1820, continued to govern itself through the ordinary New England town organization.

While the charters that were issued after the Revolution were very similar to those which had been issued during the colonial period, there was this essential difference between them: the colonial charters had been granted by the governors of the colonies; the municipal charters that were issued after the Revolution were granted by the state legislatures. This difference in the incorporating authority was destined to have an important influence on the position of the community that was incorporated. For the charter that was granted by the governor was, like the municipal charter which was granted in England by the crown, regarded as something of the nature of a contract between the executive part of the colonial government and the community incorporated. The municipal charter, on that account, was not believed to be capable of amendment except as the result of an agreement between both parties to the contract. When, however, a charter was granted by the legislature, it was regarded not so much as of the nature of a contract, but as an ordinary act of legislation which, like all acts of legisla-

1. The probable reason why the idea of incorporating cities was not adopted in New England is to be found in the vitality of the New England town. The town system of government really gave to localities all the freedom of government that they desired, and was well adapted to the needs of the various districts which, until the beginning of the nineteenth century, did not contain any very large population.

tion, was capable of amendment by the action of the legislature alone.

The municipal corporations which were established in this country during the colonial period departed in one respect from the English model. In very few instances was the council a self-perpetuating body. Indeed, Philadelphia may be said to have been the only important city in which the council was renewed by coöptation. As a general thing the people of the city were permitted by the colonial municipal charters to participate in the choice of local officers. . . . While the people were generally permitted to participate in the selection of municipal officers, no such principle as universal manhood suffrage was adopted. The power to vote for municipal officers was, as a general thing, confined to the well-to-do classes. The usual rule was to grant it to the freemen of the city, being freeholders. Thus in the Montgomerie charter of New York city the suffrage was granted to "the freemen of the said city, being inhabitants and the freeholders of each respective ward."[2]

The municipal organization provided by most of the colonial municipal charters followed very closely the English municipal organization of the eighteenth century. The governing body of the corporation was a council. This council, like the English council of the same period, consisted of a mayor, recorder, and a number of aldermen and councilmen, or assistants. The mayor, however, seems, even in the earliest charters, to have occupied a rather more important position than that which was accorded to the mayor by the English charters. In the first place, he was quite commonly the appointee of the governor of the colony.[3] In the second place, he seems to have had rather wider police powers than any other member of the council. For example, in New York and Albany he had full control of the licensing of the retail sale of liquors, and was the clerk of the markets. It may well be that the greater importance, which the mayor secured, as a result both of the peculiarity of his tenure and the rather wider powers that he possessed, was the cause of his development into the all-important mayor of the present day.

While the council thus composed was the only governing body in

2. A word of explanation is perhaps necessary with regard to the freemen of the city. Almost all the colonial charters contained provisions for bestowing the freedom of the city upon persons, either resident or non-resident. The advantages which the freemen of the city possessed in addition to that of voting was that they alone could practice any "art, trade, mystery, or manual occupation, or merchandising business" within the borough, except during the great fair. In some cases this monopoly of trade was a privilege of considerable value. For example, Albany had a monopoly of trade with the Indians, and New York at one time had a monopoly of bolting flour. In the later years of the colonial period, however, these advantages ceased to be of any particular importance, since trades were thrown open to all; and at the present time, while the freedom of the city is sometimes granted to distinguished visitors, it has come to be regarded as nothing but a compliment.

3. In some of the English cities, however, the titular officer corresponding to the early American mayor was appointed either by the crown or by some powerful nobleman.

the city, certain of its members, namely, the mayor, recorder, and the aldermen were, after the English model, vested with important judicial powers not granted to the other members of the council. The mayor, recorder, and aldermen indeed were, by the charters of some of the cities, of which New York is an example, vested with almost all the judicial powers which were exercised within the limits of the city. The only important exception to this rule was to be found in the powers possessed by the court of the colony occupying a position similar to that of the state supreme court which was the only court of general common law jurisdiction to be found.[4]

The mayor, recorder, aldermen, and councilmen, or assistants, were then to constitute the common council of the colonial municipal corporation. As a general thing provision was made in the royal charters for district representation. For example, the Montgomerie charter of New York provided that one alderman and one assistant were to be elected in each of the wards into which the city was divided. Apart from the provisions of the charter, with regard to the members of the council, the royal charters did very little toward providing for the detailed organization of the city administration. This was left to the council to arrange by ordinance. . . .

Original Sphere of Action of American Cities

The sphere of action of these early American municipal corporations was very much the same as that of the English municipal corporation of the same period. This sphere of action was quite narrow when compared with that possessed by the modern American municipal corporation. The functions possessed by the municipal authorities were more of a police and judicial than an administrative character. The judicial functions of certain members of the council have already been considered. The police functions of the council, using the word in its broad sense, were considerable. Thus the council had general authority to pass such ordinances as seemed "to be good, useful, or necessary for the good rule and government of the body corporate," subject merely to the limitation that these ordinances be "not contradictory or repugnant" to the laws of England.

The exercise of this police power, which was theoretically a very large one, was, however, very much limited by the fact that the financial resources of the corporations were very small. Some of the corporations, of which New York was a rather exceptional example,

4. It is perfectly easy to trace in the legislation of the state of New York the development, from these judicial powers of the mayor, recorder, and aldermen, of all of the courts within the city of New York which exercise civil and criminal jurisdiction, outside of the supreme court.

obtained by their charters large property rights, receiving among other things ferry, dock, and wharf rights. But in few instances was the income from the property, which a city possessed, supplemented by the right of local taxation. The result was that the income of these corporations was insufficient to defray the expenses of the very modest kind of municipal government which they carried on and resort had to be had to loans and to municipal lotteries, from whose income the debts which were incurred were discharged. At quite an early time in the history of the colonial corporations, however, the insufficiency of the revenues of the corporations resulted in an application by those bodies to the legislature for the power to levy taxes for specific purposes. The first instance of such an application is said to have been in 1676, when the corporation of New York, on its application, was authorized to levy a tax to pay off debts incurred in rebuilding one of its docks. By the middle of the eighteenth century, however, taxation became a regular source of a considerable part of the revenue of most all the colonial corporations. In some cases the power to tax was granted only for specific purposes; in other cases the power might be exercised for any of the purposes of municipal government, but limits were imposed upon the amount of money which could be raised.

The result of the narrow powers of the colonial municipal corporations was that little or no attention was paid to a long series of matters which we regard at the present time as essential parts of municipal administration. For example, little was done by the corporations to supply the cities with water. All that was usually done was for the council to pass regulations of a police character to prevent the fouling of the wells and pumps from which the people of the city obtained their water. In some cases the council appointed overseers of wells and pumps whose duty it was to keep the wells and pumps in good order. The first city in this country which attempted to establish a model waterworks plant was the city of Albany, which began its work in this direction in 1774. In the same way little or no attention was paid to charities or public schools. In Philadelphia alone was either of these matters under the control of officers provided by the city authorities. Elsewhere the poor officers were separately elected, as a general thing, in close connection with the ecclesiastical organizations, and schools were conducted by private persons or by the churches.

The position of the American municipalities at the end of the colonial period was, then, that of organizations which had been formed for the satisfaction of what were then regarded as the local needs of the district over which the corporation had jurisdiction. The conception of what were local needs was both broader and narrower than it is at the present time. It was broader in that judicial powers were regarded as sufficiently local to be delegated to the cities. During the nineteenth century these judicial powers have very largely been taken by the state into its own administration. The powers of municipal corporations were narrower than they are now, inasmuch as many, if not most, of the matters which receive attention by the municipal corporations of the present time not only did not receive attention but were not regarded as having been given into the charge of the municipal corporations by their charters. The narrowness of their powers and the rather local and *quasi*-private character of these powers were undoubtedly responsible in some degree for the conception which was held by the people of the day, that the municipal corporations were not liable to be controlled to any very great extent by the legislatures of the colonies.

Change in the Position of American Cities

The nineteenth century brought about great changes, both in the position which the city occupied in the state government, and in the organization of the city for the purpose of discharging the functions which were intrusted to it.

The position of the city has been changed from that of an organization for the satisfaction of local needs to that of a well-recognized agent of state government. The state government of the present time makes use of the city or of its officers as agents for the purposes of general state administration. In financial matters the city, when of large size, is often made the agent of the state for the assessment and collection of taxes. Indeed, the city itself is often the taxpayer of certain of the state taxes, as for example, the general property tax, and adds the amount, which it pays to the state, to the amount which it collects from the inhabitants for the purpose of paying the expenses of the city. In the colonial period, the state taxes were often collected by state officers acting within the city, but not a part of the general corporate organization. When the system of local taxation was developed, the beginning of which we have already noticed, it seemed advisable, for reasons of convenience and economy, to combine the collection of local and state taxes in the same officers. These officers were naturally the municipal officers, inasmuch as the general system of decentralized administration, which was adopted for the state as a whole, confided the care of such matters to officers chosen directly or indirectly by the localities in which the duties were performed.[5]

What has been said of the tax administration may be said also of other branches of administration, both those which were being attended

5. Within the last twenty-five years there has been somewhat of a change in this matter of taxation, and the modern tendency has been in the direction of providing separate taxes for the state, to be collected by its own officers,—taxes, for example, like the corporation tax, the succession tax, or the liquor tax, as in New York,—and a system of local taxation for the cities and other localities, which is put into the hands of local officers.

to by governmental action at the beginning of the nineteenth century, and those which have been developed during the course of the nineteenth century. Thus in cities of large size, in accordance with the principles of decentralized administration, which have been spoken of, the care of the poor has often been vested in the local corporations or officers. The same may be said of education. The schools, which, at first, were really nothing more than private schools, have been made a part of the city administration. The result of this development has been to put the city in the position not merely of an organization for the satisfaction of local needs, but also in that of an agent for the purposes of general state administration.

But while the sphere of the state agency of cities has thus vastly increased, it must not be supposed that their functions as local organizations have not also increased in importance. In the early part of the nineteenth century the city of New York began the construction of the Croton aqueduct. Later on it established a professional police and fire force. About the middle of the century it began the laying out of a park system. The streets were very commonly sewered and paved, and, indeed, by 1850 the whole sphere of municipal activity had extended far beyond the dreams of the city inhabitants of 1800. What was done in New York was very soon copied in other cities, so that at the present time almost all cities of the country, while important agents of state government, have, as a result of the enormous extension of the sphere of distinctly municipal activity, become even more important as organs for the satisfaction of local needs. . . .

Legislative Interference with Cities

This great development of the local side of municipal corporations has not, however, been accompanied by the application of the same principle that seems to have been applied to municipal corporations during the colonial period. It has been pointed out that during that period the corporations were regarded as in very large degree free from central control.[6] But about 1850 the legislatures of the states began to interfere in the government of cities. Undoubtedly one of the reasons for this interference is to be found in the more public character which had been assigned to municipal corporations. Legislative control over cities was the only state control possible under the general administrative system. Legislative control was necessary as to matters in which the cities acted as agents of the state government. Accustomed to interfere in matters which were of interest to the state government, the leg-

6. For example, Judge Spencer of the New York Supreme Court, said (Mayor *v.* Ordrenan, 12 Johns., 125) that it was the almost invariable course of procedure for the legislature not to interfere in the internal affairs of a corporation without its consent.

islatures failed to distinguish between such matters and matters which were of main, if not of exclusive, interest to the cities themselves. The legislatures were able to carry this interference to the extent to which it was carried because of the adoption of the legal theory that the municipal corporation was a mere creature of the state. Legislative interference became so great, however, that a number of states inserted provisions into the state constitutions which were intended to prevent absolutely all interference with particular matters or to prevent the legislature from adopting certain methods of interference which had proved to be particularly bad. Some states, like the state of New York, inserted in their constitutions provisions securing to municipal corporations the local selection of their own officers. But the most common method which was adopted was to prohibit all special legislation with regard to cities.

Change in the Organization of Cities

Not only has the position of the city been changed, but also its organization has been subjected to great modification. . . . Soon after the expiration of the first quarter of the nineteenth century, changes were introduced into the original municipal organization which had the result of making it conform to the system of government adopted for the state and the nation.

The result of the application to municipal organization of the principles at the bottom of the state and national governments was, in the first place, according to the mayor a position similar to that of the governor in the state government, and the president in the national government. Thus the mayor was to be chosen by the people and not by the state governor or city council. Popular election was provided in Boston and St. Louis in 1822 and in Detroit in 1824. In 1834 the mayor of New York became elective, and at the present time the principle of an elective mayor may be regarded as permanently adopted in the municipal system of the United States. In the second place, the council was treated as if it occupied a position in the city government similar to that of the legislature in the state and national governments. The council was quite frequently made to consist of two chambers. The only reason for the change that can be found is the desire to model the council upon the state legislature. . . .

By the first quarter of the nineteenth century, then, the municipal organization which had been developed was of a type modeled very closely upon the system of government in the state and the nation, and consisted of a mayor, who was elected by popular vote, and had very commonly a veto power over the resolutions of the council similar to that possessed by the president and state governor over the acts of Congress and the state legislature respectively, and a council, also elected by popular vote, which was frequently composed of two chambers.

This system of government was not, however, a satisfactory one. Prior to the making of these changes in the municipal organization, the complaints against the council were neither frequent nor severe. Very soon after the change was made they increased both in number and in vehemence. About this time the great national parties were developing throughout the country as a whole, and were reaching out in every direction for means by which to increase their power. There was no branch of the government whose possession could so much increase the power of political parties as the city governments. All the cities had, as compared with the other districts in the country, large numbers of officers and employees, and all were spending a large proportion of the money which was spent by the government authorities of the country. Either because of the inefficiency of the city governments, which certainly became quite marked soon after 1850, or because of the desire of the political parties to get control of the city governments in order to increase their power in the state and nation, changes were made in the system of city government as it existed in 1850, which resulted in the ushering in of a new period in the development of municipal organization in the United States. This new system we may speak of as the board system.

Board System of City Government

As we originally find it, the board system was little more than a system of boards independent of the city council. The origin of the system is probably to be found in the New York charter of 1849. This made provision for independent executive departments and for taking from the council almost all administrative power. The reasons for the change were somewhat the same as those for the establishment of the mayor in a position of independence over against the council. That is, it was desired to model the city organization on that of the state and national government. The influence of the democratic spirit, so prevalent about the middle of the nineteenth century, is seen in the provision of the charter of 1849, that the heads of the new executive departments were to be elected by the people of the city. The election of the heads of these departments was seen at once to be unsatisfactory, and by the charter of 1853 the power was given to the mayor to appoint, subject to the approval of the city council, the heads of all departments except the comptroller, and the corporation counsel. The example set by New York was followed by other cities. Thus Cleveland provided for elective departments in 1852; Detroit, in 1857.

Soon after the adoption of this board system, however, the legislatures of the states began to provide for the state appointment of the members of city boards. This custom on the part of the legislature began just before 1860. The first point of attack was the police department. Later on the attempt was made to introduce this system into other branches of municipal administration.

By about 1860 it may be said that in all the important cities of the United States the most important parts of the city governments were in the hands of boards largely independent of the council, the members of which were in some instances appointed by the central state government, in some instances by the mayors of the cities, either acting alone or in conjunction with the city councils, and in some cases elected by the people of the city. At the time that this system was at its height, the members of these boards were not only independent of the council, but were also practically independent of the mayor. They were independent of the mayor even where he appointed them. For, as a general thing, they could not be removed from office by the mayor except for cause. This meant that they could be removed only as the result of charges and after a hearing, and the determination of the removing authority was subject to the review of the courts.

The result of the introduction of this system was completely to disorganize the municipal administration. Each important branch of city government was attended to by a board or officer practically independent of any other municipal authority. No one mayor, because of the shortness of his term as compared with that of these officers and the members of these boards, could appoint all the city officers or all the members of any one board. The result was that the municipal organization consisted of a collection of independent authorities, and that the mayor, where the right of local appointment was secured to him, was merely an officer who could fill vacancies in the various offices which happened to occur during his term.

Finally, it is to be noticed that frequently the acts of the legislature establishing these municipal boards or commissions, provided for what are sometimes called non-partisan, at other times bi-partisan, commissions. The provision for the bi-partisan or non-partisan board took one of two forms: It was enacted either that no more than a certain number, either half or a bare majority of the members, should belong to the same political party, or that half of the members of the board should belong to each of the two leading political parties. This common provision in the acts establishing the board system is an indication that one of the reasons for its establishment was the desire of the political parties to secure the influence which resulted from the possession of power in the city administration.[7]

We may say, then, that by the year 1860 the council had in most of

7. See Wilcox, "Party Government in Cities" in *Political Science Quarterly,* XIV, p. 681.

the larger American cities ceased to be anything more than a legislative body in the city government. It had lost all its original administrative functions. These had been assumed, in the first place, by the mayor, and, in the second place, by the officers and boards, to which reference has just been made. The council had lost also important legislative powers. Among the important legislative powers which the council lost was the power it possessed, under the original charters, of organizing the details of the city administration. This power had been lost because of the fact that the new charters and acts of the legislature regulating the city government went into great detail. The assumption by the legislature of this former power of the city council had extremely bad effects. It resulted, in the first place, in the regulation of the details of city government by an authority which had little knowledge of the needs of the city. This authority was often governed in its action not by considerations which had anything to do with the welfare of the city, but by considerations of partisan politics. In the second place, the regulation of the details of municipal organization by the legislature offered a constant temptation and opportunity to interfere in matters which properly should have been left to the municipality to regulate. It cannot be doubted that the introduction of this board system, accompanied, as it was, by the assumption by the legislature of the power to regulate the details of city organization, was one of the chief causes for the great extension of the control of the legislature over municipal affairs generally.

Mayor System of City Government

But about 1880 the people of the United States seem to have awakened to the fact that the board system did not work satisfactorily; that it diffused responsibility for municipal action; that it made it impossible for the people, at any given municipal election, to exercise any appreciable control over the municipal government, and that it offered a continual temptation to the legislature to interfere in the affairs of the city. The result was an attempt to change again the municipal organization. The changes that were introduced into the system, beginning with about the year 1880, may be said to have ushered in a new period of municipal development, which we may call the mayor period. The first modification of the board system which was made in any important city charter was made in the charter of the city of Brooklyn about the year 1882. By this charter, the mayor was given the right, within twenty days after assuming office, to appoint new heads of the executive departments. The example of Brooklyn was followed by the city of New York in the year 1895. As a result of the continued success of one political party at the city elections in the years preceding 1895, all of the boards and offices of the city were practically controlled by adherents of this organization. In 1894 this organization was defeated at the polls after a campaign of great interest and excitement. It was felt by the people of the city and by the legislature of the state that, under existing conditions, the new administration could not represent the wishes of the people who had put it into power, and therefore a law was passed in 1895 giving to the mayor the right, within six months after assuming his office, to remove the heads of departments from office arbitrarily and not subject to the review of the courts.

In the meantime the mayor had received an absolute power of appointment in a number of cities, among which was the city of New York, being relieved from the necessity of obtaining the consent of the council to his appointments. Later on a number of cities, to which the city of New York was added by its recent charter of 1901, adopted the principle of arbitrary removal by the mayor throughout his entire term. The change in the municipal organization which has just been outlined was accompanied in many instances by the substitution of single commissioners for boards as department heads. The single commissioner was regarded as a necessary part of the original Brooklyn plan.

This system of city government we may call the mayor system of government. It is characterized by the fact that the mayor is vested with the absolute power of appointing and removing most of the important municipal officers. The mayor system may possibly be regarded as the coming system in the United States. But it cannot be said that it has been generally adopted throughout the country. Indeed, it is difficult to say what at the present time is the American type of municipal government. Most of the charters of the cities of the United States show the influences of the different periods of municipal development which have been outlined. Thus we find in a number of cities that the council still has a great deal of power. We find again, in a number, independent departments, the heads of which in some cases are elected by the people of the city in accordance with the ideas of democratic government so prevalent about 1850, in other cases, appointed by the central government of the state, in other cases, but in the majority of cases, appointed by the mayor and confirmed by the council. . . .

The City a Creature of the State Legislature

The character of our administrative system has several important effects on the position of the city. In the first place, the city is made by the system the creature of the state legislature. In the absence of a constitutional restriction the legislature of the state may do as it will with the cities within its jurisdiction. The charters of cities are at the present time regarded as mere statutes, which, in the absence of a constitutional limitation of the powers of the legislature, are subject to amendment by that body at any time.

The legislature then has, under our system of government, the absolute legal right to regulate municipal affairs as it sees fit. It has not only the legal right, it has also had in the past the moral right to interfere in city government. For the city became, during the course of the nineteenth century, an agent of the state government. The city has ceased to be what it once was, merely an organization for the satisfaction of local needs, and has become as well an important member of the general state governmental system. Our system of decentralized administration did not permit of the exercise by any state administrative authority of any control over the city, even where it was thus acting as an agent of the state. It was necessary, therefore, if any central control at all should be exercised, that it should be exercised by the legislature.

The City an Authority of Enumerated Powers

In the second place, the city, in the absence of a constitutional provision, has no powers not granted to it by the legislature.[8]

It may be added that the legislatures of the states have not granted wide powers to the cities, but have generally enumerated in greater or less detail the powers which cities may exercise. Thus when the city of New York wished to build and lease a rapid-transit railway it had no power to do so, and had to apply to the legislature for the necessary authority. Thus again when it wished to establish a municipal electric-lighting plant, it had no power. When it applied to the legislature for authority in this instance its application was denied.

8. No better or more authoritative statement of the powers possessed by the municipal corporations in the United States can be found than that given by Judge Dillon in his great work on municipal corporations and approved by many of the later decisions of the courts themselves (Dillon, "Law of Municipal Corporations," 4th ed., p. 145). He says: "It is a general and undisputed proposition of law that a municipal corporation possesses and can exercise the following powers and no others: First, those granted in express words; second, those necessarily or fairly implied in or incident to the powers expressly granted; third, those essential to the declared objects and purposes of the corporation—not simply convenient but indispensable. Any fair reasonable doubt concerning the existence of power is resolved by the courts against the corporation and the power is denied. Of every municipal corporation the charter or statute by which it is created is its organic art. Neither the corporation nor its officers can do any act, or make any contract, or incur any liability not authorized thereby or by some legislative act applicable thereto. All acts beyond the scope of the powers granted are void." Judge Dillon adds that while the rule "of strict construction of corporate powers is not so directly applicable to the ordinary clauses in charters or incorporating acts of municipalities as it is to the charters of private corporations . . . it is equally applicable to grants of powers to municipal and public bodies which are out of the usual range or which may result in public burdens or which in their exercise touch the right of liberty or property or, as it may be compendiously expressed, any common law right of the citizen or inhabitant" (ibid., p. 148).

In the third place, whatever may be the theoretical power of the city to enter upon any particular branch of governmental activity, the financial powers which it possesses are so limited that it is practically unable to exercise the powers of which it may be possessed without the grant to it by the legislature of the necessary financial power. That is, the American law recognizes the taxing power, from whose exercise most of the city's revenues must come, as a power of state government possessed alone by the state legislature. The city certainly does not possess it in the absence of legislative grant. The American law also does not accord to cities large powers of borrowing money in the absence of legislative authorization. In many cases the legislature has been as niggardly in its grants to cities of financial powers as it has been in the grants of other powers. . . .

Cities Have Lost Their Autonomy

It has been said that the exercise of its powers by the legislature has deprived cities of their power of local government. The result has come about in the following way: No legislature is far-seeing enough to be able to determine for all time what powers it may be expedient for a city to exercise. No legislature, even under the régime of special city charters, can give a particular city powers which will be permanently satisfactory so long as these powers are enumerated in detail. The conditions, economic and otherwise, upon which city governments are based, are continually changing. As a result of these changing conditions American cities are forced to apply continually to the legislature for new and extended local powers. Such powers are often granted retrospectively through the exercise of the power the legislature possesses to ratify illegal action.

The necessity of changing and extending local powers has brought about an immense amount of special legislation, and the legislature, accustomed to regulate by special act municipal affairs on the proposition of the various cities, and obliged to exercise through special legislation the necessary central control over matters attended to by cities which are of vital interest to the state as a whole, has got into the habit of passing special legislation with regard to purely municipal matters of its own motion not only without the consent of the local people, but often against their will, and for reasons in many cases in no way connected with their local welfare. The condition of things which has resulted from this habit of the legislature is one about which there is no difference of opinion. In those states where such central interference has been most marked the people of the cities have very largely lost interest in the municipal government, and whenever they desire to see some concrete municipal policy adopted their point of attack is the state legislature rather than any local and municipal organ. In New York city, for example, the people have become so accustomed to this method of action that they regard it as perfectly natural and normal.

The loss of local government by the cities and the resulting lack of interest of municipal citizens in the conduct of city affairs are not, however, the worst results of the actual position which the city occupies in the American political system. More serious is the fact that owing to this position it is practically impossible to secure a solution of any one of our municipal problems uninfluenced by the consideration of the effect which the solution proposed may have on questions of state and national politics.

A Reappraisal of Constitutional Home Rule

The Chicago Home Rule Commission

CONSTITUTIONAL HOME RULE, as an abstract political concept, has an undeniably attractive appeal as a technique of establishing desirable state-city relationships. That cities should have the legal power of "self-government" or the power "to regulate their own affairs" or "to conduct local government in accordance with the wishes and demands of the governed" is a principle of broad content with which it is difficult to disagree. Limited as this abstract concept is to the legal power of cities to act with independence and initiative, with freedom from irksome legislative controls, in the area of municipal affairs only, and recognizing as it does the supremacy of the state in matters in which the state may have a paramount concern, the political concept of home rule may be said to reflect a meritorious and desirable policy of power allocation between the state and its municipalities.

When, however, the abstract political concept of constitutional home rule is weighed against the legal concepts of constitutional home rule, as these have been set out in state constitutions and court decisions, the disparities are strikingly evident. The diversity of constitutional home-rule provisions; the customary reservations of constitutional and legislative restraint upon the exercise of municipal power, particularly in the all-important area of revenue; and the futility, politically and judicially conceded, of attempting to draw a sharp division between municipal or local affairs or concerns and matters of state concern—all these factors which have been previously analyzed in detail—combine to effect a dilution of the political concept of constitutional home rule to an extent which renders it a symbol almost wholly devoid of substantive content and meaning. To heighten the paradox, sincere protagonists of constitutional home rule continue to view its political concept and legal expressions as identical, with mutually consistent objectives capable of attainment. This view is apparently the result of a failure to come to

Reprinted from Modernizing a City Government *(Chicago: University of Chicago Press, 1954), pp. 309–314.*

grips with the basic difficulties inherent in the reconciliation of both concepts.

Thus, in the 1948 National Municipal Policy Statement of the American Municipal Association, the declaration is made that cities "should have the right to decide for themselves what services they require, without asking for state permission for each new undertaking," and, further, "that cities should have the authority to raise revenues from any local sources, without being required to beg for funds to pay for the services they need."

This challenging doctrine is then followed by the statement that, "while no municipality can have complete autonomy, the cities should have the maximum local authority consistent with their positions as constituent elements in a sovereign state." The coalition of these statements—the first expressing the need for a maximization of municipal autonomy and the second, recognizing that complete autonomy is unattainable, is indicative of the lack of preciseness of definition which confounds the problem. Does the first statement imply that any new services which a city may desire to undertake must be within the exclusive power of local determination, without regard to the doctrines of state concern or state pre-emption or the question of conflict with state laws? More importantly, and conceding for the purpose of analysis that a new service may unquestionably fall within the area of municipal affairs and that there exists no question of conflict with a state law, does the statement respecting the power to finance the service imply complete autonomy in the revenue field? More specifically, does it argue against the propriety of property tax-rate limitations or indebtedness limitations, the application of which may prevent the undertaking of the new service? If so, there is no indication that such is the intent. If not, to what extent should the power of self-determination be subject to such restrictions? If the statement implies power to utilize non-property revenue sources, is this power to be exercised with regard to any subject or object of taxation permissible under constitutional principles, with complete municipal freedom in the establishment of tax rates? Does it deny the validity of any legislatively imposed restraints, either as to subjects or rates of taxation, or of any legislatively prescribed limitations on the appropriation or expenditure of tax funds so raised? If so, the intention is not clearly expressed in view of the concession that complete autonomy is unattainable. If not, to what extent are such limitations desirable?

The questions posed are not irrelevant. Nor are they intended to suggest either the desirability or the undesirability of legislative restrictions on municipal revenue powers. They do, however, point out the areas of uncertainty and ambiguity which surround the abstract concept of constitutional home rule. Until these questions are resolved and the ambiguities removed, generalizations concerning municipal autonomy are largely meaningless.

This conclusion applies with equal force to municipal powers other than revenue. Until recently, the consensus of constitutional home-rule theorists was that the grant of power should be couched in general terms for fear that a detailing of specific powers would be restrictively construed by the courts to deny local authority in areas not specified. With the unhappy experience resulting from that technique, a modification in viewpoint is now evident, as indicated by the following extract from the report of the Committee on State-Local Relations of the Council of State Governments:

> It is difficult . . . to separate state from local functions. A complete specific enumeration of powers to be exercised by home rule cities is therefore impossible. Nevertheless, it seems both possible and highly desirable that some specified powers be given to localities in addition to the general grant of authority over local affairs. Rather than leaving the entire field of home rule powers to the definition of the courts, there seems no valid reason why an enumeration of powers cannot be conferred upon cities in every home rule state. In the process of this enumeration, those powers which have been the cause of the greatest litigation in the past could be carefully considered. *As a matter of public policy, they can be granted or denied to home rule localities.*[1]

Note here, also, the fatal gap. The specific powers which have been the cause of the greatest litigation are those in respect to which there is the most controversy and the least measure of agreement. These include, among others, powers of taxation for local purposes, health, sanitation, regulation of private utilities, eminent domain, and the settlement of claims against a city. It is these powers which, after careful consideration *and as a matter of public policy*, are to be granted or denied.

The question arises immediately as to what agency or group is to make this crucial determination as a matter of public policy. Is it to be the legislature? A charter commission? A panel of governmental or public administration experts in state-local relations? What criteria are they to employ in making their determinations? Will there be any assurance that their determinations will be more valid than the conflicting determinations of the courts and that they will be any less the subject of controversy? These and many other relevant questions remain unanswered in the general statement respecting the proposed change in the method of specifying constitutional home-rule powers.

Again, the point is made that there is no quarrel with the general objectives of that report. It is in the translation of the general objectives into a definitive and meaningful constitutional concept that the difficulty

1. The Council of State Governments, *State-Local Relations* (1946), pp. 171, 172 (italics ours).

lies. Until this is done, if it can be done, there is little hope that constitutional home rule will be any more effective an instrumentality in aid of municipal autonomy than it has been in the past.

The most recent attempt to redefine the constitutional home-rule concept is worthy of note as a further illustration of the extreme difficulty of investing it with any attributes of certainty. In a draft prepared by Professor Fordham for the Committee on Home Rule of the American Municipal Association,[2] municipalities would have complete autonomy in respect to "executive, legislative and administrative structure, organization, personnel, and procedure" (the areas in which constitutional home rule provisions have been most effective in establishing the supremacy of municipal laws), subject only to the requirement that the members of the legislative body be chosen by popular vote and to a further exception respecting judicial review of administrative proceedings. In the area of substantive powers, the draft proposes the abandonment of the technique of granting general and specific powers and offers a "local federalism" formula which would authorize a city adopting a home rule charter under constitutional authority to "exercise any power or perform any function which the legislature has power to devolve upon a non-home rule charter municipal corporation and which is not denied to . . . [the home-rule city] by its . . . charter, *is not denied to all home rule charter [cities] by statute and is within such limitations as may be established by statute*" (italics ours).

This proposal is designed to effect a shift in power distribution by placing the burden upon the legislature, by general laws applicable to all home-rule cities, to deny cities the authority to exercise any given power. Cities would no longer be dependent upon an express grant of power but could operate freely within the total area of municipal power, except as proscribed by the legislature. Whether such a proposal would effect its objective of expanded powers of local self-determination will depend entirely upon the legislature's desires. If, for example, the legislature enacts a general law prohibiting the exercise of any taxing power, excepting those expressly delegated by statute, a not inconceivable prospect in many states, municipal autonomy will be largely an illusion.

Other areas of uncertainty remain unresolved. Is it, for example, politically desirable as a concept of state-city relationships that the constitutional grant of home-rule powers be made subject to legislative implementation, definition, or restriction in the manner which prevails in West Virginia, Michigan, Pennsylvania, and Louisiana? Or should the grant be defined as "self-executing," emanating from the constitution and vesting in the people of the city directly, to be by them, rather than the legislature, translated into the definitive powers which their city

2. Jefferson Fordham, *Model Constitutional Provisions for Municipal Home Rule* (Chicago: American Municipal Association, 1953).

government may exercise? This is the theory which sustains the extensive municipal autonomy of California cities in revenue matters and which supports the more limited autonomy in revenue matters enjoyed by cities in Ohio and Missouri.

A related, but highly significant, aspect of this inquiry concerns the legal character of the charter adopted by constitutional home-rule cities. Should the charter be viewed as a grant of powers by the people to their government, or should it be viewed as a limitation upon their government's powers? The legal consequences flowing from this distinction are of extreme importance in respect to the measure of autonomy vested in the city government. Thus, as we have seen, California views the locally adopted charter, in revenue matters, as a limitation on power, and the crucial inquiry in respect to the exercise of a particular tax power is not whether the charter expressly permits such exercise but whether it proscribes it. On the other hand, in Texas and Missouri, among other states, the charter is viewed as a grant of powers, and the exercise of any specific tax power must be referable to an express grant. In the latter states, broadly defined grants of revenue powers have been held insufficient to sustain municipally imposed taxes, and city governments have found it necessary to seek authority from the legislature. This concept of constitutional home rule places municipalities in substantially the same legal position as municipalities in nonconstitutional home-rule states.

In respect to these issues, most of the political and legal literature on the subject of constitutional home rule is either silent or obscure— a further indication of the vagueness and uncertainty which underlies the concept. The failure to resolve these issues, in accordance with criteria and standards upon which a substantial political consensus may be reached, will continue to plague the development of constitutional home rule as a meaningful concept.

City Government in the State Courts

A Note from the Harvard Law Review

IF FIVE MEN are unable to decide whether to spend an evening playing poker or going to a movie they may put the question to a vote. If three vote to play cards and two vote to go to the movie the matter is settled. Suppose, however, that the five men are faced with the same choice on a succession of evenings and the vote is always the same. The members of the minority are likely to say that although a single night's entertainment may properly be chosen by majority vote, they would not have agreed to go along with the majority on a succession of occasions if they had realized that they would never get their way. Suppose further that on one evening there is a movie that the two in the minority particularly want to see. They are likely to feel that their special interest on this evening should be taken into account, but the system to which they have agreed has no mechanism for measuring the strength of each individual's feelings.[1]

The two men have discovered a basic fact of politics: if decision making by majority preference is to give each man a significant voice, stable coalitions able to dominate the process and deny other groups an effective role must be avoided. Suppose that on one occasion the three-man majority is split two to one over what card game to play. At this point one side may seek the help of the minority group, which may in return demand support for going to the movies on some other occasion. Enlarging the number of issues and, as a result, producing a different division in the voting group has, for the first time, given the votes of the minority some meaning, by according the two men something with which to bargain. Even if the five men voted and bargained on a large number of issues one might not be able to say that each man won an exact "fair share" of the time; but each man would be satisfied that he was winning some of the time and that his power to bargain would usually enable him to win on the issues most important to him.

1. Professor Robert Dahl has called this the "intensity" factor in decision making. See DAHL, A PREFACE TO DEMOCRATIC THEORY 48–50, 90–123 (Phoenix ed. 1963).

Reprinted from "City Government in the State Courts," 78 Harvard Law Review 1596 (1965). *Copyright (c) 1965 by The Harvard Law Review Association.*

I. The Problem of the Stable Majority

It is the hypothesis of this Note that there is a greater threat in a small city[2] than in larger political units that significant interest groups will find themselves in a position somewhat resembling that of the two men unable to go to the movies: members of certain groups may be denied an effective role in decision making because larger or politically more effective groups dominate the political process. In all but the smallest political units legislating is left to a group of elected representatives, generally a small, unicameral city council.[3] The municipal executive sometimes lacks veto power and may have little influence on policy.[4] Hence, the city is unlike federal or state governments with their series of checks and balances: the necessary and sufficient condition of control of the decision-making process is control of a group of representatives that comprises a majority of the city council and acts together for common aims.

A.

Control by Majority Faction

A majority coalition in the city council can occur when a majority of the citizenry, having a common position on a significant share of the issues before the legislature, elects a majority favorable to its interests. James Madison feared just such dominance by a unified majority:[5]

> Either the existence of the same passion or interest in a majority at the same time must be prevented, or the majority, having such coexistent passion or interest, must be rendered, by their number and local situation, unable to concert and carry into effect schemes of oppression.

Madison went on to suggest that the threat of a stable coalition of interests, capable of dominating the political process, would be greatest in a town or small city:[6]

> The smaller the society, the fewer probably will be the distinct parties and interests composing it; the fewer the distinct parties and interests,

2. This Note is concerned with a danger that increases as the size of the city diminishes rather than an evil that can be predicated of an exact number of cities. Consequently, it is not possible to give a precise definition of "small city." Most of the theoretical political factors with which the Note is concerned, however, probably cease to play an important role when a city's population rises above 100,000.

3. See KNEIER, CITY GOVERNMENT IN THE UNITED STATES 221 (3d ed. 1957).

4. See *id.* at 249; BABCOCK, STATE AND LOCAL GOVERNMENT AND POLITICS 120 (2d ed. 1956); GRANT & NIXON, STATE AND LOCAL GOVERNMENT IN AMERICA 315 (1963).

5. THE FEDERALIST No. 10, at 81 (New Am. Lib. ed 1961).

6. *Id.* at 83.

the more frequently will a majority be found of the same party; and the smaller the number of individuals composing a majority, and the smaller the compass within which they are placed, the more easily will they concert and execute their plans of oppression.

To state the Madisonian proposition somewhat more broadly, the danger of a stable coalition increases as the size of the political unit decreases because the areas of disagreement become fewer and the divisions in the population consequently become more fundamental and permanent. In the first place, a small city's population may include a small number of ethnic, economic, and social groups. A group of local businessmen is found in almost every city; other groups may include laborers who work at one or a few local factories, wealthier families living on incomes derived from outside the city, perhaps a university community, a large group of retired couples, or a number of people who are unemployed.

Though the individuals in each of these groups may disagree widely on matters of state or national policy, they will often have similar expectations from the city and share a common view of the proper role of their city government.[7] Most major issues in a small city tend to divide the people who hold one set of expectations from those who hold another so that individuals with the same basic interest will often be allied on a large proportion of civil questions: for the businessman the city is the source of livelihood; for some residents the city is a source of social and cultural opportunities; for others it may be merely an economical place to live; one might expect individuals holding such different views to differ on a large proportion of the issues with which city government deals.

.A variety of studies of individual communities indicate that one interest group is often able to impose its conception of the community on the entire populace.[8] Local business interests seeking to attract new

7. For an exposition of categories of expectations of various classes, see WILLIAMS & ADRIAN, FOUR CITIES 23-32 (1963). See also BANFIELD & WILSON, CITY POLITICS 53-56 (1963).

8. The word "variety" in this sentence could be underscored. Urban sociology, as a science, is plagued by major disagreements among scholars—not only about what the answers are, but about what the questions are. Some have regarded influential individuals as the key to small-city politics; others have explored the city's social structure, economic structure, or political organization, each observer believing his approach to be the one that best describes how city decisions are made. A comprehensive bibliographic work on recent studies of city politics—and a work that illustrates this variety of approaches—is PRESS, MAIN STREET POLITICS (1962). The studies do tend to find a rigid pattern of influence; as a result the character of the city is determined by a dominant group and channels of influence are few; presumably groups that cannot enter those channels find it difficult to be heard. See especially HUNTER, COMMUNITY POWER STRUCTURE (1953); LYND & LYND, MIDDLETOWN (1929); Mills, *The Middle Classes in Middle-Sized Cities*, 11 AM. SOCIOLOGICAL REV. 520 (1946); Stewart, *A Study of Influence in Southtown: II*, 10 SOCIOMETRY 273 (1947). *But see* Polsby, *The Sociology of Community Power: A Reassessment*, 37 SOCIAL FORCES 232 (1959) (questioning whether local power structure in fact remains stable from issue to issue).

industry, or upper middle class families favoring amenities to make the city "a nice place to live," or small property owners who wish to avoid raising the tax level may dictate the outcome of virtually every major issue.[9] The formation of relatively stable majorities has the converse effect of rendering minorities powerless. A group effectively disfranchised by its minority position may find that community services in its part of town remain marginal.[10] A large industrial concern may find itself financing bowling alleys and elaborate public buildings.[11]

The factors that divide public opinion in a city—residence, economic status, ethnic group membership, number of children per voter, and so forth—tend to coincide. To illustrate, a proposed federal measure that favors one geographical area is likely to produce a different division of opinion from a measure assisting all people of a certain economic status, but a geographical issue in city politics often produces the same alignment of voters as an economic issue because people of the same economic status often live in the same area of the city.

There are, of course, disagreements within municipal interest groups; but there is also pressure to resolve disputes within the group so that individuals will not resort to bargaining with outsiders who will, in return, demand things to which the group as a whole is opposed. The ability of the group to stick together and work out internal differences is enhanced by the intimacy of city life. People with common interests may be friends, coworkers, and neighbors; the leaders of an interest group have easy access to their followers. And in very small cities the intimacy of city life may weaken opposition to the dominant group in another way: the desire to avoid confrontations that, in a small town, must be personal as well as political, may lead people to acquiesce in the decisions of acknowledged leaders even when these decisions do not reflect their own preferences.[12]

The absence of "slack" in the legislative process itself may also make it difficult for minorities to gain an effective bargaining position. In Congress, large numbers of legislators are often not unalterably committed, by predilection or by the impact of a decision on their constituents, to one side of a particular issue. As a result, a significant minority that feels strongly about a particular issue may be able to gain votes of the uncommitted by promising assistance on other matters about which the minority is less concerned. In a small city legislature there may be far fewer uncommitted votes on each issue. For example, the impact of every expenditure on the constituents of each legislator is relatively easy for both him and them to calculate. A legislative majority committed to the "low tax principle" is often particularly powerful be-

9. See WILLIAMS & ADRIAN, FOUR CITIES 271–78 (1963).

10. KIMBALL & PEARSALL, TALLADEGA STORY 163–72 (1954), reprinted in WILLIAMS & PRESS, DEMOCRACY IN URBAN AMERICA 346–53 (1961).

11. *Cf.* ADRIAN, GOVERNING URBAN AMERICA 155–60 (2d ed. 1961).

12. See BANFIELD & WILSON, CITY POLITICS 25–26 (1963).

cause the tax impact of every expenditure is sufficiently apparent to keep individual legislators from being wooed away on individual issues. An example of dominance by economy-minded property owners is found in the town that Arthur Vidich and Joseph Bensman studied and called Springdale, New York:[13]

> Hardly a meeting of the village board passes without some action being justified on the basis of the low tax principle—services are curtailed to avoid a tax raise, purchases of new equipment are postponed in order to avoid expenditures, the trustees complain to each other if street lights are not turned off at sunrise . . . .

There are people who want the town to try to attract new industry, or to provide adequate roads or street lighting, but their point of view plays no part in decision making.[14]

B.
The Central Group Within the Stable Majority

Frequently a stable majority coalition consists of two main groups, a core of people who want the city's decisions to follow certain lines and a larger group that gives the leaders votes and political support for reasons that have little to do with the major decisions of city government. This Note is not concerned with the man who trades away his vote for small favors: he is participating in the political process even if he is participating foolishly. We are concerned, however, with those who feel strongly about city decisions but have no voice in making them, and one of the reasons why such excluded groups are likely to exist is that a clique that does have political concerns can often gain support from people who do not care.

At least since Lincoln Steffens,[15] observers have argued that the trouble with municipal politics is that people do not care about the city. The statement of a Chicago precinct captain in 1950 illustrates the effect of this unconcern: "I help my people get relief and driveway permits. . . . The only return I ask is that they register and vote. If they have their own opinions on certain top offices, I just ask them to vote my way on lower offices where they usually have no preferences anyway."[16] These remarks illustrate two factors that make possible an "economy of promises" in city politics. The first is the failure of many people who vote in state and national elections to vote in city elections

---

13. VIDICH & BENSMAN, SMALL TOWN IN MASS SOCIETY 117 (1958).
14. See *id.* at 122–24.
15. STEFFENS, THE SHAME OF THE CITIES 1–18 (Am. Cent. ed. 1960).
16. Quoted in Myerson & Banfield, *A Machine at Work,* in URBAN GOVERNMENT 135, 141 (Banfield ed. 1961).

or even to inform themselves about city affairs.[17] When combined with the small size of the electorate, this apathy often assures a political victory, without commitments to large numbers of voters, to an organization that can get a core of people to register and vote. Even if voter apathy were equal in national, state, and local elections, it would be far more significant in local elections, for a local politician may know his constituents personally and can more easily isolate the individuals, families, and groups that will determine the outcome of an election.

The precinct captain's remarks also suggest that politicians in many cities may be able to command support for a relatively low political price from people who do vote. The closeness of the representative (or his political associates) to the constituency may enable him to gain favor more by personal contact and less by appeal to group interests than his state or national counterparts. And the closeness of the representative to the constituency lowers the price for political victory in another way: a politician needs to offer a man or a group less when he knows exactly what it wants.

The ethnic background of voters may also play a particularly large role in city politics. Some critics of local government who blamed large immigrant or racial groups for giving a power base to unscrupulous politicians thought only of the supposed lack of political sophistication of these groups. At this point in our history it is probably more accurate to say simply that ethnic lines tend to influence voting patterns whether or not the group is "politically sophisticated."[18]

II. Judicial Review of Municipal Ordinances

Distrust of municipal democracy is imbedded deep in American political thinking. Both Jefferson[19] and Madison[20] speculated that cities could not govern themselves equitably. Some early state decisions limited local powers in order "to prevent the minority from being at the disposal of the majority."[21] Years later, when cities were troubled by corruption, observers like Lincoln Steffens[22] and James Bryce[23] proclaimed the failure of the municipal political process. Criticism of cities reached its height in the late nineteenth century reform movement. "[T]he city governments of the United States," one reformer said, "are

17. KNEIER, *op. cit. supra* note 3, at 335–39. See also ADRIAN, *op. cit. supra* note 11, at 6–7, 91–98; BANFIELD & WILSON, CITY POLITICS 231–34 (1963).

18. BANFIELD & WILSON, CITY POLITICS 51–53, 229–31 (1963); DAHL, WHO GOVERNS? 52–59 (1961).

19. JEFFERSON, NOTES ON THE STATE OF VIRGINIA 303–04, in 3 JEFFERSON'S WRITINGS 269 (Ford ed. 1894).

20. See THE FEDERALIST No. 10.

21. See Stetson v. Kempton, 13 Mass. 272, 284 (1816).

22. STEFFENS, *op. cit. supra* note 15, at 1–18.

23. 2 BRYCE, THE AMERICAN COMMONWEALTH 105–09 (2d ed. 1891).

the worst in Christendom."[24] The reformers often assumed that the evils of the city, corruption and the exclusion of important interests from political participation, resulted from the fact that city people—in particular, laborers who had never been exalted by working the soil and immigrant groups from countries where democracy was unknown— lacked the personal qualities necessary for self-government.[25]

The reformers' solution to city problems was to reform the political system itself. Two groups of reformers—to some extent two generations —reached different solutions. The first generation argued that a city should be run like a business, that competence and honesty were the only requirements for good civic leadership, and that the solution lay in a professional, apolitical management group that would seek the "common good" instead of devoting itself to special interests.[26] It has been suggested, however, that the proponents of this plan were often (perhaps with the best of motives) advocating a version of the common good with which significant sections of the community might properly disagree.[27] A later generation of reformers thought that not enough attention was being paid to the popular will, and that politics should not be abandoned but rather improved and expanded. This was the era of the advocates of referendum and initiative, of recall and proportional representation.[28]

While the reformers debated the problems of the city, an external check on municipal democracy was created by expanding the role of state courts. In 1872, the year of the Boss Tweed scandal, New York passed a statute conferring standing on residents, as taxpayers,[29] to secure review of municipal legislation in a state court,[30] and taxpayers have been given standing to challenge municipal action in almost every American jurisdiction.[31] A taxpayer still has no standing to seek review of federal legislation[32] and one might speculate that this difference in requirements for standing indicates a difference in attitude about the judiciary's role at different levels of government. Variance in standing requirements has been explained in terms of the supposedly more direct impact of city expenditures on the individual taxpayer;[33] but taxpayer suits are often allowed when not even a minimal pocketbook effect is shown, as when the act challenged involves no increase in expendi-

---

24. White, *The Government of American Cities* (1890), in URBAN GOVERNMENT 213 (Banfield ed. 1961).

25. See HOFSTADTER, THE AGE OF REFORM 174–86 (Vintage ed. 1960).

26. White, *supra* note 24, at 213.

27. See URBAN GOVERNMENT 209–12 (Banfield ed. 1961).

28. See BABCOCK, *op. cit. supra* note 4, at 79–82.

29. An Act for the protection of taxpayers against the frauds, embezzlements, and wrongful acts of public officers and agents, 1 N.Y. Sess. Laws 1872, ch. 161; see Ayers v. Lawrence, 59 N.Y. 192 (1874), connecting the statute with the activities of Tweed.

30. See Note, *Taxpayers' Suits: A Survey and Summary*, 69 Yale L.J. 895, 899 (1960).

31. *Id.* at 895.

32. Frothingham v. Mellon, 262 U.S. 447 (1923).

33. See *id.* at 486–87.

tures.[34] If a defendant city challenges the plaintiff's standing on the ground that he will not be affected, qua taxpayer, by the municipal act, the courts usually answer that a citizen has an interest in "good government."[35] A taxpayer, of course, has an interest in good government at all levels: it is the court's readiness to play a larger role in protecting this interest on the municipal level that is demonstrated by the willingness to review municipal ordinances without a showing of substantial impact on rights personal to the plaintiff.

A.
The Standards of Review

In responding to the demand for good government the courts also adopted broad standards of review that contrast dramatically with the restraint exercised in the review of federal and state legislation. The theory of separation of powers, each branch playing a distinct role and complementing the other branch without infringing on the other's areas of special competence, has defined and limited the task of courts reviewing state and federal legislation; courts reviewing municipal legislation have not accepted such narrow restraints on their role in decision making, and the comparison is instructive.

I. JUDICIAL RESTRAINT IN REVIEWING FEDERAL AND STATE LEGISLATION. A fundamental principle of democracy is that the people or their representatives should decide most questions of public policy. Yet we have not trusted the people to make decisions in all areas, and our democracy has always been tempered by limits on the power of the people's representatives. Broadly, the limits are of two kinds: first, checks within the lawmaking process (such as the requirement of concurrence by two houses and the provision of an executive veto);[36] and second, limits on the types of decisions entrusted to legislative bodies. Legislatures are restricted in making decisions that will affect persons who are either unrepresented or inadequately represented. For example, the concepts of privileges and immunities and full faith and credit seem in part designed to protect nonresidents of a given state from the acts of that state's legislature; and one justification for limiting Congress to questions of national and interstate importance is that the people of a given state will be better represented on intrastate questions if these latter questions are decided by a body responsible solely to the state's residents.[37] Finally, certain substantive rights are protected from legis-

---

34. See, *e.g.*, Wirin v. Parker, 48 Cal. 2d 890, 313 P.2d 844 (1957); Howard v. City of Boulder, 132 Colo. 401, 290 P.2d 237 (1955).

35. See Howard v. City of Boulder, *supra* note 34.

36. THE FEDERALIST No. 51 and No. 62 (Madison).

37. *Cf.* Acton, *The History of Freedom in Antiquity* (1877), in THE HISTORY OF FREEDOM AND OTHER ESSAYS 1, 20 (1909).

lative action because they are not thought appropriate for majority decision.

The task of a court reviewing legislation is to police the boundaries that have been placed around legislative action without undermining the basic assumption that the people's representatives are the best qualified and safest group to which to entrust most decisions:[38]

> If what is done by Congress is manifestly in excess of the powers granted to it, then upon the courts will rest the duty of adjudging that its action is neither legal nor binding upon the people. But if what Congress does is within the limits of its power, and is simply unwise or injurious, the remedy is that suggested by Chief Justice Marshall in *Gibbons v. Ogden,* when he said: "The wisdom and the discretion of Congress, their identity with the people, and the influence which their constituents possess at elections, are, in this, as in many other instances, . . . the sole restraints on which they have relied, to secure them from its abuse. They are the restraints on which the people must often rely solely, in all representative governments."

Courts have limited their own participation in the decision-making process not only out of respect for the doctrine of separation of powers but also out of respect for their own fallibility and for the inherent limitations of judicial procedure. A tribunal may give great weight to the opinion of a coordinate legislature that a law is constitutional.[39] Courts have recognized that they can answer only questions that may be decided on the basis of accessible facts and precedent, legal expertise and human reason, and have refused to review legislative judgments that raise questions beyond judicial competence.[40] The Supreme Court has refused to examine the motives of federal or state legislators, in part because of the difficulty of obtaining facts, of "psychoanalyzing the legislature," in part because it is difficult to set standards for deciding what evidence would justify striking down a statute.[41]

2. STATE COURTS, CITY LEGISLATURES, AND THE DOCTRINE OF SEPARATION OF POWERS. A rigorous doctrine of separation of powers between state courts and municipal legislatures has not evolved. one reason for this is that cities, as administrative subdivisions of the states in which they are located,[42] possess only the powers granted by the state.[43] Thus, the basic assumption that policy decisions should be made by legislators responsible to the people is not entirely applicable. City legislators are responsible not only to city residents but to the state. State courts, which can treat city councils as subordinate agencies rather than

38. Champion v. Ames, 188 U.S. 321, 363 (1903).
39. See Thayer, *The Origin and Scope of the American Doctrine of Constitutional Law,* 7 HARV. L. REV. 129, 144 (1893).
40. See, *e.g.,* Korematsu v. United States, 323 U.S. 214, 218 (1944); Commercial Trust Co. v. Miller, 262 U.S. 51, 57 (1923).
41. See Fletcher v. Peck, 10 U.S. (6 Cranch) 87 (1810).
42. See City of Trenton v. New Jersey, 262 U.S. 182, 185–86 (1923); BABCOCK, *op. cit. supra* note 4, at 123.
43. See KNEIER, *op. cit. supra* note 3, at 163.

co-equal branches of government, then have the leeway to determine that local legislatures have acted contrary to state policy.

Reformers hoped that home rule—meant to give cities broad authority over intracity affairs—would undercut the principle that every city decision is basically a decision of state policy made by a subordinate agency. This has not always happened: while in some of the twenty-seven states that have home rule[44] cities are given broad discretion, one commentator has observed that "after nearly a century of experience with home rule, no definition of the extent of municipal initiative has evolved."[45] Courts have sometimes used their power to determine whether a city has stayed within its home-rule grant in much the same way that courts in non-home-rule states decide whether municipal decisions conform to state policy.[46] In determining whether home rule gives a city the power to make a certain decision, courts sometimes look to decisions in non-home-rule states and to pre-home-rule decisions in the same state.[47]

One important fact in the relation of state courts to local legislatures is the number of city decisions that affect nonresidents. State courts must protect nonresidents, who have no voice in city politics, from the effects of such decisions. The courts have found in this duty a powerful tool with which to narrow the range of municipal power: for example, local traffic regulation has been held not to be a matter for local decision, probably because it affects nonresidents.[48]

One of the major groups in the municipal reform movement was rural, presumably composed of people whose lives were affected in new ways by the growth of cities after the Civil War. This nonresident pressure may have been one factor that led courts to interpret municipal powers strictly. It is apparent, however, that a city cannot be deprived of power to pass any ordinance affecting nonresidents; hence it is necessary to decide when the risk of infringing upon nonresident interests is so great that the city should not be permitted to make a particular decision.[49] Judicial efforts to protect nonresidents from the effects of city decisions perhaps provided the impetus for judicial protection of interests within the city itself. Whatever the precise historical roots, state courts in the late nineteenth century began to formulate standards of review that made them, in effect, active participants in municipal policy making.

3. THE ANNOUNCED STANDARDS OF JUDICIAL REVIEW. State courts have articulated standards of review of municipal ordinances that

44. See Sandalow, *The Limits of Municipal Power Under Home Rule: A Role for the Courts,* 48 MINN. L. REV. 643, 645 (1964).

45. *Id.* at 671.

46. See BANFIELD & WILSON, CITY POLITICS 66–67 (1963).

47. See, *e.g.,* People *ex rel.* Wilshire v. Newman, 96 Cal. 605, 31 Pac. 564 (1892).

48. See Pipoly v. Benson, 20 Cal. 2d 366, 125 P.2d 482 (1942).

49. See Ferran v. City of Palo Alto, 50 Cal. App. 2d 374, 122 P.2d 965 (Dist. Ct. App. 1942); *Ex parte* Blois, 179 Cal. 291, 176 Pac. 449 (1918).

differ greatly from the standards used by courts reviewing federal and state legislation. In the first place, grants of municipal power are strictly interpreted. The American towns that de Tocqueville had described as "independent in all that concerns themselves alone,"[50] were pictured rather differently at the end of the nineteenth century in John F. Dillon's treatise on Municipal Corporations:[51]

> It is a general and undisputed proposition of law that a *municipal corporation possesses and can exercise the following powers and no others:* First, those granted in *express words;* second, those *necessarily or fairly implied* in or *incident* to the powers expressly granted; third, those *essential* to the accomplishment of the declared objects and purposes of the corporation,—not simply convenient, but indispensable. Any fair, reasonable, substantial doubt concerning the existence of power is resolved by the courts against the corporation, and the power is denied.

In explanation of this rule Dillon stated that reasonable doubts should be determined "in favor of the State or general public, and against the State's grantee."[52] Perhaps a presumption of validity is inappropriate for cases in which nonresidents are affected by the legislation in question, but Dillon's rule purported to summarize the existing law for all situations and, perhaps more significant, provided support for strict interpretation in subsequent cases, frequently cases involving no nonmunicipal interests.

State courts have found ways other than the strict interpretation of constitutional or statutory powers to limit municipal authority. Courts have used the doctrine that tax money must be spent for a public purpose to prevent cities from entering upon commercial activities that would at least arguably serve the public but would not do so in a way that the court believes to be among the city's proper functions.[53] It has been held that a municipal ordinance may not violate state "common law" or "public policy"[54] and must be "reasonable."[55] These standards reflect a special attitude toward municipal legislation:[56]

50. 1 DE TOCQUEVILLE, DEMOCRACY IN AMERICA 68 (Bradley ed. 1945). On the relative independence of early cities, see also Mayor, Alderman & Commonalty v. Ordrenan, 12 Johns. R. 122, 124 (N.Y. Sup. Ct. 1815); MCBAIN, THE LAW AND THE PRACTICE OF MUNICIPAL HOME RULE 3–12 (1916).

51. 1 DILLON, COMMENTARIES ON THE LAW OF MUNICIPAL CORPORATIONS § 237 (5th ed. 1911) (footnotes omitted.)

52. *Id.* § 239.

53. See Kneier, *Municipal Functions and the Law of Public Purpose,* 76 U. PA. L. REV. 824 (1928).

54. See generally 5 MCQUILLIN, MUNICIPAL CORPORATIONS § 15.21 (3d ed. 1949).

55. See generally *id.* ch. 18.

56. Hopkins v. City of Richmond, 117 Va. 692, 708, 86 S.E. 139, 144 (1915). *Compare* 5 MCQUILLIN, *op. cit. supra* note 54, § 18.02, *with* id. § 18.03. Sometimes courts fortify declarations of the invalidity of ordinances by holding legislation *unconstitutionally* unreasonable rather than simply unreasonable. In the absence of a constitutional provision demanding reasonableness, the two characterizations would seem equivalent.

[W]hat the [state] legislature distinctly says may be done cannot be set aside by the courts because they may deem it unreasonable, or against sound policy. But where the power to legislate in a given subject is conferred [on a city], and the mode of its exercise is not prescribed then the ordinance passed in pursuance thereof must be a reasonable exercise of the power, or it will be pronounced invalid.

The distinction between the judicial approaches to state legislation and local legislation is well reflected in two Missouri decisions. Although the state and the city of St. Louis both have the legislative power to abate nuisances, the state alone has been held to have general power to declare things to be nuisances that were not so at common law.[57] A municipal abatement is subject to review to determine whether, taking into account the interests involved, the legislature reached a reasonable and proper resolution of the merits of the particular question.[58]

State courts may receive evidence showing what considerations entered into the city council's decision, and will occasionally strike down an ordinance proper on its face if the court concludes that it was in fact intended to achieve something the court considers improper. Thus when the City of Miami Beach passed an ordinance prohibiting use of cooking devices in single-family hotel or apartment units containing less than four hundred square feet of floor space, the ordinance was held both unreasonable and unconstitutional.[59] The city contended that the ordinance was (1) a safety measure and (2) a way of establishing minimum floor space for family living. Not believing this, the court said:[60]

> Taking into account the identity of the protagonists for the enactment and enforcement of this ordinance, namely, the Miami Beach Apartment Association, the contents of the minutes of the city Council of Miami Beach, the arbitrary and nowhere justified criteria of four hundred (400) square feet of floor space, the limited application of the ordinance, the effect of the ordinance upon competing groups in the tourist accommodation business, . . . it is patent and beyond real debate that the sole aim of the ordinance was to interfere with business competition and the operation of natural economic laws in a discriminatory manner.

B.

A Theory of the Role of the Courts

Distrust of city governments and the willingness of state courts to play a large role in regulating municipal decision making are matters of record. The relation between court decisions in individual cases and

57. State v. Tower, 185 Mo. 79, 91, 84 S.W. 10, 11 (1904).
58. City of St. Louis v. Heitzeberg Packing & Provision Co., 141 Mo. 375, 42 S.W. 954 (1897).
59. Fox v. Bancroft Hotel Associates, 128 So. 2d 771 (Fla. Dist. Ct. App. 1961).
60. *Id.* at 773.

the underlying weaknesses of the municipal political process is a matter of theory that can perhaps be best explored by examining individual cases in the light of the political factors that might move a court to strike down a particular municipal decision. Because a court's decision is usually explained in terms of the "announced standards," it is often necessary to speculate when explaining a particular holding in terms of the relation of a given ordinance to the problems in the municipal political process. Nevertheless, one finds that the most satisfactory explanation of many holdings is that the court felt that certain interests might not be afforded adequate consideration in the municipal legislature, or obviously had not received such consideration in a particular instance.

I. ISSUES THOUGHT INAPPROPRIATE FOR LOCAL DECISION MAKING. The reason this Note has advanced for distrust of the municipal legislative process is the danger that one group of community interests will dominate that process. This suggests that a court that is trying to decide what issues are appropriate for local decision might be moved by the consideration that certain classes of issues are likely to involve stable divisions in the community and that in a series of such issues one of the sections of the community is likely not to receive its due. An obvious cleavage in most communities is that between commercial interests and residential or taxpayer interests, and in fact municipal powers appear to be most strictly construed when the city is attempting to decide questions that divide these groups.

The doctrine that tax money may be used only for a public purpose has been used to prevent cities from benefiting residents at the expense of a commercial enterprise, and vice versa.[61] The doctrine has been explained in bewildering and mystical terms: the question is whether the proposed municipal activity is "essentially public" or "essentially private" but the answer to the question has "no relation to the urgency of the public need, or the extent of the public benefit which is to follow."[62] The line that has in fact been drawn seems to divide those local problems on which action by the city as a unit is essential from those activities for which unified action is less essential *and* in which there is a danger that a commercial enterprise will be unduly harmed or benefited. Thus a city can supply water, which must run through pipes,[63] but it was held (in an age before power refrigeration) that the city could not undertake to supply ice even if it determined that existing commercial sources were inadequate.[64]

The doctrine of "public policy" has been similarly used to prevent the city from choosing between residential and commercial interests. An ordinance prohibiting the construction of a gasoline service station

---

61. See Kneier, *supra* note 53, at 824.
62. People *ex rel.* Detroit & H.R.R. v. Township Bd., 20 Mich. 452, 485 (1870).
63. See City of Augusta v. Augusta Water Dist., 101 Me. 148, 63 Atl. 663 (1906).
64. Union Ice & Coal Co. v. Town of Ruston, 135 La. 898, 66 So. 262 (1914).

in a place where two-thirds of the buildings within a three hundred foot radius were residential was held contrary to public policy.[65] Requiring consent of three-fourths of the residents of a residential block before a billboard could be erected was found similarly improper.[66] Ordinances requiring barbershops to close on Sundays[67] and forbidding sale of fireworks[68] were held to conflict with state policies of not restricting lawful uses of property.

2. PARTICULAR ORDINANCES THAT BURDEN MINORITIES. If a court finds that it is within the power of the city to deal with a particular question, it may yet feel that the actual decision made by the city reflects inadequate consideration of a minority interest. In theory, the legislature, effectively controlled by one interest group, may have done either of two things: it may have passed an ordinance that is "uneconomic" from the point of view of the total wealth of the community—the burdens placed on one group of citizens are larger than the benefits that accrue to others; or the ordinance may be "economic" yet "unfair" if too large a burden is placed on one or a few persons. Thus suppose one man has a factory worth one million dollars and the city passes a zoning ordinance that forces the factory out of business: a court may feel either (1) that the resulting gain to the community—to surrounding property values and other interests—simply does not equal one million dollars, or (2) that it is probably beneficial to the city as a whole to remove the offending factory, and yet it is not proper to impose the whole cost of this city improvement upon a single factory owner, in other words, that it is not proper for the city to make a major, indirect, and arbitrary redistribution of wealth. In this hypothetical situation the distinction between an uneconomic ordinance and an unfair ordinance is that in the former case the city should not be permitted to close the factory at all and in the latter it should be permitted to do so only if it compensates the owner. Unfortunately courts have generally failed to distinguish these two problems when calling an ordinance "unreasonable," and have usually indicated only that the test of reasonableness involves a weighing of the civic objective and the burden placed on individuals:[69]

> [The reasonableness of an ordinance is] a question for the court, and there is no specific formula by which . . . reasonableness can be tested. However, the court will consider all the circumstances; not only what has been done under the ordinance but what may be done, *the objects sought to be attained and the necessity which exists for the ordinance.*

65. People *ex rel.* Russell v. Andrews, 339 Ill. 157, 171 N.E. 137 (1930).

66. City of Chicago v. Gunning Sys., 214 Ill. 628, 73 N.E. 1035 (1905).

67. City of Marengo v. Rowland, 263 Ill. 531, 534, 105 N.E. 285, 286 (1914).

68. King v. City of Louisville, 207 Miss. 612, 42 So. 2d 813 (1949).

69. National Linen Serv. Corp. v. City of Norfolk, 196 Va. 277, 281, 83 S.E.2d 401, 404 (1954) (Emphasis added). See generally 5 McQUILLIN, *op. cit. supra* note 54, § 18.06.

Municipal attempts to require laundries remaining open at night to employ a night watchman after 11:00 P.M.,[70] or to limit the number of gasoline service stations within a particular fire district[71] have been struck down because the court disagreed with the conclusion that the legislature reached after "balancing the interests." The City of Port Chester, after receiving authority to regulate sales of merchandise on the streets, passed an ordinance prohibiting sale of newspapers on public streets between 9:00 P.M. and 7:00 A.M., but the New York Court of Appeals found this unreasonable and unconstitutional.[72] Whatever the city stood to gain by the ordinance probably did not equal the burden placed upon roving newsboys. When a city prohibited "rope-geared, hydraulic elevators" under its power to enact safety ordinances the ordinance was declared unreasonable because the reviewing court was not convinced that such elevators were sufficiently unsafe to justify the harm caused property owners by the prohibition.[73] It is difficult to determine whether the court thought that even a prospective prohibition of such elevators would be "uneconomic"—imposing an unjustified cost on future builders—or that a retrospective prohibition would be uneconomic since it was not worth the cost of replacing the elevators, or that the prohibition was unfair as it stood but would be permissible if the city assumed the cost of replacement. An ordinance requiring restaurants to supply disposable paper towels in their restrooms was struck down when the court was not satisfied that these towels were sufficiently more sanitary than cloth towels to justify the harm to a linen firm.[74] Since there is a substantial argument, made by the city, that a disposable towel is preferable to one that is, in practice if not in theory, reusable, the holding seems hard to justify.

Often a holding that purports to rest on a "literal" reading of a city's authorization appears to be based in large part on the court's conclusion that a city's objective places too great a burden on a single section of the population. A town authorized to license and regulate taxicabs and "to make ordinances . . . for the better government of the town" discovered that it could not require taxicab operators to carry liability insurance; the court held that the ordinance was not literally "regulation" and was not related to "better government."[75] New York City found, in 1942, that it had no power to prohibit street peddling although it had been granted power to control use of its streets and to regulate business within its limits.[76] Cities permitted to abate nuisances have

70. Heard v. Bolton, 107 Ga. App. 863, 131 S.E.2d 835 (1963).
71. Town of Clinton v. Standard Oil Co., 193 N.C. 432, 137 S.E. 183 (1927).
72. People v. Kuc, 272 N.Y. 72, 4 N.E.2d 939 (1936).
73. Streb v. City of Rochester, 32 Misc. 2d 29, 222 N.Y.S.2d 813 (Sup. Ct. 1961).
74. National Linen Serv. Corp. v. City of Norfolk, 196 Va. 277, 83 S.E.2d 401 (1954).
75. State v. Gulledge, 208 N.C. 204, 179 S.E. 883 (1935).
76. Good Humor Corp. v. City of New York, 264 App. Div. 620, 36 N.Y.S.2d 85 (1942), aff'd, 290 N.Y. 312, 49 N.E.2d 153 (1943).

sometimes found their power to change the operations of existing com-
merical enterprises small indeed: smoke[77] and storage of gasoline in
bulk, for example, have been held not to be nuisances.[78]

A holding that a city is not authorized to make a certain decision
may reflect the court's conclusion that, on this issue, the interest in
allowing each person to act as he sees fit outweighs any practical advantages of action by the community as a whole. A city empowered
to appoint officers who may, "in the opinion of the city council be necessary for the . . . advantage of commerce and trade" was held not to
have power to appoint an advertising agent for the purpose of publicizing the city as a resort; one might speculate that the court thought
that this kind of commerce should not be furthered by public expenditures because some members of the community might object to the
expansion of the resort trade.[79]

The opinions in these cases give no indication that the courts had
heard evidence that the interest harmed by the ordinance in question
had been consciously or unconsciously disregarded in the legislature's
deliberations. Yet it is difficult to justify a holding that the legislature
reached the wrong result when weighing local interests unless one
adopts an analysis such as the following: there is some independent
probability that, say, the owners of buildings with "rope-geared hydraulic
elevators"—who may be the owners of most or all of the buildings in
an old section of town—have little influence in city politics; the value
of removing such elevators is marginal and the burden of installing new
ones is great; hence it may be deduced that were the owners of these
buildings wielding their share of influence in city decisions they would
have fought this ordinance down.

3. UNFAIRNESS IN THE DECISION-MAKING PROCESS. On occasion
there is direct evidence that one interest suffered from discrimination in
the legislature's deliberations. In such a case a court may feel (1) that
an ordinance should be struck down, regardless of its merits, because
the city's decision was improperly reached, or (2) that legislative discrimination, taken in combination with a strong but not conclusive case
that the ordinance is "uneconomic," or "unfair," should suffice. Margate
City had passed a zoning ordinance in 1930, permitting two-family
houses in a certain unimproved area; in 1947, when the land was still
unimproved, a new ordinance was passed permitting only one-family
dwellings to be built. The court heard evidence that plaintiff was a land
developer who had bought a section of the land shortly before it was
rezoned and concluded that the ordinance was "hurriedly adopted for
the specific purpose of preventing prosecutor from carrying out its

77. City of St. Louis v. Heitzeberg Packing & Provision Co., 141 Mo. 375, 42 S.W.
954 (1897).
78. City of Miami Beach v. Texas Co., 141 Fla. 616, 194 So. 368 (1940).
79. State v. City of Cape May, 66 N.J.L. 544, 49 Atl. 584 (Sup. Ct. 1901).

known plans . . ."[80] This did not mean that the motive for passing the ordinance was personal dislike of the plaintiff: the city contended that it had a real interest since its own economic burdens (additional schools, police, fire, and other city services that would have to be supplied to the new area) would exceed the tax revenue the area would yield. In this case, the court appears unable to reach a defensible conclusion about whether or not the ordinance on its face is "unfair" or "uneconomic," and consequently relies in part on the fact that the legislature seems to have given no consideration to the developer's interest.

A court may conclude that the legislative history of an ordinance evidences not merely disregard of a particular interest but a positive effort to harm one group. Although the opinion is slightly cryptic, the Miami Beach case quoted above is an example of this: apparently one group of hotel owners had contrived the passage of an ordinance that would damage the business of competing groups.

We have examined three factors that might move a court to disallow a municipal ordinance: (1) the feeling that a certain kind of issue lends itself to abuse and therefore the city should not be permitted to consider it; (2) the feeling that a decision actually made is clearly unfair regardless of how it was reached; (3) the feeling that the actual process that led to a municipal decision involved elements that prejudiced the interests of a particular group. These are not distinct categories but points on a spectrum. A court would probably be more likely to conclude that an ordinance is in a "dangerous class" when it thinks the ordinance before it is unfair; it would be more likely to find that an ordinance is unfair when it suspects that a class of people received no consideration in the legislature and, conversely, it would be more likely to question whether adequate consideration was given to burdened interests when it thinks that the ordinance that resulted is unfair. Indeed, there is judicial language that indicates reliance on a combination of these factors. It has been said, for example, that a court will not explore what motivated a legislature to exercise its discretion in a particular case unless the effect of an ordinance indicates "such an abuse of that discretion that it may be said to be no exercise of discretion at all."[81]

III. The Effectiveness of the Courts

State courts have undertaken to act in an area laden with political problems; they have often acted without being aware of the intricacy of the questions raised when a court tries to decide, without substantial

---

80. DeMott Homes at Salem v. Margate City, 136 N.J.L. 330, 334, 56 A.2d 423, 426 (Sup. Ct. 1947), aff'd per curiam, 136 N.J.L. 639, 57 A.2d 388 (Ct. Err. & App. 1948).

81. People *ex rel.* Burton v. Corn Prods. Ref. Co., 286 Ill. 226, 121 N.E. 574 (1918) (dictum); *cf.* Grogan v. De Sapio, 15 N.J. Super. 604, 83 A.2d 809 (Super. Ct. 1951).

guidance from a constitution or a legislature, whether a decision of a municipal legislature should be permitted to stand. Something of the complexity of this question may be indicated by examination of the ways a court might handle the problem of the five men whom we left trying to decide whether to play poker or go to the movies. Four approaches to that problem suggest themselves: (1) a court could order (or permit) the men to continue deciding by majority vote; (2) the court could order the men to submit their dispute to a higher authority (for example, their wives) for decision; (3) the court could order the group to split up; (4) the court could itself dictate the solution it thought appropriate. Each of these possibilities involves a problem. Solutions (2) and (4) may be undesirable because they involve taking the decision out of the hands of the people most directly concerned. Solution (3) may be undesirable for the reason that it is not possible to play poker with just the three men who would like to play, and consequently a decision that each man shall go his own way would make the choice of the majority, playing poker, impossible. Solution (1) means, as outlined above, that the two men never get to the movies.

These four approaches may be likened to four possible responses to an act of a city council. One might feel (1) that the city should be able to decide a question through its political process; (2) that a higher authority—the state legislature—should decide it; (3) that the decision should not be made collectively but each man should be left to deal with the matter as he wishes; or (4) that a particular decision is simply wrong and should be reversed on its merits. A court's reaction may involve some combination of possibilities: it may believe, for example, that a collective decision might be made by the state legislature, but unless the state legislature chooses to act the matter should be left to individuals.

Unfortunately, courts have not always articulated which response, or combination of responses, they are making. The rule of strict construction of municipal powers, for example, has been used in cases in which the court seems to be moved by a feeling that a particular decision is the wrong solution to a problem, rather than a solution to a problem with which the city is not permitted to deal. If the courts made a greater attempt to articulate the distinction between cases in which they are simply denying the city power to deal with a certain problem and cases in which they are rejecting a particular city solution they would be forced (1) to deal with the complex theoretical problems involved in deciding how decisions are to be made and (2) to explain, when they reject a particular ordinance as unfair or uneconomic, the exact grounds of their rejection.

Like the suggested solutions to the five-man problem, each of the approaches to the problem of how civic decisions should be made has its particular shortcoming. To decide that a local question should be answered at a higher level one must overcome the argument that local people will be better informed about local problems and local feeling and will have greater incentive to act. The counterargument is that while problems and individual feelings will be more thoroughly understood on the local level, interest groups may receive fairer treatment on the state level, where there is likely to be greater objectivity and where certain interests may, in connection with similar interests throughout the state, be able to participate more effectively in the decision-making process. For example, should state or local authorities be empowered to declare nuisances? While local authorities will be in a better position to weigh the interests on each side in a particular case, there is a danger that the owner of a single factory, for example, may have no political power in the city. People similarly situated throughout the state may be able to bring their side of the story before the state legislature.

The question whether a certain problem should be handled by the city or by private action alone involves balancing the interest in unanimous participation against the individual's interest in withholding participation: certain legitimate objectives may be pursued most effectively by the city as a whole, but it does not necessarily follow that a majority favoring those objectives should be able to impose its wishes on a minority. While a program might be most effective if the resources of the community as a whole were available, it may seem proper to leave the individuals in the majority to act privately rather than force the members of the minority to contribute to—and to make more effective—a program to which they are opposed.

If a court is trying to decide whether to defer to a city council or impose its own views on a particular question of civil policy, another problem is presented. If a city passes, for example, a building safety ordinance that places a severe burden on builders, a court may think that, on balance, the burden far outweighs a slight (and perhaps dubious) increase in safety. But before the court can hold that the ordinance is unreasonable it must decide, explicitly or implicitly, that it should not defer to the legislature's judgment. The conflicting considerations are (1) that the legislature is often better equipped to handle such an issue but (2) that the legislature may not have been fair to an interest that has little political power.

A.

The Difficulty of Examining the Legislative Process

It has been argued that there is a danger in any legislative process that one group may be able to dominate decision making and avoid considering or bargaining with outside interests. Ideally, it would be possible to examine the process to determine whether, in any particular instance, minority interests have received adequate consideration. But legislating is a process of creative bargaining and therefore this ideal solution is not always possible. To accumulate all the evidence and weigh all the interests involved in a city expenditure or zoning ordinance or tax requires a procedure free from the restrictions of formal rules of evidence and the limitations imposed by the narrow interests of the two parties before the court, which may not reflect the full range of community sentiment.[82]

It is difficult in practice to determine whether the legislature has reached a fair compromise of interests on a particular issue. The process of weighing interests and bargaining requires a number of decision makers representing different community sentiments, who can measure each project's worth to the community as a whole by engaging in political barter. The difficulty a judge would have in evaluating such a process is illustrated by the fact that a satisfactory decision may be reached by the legislature as a whole even when some (or all) of the individual legislators are not entirely satisfied. Further, legislation requires creativity, for legislators must often approve measures that they think will benefit constituents even when the constituents have not expressed interest in the legislation.[83] In sum, an attempt to determine whether a particular interest was given adequate consideration must fail because there are neither standards of "adequate consideration" nor ways of measuring how much consideration was actually given to a particular interest in the course of the legislative process.

Courts nevertheless are occasionally able to see that an *improper* consideration entered into the legislature's deliberations. When an adequate definition of "improper consideration" is available and when it is possible to determine the role of the improper consideration, a court can act. Thus a court may reasonably invalidate an ordinance if a city councilman has taken a bribe or if he has voted for an ordinance whose principal effect is to benefit his own property.[84] But when the argument is that the legislature as a whole consciously discriminated against a particular group, adequate procedures for evaluating the argument are usually lacking. Probing the conscience of government officials is a discomforting process at best and it is usually an unrewarding one, yielding ambiguous results. An ordinance itself may not provide clear evidence of the motive for its passage. When the city of Atlanta

82. *Cf.* Pennsylvania v. West Virginia, 262 U.S. 553, 618–23 (1923) (Brandeis, J., dissenting); HART & SACKS, THE LEGAL PROCESS 662–69 (tentative ed. 1958).

83. See generally *id.* at 708–13.

84. Statutes providing standards for disqualifying municipal legislators from voting on particular issues have been interpreted to give the courts authority to strike down legislation for which a disqualified councilman voted. See, *e.g.*, N.Y. PEN. LAW § 1868, and Schenectady Illuminating Co. v. Board of Supervisors, 88 Misc. 226, 151 N.Y.S. 830 (Sup. Ct. 1914), *aff'd*, 166 App. Div. 758, 151 N.Y.S. 1012 (1915); N.J. STAT. ANN. § 40:55–1.4 (Supp. 1964), and Bracey v. City of Long Branch, 73 N.J. Super. 91, 179 A.2d 63 (Super. Ct. 1962).

passed an ordinance prohibiting the sale of jewelry from 6:00 P.M. to 6:00 A.M., it was challenged on the ground that it was designed to protect some jewelers from the competition of stores catering to the after-dinner trade. The city offered in support of the ordinance the questionable rationale that it had been passed to prevent customers from being swindled (presumably it would accomplish this by restricting sales to daylight hours). The court refused to strike the ordinance down.[85] It could not determine which purpose each legislator had in mind, and it was not possible to tell from the face of the ordinance whether the purpose was proper.

"Improper purpose" is apt, moreover, to be a difficult thing to define. Suppose it is shown that a zoning ordinance was passed with the votes of members of the city council whose own property—or the property of people who contributed heavily to their political campaigns—would be benefited thereby. Acting upon self-interest is of the essence of the political process. Constituents are expected to seek benefits for themselves, and in the absence of laws regulating contact between a representative and his supporters, the line between a proper and an improper response on the part of a legislator is difficult to draw. Further, when a legislator's own interests are part of the larger interests of a section of the community it may be difficult to separate personal from political motivation; the phrase that courts often use—"a man should not be a judge in his own cause"—does not help when the man's own cause is also that of a larger group.

The rule that legislative motive is relevant only in "quasi-judicial" or "administrative" cases[86] would seem to indicate recognition of the difficulty of finding the "real motive" of legislators.[87] Ordinances called quasi-judicial are those whose effects are narrow in scope. When the number of affected interests is small it may be easy to analyze the process by which a decision was reached. The narrow impact will often make the "true purpose" easy to isolate and the decision will often involve no interests not represented before the court.

B.

The Difficulty of Evaluating Ordinances

Since it is rarely possible for a court to determine either that inadequate consideration was given to one interest or that improper considerations entered into the legislature's deliberation, a real attempt to ensure that individuals and groups are treated fairly must be based on an examination of the substance of ordinances. State legislatures, by

85. Clein v. City of Atlanta, 164 Ga. 529, 139 S.E. 46 (1927).
86. See 5 McQuillin, *op. cit. supra* note 54, § 16.91.
87. See 75 Harv. L. Rev. 423–26 (1961); *cf.* 57 Mich. L. Rev. 423–26 (1959).

imposing substantive limitations on municipal power, outline the areas in which local decision making is permitted. Yet grants of municipal power are usually broadly drawn, and courts must answer the hard questions. Cities may be authorized to provide for "health, safety, and welfare," or "good government," or the "promotion of trade and commerce"; to regulate "business" or "streets." A court can examine an ordinance to see whether it is arguably related to "promotion of trade and commerce" in the same way a court can determine whether a federal law does or does not regulate interstate commerce. Yet a court cannot construe statutory grants of power so as to leave to the city exactly those questions that are appropriate for municipal decision unless it has guidance from the state legislature. The judiciary is not competent to determine the proper allocation of political power—to build a framework for government. Thus, if a city council undertakes an advertising campaign to make the city a resort town and the city is authorized to promote "trade and commerce," the council's action seems to come within a literal reading of the authorization. A tribunal may believe that the city should not have power to make so far-reaching a change in the city's life—it may even doubt that the legislature intended the city to have such a power—but the court cannot draw clear and rational lines indicating what activities in promotion of trade and commerce are "too far-reaching" because that requires a judgment based not on principles of law but on theories of political science.

Another way in which courts seek to protect minority interests is by striking down ordinances as unreasonable. A court may conclude, for example, that a restriction of the use of certain property is not justified on the basis of a fair weighing of the interests involved. The weighing of interests in larger political bodies is usually impossible. There is a chance, for example, that the interests of various localities have been given inadequate consideration in national decisions on defense spending. But the range of choices is too wide and the weight of various considerations too imponderable to permit effective judicial review. With a small city, the courts are often in a better position to determine whether an ordinance reflects a fair balancing of interests. The impact of much municipal legislation is far more narrow than the impact of state or federal legislation. A city zoning ordinance or property or occupation tax, an ordinance to promote health and safety or abate a nuisance will generally result in clear and calculable burdens and benefits for small numbers of people. Consequently, when the arguments for and against a particular ordinance are presented, a court will often be able to conclude (1) that the interests are not too imponderable to balance and (2) that there are no significant interests that have not been presented in the litigation.

Courts should pay more attention than has been their wont, however, to the difference between the problem that an ordinance is "un-economic" and the problem that it is "unfair." It is difficult, except in the rare case when burdens and benefits are clear and calculable, to decide whether an ordinance is "economic"—whether it produces a net gain or loss for the community. The overall wisdom of a zoning ordinance or safety regulation, for example, may be impossible to judge. Courts could go much further than they have, however, in articulating standards of fairness, rules for deciding when an ordinance (whether wise or not) simply imposes too great a burden on one group in the city. The fairness of charging a small group of property owners for a benefit to the whole community may often be judged: the question whether a burden is so large that it ceases to be one of the random and incidental costs of living in society is generally not imponderable.

There is one final, obvious limitation on the ability of courts to correct municipal unfairness. They can act only when a judicial remedy will be effective. A continual domination of the political bargaining process will not even give rise to a justiciable issue when, for example, the dominant coalition is devoted to avoidance of expenditures and the problem is council inaction rather than action. And even when there is an ordinance to challenge, a court can act only by partially or totally invalidating it, and this remedy is unsatisfactory when an ordinance, despite its limitations, performs an arguably useful function.

IV. Conclusion

Courts are competent to decide whether a particular fact situation is governed by a particular rule of law, and to adjudicate well-defined conflicts between opposing interests. Judges may determine whether a municipal ordinance falls within statutory authorization, or violates a constitutional or statutory provision, if they receive sufficient guidance from the authorizing or limiting document itself together with traditional canons of construction. A court can act under a clear rule that states when evidence of corruption is sufficient to justify striking down an ordinance. Or a court may evaluate the balance of interests that a municipal legislature has made when the conflict between these interests is clear and simple. But a court cannot decide what kinds of problems it is appropriate for a city council to consider; nor can it determine in every case whether the legislative process as a whole or the individuals who participate in it are doing their jobs properly. In an era of expanding municipal responsibility, the need for rational answers to questions about the proper limits on municipal power and proper restrictions on exercise of that power must be answered by a body whose special competence is politics rather than law.

"One-Man, One-Vote" Applies to Local Government[*]

SUPREME COURT OF THE UNITED STATES

No. 39.—OCTOBER TERM, 1967.

Hank Avery, Petitioner,	
v.	On Writ of Certiorari to the
Midland County, Texas, et al.	Supreme Court of Texas.

[April 1, 1968.]

MR. JUSTICE WHITE delivered the opinion of the Court.

Petitioner, a taxpayer and voter in Midland County, Texas, sought a determination by this Court that the Texas Supreme Court erred in concluding that selection of the Midland County Commissioners Court from single-member districts of substantially unequal population did not necessarily violate the Fourteenth Amendment. We granted review, 388 U.S. 905 (1967), because application of the one man, one vote principle of *Reynolds* v. *Sims*, 377 U.S. 533 (1964), to units of local government is of broad public importance. We hold that petitioner, as a resident of Midland County, has a right to a vote for the Commissioners Court of substantially equal weight to the vote of every other resident.

Midland County has a population of about 70,000. The Commissioners Court is composed of five members. One, the County Judge, is elected at large from the entire county, and in practice casts a vote only to break a tie. The other four are chosen from districts. The size of those districts, according to the 1963 population estimates that were relied upon when this case was tried, was respectively 67,906, 852, 414, and 828. This vast imbalance resulted from placing in a single district virtually the entire city of Midland, Midland County's only urban center, in which 95% of the county's population resides.

The Commissioners Court is assigned by the Texas Constitution and by various statutory enactments with a variety of functions. According to the commentary to Vernon's Texas Statutes, the court:

> "is the general governing body of the county. It establishes a courthouse and jail, appoints numerous minor officials such as the county health officer, fills vacancies in the county offices, lets contracts in the name of the county, builds roads and bridges, administers the county's public welfare services, performs numerous duties in regard to elections, sets the county tax rate, issues bonds,

---

[*] *Excerpted by Professor Robert G. McCloskey, Harvard University especially for this book.*

adopts the county budget, and serves as a board of equalization for tax assessments."[1]

The court is also authorized, among other responsibilities, to build and run a hospital, an airport, and libraries. It fixes boundaries of school districts within the county, may establish a regional public housing authority, and determines the districts for election of its own members.

In *Reynolds* v. *Sims, supra,* the Equal Protection Clause was applied to the apportionment of state legislatures. Every qualified resident, *Reynolds* determined, has the right to a ballot for election of state legislators of equal weight to the vote of every other resident, and that right is infringed when legislators are elected from districts of substantially unequal population. The question now before us is whether the Fourteenth Amendment likewise forbids the election of local government officials from districts of disparate size. As has almost every court which has addressed itself to this question, we hold that it does.

The Equal Protection Clause reaches the exercise of state power however manifested, whether exercised directly or through municipal subdivisions of the State.

"Thus the prohibitions of the Fourteenth Amendment extend to all action of the State denying equal protection of the laws; whatever the agency of the State taking the action. . . ." *Cooper* v. *Aaron,* 358 U.S. 1, 17 (1958).

Although the forms and functions of local government and the relationships among the various units are matters of state concern, it is now beyond question that a State's political subdivisions must comply with the Fourteenth Amendment. The actions of local government *are* the actions of the State. A city, town, or county may no more deny the equal protection of the laws than it may abridge freedom of speech, establish an official religion, arrest without probable cause, or deny due process of the law.

When the State apportions its legislature, it must have due regard for the Equal Protection Clause. Similarly, when the State delegates lawmaking power to local government and provides for the election of local officials from districts specified by statute, ordinance, or local charter, it must insure that those qualified to vote have the right to an equally effective voice in the election process. If voters residing in oversize districts are denied their constitutional right to participate in the election of state legislators, precisely the same kind of deprivation occurs when the members of a city council, school board, or county governing board are elected from districts of substantially unequal population. If the five senators representing a city in the state legislature may not be elected from districts ranging in size from 50,000 to 500,000, neither is it permissible to elect the members of the city council from those same districts. In either case, the votes of some residents have greater weight

1. Interpretive Commentary, Vernon's Ann. Tex. Const., Art. V, § 18 (1955).

than those of others; in both cases the equal protection of the laws has been denied.

That the state legislature may itself be properly apportioned does not exempt municipalities from the Fourteenth Amendment. While state legislatures exercise extensive power over their constituents and over the various units of local government, the States universally leave much policy and decision making to their governmental subdivisions. Legislators enact many laws but do not attempt to reach those countless matters of local concern necessarily left wholly or partly to those who govern at the local level. What is more, in providing for the governments of their cities, counties, towns, and districts, the States characteristically provide for representative government—for decision making at the local level by representatives elected by the people. And, not infrequently, the delegation of power to local units is contained in constitutional provisions for local home rule which are immune from legislative interference. In a word, institutions of local government have always been a major aspect of our system, and their responsible and responsive operation is today of increasing importance to the quality of life of more and more of our citizens. We therefore see little difference, in terms of the application of the Equal Protection Clause and of the principles of *Reynolds* v. *Sims*, between the exercise of state power through legislatures and its exercise by elected officials in the cities, towns, and counties.[2]

We are urged to permit unequal districts for the Midland County Commissioners Court on the ground that the court's functions are not sufficiently "legislative." The parties have devoted much effort to urging that alternative labels—"administrative" versus "legislative"—be applied to the Commissioners Court. As the brief description of the court's functions above amply demonstrates, this unit of local government cannot easily be classified in the neat categories favored by civics texts. The Texas commissioners courts are assigned some tasks which would normally be thought of as "legislative," others typically assigned to "executive" or "administrative" departments, and still others which are "judicial." In this regard Midland County's Commissioners Court is representative of most of the general governing bodies of American

2. Inequitable apportionment of local governing bodies offends the Constitution even if adopted by a properly apportioned legislature representing the majority of the State's citizens. The majority of a State—by constitutional provision, by referendum, or through accurately apportioned representatives—can no more place a minority in oversize districts without depriving that minority of equal protection of the laws than they can deprive the minority of the ballot altogether, or impose upon them a tax rate in excess of that to be paid by equally situated members of the majority. Government—National, State, and local—must grant to each citizen the equal protection of its laws, which includes an equal opportunity to influence the election of lawmakers, no matter how large the majority wishing to deprive other citizens of equal treatment or how small the minority who object to their mistreatment. *Lucas* v. *Colorado General Assembly,* 377 U.S. 713 (1964), stands as a square adjudication by this Court of these principles.

cities, counties, towns, and villages.[3] One knowledgeable commentator has written of "the states' varied, pragmatic approach in establishing governments." R. Wood, in E. Redford *et al.*, Politics and Government in the United States 891–892 (1965). That approach has produced a staggering number of governmental units—the preliminary calculation by the Bureau of the Census for 1967 is that there are 81,304 "units of government" in the United States—and an even more staggering diversity. Nonetheless, while special purpose organizations abound and in many States the allocation of functions among units results in instances of overlap and vacuum, virtually every American lives within what he and his neighbors regard as a unit of local government with general responsibility and power for local affairs. In many cases citizens reside within and are subject to two such governments, a city and a county.

The Midland County Commissioners Court is such a unit. While the Texas Supreme Court found that the Commissioners Court's legislative functions are "negligible," the court does have power to make a large number of decisions having a broad range of impacts on all the citizens of the county. It sets a tax rate, equalizes assessments, and issues bonds. It then prepares and adopts a budget for allocating the county's funds, and is given by statute a wide range of discretion in choosing the subjects on which to spend. In adopting the budget the court makes both long-term judgments about the way Midland County should develop—whether industry should be solicited, roads improved, recreation facilities built, and land set aside for schools—and immediate choices among competing needs.

The Texas Supreme Court concluded that the work actually done by the Commissioners Court "disproportionately concern[s] the rural areas." Were the Commissioners Court a special purpose unit of government assigned the performance of functions affecting definable groups of constituents more than other constituents, we would have to confront the question whether such bodies may be apportioned in ways which give greater influence to the citizens most affected by the organizations' functions. That question, however, is not presented by this case, for while Midland County authorities may concentrate their attention on rural roads, the relevant fact is that the powers of the Commissioners Court include the authority to make a substantial number of decisions that affect all citizens, whether they reside inside or outside the city limits of Midland. The Commissioners maintain buildings, administer welfare services, and determine school districts both inside and outside

---

3. Midland County is apparently untypical in choosing the members of its local governing body from districts. "On the basis of reliable figures, coupled with rough estimates from samplings made of the situations in various States, it appears that only about 25 percent of . . . local government governing boards are elected, in whole or in part, from districts or, while at large, under schemes including district residence requirements." Brief for the United States as Amicus Curiae, p. 22, n. 31, filed in *Sailors* v. *Board of Educ.*, 387 U.S. 105 (1967), and the other 1966 Term local reapportionment cases.

the city. The taxes imposed by the court fall equally on all property in the county. Indeed, it may not be mere coincidence that a body apportioned with three of its four voting members chosen by residents of the rural area surrounding the city devotes most of its attention to the problems of that area, while paying for its expenditures with a tax imposed equally on city residents and those who live outside the city. And we might point out that a decision not to exercise a function within the court's power—a decision, for example, not to build an airport or a library, or not to participate in the federal food stamp program—is just as much a decision affecting all citizens of the county as an affirmative decision.

The Equal Protection Clause does not, of course, require that the State never distinguish between citizens, but only that the distinctions that are made not be arbitrary or invidious. The conclusion of *Reynolds* v. *Sims* was that bases other than population were not acceptable grounds for distinguishing among citizens when determining the size of districts used to elect members of state legislatures. We hold today only that the Constitution permits no substantial variation from equal population in drawing districts for units of local government having general governmental powers over the entire geographic area served by the body.

This Court is aware of the immense pressures facing units of local government, and of the greatly varying problems with which they must deal. The Constitution does not require that a uniform straitjacket bind citizens in devising mechanisms of local government suitable for local needs and efficient in solving local problems. Last Term, for example, the Court upheld a procedure for choosing a school board that placed the selection with school boards of component districts even though the component boards had equal votes and served unequal populations. *Sailors* v. *Board of Educ.*, 387 U.S. 105 (1967). The Court rested on the administrative nature of the area school board's functions and the essentially appointive form of the scheme employed. In *Dusch* v. *Davis*, 387 U.S. 112 (1967), the Court permitted Virginia Beach to choose its legislative body by a scheme that included at-large voting for candidates, some of whom had to be residents of particular districts, even though the residence districts varied widely in population.

The *Sailors* and *Dusch* cases demonstrate that the Constitution and this Court are not roadblocks in the path of innovation, experiment, and development among units of local government. We will not bar what Professor Wood has called "the emergence of a new ideology and structure of public bodies, equipped with new capacities and motivations. . . ." R. Wood, 1400 Governments, at 175 (1961). Our decision today is only that the Constitution imposes one ground rule for the development of arrangements of local government: a requirement that units with general governmental powers over an entire geographic area not be apportioned among single-member districts of substantially unequal population.

The judgment below is vacated and the case is remanded for disposition not inconsistent with this opinion.

It is so ordered.

MR. JUSTICE MARSHALL took no part in the consideration or decision of this case.

MR. JUSTICE HARLAN, dissenting.

I could not disagree more with this decision, which wholly disregards statutory limitations upon the appellate jurisdiction of this Court in state cases and again betrays such insensitivity to the appropriate dividing lines between the judicial and political functions under our constitutional system.

I.

[The Justice here argues that the Supreme Court should have refused to accept jurisdiction in this case.]

II.

On the merits, which I reach only because the Court has done so, I consider this decision, which extends the state apportionment rule of *Reynolds* v. *Sims*, 377 U.S. 533, to an estimated 80,000 units of local government throughout the land, both unjustifiable and ill-advised.

I continue to think that these adventures of the Court in the realm of political science are beyond its constitutional powers, for reasons set forth at length in my dissenting opinion in *Reynolds*, 377 U.S., at 589 *et seq*. However, now that the Court has decided otherwise, judicial self-discipline requires me to follow the political dogma now constitutionally embedded in consequence of that decision. I am not foreclosed, however, from remonstrating against the extension of that decision to new areas of government. At the present juncture I content myself with stating two propositions which, in my view, stand strongly against what is done today. The first is that the "practical necessities" which have been thought by some to justify the profound break with history that was made in 1962 by this Court's decision in *Baker* v. *Carr*, 369 U.S. 186, are not present here. The second is that notwithstanding *Reynolds* the "one man, one vote" ideology does not provide an acceptable formula for structuring local governmental units.

A.

The argument most generally heard for justifying the entry of the federal courts into the field of state legislative apportionment is that since state legislatures had widely failed to correct serious malapportionments in their own structure, and since no other means of redress had proved available through the political process, this Court was entitled to step into the picture. While I continue to reject that thesis as furnishing an excuse for the federal judiciary straying outside its proper constitutional role, and while I continue to believe that it bodes ill for the country and the entire federal judicial system if this Court does not firmly set its face against this loose and short-sighted point of view, the important thing for present purposes is that no such justification can be brought to bear in this instance.

No claim is made in this case that avenues of political redress are not open to correct any malapportionment in elective local governmental units, and it is difficult to envisage how such a situation could arise. Local governments are creatures of the States, and they may be reformed either by the state legislatures, which are now required to be apportioned according to *Reynolds,* or by amendment of state constitutions. In these circumstances, the argument of practical necessity has no force. The Court, then, should withhold its hand until such a supposed necessity does arise, before intruding itself into the business of restructuring local governments across the country.

There is another reason why the Court should at least wait for a suitable period before applying the *Reynolds* dogma to local governments. The administrative feasibility of judicial application of the "one man, one vote" rule to the apportionment even of state legislatures has not yet been demonstrated. A number of significant administrative questions remain unanswered,[1] and the burden on the federal courts has been substantial. When this has thus far been the outcome of applying the rule to 50 state legislatures, it seems most unwise at this time to extend it to some 80,000 units of local government, whose bewildering variety is sure to multiply the problems which have already arisen and to cast further burdens, of imponderable dimension, on the federal courts. I am frankly astonished at the ease with which the Court has proceeded to fasten upon the entire country at its lowest political levels the strong arm of the federal judiciary, let alone a particular political ideology which has been the subject of wide debate and differences from the beginnings of our Nation.[2]

B.

There are also convincing functional reasons why the *Reynolds* rule should not apply to local governmental units at all. The effect of *Reynolds* was to read a long debated political theory—that the only per-

1. One such question is the extent to which an apportionment may take into account population changes which occur between decennial censuses. Cf. *Lucas* v. *Rhodes,* 389 U.S. 212 (dissenting opinion of this writer). Another is the degree of population variation which is constitutionally permissible. See *Swann* v. *Adams,* 385 U.S. 440; cf. *Rockefeller* v. *Wells,* 389 U.S. 421 (dissenting opinion of this writer).

2. See the dissenting opinion of Mr. Justice Frankfurter in *Baker* v. *Carr,* 369 U.S. 186, 266, 300–324.

missible basis for the selection of state legislators is election by majority vote within areas which are themselves equal in population—into the United States Constitution, thereby foreclosing the States from experimenting with legislatures rationally formed in other ways. Even assuming that this result could be justified on the state level, because of the substantial identity in form and function of the state legislatures, and because of the asserted practical necessities for federal judicial interference referred to above, the "one man, one vote" theory is surely a hazardous generalization on the local level. As has been noted previously, no "practical necessity" has been asserted to justify application of the rule to local governments. More important, the greater and more varied range of functions performed by local governmental units implies that flexibility in the form of their structure is even more important than at the state level, and that by depriving local governments of this needed adaptability the Court's holding may indeed defeat the very goals of *Reynolds*.

The present case affords one example of why the "one man, one vote" rule is especially inappropriate for local governmental units. The Texas Supreme Court held as a matter of Texas law:

> "Theoretically, the commissioners court is the governing body of the county and the commissioners represent all the residents, both urban and rural, of the county. But developments during the years have greatly narrowed the scope and function of the commissioners court and limited its major responsibilities to the non-urban areas of the county. It has come to pass that the city government . . . is the major concern of the city dwellers and the administration of the county is the major concern of rural dwellers."

Despite the specialized role of the commissioners court, the majority has undertaken to bring it within the ambit of *Reynolds* simply by classifying it as "a unit of local government with general responsibility and power for local affairs." Although this approach is intended to afford "equal protection" to all voters in Midland County, it would seem that it in fact discriminates against the county's rural inhabitants. The commissioners court, as found by the Texas Supreme Court, performs more functions in the area of the county outside Midland City than it does within the city limits. Therefore, each rural resident has a greater interest in its activities than each city dweller. Yet under the majority's formula the urban residents are to have a dominant voice in the county government, precisely proportional to their numbers, and little or no allowance may be made for the greater stake of the rural inhabitants in the county government.

This problem is not a trivial one and is not confined to Midland County. It stems from the fact that local governments, unlike state governments, are often specialized in function.[3] Application of the *Reynolds*

3. See generally Anderson & Weidner, State and Local Government 85–103 (1951).

rule to such local governments prevents the adoption of apportionments which take into account the effect of this specialization, and therefore may result in a denial of equal treatment to those upon whom the exercise of the special powers has unequal impact. Under today's decision, the only apparent alternative is to classify the governmental unit as other than "general" in power and responsibility, thereby, presumably, avoiding application of the *Reynolds* rule. Neither outcome satisfies *Reynolds*' avowed purpose: to assure "equality" to all voters. The result also deprives localities of the desirable option of establishing slightly specialized, elective units of government, such as Texas' county commissioners court, and varying the size of the constituencies so as rationally to favor those whom the government affects most. The majority has chosen explicitly to deny local governments this alternative by rejecting even the solution of the Texas Supreme Court, which held that the present county apportionment was impermissible but would have allowed the new apportionment to reflect factors related to the special functions of the county commissioners court, such as "land areas, geography, miles of county roads, and taxable values," as well as population.

Despite the majority's declaration that it is not imposing a "straitjacket" on local governmental units, its solution is likely to have other undesirable "freezing" effects on local government. One readily foreseeable example is in the crucial field of metropolitan government. A common pattern of development in the Nation's urban areas has been for the less affluent citizens to migrate to or remain within the central city, while the more wealthy move to the suburbs and come into the city only to work.[4] The result has been to impose a relatively heavier tax burden upon city taxpayers and to fragmentize governmental services in the metropolitan area.[5] An oft-proposed solution to these problems has been the institution of an integrated government encompassing the entire metropolitan area.[6] In many instances, the suburbs may be included in such a metropolitan unit only by majority vote of the voters in each suburb.[7] As a practical matter, the suburbanites often will be reluctant to join the metropolitan government unless they receive a

4. See, *e.g.*, Anderson & Weidner, *supra*, at 171–174; United States Advisory Commission on Intergovernmental Relations for use of House Committee on Government Operations, 87th Cong., 1st Sess., Governmental Structure, Organization, and Planning in Metropolitan Areas 7 (Comm. Print 1961).

5. See, *e.g.*, United States Advisory Commission on Intergovernmental Relations, Alternative Approaches to Governmental Reorganization in Metropolitan Areas 8–9 (1962); United States Advisory Commission on Intergovernmental Relations for use of House Committee on Government Operations, 87th Cong., 1st Sess., Governmental Structure, Organization and Planning in Metropolitan Areas 15–16 (Comm. Print 1961).

6. See, *e.g.*, Anderson & Weidner, *supra*, at 174–179; United States Advisory Commission on Intergovernmental Relations, Alternative Approaches to Governmental Reorganization in Metropolitan Areas (1962).

7. See, *e.g.*, United States Advisory Commission on Intergovernmental Relations, State Constitutional and Statutory Restrictions upon the Structural, Functional, and Personnel Powers of Local Government 38, 44–53 (1962).

share in the government proportional to the benefits they bring with them and not merely to their numbers.[8] The city dwellers may be ready to concede this much, in return for the ability to tax the suburbs. Under the majority's pronouncements, however, this rational compromise would be forbidden: the metropolitan government must be apportioned solely on the basis of population if it is a "general" government.

These functional considerations reinforce my belief that the "one man, one vote" rule, which possesses the simplistic defects inherent in any judicially imposed solution of a complex social problem, is entirely inappropriate for determining the form of the country's local governments.

No better demonstration of this proposition could have been made than that afforded by the admirable analysis contained in the dissenting opinion of my Brother FORTAS. But, with respect, my Brother's projected solution of the matter is no less unsatisfactory. For it would bid fair to plunge this Court into an avalanche of local reapportionment cases with no firmer constitutional anchors than its own notions of what constitutes "equal protection" in any given instance.

With deference, I think that the only sure-footed way of avoiding, on the one hand, the inequities inherent in today's decision, and on the other, the morass of pitfalls that would follow from my Brother FORTAS' approach, is for this Court to decline to extend the constitutional experiment of *Reynolds*, and to leave the structuring of local governmental units to the political process where it belongs.

Mr. Justice Fortas, dissenting.

[The Justice here argues that the Supreme Court should have refused to accept jurisdiction in this case.]

I am in fundamental disagreement. I believe, as I shall discuss, that in the circumstances of this case equal protection of the laws may be achieved—and perhaps can only be achieved—by a system which takes into account a complex of values and factors, and not merely the arithmetic simplicity of one equals one. *Dusch* and *Sailors* were wisely and prudently decided. They reflect a reasoned, conservative, empirical approach to the intricate problem of applying constitutional principle to the complexities of local government. I know of no reason why we now abandon this reasonable and moderate approach to the problem of local suffrage and adopt an absolute and inflexible formula which is potentially destructive of important political and social values. There is no reason why we should insist that there is and can be only one rule for voters in local governmental units—that districts for units of local government must be drawn solely on the basis of population. I

8. See Weinstein, The Effect of the Federal Reapportionment Decisions on Counties and Other Forms of Municipal Government, 65 Col. L. Rev. 21, 37 and n. 67 (1965); cf. United States Advisory Commission on Intergovernmental Relations, Factors Affecting Voter Reactions to Governmental Reorganization in Metropolitan Areas 26–27 (1962).

believe there are powerful reasons why, while insisting upon reasonable regard for the population-suffrage ratio, we should reject a rigid, theoretical, and authoritarian approach to the problems of local government. In this complex and involved area, we should be careful and conservative in our application of constitutional imperatives, for they are powerful.

Constitutional commandments are not surgical instruments. They have a tendency to hack deeply—to amputate. And while I have no doubt that, with the growth of suburbia and exurbia, the problem of allocating local government functions and benefits urgently requires attention, I am persuaded that it does not call for the hatchet of one man-one vote. It is our duty to insist upon due regard for the value of the individual vote but not to ignore realities or to by-pass the alternatives that legislative alteration might provide.

I.

I agree that application of the Equal Protection Clause of the Constitution, decreed by this Court in the case of state legislatures, cannot stop at that point. Of course local governmental units are subject to the commands of the Equal Protection Clause. *Cooper* v. *Aaron*, 358 U.S. 1, 17 (1958). That much is easy. The difficult question, and the one which the Court slights is, what does the Equal Protection Clause demand with regard to local governmental units?

III

I have said that in my judgment we should not decide this case but should give Texas a chance to come up with an acceptable result. Texas' own courts hold that the present system is constitutionally intolerable. The 1963 population estimates relied upon in this case show that the City of Midland with 67,906 people has one representative, and the three rural districts, each of which has its own representative, have 852, 414, and 828 people respectively. While it may be that this cannot be regarded as satisfying the Equal Protection Clause under any view, I suggest that applying the Court's formula merely errs in the opposite direction: Only the city population will be represented, and the rural areas will be eliminated from a voice in the county government to which they must look for essential services. With all respect, I submit that this is a destructive result. It kills the very value which it purports to serve. Texas should have a chance to devise a scheme which, within wide tolerance, eliminates the gross under-representation of the city, but at the same time provides an adequate, effective voice for the nonurban, as well as the urban, areas and peoples.[1]

1. Cf. Weinstein, The Effect of the Federal Reapportionment Decisions on Counties and Other Forms of Municipal Government, 65 Col. L. Rev. 21, 40–49 (1965).

MR. JUSTICE STEWART, dissenting.

I would dismiss the writ as improvidently granted for the reasons stated by MR. JUSTICE HARLAN and MR. JUSTICE FORTAS.

Since the Court does reach the merits, however, I add that I agree with most of what is said in the thorough dissenting opinion of MR. JUSTICE FORTAS. Indeed, I would join that opinion were it not for the author's unquestioning endorsement of the doctrine of *Reynolds* v. *Sims*, 377 U.S. 533. I continue to believe that the Court's opinion in that case misapplied the Equal Protection Clause of the Fourteenth Amendment— that the apportionment of the legislative body of a sovereign State, no less than the apportionment of a county government, is far too subtle and complicated a business to be resolved as a matter of constitutional law in terms of sixth-grade arithmetic. My views on that score, set out at length elsewhere,* closely parallel those expressed by MR. JUSTICE FORTAS in the present case.

* Lucas *v.* Colorado General Assembly, *377 U.S. 713, 744 (dissenting opinion).*

The Effect of State Reapportionment on the Cities

William J. D. Boyd[*]

THE SUBURBS and, in the long run, only the suburbs will gain in the upheaval resulting from reapportionment of state legislatures on the basis of population. Rather than being dominated by the big cities, as is commonly supposed, the new legislatures will see suburban representatives increase the most in number.

Actually, there will be very few states in which one segment of the population will have a clear-cut majority. Where this does happen, it will continue to be the rural population that prevails, as in Mississippi, the two Dakotas, South Carolina and Vermont. In other states, suburbanites will hold the balance of power between rural and big-city forces.

Analysis of population trends of the big cities in recent decades discloses the following facts:

1. All suburban areas are gaining in population.

2. Most big cities are losing population.

3. Almost one-half of the big cities already have less population than their suburbs; by 1970, the overwhelming majority will have less.

4. No city contains as much as 50 per cent of the population of its state.

5. All cities which contain as much as 15 per cent of their states' population have shown a percentage decline over the last 30 years.

Table 1 shows the 23 metropolitan centers in the United States that have populations of a million or more (Washington, D.C., not being located in a state, is not included). In six of these, the metropolitan area spills over into at least one adjoining state, so only that metropolitan-area population is shown which is within the same state as the

[*] Mr. Boyd is senior associate of the National Municipal League and for the last three years has been in charge of its activities on apportionment. Author of the League publication, *Patterns of Apportionment,* and of an article in the NATIONAL CIVIC REVIEW (November, 1964, page 530), he is also editor of the REVIEW's Representation department.

Reprinted from the National Civic Review *(June, 1965). Used by permission of the National Municipal League.*

TABLE I   1960 Population 23 Largest Metropolitan Areas

Metropolitan Area	1960 Total Population	Central-City Population	Percentage Increase or Decrease since 1950	Suburban Population	Percentage Increase since 1950
New York City	10,694,633*	7,781,984	− 1.4	2,912,649*	+ 75.0*
Los Angeles-Long Beach	6,742,696	2,823,183	+27.1	3,919,513	+ 82.6
Chicago	6,220,913*	3,550,404	− 1.9	2,670,509*	+ 71.5
Detroit	3,762,360	1,670,144	− 9.7	1,589,011*	+ 48.4
Philadelphia	3,591,523*	2,002,512	− 3.3	2,092,216	+ 79.3
San Francisco-Oakland	2,783,359	1,107,864	− 4.5	1,675,495	+ 55.0
Boston	2,589,301	697,197	−13.0	1,892,104	+ 17.6
Pittsburgh	2,405,435	604,332	−10.7	1,801,103	+ 17.2
Cleveland	1,796,595	876,050	− 4.2	920,545	+ 67.2
Baltimore	1,727,023	939,024	− 1.1	787,999	+ 72.9
Newark	1,689,420	405,220	− 7.6	1,284,200	+ 24.7
St. Louis	1,572,905*	750,026	−12.5	822,879*	+ 73.5
Minneapolis-St. Paul	1,482,030	796,283	− 4.4	685,747	+115.7
Buffalo	1,306,957	532,759	− 8.2	774,198	+ 52.1
Houston	1,243,158	938,219	+57.4	304,939	+ 44.8
Milwaukee	1,194,290	741,324	+16.3	452,966	+ 41.7
Paterson-Clifton-Passaic	1,186,873	279,710	+ 6.9	907,163	+ 47.6
Dallas	1,083,601	557,087	+19.1	550,126	+ 45.9
Seattle	1,107,213	679,684	+56.4	403,917	+ 30.7
San Diego	1,033,011	573,224	+71.4	459,787	+108.7
Atlanta	1,017,188	487,455	+47.1	529,733	+ 33.9
Cincinnati	864,121*	502,550	− 0.3	361,671*	+ 64.4*
Kansas City, Missouri	730,206*	475,539	+ 4.1	254,667*	+ 96.5*

* Includes only that suburban population located within the same state as the major central city (or cities).

central city. Because of such adjustments, both the Cincinnati and Kansas City (Missouri), metropolitan areas fall below a million in population.

From 1950 to 1960, the suburban areas around every one of these 23 cities increased in population, even in those states such as Massachusetts in which population increased less rapidly than the national average. Fifteen of the central cities had an actual loss of population and only five of the 23 managed to increase as rapidly as the statewide average.

In addition, during the decade 1950 to 1960, suburban growth was so rapid that eleven of the 23 cities are now smaller than their suburbs which are located within the same state. Population trends indicate that by 1970 about a half-dozen more will become smaller than their suburbs. By 1980, only New York, Dallas and Houston should remain more populous than their surrounding suburbs.

Continued growth of central cities in Texas is easily explained, for they may readily annex any adjacent unincorporated territory. In this way, they swallow their suburbs almost as fast as the latter are created, unless the new areas rapidly incorporate as municipalities. Politically, this has had the advantage of keeping available to a city the business and professional leadership which so many of the older cities of the eastern seaboard have long since lost to the suburbs.

New York City, while steadily losing population to its suburbs, is so situated that its metropolitan area covers parts of three states. Therefore, although it is steadily declining in relation to its suburbs, including those within the state, the total population of the city will probably remain larger than those New York suburbs for some years.

TABLE 2 *Percentage Total State Population (1930 to 1960) of Central Cities on Table 1 Containing 15 Per Cent or More of Their State's Total Population*
(Ranked according to the size of the central city)

City	1960	1950	1940	1930	Change since 1930 in Percentage of Total State Population
New York City	46.4	53.2	55.3	55.1	− 8.7
Chicago	35.2	41.6	43.0	44.2	− 9.0
Los Angeles	15.8	18.6	21.8	21.8	− 6.0
Philadelphia	17.7	19.7	19.5	20.3	− 2.6
Detroit	21.3	29.0	30.9	32.4	−11.1
Baltimore	30.3	40.5	47.2	49.3	−19.0
Minneapolis-St. Paul	23.3	27.9	27.9	28.7	− 5.4
St. Louis	17.4	21.7	21.6	22.6	− 5.2
Milwaukee	18.8	18.6	18.7	19.7	− .9
Seattle	19.5	19.7	21.2	23.4	− 3.9

PERCENTAGE TOTAL STATE POPULATION (1930 to 1960) OF CENTRAL CITIES ON TABLE 1 CONTAINING 15 PER CENT OR MORE OF STATE'S POPULATION

	New York	Chicago	Los Angeles	Philadelphia	Detroit	Baltimore	Minneapolis-St. Paul	St. Louis	Milwaukee*	Seattle
% Change	— 8.7	— 9.0	— 6.0	— 2.6	—11.1	—19.0	— 5.4	— 5.2	.9	— 3.9

*Major annexations made during 1950-1960

When the New York legislature is reapportioned on the basis of population, however, New York City will gain only four assemblymen. Suburban Nassau County alone will gain six and still more will go to Suffolk and Westchester Counties. In percentage terms, New York City will gain about 6 per cent more in representation. Nassau and Suffolk Counties will each make a 100 per cent gain. Following the 1970 census, the city should lose more seats than the number gained in 1965.

Table 2 and the chart dramatically show what has happened to central cities since 1930. They list all those from Table 1 which contain 15 per cent or more of the total population of their states. Only ten cities fall into this category. Without exception, the percentage of the state's population living within the city's borders has declined. The 30-year downward curve is so uniform and so pronounced that it establishes beyond question that the danger of big-city dominance is gone forever.

New York City presents one of the most interesting examples. The city presently contains a smaller percentage of the state's population than it did in 1900. Since World War II, the trend has been so consistently downward that in the last decade the city actually lost in absolute population terms as well as in percentage terms. This phenomenon is unlikely to continue, but all indications are that, in percentage terms, the decline of the city may become more rapid than in past decades even if the city does increase in absolute population once more. (Note that Los Angeles, while gaining 500,000 during the last decade, actually declined in comparison with total statewide growth.)

*   *   *

There are a few cities not shown on either of the tables (cities in metropolitan areas with less than a million population or those which have less than 15 per cent of their states' total populations) that are continuing to grow. Here, too, however, suburban areas are growing more rapidly than the central cities. This development is most common in states experiencing major growth, such as California, Florida and Arizona. Arizona's annexation laws, like those in Texas, allow central cities to annex so much of their suburban areas that the former did outstrip the areas beyond their new limits for a time. This trend, however, seems to have halted. While Phoenix and Tucson continue to grow, incorporated areas outside their limits are expanding at an even more rapid rate.

The vast open spaces within the boundaries of the new cities of California and Florida are filling up. The great boom, therefore, is taking place beyond city limits. In both of these states, every one of the metropolitan areas, even those of rather insignificant size, is characterized by big suburban rather than urban populations.

Finally, not only the intense rivalry between the central city and its suburbs but also inter-city rivalry works to block any power grab by big-city machines. Historically, San Francisco and Los Angeles, St. Louis and Kansas City, Phoenix and Tucson, Dallas and Fort Worth have provided the greatest enmities and jealousies in their respective state legislatures. (The recent bitter squabble in the New York state legislature among its new Democratic leaders even shows a division within New York City.)

No central city contains the necessary 50 per cent of the people to dominate the state. It is now apparent that no city will ever attain that dominance. The United States is an urban nation, but it is not a big-city nation. The suburbs own the future.

Under current reapportionment changes, many large cities will gain some additional representatives in their state legislatures but in most cases their own suburbs will gain *more*, and after the 1970 census, almost all central cities will lose some of the seats gained now. Without exception, those seats will go to the suburbs. Big-city politicians, rather than dominating future state legislatures, are going to find they have more numerous and articulate opponents in their new suburban rivals than ever before.

METROPOLITAN ORGANIZATION

Metropolitan Districts

John C. Bollens

THE USE of metropolitan districts in the metropolitan areas of the United States is increasing. In operation in more than one-fourth of such areas, they are proportionately most prevalent in concentrations of 500,000 or more people. Approximately three-fourths of the thirty-three most populous areas have at least one metropolitan district, and it is not unusual for them to have more than one. Geographical location has constituted no barrier, for these districts are found in metropolitan areas in all sections of the United States. Although appearing in Philadelphia as early as 1790 and in such areas as Chicago and Portland, Oregon, in the latter part of the nineteenth century, metropolitan districts are largely a post-World War I development.[1] Once established, most of them have given indications of being permanent or long-lived. In contrast to many other types of districts, few of them have become inactive or been abolished or merged.

Collectively, metropolitan districts are concerned with a wide range of activities and have eliminated or mitigated some of the most important problems of specific metropolitan areas. Although their most frequent services have to do with port facilities, sewage disposal, water supply, and parks, they also own and operate bridges, tunnels, airports, housing, libraries, and mass transit facilities; furnish public health

1. For details on early metropolitan districts, see Paul Studenski, *The Government of Metropolitan Areas in the United States* (New York: National Municipal League, 1930), pp. 256–265. Several districts discussed by Mr. Studenski are not independent or are less than metropolitan in jurisdiction.

Reprinted from Special District Governments in the United States (*Berkeley: University of California Press, 1957*), *pp. 67–71 and 87–92.*

services, regional planning, power, ice, gas, and coke; regulate naviga-
tion channels; and control water to prevent disasters. They emphasize
service rather than regulatory functions. Certain functions considered by
many people to be metropolitan are not provided by any metropolitan
district. The most notable omissions are fire protection and law enforcement.

Mostly Single-Purpose

An overwhelming majority of these districts are legally limited to
supplying a single service. Prominent examples among the relatively few
districts that perform more than one function are the Port of New York
Authority, the Hartford County (Connecticut) Metropolitan District, the
Bi-State Development District (St. Louis metropolitan area), and the
East Bay Municipal Utility District (San Francisco-Oakland metropolitan
area). Although it has happened that one or more functions of these
districts were authorized after their establishment, generally neither
metropolitan districts nor their residents have shown much interest in
assuming new obligations. Very few metropolitan districts have therefore increased functionally through subsequent authorization by the
state legislature, or through the exercise of other powers originally
granted them. The usual pattern has been to have one metropolitan
district carry out one function, and to establish other metropolitan
districts for additional single purposes if sufficient concern develops. As
a result, no metropolitan district is presently serving as a comprehensive multifunctional metropolitan government. Instead, all of them
are operating as limited governments of metropolitan jurisdiction.

Large and Flexible Areas

Metropolitan districts have large areas, and on the average are
larger than any other kind of special district. Some districts in rural sections, for example, are very extensive, but others contain only a fraction
of a square mile or a few square miles. On the other hand, the territory of metropolitan districts is consistently measured in tens or hundreds of square miles and in some instances exceeds a thousand square
miles. Then, too, since metropolitan districts have jurisdiction in densely
settled areas, they usually encompass a large number of general and
special district governments. Furthermore, the territory of some of them
crosses state boundaries, a feature foreign to most special districts and
to all general governments except the national government. Some metropolitan districts have grown substantially through annexation. An
illustration is the Metropolitan Sanitary District of Greater Chicago

which has almost tripled its original size of 185 square miles. Thousands, sometimes millions, of people reside within each metropolitan district and use or benefit from its service. In addition, many nondistrict residents benefit from the operations of certain functional kinds of metropolitan districts, such as those operating parks, mass transit, and ports.

Sometimes Big Government

Although performing only one or a few functions, some metropolitan districts are very large governmental operations, and may even be larger than state governments in some respects. The Chicago Transit

The Largest Nonschool Districts

District	Number of employees, October, 1952	Revenue for fiscal year 1952 ($ thousands)	Total long-term outstanding debt, 1952 ($ thousands)
Metropolitan Districts			
Chicago Transit Authority	17,472	119,064	137,400
Metropolitan Transit Authority (Boston)	7,652	50,004	131,054
Port of New York Authority	3,745	57,097	241,688
Metropolitan Sanitary District of Greater Chicago	1,882	29,246	141,164
Indianapolis Utilities District	1,230	21,828	11,785
East Bay Municipal Utility District (eastern section of San Francisco Bay area)	1,208	17,708	69,530
Omaha Public Power District	1,116	17,942	71,528
Omaha Metropolitan Utility District	1,007	10,515	......
Other Districts			
Chicago Park District	3,935	27,497	66,230
Washington Suburban Sanitary District (Maryland)	1,398	8,550	75,032
Consumers Public Power District (Nebraska)	1,193	13,775	40,698
Imperial Irrigation District (California)	1,040	10,946	62,412
Totals	42,878	384,172	1,048,521
Per cent of nonschool district totals	35	38	28

Source: *Special District Governments in the United States,* U.S. Bureau of the Census, Governments Division, State and Local Government Special Studies No. 33 (Washington: 1954), p. 3. The Chicago Park District is coterminous with the city limits of Chicago; the Washington Suburban District operates in part of the Washington Metropolitan area; and the Consumers Public Power District is state-wide. Of the twelve districts, only the Imperial Irrigation District operates entirely outside a metropolitan area.

Authority, for example, outranked seventeen states in number of employees and twelve states in annual revenue in the fiscal year 1952. At the same time, the Port of New York Authority had more long-term outstanding debts than each of thirty-nine individual states.[2] Metropolitan districts with the most extensive operations also stand out in comparison with other districts. Of the twelve largest nonschool districts, eight are metropolitan and three others are located in metropolitan areas but are less than metropolitan territorially (see table). These are the most important metropolitan districts in terms of operations, but in addition there are a number of others that are significant in one or more of the categories of personnel, revenue, and debt. These others similarly demonstrate the high relative operational importance of metropolitan districts, especially among nonschool special units. . .

Variations and Limitations

. . . [T]here is wide variation in the features of metropolitan districts despite their relatively limited number. This can be seen by recalling the formation, governing board composition, and financing characteristics of the districts presented as case studies. Even functionally similar districts operating in metropolitan areas in the same state may have marked differences. The Metropolitan Water District of Southern California and the East Bay Municipal Utility District supply water to residents of different California metropolitan areas. The former is largely financed by property taxation, the latter depends upon service charges. There are frequently great differences between two metropolitan districts in the same metropolitan area. For example, the formation procedure and the method of selecting the governing body of the Metropolitan Sanitary District of Greater Chicago and the Chicago Transit Authority contrast sharply.

Metropolitan districts differ appreciably in the proportion of the metropolitan area or population which they include, although all of them encompass at least a major part of one or the other. Beyond this, however, there is frequently little similarity. Some districts, such as the Huron-Clinton Metropolitan Authority, extend outside the metropolitan area into nonmetropolitan land, whereas the Metropolitan Water District of Southern California contains most of one metropolitan area and parts of two others. By contrast, the Metropolitan Sanitary District of Greater Chicago includes about one-half the territory and most of the population of only the core county of a metropolitan area. This district, as a result of territorial limitations, cannot prevent sewage dumping in the portion

2. *Special District Governments in the United States,* U.S. Bureau of the Census, Governments Division, State and Local Government Special Studies No. 33 (Washington: 1954), p. 3.

of the metropolitan area which is outside district boundaries. Its geographical limits lessen its functional effectiveness. Most metropolitan
districts contain less than the entire metropolitan area.

Although metropolitan districts collectively engage in many functions, in no metropolitan area are all or even nearly all metropolitan
functions handled by metropolitan districts. Such units are therefore
solving only part of the over-all metropolitan problem. As noted previously, most metropolitan districts have not increased their functions
since their establishment. Generally when they have grown in this
manner they have taken on functions closely related to their initial
functions. For example, the Port of New York Authority has enlarged its
operations, but within the original field of transportation, and the East
Bay Municipal Utility District, which started by supplying water, has
added sewage disposal.

Control and Complexity

One of the most striking features of metropolitan districts is
the fact that metropolitan residents lack determination of and control
over certain important aspects of the districts. This situation is not an
isolated one, but appears with some frequency, especially in metropolitan
districts containing territory in two states. Establishing a district by state
legislative or judicial action, permitting the district directors to issue
bonds on their own decision, effectuating annexations through state
laws, and having members of the governing body chosen by a governor
or a judge whose constituency is wider than that of the metropolitan
area are important examples of the remoteness of some districts from
the voters of metropolitan areas. A number of metropolitan districts
utilize one or two of these procedures, but interstate metropolitan districts use all of them. Metropolitan districts with territory in two states
are created by the adoption of similar laws by two state legislatures,
approval by Congress, and the completion of an interstate compact. The
members of the governing body are appointed by the respective governors and occasionally some of them are ex officio state officials. The
governing body may issue bonds through its own unilateral action. The
district area can be enlarged by amendment of the interstate compact.
How can such districts, which operate in metropolitan areas and
materially affect the local people, be held sufficiently accountable by the
metropolitan population? The only possible regular channel of control
is through the legislature or the governor, but such a route is often too
circuitous to be effective.

With a substantial number of metropolitan areas already territorially interstate and more about to become so, district government is
likely to be used more frequently. So far the uniform district pattern in

interstate situations has been detachment from responsibility to the people most intimately affected by such governments. There is of course no logical reason why districts in these circumstances cannot be organized under a system calling for direct metropolitan determination and control. Such a procedure would, however, require a reshaping of the established mold.

These interstate metropolitan districts, and certain other metropolitan districts subject to repeated amendment by state law, seem to represent a hybrid level of government, neither truly local nor state. They are local governments principally in the sense that they function in a local area. At the same time they are operationally separated from the area they serve, or are affected by major changes initiated by the state legislature, which may or may not be directly responsive to the desires of the metropolitan people. These districts are very close to being adjuncts of the state government, a matter of concern to persons who want the approaches to metropolitan difficulties to be locally determined and locally accountable.

Another prominent feature of metropolitan districts is the complexity of their composition or functioning. This handicap, found in more than a few of these districts, renders metropolitan determination and control less effective. The Metropolitan Water District of Southern California is a prominent example, for the composition of its governing body, the distribution of voting power, the requirement of bloc voting, and the methods of annexing territory combine to make it an extremely complicated system. Furthermore, there is a stratification of governments within governments as major parts and subordinate parts of this metropolitan operation. For example, in San Diego County the Crest Public Utility District and the cities of La Mesa and El Cajon are part of the La Mesa, Lemon Grove, and Spring Valley Irrigation District, which in turn is a constituent member of the Metropolitan Water District of Southern California. A similar intricate pyramiding exists in Orange County, and numerous other areas within the metropolitan district are slightly less involved. There is no question that metropolitan determination and control were conceived as being part of the original arrangement, but the intricacies that have developed severely dilute the possibilities of their full and consistent attainment.

The complexity usually centers around the composition of the governing body. In the Chicago Transit Authority three of the seven members are appointed by the governor with the consent of the state senate and the approval of the mayor of Chicago. One of these three must reside outside the Chicago city limits. The remaining four are appointed by the mayor of Chicago with the consent of the city council and the sanction of the governor. The Milwaukee Metropolitan Sewerage District has two governing bodies, a city commission and a metropolitan commission. The city commission, consisting of five appointees of the mayor of Milwaukee, builds and operates intercepting sewers and the sewage plant inside Milwaukee and operates sewers outside the city in the district. The metropolitan commission, whose three members are selected by the governor, is responsible for the building of main sewers outside Milwaukee. Special districts should not be so complicated as to negate the worthy objectives of understanding and interest by metropolitan residents.

Criticism and Potentialities

Strong objections to metropolitan districts are frequently raised, but some of them, of course, are based on specific situations and hence do not apply to all districts. Two of the most common criticisms are that districts are too remote from public influence and regulation, and that they have substituted control by a professional administrative guild of experts and an allied interest group for public control.[3] Also often stated are complaints about the limitations on types of district activities which result from mandatory reliance on nontax sources for financing, and about the lack of intergovernmental coöperation and coördinated planning. A more general objection to districts focuses on the effects of restricting their functional scope. It is argued that this type of functional consolidation, without any alteration of existing governmental areas, is simply a makeshift or expedient and lacks sufficient comprehensiveness to meet the many difficulties of the metropolitan problem. Putting the argument in the form of a medical analogy, a long-time analyst observed that "If a patient were suffering from cataracts, heart disease, diabetes and an infected toe, amputating the toe might enable him to walk around for a while but it could not be considered a really important step toward restoring him to health. Just so with [metropolitan] districts and the metropolitan problem."[4] The limited scope of each district therefore leads to further profusion of governmental units which increases the confusion of citizens. In addition, utilization of the metropolitan district device in a restricted manner takes the impetus and interest away from more thorough approaches by alleviating the most pressing difficulties.

In view of this general censure of metropolitan districts, it is significant that for a long time there have been expressions of interest in a remedial measure. This is the idea of broadening the range of functions so as to make metropolitan districts multipurpose operations. So far, however, districts of limited purpose have shown little inclination to

3. The latter point is stressed by Victor Jones in his talk, "Methodology in the Study of Metropolitan Areas," which appears in *The Study of the Metropolitan Region of Chicago: Objectives and Methodology* (Evanston: Northwestern University Department of Political Science, 1952), p. 10.

4. Thomas H. Reed, "The Metropolitan Problem—1941," *National Municipal Review*, 30 (July, 1941), 407.

seek authorization for additional services. Furthermore, in the relatively few district laws that allow the performance of several functions, most districts undertake only one. The same is true of the even rarer districts which may legally perform numerous diversified functions. Nevertheless, interest in creating new multipurpose metropolitan districts continues, as does optimism that some of the established districts will evolve into such governments.

The ease of establishing metropolitan districts, in contrast to the difficulty of achieving other types of metropolitan integration, makes this approach extremely inviting. In addition, public acceptance of the district idea does not seem to lessen with the granting of more than one function, probably because most metropolitan districts vested with multiple functions perform only one at the outset. This technique, unconsciously used for the most part, may well be a key strategy which advocates of multipurpose metropolitan districts should deliberately use. Will this transformation of the metropolitan district mechanism be attempted in efforts to accomplish metropolitan integration? An affirmative answer seemingly has broad implications for the future.

The apparent political feasibility of establishing multipurpose metropolitan districts, and the attractiveness of forming some type of metropolitan government, should not cause important parts of the plan to be overlooked. There should be metropolitan determination and control of metropolitan districts. There should also be an adequate and equitable financial base. Many metropolitan districts of limited functional scope do not adequately meet these standards. The question of success or failure in adoption of a plan should not overshadow the careful formulation of its proper elements, for governments tend to be permanent, and original provisions are sometimes difficult to change. Therefore, although the idea of multipurpose metropolitan districts may be very applicable in specific situations, the details of such proposals are highly important and should not be neglected in the early stages.

What Is a "Metropolitan Problem"?

Oliver P. Williams, Harold Herman, Charles S. Liebman, and Thomas R. Dye

Metropolitan Problems

THE TERM "metropolitan problem" has often been affixed to any situation requiring cooperation or interaction between adjacent units of government in urban areas. Problems are usually identified on a service basis, and there is hardly any governmental activity which has not been identified as constituting a metropolitan problem. The advocacy of metropolitan government is, for some, based merely on the belief that almost every activity has an intergovernmental aspect.

Some writers have distinguished between *metropolitan problems* and *problems in a metropolitan area*. This observation contains a very sound insight, but it lacks specificity. The following classification attempts to make explicit the crucial distinction between the two. The distinction is based on the recognition that the major characteristic of metropolitan areas is the coincidence of spatial specialization and autonomous local governing units. A metropolitan problem is one that, unlike other intergovernmental problems, results from this coincidence.

Problem One: Maintaining the System

If people want to work in one community, sleep in another, shop in a third, and play in a fourth; if high-status persons want to reside apart from those of low status; if smoky factories are to be separated from homes; in short, if spatial specialization is to exist within a metropolitan economy—then basic services necessary for the development of each subarea and means through which they may be accessible to one another, must be provided.

Transportation and communication are the primary avenues of maintaining accessibility. The latter is provided primarily through the private sector of our economy, the former is shared by private and pub-

Reprinted from Suburban Differences and Metropolitan Problems (*Philadelphia: University of Pennsylvania Press, 1964*), *pp. 299–305.*

lic management, with government playing an increasingly important role. But transportation is not the only service through which government makes the system feasible. Certain basic utilities, such as water and sewage disposal, are often requisites for urban development. If they cannot be locally provided, and if a larger service area is a technical or financial necessity for continued development, then autonomy in policy formulation must give way to integrated mechanisms if the component units are to survive. Thus we characterize as a truly metropolitan problem the *maintenance of services providing the supports necessary for the continued existence of areal specialization.*

Problem Two: Unequal Distribution of Resources and Services

In every metropolitan area, there are "have" and "have not" communities, with the core city often being the most advertised of the "have nots." Such disparities are largely a by-product of the system of areal specialization. Of course there always have been, and probably always will be, differences in individual and community wealth. In a metropolitan context, such differences are aggravated by the efficiency with which the system of differentiation is maintained. Moreover, the multiplicity of local governing units, when imposed upon specialized populations, affects their ability to reconcile differences between groups. It is in this sense that we take exception to views such as that of Banfield and Grodzins who argue that housing is not a metropolitan problem. We agree that the structure of metropolitan government is not the *cause* of slums or blight; we agree that the mere existence of different housing standards does not constitute a problem; but we disagree with their belief that alterations in governmental structure will not alter housing policies. Such alteration can distribute the burden of housing costs over wider areas, it can impose higher minimum standards, it can organize leadership that is lacking in those areas where housing is poorest, it can attack the roots of the social and economic differences that segregate the poor and dictate their housing. It can do all this if one recognizes the extent to which urban differentiation affects the distribution of the supply of housing and the costs of remedying its inadequacies, and if one holds government responsible for producing change.

Our disagreement with Banfield and Grodzins is similar to that between the professionals and local politicians. As we have seen, some Suburbs may choose to deemphasize or do without some services. Although we did not specifically probe this question, we suspect that some working-class Suburbs would willingly forego basic health services, for example, if commensurate tax savings would accrue. Thus the existence of different service standards reflect both differences in burdens associated with supplying financial support and differences in the preferences of specialized populations. Whether or not the local people approve of the differentials, disparities in services result. Professionals will identify such disparities as metropolitan problems when local officials and residents will not.

There is still another basis for labelling inequities in resources and services a metropolitan problem. When upper-middle-class suburbs draw off leadership, and, more particularly, wealth from the rest of the system, the remaining areas are impoverished thereby. As a result the cost and burden of providing services vary throughout the metropolitan area. The attainment of a recognized minimum standard becomes excessively costly to some communities and so an acceptable standard of service is not always provided throughout the area.

Thus we characterize as a metropolitan problem *the unequal distribution of resources and services that result from the process of specialization.*

Problem Three: Border Relationships

Contiguous units of government must engage in many reciprocal relations merely as a result of their proximity to one another. This is as true for rural as urban areas. The fleeing criminal crossing municipal boundaries is a clear example. Such fugitive pursuit problems are common to all governments; yet we frequently refer to this situation as metropolitan when it occurs in an urban environment, but not when it occurs in rural areas. River pollution evokes upstream-downstream conflicts regardless of whether the jurisdictions involved are urban or rural. Factories in rural areas may poison animals and plants with discharges of noxious fluids or fumes. That such discharges affect more than one political jurisdiction does not make the problem metropolitan.

The politics of mere propinquity does not constitute a truly metropolitan problem, since it is unrelated to the fundamental metropolitan characteristic—areal specialization. For this reason, cooperative demands that emanate simply from border relationships represent pseudo-metropolitan issues. Success in initiating and maintaining cooperation on matters such as fugitive-search systems, police-radio networks, common streets, minor utility exchanges, etc., should not be viewed as symbols of metropolitan fraternalism which are precursors of true union.

It should be added, however, that the density and greater activity of urban governments increases the number of border contacts between municipalities in metropolitan areas. While urbanism may thus generate a high level of municipal interaction, the qualitative nature of border policies is not thereby changed. These policies deal with problems that are distinct from those of system maintenance and resource and service inequities. Generally, border problems are easily solved until money is required. At that time, the nature of the problem changes, as questions of the proration of costs and obligations arise.

The three classes of problems described above are not mutually exclusive. It is difficult to conceive of any governmental policy or service without some overtones that would qualify it for inclusion in all three categories. Moreover, the importance of the three, and the degree to which they are popularly recognized at any one time, differ. Proposals offered as solutions to metropolitan problems are received and judged in accordance with how problems are perceived and what interest they evoke. A proposal for a joint sewer authority may at the same time be perceived as relating to (1) maintenance of the system (2) service and resource inequities or (3) a border problem of contiguous urbanized communities. How individual municipalities will react to the proposal is conditioned largely by what problem they view it as solving and what problems they feel may result from the proposal. Nevertheless, some policy areas tend to fall in one category more frequently than in another.

Transportation would undoubtedly head any list of policies related to the maintenance of the system of metropolitan specialization. While some integrated means of planning and managing transportation systems are increasingly being employed, their consequences are such as to profoundly influence the manner in which communities specialize, their relationships to other communities and area-wide distributions of wealth. Thus while municipalities depend upon a more-or-less integrated transportation system for their accessibility to complementary municipalities, it is with the greatest reluctance that they relinquished control over transportation policy. But they have relinquished it.

In nearly every metropolitan area, state highway departments have always supplied a modicum of coordination over the highway network. In the Philadelphia area, transportation planning and operation is sufficiently recognized as metropolitan in character that the county and state governments have assumed jurisdiction over it. The creation of a regional transportation-planning agency sustained mostly by federal funds, and the signing of intercounty and interstate agreements on transit development reflect recognition of the essential integrative role of transportation. Municipal activity is becoming confined to lobbying before these higher units of government.

Water and sewage disposal systems are second only to transportation in providing support to the metropolitan system. It has been possible to secure cooperation from very diverse Suburbs for the provision of both these utilities. Cooperative arrangements between Philadelphia and the Suburbs are also common. Indeed, the only firm cooperative arrangements involving financial obligations between the Suburbs and the central city have concerned transportation, sewage disposal, or water.

In considering metropolitan problems which result from inequities, it must be recognized that the seeking of specialized areas by home-owners or businesses is the very cause of the "problem." To attempt to redress inequities on a voluntary basis is largely unrealistic. Wealth-sharing plans have never achieved great popularity among those who enjoy favored positions. Furthermore, in most areas, resolving inequities is not essential to maintaining the system. The fact that older industrial centers may, in the process of social integration, end up with indigent populations for whom they cannot provide is, if of any interest to Main Line residents, perhaps welcomed by them. The very existence of inequities testifies to the success of specialization. Re-distributions of resources and services are the most difficult area in which to achieve metropolitan agreement, in part because they are closely related to social inequalities.

The redistribution achieved by the state's school-subsidy program is the result of pressures applied from the outside. Hard-pressed Suburbs can find many other hard-pressed districts with which to ally in the state legislature, and the resulting redistribution encompasses not only metropolitan areas but the entire state. Service inequities peculiar to urban areas have found less favorable reception in state capitals; hence grants-in-aid for municipal services are a rarity in comparison with school grants.

The Basic Conflict of Metropolitan Government

The question of structuring metropolitan government reflects the basic dualism characteristic of metropolitan areas: the existence of specialization and the need for integrative mechanisms. Most metropolitan proposals are caught between these centrifugal and centripetal elements of the system. The fact that one cannot have specialization without integration does not furnish a basis for agreement. It only assures that questions touching on these two facets of the system will continually be raised and not permanently ignored. Thus the metropolis furnishes an inexhaustible political agenda for discussion by political leaders, political scientists, and urbanists.

The underlying normative question implicit in any proposal for structuring government in a metropolitan area is whether the proposed government is designed to maintain or to modify the system. In the past, those who have advocated consolidation as the ultimate "solution to the metropolitan problem" have, in effect, sought a comprehensive modification of the existing system of areal specialization. So, too, have some of the "Garden City" planners, who, although they would not consolidate, would decentralize the metropolis into economically though not socially, specialized subareas. On the other hand, the narrowly designed, single-purpose special district or authority and the intermunicipal contract concepts have been conceived so as to have as small a disturbing effect on the status quo as possible.

Of the two extreme suggestions for structuring government in metropolitan areas, proposals closer to the latter have been most successful. Metropolitan politics in the United States, as well as in Philadelphia, have never really encompassed a radical revamping of the metropolis as a system of specialization. Why should it? It is unrealistic to expect citizens to acquiesce voluntarily in giving up the prized values of urban differentiation. Thus, while the general-purpose, consolidated metropolitan government has had little acceptance, the special-purpose government has been used frequently. The criticism directed toward this latter development has been that we are in danger of assembling such a complex of special-purpose governments that the problem of policy coordination will be intensified rather than reduced. Such fears are well grounded.

Frequently, the quest for a solution to metropolitan problems is a quest for a governmental structure as politically acceptable as the special district and yet as comprehensive as consolidation. Such solutions do not exist. Moreover, the quest is perhaps misguided. While centralization or decentralization do affect such questions as economy, efficiency, and speed of action, the true test of the adequacy of a metropolitan governmental system is whether it can so structure the political process of negotiation and compromise as to deal effectively and adequately with metropolitan problems.

In the absence of a local political arena in which the demands for integrative services and the claims for greater equities can be arbitrated, such issues are often taken to the state capital and increasingly to Washington. The integrative demands take the form of requests for special regional agencies. Redressing inequities occurs through grants-in-aid. To achieve either goal, parties in the metropolitan area must gain allies or at least still opposition from parties outside the immediate region. The strategy with regard to the state capital or Washington is much the same—the use of political party organizations to form a coalition of urban interests with their nominally affiliated partisan colleagues from non-urban territories. While the procedure varies from state to state, most of the essential metropolitan decisions are made outside the metropolitan area.

In part, this locus for decision-making is an outgrowth of the legal foundations upon which our federal system rests. In part, it is the inevitable outcome of the search for outside coalitions that has been fostered by the inability to gain consensus within the area.

The Desirable and the Possible

Edward C. Banfield and
Morton Grodzins

IN MANY DISCUSSIONS of metropolitan organization, there is a strong bias toward simplicity, uniformity, and symmetry of structure. It is often taken for granted that the presence of a large number of independent local governments in a single area means waste and duplication. That there may be even administrative advantages in decentralization is often overlooked entirely. Beyond problems of efficiency and economy, issues of community independence, sociability, and status are involved. Technical considerations concerning optimum areas for given services must compete for priority with political issues concerning the best organization for the public control of public officials. Issues of philosophy intrude: when does self-government in one locality impede self-government in another? Values of local control compete with values of area efficiency. A consideration of what is desirable in the way of organization ought to take into account the full range of problems. Intangibles—for example, the suburbanite's satisfaction in remaining apart from the central city—should be accorded some value. If a careful accounting is made with all relevant factors taken into consideration, the present "Balkanization" of government in the metropolitan areas may not be as undesirable as it is often made to appear. At any rate, arguments in favor of metropolitan integration on the grounds of administrative efficiency must compete with other arguments that favor independence and separateness.

When the needed distinction is made between "problems which exist in metropolitan areas" and "problems which exist by virtue of the inadequacies of governmental structure in the metropolitan areas," the latter are relatively few. Transportation is probably the most common and the most pressing of the real metropolitan-area problems. Other common and important problems are air-pollution control and civil defense, and in some areas, water supply and waste disposal. Opinion, rather than technical considerations, may add other functions to this list. Even the few named do not require the same jurisdiction, a fact which makes it extremely difficult to say what the boundaries of an all-purpose general government should be. Moreover, there is no reason in technology why most of these functions cannot be carried on effectively by metropolitan governments which do not have general jurisdiction, or by several governments acting collaboratively.

Deep and persistent political conflicts divide the populations of most metropolitan areas. The conflict between the central city and the suburban ring—which also is a conflict between lower-classes and middle-classes and between Negroes and whites—in most places rules out any immediate possibility of "one local government for one local area." The sharpness of these conflicts makes it doubtful in some places whether metropolitan-area government would be immediately desirable even if it were possible. Though the argument for larger areas in the long run is a persuasive one, it is hard to say whether short-run conflicts are better managed if the parties to them are members of the same or of different political communities. But this question is not a practical one under present circumstances. The fact is that sweeping programs of governmental integration will be politically impossible in most metropolitan areas for a long time to come. Those who push for perfectionist schemes can do the cause of reform more harm than good. The very energy poured into allegedly "ideal" solutions diverts attention from less symmetrical but no less desirable steps. And in exciting opposition to grandiose schemes of complete integration, proponents of such schemes also stimulate opposition to the lesser alternatives.

Where strong political conflicts either do not exist or can be overcome, there may be progress toward genuine area-wide government. Large-scale annexations of territory to the central cities are least likely. Some form of urban federalism or some variant of city-county consolidation may be practicable. Of the latter, the "urban-county" idea is probably most feasible. The essence of this plan is the transfer of area-wide functions to the county and the transformation of the county into a government of general competence. State action to facilitate such transfers and to establish county structure as an effective organization for policymaking and administration is essential if the urban-county plan is to have a chance of substantial success.

If the twin questions of what is desirable and what is possible in metropolitan organization are considered in all their complexity, it will be apparent that no single scheme of reform will be applicable everywhere. Every metropolitan area presents a special case, and only detailed consideration of the intricacies and idiosyncrasies of a specific local situation can produce a "plan" that is both desirable and feasible. Recommendations found in reports like this one have their uses, but they are no substitute for the arduous process of local study, discussion, negotiation, and compromise.

A "Model" for Action

The considerations outlined above lead to a "model" for action: a description in general terms of the means by which housing may be improved through changes in the structure of government in a "typical" —and therefore nonexistent—metropolitan area. The aim of the plan is to meet genuine area-wide housing needs with area-wide solutions while maintaining personal and community discretion. In the light of political and social obstacles to sweeping plans of governmental integration, the model places emphasis upon collaboration and the exchange of contractual services among independent governmental units. From the start, this creates a *de facto* local confederation; in the long run it looks forward to a scheme of local federalism.

The impulse for governmental reorganization affecting housing may come for reasons only indirectly related to housing: as a consequence of new transportation needs, or civil defense, or flood control, for example. Furthermore, the persons responsible for initiating structural change may be variously situated. They may be leaders of civic groups, powerful businessmen, members of a state commission, or state legislators. Whatever the immediate causes of reorganization and whoever the initiators, success of any plan will depend crucially upon the mayor of the central city. Even where others play the leading role, the mayor's acquiescence is mandatory. Where the central-city mayor opposes reorganization, it will fail. Where he supports it fully, chances for success are at their best. The central-city mayor is therefore the leading figure in the model.

What gives the central-city mayor his central role? The core city has more at stake in truly metropolitan matters than do the other governments. The biggest of the local governments, it is more likely to have the resources—financial, technical, and political—to initiate and carry on effective action. Moreover the mayor of the central city has a constituency large enough and diverse enough in its interests to permit him to view matters in metropolitan scale. A portion of this constituency, including heavy investors in downtown business districts, may demand rather than merely permit this course of action.

The mayor and his associates are therefore able to play the part of regional statesmen. That is to say, they can think in terms of the whole metropolitan area and when necessary can sacrifice the short-run special interests of the central city to its less immediate, but no less real, interest in the welfare of the area as a whole.

It is not unreasonable to expect statesmanship of this kind from the mayors of central cities. No doubt, in many cases nothing of the sort is to be expected. But in others—New York, Chicago, Philadelphia, Milwaukee, Denver, and St. Louis come to mind especially—action along these lines has already been taking place with encouraging results.

As the center and energizing force of metropolitan organization, the mayor of the central city will seek actively to bring the other units of government into the necessary cooperative relations. He will not do this merely by preaching or persuasion. The proposed model does not assume that the lesser officials of the metropolitan area will also be statesmen (though it does not rule out that possibility). In many cases the mayors of suburban towns or the county commissioners will be unwilling to cooperate in matters which offer no advantages to their jurisdictions. This unwillingness is not due solely to the lesser stature of the small-town official, although this may be a contributing factor. The decisive consideration is that the official elected by a relatively small and homogeneous constituency does not have the independence which would allow him to forego an immediate point for a more remote one, or to find support from one important constituency group when damned by another.

The mayor of the central city will not be without ability to impress others with the importance of cooperation. The merchants, bankers, real estate brokers, and other businessmen of the central cities suffer badly—in higher taxes, in lower income, and in difficulties of getting and keeping personnel—when property values decline in the core cities. Many of these leaders are influential residents of the suburbs, and often their interests, both economic and social, spill over the central-city boundary lines. Their civic groups are most often organized on a wider-than-single-city basis and have considerable influence in the affairs of many local governments. With the requisite leadership from the mayor, these citizens and their voluntary organizations may be mobilized to support area-wide collaborative activities. (An effort to enlist them in grandiose programs of governmental integration is far less likely to succeed; these are the very people to whom, in their role as family heads and homeowners, suburban independence is most important.) To utilize already existing voluntary groups is to maximize the effectiveness of such a citizen effort.

The governor's office can also be expected to help. Many governors in the past, in the words of Mayor Zeidler of Milwaukee, have been "not only indifferent to the problems of the central cities but also hostile to them." But, to a rapidly increasing extent, the populations of states are metropolitan-area populations. In almost every state, the governor has especially close ties to the rural areas—to "upstate" and "downstate"—but his electoral base is more and more bringing him into the orbit of metropolitan interests. And as those interests are mobilized and made effective by the central-city mayor, the governor's cooperation can be assured. Downstate opposition need not always be anticipated. The possible economies in state expenditures that may accompany collaborative action of local governments in metropolitan areas may, on the contrary, produce downstate support. A combination of rural and suburban opposition will be fatal to the governor's cooperation with the central-city mayor; but if suburban cooperation is achieved, the governor's will follow.

If he is to play his role on the metropolitan scene with full effect, the governor must have at his command more substantial staff aides than he has at present, and the state legislature must supply him with requisite programmatic tools. One important device available to him is the state grant-in-aid. State aid for such functions as sewage disposal, storm drainage, and water supply—and for housing and urban renewal as well—can be made contingent upon appropriate administrative collaboration at the metropolitan level. No such state requirements will appear spontaneously. They require political encouragement; and they have little chance of being passed without prior agreement of city and suburban leaders. The economies and program advances made possible by collaborative action are patent arguments for both the initial agreements and the state legislation itself. In short, with vigorous leadership from political leaders of the central cities, state aid can be used to promote an emerging federalism of the multiple governments in the metropolitan areas.

The mayor cannot hope for success in metropolitan arrangements by mobilizing citizen support or by lobbying at the state house. These are important adjuncts, not his principal weapons. In the main, he must rely upon direct negotiations with officials of other local governments. His bargaining position is good because he has power to give or withhold benefits which the smaller places want. Most of the local governments on the periphery of the central city need something from it. They want water and sewer lines extended. They want rapid transport to places of work. They want to use city parks and playgrounds. They want planning assistance.

If the mayor accommodates the suburbs overgenerously, he will not advance the cause of metropolitan collaboration. Once the petitioners get what they want, they are likely to be more indifferent to the needs of the central city than ever before. The mayor will do most for metropolitan organization if he drives a hard bargain. The suburb may have water from the central city at a fair price—but only if it first agrees to subdivison regulations consistent with the requirements of metropolitan development. The suburb may have its policemen trained in the central city and it may use the central city's crime laboratory—but only after it agrees to a plan for exchanging information about fugitives. The central city will agree to help support a planning staff—but only on the understanding that some of the planners will work on a metropolitan highway system while others do zoning chores for the suburbs.

Here again there is nothing new. Many central cities have brought an element of order into metropolitan relations in just such ways. The compact between Denver and its suburbs is a case in point. Salt Lake City is in an excellent position to bring about the orderly development of the entire county through bargaining with the smaller communities, because it controls the water supply. Grand Rapids has established uniform subdivision regulations on its peripheries by negotiating an agreement with suburbs concerning water, sewer, and other services.

Specialists in public administration frequently object to the creation of special-function districts because they further complicate the already complicated structure of metropolitan government. This is not a weighty objection if such special governments are utilized only for genuine area-wide problems. As noted previously, there are not many functions that really require a metropolitan jurisdiction. A more relevant objection to special-district governments, as they are usually constituted, is that they remove needed bargaining power from the mayors of the central cities. And this, even if special districts are few in number, becomes a towering obstacle to general inter-community collaboration over a wide range of problems. A suburb that has its water supplied by an independent agency can cease to cooperate without penalty in other functions. The solution for this difficulty is apparent: when special-function governments are established, they should be governed not by separate, independent boards but by the regular political heads of the governments concerned. The mayor of the largest city on such a board will find his effectiveness augmented in fostering general area-wide collaboration; where independent boards are established, this effectiveness is diminished.

In the absence of metropolitan government, metropolitan planning has an important, but not decisive, role. In the proposed model, there is not a single plan for an entire metropolitan region; rather, there are several. The mayor's office must obviously contain a planning staff; so must the governor's. Other planning groups will exist in the special-function districts. The important point is not to leave planning in limbo. It must be attached to the arms of action—all of them. In the long run, this may mean that the most decisive planning comes from the largest general-purpose government. But it may also develop as an adjunct to a special-purpose government for handling water, sewers, or transportation. The latter development will produce unified planning over a broad range of problems if political control runs, as has been suggested, to the offices of general government in the area concerned.

The mayor's bargaining for specific area-wide programs should be geared to his larger purpose of achieving a more comprehensive regional organization. Where more than one local cooperative arrangement exists between two or more communities, efforts should be made to combine them into a single contract and to use common administrative machinery. As William Rafsky, Philadelphia Development Coordinator, has written, "Thus cumbersome and overlapping devices are avoided, and the concept of broad regional cooperation is advanced."[1] More than this, the steady accretion of cooperative programs, fitted together through the normal push and haul of political bargaining, provides an organic method of constructing, through time, a new form of metropolitan federalism. Special staffs from the core cities, augmented by representatives of other communities, should be assigned to cultivate this development, performing, at least initially, planning and professional services for suburban areas for which no return is expected. Simultaneously—or as a second step—central cities can make available on a cost basis to small municipalities and other local units such services as those governments cannot easily provide for themselves—for example, a comprehensive plan for a suburban village; central purchasing services for a school district; or an application for Federal aid on behalf of a county. Here, as elsewhere, the advantages of collaboration are best demonstrated by collaborative action, and the central city mayor must display initiative and resourcefulness in matters of small importance if he is to make progress toward his larger goals. It bears repeating that he will find substantial political support for such efforts.

These suggestions obviously do not add up to a "solution" to the metropolitan-organization problem. There is no solution in any absolute or final sense. There is, however, the possibility of moving step by step from where metropolitan organization now is to where it ought to be. The advantage of the proposed model is that it can accomplish some things immediately while simultaneously traveling toward a more comprehensive regional organization. In both the short and long run, the model takes account of the importance of community discretion and local freedoms. It recognizes that some joint programs will appear unpalatable at times to some communities, and that joint voluntary action adversely affecting the interests of any given community will not be achieved through simple exhortation or come about easily as one in a series of contractual relationships. It recommends that such difficulties be met through the usual political processes of bargaining and compromise within a large framework of intent: that of sharing joint functions through some sort of local federalism. The program can only succeed if it has energetic leadership from central-city mayors and other political leaders. With such leadership it can find support from the governor, from business and social groups, and from professional planners and administrators. The advances that are to be made through this scheme of development may be slow; but they have the positive virtue of respecting local options and the negative one of avoiding the complete failure that may follow insistence upon politically unattainable "ideal" programs.

1. Personal communication to the authors. They are indebted to Mr. Rafsky for several suggestions incorporated into this section. They have also profited from a memorandum by Luther Gulick. But neither Mr. Rafsky nor Mr. Gulick should be charged with responsibility for the "model" or any of its details.

Needed: A New Layer of Local Self-Government

Luther Gulick

A STRIKING CHARACTERISTIC of the new metropolitan pattern of settlement in the United States is its amorphous structure, dynamism and unprecedented scale. The metropolitanized sections of the country now contain well over 60 per cent of the total population, while single "clusters" have three million, five million, or as many as 23 million human beings. In geographic extent the individual complexes run to as much as 18 thousand square miles.

The scale of what exists and is coming on top is so colossal that we are carried into a new dimension, a new world.

There are three aspects of scale and growth which must concern us as we think about the organization of government in the metropolitan regions. These are the management problems, the cost problems, and the problems of democracy.

From the standpoint of *management*, scale and dynamism are extremely significant. With large scale we can no longer rest back on simple, inherited, amateur, informal, and voluntary approaches to government. As in other large-scale operations, we will be forced to define functions, divide the work, formalize structures and interrelations, professionalize the staffs, and institutionalize activities and communications. With growth also there will be more and more subdivison of work and in consequence a parallel development of integration through formalized co-ordination and control.

These shifts from the "beautiful simplicity of the past" to institutionalized management, forced on us by scale, are not all losses for the community. In most cases, there is at the same time a marked increase in the quality of service and the skill and competence of management.

There are those who think that our bigger cities are already "too big to govern effectively." A little analysis will show, however, that it is

Reprinted from the Annals of the American Academy of Political and Social Science, 314 (November 1957), 57–65, where it appeared under the title "Metropolitan Organization," by permission of the publisher.

not the size that creates the "impossible" situation. The biggest cities are smaller than the states and nations of which they are a part, yet no one says the state or the nation is too big to govern effectively. The problem is not the size; the problem is adjustment of management devices to the size which is forced upon us by events. And when it comes to this, it will be recognized that we now know how to deal with size. We have the organizational and managerial knowledge and tools. There is no reason for running away from scale.

As to the *costs of scale* it is generally believed that most per capita costs increase with size because people who live in big urban centers need more service and protection. Fortunately, there are also certain *economies of scale*. When quality and costs are compared, it is clear that costs of scale are partly neutralized by the economies of scale so that there appear to be no economic "laws" which will automatically limit the scale of metropolitan operations.

A great deal needs to be known also concerning the effect of scale on *democracy*. Particularly when we deal with local government it is fashionable to think and talk about little communities. Most of our "democratic dogmas," developed through our early history, sentimental-ize over this kind of small-scale democracy. While everyone recognizes that with size we cannot have direct democracy but must move to rep-resentative institutions, they do so with nostalgic regret. However, no one has drawn up a clear statement of "the democracy of scale" nor given our people a dogma of big democracy by which they can authenticate their present-day institutions.[1] We still measure big democracies with the yardstick of the town meeting and test their democratic validity by the words of Jefferson and de Tocqueville. This is a philosophical blunder based on the scale fallacy.

Scale cannot be avoided now. Either we develop a clear philosophy and machinery for large scale democracy or we inflict on our people and their leaders a painful sense of frustration and guilt. The truth is, the tests for ideal self-government in a large population which is wide-spread geographically, but knit together in a new structured web of economic, social, and communicational existence, must be radically dif-ferent from the tests for small-scale democracy.

Does the Metropolitan Area Need a "Government"?

Every metropolitan area in the United States has many govern-ments and much governmental activity. Many of the activities are fed-eral, still more are state, and both operate through their several inde-

1. However, a good start has been made by Paul H. Appleby in his *Big Democracy* (New York: Alfred A. Knopf, 1945).

pendent departments. In addition there are the activities of the cities, counties, "authorities," villages, towns, school, and other districts.

Even with all these governments severally at work, with the added influence of countless voluntary agencies, and with many intergovernmental arrangements and contracts, there are a number of clearly unmet requirements in most areas.

The unmet needs give a clue to what is required. They differ from place to place. In some areas the work which falls between the many jurisdictions is water supply; in others it may be waste disposal, pollution control, education or housing, health, crime or flood and fire protection. Generally, there is an imbalance of local financial resources with resulting luxury for some and tax deficiences for others. But everywhere there is chaos as to the major circulation system and pattern including highways, railroads, air facilities, mass transportation, and provision for traffic.

It is now evident that there are inherent reasons why such problems cannot be handled effectively by bits and pieces, each in the hands of independent jurisdictions.

And when it comes to zoning, land use regulation, and the system for circulation and traffic, the underlying problems become impossible of rational attack unless there is a single center for co-ordinated analysis, planning, and action. It is inherently impossible to "solve the traffic problem" within boundaries which are less than those of the normal area of circulation, that is, the entire metropolitan area; nor by separate and competing jurisdictions; nor by ignoring the fact that land uses and the transportation system and pattern are two sides of the same coin.

This statement does not prove that there must be "a single metropolitan government." It suggests, rather, that there must be several new area-wide governmental activities.

Some of these might be assigned to the federal government. The minimum civilized standards might be set and enforced by various federal and state departments. The states might be required to take over the broader metropolitan regional land use controls and to develop and enforce the general pattern of the highway system, controlling federal and state highway funds to this end. Tax difficulties and imbalances may be dealt with through state aid and various equalization formulas. And where some special service is required, like a single great sewage treatment plan or an interjurisdictional bridge or transit system, an "authority" may be set up with its own sources of support from charges or tolls.

Thus it may be possible to design governmental machinery to deal with each and every present need of the metropolitan regions without setting up any specific "metropolitan government." This *ad hoc* approach with a separate metropolitan agency of some sort for each metropolitan job is possible.

What does such an *ad hoc* approach lack? It lacks two very important elements:

First, the *ad hoc* approach lacks comprehensiveness. If we rely on existing state and federal departments each to take care of one or more of the area-wide needs of the metropolitan regions or set up special new agencies or authorities each to perform a specific service, it is evident that this arrangement cannot give a comprehensive or integrated treatment of the several metropolitan needs. Nor would fiscal resources be interrelated or pooled. There would be no possibility of over-all planning, integration, or mutual adjustment and compromise. Each activity would go it alone, and there would be nobody to hold things in balance or to tackle a new development not originally provided for.

Second, the *ad hoc* approach makes self-government by the people of the metropolitan area as concerns their own metropolitan problems impossible as a practical matter. The state and federal agencies are democratically but distantly responsible to their larger electorates, not specifically to the metropolitan area. In fact, metropolitan areas are markedly underrepresented in most state legislatures and in the national political structure. The *ad hoc* agencies and authorities are legally parts of the state government, though in fact floating around in a sort of irresponsible political limbo. Even if such *ad hoc* agencies were made responsible entirely to local electorates, they would confront the electorates competitively with unresolved problems of balance and priorities in a form with which large-scale constituencies cannot deal directly.

These two inescapable deficiencies of the *ad hoc* approach, both of which are greatly accentuated by scale, lead one to explore the possibility of designing one or more governmental "models" planned to give the metropolitan area a government which is comprehensive as to area-wide matters and gives the region at the same time a large measure of local democratic self-government.

Structure of Required Metropolitan Government

The design of such a governmental structure for any metropolitan area must be settled after functions and locale are known. But we need to keep a few central desiderata clearly in mind. These may be noted as:

1] The need to put together within a single viable political boundary the people and the territories which have to be together to work out the local problems of the metropolitan area. By this engineered strategy we make it possible for the people to think, debate, act, and work together politically as a community; and we create the political habitat within which responsible political leadership will arise.

2] The need to achieve geographic, social, and economic comprehensiveness so that the metropolitan government may not be confronted by the impossible task of building half a bridge, regulating traffic on one part of a through highway, controlling land use for one side of a street, or fighting to hold down crime in half of a slum.

3] The need to create workable joint and balanced action between interrelated activities like water supply and waste disposal; crime control, traffic regulation, and recreation; building permits and fire prevention; housing, health, and welfare; and especially to tie together in one package the control over developing land use and density and the control over the major pattern of circulation.

4] The need to create a governmental representative body drawn from the metropolitan area as a whole to which may be given both the legal and the pragmatic power to consider each and every major metropolitan problem on an integrated basis, to devise remedial programs, to listen to all shades of opinion, to develop compromises and community agreements, and then to take action to carry out the decisions made and to require compliance with these decisions not only from individuals and private groups but from subordinate municipal corporations concerning area-wide metropolitan matters.

5] The need to protect the local communities, natural neighborhood subdivisions, and incorporate units against being swallowed up and destroyed by the metropolis and its government in the performance of their separable local activities and in the maintenance of their desired above-standard services and environments.

6] The need to develop a fiscal system for the metropolitan government in its own right, so that (a) the wealth, power, and credit of the area as a whole may be mobilized for the solution of the over-all problems of the area; (b) the sudden new wealth created through the activities of the metropolitan government may make a fair contribution toward the costs; and (c) the fortuitous tax resources of one lucky subregion may contribute to support the basic community requirements of another small subunit which has no such metropolitan windfall.

7] The need to equip the metropolitan government with suitable arms for (a) analysis, comprehensive and balanced planning, and compromise development; (b) policy decision-making; and (c) execution, management, and enforcement. And finally,

8] The need to remember that we are not working with eternal and fixed boundaries, but with volatile, dynamic, and expanding settlements; that we are always striving in the United States to keep government and political decisions "close to the people."

There are situations in which these eight requirements may be met within reason without creating a new layer of metropolitan government. Where this is the case, it goes without saying that we should develop and adapt existing machinery to do the job, turning to new creations only where this is the best and only way out.

Approaching our problem from this point, it will be found that there are situations, as noted above, in which we can turn to the federal government, to the states, to the counties, and to existing *ad hoc* agencies or to interjurisdictional contracts to handle the activities now called for.

Where none of these devices is available or adequate to meet the requirements we have laid down above, we shall need entirely new political invention.

With this in mind, four such "inventions" are here sketched, with no claim that they are original with the author. These are:

1]   The creation of a state department of local affairs with an independent bureau or "desk" for each major metropolitan area within the state.

2]   The reconstruction of the county so that the county may become the metropolitan government of its region.

3]   The creation of a new limited purpose metropolitan service agency with a built-in power to expand as to functions, finance, and representation.

4]   The creation of a new layer of local government above the existing localities and below the state to be known as the metropolitan council of XYZ, having the authority and financial power to deal with broad but specified metropolitan activities.

These four inventions are not necessarily mutually exclusive, though 2 and 3 would not be needed where a metropolitan council is established. The four proposals are briefly discussed in the following paragraphs.

A State Department of Local Affairs

The proposed state department of local affairs would take over responsibility for handling all general relations of the state with county, city, village, town, and special district governments, and with their officials. The new department would collect local statistics, especially financial statistics, make administrative surveys and financial audits, offer "efficiency" advice and assistance, and would carry on extensive officer training and in-service-training programs for local elective and appointed personnel. The department would work directly with existing associations of local officials, participate in conferences, and defend the interests of the local governments as a group before the legislature and with all administrative departments.

Such a state department would not take the place of the state department of education in dealing with the local schools nor of the health department, the welfare department, the highway department, the state planning department, the tax department, or any other functional department in its specialized and professional functions. But the state department of local affairs would be concerned with the general impact of these specialized departments on local governments as such.

Under this concept, it would be desirable to set up in the proposed department a separate "desk" for each major metropolitan area of the state and to appoint to this desk a man of broad experience and competence. He would not only "clear" all state activities concerning their combined impact on "his metropolitan area" but would work directly with the local governments of his area. On occasion he would call their officials together for conference in order to develop the maximum co-operation and participation in the local solution of metropolitan problems and the fullest possible reflection of local needs and desires in all state decisions.

Co-operation in planning, the establishment of standards, and the development of services and compacts across state lines concerning metropolitan problems would be a responsibility of the "desk" and the department.

Under this plan, it would be most helpful if the local governments would set up voluntary regional councils like that developed in the New York tri-state region some years ago under the chairmanship of Mayor Robert F. Wagner.

The Metropolitan County

A second possible approach is the complete reconstruction of the county government in densely populated regions so that it may add to its existing functions and become "the metropolitan government" of its area. Where the county already has an adequate geographical extent and a reasonable level of political responsibility and administrative competence, this might well meet the eight requirements stated above.

The major disadvantage of using the county as the foundation for metropolitan government is that the county is generally imbedded constitutionally in the state administrative, representational, and political structure. Its boundaries are most inflexible and its operation can be raised in managerial competence only with the greatest effort.

Wherever the county is used as the metropolitan government, issues of political representation arise as in the case of the new Dade County charter (Miami, Florida). Such a county falls into the same category as the great metropolitan city, or the city-county, in terms of political representation. The governing body must, preferably, be so designed as to represent the voters directly either by election at large, by districts, or by some combination of these methods. The size of the county council must be articulated to the form of county government. If a county manager is used, the council would be small and representative. If the county mayor is elected and assisted by an appointive chief administrative officer, then the council can be designed more freely in regard to size and method of election. However structured in detail, the design of such a federated county council should be based on the representative system already tested in our great cities and city-counties and tailored to the political needs of the specific area.

The Open-Ended Metropolitan Commission

A third possible approach is the creation of a limited-purpose special "authority," service unit or commission designed to cover a large metropolitan area and to perform from the beginning some needed service, such as water supply or airport construction and operation, with the authority to add to its functions and powers of local action.

The recently enacted law in the State of Washington, the Metropolitan Council Act, is along this line although its possible added functions are rather narrowly limited. Presumably these could be extended by the state legislature in future years if occasion warrants.

Where this approach is adopted, it would seem important to establish something more than a small board of directors appointed by the governor, as is so often the case. If the board is to make extensive policy decisions as to planning, land use controls, and the general pattern of the transportation system, it is not likely that a small specifically chosen board can be effective.

A New Metropolitan Council

A fourth approach is the creation of an entirely new layer of local self-government, what we may call a metropolitan council.

This would be, first of all, a legislative body. It would be designed to bring together officially and regularly all of the major local governmental interests and problems of the metropolitan area so that the regional governmental shortfalls may be fully considered; remedial and developmental programs may be evolved with adequate planning; compromises arrived at, and decisions made and carried out.

These are primarily "policy" assignments; they are the stuff of politics.

We know from much experience that such functions cannot appropriately be left to experts or bureaucrats working alone. This kind of work calls for politically sensitive and responsible "representatives."

We know also that the real essence of the problem is the laying of the political foundation for the development of the metropolitan community as a political reality with rising political leadership, political education, and political following. This alone will make possible effective and balanced political action and community commitment for the metropolitan area as a whole.

Because of scale, we must have representative institutions, and for these to work we must have political leadership and political action. It is to this end that we need a political entity coextensive with the area and consequently a metropolitan political constituency.

Furthermore, we know that it is generally safer to build political institutions on what we already have, rather than to wipe the slate clean and start all over again.

From these considerations it follows that the membership of the metropolitan council should be made up initially from the chief elected officials of the local governments of the region which is being brought together. This would include, in most situations, the mayors of the larger cities and incorporated units and the chief elected official of each county compromised in the "metropolitan area." It might be desirable to add to this group a number of specifically elected representatives and a president of the metropolitan council to be elected at large, although these developments might well be postponed until the region is ripe for this type of leadership and direct representation.

The metropolitan council would establish a strong and well-staffed program development and planning unit, placing this directly under its chairman or president. The council would set up several special working committees for which the program and planning unit would furnish an appropriate staff.

The metropolitan council would do its administrative work, such as building a bridge or a water works or running a sewage treatment plant or a transit system, by using existing regional and local operating agencies as far as possible. Where no agency exists which can handle the operation, the council would by ordinance create such an administration. This could be done by setting up "an authority" or by creating an operating department under a manager to be appointed by the council president. Where one or more authorities or special district bodies exist already within the boundaries of the metropolitan council, these could be continued as they are, bringing certain of their powers under the supervision of the council.

Especially important is the definition of the responsibility of the metropolitan council. The effort would be made to assign to the council the over-all, interunit metropolitan matters and activities and to guarantee to the existing and underlying governmental units the responsibility to carry on their normal non-metropolitan local activities. This can only be approached through trial and error: With a general statement of this principle, the listing of the arrangements with reference to a number of the more obvious services where the division of work is required, and by authorizing the localities which so desire to protect their unique advantages and to have local services of a higher standard than those of their neighbors.

While many of the metropolitan services and facilities developed by the metropolitan council will be "self-supporting" on the basis of prices and tolls collected, the council should not be required to rely solely on such receipts.

As to metropolitan areas which extend across state lines, as is already true of more than a score of such metropolises, the metropolitan council would be set up by joint action of the states involved, presumably utilizing the inter-state compact procedure. In such cases the original compact should provide for territorial extension and for functional and fiscal modifications without requiring congressional reconsideration. As to modifications which do not change the arrangement fundamentally, it would be desirable for the contracting states to leave these to the area concerned, rather than to require the state legislatures to review the arrangement again.

Each such interstate metropolitan compact will have to be tailor-made, primarily because of the required fiscal provisions. The present local government provisions, court decisions, and tax and debt systems are so diverse among neighboring states, that a great deal of constitutional ingenuity will be required to develop workable arrangements in all cases. It may even be necessary to consider the in-state members of an inter-state metropolitan council as a separate "municipal corporation" with the right to act concerning matters within its state along lines agreed on jointly in the metropolitan council.

Character of the Council

The metropolitan council as thus conceived is, first, an old-fashioned American "body of overseers" with authority limited to the over-all interests, concerns, and problems of the defined metropolitan region. It is democratically constituted from locally elected officials, with the eventual addition of directly elected members. As such it is also a federation of the existing local governments. The council is initially primarily a policy-developing and adopting body; that is, a legislative agency. However, the council is given the authority, as are local legislatures generally, to develop such administrative units as may be required, using existing agencies as far as this is possible, or to create new units where necessary.

Under this proposal, the existing local governments—the cities, counties, towns, villages, and special districts—could be continued as they now are in relation to their local functions. Only the metropolitan aspects of functions would come under the oversight of the metropolitan council. At the same time, the existing local jurisdictions would be authorized to shift to the council by mutual consent any activities which they wish to handle in this way.

This proposal is not only elastic in its boundaries since it is not tied by definition to a specific set of existing city or county boundaries, but is extensible across state lines, following precedents already well established in many jurisdictions for more limited activities.

Under this proposal, finally, there is brought into legal and political existence what is now evolving naturally as a matter of social and economic life; namely, the metropolitan community. With a representative council, this emergent community is given political being. The metropolitan area becomes a single constituency for metropolitan representation, for metropolitan policy discussion, for metropolitan administration, and above all, for metropolitan political leadership and political action. While this in no way supersedes existing governmental organizations, it fills the vacuum and makes it possible for the rising metropolis to deal effectively and democratically with its now unmet metropolitan needs.

A Proper Role
for the Federal Government

Robert H. Connery and
Richard H. Leach

AS THE FEDERAL GOVERNMENT moves to act on the metropolitan area problem, it begins with a severe handicap. It lacks knowledge, first of all, of the extent and complexity of the problem the nation faces. Not only is there no basis of fact regarding the total impact of its many activities in metropolitan areas on which to build, but its statistical procedures are not designed to produce the raw data for metropolitan areas as such, from which the basic facts can be derived. Even in its collection of urban data, there are a number of obvious gaps. The definition of a standard metropolitan area used by the Bureau of the Census still needs to be revised. Even the new definition of a "Standard Metropolitan Statistical Area" is built on a county basis. But counties which impinge on metropolitan areas often have a vast hinterlnad of sparsely settled rural territory which is far from being metropolitan in any sense of the term. San Bernardino County in southern California is a good example. Whereas the western end of the county is in fact part of the Los Angeles urban complex, the eastern part runs two hundred miles back into the desert. Yet all of it, by the Bureau of the Census definition, is part of the Los Angeles metropolitan area.

Moreover, knowledge is lacking about what happens when a federal program is put into effect in a metropolitan area so far as the total resources and social structure of the community are concerned, and even less is known about the total effect of a series of federal programs on a single metropolitan area. This was pointed out emphatically in the Kestnbaum report. Part of the trouble results from not knowing exactly how much federal money is spent in individual metropolitan areas. These data are available in the files of the operating agencies, but have never been put together in terms of metropolitan areas. As a preliminary step, exact data should be gathered on federal expenditures in major metropolitan areas over the past decade. Subsequently, a study should be made of the total impact of federal programs on government in metropolitan areas.

Because exact data are lacking, as this study has repeatedly emphasized, all recommendations for action to solve metropolitan problems must be predicated on a great deal of assumption. Nor is it possible, for the same reason, to spell out in great detail what should be done. A more solid basis of factual knowledge than is now available would be required for such a project. The recommendations which follow are therefore based, of necessity, on the facts which are most clearly evident.

There is reason to believe that federal programs are piling up on each other faster than metropolitan areas can digest them. Each is planned separately, and there is no correlation among them. Programs are launched in isolation, without reference to their impact on the areas to which they are directed. As a consequence, federal programs are badly co-ordinated so far as metropolitan areas are concerned, both among themselves and in terms of state and local programs in the same areas. Federal programs having a bearing on metropolitan problems should be re-examined in order to assure better co-ordination and to provide the maximum flexibility and a minimum of standardization as to detail and procedure.

Moreover, the federal government in its grant-in-aid programs should encourage the creation of larger units of government to fit present social and economic realities in metropolitan areas. In particular, it ought not to require the continued existence of outmoded local governmental units by limiting its grants to cities when action over a larger area is needed. The example set in the housing program, to provide assistance for broad over-all metropolitan planning, should be followed in other areas. The federal government should assist in the preparation of plans by providing technical aid, information, and financial assistance, and it should require all federal and federal grant-in-aid programs, including highways and recreation, as well as housing and urban renewal, to be related to comprehensive metropolitan plans.

Federal programs for the most part are concerned with unrelated physical things—buildings, highways, airports—but there is a magnificent unconcern about the people who are displaced by these activities. The elimination of slums, for example, is going on at such breakneck speed that many more people are left homeless than ever before, crowding is getting worse, and delinquency is increasing. To be sure, one cannot make omelets without breaking eggs, but the life of a community is as important as its physical development, and both should be taken into account. Moreover, it should be recognized that massive urban relocation breaks up long-established community patterns. Replacing slum dwellings with new and sterile housing projects which offer no encouragement to rebuilding community life will have serious repercussions on metropolitan living. The relocation of these displaced people and the solution of all the social problems their movement entails should be the joint responsibility of the federal government and the local communities.

In interstate metropolitan areas, the federal government should recognize its special responsibilities by offering incentives to the states involved to cooperate with one another and with the federal government in attacking particular problems on an area-wide basis. The states should be encouraged to make broader use of all sorts of co-operative arrangements, including interstate compacts, in attacking metropolitan area problems. Congress could do much to encourage the use of compacts by simplifying its own legislative procedures for dealing with them and by the passage of general permissive legislation. The federal government should give the nation a good example by speedily implementing the recommendations of the Bible Committee for the Washington metropolitan area. It should also grant the District of Columbia greater freedom to solve its own problems, and by a policy of self-restraint should refrain from constant interference with local policy formation in the District.

With regard to international metropolitan areas, the federal government should recognize that such areas have many of the same governmental problems that domestic metropolitan areas have, and it ought to facilitate the creation of local planning agencies or other appropriate devices for each of these areas. Moreover, since many problems of these areas will still have to be handled through ordinary diplomatic channels, the federal government should make certain that the International Commissions and the Department of State have personnel on their staffs who are familiar with metropolitan government and its problems.

Under the American system of government, unless the President provides leadership, no great amount of progress can be made in solving any problem. None of the recent presidents have been concerned with government in metropolitan areas; their neglect has affected both the legislative and the executive branches, and has been felt from top to bottom of the administrative pyramid and far beyond into the tentacles of the operating agencies. Presidential interest in metropolitan areas must be aroused before effective action can be expected. Lacking presidential leadership, Congress has been slow to appreciate the magnitude of the problem. Consequently, it has not given a high priority to considering ways in which the federal government could aid in solving it. Structural changes, such as those suggested below, can provide for better integration of federal programs, but mere structural change cannot make its maximum contribution until both the President and Congress have been made fully conscious of their responsibilities for action.

Urban needs have not received anything like the recognition that has been given to agriculture and the needs of rural areas because in many federal agencies there is a conspicuous lack of people with training and experience in the government problems of metropolitan areas. One of the reasons American agriculture has made the great strides it has in less than a century is that the federal government has recognized its importance by recruiting thousands of agricultural specialists. To date, not even the beginnings of anything comparable have been developed for metropolitan needs, although almost two-thirds of the population of the United States now live in metropolitan areas. The federal government does not lack skilled engineers to build urban highways or airports to serve urban areas, but it does lack personnel who are skilled in the general problems of urban government. Special urban units should be established and those already in existence should be strengthened in the federal agencies whose programs particularly concern metropolitan areas.

One of the structural changes which are needed is the establishment of a staff agency to furnish the President with continuous staff assistance on metropolitan problems. Stated briefly, a Council on Metropolitan Areas should be established by statute in the Executive Office of the President. The Council should consist of three to five full-time members, one of whom should be designated as chairman and be assigned broad administrative authority over the work of the Council. In addition to such day-to-day duties as the President might assign it, the Council should organize a program of continuing research on the impact of federal programs on metropolitan areas. Though the Council should have no authority to co-ordinate federal programs, it should have power to collect data, ask questions, and make recommendations to the President. It should keep abreast of developments in the field through the device of regional desks rather than by means of permanently established field offices. An advisory group representing private research bodies as well as state and local governmental units and interested professional groups should be appointed to consult with the Council in the performance of its duties.

The federal government's program for metropolitan areas should be firmly anchored in the structure of Congress as well as in the White House. This can best be accomplished by requiring the President to submit an annual report to Congress on metropolitan problems, just as he does on the economic state of the nation, and by creating an appropriate Committee on Metropolitan Problems to which the President's report could be referred for study and action. These devices have been used successfully with regard to economic matters, and they could be used with equal success here. The creation of such a committee, however, should not deter the present House Subcommittee on Intergovernmental Relations (the Fountain Subcommittee) from continuing its studies of intergovernmental problems in general, with special attention to the important problem of federal-state relations.

III

The Machine
and Its Reform

A "MACHINE" is a party organization held together and motivated by desire for personal gain rather than by political principle or ideology. To the poor in the slums, who are its chief support at the polls, it is a source of jobs, petty favors, and protection. To its precinct and ward workers, it is a source of soft jobs, careers in minor elective office, and favors—an "in"—at city hall. To the few who control it, it is a way of making money.

Perhaps the machine should be spoken of in the past tense. Chicago is the only large city still run by one, and (as a reading in Section V shows) the character of that machine is changing rapidly. Fragments of machines survive in various stages of deterioration in many cities. Some of these have a good deal of vitality and power, even though not enough to take control of the city, and it is not altogether out of the question that a change of conditions—the onset of a major depression, for example—might return them to power in a few central cities where the number of low-income Negroes, Puerto Ricans, and white hillbillies is very large. As a general phenomenon of urban politics, however, the machine is a thing of the past. The immediate causes of its decline were the introduction of merit systems (which eliminated most of the patronage at the disposal of the bosses), full employment and rising national income (which vastly depreciated the value of such patronage as remained), the development of professionalized welfare services under the New Deal, and the structural reorganization of city governments. But a more general and long-term cause was the changing class character of the urban electorate. Middle-class people do not want and will not tolerate the boss and his "gravy train," and they have recently come to be in the majority in almost every city.

For a long time the machine was a conspicuous and powerful institution in American life. Between the Civil War and the Second World War all large cities and many small ones were at one time or another in the grip of machines. The bosses of the big city machines were leading figures in state and national politics. Whatever its present or future role, the machine is well worth study because of the part it has played in our history.

There is, however, a further and perhaps more important reason for studying it. Every political party (like every other formal organization) must maintain what Chester I. Barnard calls an "equilibrium of incentives." That is, it must offer a combination of inducements (in the case of the machine, "friendship," jobs, favors, protection, money) that will elicit from various classes of actors (voters, precinct captains, ward leaders, elective officials) the actions the organization requires; it must then use these actions to replenish its supply of inducements so that it may elicit more actions, and so on. Because of its heavy reliance upon personal, material inducements, the machine represents an extreme— and therefore analytically interesting—type of organization. Analysis of the extreme type is likely to be productive of insights into the "equilibrium of incentives" of other kinds of party organization, including those that are very unlike it. All of the readings of this section contribute in some way to an understanding of the machine as a system of incentives.

The first two readings offer general views of the machine. Martin Meyerson and Edward C. Banfield describe the Chicago machine as it was during the transitional period between the retirement of Mayor Kelly and the rise of Mayor Daley. Lord Bryce's classic account is of machines as they were in many large cities at the turn of the century. The reader will find that the Chicago machine of the mid-1950's was strikingly like its predecessors.

George Washington Plunkitt, who started life as a butcher boy and became a millionaire during forty years of service as a Tammany office-holder, explains how the machine gets votes. The secret is that it asks for something of little or no value to the donor: note that Plunkitt's cousin Tommy "didn't take any particular interest in politics" and that his vote was therefore Plunkitt's for the asking. The Plunkitt reading incidentally conveys an impression of the amiable cynicism of the professional machine politician; perhaps William L. Riordan, the newspaperman who edited Plunkitt, gilded the lily a bit. In the next reading,

Oscar Handlin, an historian, describes the bond between the immigrant and the ward boss. He says that the control of the boss rested on several grounds: the jobs at his disposal, the feelings of group loyalty that were focused upon him, his social role as a spokesman for the immigrant, and his having favors to give and being fair in the giving of them.

The next three readings describe the internal economy of the machine at a higher level of hierarchy. Frank R. Kent, for many years a writer for the Baltimore *Sun*, discusses two aspects of the mechanics of control: the use of primary elections and the picking of the ticket. William Foote Whyte, a sociologist, tells how the politician uses his stock of resources to create the largest possible amount of support, how he uses the support to augment his influence, how he sells the influence for cash to buy more support, and so on in the endless cycle of organizational maintenance. Edward N. Costikyan, a former Tammany leader, brings the discussion up to date with an account of how Democrats are motivated in New York nowadays.

Corrupt and wasteful as it was, the machine served some socially valuable functions. Robert K. Merton, a sociologist, says that to understand its role we must look at the social circumstances that prevent other institutions from fulfilling essential social functions (the "structural context") and at the subgroups whose needs would remain unfulfilled if it were not for latent (i.e. unintended and unrecognized) functions performed by the machine. He lists several of these. The machine, he says, was an antidote to the constitutional dispersal of power. [It humanized and personalized assistance to the needy. It gave business, including illicit business, the privileges it needed to survive. It provided a route of social mobility for some to whom other routes were closed.] Unless due recognition is given to the importance of these and other functions, Merton warns, attempts at reform are likely to be "social ritual rather than social engineering." Mr. Dooley (Finley Peter Dunne, the humorist) follows a similar line in explaining why "rayformers" almost always fail and why he doesn't like them—"or anny other raypublican."

How to eliminate the machine and make democracy work has been the subject of a great deal of theory, a representative sample of which is presented in the second half of this section. Some of the theorists of reform anticipated Merton's functional approach. Thus Henry Jones Ford, writing more than half a century before Merton, makes much of the constitutional dispersal of power. The cities are corrupt, he says, because the executive and legislative functions are disconnected; corruption, under the circumstances, is an indispensable mechanism for overcoming an otherwise unworkable decentralization. Lincoln Steffens, the best known of the muckraking journalists, emphasizes another latent function of the machine, that of affording privileges to business, especially legitimate business. Politicians, he said, are corrupt because they are bribed by businessmen; businessmen offer bribes because they "have to." The cure, manifestly, was to change the system (the structural context, as Merton would say). "Abolish privilege" was the advice that Steffens, a man who prided himself on his realism, gave. Jane Addams, the founder of Hull House, wrote informatively of the way the machine humanized assistance to the needy and gave opportunities for social mobility. In the pages reprinted here, she dwells on a related theme: the difference between the moral perspectives of the lower and the middle classes. The machine politician, she says, personifies the lower-class ideal of moral goodness, an ideal lacking sophistication because it is "individual" rather than "social" in reference. Perhaps exemplifying the moral standards of a class is still another social function of the machine. Mr. Costikyan, the politician, points out that in recent years the power to exercise discretion in the distribution of governmental privileges has to a large extent shifted from the politician to the bureaucrat. Power, he says, always attracts the corrupt (a proposition which differs in an interesting way from Lord Acton's famous dictum about power tending to corrupt).

THE NATURE AND FUNCTIONS
OF THE MACHINE

A Machine at Work

Martin Meyerson and
Edward C. Banfield

THE CITY COUNCIL, the body which would have to pass upon any sites proposed by the Authority, consisted of 50 aldermen, with the mayor as presiding officer. The aldermen were elected for four-year terms from wards of roughly 25,000 to 65,000 registered voters, only about a third of whom usually voted in aldermanic elections. (The number who voted in mayoralty elections was about twice as great.) Nominally the office of alderman was non-partisan. Actually, however, no one could win an election without the support of a powerful organization and (with some rare exceptions) the only powerful political organizations in the wards were the Democratic and Republican parties. An alderman who did not have the support of his party "machine" ordinarily had no hope of reelection.

The Democratic "machine" had ruled Chicago since 1923. Catholics were in control of it; since 1930, with a few exceptions, they had held the major city offices: the mayor, city treasurer, county clerk, more than half of the county commissioners, and two-thirds of the aldermen were Catholics.[1] And among the Catholics it was those of Irish extraction who were dominant in politics: one-third of the Council, including most of its leaders, were Irish-Catholics. The other aldermen were mostly of Polish,

1. William R. Gable, "The Chicago City Council: A Study of Urban Politics and Legislation," unpublished dissertation, Department of Political Science, University of Chicago, Chicago, 1953, p. 13.

Reprinted from Politics, Planning, and the Public Interest (*New York: The Free Press, 1955*), *pp. 64–75.*

Italian, Bohemian, Lithuanian, Slovak, or Greek extraction (in descending order of importance, these were the principal nationality groups in the Democratic party) or of German extraction (these were Republicans).[2] A few aldermen were Jews (unlike the Poles, Italians, and other ethnic minorities, the Jews did not usually endeavor to be recognized as a group on the party slate or in the award of patronage).[3] Two were Negroes. The numerical importance of the Irish in the Council was to be accounted for not so much by their numbers in the electorate as by the fact that in wards where no one ethnic group had a clear majority they made the most acceptable compromise candidates. As one politician explained to an interviewer, "A Lithuanian won't vote for a Pole, and a Pole won't vote for a Lithuanian. A German won't vote for either of them—but all three will vote for a 'Turkey' (Irishman)."[4]

A few of the aldermen aspired to higher political office, especially (among those who were lawyers) to judgeships, but most of them were in the business of being aldermen as other men are in the business of selling shoes. Being an alderman was supposed to be a full-time occupation, but the salary was only $5,000, so most aldermen supplemented their salaries by selling something—most often insurance or legal service (more than half of them were lawyers). Being an alderman was, of course, very good for business.

Ordinarily, even if he were so inclined, an alderman could not concern himself deeply with the larger issues of city government or take a city-wide view of important problems. If he wanted to stay in office, he had to devote all of his available time and attention to the affairs of the groups that made up his ward. He was in the Council to look after the special interests of his ward and to do favors for his constituents: to get streets repaired, to have a playground installed, to change the zoning law, to represent irate parents before the school authorities, and so on. In addition to activities of this kind, he had to take an interest in the social life of his ward—to appear at weddings, funerals, and neighborhood occasions, and to say a few well chosen words and make a

2. John P. White, "Lithuanians and the Democratic Party, A Case Study of Nationality Politics in Chicago and Cook County," unpublished Ph.D. dissertation, Political Science Department, University of Chicago, Chicago, 1953, p. 25.

3. *Ibid.*, p. 28.

4. *Ibid.*, p. 64. A candidate's ethnicity was often a decisive asset or liability; in mixed wards he was most fortunate if his name was such that he could be presented as belonging to more than one ethnic or nationality group. Thus, Alderman Benjamin M. Becker's ward committeeman introduced him to voters of German extraction as of German extraction, stressed to voters of Swedish origin that Becker's wife had lived in Sweden and must have Swedish blood herself, pointed out to Catholics that Becker was a graduate of the DePaul University College of Law and a teacher there (thus implying that he was a Catholic), and presented him to Jews as a Jew. If the Catholics were fooled, no great injustice was done, for Becker's predecessor as alderman for many years was Dr. Joseph Ross, a Catholic whom the Jews assumed was a Jew. [Interview document.]

small donation when called upon. If he had any time left, he might think about the problems of the city as a whole. But whatever he thought, he was expected to work for his ward first.

From a formal standpoint, the 50 aldermen governed Chicago.[5] The Council made appropriations for all municipal purposes, it awarded franchises to and regulated the rates of public utility companies, it passed on appointments presented by the mayor, and (within the authority given it by the state) it could create new city departments at will. The mayor could send or read messages to the Council, he could vote when there was a tie (or when more than one-half of the aldermen had already voted for a measure), and he had a veto (including an item veto over appropriations acts) which could be overridden by a two-thirds vote. In principle, each alderman was the independent agent of his ward. From a formal standpoint, then, the Council was a good deal like a league of independent nations presided over by a secretary-general.

In fact, however, there existed two sets of informal controls by which the aldermen's independence was very much limited and qualified. One set of controls was the leadership of the Council itself. Half a dozen of the most powerful Democratic aldermen—the "Big Boys," they were sometimes called—working usually with the mayor, effectively controlled the whole Council when matters of interest to them or to the mayor were at stake. They did this in part by controlling committee assignments. Unless an alderman could get on an important committee, his power in the Council was small. And unless he cooperated with the chairmen of the important committees and especially with the chairman of the Finance Committee (whose salary was $8,500, who was provided a limousine with a police chauffeur, and who had an office second only to the mayor's in splendor), he could not hope to get anything done for his ward. Any measure that required an appropriation had to go to the Finance Committee, and so, as one alderman explained, the chairman of that committee "sits at the gate of accomplishment for any alderman. . . ."[6] Indeed, if an alderman fell foul of the Finance Committee chairman or of any of the "Big Boys" he might be punished by having some city service to his ward reduced or suspended. On the other hand, even if he were a Republican, he could expect generous treatment from the leadership if he "played ball."

The other set of informal controls operated through the party or machine. An alderman had to stay in favor with his ward committeeman —i.e., the party leader in his ward—or else be the committeeman himself. The ward committeeman made all of the important decisions for

---

5. The city could exercise only those powers doled out to it by the state legislature, however, and so it might be more accurate to say that the city was governed by the state. See Barnet Hodes, "The Illinois Constitution and Home Rule for Chicago," 15 *Chicago Law Review* 78 (1947).

6. Interview document.

the party within the ward. The Committeeman was elected in the primary every four years (usually he could keep an opponent off the ballot by raising technical objections to his petitions) and so his power rested in part upon a legal foundation. From a legal standpoint, he was entitled to receive and disburse party funds, to manage campaigns, and to represent the leaders of the party within the ward. In fact he was commonly the "boss" of the ward; the party organization in the ward "belonged" to him. He decided who would run on the party's ticket within the ward, he appointed and dismissed precinct captains at will, and he dispensed patronage. As a member of the City and County Central Committees of his party, he particiapted in selecting its candidates for all city, county, and state offices and for Congress. (Half of Illinois' 26 Congressional districts were in greater Chicago.) In each of the party governing bodies his vote was in proportion to the total primary vote for his party in the last election; this of course gave him an incentive to "turn in" the biggest vote possible.

No salary went with the office of committeeman, but most of the committeemen held one or more public jobs and some of them ran businesses which were profitable because of their political connections.

William J. Connors, Democratic boss of the 42nd ward (the district described by Zorbaugh in *The Gold Coast and the Slum*),[7] may be taken as reasonably representative of at least some other ward committeemen. In 1950 Connors, who was in the insurance business, was on the public payroll in two capacities: as a state senator and as a bailiff of Municipal Court. His way of running his ward was described as follows:

> That Connors provides well for his workers is undeniable. Not only does he have a great many jobs to distribute, but he is a source of funds if any of his men need to borrow. He supports them when they are in difficulty with the law, as sometimes happens, and takes an interest in their family affairs. His relationship with them is that of a benevolent despot. He holds the power to withdraw their source of livelihood and to banish them from active work in the party and from their power positions in the community. He is the sole dispenser of the campaign funds from the party superstructure and the candidates. He may establish the assessments of the jobholders at any rate he desires without consulting them. He makes the party commitments to the county and city organs without a canvass of the captains' opinions and then demands complete obedience to these decisions. He may move a captain from one precinct to another at his discretion and is, of course, the sole source of patronage distribution.
>
> The committeeman generals his workers much like a military leader might. He plots the strategy of the campaign, estimates the difficulties that may be encountered, and decides the amount and allocation of money to be spent. He shifts captains from one point to another when

7. Harvey W. Zorbaugh, *The Gold Coast and the Slum*, University of Chicago Press, Chicago, 1929, p. 287.

called for. He attempts to build good precincts over a long period of time. Such building requires several years and may involve extensive trials and changes. Jobs are distributed not only on the basis of the effectiveness of the captain but in regard to the total effects such distribution may have. It happens occasionally that a strong Democratic captain has a smaller number of jobs allotted to him than one who is attempting to build up a Democratic precinct in the face of strong Republican competition. Thus in one precinct which casts a heavy Democratic vote, there are only two jobs besides the captain's, while another precinct that turns in only a slight Democratic majority is staffed by nine jobholders in addition to the captain.

The committee respects the unity of the precinct organization and the authority of the captain and his workers. As long as the captain's activities are successful and his conduct does not threaten the party's vote-getting power, Connors does not interfere with the internal structure. The captain selects his own assistants and nominates his choices to receive public jobs. He assumes the responsibility for building an effective precinct organization. He decides how party funds allocated to him will be distributed and to a certain extent how they will be obtained. He and his men must share the responsibility of contributing whatever additional money is necessary beyond that sent from the party's headquarters. Connors respects the autonomy of the captain in this area of personal influence. Captains may or may not distribute campaign literature, pay cash for votes, engage in fraudulent activities, or arrange precinct meetings of the voters. The only important check on the captain's conduct is the final tabulation of votes at each election.[8]

Any ward committeeman who cared to could have himself nominated alderman. If he chose not to run for office himself (like Connors, he might prefer to be on the public payroll in another capacity), he made sure that the candidate was someone who would work closely with him in ward affairs and offer no challenge to his control of the organization. "Naturally," an alderman once explained, "he (the ward committeeman) doesn't want to get a man who will build himself into a power so he can take the organization away from the committeeman. If the alderman doesn't do what the ward committeeman wants him to do, then the committeeman will dump him at the next election."[9] Some committeemen treated their aldermen as errand boys, others paid little attention to them, and still others treated them as friends, partners, and collaborators.[10]

If an alderman became powerful enough, he might unseat his committeeman and become the ward boss himself. But even in this case he

8. Leonardo Neher, "The Political Parties in Chicago's 42nd Ward," unpublished dissertation, Department of Political Science, University of Chicago, Chicago, 1952, pp. 65–66.

9. W. R. Gable, *op. cit.*, p. 74.

10. James A. Rust, "The Ward Committeeman in Chicago," unpublished dissertation, Department of Political Science, University of Chicago, Chicago, 1953, p. 56.

could not be independent of the machine. The leaders of the Central Committee could bring him into line by withholding patronage or discharging public employees from his ward, by denying him financial support from the party's general coffers at election time, or by allowing an investigation of graft and corruption to take place in his ward. If it saw fit, the Central Committee could destroy a ward organization—and thus a ward committeeman—by these means, but it could do so, of course, only at the cost of impairing, at least temporarily, the effectiveness of the machine. Since its purpose was to win elections, a major concern of the machine was "harmony." Only if a committeeman failed to support the party's slate was he likely to be disciplined severely. If they wanted a favor from him, party leaders would offer him a favor —usually patronage—in return.

To increase their power *vis-à-vis* the Central Committee leadership, ward committeemen formed factional alliances or "blocs." Usually these alignments were on a geographical basis—thus, for example, there were South Side and West Side blocs of ward committeemen.

In order to maintain itself and to accomplish its purposes, any organization must offer incentives of the kinds and amounts that are necessary to elicit the contributions of activity it requires. It must then use these contributions of activity so as to secure a renewed supply of resources from which further incentives may be provided—it must, in other words, maintain what Chester Barnard has called an "economy of incentives" or else cease to exist.[11]

In Chicago a political machine distributed "gravy" to its officials, its financial backers, and to the voters. In this way it induced them to contribute the activity it required—to ring doorbells on election day, to give cash, and to go to the polls and vote for its candidates—and in this way it gained possession, through its control of the city or county government, of a renewed supply of "gravy."

As the word "gravy" suggests, the incentives upon which the machines relied were mainly material. Some prestige attached to being a ward politician; there was "fun" in playing the political "game"; there was satisfaction in being "on the inside"; and sometimes there was even an ideological commitment to an issue, the party, or a candidate. But these non-material incentives were not ordinarily strong enough to elicit the amount and kind of activity that a machine required from its workers. "What I look for in a prospective captain," a ward committeeman told an interviewer, "is a young person—man or woman—who is interested in getting some material return out of his political activity. I much prefer this type to the type that is enthused about the 'party cause'

11. Chester I. Barnard, *The Functions of the Executive,* Harvard University Press, Cambridge, 1938, Ch. XL. Barnard discusses the special case of the political organization on pp. 156–157.

or all 'hot' on a particular issue. Enthusiasm for causes is short-lived, but the necessity of making a living is permanent."[12]

The "material return" that the party offered a worker was generally a job on the public payroll. Committeeman Connors, for example, had at his disposal in 1952 an estimated 350 to 500 jobs and the total public payroll to Democratic workers in his ward was conservatively estimated at $1,320,000.[13]

Although jobs were the most visible of the material returns the party gave its workers, other opportunities to make money may have been more valuable. An alderman or committeeman who was a lawyer, an insurance man, or a tavern owner could expect to profit greatly from his association with the party. Whether he was profiting lawfully or unlawfully it was often impossible to tell. Alderman Sain and his ward committeeman, County Commissioner John J. Touhy, for example, were partners in an insurance business. "We handle a lot of business, no question about it," Touhy once blandly told a reporter. "I assume its just good business in the ward to carry insurance with us."[14]

Even with the voters the machine did not make its appeal on the basis of issues or ideology. It offered them certain non-material incentives—chiefly the friendship and protection of its precinct captains—but in the main with them, as with the party workers, it relied upon "gravy." Just as it gave its workers jobs and opportunities to make money in exchange for their services, so it gave its loyal voters "favors"—special services and preferential treatment at the hands of its members and dependents who held city or county jobs—in exchange for their votes.

The party's agent in exchanging friendship and favors for votes was the precinct captain.[15] In 1950 a representative captain described his work as follows:

> I am a lawyer and prosecuting attorney for the City. I have spent 19 years in precinct work and have lived and worked in my present precinct for three and a half years.

12. H. Dicken Cherry, "Effective Precinct Organization," unpublished dissertation, Department of Political Science, University of Chicago, Chicago, 1952.

13. Leonardo Neher, *op. cit.*, p. 76.

14. *Chicago Daily News*, August 27, 1949. Some years earlier the *Chicago Daily News* compiled a list of the ordinances introduced by Sain over a five-month period and then inquired of the people who were specially benefited by these ordinances whether they had recently bought insurance of the firm of Touhy and Sain. It turned out that many of them had. (September 24, 1940.)

15. In a vivid account by David Gutmann, the Chicago precinct captain is described as a "salesman." Mr. Dolin [the precinct captain] is a go-between between his party, which has services and favors to sell the public in exchange for the public's votes, and the public, or at least the segments of it which are willing to exchange their votes for services—often enough to swing a close election. In this relationship the vote stands for currency, the party is the manufacturer or the supplier, the public is the consumer, and Mr. Dolin the door-to-door salesman. . . . To the party the vote has 'commodity' or exchange value, in that it represents a fraction of the total sum of votes needed by the party to gain exclusive control over the 'tons' of patronage whereby it holds power, and to gain access to the financial resources of the community." [David Gutmann, "Big-Town Politics: Grass-Roots Level," *Commentary*, 17:1, February 1954, p. 155.]

I try to establish a relationship of personal obligation with my people, mostly small shopkeepers and eighty per cent Jewish. I spend two or three evenings a week all year round visiting people, playing cards, talking, and helping them with their problems. My wife doesn't like this, but it is in my blood now. I know ninety per cent of my people by their names.

Actually I consider myself a social worker for my precinct. I help my people get relief and driveway permits. I help them on unfair parking fines and property assessments. The last is most effective in my neighborhood.

✳The only return I ask is that they register and vote. If they have their own opinions on certain top offices, I just ask them to vote my way on lower offices where they usually have no preferences anyway.

I never take leaflets or mention issues or conduct rallies in my precinct. After all, this is a question of personal friendship between me and my neighbors. I had 260 promises for Korshak in this primary.

On election day I had forty or fifty people help me because this was a "hot" campaign. All they had to do was to get out their own family and friends. I used to lease an apartment near the poll where I gave out drinks and cigars, but I don't do this any more.

I stayed inside the poll most of election day, especially during the vote counting. If something went wrong, you could have heard me yell all over the precinct. Actually there isn't as much fraud now as there used to be.

Abner (the PAC candidate) was not really a threat in my precinct. He had seven workers but they contacted only their friends. No one feels obligated to them and they worked only during the campaign. Abner's campaigners were naive. They expected to influence people by issues, and they relied on leaflets and newspaper publicity which is not effective. Besides, Abner (Negro) is not hard to beat in a white precinct. I just carried a picture of both candidates around with me.

I can control my primary vote for sure because I can make the party regulars come out. I don't encourage a high vote here, just a sure vote. In the general election there is much more independent voting, and I can't be sure of control.[16]

In the conservation areas, especially, the precinct captain was often active in the neighborhood improvement association and a leader in efforts to keep "undesirable people" out of the neighborhood. An interviewer who spoke to 30 precinct captains in 1951 found that 16 of them had been approached by voters who wanted help in preventing Negroes and Jews from moving into the neighborhood. Some of these captains invented slogans and ran campaigns on an issue such as: "The —————— neighborhood is a good clean neighborhood. Let's keep it that way!" A captain was likely to learn about it almost immediately if a landlord rented to an "undesirable"; very often the captain would go

16. Quoted in Fay Calkins, *The CIO and the Democratic Party,* University of Chicago Press, Chicago, 1952, pp. 67–68.

to the landlord to urge in the name of civic pride that he discriminate and to point out that property values would decline if he did not.

In heavily Democratic precincts the owners of rooming houses sometimes consulted with their precinct captains about new roomers and assisted the party workers with their canvass at election time. In some cases these owners refused to permit Republican workers to enter their buildings. The loyalty of the rooming house owner to the Democratic party was not a matter of ideology: the owner who did not cooperate with the precinct captain could expect a visit from the city building inspector the next day.[17]

In addition to the services of party workers and voters, the machine needed cash. (It usually cost about $40,000 to elect an alderman.) This it raised by assessing the salaries of people who owed their jobs to the party, from the proceeds of ward-sponsored affairs such as picnics, boxing matches, and golf days, and in contributions from individuals and organizations who wanted to be on good terms with the party or, perhaps, even to help its candidates win.[18] These were all considered legitimate sources of revenue. In some wards, however, money was raised by promising favors or threatening injury to business interests, especially to those interests—e.g., taverns, hotels, and nightclubs—which were subject to inspection and licensing laws. Business people who wanted favors—a change in the zoning law, a permit to operate a tavern, a tax adjustment, and so on—were expected to pay for them in cash. In some wards there was even said to be a fixed schedule of prices for such favors. Whether the money so received went to support the party or to support personally the ward committeeman, the alderman, and their cronies was seldom clear; indeed, in many wards no real distinction could be made between the coffers of the party and the pockets of the boss: the ward organization "belonged" to the boss.[19]

The most profitable favors were of course those done for illegal enterprises. In giving protection to gambling joints, unlawful taverns, and houses of prostitution some politicians joined with racketeers to form a criminal syndicate.[20] A by-product of their activity was the syste-

17. H. D. Cherry, *op. cit.*, pp. 67–68.

18. Neher, *op. cit.*, p. 92.

19. If he thought the transaction was likely to be profitable, the ward boss might sell the services of his organization to the opposition. He might be criticized for doing this, but he was not likely to be unseated; after all, the organization "belonged" to him.

20. ". . . the criminal syndicate," according to Aaron Kohn, chief investigator for the Emergency Crime Committee of the City Council, "can be described as consisting of political officials, having the power and responsibility to enforce the laws, who maliciously withhold that power in exchange for money and support from hoodlums, vice operators, professional gamblers, and other community enemies, to aid them in their political ambitions." Independent Voters of Illinois, *The Kohn Report; Crime and Politics in Chicago*, Chicago, 1953, p. iii. However, after two months' inquiry a grand jury in the Spring of 1954 gave up its efforts to uncover specific links between crime and

matic corruption of the police force; in one way or another officers were either bribed or discouraged from doing their duty. "After you find out how many places are protected by the ward politicians," a patrolman of long service told an investigator, "you just stay out of the way so you won't be around when something happens."[21]

The machines were most effective in delivering votes in the precincts where they were most corrupt. In general, these were in the "skid-row" districts and the slums, where votes were cheapest and illegal activities most numerous. The "river wards" in the decaying center and on the West Side of the city were the most solidly organized and the most corrupt. Here "social absenteeism"—the departure of socially articulate leaders of the community—had reached such a point that the machine politicians had the field to themselves.[22] It was almost unthinkable that an alderman in one of these wards might lose at the polls because he took an unpopular stand on an issue. If he lost, it was because his committeeman "dumped" him, because the committeeman sold out to the opposition, or because the opposition managed to build a more powerful machine, but it was not because the voters disliked his stand on any issues. These "river wards" were in sharp contrast to the so-called "newspaper wards" particularly on the North Side where voters usually split the ticket in the way a newspaper advised. The aldermen in the "river wards" could afford to be contemptuous of the newspapers; in their wards editorials were words wasted.

Although corruption in varying degrees was widespread in both parties, it was by no means universal in either. Some Democratic and some Republican wards were probably almost entirely "clean" and even in wards which were not "clean" there were aldermen and other officials who were not parties to the "deals" that were made in the back rooms. The honest aldermen, however, got little credit or encouragement from the voters. Many people seemed to think that all politicians were corrupt and that if an alderman did not use his office for personal profit it was because he was a fool. When a North Side alderman bought his boy a football suit and helmet the other children in the neighborhood said, "Look at the alderman's son," suggesting ill-gotten funds. The alderman himself drove a two-year-old Dodge instead of the Cadillac that he could well afford, but even this did not convince his constituents that he was

---

politics in Chicago. "If an alliance exists," the jurors said, "it might be disclosed with funds to conduct undercover work. . . ." *Chicago Sun-Times,* May 1, 1954.

21. Independent Voters of Illinois, *The Kohn Report; Crime and Politics in Chicago,* Chicago, 1953, p. 10.

22. See the discussion of social absenteeism in Morris Janowitz, *The Community Press in an Urban Setting,* The Free Press, Glencoe, Illinois, 1952, p. 214. Janowitz notes that social absenteeism contributes to the decay of the ideological element in politics, thus creating "a new kind of hoodlumism in politics" and making possible sudden shifts from one party to another which have no significance in terms of the traditional political allegiances.

honest.[23] This widespread cynicism tended, perhaps, to give the aldermen a low conception of their calling and to encourage irresponsibility on their part.

Some of the honest men, the Mayor among them, did less than they might have done to put a stop to corruption. The fact was that they needed for themselves or for their party the support of the powerful bosses in the corrupt wards. So, for that matter, did many other interests, both liberal and conservative, in city, state, and nation.

23. Interview document. As this study went to press a committee of the Chicago Bar Association filed charges against this very alderman after the *Sun-Times* had accused him of fee-splitting in zoning cases.

Rings and Bosses

James Bryce

THE READER WILL ASK, How is the Machine run? What are the
inner springs that move it? What is the source of the power the committees wield? What force of cohesion keeps leaders and followers together? What kind of government prevails among this army of professional politicians?

The source of power and the cohesive force is the desire for office,
and for office as a means of gain. This one cause is sufficient to
account for everything, when it acts, as it does in these cities, under
the condition of the suffrage of a host of ignorant and pliable voters.

Those who in great cities form the committees and work the machine are persons whose chief aim in life is to make their living by
office. Such a man generally begins by acquiring influence among a
knot of voters who live in his neighbourhood, or work under the same
employer, or frequent the same grogshop or beer saloon, which perhaps
he keeps himself. He becomes a member of his primary, attends regularly, attaches himself to some leader in that body, and is forward to
render service by voting as his leader wishes, and by doing duty at
elections. He has entered the large and active class called, technically,
"workers," or more affectionately, "the Boys." Soon he becomes conspicuous in the primary, being recognized as controlling the votes of
others—"owning them" is the technical term—and is chosen delegate to
a convention. Loyalty to the party there and continued service at elections mark him out for further promotion. He is appointed to some
petty office in one of the city departments, and presently is himself
nominated for an elective office. By this time he has also found his way
on to the ward committee, whence by degrees he rises to sit on the central committee, having carefully nursed his local connection and surrounded himself with a band of adherents, who are called his "heelers,"
and whose loyalty to him in the primary, secured by the hope of
"something good," gives weight to his words. Once a member of the
central committee he discovers what everybody who gets on in the world

Reprinted from The American Commonwealth (*London and New York: Macmillan & Company, 1889*), *Vol. II, Ch. 63.*

discovers sooner or later, by how few persons the world is governed. He is one of a small knot of persons who pull the wires for the whole city, controlling the primaries, selecting candidates, "running" conventions, organizing elections, treating on behalf of the party in the city with the leaders of the party in the State. Each of this knot, which is probably smaller than the committee, because every committee includes some ciphers put on to support a leader, and which may include one or two strong men not on the committee, has acquired in his upward course a knowledge of men and their weaknesses, a familiarity with the wheels, shafts, and bands of the party machine, together with a skill in working it. Each can command some primaries, each has attached to himself a group of dependents who owe some place to him, or hope for some place from him. The aim of the knot is not only to get good posts for themselves, but to rivet their yoke upon the city by garrisoning the departments with their own creatures, and so controlling elections to the State legislature that they can procure such statutes as they desire, and prevent the passing of statutes likely to expose or injure them. They cement their dominion by combination, each placing his influence at the disposal of the others, and settle all important measures in secret conclave.

Such a combination is called a Ring.

The power of such a combination is immense, for it ramifies over the whole city. There are, in New York City, for instance, over ten thousand persons employed by the city authorities, all dismissible by their superiors at short notice and without cause assigned. There are two thousand five hundred persons employed in the Custom-House, Post-Office, and other branches of the Federal service, most of whom are similarly dismissible by the proper Federal authority; and there are also State servants, responsible to and dismissible by the State authority. If the same party happens to be supreme in city politics, in the Federal government, and in the State government, all this army of employés is expected to work for the party leaders of the city, in city primaries, conventions, and elections, and is virtually amenable to the orders of these leaders.[1] If the other party holds the reins of Federal government, or of both the Federal government and State government, then the city wire-pullers have at any rate their own ten thousand or more, while other thousands swell the army of "workers" for the opposite party. Add those who expect to get offices, and it will be seen how great and how disciplined a force is available to garrison the city and how effective it becomes under strict discipline. Yet it is not larger than is needed, for the work is heavy. *Tantae molis erat Romanam condere gentem.*

In a Ring there is usually some one person who holds more strings in his hand than do the others. Like them he has worked himself up to power from small beginnings, gradually extending the range of his in-

1. Assuming, as one usually may, that the city leaders are on good terms with the Federal and State party managers.

fluence over the mass of workers, and knitting close bonds with influential men outside as well as inside politics, perhaps with great financiers or railway magnates, whom he can oblige, and who can furnish him with funds. At length his superior skill, courage, and force of will make him, as such gifts always do make their possessor, dominant among his fellows. An army led by a council seldom conquers: it must have a commander-in-chief, who settles disputes, decides in emergencies, inspires fear or attachment. The head of the Ring is such a general. He dispenses places, rewards the loyal, punishes the mutinous, concocts schemes, negotiates treaties. He generally avoids publicity, preferring the substance to the pomp of power, and is all the more dangerous because he sits, like a spider, hidden in the midst of his web. He is a Boss.

Although the career I have sketched is that whereby most Bosses have risen to greatness, some attain it by a shorter path. There have been brilliant instances of persons stepping at once on to the higher rungs of the ladder in virtue of their audacity and energy, especially if coupled with oratorical power. The first theatre of such a man's successes may have been the stump rather than the primary: he will then become potent in conventions, and either by hectoring or by plausible address, for both have their value, spring into popular favour, and make himself necessary to the party managers. It is of course a gain to a Ring to have among them a man of popular gifts, because he helps to conceal the odious features of their rule, gilding it by his rhetoric, and winning the applause of the masses who stand outside the circle of workers. However, the position of the rhetorical boss is less firmly rooted than that of the intriguing boss, and there have been instances of his suddenly falling to rise no more.

A great city is the best soil for the growth of a Boss, because it contains the largest masses of manageable voters as well as numerous offices, and plentiful opportunities for jobbing. But a whole State sometimes falls under the dominion of one intriguer. To govern so large a territory needs high abilities; and the State boss is always an able man, somewhat more of a politician, in the European sense, than a city boss need be. He dictates State nominations, and through his lieutenants controls State and sometimes Congressional conventions, being in diplomatic relations with the chief city bosses and local rings in different parts of the State. His power over them mainly springs from his influence with the Federal executive and in Congress. He is usually, almost necessarily, a member of Congress, probably a senator, and can procure, or at any rate can hinder, such legislation as the local leaders desire or dislike. The President cannot ignore him, and the President's ministers, however little they may like him, find it worth while to gratify him with Federal appointments for persons he recommends, because the local votes he controls may make all the difference to their own prospects of getting some day a nomination for the presidency. Thus he uses his

Congressional position to secure State influence, and his State influence to strengthen his Federal position. Sometimes however he is rebuffed by the powers at Washington and then his State thanes fly from him. Sometimes he quarrels with a powerful city boss, and then honest men come by their own.

It must not be supposed that the members of Rings, or the great Boss himself, are wicked men. They are the offspring of a system. Their morality is that of their surroundings. They see a door open to wealth and power, and they walk in. The obligations of patriotism or duty to the public are not disregarded by them, for these obligations have never been present to their minds. A State boss is usually a native American and a person of some education, who avoids the grosser forms of corruption, though he has to wink at them when practised by his friends. He may be a man of personal integrity.[2] A city boss is often of foreign birth and humble origin; he has grown up in an atmosphere of oaths and cocktails: ideas of honour and purity are as strange to him as ideas about the nature of the currency and the incidence of taxation: politics is merely a means for getting and distributing places. "What," said an ingenuous delegate at one of the National Conventions at Chicago in 1880, "what are we here for except the offices?" It is no wonder if he helps himself from the city treasury and allows his minions to do so. Sometimes he does not rob, and, like Clive, wonders at his own moderation. And even he improves as he rises in the world. Like a tree growing out of a dust heap, the higher he gets, the cleaner do his boughs and leaves become. America is a country where vulgarity is scaled off more easily than in England, and where the general air of good nature softens the asperities of power. Some city bosses are men from whose decorous exterior and unobtrusive manners no one would divine either their sordid beginnings or their noxious trade. As for the State boss, whose talents are probably greater to begin with, he must be of very coarse metal if he does not take a polish from the society of Washington.

A city Ring works somewhat as follows. When the annual or biennial city or State elections come round, its members meet to discuss the apportionment of offices. Each may desire something for himself, unless indeed he is already fully provided for, and anyhow desires something for his friends. The common sort are provided for with small places in the gift of some official, down to the place of a policeman or doorkeeper or messenger, which is thought good enough for a common "ward worker." Better men receive clerkships or the promise of a place in the custom-house or post-office to be obtained from the Federal authorities. Men still more important aspire to the elective posts, seats in the State legislature, a city aldermanship or commissionership, perhaps even a seat in Congress. All the posts that will have to be filled at the coming

2. So too a rural boss is often quite pure, and blameworthy rather for his intriguing methods than for his aims.

elections are considered with the object of bringing out a party ticket, *i.e.*, a list of candidates to be supported by the party at the polls when its various nominations have been successfully run through the proper conventions. Some leading man, or probably the Boss himself, sketches out an allotment of places; and when this allotment has been worked out fully, it results in a Slate, *i.e.*, a complete draft list of candidates to be proposed for the various offices.[3] It may happen that the slate does not meet everybody's wishes. Some member of the ring or some local boss—most members of a ring are bosses each in his own district, as the members of a cabinet are heads of the department of state, or as the cardinals are bishops of diocese near Rome and priests and deacons of her parish churches—may complain that he and his friends have not been adequately provided for, and may demand more. In that case the slate will probably be modified a little to ensure good feeling and content; and will then be presented to the Convention.

But there is sometimes a more serious difficulty to surmount. A party in a State or city may be divided into two or more factions. Success in the election will be possible only by uniting these factions upon the same nominees for office. Occasionally the factions may each make its list and then come together in the party convention to fight out their differences. But the more prudent course is for the chiefs of each faction to arrange matters in a private conference. Each comes wishing to get the most he can for his clansmen, but feels the need for a compromise. By a process of "dickering" (*i.e.*, bargaining by way of barter), various offers and suggestions being made all round, a list is settled on which the high contracting parties agree. This is a Deal, or Trade, a treaty which terminates hostilities for the time, and brings about "harmony." The list so settled is now a Slate, unless some discontented magnate objects and threatens to withdraw. To do so is called "breaking the slate." If such a "sore-head" persists, a schism may follow, with horrible disaster to the party; but usually a new slate is prepared and finally agreed upon. The accepted Slate is now ready to be turned by the Machine into a Ticket, and nothing further remains but the comparatively easy process of getting the proper delegates chosen by packed primaries, and running the various parts of the ticket through the conventions to which the respective nominations belong. Internal dissension among the chiefs is the one great danger; the party must at all hazards be kept together, for the power of a united party is enormous. It has not

---

3. A pleasant story is told of a former Boss of New York State, who sat with his vassals just before the convention, preparing the Slate. There were half a dozen or more State offices for which nominations were to be made. The names were with deliberation selected and set down, with the exception of the very unimportant place of State Prison Inspector. One of his subordinates ventured to call the attention of the Boss to what he supposed to be an inadvertence, and asked who was to be the man for that place, to which the great man answered, with an indulgent smile, "I guess we will leave *that* to the convention."

only a large but a thoroughly trained and disciplined army in its office-holders and office-seekers; and it can concentrate its force upon any point where opposition is threatened to the regular party nomination.[4] All these office-holders and office-seekers have not only the spirit of self-interest to rouse them, but the bridle of fear to check any stirrings of independence. Discipline is very strict in this army. Even city politicians must have a moral code and moral standard. It is not the code of an ordinary unprofessional citizen. It does not forbid falsehood, or malversation, or ballot stuffing, or "repeating." But it denounces apathy or cowardice, disobedience, and above all, treason to the party. Its typical virtue is "solidity," unity of heart, mind, and effort among the workers, unquestioning loyalty to the party leaders, and devotion to the party ticket. He who takes his own course is a Kicker or Bolter; and is punished not only sternly but vindictively. The path of promotion is closed to him; he is turned out of the primary, and forbidden to hope for a delegacy to a convention; he is dismissed from any office he holds which the Ring can command. Dark stories are even told of a secret police which will pursue the culprit who has betrayed his party, and of mysterious disappearances of men whose testimony against the Ring was feared. Whether there is any foundation for such tales I do not undertake to say. (But true it is that the bond between the party chiefs and their followers is very close and very seldom broken.) What the client was to his patron at Rome, what the vassal was to his lord in the Middle Ages, that the heelers and workers are to their boss in these great transatlantic cities. They render a personal feudal service, which their suzerain repays with the gift of a livelihood; and the relation is all the more cordial because the lord bestows what costs him nothing, while the vassal feels that he can keep his post only by the favour of the lord.

European readers must again be cautioned against drawing for themselves too dark a picture of the Boss. He is not a demon. He is not regarded with horror even by those "good citizens" who strive to shake off his yoke. He is not necessarily either corrupt or mendacious, though he grasps at place, power, and wealth. (He is a leader to whom certain peculiar social and political conditions have given a character dissimilar from the party leaders whom Europe knows. It is worth while to point out in what the dissimilarity consists.

A Boss needs fewer showy gifts than a European demagogue. His special theatre is neither the halls of the legislature nor the platform, but the committee-room. A power of rough and ready repartee, or a turn for florid declamation, will help him; but he can dispense with both. What he needs are the arts of intrigue and that knowledge of men which teaches him when to bully, when to cajole, whom to attract by the hope

---

4. As for instance by packing the primaries with its adherents from other districts, whom a partisan chairman or committee will suffer to be present and perhaps to vote.

of gain, whom by appeals to party loyalty. Nor are so-called "social gifts" unimportant. The lower sort of city politicians congregate in clubs and bar-rooms; and as much of the cohesive strength of the smaller party organizations arises from their being also social bodies, so also much of the power which liquor dealers exercise is due to the fact that "heelers" and "workers" spend their evenings in drinking places, and that meetings for political purposes are held there. Of the 1007 primaries and conventions of all parties held in New York City preparatory to the elections of 1884, 633 took place in liquor saloons. A Boss ought therefore to be hail fellow well met with those who frequent these places, not fastidious in his tastes, fond of a drink and willing to stand one, jovial in manners, and ready to oblige even a humble friend.

The aim of a Boss is not so much fame as power, and not so much power over the conduct of affairs as over persons. Patronage is the sort of power he seeks, patronage understood in the largest sense in which it covers the disposal of lucrative contracts and other modes of enrichment as well as salaried places. The dependents who surround him desire wealth, or at least a livelihood; his business is to find this for them, and in doing so he strengthens his own position.[5] It is as the bestower of riches that he holds his position, like the leader of a band of condottieri in the fifteenth century.

The interest of a Boss in political questions is usually quite secondary. Here and there one may be found who is a politician in the European sense, who, whether sincerely or not, purports and professes to be interested in some principle or measure affecting the welfare of the country. But the attachment of the ringster is usually given wholly to the concrete party, that is to the men who compose it, regarded as office-holders or office-seekers; and there is often not even a profession of zeal for any party doctrine. As a noted politician happily observed to a friend of mine, "You know, Mr. R., there are no politics in politics." Among bosses, therefore, there is little warmth of party spirit. The typical boss regards the boss of the other party much as counsel for the plaintiff regards counsel for the defendant. They are professionally opposed, but not necessarily personally hostile. Between bosses there need be no more enmity than results from the fact that the one has got what the other

5. "A Boss is able to procure positions for many of his henchmen on horse-railroads, the elevated roads, quarry works, etc. Great corporations are peculiarly subject to the attacks of demagogues, and they find it greatly to their interest to be on good terms with the leader in each district who controls the vote of the assemblyman and alderman; and therefore the former is pretty sure that a letter of recommendation from him on behalf of any applicant for work will receive most favourable consideration. The leader also is continually helping his supporters out of difficulties, pecuniary and otherwise: he lends them a dollar now and then, helps out, when possible, such of their kinsmen as get into the clutches of the law, gets a hold over such of them as have done wrong and are afraid of being exposed, and learns to mix bullying judiciously with the rendering of service."—Mr. Theodore Roosevelt, in an article in the *Century* magazine for November 1886.

wishes to have. Accordingly it sometimes happens that there is a good understanding between the chiefs of opposite parties in cities; they will even go the length of making (of course secretly) a joint "deal," *i.e.*, of arranging for a distribution of offices whereby some of the friends of one shall get places, the residue being left for the friends of the other. A well-organized city party has usually a disposable vote which can be so cast under the directions of the managers as to effect this, or any other desired result. The appearance of hostility must, of course, be maintained for the benefit of the public; but as it is for the interest of both parties to make and keep these private bargains, they are usually kept when made, though of course it is seldom possible to prove the fact.

The real hostility of the Boss is not to the opposite party, but to other factions within his own party. Often he has a rival leading some other organization, and demanding, in respect of the votes which that organization controls, a share of the good things going. The greatest cities can support more than one faction within the same party; thus New York has long had three democratic organizations, two of which are powerful and often angrily hostile. If neither can crush the other, it finds itself obliged to treat, and to consent to lose part of the spoils to its rival. Still more bitter, however, is the hatred of Boss and Ring towards those members of the party who do not desire and are not to be appeased by a share of the spoils, but who agitate for what they call reform. They are natural and permanent enemies; nothing but the extinction of the Boss himself and of bossdom altogether will satisfy them. They are moreover the common enemies of both parties, that is, of bossdom in both parties. Hence in the ring-governed cities professionals of both parties will sometimes unite against the reformers, or will rather let their opponents secure a place than win it for themselves by the help of the "independent vote." Devotion to "party government," as they understand it, can hardly go farther.

This great army of workers is mobilized for elections, the methods of which form a wide and instructive department of political science. Here I have to refer only to their financial side, because that is intimately connected with the Machine. Elections need money, in America a great deal of money. Where, then, does the money come from, seeing that the politicians themselves belong to, or emerge from, a needy class?

The revenues of a Ring, that is, their collective, or, as one may say, corporate revenues, available for party purposes, flow from five sources.

I. The first is public subscriptions. For important elections such as the biennial elections of State officers, or perhaps for that of the State legislature, a "campaign fund," as it is called, is raised by an appeal to wealthy members of the party. So strong is party feeling that many respond, even though they suspect the men who compose the Ring, disapprove its methods, and have no great liking for the candidates.

II. Contributions are sometimes privately obtained from rich men who, though not directly connected with the Ring, may expect something from its action. Contractors, for instance, have an interest in getting pieces of work from the city authorities. Railroad men have an interest in preventing State legislation hostile to their lines. Both, therefore, may be willing to help those who can so effectively help them. This source of income is only available for important elections. Its incidental mischief in enabling wealth to control a legislature through a Ring is serious.

III. An exceptionally audacious Ring will sometimes make an appropriation from the city or (more rarely) from the State treasury for the purposes not of the city or the State, but of its own election funds. It is not thought necessary to bring such an appropriation[6] into the regular accounts to be laid before the public; in fact, pains are taken to prevent the item from appearing, and the accounts have often to be manipulated for that purpose. The justification, if any, of conduct not authorized by the law, must be sought in precedent, in the belief that the other side would do the same, and in the benefits which the Ring expects to confer upon the city it administers. It is a method of course available only when Ring officials have the control of the public funds, and cannot be resorted to by an opposition.

IV. A tax is levied upon the office-holders of the party, varying from one to four or even five per cent upon the amount of their annual salaries. The aggregate annual salaries of the city officials in New York City amount to $11,000,000 (£2,200,000 sterling), and those of the two thousand five hundred Federal officials, who, if of the same party, might also be required to contribute,[7] to $2,500,000 (£500,000 sterling). An assessment at two per cent on these amounts would produce over £45,000 and £10,000 respectively, quite a respectable sum for election expenses.[8] Even policemen in cities, even office boys, and workmen in Federal dockyards, have been assessed by their respective parties. As a tenant had in the days of feudalism to make occasional money payments to his lord in addition to the military service he rendered, so now the American vassal must render his aids in money as well as give knightly service at the primaries, in the canvass, at the polls. His liabilities are indeed heavier than those of the feudal tenant, for the latter could relieve himself from duty in the field by the payment of scutage, while under the Machine a money payment never discharges from the obliga-

6. The practice of openly taking from Parliament a sum for secret service money, which was usually applied by the government in power for electioneering purposes, has just been finally extinguished (1887) in England. A sum is still voted for foreign secret service. In England, however, the money was regularly voted each session for the purpose, and though no account was rendered, it was well understood how it went.

7. Federal officials, would, as a rule, contribute only to the fund for Federal elections; but when the contest covered both Federal and city offices the funds would be apt to be blended.

8. To make the calculation complete we should have to reckon in also the State officials and assessments payable by them.

tion to serve in the army of "workers." As in the days of the Anglo-Norman kings, forfeiture and the being proclaimed as "nithing" is the penalty for failure to discharge the duties by which the vassal holds. Efforts which began with an order issued by President Hayes in 1877 applying to Federal offices, have lately been made to prevent by administrative action and by legislation the levying of this tribute on officials, but they have not as yet proved completely successful, for the subordinate fears to offend his superiors.

V. Another useful expedient has been borrowed from European monarchies in the sale of nominations and occasionally of offices themselves.[9] A person who seeks to be nominated as candidate for one of the more important offices, such as a judgeship or a seat in the State Senate, or in Congress, is often required to contribute to the election fund a sum proportioned to the importance of the place he seeks, the excuse given for the practice being the cost of elections; and the same principle is occasionally applied to the gift of non-elective offices, the right of appointing to which is vested in some official member of a Ring—*e.g.* a mayor. The price of a nomination for a seat in the State legislature is said to run from $500 up to $1000, and for one of the better judgeships as high as $5000; but this is largely matter of conjecture.[10] Of course much less will be given if the prospects of carrying the election are doubtful: the prices quoted must be taken to represent cases where the party majority makes success certain. Naturally, the salaries of officials have to be raised in order to enable them to bear this charge, so that in the long run it may be thrown upon the public; and a recent eminent boss of New York City defended, before a committee of the legislature, the large salaries paid to aldermen, on the ground that "heavy demands were made on them by their party."

9. As judicial places were sold under the old French monarchy, and commissions in the army in England till sixteen years ago.

10. "A judgeship," says Mr. F. W. Whitridge, "costs in New York about $15,000; the district attorneyship the same; for a nomination to Congress the price is about $4000, though this is variable; an aldermanic nomination is worth $1500, and that for the Assembly from $600 to $1500. The amount realized from these assessments cannot be exactly estimated, but the amount raised by Tammany Hall, which is the most complete political organization, may be fixed very nearly at $125,000 (£25,000). This amount is collected and expended by a small executive committee who keep no accounts and are responsible only to each other."—Article "Assessments," in *Amer. Cyclop. of Political Science*.

How to Get a Political Following

George Washington Plunkitt
Recorded by William L. Riordan

"THERE'S THOUSANDS of young men in this city who will go to the polls for the first time next November. Among them will be many who have watched the careers of successful men in politics, and who are longin' to make names and fortunes for themselves at the same game. It is to these youths that I want to give advice. First, let me say that I am in a position to give what the courts call expert testimony on the subject. I don't think you can easily find a better example than I am of success in politics. After forty years' experience at the game I am—well, I'm George Washington Plunkitt. Everybody knows what figure I cut in the greatest organization on earth, and if you hear people say that I've laid away a million or so since I was a butcher's boy in Washington Market, don't come to me for an indignant denial. I'm pretty comfortable, thank you.

"Now, havin' qualified as an expert, as the lawyers say, I am goin' to give advice free to the young men who are goin' to cast their first votes, and who are lookin' forward to political glory and lots of cash. Some young men think they can learn how to be successful in politics from books, and they cram their heads with all sorts of college rot. They couldn't make a bigger mistake. Now, understand me, I ain't sayin' nothin' against colleges. I guess they'll have to exist as long as there's bookworms, and I suppose they do some good in a certain way, but they don't count in politics. In fact, a young man who has gone through the college course is handicapped at the outset. He may succeeed in politics, but the chances are 100 to 1 against him.

"Another mistake; some young men think that the best way to pre-pare for the political game is to practise speakin' and becomin' orators. That's all wrong. We've got some orators in Tammany Hall, but they're chiefly ornamental. You never heard of Charlie Murphy delivering a speech, did you? Or Richard Croker, or John Kelley, or any other man

Reprinted from Plunkitt of Tammany Hall (*New York: McClure Philips & Co.,* *1905*), *pp. 11–18 and 46–53.*

who has been a real power in the organization? Look at the thirty-six district leaders of Tammany Hall to-day. How many of them travel on their tongues? Maybe one or two, and they don't count when business is doin' at Tammany Hall. The men who rule have practised keepin' their tongues still, not exercising them. So you want to drop the orator idea unless you mean to go into politics just to perform the sky-rocket act.

"Now, I've told you what not to do; I guess I can explain best what to do to succeed in politics by tellin' you what I did. After goin' through the apprenticeship of the business while I was a boy by workin' around the district headquarters and hustlin' about the polls on election day, I set out when I cast my first vote to win fame and money in New York city politics. Did I offer my services to the district leader as a stump-speaker? Not much. The woods are always full of speakers. Did I get up a book on municipal government and show it to the leader? I wasn't such a fool. What I did was to get some marketable goods before goin' to the leaders. What do I mean by marketable goods? Let me tell you: I had a cousin, a young man who didn't take any particular interest in politics. I went to him and said: 'Tommy, I'm goin' to be a politician, and I want to get a followin'; can I count on you?' He said: 'Sure, George.' That's how I started in business. I got a marketable commodity—one vote. Then I went to the district leader and told him I could command two votes on election day, Tommy's and my own. He smiled on me and told me to go ahead. If I had offered him a speech or a bookful of learnin', he would have said, 'Oh, forget it!'

"That was beginnin' business in a small way, wasn't it? But that is the only way to become a real lastin' statesman. I soon branched out. Two young men in the flat next to mine were school friends. I went to them, just as I went to Tommy, and they agreed to stand by me. Then I had a followin' of three voters and I began to get a bit chesty. Whenever I dropped into district headquarters, everybody shook hands with me, and the leader one day honored me by lightin' a match for my cigar. And so it went on like a snowball rollin' down a hill. I worked the flat-house that I lived in from the basement to the top floor, and I got about a dozen young men to follow me. Then I tackled the next house and so on down the block and around the corner. Before long I had sixty men back of me, and formed the George Washington Plunkitt Association.

"What did the district leader say then when I called at head-quarters? I didn't have to call at headquarters. He came after me and said: 'George, what do you want? If you don't see what you want, ask for it. Wouldn't you like to have a job or two in the departments for your friends?' I said: 'I'll think it over; I haven't yet decided what the George Washington Plunkitt Association will do in the next campaign.' You ought to have seen how I was courted and petted then by the leaders of the rival organizations. I had marketable goods and there was bids for them from all sides, and I was a risin' man in politics. As time went on, and my association grew, I thought I would like to go to the Assembly. I just had to hint at what I wanted, and three different organizations offered me the nomination. Afterwards, I went to the Board of Aldermen, then to the State Senate, then became leader of the district, and so on up and up till I became a statesman.

"That is the way and the only way to make a lastin' success in politics. If you are goin' to cast your first vote next November and want to go into politics, do as I did. Get a followin', if it's only one man, and then go to the district leader and say: 'I want to join the organization. I've got one man who'll follow me through thick and thin.' The leader won't laugh at your one-man followin'. He'll shake your hand warmly, offer to propose you for membership in his club, take you down to the corner for a drink and ask you to call again. But go to him and say: 'I took first prize at college in Aristotle; I can recite Shakespere forwards and backwards; there ain't nothin' in science that ain't as familiar to me as blockades on the elevated roads and I'm the real thing in the way of silver-tongued orators.' What will he answer? He'll probably say: 'I guess you are not to blame for your misfortunes, but we have no use for you here.' "

To Hold Your District—Study Human Nature and Act Accordin'

"There's only one way to hold a district; you must study human nature and act accordin'. You can't study human nature in books. Books is a hindrance more than anything else. If you have been to college, so much the worse for you. You'll have to unlearn all you learned before you can get right down to human nature, and unlearnin' takes a lot of time. Some men can never forget what they learned at college. Such men may get to be district leaders by a fluke, but they never last.

"To learn real human nature you have to go among the people, see them and be seen. I know every man, woman, and child in the Fifteenth District, except them that's been born this summer—and I know some of them, too. I know what they like and what they don't like, what they are strong at and what they are weak in, and I reach them by approachin' at the right side.

"For instance, here's how I gather in the young men. I hear of a young feller that's proud of his voice, thinks that he can sing fine. I ask him to come around to Washington Hall and join our Glee Club. He comes and sings, and he's a follower of Plunkitt for life. Another young feller gains a reputation as a base-ball player in a vacant lot. I bring him into our base-ball club. That fixes him. You'll find him workin' for my ticket at the polls next election day. Then there's the feller that likes rowin' on the river, the young feller that makes a name as a waltzer on his block, the young feller that's handy with his dukes—I rope them all in by givin' them opportunities to show themselves off. I don't trouble them with political arguments. I just study human nature and act accordin'.

"But you may say this game won't work with the high-toned fellers, the fellers that go through college and then join the Citizens' Union. Of course it wouldn't work. I have a special treatment for them. I ain't like the patent medicine man that gives the same medicine for all diseases. The Citizens' Union kind of a young man! I love him! He's the daintiest morsel of the lot, and he don't often escape me.

"Before telling you how I catch him, let me mention that before the election last year, the Citizens' Union said they had four hundred or five hundred enrolled voters in my district. They had a lovely headquarters, too, beautiful roll-top desks and the cutest rugs in the world. If I was accused of havin' contributed to fix up the nest for them, I wouldn't deny it under oath. What do I mean by that? Never mind. You can guess from the sequel, if you're sharp.

"Well, election day came. The Citizens' Union candidate for Senator, who ran against me, just polled five votes in the district, while I polled something more than 14,000 votes. What became of the 400 or 500 Citizens' Union enrolled voters in my district? Some people guessed that many of them were good Plunkitt men all along and worked with the Cits just to bring them into the Plunkitt camp by election day. You can guess that way, too, if you want to. I never contradict stories about me, especially in hot weather. I just call your attention to the fact that on last election day 395 Citizens' Union enrolled voters in my district were missin' and unaccounted for.

"I tell you frankly, though, how I have captured some of the Citizens' Union's young men. I have a plan that never fails. I watch the City Record to see when there's civil service examinations for good things. Then I take my young Cit in hand, tell him all about the good thing and get him worked up till he goes and takes an examination. I don't bother about him any more. It's a cinch that he comes back to me in a few days and asks to join Tammany Hall. Come over to Washington Hall some night and I'll show you a list of names on our rolls marked 'C.S.' which means, 'bucked up against civil service.'

"As to the older voters, I reach them, too. No, I don't send them campaign literature. That's rot. People can get all the political stuff they want to read—and a good deal more, too—in the papers. Who reads speeches, nowadays, anyhow? It's bad enough to listen to them. You ain't goin' to gain any votes by stuffin' the letter boxes with campaign documents. Like as not you'll lose votes, for there's nothin' a man hates more than to hear the letter-carrier ring his bell and go to the letter-box expectin' to find a letter he was lookin' for, and find only a a lot of printed politics. I met a man this very mornin' who told me he voted the Democratic State ticket last year just because the Republicans kept crammin' his letter-box with campaign documents.

"What tells in holdin' your grip on your district is to go right down among the poor families and help them in the different ways they need help. I've got a regular system for this. If there's a fire in Ninth, Tenth, or Eleventh Avenue, for example, any hour of the day or night, I'm usually there with some of my election district captains as soon as the fire-engines. If a family is burned out I don't ask whether they are Republicans or Democrats, and I don't refer them to the Charity Organization Society, which would investigate their case in a month or two and decide they were worthy of help about the time they are dead from starvation. I just get quarters for them, buy clothes for them if their clothes were burned up, and fix them up till they get things runnin' again. It's philanthropy, but it's politics, too—mighty good politics. Who can tell how many votes one of these fires bring me? The poor are the most grateful people in the world, and, let me tell you, they have more friends in their neighborhoods than the rich have in theirs.

"If there's a family in my district in want I know it before the charitable societies do, and me and my men are first on the ground. I have a special corps to look up such cases. The consequence is that the poor look up to George W. Plunkitt as a father, come to him in trouble—and don't forget him on election day.

"Another thing, I can always get a job for a deservin' man. I make it a point to keep on the track of jobs, and it seldom happens that I don't have a few up my sleeve ready for use. I know every big employer in the district and in the whole city, for that matter, and they ain't in the habit of sayin' no to me when I ask them for a job.

"And the children—the little roses of the district! Do I forget them? Oh, no! They know me, every one of them, and they know that a sight of Uncle George and candy means the same thing. Some of them are the best kind of vote-getters. I'll tell you a case. Last year a little Eleventh Avenue rosebud whose father is a Republican, caught hold of his whiskers on election day and said she wouldn't let go till he'd promise to vote for me. And she didn't.

The Attachment of the Immigrant to the Boss

Oscar Handlin

AS A BOY in Brooklyn, "Hughey" McLaughlin was already a leader among his cronies. Big and strong, handy with his fists in a fight, he commanded the respect of the lads who hung around the firehouse. One employment after another was not quite to his taste; but in the neighborhood he was well known, and favorably. In 1855 his opportunity came. Taken on at the Navy Yard, he was put in charge of a group of workers, a gang, with the title of Boss Laborer, soon shortened to Boss.

These were the essential elements. To hold his own position it was necessary that he retain the favor of the political authority that appointed him. He did so by the ability to deliver a certain number of votes. And he was able to deliver those votes because he controlled a fund of desirable jobs. In time, McLaughlin extended the scope of his operations from the Navy Yard to the whole municipality. The relationship between votes and jobs remained the same.

Throughout the country in the great cities, other bosses became the heads of other gangs. Some had assembled followings as foremen or contractors, others by growing up in a district where they exercised continuing leadership as a gang of boys grew up to be a gang of voters. Everywhere the connection between these allegiances and the opportunity to work was plain. In an economy that condemned the immigrants to unskilled labor a large percentage of the available jobs were directly or indirectly dependent upon political favor. Aqueducts and streets the city built for itself; trolley, gas, telegraph, and electric lines were laid by companies franchised by the city; and every structure, as it went up, was inspected by the city. One pair of hands was much like another when it held the shovel; the employers of unskilled labor were wise enough to treat indulgently the wishes of the municipal officials in whose power it was to let contracts or grant permits.

The job was at the center of the boss's attractiveness. But he was also able to call forth a more general sense of attachment. Often the feelings of group loyalty focused upon him. He was a member of many associations, made friends on every block. In the columns of their own newspapers his name appeared frequently. His achievements cast their reflected glory on the whole community and he in turn shared its sense of solidarity. In that respect he stood at an advantage over every competitor for the immigrants' leadership. He had sprung from them and substantially remained one with them.

Furthermore, he spoke for them. After the Civil War as the national parties in election after election chewed over the same stale issues, a great dullness settled down over their campaigns. Few people cared to take the trouble to distinguish how the position of the Democrats differed from that of the Republicans on civil service reform or the tariff. Few even bothered to learn what those problems were about. These were remote and abstract questions that did not directly touch on their own lives. The immigrant might sometimes read an article on such a matter in his newspaper but was less likely to be persuaded by any intrinsic ideas on the subject than by the character of the persuader. If a trusted source said that when a Democrat is President misery comes, that if the Republicans win the factories will open, the new citizen was likely to accept the statement without cavil.

The local issues were the important ones. Whether there should be a new public bathhouse in Ward Twelve, whether the city should hire extra laborers, seemed questions of no moment to the party statesmen. To the residents of the tenement districts they were critical; and in these matters the ward boss saw eye to eye with them. *Jim gets things done!* They could see the evidence themselves, knew the difference it made in their own existence.

The boss took command of the group in political matters. The old-line nationalist leaders still commanded the respect of their fellow countrymen but could not compete with the boss for votes. That fact Bourke Cockran discovered, in New York, when he met the opposition of Croker of Tammany Hall. Patrick Collins learned the same lesson in Boston, and an identical moral was pointed in other cities throughout the country. The machine gave form to the immigrant vote.

The ambitious politician, however, could not get very far if his power rested only on the loyalty of a bloc of immigrant followers. The instability of settlement prevented the consolidation of control on that basis. Tammany could not be sure how long its dominance of the East Side wards would last, or Lomasney in Boston of the West End, when the original Irish residents moved out and their place was taken by Jews and Italians. The successful chieftains were those who expanded their roles beyond the little group within which they had grown to power.

Hugh McLaughlin had perceived this. In his White House Saloon or in his office on Willoughby Street, he had made himself available to all comers. On the corner in Boston where his boyhood gang had whiled away the time, Martin Lomasney built the Hendricks Club. By the century's end, behind the whitened windows of an empty store, in the back room of a saloon, upstairs above the dance hall—under a variety of designations there was in every ward a place where a man could go and see the boss, or see someone who would in turn see the boss.

I think that there's got to be in every ward a guy that any bloke can go to when he's in trouble and get help—not justice and the law, but help, no matter what he's done. The old man reminisces as the incidents of a long career come back. What requests had not been made of him! And often enough he'd stepped in without waiting to be asked. Time and again one of the boys would let him know: the poor fellow had allowed his payments to lapse and now the widow had not the burial money; or, the furniture was being put out in the street and them with no place to go and the wife ailing at that. Baskets at Christmas, picnics, boat rides on the river or lake, and a ready purse at the mention of any charitable collection—these were all within his realm of obligations.

But mostly he had intervened at the points at which his people encountered the difficulties of the law. Between the rigid, impersonal rulings of the statute and the human failings of those ignorant of its complexities he stood as mediator. The poor lad who had an extra glass and by some half-remembered encounter ended the night in jail, the shopkeeper whose stand edged beyond the legal limit onto the sidewalk, turned to him whose contact set matters straight. They had all sat there explaining their troubles, the liquor dealer and the peddler worried about licenses, the contractor and the real-estate owner involved in deals with the city. They had come to him because they knew he was *fair* with his favors.

Those vain fools up on the hill had laughed and then seethed with indignation when he had torn the legislature apart so that wretched Italian could vend his peanuts on the grounds. The fulminations against "peanut politics" had been all to the good. They had confirmed the popular impression that he championed the little men against the big, the humble against the proud. Hundreds who themselves never had the occasion to turn to him firmly believed in his accessibility. The image, his own and theirs, was that of the kindly overlord, the feudal noble translated from the manor to the ward—above the law and therefore capable, if properly approached, of doing better justice than the law.

There was a price, of course. An exception made for one lawbreaker could be made for another; if the frightened peddler could get off, so too could the swaggering tough. After all, the turkeys in the baskets, the bubbling kegs of beer at the ends of the long picnic tables, all cost money. Whose money?

There were persons who would pay the bill. The thriving gambling industry of the 1870's stood on a tenuous relationship with the police. With expanded operations and greater capital investments, the operators of the keno, faro, and policy games could not tolerate a situation in which they were at the mercy of the extortions of every precinct lieutenant and his underlings. Nor would saloonkeepers willingly expose themselves to the assaults of temperance fanatics with their zealous insistence upon awkward closing hours or even upon total prohibition. An accommodating boss like Mike McDonald in Chicago provided protection in return for moderate occasional contributions from some two thousand gamblers in Chicago.

This source of support was not very secure, however. With time, the big promoters moved into the shadowland of legality and became less dependent upon protection. Some advanced to the ownership of bucket shops or indeed to the dignity of brokerage offices; others began to make book on horse racing and prize fighting, now legitimate enterprises. The older forms of speculation catered increasingly to the less profitable poor and were left to the attention of the petty promoter, from whom not much could be drawn in the ways of assessments.

Some bosses and their wives were, at the same time, stricken with social aspirations. Having made their way in the world, they wanted the visible symbols of having done so. Mike McDonald had made Carter Harrison mayor. Why should not the one be as respectable as the other? Unfortunately there were limits to the enjoyment of success; when McDonald moved to a fine suburb and began to play the gentleman, he lost his following and was unseated by Bathhouse John Coughlin and Hinky Dink Mike Kenna, two ungentle characters still close to the source of the votes.

If it was unsafe to desert one's proper district, at least some leaders hoped to surround themselves with other forms of respectability. They preferred not to deal with gamblers and saloonkeepers, but with nice people. And by this time there were some nice people quite eager to deal with the wielders of political influence. The perspicacious boss could become the familiar of the banker and the traction magnate, be taken to lunch in a good club (though not made a member), and puff his chest in the company of the financially mighty. Within the grant of government in these years were all sorts of profitable franchises, for laying trolley tracks, for building subways and electric and water lines, for the disposing of garbage. The interests concerned with these privileges were willing to aid the co-operative politician, aid to such an extent that he would not any longer be dependent on his emoluments from faro or overhours beer. The New York Dutch had a word for it, *boedel.*

Boodle was honest graft. When they floated the gas company they set aside a block of shares for the good fellows. No cash down—their credit was good. When the franchise came through and the stock prices rose in the market, the shares could be sold, the original purchase price paid, and a tidy balance would be left for the deserving. Or even if the capitalists were forced to lay out a flat sum without these complexities, that didn't hurt anyone. Such practices were not too far from the ordinary practices of legitimate business to offend any but the most tender consciences. Occasional revelations by shocked reformers did not alienate the boss's constituency; they merely endowed him with the additional romantic aspects of a Robin Hood.

Rivalry, not moral disapproval, provoked the serious troubles. In many matters the municipality shared jurisdiction with the state; and in the halls of the legislature, the city machines ran head-on into collision with the politicians who had long operated on a statewide basis These men had not the assistance of the formal organization of the machine, but they had earlier consolidated their positions through alliances of key officeholders. Generally they were native American, as was the bulk of their following; and they drew their support from the farming areas and from the small towns. In most parts of the country they had the advantage of an anachronistic distribution of power which favored the rural at the expense of the urban districts. Years of bitter struggle followed the appearance of the immigrant organizations, as the state party chieftains attempted to mobilize minority national blocs to undermine the authority of their metropolitan competitors. In New York and Massachusetts, for instance, the Republicans attempted to woo the Italians and Jews to break the hold of the Irish Democrats on the city vote.

In time, however, there was an accommodation. Spheres of influence were defined and divided. Live and let live. Perhaps the appearance on the scene after 1900 of a crew of miscellaneous reformers and liberal independents drove the various manipulators of power into a union of convenience. In any case, shortly after 1910 the old acerbity was dulled and an era of more peaceful relationships ensued.

How the Boss Runs
the Organization

Frank R. Kent

The Importance of Primaries

(RIGHT HERE is the place to explain exactly why the primaries are so much more vital than the general election to the precinct executive)

The same reasons that make this statement apply to the precinct executive, make it equally apply to the ward executive, the district leader, the boss, the machine as an entirety, and the country as a whole.

Unless these facts are clearly understood at the start, there can be no real grasp of machine power, methods, and control. No political knowledge is worth anything unless they are comprehended.

To think that the general election is more important than the primary election, as most voters do, is to magnify the wrong side of the political picture. It ought to be reversed, and instead of, as now, many more voters voting in the general election than in the primaries, the public interest should be concentrated on the primaries first, and the general election second. As things stand to-day, the popular tendency is to regard primaries as the particular concern of the politicians, and not of real interest to the average voter. The result is that often an absurdly small proportion of the qualified voters participate in the primaries.

There could not be a greater mistake. This lack of appreciation of what the primaries really mean, and the general neglect to participate in them, plays directly into the hands of the machine. It makes it ridiculously easy for the machine, through the precinct executives, to control the situation. It actually permits the machine to run the country)

The reasons this is true are simple enough. Primaries are really the key to politics. There is no way for party candidates to get on the general election ballot except through the primaries. Primaries are the exclusive gate through which all party candidates must pass. Control of that gate in any community means control of the political situation in

Reprinted from The Great Game of Politics *by Frank R. Kent (New York: Doubleday & Company, 1923), pp. 6–13 and 103–111. Copyright 1923, Doubleday & Company. Reprinted by permission of the publisher.*

that community. It makes no difference whether the candidates who pass through that gate are knocked down in the general election or not, the next set of candidates must pass through the primary gate just the same. It ought to be plain, then, that so long as the machine controls the primaries, it is in a position to limit the choice of the voters in the general election to its choice in the primaries. That is the real secret of its power, and, so long as it holds that power, it cannot be put out of business. Defeating its candidates in the general election not only does not break its grip, it often does not make even a dent in it. It can and does continue to function after a general election defeat just as it did before. The only place a machine can be beaten is in the primaries. So long as it can nominate its candidates, so long is it an unbeaten machine. This is a government by parties, and under our system parties are essential to government. In all the states the two big parties—the Democratic and Republican—are recognized by law. These laws provide that these parties shall hold primaries, which are preliminary elections, participated in exclusively by party voters, for the purpose of nominating party candidates. The only way in which candidates may get on the ballot at the general election, other than through direct nomination in the primaries, or through nominations by conventions composed of delegates chosen in the primaries, is by petition signed by a designated number of voters. This gives a candidate a place on the ballot as an "outsider" and is rarely resorted to because of the extremely small chances of success of such candidate. Nothing short of a political tidal wave or revolution can carry an independent candidate to success. He may pull sufficient votes from one side or the other to bring about the defeat of one of the regular party nominees, but his own election is a thing so rare as to be almost negligible.

The fact that I wish to drive home now is that all over the country 99 per cent of all candidates for all offices are nominated as a result of primaries. The obvious and inescapable deduction is that in 99 per cent of all elections, the choice of the voters in the general election is limited to the choice of the voters in the primary elections. When the full significance of that statement sinks in, the tremendous importance of the primaries will be better appreciated. It ought to be clear that the man who votes in the general election and not in the primaries loses at least 50 per cent of the value and effectiveness of his vote as compared to the man who votes in both. Before a candidate for any office can be elected, except the rare independents who escape the primaries and go on the general ballot by petition, he must first be nominated. In 99 per cent of the cases, nominations are made in the primaries. In 1 per cent of them they are made by petition. In the face of these facts, it would appear distinctly in the interest of every voter to be a primary election voter. The truth is, however, that the one class that regularly votes in the primaries is the machine voters—and, of course, they control, and always will control, under these conditions.

It is not too much to say that the great bulk of the men holding municipal, state, and federal offices throughout the country to-day were elected or appointed to these offices because of the support of the party organizations or machines. They are exactly the same thing. There are in the United States more than 2,000,000 political jobholders of one kind or another. They range all the way from the President of the United States to the city street sweeper.

Nearly all of these are strictly organization men. Practically all of them vote strictly party tickets with unvarying regularity. Moreover through family or other ties, every one of them is able to influence from two to ten votes beside his own. Some of them, of course, control a great many more. Five is the average. This means a powerful army. It is a lot of votes. They are divided between Republicans and Democrats, but the number is great enough to give each an exceedingly formidable force. They constitute the shock troops of the organization—the rank and file of the machines.

The potent thing politically about these machine men is that they vote. That is the real secret of machine power. They do not talk politics and then fail to register. Nor do they register and then fail to vote. Nor do they, when they vote, spoil their ballots. Every election day, regardless of wind or weather, "hell or high water," they march to the polls, cast their straight organization ballots, and they are counted. As voters they are 100 per cent effective. Besides, they see that the voters they are supposed to influence or control likewise go to the polls. Voting is a business matter with them and they attend to it.

But the overwhelming big thing is that they are primary-election voters—not merely general-election voters. No clear comprehension of politics can possibly be had until these basic facts are grasped:

First, all candidates of the two great parties must first be nominated as a result of primaries. There is no other way for them to get on the ballot.

Second, it is more important to the machine to nominate its candidates than to elect them.

Third, that the primaries are the instrument that gives the organization its legal status, and that it is, therefore, the only instrument through which it can be destroyed.

Fourth, that in the general election, the two party machines compete in getting the vote to the polls, and thus largely nullify each other's effectiveness. In the primaries the machines have no organized competition. Hence they become enormously effective and, so long as the average voter fails to participate, are practically invincible.

Fifth, in nearly all states, Republicans are barred from voting in Democratic primaries and Democrats must keep out of Republican primaries, which means that each party machine in the primaries is free from conflict with the other party machine.

Sixth, not only are the nominations made in the primaries, but members of the state central committee, control of which is the key to the whole machine, are elected in the primaries.

This is not the place to go into a detailed account of primary election variations in the different states. Some data concerning exceptions to the general rules here laid down are given in the Appendix to this book, but in the main the statements made in this chapter apply to the country as a whole.

When these things are considered, it ought to be plain why the primaries are so vital to the machine, and why it is a matter of political life and death to the precinct executive to carry his precinct in the primaries. The machine can lose its candidate time after time in the general election without greatly diminishing its strength or loosing the grip of its leaders. Of course, it is disheartening to the rank and file and it greatly lessens the number and quality of the political pies for distribution to the faithful. It could not be kept up too long without causing a revolt in the organization, but, I repeat, the machine cannot be smashed by defeating its candidate at the election.

But if it loses in the primaries, it is out of business. Any organization that cannot carry the primary election is a defunct organization. It either politically disappears or it makes peace and amalgamates with the faction that defeated it. In rare cases it waits for the wind of public sentiment that blew it over to die down, picks up the pieces, and crawls back into the saddle. But no political machine or precinct executive could possibly survive two primary defeats.

Apart from the lack of competition, it must be evident that the reason the machine is so much more potent in the primaries is that the total number of voters is so much smaller. The smaller the vote the more dominant the machine. Only the voters of one party are permitted to vote in that party's primaries. All the members of any political machine are members of one party, and they all vote. Hence, in the primaries the machine polls its full strength, while the number of voters outside of the machine who can vote is very much cut down. It ought to be plain that every party voter outside of the machine who refrains from voting in the primaries adds to the strength of the precinct executive—which means the machine—by just that much.

It also ought to be plain that the man who poses as an independent in politics and declines to affiliate with either party, thus disqualifying himself as a primary voter, has greatly lessened his individual importance as a political factor as well as added to the strength of the machine.

He can be as independent as he pleases in the general election. He can refuse to vote for the party nominees if they do not suit him, but if he does not vote in the primaries, those who do are picking the men for whom he must vote, for or against, in the general election.

Boiled down, it comes to this: so long as the primaries are controlled by machines, the general-election voter, no matter how independent he may be, 99 per cent of the time is limited in his choice to two machine selections. There is no getting away from that fact.

Picking the Ticket

Placing just as much of his machine as he possibly can on the payroll is the primary purpose of the boss.

That is the fundamental idea back of a political organization. That is its *raison d'etre*. All the labour and expense of building it up, all the time and trouble of controlling the primaries, all the fighting and working to elect the ticket after it has been nominated, from the machine standpoint, would be aimless and futile and foolish, if success were not to be rewarded with something more than the mere satisfaction of winning. If, after the machine has sweated, fought, and bled to nominate and elect a set of party candidates, somebody else is to get the jobs —why, what is the use?

[Political organizations run politics because of the lack of active interest and clear understanding upon the part of the ordinary citizen. This general political inertia, these hazy and confused political ideas, this tendency to think of politics as something low and slimy, which ought to be left to the politicians—particularly the primaries—these are the things that make machines possible and powerful. In proportion as the average voter becomes interested and informed, the bulk and power of the machine decreases.]

Under our party system, as has been shown, some sort of unofficial organization is essential to the orderly conduct of elections and the proper functioning of the Government. There has to be some human agency to do the actual party work of filling tickets, arranging details, providing election officials, bringing forward candidates, preparing for registration. These things do not do themselves. Nor can the state do them all. They call for voluntary activity upon the part of some one— and those who volunteer naturally form an organization and develop leaders. The whole thing is human and natural and inevitable. Nor can it be expected that the men who take over this work do so from patriotic or public-spirited motives. [They take it over from purely practical and selfish motives and because there is an opportunity there for place, power, and money.]

The point is that, although an organization of some sort is essential, under ideal conditions, with every citizen politically informed, and active enough to vote, the organization would be a simple, slender, inexpensive affair, easy to reward through proper patronage recognition without imposing a real burden on the taxpayers. Under existing conditions, with the voters lax, uninformed, inactive, and numerously not voting in every community—particularly in the primaries—the machine grows great and powerful, tremendously costly to the taxpayers, and develops bosses who are able to demand and get a far larger proportion of the positions under city, state, and federal governments than is good for them, for the state, the city or the country. [The basic truth is that the boss will go just so far in the patronage matter as he can— and the distance he can go is exactly measured by the indifference of the voters.] Under conditions as they exist to-day in the big cities of the country, he goes very far, indeed. It becomes his chief occupation—this placing of his followers on the public payroll.

But that is not all he has to do. There are two things expected of him as boss—the nomination in the primaries of candidates friendly to the organization and the election of these candidates. It is here that the boss shows his quality. So long as more than half the qualified voters fail to vote, the kind of machine described in these pages has the power to put over in the primaries practically any one it wants. It would be possible, for instance, in either New York, Philadelphia, Chicago, Boston, Baltimore, St. Louis, or Cleveland for the bosses to nominate almost any old "Muldoon" for mayor that they might choose—but electing him is another matter. There is no sense in putting up a candidate in the primaries merely to have him knocked down in the general election.

It is true that, so long as he holds control of the primaries, the boss still has his machine, but no machine will indefinitely follow a funeral director—and no boss not a fool would deliberately court defeat through a too-brazen exhibition of primary power. What he does is to try so to load the ticket in the primary with the precise proportion of "Muldoons" that can get by in the general election—but no more. Almost always, in the framing of the ticket which the machine supports in the primary, the boss looks for men of sufficient standing and independence not only to command a certain degree of public respect and support but also to enable him to nominate "Muldoons" for the bulk of the places without arousing a dangerous popular resentment.

It is a matter of judgment. [The boss wants a ticket that will win, but, at the same time, he wants candidates, who when they win, will not turn around and kick him and his machine out of City Hall.] How far he has to go in taking chances with independent men on the machine ticket depends upon the strength of his party in the city, the temper of the people, and the weight, disposition, and force of the newspapers. It has been shown how the nominations for the legislatures, the city councils, and the smaller or more numerous officers are made through the ward executives—and how it is easy in these instances to "get by" with tried and true deliverable machine men.

It is when it comes to picking the head of the ticket—the candidates for mayor or governor or judge—that the boss uses care and judgment. It is by the head of the ticket usually that the public judge the whole thing. If the head of the ticket is a good, strong man of standing and known integrity, or if some of the more conspicuous of the candidates are of this type, the rest of the ticket can be and is with impunity loaded down with "Muldoons."

In political circles this practice of putting a few of the conspicuously higher type on to leaven the organization loaf is known as "perfuming the ticket" or putting a "clean collar on the dirty shirt." In other words, the machine ticket is as clean as—and no cleaner than—the sentiment of the people of the community compels it to be. That is to say once more what has already been said in these pages a number of times—the quality of the ticket is exactly measured by the tolerance of the voters. Everything about the machine—everything in politics—is measured by this same yardstick, and it cannot be said too often. It is the heart of the whole thing from beginning to end.

There are various ways in which the boss, or bosses—because in some cities like Philadelphia and Norfolk the machine is run by a little oligarchic group of bosses, rather than by one man—get the "clean collar" or "perfumery." Sometimes he has nothing at all to do with bringing the candidate out, but places his machine behind a man who announces himself, without reference to the boss or the machine, but who looks like the strongest proposition in sight, and a dangerous one to beat in the primaries. It may be a matter of expediency, or to avoid a bruising fight, or to placate popular sentiment, or purely a question of finances.

Sometimes the boss manoeuvres the appointment of a group of prominent business men affiliated with the party, who canvass the field and induce some respectable citizen to enter with the assurance of a machine support, which leaves him unpledged and uncompromised. Sometimes the man thus chosen is friendly to the machine; sometimes not. There are no rules about this part of the game. It is purely a matter of what can be done, and depends upon the character of the candidate, the exigencies of the situation, the necessities of the machine, the political complexion of the community. There are times and places when the boss can himself inspire a mayoralty candidacy without the necessity of a camouflaged committee or any other set of false whiskers. The disadvantage of this, however, is that it is apt to make the boss and the machine more directly the campaign issue than is safe.

This fact may be set down as sure—whatever way the boss may get his candidate, he tries to pick one whom he can elect.

Right here it ought, in fairness to the boss, to be said that, even if he had a free hand and did not operate under the restraint of public sentiment, in only rare cases would he go the limit in putting up wholly unfit or really bad men for conspicuous places. The boss may, and often does, live like a leech, on the public purse, but, in spite of being a boss, he is also a citizen of his community, and there are mighty few of them who have not some sort of civic sense of right and wrong. His is not at all the civic view of the reformer, perhaps, but it is a distinct civic sense just the same. It is an unusual boss who does not take pride when his machine-made mayor turns out to be a good public official, and equally unusual that he is not disgusted when he commits some disgraceful or scandalous act.

There have been instances in most cities where the boss has sold out to the other side, "laid down" or "thrown the election," but they are rare. Often machines coöperate and help one another in the primaries. That is sensible and easy, but it is neither sensible nor easy in the general election. In the first place, the ward and precinct executives, very many of whom are decent fellows who play the game on the level, according to their lights, revolt against treachery. In the second place, if there is a chance to win they want to win, because to lose means hard times and no jobs. In the third place, the boss cannot "throw an election" without a good many people knowing about it and raising a howl that may split his machine.

Some of the cogs in the machine in a hard fight, with money on both sides, go crooked. District leaders and executives of the lower type may jump the track, but rarely the boss, and when there is treachery in the ranks it is sternly punished by the boss. All of this does not prevent an occasional general "sell out," but in these days it is rapidly getting almost as dangerous to "buy" as well as to "sell." Men are apt to hesitate before they give to the necessarily unscrupulous person with whom they must deal the power such knowledge affords him.

Now, when the boss gets his "clean collar" it is the simplest and easiest thing imaginable to swing the machine back of him. The balance of the ticket has been made up through recommendations of the ward executives and district leaders, by giving recognition to the various elements with voting strength sufficient to make it inexpedient to ignore them, or to individuals powerful enough to compel recognition, and to sections of the city which will resent being left unrepresented on the ticket. In some cases candidates are put on because of their ability, or the ability of their friends, to contribute to the campaign fund, and sometimes for purely personal reasons. Sometimes, too, it is a matter of luck with a candidate—lack of opposition, or a last-minute demand for a man. Take any machine ticket in any city and it is a queer conglomeration containing some of the best and some of the worst types in town—and put there through all sorts of influence and for all sorts of reasons.

When it is completed the boss closes the gate and "sends the word down the line." All this consists of is a curt phrase to the ward executives and the district leaders as they come in to see him at headquarters.

"It's Smith," says the boss, or "It's Jones," "go to it." In many cases, that is all he does say. Sometimes after the "It's Smith," the boss says, "What can you do down your way?" or "What will your ward give?" or "You ought to give him 1,000 majority," or some such thing. The ward executive is likely to reply, "All right, boss," and get out, or he may tell the boss about the sentiment of his people or express his judgment as to the selection's strength or weakness in his ward or district, but it is always an exceedingly brief conversation. There is no argument. What the boss says goes.

A bolter is an extremely rare bird in a well-run machine with a real boss. Once he gets the "word" the ward executive or district leader hurries off, calls a meeting of his ward club, and passes the "word" along that night to his precinct executives. Inside of twenty-four hours after the boss decides the whole machine, from top to bottom, has got the "word" and begins to function. The ward clubs meet and indorse the ticket, the business of lining up the office-holders begins, the candidates open up headquarters and the campaign is under way.

Sometimes the boss decides weeks in advance. Sometimes it is only a few days before the primaries when the decision is given out, but it makes no difference—the machine can be swung in line just the same. The executives prefer to know as far ahead as possible, because it gives a better chance to iron out the rough spots, and checks freelance candidates from tying up and committing precinct executives, and making inroads on the organization forces. But the manner in which, at short notice, the vast bulk of the machine workers can be swung in behind the boss's candidate is a marvellous illustration of discipline, when the looseness of the organization construction is considered and the varieties of human beings taken into account.

The Nature of Political Obligations

William Foote Whyte

THE CORNERVILLE POLITICAL ORGANIZATION can best be described as a system of reciprocal personal obligations. The nature of the obligations may be understood by observing the situations in which they arise, the actions which create them, and the actions which are required to discharge them.

Everyone recognizes that when a politician does a favor for a constituent, the constituent becomes obligated to the politician. Depending upon the importance of the favor, the obligation may be discharged by voting for the politician or by performing more important services for him. The politician need not bring the whole weight of his personal influence to bear in obtaining each favor for his constituents. When dealing with authorities, the person who speaks English poorly or not at all has an obvious need for an interpreter, and even the corner boy who has grown up speaking English tends to be inarticulate when he is out of his own sphere. Besides, the uninitiated do not understand the complex organization of government and do not know how to find the channels through which they can obtain action. In some cases the constituent has an undeniable claim to a certain benefit and may secure it simply by appearing before the proper authority and stating his case. Nevertheless, the person who does not know where to go or how to speak for himself must ask for a guide and spokesman, and the politician who serves in that capacity performs a real service, which results in the creation of an obligation.

The politician becomes obligated to those who support his campaign, and the high cost of political activity tends to put a premium on financial support. The more the politician can contribute to the support of his own political activity, the freer he will be from this particular type of obligation. This may account for the fact that the undertaker-politician is less closely tied to the racketeers than is the lawyer-

Reprinted from Street Corner Society *by William Foote Whyte (Chicago: University of Chicago Press, 1943), pp. 240–246, by permission of The University of Chicago Press.*

politician, for whom the racketeers are the most important clients as well as the largest campaign contributors.

[Discussion of the campaign indicates the different ways in which money may be spent but does not show how the politician decides into which particular channels to pour his funds. In practice the politician spends most of his money in areas where he lacks popular support.]

Fiumara's campaign of 1937 provides an illustration of this sort of behavior. For years Joseph Maloney had been so firmly intrenched as alderman that most Italian politicians concentrated their attention upon other offices. At this time Fiumara was just another undertaker to the voters of the ward. When he opened his campaign, he set about winning over the various Italian and other non-Irish groups. He paid clubs for their indorsements and in addition financed election parties in their quarters. He gave out money to be spent in his interest. His expenditure, locally reported as $6,400, was unparalleled in the history of Ward 4 aldermanic contests, and some of it may have been wasted, but it served to establish Fiumara as Boss Maloney's chief rival for the office. In his first campaign Fiumara polled over three thousand votes and ran second to Maloney. Without such lavish financing, Fiumara would have been only one more minor competitor, and he would have had no chance to defeat the Cleveland Club boss in 1939.

Even so free a spender as Fiumara does not spread his money evenly. He tries to win as much Italian support as he can without spending money. In the election of 1939 most of the Fiumara poll workers in Cornerville served as volunteers. Maloney and Kelly, who had little support in Cornerville, paid five dollars each to their poll workers in that section. That is the situation in general. Where a politician has established a chain of personal obligations, he spends little, and where he lacks such a chain he concentrates his funds.]

The politician who must pay cash for a large proportion of his support may offset this by charging his constituents for favors. This practice has become increasingly common.

In order to get a job, to have a case fixed, or to obtain some other favor, one is required to pay a sum of money which varies with the importance of the favor. The ward politician does not keep all this himself. He must pay someone who has the power to grant the favor. If it is an important favor which must be performed by a man near the top of the political hierarchy, the money passes through an intermediary. The ward politician pays the "bag man," who turns the money over to the "big shot." All important politicians who operate according to this system have trusted friends who serve as graft collectors in order to protect their superiors from prosecution. It is understood in Cornerville that the constituent's money is not paid in full to the big shot. The ward politician takes his "cut" and the bag man does likewise. If the favor is performed, the constituent is not expected to interest himself in the fate of his money. Not all Ward 4 politicians work on this basis. There are some, like George Ravello, who refuse to accept cash payment for their political services.

[The nature of the obligations existing between politicians and their constituents depends upon whether the services performed on either side are paid for or furnished free of charge. The constituent who pays for a favor feels less obligated than the one who is not charged. Money need not entirely destroy the basis of personal obligation. That depends to a certain extent upon the size of the payment and the importance of the favor. The constituent may say to himself: "I paid the politician for getting me a job, but, still, jobs are in demand; there are plenty of others who would have paid what I did and more for this job; the politician was a good fellow to do this for me, and I'll be with him at the next election." Nevertheless, the obligation is not so secure when money passes from constituent to politician. /

As Joseph Maloney expressed it in attacking his rival, Mike Kelly, in the campaign of 1939:

> There is one candidate that has promised at least two hundred jobs. How is he going to deliver them? He's got men with him, yes, they've all got their price, but they should realize that when they get their price the obligation is discharged.

One of the corner boys expressed his opinion in this way:

> Sometimes them politicians want to give you money if you work for them. Then when you come up to them after for a job, they say, "What's the matter, didn't I pay you?". . . . If you're smart, you don't take the money, and then maybe you got a chance to get something.

Many take the opposite view. Tony Cataldo, Carlo, and several other members of the Cornerville S. and A. held that the corner boys should recognize that they were not going to get anything after the election anyway and that therefore they should demand cash in advance. The politician would then not be obligated to them for their support, but, if they had received the money, they would be satisfied.

[If the politician uses money to secure a large part of his support, he frees himself from his obligations to those constituents. Lacking strong personal ties, they may turn against him after the election, but in the next campaign he can win them over with money once more, or, if they desert him permanently, he can find other groups which will respond to the same incentive. /

The effectiveness of cash payments in securing votes should not be overemphasized. The corner boys' attitude toward money in politics is something like this: Politics is a racket; the politician is just trying to use us to get something for himself; we might as well promise him anything and get all we can out of him; then we'll do what we want to do anyway.] In this connection it is pertinent to recall the speech made in the Cornerville S. and A. Club by the Fiumara supporter who advised the boys: "Don't be chumps. Take their dough. You can use it, but then go in and vote for Fiumara." The political obligation depends not alone upon a favor done by the politician but upon the personal contacts between the politician and his constituents. Where these are lacking, money cannot fill the gap.]

This discussion should not give the impression that the politician is free to select his course of action. If he has not been able to establish a sufficiently extensive network of obligations before the campaign, he will have to use money freely in order to win support. If, when elected, he cannot raise sufficient funds in other ways, he may have to take money for the favors he does. Since many of his superiors operate on a cash basis, he may be forced to do likewise. One of the reasons given for George Ravello's failure to secure more jobs and favors for his constituents was his unwillingness to arrange for their purchase. In his first term he asked certain big shots for favors and was told that they could be had for a price. When word got around that Ravello would not pay, the big shots simply told him that the favors could not be done.

This does not mean that all important favors must be paid for. The relations between politicians, like those between the politician and his constituents, are based upon personal nonfinancial obligations as well as upon cash payments. By refusing to pay cash, the politician cuts himself off from some but not all the available favors.

According to Cornerville standards, the politician who does a favor for friendship is considered morally superior to one who does it for money. Similarly, the constituent who shows his devotion to the candidate's cause by contributing freely to his campaign fund is superior to the man who tries to buy a special favor. Favors should be reciprocated out of personal loyalty, as they are in the corner gang.

Although political organizations have changed profoundly in recent years, most Cornerville people continue to believe in these standards. Still, cash in advance has a powerful appeal, and people do not always support the candidate for whom they have the most respect. Since more and more of the ward candidates have taken to a cash basis, their constituents have less choice in the matter of obtaining favors. They feel that it is better to pay for a favor than to get no favor at all.

So far, obligations and favors have been discussed in personal terms. It is believed in Cornerville as well as elsewhere that the politician has an obligation to his community to secure parks, playgrounds, and other improvements contributing to the general welfare. Cornerville people complain bitterly that their representatives have failed to meet this obligation. Brief inspection is all that is needed to convince one that the district has fared worse than others in obtaining such improvements.

Cornerville people have a variety of explanations for this condition.

They say that the politicians sell them out, that the politicians are not interested in improving the district, or that they do not want to do too much for fear that the people will be able to get along without them. These expressions of sentiment throw little light upon the question. We should not expect a politician who sincerely desires to obtain improvements to lose interest in this goal as soon as he is elected. Even if he were only interested in graft, there can be more graft in a public improvement project than in anything else.

Evidently, the explanation must be made in different terms. The politician-constituent and politician-politician personal relations provide a clue.

It would be pleasing to people in general to have public improvements, but the political structure is not based upon people in general. The politician has obligations to particular people, and he maintains his organization by discharging a certain number of these obligations.

The politician must concentrate his efforts where there are the most pressing demands. If a man wants three things—to keep out of jail, to get a job, and to have new play space for his children—he will not ask for them all at once. First, he wants to secure his freedom and then a means of obtaining money. If the politician can do these favors for him, he will be satisfied and probably will not mention the park at all, for the constituents realize that what they can ask from a politician depends upon what they can do for him.

The constituents feel that people in general have a right to community improvements and therefore they do not look upon them as personal favors. The man who has a job and has no trouble with the law does not make the effort to establish close personal relations with the politician in order to obtain community improvements.

When he is asked to fix a pinch for a corner boy or to use his influence to protect the racketeers, the politician must make the connections with the police and the district attorney which such action requires. The closest possible connections with these people will not aid him toward obtaining community improvements because they have no jurisdiction in such matters. When he is asked to get a man on the relief rolls, he must make connections with the authorities who handle such matters, and they also have nothing to do with initiating community improvements. When he is asked to get a man a political job, he must try to make connections with the important figures in the administration, and there he comes into contact with the people who have power over improvements. But he cannot ask for everything. It is well understood in politics that one politician cannot ask a great deal of another unless he can perform important services in return. If he asks too much, the connection breaks down, and he can get nothing.

The New-Fashioned Machine

Edward N. Costikyan

EVERY LOCAL POLITICAL LEADER in an urban area must have a permanent headquarters to which supporters and suppliants alike may go to see him. In New York County, there are in normal circumstances thirty-three such local headquarters.[1] They are the regular Democratic clubs of their respective areas.

Each club pays for its own rent, telephone bills, mailings, insurance, typewriters, addressograph and addressograph plates. It must pay for whatever social events it sponsors, and for its own charities.

The hardest organization in the world to manage and lead is such a volunteer organization. Neither executives nor envelope-stuffers are paid. Dereliction in duty cannot be controlled by discipline nor by the threat of discharge. Even if the miscreant is a public employee by reason of the club's help, there is little that can be done; the city will not fire people because they fail to get out a political mailing or to ring doorbells even after they have promised, or even volunteered, to do so.

Once one of our club leaders insisted that at a particular election *every* captain be at his polling place at 6:00 A.M. sharp. We were then still an insurgent club. Our captains had no real function to perform at 6:00 A.M., since our Regular Democratic counterparts had their own staff of captains ready to handle early morning election-day details such as making sure the polls opened on time. Our captains knew it, and few were inclined to rise at 5:00 A.M. in order to show the flag when no one else would be awake to see it. I knew this, and declined to issue the 6:00 A.M. directive.

"But they *have* to come," I was told.

"What if they ask why, and there's no good reason to be there?" I asked.

---

1. In 1955 the party adopted rules which, defying all natural law, declared each district would be headed by two co-equals, one male and one female. In 1963 in three districts, the male from one club and the female from its opposition club won. So in those districts there are two co-equal headquarters, making the county total 36 for 33 leadership districts. But the number may vary every two years. In 1965, due to reapportionment the total was 39 districts.

"Then fire them."

"Yeah," I said, "fire them and then what do we do?"

To this there was no answer. There was no waiting line of anxious applicants begging for appointment to a captaincy. In fact, over half the districts then had no captains. This is the unanswerable problem when one seeks efficiency in a modern volunteer political party—if you fire someone, then what do you do?

Even if every public jobholder who failed to carry out his political duties could be fired, one still could not maintain discipline. The maximum percentage of jobholders among the captains and workers in any club in New York County is about 35 percent—and that is very unusual. More often it's between 10 and 20 percent and frequently less. Even if job threats could insure discipline in this minority, little would be achieved. A 35 percent container—like a sieve—carries little water.

These being the facts, other techniques must be used. Appeals to idealism, personal friendship, supposed obligations—all of these are among the tools. But essentially the leader must create a spirit that can produce a desire to follow through among his supporters. To sustain such a spirit is the heart of the matter. Even with it, running a club of this kind is a difficult and perpetually challenging task. The investment of time is incredible. Privacy, to a considerable extent, evaporates.

Budgets vary—from as low as $4,000 to as high as $30,000 a year. Memberships vary—from under 200 to over 4,000. The number of voters represented varies from under 10,000 to over 50,000. The degree of activity varies. In each case, the leader's responsibility is to keep the local headquarters open and functioning. Prospective new members must be sought and, once inveigled into the headquarters, welcomed. Someone else may have done the inveigling, but the leader had better personally show his happiness at their presence.

The headquarters usually looks dingy and needs repainting, which means money or labor or both. The leader must be prepared to see that the money or labor is there (or do it himself).

The Membership Committee is planning a new-member's party. The leader must be available.

The club's bank account is low and someone must be stimulated to set up a fund-raising affair. The leader's counsel is sought as to the best money-raising device to try this time.

Regular monthly membership meetings require a continuing supply of reasonably interesting speakers on important issues. Can the leader get the commissioner of correction or housing or something?

There is a growing feud between two key officers in the club. Will the leader talk to them and straighten them out?

Complaints are flowing in (to the leader) that club members are not receiving club mailings. The leader finds out that two volunteers, each looking to the other, have fallen five months behind in keeping the membership lists current.

So-and-so has moved out of the district, and no one is handling such-and-such committee. Does the leader have any ideas as to who might take over?

The treasurer has been away, the bills for annual dues (usually five or six dollars, with optional higher amounts for "sustaining members") have not been sent out, and the treasury is low. Where can we find some funds, borrowed or otherwise, for last month's rent?

The theater-benefit committee must put down a thousand-dollar deposit by next Tuesday. Can the leader suggest ten people to be asked to lend a hundred apiece?

And so it goes. The leader is always the first and last resort.

A good leader delegates—and then redelegates when the original delegatee flops. As a result, as time passes, more and more of the internal work is undertaken by the club president and other officers. But still the problems continue, and when they remain unsolved on the way up, they end in the leader's hands.

Every problem—paint, heat, rent, telephone, mailing costs, repairs, robberies, fires, insurance, location, cleaning—at one time or another are the leader's ultimate responsibility. Indeed, the hallmark of a real political leader is whether he has swept out his own clubhouse—*while he was the leader!* There's nothing like it to stimulate the club members and, if I may say so, to clean up the headquarters the way they should be cleaned up.

The final club problem is *knowing* the members. They come and go. There are as many as a hundred new members a year. A leader who wants to survive must make sure that he spends enough time learning who they are, and meeting them, becoming *their* leader as well as the club's!

The Constituents

The second major area of the leader's activity is dealing with constituents. Depending upon the area serviced, a leader may have a heavy or light load of constituents *every* Monday and to a lesser extent, Thursday night, fifty-two weeks a year.

In some areas of New York, fifty to a hundred constituents arrive each week for help from the leader. In areas like mine, the number has varied—five to ten a week at the beginning, when the area was 60 percent tenements; one to two a week at the most now that the district is 80 percent middle, upper-middle, and luxury housing.

What do these people want?

Basically they want help with problems that are frequently impossible to solve and frequently quite simple.

Tenant disputes with landlords were once the bulk of our problem.

the apartment hasn't been painted in six years; there's no heat; the plaster is broken; we need new windows; there are no lights in the halls. Sometimes it's worse: the landlord wants a rent increase; the building is going to be torn down and the landlord says I've got to get out; I was late on the rent and I have this eviction notice.

These problems, calling for various degrees of activity—from a phone call or a form to representing a tenant in court—are handled as the problem demands, either by the leader or his associates.

I always insisted that if anything more than routine form-filling or telephoning was necessary, one of the attorneys in the club assume the personal responsibility of becoming the attorney for the complainant—or else let someone else do the job.

On only two occasions did a constituent ask me to "talk to the judge," both times about a housing matter. One was a landlord. The other a tenant. In both cases I said no. In both cases, justice was done. Indeed, the tenant, who won her case without intervention, became a committed party worker and a firm believer in a nonpolitical judiciary.

There are constituents with problems in the criminal courts. A sixteen-year-old son was arrested; one of the club members, who was a good criminal lawyer, took that one on—and the boy was acquitted. The sister-in-law of a club officer was arrested for shoplifting and was on her way to night court when the leader was advised. The leader dropped everything, went to court, and ultimately worked out a disposition with the complaining witness.

A local neighborhood hotspot had repeated trouble with the State Liquor Authority, whose inspectors seemed to be harassing the place looking for a shakedown. Did the leader know anyone at the S.L.A.? He didn't, but he knew a leader who did, the complaint of harassment was made, and the harassment ceased.

A constituent on welfare had violated the rules, taken a parttime job, and picked up an extra three hundred dollars over a four-month period. Welfare had found out and was demanding he repay the three hundred, but he didn't have it. There were criminal charges pending. Could the leader help? He could. A couple of phone calls to the appropriate authorities in the Welfare Department resulted in the obvious conclusion that the money simply wasn't there and that it wouldn't help anyone to send the man to jail. That was over ten years ago—and the man has been in no trouble since.)

A constituent had lost his job in an advertising agency at the age of forty-five, his unemployment insurance had run out, so had his savings. Wasn't there some place his obvious talents could be used? There was. A city agency needed a skilled economic researcher at $6,500 a year.

A constituent had taken a civil-service exam and passed it, but an ancient matrimonial dispute had led the appointing authority to reject him. Could he get a chance to explain the whole matter in person? He could (though he didn't get the job).

A group of constituents were fighting the installation of a commercial parking garage in a residential building. Could the leader appear at the hearing before the zoning authority? He couldn't, but the club president could.

The residents of a building were going crazy because of excavation for a new apartment house across the street. The racket started at 7:00 A.M. every day, including Saturdays. Could the leader get the contractor to lay off on Saturdays? He could.

A constituent wanted to organize a program to plant trees down one street. Would the leader get permission—and some money—from the landowners? He would.

A taxi driver had three moving-traffic violations and was about to lose his license. Can we help? Not much.

A family found their welfare allowance wholly inadequate. Could the leader help? He could, if only to the extent of speeding a review of the allowances.

And so it goes, week in and week out, year after year.

A relatively small number seek jobs; many—often proprietors of single-man enterprises—seek relief from jury duty; once the general counsel of a major oil company (a Republican, by the way, although we never asked anyone their party affiliation—a constituent is a constituent) sought help because a new street light had been put up outside his third-story bedroom window on Beekman Place. It was shining in his eyes all night. Couldn't a shield be placed on the back of the light? It was—and it was carefully adjusted one evening, while the venerable gentlemen stuck his head out the window and shouted directions to the man on the ladder.

In other districts the problems will differ. Getting new street lighting; placing traffic lights where constituents—not traffic engineers—think them necessary; dealing with school location and other education problems; securing better parks, or getting existing parks cleaned up; law-enforcement problems and better police protection.

Indeed, every variety of problem that affects his district finds its way to the district leader. A composite of the problems brought to district leaders is a composite of the problems that affect the city.

In a tiny percentage—far less than one percent of the problems, in my experience—something illicit is sought: the fixing of a case or the calling-off of an inspector who insists that a sidewalk be repaired. In twelve years of handling these problems, I can remember only one case where I was offered a pay-off, three cases where communication with a judge or hearing officer was sought, and one other case of proposed misconduct. That's a low percentage, in light of the legends about politicians.

As a general rule, no one who asks for help from the club is expected to pay for it. Indeed, the ranks of former politicians are heavy-laden with unimaginative types who thought it appropriate to receive a slight token of appreciation for each favor undertaken, let alone satisfactorily performed.

The requests are of all degrees of difficulty. In many cases, the only answer that can be given ("I want a five-room apartment in a city housing project, and my income is ten thousand a year") is "Sorry, nothing can be done." In other cases—for example, when an aged couple, seeking a city housing-project apartment, is perplexed by a one-year delay after due application,—the answer may be "We'll see what's wrong and what can be done."

Very rarely indeed can the district leader say "Yes, it will be done." Perhaps in only one-third of the cases can anything be done— and for those cases months may be needed. And yet the district leader and his associates, who frequently take on responsibility for following through on problems, must make friends while doing no more than "their best," with no better than a one-third record of success except in purely routine matters. Dealing with constituents soon develops in the leader both a broad knowledge of government and considerable tact and diplomatic skill.

And when a local issue erupts that places the local community in conflict with city or state government—such as the proposal for the Lower Manhattan Expressway, which Robert Moses and various labor unions supported and which the local residents opposed; the destruction of a local hospital, which the hospital commissioner proposed and the local hospital residents opposed; the closing of Washington Square Park to traffic, which was generally opposed by the city but violently supported by local residents; and so on—the party leader must be prepared to be the community spokesman, especially if he has an opponent or potential opponent for the leadership, who will be delighted to become the spokesman if the leader is silent.

Basically the leader cushions the impact of government upon his constituents and provides a pipeline for his constituents to the bureaucracy at the heart of every urban center.

Instead of the tenant calling a telephone number for the nth time to make a complaint about the absence of heat on a freezing day in January, the leader calls or goes to see a deputy clerk he knows—and that impossible temperature and the freezing tenants become a far more human problem, and far more likely to receive attention than if they were merely one address on a long list of telephoned complaints. The political rewards for effective handling of such problems are simple: votes for the leader and his club's candidates when, every two years, they run for re-election to party office, and, it is hoped, votes for the party's candidates for public office on every election day.

The first reward is far surer. When someone has been helped—or even treated decently—he doesn't forget the man or the club that helped him. Translating that memory into a vote for a President or governor or mayor or even an assemblyman is a far chancier business. But chancy or not, this is an essential part of the duty of a district leader. And his willingness to devote his time to this kind of activity is one of the credentials he must possess if he wishes to be accepted as a political leader who is entitled to be heard by other leaders when candidates are being nominated and policies being decided.

This description of tasks undertaken for constituents is not a careful distillation of the legitimate from the illegitimate ones. The percent of illegitimate requests to which the author was subjected was minuscule. True, other leaders might attract more illicit requests and might accept the assignments. I can issue no guarantees of probity for all politicians. But my experience tells me that the percentage of misconduct among political leaders in this area is relatively insignificant. For example, as pointed out in Chapter 26, the locus of corruption (to the extent that there is corruption) has shifted. The politician is no longer the middle-man. Public officials amenable to corruption can be approached directly, and with less exposure. Why use an unnecessary middleman?

Moreover, most of the problems that concern constituents do not require illicit intervention. So why do it?

Indeed, the myth of the corruptibility of the political leaders is, I am convinced, to a large extent and in a substantial majority of cases a relic from ancient history and a carefully exploited legend designed to immobilize and minimize the significance of political leaders.

After all, many a civic leader and many a public official makes his reputation by periodically denouncing "the politician," "the bosses," and "the political hacks." Yet the evidence of graft and misconduct in recent years has in almost all cases involved civil servants and public officeholders—not political leaders—who have gone wrong.

The Campaign

The final area of the leader's principal local activity is the management of the party's general election campaign in his area.

He has thirty election districts? He *must* have thirty captains—one for each district. If there are thirty captains but six are no good, he must find six new ones and ease the old ones out without too much of a fuss.

Every year one or two captains retire. They must be replaced—by trained people.

Does Captain A have enough help? How can we get him or her a couple of assistants? The Fourteenth E.D. has two good co-captains sharing the district. They've developed to the point that either one can handle it alone—if he or she will. Can we move one over to the Sixteenth E.D.?

✓ Last year's campaign chairman, who deals directly with the captains and handles the execution of the campaign, has gotten too busy in his law practice, or has gotten married, or has moved. Whom shall we put in his place?

We will want to send out two mailings the week before election day—one to Democratic registrants and one to Republicans. Can we put X in charge of getting the 25,000 envelopes (or 50,000, or 75,000) addressed during the summer?

Who will write our local literature? What should it say?

How about a telephone campaign the last two weeks? Can we get so-and-so to organize that?

We need a mailing to new residents to tell them where to register, so we'll need someone to canvass all the new buildings before September 1 to get the names of new tenants.

And so on and on. By September 1, the campaign machinery must be set up. By September 30, it must be rolling. After that it's too late to start concocting new campaign plans, or even to do much more than feed the machinery that has been set up, to oil it, and to make minor adjustments and replacements.

All year round, therefore, as the leader meets new members, as he deals with constituents, he notes those who might be helpful in a campaign and passes on the names to the campaign chairman. The campaign chairman looks about too. The club president, the secretary, vice-president, ex-leaders, ex-presidents—they all look, and suggest. The campaign chairman assigns people to specific tasks or areas. One out of three delivers. Those who don't are forgiven, but then are forgotten as campaigners.

The campaign chairman keeps a chart; it shows captains and workers in each election district. Regularly the leader checks it. "We're light in the Eleventh. There's a fellow named so-and-so who was in to get some help who might work out. Why don't you try him?" And so the list grows. By election day there is, besides the captain, a list of five or six workers per election district. Two to four of them, moreover, are really prepared to work all day getting Democratic voters to the polls. The district is "manned"!

On election day, while voters sleep, the leaders and the campaign chairman and the lawyers and the captains and workers rise at 5:00 A.M. By 6:00 A.M. the leaders—male and female—are on the way around the polls to see they are open, manned by captains, functioning, peaceful, and happy.

All day long, the leaders check the polls—the voter turnout, the captains' attitudes, the morale. Where a district is light when it shouldn't be, the leaders or the campaign chairman find the captain and jack him up.

When there are legal problems at the polls, a lawyer is sent. When a machine breaks, the leader or the law chairman calls the Board of Elections again and again—until it's fixed. If a voter is denied the right to vote, one of the lawyers gets him a cab, and soon he's on his way to the Supreme Court to apply for a legal order authorizing him to cast his ballot.

When night falls, the leader gives his captains a last push to get out the Democrats, and then awaits the closing of the polls and the reports of the results.

The first four election districts often give the experienced leader a clue to the results—win, lose, or too close to tell. By 1:00 A.M. the results are finally in—good or bad.

The next morning—bright, early, and perhaps groggily—the leader and the campaign chairman and the captains are at work earning their livings, while their nonpolitical co-workers comment how nice it was to have had a day off. That night the leader may very well be at his headquarters—especially after a licking—surveying the wreckage, putting the election figures in the desk drawer so that they'll be available for later analysis, cleaning up the headquarters.

The week after election day, the leaders and the campaign managers go over the results and compare them with those of prior years. There was a new captain in the Fifteenth E.D. and that district went Democratic for the first time in ten years ("That guy looks good—I hope we can keep him interested"); the margin keeps going up in the Eighteenth; according to the captain in the Nineteenth, Y was a great help—maybe Y could take on a district.

And so the planning starts for the next year's campaign. More people, new people, different people. But the machinery is permanent, although the people who man it change and change and change.

There are "promotions"—a captain becomes assistant campaign manager, and then campaign manager, and then club president—and then perhaps district leader. Or a captain, after two or three or four (or ten) years grows tired of the drudgery, the stairs to climb, the doorbells to ring, and retires.

Out of the shifting but steady process grows a small, semipermanent, semiautonomous political institution—the leader's political home, and usually his successor's political home. The club is the symbol of his district. It is his headquarters, his meeting place, his responsibility, his ticket of admission to the meetings where candidates are selected and political policy made.

The Latent Functions
of the Machine

Robert K. Merton

. . . IN LARGE SECTORS of the American population, the political machine or the "political racket" are judged as unequivocally "bad" and "undesirable." The grounds for such moral judgment vary somewhat, but they consist substantially in pointing out that political machines violate moral codes: political patronage violates the code of selecting personnel on the basis of impersonal qualifications rather than on grounds of party loyalty or contributions to the party war-chest; bossism violates the code that votes should be based on individual appraisal of the qualifications of candidates and of political issues, and not on abiding loyalty to a feudal leader; bribery and "honest graft" obviously offend the proprieties of property; "protection" for crime clearly violates the law and the mores; and so on.

In view of these manifold respects in which political machines, in varying degrees, run counter to the mores and at times to the law, it becomes pertinent to inquire how they manage to continue in operation. The familiar "explanations" for the continuance of the political machine are not here in point. To be sure, it may well be that if "respectable citizenry" would carry through their political obligations, if the electorate were to be alert and enlightened; if the number of elective officers were substantially reduced from the dozens, even hundreds, which the average voter is now expected to appraise in the course of local, county, state and national elections, if the electorate were activated by the "wealthy and educated classes without whose participation," as the not-always democratically oriented Bryce put it, the best-framed government must speedily degenerate," if these and a plethora of similar changes in political structure were introduced, perhaps the "evils" of the political machine would indeed be exorcized. But it should be noted that these changes are not typically introduced, that political machines have the phoenix-like quality of arising strong and

Reprinted from Social Theory and Social Structure (*rev. ed.; New York: The Free Press, 1957, pp. 71–81.*

unspoiled from their ashes, that, in short, this structure exhibits a notable vitality in many areas of American political life.

Proceeding from the functional view, therefore, that we should *ordinarily* (not invariably) expect persistent social patterns and social structures to perform positive functions *which are at the same time not adequately fulfilled by other existing patterns and structures*, the thought occurs that perhaps this publicly maligned organization is, *under present conditions*, satisfying basic latent functions. A brief examination of current analyses of this type of structure may also serve to illustrate additional problems of functional analysis.

SOME FUNCTIONS OF THE POLITICAL MACHINE. Without presuming to enter into the variations of detail marking different political machines—a Tweed, Vare, Crump, Flynn, Hague are by no means identical types of bosses—we can briefly examine the functions more or less common to the political machine, as a generic type of social organization. We neither attempt to itemize all the diverse functions of the political machine nor imply that all these functions are similarly fulfilled by each and every machine.

The key structural function of the Boss is to organize, centralize and maintain in good working condition "the scattered fragments of power" which are at present dispersed through our political organization. By this centralized organization of political power, the boss and his apparatus can satisfy the needs of diverse subgroups in the larger community which are not adequately satisfied by legally devised and culturally approved social structures.

To understand the role of bossism and the machine, therefore, we must look at two types of sociological variables: (1) the *structural context* which makes it difficult, if not impossible, for morally approved structures to fulfill essential social functions, thus leaving the door open for political machines (or their structural equivalents) to fulfill these functions and (2) the subgroups whose distinctive needs are left unsatisfied, except for the latent functions which the machine in fact fulfills.

STRUCTURAL CONTEXT. The constitutional framework of American political organization specifically precludes the legal possibility of highly centralized power and, it has been noted, thus "discourages the growth of effective and responsible leadership. The framers of the Constitution, as Woodrow Wilson observed, set up the check and balance system 'to keep government at a sort of mechanical equipoise by means of a standing amicable contest among its several organic parts.' They distrusted power as dangerous to liberty: and therefore they spread it thin and erected barriers against its concentration." This dispersion of power is found not only at the national level but in local areas as well. "As a consequence," Sait goes on to observe, "when *the people or par-*

ticular groups among them demanded positive action, no one had adequate authority to act. The machine provided an antidote."[1]

The constitutional dispersion of power not only makes for difficulty of effective decision and action but when action does occur it is defined and hemmed in by legalistic considerations. In consequence, there develops "a much *more human system* of partisan government, whose chief object soon became the circumvention of government by law. . . . The lawlessness of the extra-official democracy was merely the counterpoise of the legalism of the official democracy. The lawyer having been permitted to subordinate democracy to the Law, the Boss had to be called in to extricate the victim, which he did after a fashion and for a consideration."[2]

Officially, political power is dispersed. Various well-known expedients were devised for this manifest objective. Not only was there the familiar separation of powers among the several branches of the government but, in some measure, tenure in each office was limited, rotation in office approved. And the scope of power inherent in each office was severely circumscribed. Yet, observes Sait in rigorously functional terms, "Leadership is necessary; and *since* it does not develop readily within the constitutional framework, the Boss provides it in a crude and irresponsible form from the outside."[3]

Put in more generalized terms, *the functional deficiencies of the official structure generate an alternative (unofficial) structure to fulfill existing needs somewhat more effectively.* Whatever its specific historical origins, the political machine persists as an apparatus for satisfying otherwise unfulfilled needs of diverse groups in the population. By turning to a few of these subgroups and their characteristic needs, we shall be led at once to a range of latent functions of the political machine.

FUNCTIONS OF THE POLITICAL MACHINE FOR DIVERSE SUBGROUPS. It is well known that one source of strength of the political machine derives from its roots in the local community and the neighborhood. The political machine does not regard the electorate as a vague, undifferentiated mass of voters. With a keen sociological intuition, the machine recognizes that the voter is primarily a man living in a specific neighborhood, with specific personal problems and personal wants. Public issues are abstract and remote; private problems are extremely concrete and immediate. It is not through the generalized appeal to large public concerns that the machine operates, but through the direct, quasi-feudal relationships between local representatives of the machine and voters in their neighborhood. Elections are won in the precinct.

1. Edward M. Sait, "Machine, Political," *Encyclopedia of the Social Sciences*, IX, 658b [italics supplied].
2. Herbert Croly, *Progressive Democracy* (New York, 1914), p. 254, cited by Sait, *op. cit.*, 658b.
3. Sait, *op. cit.*, 659a.

The machine welds its link with ordinary men and women by elaborate networks of personal relations. Politics is transformed into personal ties. The precinct captain "must be a friend to every man, assuming if he does not feel sympathy with the unfortunate, and utilizing in his good works the resources which the boss puts at his disposal."[4] The precinct captain is forever a friend in need. In our prevailingly impersonal society, the machine, through its local agents, fulfills the important social *function of humanizing and personalizing all manner of assistance* to those in need. Foodbaskets and jobs, legal and extra-legal advice, setting to rights minor scrapes with the law, helping the bright poor boy to a political scholarship in a local college, looking after the bereaved—the whole range of crises when a feller needs a friend, and, above all, a friend who knows the score and who can do something about it—all these find the ever-helpful precinct captain available in the pinch.

To assess this function of the political machine adequately, it is important to note not only the fact that aid *is* provided but *the manner in which it is provided.* After all, other agencies do exist for dispensing such assistance. Welfare agencies, settlement houses, legal aid clinics, medical aid in free hospitals, public relief departments, immigration authorities—these and a multitude of other organizations are available to provide the most varied types of assistance. But in contrast to the professional techniques of the welfare worker which may typically represent in the mind of the recipient the cold, bureaucratic dispensation of limited aid following upon detailed investigation of *legal* claims to aid of the "client," are the unprofessional techniques of the precinct captain who asks no questions, exacts no compliance with legal rules of eligibility and does not "snoop" into private affairs.

For many, the loss of "self-respect" is too high a price for legalized assistance. In contrast to the gulf between the settlement house workers who so often come from a different social class, educational background and ethnic group, the precinct worker is "just one of us," who understands what it's all about. The condescending lady bountiful can hardly compete with the understanding friend in need. In *this struggle between alternative structures for fulfilling the nominally same function* of providing aid and support to those who need it, it is clearly the machine politician who is better integrated with the groups which he serves than the impersonal, professionalized, socially distant and legally constrained welfare worker. And since the politician can at times influence and manipulate the official organizations for the dispensation of assistance, whereas the welfare worker has practically no influence on the political machine, they only add to his greater effectiveness. More colloquially and also, perhaps, more incisively, it was the Boston ward-leader, Martin Lomasny, who described this essential function to the curious Lincoln

4. *Ibid.*

Steffens: "I think," said Lomasny, "that there's got to be in every ward somebody that any bloke can come to—no matter what he's done—and get help. *Help, you understand; none of your law and justice, but help.*"[5]

The "deprived classes," then, constitute one subgroup for whom the political machine clearly satisfies wants not adequately satisfied in the same fashion by the legitimate social structure.

For a second subgroup, that of business (primarily "big" business but also "small") the political boss serves the function of providing those political privileges which entail immediate economic gains. Business corporations, among which the public utilities (railroads, local transportation companies, communications corporations, electric light) are simply the most conspicuous in this regard, seek special political dispensations which will enable them to stabilize their situation and to near their objective of maximizing profits. Interestingly enough, corporations often want to avoid a chaos of uncontrolled competition. They want the greater security of an economic czar who controls, regulates and organizes competition, providing this czar is not a public official with his decisions subject to public scrutiny and public control. (The latter would be "government control," and hence taboo.) The political boss fulfills these requirements admirably.

Examined for a moment apart from any "moral" considerations, the political apparatus of the Boss is effectively designed to perform these functions with a minimum of inefficiency. Holding the strings of diverse governmental divisions, bureaus and agencies in his competent hands, the Boss rationalizes the relations between public and private business. He serves as the business community's ambassador in the otherwise alien (and sometimes unfriendly) realm of government. And, in strict business-like terms, he is well-paid for his economic services to his respectable business clients. In an article entitled, "An Apology to Graft," Steffens suggested that "Our economic system, which held up riches, power and acclaim as prizes to men bold enough and able enough to buy corruptly timber, mines, oil fields and franchises and 'get away with it,' was at fault."[6] And, in a conference with a hundred or so of Los Angeles business leaders, he described a fact well known to all of them—the Boss and his machine were an *integral part* of the organization of the economy. "You cannot build or operate a railroad, or a street railway, gas, water, or power company, develop and operate a mine, or get forests and cut timber on a large scale, or run any privileged business, without corrupting or joining in the corruption of the government. You tell me privately that you must, and here I am telling you semi-publicly that you must. And that is so all over the country. And that means that we have an organization of society in which, *for some*

5. *The Autobiography of Lincoln Steffens* (Chautauqua, N.Y.: Chautauqua Press, 1931), 618.
6. *Autobiography of Lincoln Steffens*, 570.

reason, you and your kind, the ablest, most intelligent, most imaginative, daring, and resourceful leaders of society, are and must be against society and its laws and its all-around growth."[7]

Since the demand for the services of special privileges are built into the structure of the society, the Boss fulfills diverse functions for this second subgroup of business-seeking-privilege. These "needs" of business, as presently constituted, are not adequately provided for by "conventional" and "culturally approved" social structures; consequently, the extra-legal but more-or-less efficient organization of the political machine comes to provide these services. To adopt an *exclusively* moral attitude toward the "corrupt political machine" is to lose sight of the very structural conditions which generate the "evil" that is so bitterly attacked. To adopt a functional outlook on the political machine is not to provide an apologia, but a more solid base for modifying or eliminating the machine, *providing* specific structural arrangements are introduced either for eliminating these effective demands of the business community or, if that is the objective, of satisfying these demands through alternative means.

A third set of distinctive functions fulfilled by the political machine for a special subgroup is that of providing alternative channels of social mobility for those otherwise excluded from the more conventional avenues for personal "advancement." Both the sources of this special "need" (for social mobility) and the respect in which the political machine comes to help satisfy this need can be understood by examining the structure of the larger culture and society. As is well known, the American culture lays enormous emphasis on money and power as a "success" goal legitimate for all members of the society. By no means alone in our inventory of cultural goals, it still remains among the most heavily endowed with positive affect and value. However, certain subgroups and certain ecological areas are notable for the relative absence of opportunity for achieving these (monetary and power) types of success. They constitute, in short, sub-populations where "the cultural emphasis upon pecuniary success has been absorbed, but where there is *little access to conventional and legitimate* means for attaining such success. The conventional occupational opportunities of persons in (such areas) are almost completely limited to manual labor. Given our cultural stigmatization of manual labor, and its correlate, the prestige of white-collar work, it is clear that the result is a tendency to achieve these culturally approved objectives *through whatever means are possible.* These people are on the one hand, "asked to orient their conduct toward the prospect of accumulating wealth [and power] and, on the other, they are largely denied effective opportunities to do so institutionally."

7. *Ibid.,* 572–573.

It is within this context of social structure that the political machine fulfills the basic function of providing avenues of social mobility for the otherwise disadvantaged. Within this context, even the corrupt political machine and the racket "represent the triumph of amoral intelligence over morally prescribed 'failure' when the channels of vertical mobility are closed or narrowed *in a society which places a high premium on economic affluence, [power] and social ascent for* all *its members*."[8] As one sociologist has noted on the basis of several years of close observation in a "slum area":

> The sociologist who dismisses racket and political organizations as deviations from desirable standards thereby neglects some of the major elements of slum life . . . . He does not discover the functions they perform for the members [of the groupings in the slum]. The Irish and later immigrant peoples have had the greatest difficulty in finding places for themselves in our urban social and economic structure. Does anyone believe that the immigrants and their children could have achieved their present degree of social mobility without gaining control of the political organization of some of our largest cities? The same is true of the racket organization. *Politics and the rackets have furnished an important means of social mobility for individuals, who, because of ethnic background and low class position,* are blocked from advancement in the "respectable" channels.[9]

This, then represents a third type of function performed for a distinctive subgroup. This function, it may be noted in passing, is fulfilled by the *sheer* existence and operation of the political machine, for it is in the machine itself that these individuals and subgroups find their culturally induced needs more or less satisfied. It refers to the services which the political apparatus provides for its own personnel. But seen in the wider social context we have set forth, it no longer appears as *merely* a means of self aggrandizement for profit-hungry and power-hungry *individuals*, but as an organized provision for *subgroups* otherwise excluded or restricted from the race for "getting ahead."

Just as the political machine performs services for "legitimate" business, so it operates to perform not dissimilar services for "illegitimate" business: vice, crime and rackets. Once again, the basic sociological role of the machine in this respect can be more fully appreciated only if one temporarily abandons attitudes of moral indignation, to examine with all moral innocence the actual workings of the organization. In this light, it at once appears that the subgroup of the professional criminal, racketeer, gambler, has basic similarities of organization, demands and operation to the subgroup of the industrialist, man of business, speculator. If there is a Lumber King or an

8. Merton, *op. cit.*, 146.
9. William F. Whyte, "Social Organization in the Slums," *American Sociological Review*, Feb. 1943, 8, 34–39 (italics supplied).

Oil King, there is also a Vice King or a Racket King. If expansive legitimate business organizes administrative and financial syndicates to "rationalize" and to "integrate" diverse areas of production and business enterprise, so expansive rackets and crime organize syndicates to bring order to the otherwise chaotic areas of production of illicit goods and services. If legitimate business regards the proliferation of small enterprises as wasteful and inefficient, substituting, for example, the giant chain stores for the hundreds of corner groceries, so illegitimate business adopts the same businesslike attitude, and syndicates crime and vice.

　Finally, and in many respects, most important, is the basic similarity, if not near-identity, of the economic role of "legitimate" business and "illegitimate" business. *Both are in some degree concerned with the provision of goods and services for which there is an economic demand.* Morals aside, they are both business, industrial and professional enterprises, dispensing goods and services which some people want, for which there is a market in which goods and services are transformed into commodities. And, in a prevalently market society, we should expect appropriate enterprises to arise whenever there is a market demand for given goods or services.

　As is well known, vice, crime and the rackets *are* "big business." Consider only that there have been estimated to be about 500,000 professional prostitutes in the United States, and compare this with the approximately 200,000 physicians and 200,000 nurses. It is difficult to estimate which have the larger clientele: the professional men and women of medicine or the professional men and women of vice. It is, of course, difficult to estimate the economic assets, income, profits and dividends of illicit gambling in this country and to compare it with the economic assets, income, profits and dividends of, say, the shoe industry, but it is altogether possible that the two industries are about on a par. No precise figures exist on the annual expenditures on illicit narcotics, and it is probable that these are less than the expenditures on candy, but it is also probable that they are larger than the expenditure on books.

　It takes but a moment's thought to recognize that, *in strictly economic terms*, there is no relevant difference between the provision of licit and of illicit goods and services. The liquor traffic illustrates this perfectly. It would be peculiar to argue that prior to 1920 (when the 18th amendment became effective), the provision of liquor constituted an economic service, that from 1920 to 1933, its production and sale no longer constituted an economic service dispensed in a market, and that from 1934 to the present, it once again took on a serviceable aspect. Or, it would be *economically* (not morally) absurd to suggest that the sale of bootlegged liquor in the dry state of Kansas is less a response to a market demand than the sale of publicly manufactured liquor in the neighboring wet state of Missouri. Examples of this sort can of course be multiplied many times over. Can it be held that in European countries, with registered and legalized prostitution, the prostitute contributes an economic service, whereas in this country, lacking legal sanction, the prostitute provides no such service? Or that the professional abortionist is in the economic market where he has approved legal status and that he is out of the economic market where he is legally taboo? Or that gambling satisfies a specific demand for entertainment in Nevada, where it is one of the largest business enterprises of the largest city in the state, but that it differs essentially in this respect from movie houses in the neighboring state of California?

The failure to recognize that these businesses are only *morally* and not *economically* distinguishable from "legitimate" businesses has led to badly scrambled analysis. Once the economic identity of the two is recognized, we may anticipate that if the political machine performs functions for "legitimate big business" it will be all the more likely to perform not dissimilar functions for "illegitimate big business." And, of course, such is often the case.

The distinctive function of the political machine for their criminal, vice and racket clientele is to enable them to operate in satisfying the economic demands of a large market without due interference from the government. Just as big business may contribute funds to the political party war-chest to ensure a minimum of governmental interference, so with big rackets and big crime. In both instances, the political machine can, in varying degrees, provide "protection." In both instances, many features of the structural context are identical (1) market demands for goods and services; (2) the operators' concern with maximizing gains from their enterprises; (3) the need for partial control of government which might otherwise interfere with these activities of businessmen; (4) the need for an efficient, powerful and centralized agency to provide an effective liaison of "business" with government.

Without assuming that the foregoing pages exhaust either the range of functions or the range of subgroups served by the political machine, we can at least see that *it presently fulfills some functions for these diverse subgroups which are not adequately fulfilled by culturally approved or more conventional structures.*

Several additional implications of the functional analysis of the political machine can be mentioned here only in passing, although they obviously require to be developed at length. First, the foregoing analysis has direct implications for *social engineering.* It helps explain why the periodic efforts at "political reform," "turning the rascals out" and "cleaning political house" are typically short-lived and ineffectual. It exemplifies a basic theorem: *any attempt to eliminate an existing social structure without providing adequate alternative structures for fulfilling the functions previously fulfilled by the abolished organization is doomed to failure.* (Needless to say, this theorem has much wider bearing than the one instance of the political machine.) When "political reform" confines itself to the manifest task of "turning the rascals out," it is engaging in little more than sociological magic. The reform may for a time bring new figures into the political limelight; it may serve the casual social function of re-assuring the electorate that the moral virtues remain intact and will ultimately triumph; it may actually effect a turnover in the personnel of the political machine; it may even, for a time, so curb the activities of the machine as to leave unsatisfied the many needs it has previously fulfilled. But, inevitably, unless the reform also involves a "reforming" of the social and political structure such that the existing needs are satisfied by alternative structures or unless it involves a change which eliminates these needs altogether, the political machine will return to its integral place in the social scheme of things. *To seek social change, without due recognition of the manifest and latent functions performed by the social organization undergoing change, is to indulge in social ritual rather than social engineering.* The concepts of manifest and latent functions (or their equivalents) are indispensable elements in the theoretic repertoire of the social engineer. In this crucial sense, these concepts are not "merely" theoretical (in the abusive sense of the term), but are eminently practical. In the deliberate enactment of social change, they can be ignored only at the price of considerably heightening the risk of failure.

A second implication of our analysis of the political machine also has a bearing upon areas wider than the one we have considered. The "paradox" has often been noted that the supporters of the political machine include both the "respectable" business class elements who are, of course, opposed to the criminal or racketeer and the distinctly "unrespectable" elements of the underworld. And, at first appearance, this is cited as an instance of very strange bedfellows. The learned judge is not infrequently called upon to sentence the very racketeer beside whom he sat the night before at an informal dinner of the political bigwigs. The district attorney jostles the exonerated convict on his way to the back room where the Boss has called a meeting. The big business man may complain almost as bitterly as the big racketeer about the "extortionate" contributions to the party fund demanded by the Boss. Social opposites meet—in the smoke-filled room of the successful politician.

In the light of a functional analysis all this of course no longer seems paradoxical. Since the machine serves both the businessman and the criminal man, the two seemingly antipodal groups intersect. This points to a more general theorem: *the social functions of an organization help determine the structure (including the recruitment of personnel involved in the structure), just as the structure helps determine the effectiveness with which the functions are fulfilled.* In terms of social status, the business group and the criminal group are indeed poles apart. But status does not fully determine behavior and the inter-relations between groups. Functions modify these relations. Given their distinctive needs, the several subgroups in the large society are "integrated," whatever their personal desires or intentions, by the centralizing structure which serves these several needs. In a phrase with many implications which require further study, *structure affects function and function affects structure.*

Mr. Dooley on Why Rayformers Fail

F. P. Dunne

"WHY IS IT," asked Mr. Hennessy, "that a rayform administhration always goes to th' bad?"

"I'll tell ye," said Mr. Dooley. "I tell ye ivrything an' I'll tell ye this. In th' first place 'tis a gr-reat mistake to think that annywan ra-aly wants to rayform. Ye niver heerd iv a man rayformin' himsilf. He'll rayform other people gladly. He likes to do it. But a healthy man'll niver rayform while he has th' strenth. A man doesn't rayform till his will has been impaired so he hasn't power to resist what th' pa-apers calls th' blandishments iv th' timpter. An' that's thruer in politics thin annywhere else.

"But a rayformer don't see it. A rayformer thinks he was ilicted because he was a rayformer, whin th' thruth iv th' matther is he was ilicted because no wan knew him. Ye can always ilicit a man in this counthry on that platform. If I was runnin' f'r office, I'd change me name, an' have printed on me cards: 'Give him a chanst; he can't be worse.' He's ilicted because th' people don't know him an' do know th' other la-ad; because Mrs. Casey's oldest boy was clubbed be a polisman, because we cudden't get wather above th' third story wan day, because th' shtreet car didn't stop f'r us, because th' Flannigans bought a pianny, because we was near run over be a mail wagon, because th' saloons are open Sundah night, because they're not open all day, an' because we're tired seein' th' same face at th' window whin we go down to pay th' wather taxes. Th' rayformer don't know this. He thinks you an' me, Hinnissy, has been watchin' his spotless career f'r twenty years, that we've read all he had to say on th' evils iv pop'lar sufferage befure th' Society f'r the Bewildermint iv th' Poor, an' that we're achin' in ivry joint to have him dhrag us be th' hair iv th' head fr'm th' flowin' bowl an' th' short card game, make good citizens iv us an' sind us to th' pinitinchry. So th' minyit he gets into th' job he begins a furyous attimpt to convart us into what we've been thryin' not to be iver since we come into th' wurruld.

"In th' coorse iv th' twenty years that he spint attimptin' to get

Reprinted from Observations by Mr. Dooley (*New York: Harper & Bros., 1906*), *pp. 167–172.*

office, he managed to poke a few warrum laws conthrollin' th' pleasures iv th' poor into th' stachoo book, because no wan cared about thim or because they made business betther f'r th' polis, an' whin he's in office, he calls us th' Cap'n iv the polis an' says he: 'If these laws ar-re bad laws th' way to end thim is to enfoorce thim.' Somebody told him that, Hinnissy. It isn't thrue, d'ye mind. I don't care who said it, not if 'twas Willum Shakespere. It isn't thrue. Laws ar-re made to throuble peoplc an' th' more throuble they make th' longer they stay on th' stachoo book. But th' polis don't ast anny questions. Says they: 'They'll be less money in th' job but we need some recreation,' an' that night a big copper comes down th' sthreet, sees me settin' out on th' front stoop with me countenance dhraped with a tin pail, fans me with his club an' runs me in. Th' woman nex' dure is locked up f'r sthringin' a clothes line on th' roof, Hannigan's boy Tim gets tin days f'r keeping a goat, th' polis resarves are called out to protict th' vested rights iv property against th' haynyous pushcart man, th' stations is crowded with felons charged with maintainin' a hose conthrary to th' stachoos made an' provided, an' th' tindherline is all over town. A rayformer don't think annything has been accomplished if they'se a vacant bedroom in th' pinitinchry. His motto is 'Arrest that man.'

"Whin a rayformer is ilicted he promises yc a business adminis-thration. Some people want that but I don't. Th' American business man is too fly He's all right, d'ye mind. I don't say annything again' him. He is what Hogan calls th' boolwarks iv pro-gress, an' we cudden't get on without him even if his scales are a little too quick on th' dhrop. But he ought to be left to dale with his akels. 'Tis a shame to give him a place where he can put th' comether on millions iv people that has had no business thrainin' beyond occasionally handin' a piece iv debased money to a car conductor on a cold day. A reg'lar pollytician can't give away an alley without blushin', but a business man who is in pollytics jus' to see that th' civil sarvice law gets thurly enfoorced, will give Lincoln Park an' th' public libr'y to th' beef thrust, charge an admission price to th' lake front an' make it a felony f'r annywan to buy stove polish outside iv his store, an' have it all put down to public improvemints with a pitcher iv him in th' corner stone.

"Fortchnitly, Hinnissy, a rayformer is seldom a business man. He thinks he is, but business men know diff'rent. They know what he is. Hc thinks business an' honesty is th' same thing. He does, indeed. He's got thim mixed because they dhress alike. His idee is that all he has to do to make a business administhration is to have honest men ar-round him. Wrong. I'm not sayin', mind ye, that a man can't do good work an' be honest at th' same time. But whin I'm hirin' a la-ad I find out first whether he is onto his job, an' afther a few years I begin to suspect that he is honest, too. Manny a dishonest man can lay brick sthraight an' manny a man that wudden't steal ye'er spoons will break ye'er furniture. I don't want Father Kelly to hear me, but I'd rather have a competint man who wud steal if I give him a chanst, but I won't, do me plumbin' thin a person that wud scorn to help himsilf but didn't know how to wipe a joint. Ivry man ought to be honest to start with, but to give a man an office jus' because he's honest is like ilictin' him to Congress because he's a pathrite, because he don't bate his wife or because he always wears a right boot on th' right foot. A man ought to be honest to start with an' afther that he ought to be crafty. A pollytician who's on'y honest is jus' th' same as bein' out in a winther storm without anny clothes on.

"Another thing about rayform administhrations is they always think th' on'y man that ought to hold a job is a lawyer. Th' raison is that in th' coorse iv his thrainin' a lawyer larns enough about ivrything to make a good front on anny subject to annybody who doesn't know about it. So whin th' rayform administhration comes in th' mayor says: 'Who'll we make chief iv polis in place iv th' misguided ruffyan who has held th' job f'r twinty years?' 'Th' man f'r th' place,' says th' mayor's adviser, 'is Arthur Lightout,' he says. 'He's an ixcillent lawyer, Yale, '95, an' is well up on polis matthers. Las' year he read a paper on "The fine polis foorce iv London" befure th' annyal meetin' iv th' S'ciety f'r Ladin' th' Mulligan Fam'ly to a Betther an' Harder Life. Besides,' he says, 'he's been in th' milishy an' th' foorce needs a man who'll be afraid not to shoot in case iv public disturbance.' So Arthur takes hold iv th' constabulary an' in a year th' polis can all read Emerson an' th' burglars begin puttin' up laddhers an' block an' tackles befure eight A.M. An' so it is on ivry side. A lawyer has charge iv the city horseshoein', another wan is clanin' th' sthreets, th' author iv 'Gasamagoo on torts' is thryin' to dispose iv th' ashes be throwin' thim in th' air on a windy day, an' th' bright boy that took th' silver ware f'r th' essay on *ne exeats* an' their relation to life is plannin' a uniform that will be sarviceable an' constitchoochinal f'r th' brave men that wurruks on th' city dumps. An' wan day th' main rayformer goes out expictin' to rayceive th' thanks iv th' community an' th' public that has jus' got out iv jail f'r lettin' th' wather run too long in th' bath tub rises up an' cries: 'Back to th' Univarsity Settlemint.' Th' man with th' di'mon' in his shirt front comes home an' pushes th' honest lawyers down th' steps, an' a dishonest horse shoer shoes th' city's horses well, an' a crooked plumber does th' city's plumbin' securely, an' a rascally polisman that may not be avarse to pickin' up a bet but will always find out whin Pathrolman Scanlan slept on his beat, takes hold iv th' polis foorce, an' we raysume our nachral condition iv illagal merrimint. An' th' rayformer spinds th' rest iv his life tellin' us where we are wrong. He's good at that. On'y he don't undherstand that people wud rather be wrong an' comfortable thin right in jail."

"I don't like a rayformer," said Mr. Hennessy.

"Or anny other raypublican," said Mr. Dooley.

THEORIES OF REFORM

Separation of Powers Necessitates Corruption

Henry Jones Ford

THAT THE CORRUPTION of local politics is the natural outcome of democratic institutions is the explanation one is apt to get in private talk with party managers. It is not propounded as a theory, but frankly recognized as a condition which must be dealt with on the principle that what can't be cured must be endured. Good and bad go together in most of the affairs of life, and democratic government is no exception to the general rule. It is in the main good, because it secures attention to the wants and desires of the common people, but at the same time it subjects the transaction of government to the play of their passions and appetites. Despite the railing of purists and idealists, the general result is not so bad; the public business in one way or another does get on and social interests are tolerably well protected. It is true that a great deal of grafting goes on, but if there is a strong boss and a solid machine it is kept within bounds and business interests can know just what they can depend upon. It costs a great deal of money to run politics, and in one way or another the public offices must meet the cost of filling them under the system of popular election. The best and really cheapest way of treating the problem is through the boss system, which controls the selection of candidates and determines public policy by putting it upon a business basis.

Reprinted from Annals of the American Academy of Political and Social Science, *March 1904, pp. 202–203 and 207–216, where it appeared under the title, "Principles of Municipal Organization."*

This opinion is held not only by party managers but also prevails among hard-headed business men who face facts as they find them. They support ring rule as a practical necessity; that is to say, they believe that some sort of a firm political control superior to and exercising authority over the regular constitution of municipal government is necessary to prevent the government from being simply almoner and pander to the mob, and to make it considerate of business and social interests about which the ordinary run of people know little and care less. Unless there is a boss, government lacks consistency and purpose; there are no settled conditions upon which enterprise can rest; no competent authority with which business interests can negotiate. The occasional interregnums which occur between the downfall of one boss and the rise of another are always a period of political demoralization and contention. While not enunciated as a distinct principal, yet the tone of comment one hears in discussion of municipal politics among practical men of affairs implies that corruption is the natural defence of society under democratic conditions of government.

It must be admitted that close contact with actual conditions is apt to lead to a practical conclusion of this kind. No one who ever knew a boss as he is can doubt that he constantly acts under stress of circumstances which he did not create and which his disappearance would not remove. The individual boss frequently disappears; the boss system remains and is a normal characteristic of American municipal politics. The combinations which the boss makes and by which he maintains his ascendency are his own, but he must play the game on the board and with the pieces he finds. I have heard a boss speak in tones of unfeigned scorn of city councilmen who were reputed to be his own agents. When asked why he took up with such people, he described the posture of politics in their wards to show that in joining interests with them he had done the best he could under the circumstances. The poor material furnished by the working of local representation is not unfrequently a subject of remark in the private talk of a boss, but without complaint, for it is the characteristic of the type and the secret of its strength to respond with simple directness to actual conditions, and to base measures on the realities. It is proof of great efficiency of character when a boss is able to maintain himself upon his slippery throne.

The notion that democratic politics are necessarily vile has abundant philosophic support. It pervades the Federalist and was fairly rampant in the convention which framed the Constitution of the United States. If one consults Calhoun's analysis of the tendencies of "the government of the numerical majority," his prophecy seems startling in its accurate anticipation of the present evils of our politics. As an exercise in dialectics it would be possible to produce a copious thesis in support of Talleyrand's cynical definition of democracy as an aristocracy of blackguards, but there would be a fatal flaw in the argument.

For one thing, the marked difference which exists in this country between national and municipal administration, which have a common base in the character of the people, would not be accounted for. Dialectic skill might perhaps get around that, but the working of democratic institutions elsewhere furnishes facts absolutely irreconcilable with the thesis. If corruption is a character mark of democracy, why is it not displayed in the municipal institutions of Canada, England, Switzerland, and Australia? They are far more democratic than those of this country; the policy of government is immediately subject to popular control; checks which we think necessary to guard against results of popular impulse do not exist; mayors have no veto power and all power is amassed in the city council, but there is no boss system, no machine to run the administration, and honesty is the normal characteristic of the system. Although there is complaint as to the character and tendencies of municipal government, it does not relate to integrity of administration but to its scope and purpose. That democratic government should be successful in securing a faithful stewardship of public resources is assumed as a natural consequence of the system; where it works badly is in the ideas it engenders of the social application of these resources, and some alarm is expressed as to the results of the tendency of municipal government to enlarge its functions. Not content with managing markets, water supply, lighting, and street railways, it is taking on lodging-houses and even dance-halls. . . .

Defect in the Organization of Government

We now take up . . . the possibility that the cause of failure may be defect in the organization of government. On first thought it might seem to be impracticable to submit this hypothesis to the test of facts, so many experiments have been tried in municipal charters and so many varieties exist. Upon this score alone one might feel justified in rejecting the supposition offhand, since if the trouble lay in defect of organization surely it would have been gotten at in the course of so much anxious effort. We are, however, bound by our plan to discard all assumptions and to proceed with scientific precision. Since American varieties of municipal government unite in common failure, we need not consider them in detail. Whatever the cause may be, it is generic. Furthermore, we must conclude that this generic cause will manifest itself as a generic difference when American municipal government is compared with municipal government in other civilized countries. Now when the comparison is made, what generic difference appears? Nearly all cities here and abroad have their own peculiarities, and a survey of the general field reveals great variety of organization. The only difference which appears to be generic is this, that whereas everywhere else the executive and legislative departments are connected, in the United States they are disconnected. It further appears that whatever evils or defects may accompany the connection of the executive and legislative departments in one organ of municipal sovereignty, the boss system is unknown wherever that principle of organization obtains, no matter in what country we look for examples. It is a phenomenon characteristic of and peculiar to municipal government organized upon the principle of separating the executive and legislative functions by embodying them in distinct organs of authority. The logical conclusion is that the principle of corruption in American municipal government is this disconnection of the executive and legislative functions.

On reaching this conclusion one instinctively revolts from it, because it seems to attack the fundamental principle of American constitutional law,—the principle of the separation of the powers of government. Moreover, one finds that the idea which pervades theories of municipal reform is the necessity of sharper division and more effectual separation of the executive and legislative functions. This idea is the cardinal principle of reform advocated in the municipal programme adopted by the National Municipal League, and so high an authority as Professor Goodwin argues that it is a principle based upon the laws of psychology, governing all conscious activities. It would seem to be a supposition too monstrous to be entertained that the whole theory upon which American institutions of government are founded is malign, and that the anxious studies of reformers have so grievously miscarried as to prompt them to select the fundamental case of corruption as the cardinal principle of municipal organization. But, on the other hand, the conclusion in which our inquiry has resulted has been reached by logical inference, so that the need is suggested of close scrutiny to determine whether the apparent conflict really exists.

Separation of the Powers of Government

What is meant by the separation of the powers of government? If it means simply that the executive, legislative, and judicial powers shall be separately constituted, there is no radical divergence between American institutions and those of other civilized countries. The generic difference which has been noted lies in this: outside of the United States it is the practice to join together in one organ of government and thus indissolubly connect in their operations the separately constituted powers of government; in the United States it is the practice not only to constitute these powers separately, but also to disconnect them in their operation by embodying them in separate organs of government. For instance, in Toronto the people elect a mayor to be head of the executive government; they also elect a board of controllers upon a general ticket to represent the community as a whole, and in addition members of the city council are elected in every ward to represent the interests of locality. Each of these separately constituted bodies have their special powers and functions which are sharply defined, but they meet and act together as the city council, the organ of municipal sovereignty, whose determinations are final and conclusive. The mayor presides, but he has only his own vote, and has no veto power. He does not even appoint the committees, that being the province of the ward representatives; but the mayor is *ex officio* a member of the board of controllers and of every committee. The controllers, as representatives of the community as a whole, are the medium through which the reports of council committee are submitted to the city council, and the recommendations of the controllers form the subject of legislative action. All appointments to office in the service of the corporation are made by the nomination of the mayor and controllers subject to the approval of the city council. At every point in the organization of the city government the executive and legislative functions, while separate and distinct in constitution, are connected so that they operate as a reciprocal control. While the means by which the executive authority and the legislative authority is separately constituted varies in different countries, the usual English and Swiss practice being to form the executive administration through the action of the legislative body, yet the two functions are always sharply distinguished and separately constituted, but are at the same time invariably connected.

In the United States the authority of the mayor is not only separate and distinct from that of the legislative branch, but is altogether disconnected by being made also a separate organ of government. The legislative authority is embodied in the city council, organized as a separate organ of government. In many cities it is divided into two branches so that one may be a check upon the other, and a further check is provided by giving the mayor a veto over the acts of the city council. It is frequently the case that such offices as those of treasurer and controller are separately constituted and independently organized. The process of separate organization is in some cases—as, for instance, in Ohio municipal corporations—carried out to such an extent that important branches of executive authority, such as police control, fire department administration, and the management of public works, are separately embodied.

The Views of the Fathers

The essential difference between the two systems in organic principle is not in the separate constitution of different powers of government, but in the fact that one system connects them while the other disconnects them. Is it contrary to the principles of the separation of powers to connect them? It is generally assumed that it is. While the point was not considered in the discussion attending the adoption of the programme of the National Municipal League, the tone of the discussion and the recommendations made assume that this principle requires the embodiment of executive and legislative authority in separate organs of government. Nevertheless, there is conclusive evidence that no such assumption was made by the framers of the Constitution of the United States, and indeed, that it is contrary to their ideas of the meaning of the principle of the separation of the powers. Their ideas are not to be inferred from the relations between the executive and the legislative departments as they now stand in our national government, for, as is well known to students of our constitutional history, they contemplated a much closer connection than that which now exists. It fortunately happens that this very point was discussed in the *Federalist*. In numbers 47 and 48 Madison argues that the principle of the separation of powers "does not require that the legislative, executive, and judiciary departments should be wholly unconnected with each other." Not content with this negative statement of the case, he goes on to say that "unless these departments be so far connected and blended as to give to each a constitutional control over the others, the degree of separation which the maxim requires, as essential to a free government, can never in practice be duly maintained." The profound truth of this observation is conspicuously attested by the present condition of government in this country. Any one possessing insight into actual conditions knows that executive and legislative functions are not really separate in practice. Members of legislative and city councils habitually extort surrender to them of executive function, especially as regards appointments to office, and are enabled to do so because the executive department, being disconnected from the legislative department, has no way of securing consideration of public business save by the favor of members. The same is true as regards the national government also, but presidential authority is a force of such high tension that it tends to establish a regular connection although subject to interruptions which cause jarring vibrations through the whole frame of government. The connection is, however, sufficiently constant to preserve the national government from the system of boss control which is the natural adjunct of state and municipal government. When those functions of government whose concerted action is essential to administration are connected, there is no room for the boss system, and it has never been developed under such circumstances. The conditions are such that actual control can be developed only inside the formal constitution of government and not outside of it. Hence in the municipal institutions of other countries having fairly representative institutions there appears, instead of the irresponsible boss ruling from the outside by combinations of class interest, the responsible leader basing his control upon the support of public opinion. The variation in the practical application of the principle of separate powers which has such disastrous results in the United States, so far from being constitutional doctrine, is the result of departure from it, and the consequence has been just as Madison predicted,—the destruction of constitutional separation in actual practice.

The Psychological Basis

Let us now proceed to consider the principle itself, to see whether analysis of its nature will enable us to determine how it should be construed. Professor Goodnow has suggested that it has a psychological foundation. He says:

"It is a distinction based upon a sound psychology. In the case of a single sentient being the will must be formulated, if not expressed, before its execution is possible. In the case of political bodies, which are more and more coming to be recognized as subject to psychological law, not only must the will or policy be formulated before it can be executed, but also the very complexity of their operations makes it almost impossible to intrust the same authority as well with the execution as with the determination of the public policy."[1]

Following out this line of reasoning, which is extremely valuable and suggestive, Professor Goodnow distinguishes between the formation of policy, which he regards as the legislative function, and the execution of policy or the administration function, and he concludes that these two functions should be separately constituted in any proper organization of government. "The failure to distinguish legislation from administration" he considers to be the root of trouble in our municipal institutions. The proper connection of these functions is not considered, but the subject is treated in a way which assumes that separation means also disconnection. This assumption, moreover, affects the statement of psychological principle which appears to have been unconsciously warped to fit the case. If we consider the volitional process it will be seen that while there is a separation of function it is not exactly such as Professor Goodnow has delineated. A man sees something he would like to buy, doubts whether he can afford it, decides to gratify his inclination, and makes the purchase. The totality of his action is made up of volitional and inhibitory impulses, but his resolution and the execution thereof are both stages of volition. The will participates in what Professor Goodnow designates as the policy-forming function, which, psychologically speaking, is not a function at all, but a process in which the volitional and inhibitory impulses participate in conjunction. The

1. *A Municipal Programme.* The Macmillan Co., page 74.

distinction suggested by psychological law is not between administration and legislation, but between administration and control, corresponding to the volitional and inhibitory functions of mental activity, and as those functions meet together in determinations of conduct, so administration and control should be connected in legislation.

If the organization of municipal government outside of the United States be examined, it will be found that it conforms to these psychological principles. Administration and control are separately constituted, but meet together in the city council. In practice, administrative experience furnishes the legislative impulse. The organs of administration conceive and mature the legislative proposals, a process conforming to the psychological law that perception is developed through the agency of special organs. The administration submits its legislative proposals to the city council, representing the function of control, assists deliberation by explanation and advice, and thus determinations of conduct are reached in strict conformity to psychological law, through the interaction of the volitional and inhibitory functions.

We have all about us illustrations of the same principle in the business world. There administration and control are invariably connected, distinguished as the management and the directory, which meet in determination of policy. It is the function of the management to plan the operations of the concern as well as execute them, subject to the approval of the board of directors. Is it a question of entering a new field, adopting new processes, enlarging the plant, providing fresh capital? The management conceives and formulates the measures and submits them to the board of directors for approval. What may be called the legislative initiative of the management is justly regarded as its most important and valuable function.

If, however, the organic connection of the separately constituted functions of administration and control is a principle founded upon psychological law, it must be immutable in its operation, whether or not it be recognized or provided for in the intentional structure of government. Although the generic type of American municipal institutions violates that principle, yet if the principle is sound the actual operations of government should conform to it. That is invariably what we do see if able to see things as they really are. The vital principle of the boss system is that it furnishes this connection between the executive and legislative departments. It has grown up in satisfaction of practical necessities of government, and it is peculiar to our institutions because they disconnect what must in some way or another be joined in carrying on administration. This is the secret of the normal tendency of municipal government towards corruption; it is so constituted that it cannot be carried on without corruption. In the national government this tendency is mitigated by the fact that executive authority has escaped the disintegration to which it has been subjected in State and municipal government. Functions which in the latter are separately constituted are in the national government united in one executive authority, making it so massive that it attracts legislative initiative despite the formal disconnection, and "the policy of the administration" is ordinarily the informing principle of legislative activity, but in this field also defect of regular connection is the source of continual evil.

The Course of Improvement

In further illustration of the operation of this principle despite failure to recognize it, observe that such reforms of municipal government as have resulted in real improvement have really connected the executive and legislative powers. The New York and Baltimore city charters are typical examples of this process. Both the formulation of public policy and the execution of public policy have been concentrated in the executive department which fixes the tax levy, frames the appropriations, determines the conditions and terms of legislative grants, and in general decides upon ways and means. A pretence is made of retaining the usual disconnection through the separate organization of the city council, but it has become an atrophied organ of government. While there is a formal reference to the city council of the determinations of the governing body, yet its authority is so reduced that all it amounts to is a limited veto power. It has become the practice of the New York city council to treat its authority frankly as such, allowing appropriations to become law by lapse of the time in which the city council has power to act, and interfering only for the purpose of negativing some particular appropriation when exertions of political influence temporarily energize council proceedings. The practical benefits of the system causes its violation of traditional theory to be ignored. The enormous gains it makes for the public in the granting of franchises has excited general notice and has stirred up angry agitations for like benefits in other cities, which, however, they will never secure until they adopt like methods. These gains are essentially economies introduced by dispensing with the boss and the machine as the basis of administrative connection. By abolishing their office, its emoluments have been turned into the public treasury. There is, however, a principle of evil still at work, in that the system, although a vast improvement over the old one, aggrandizes the administrative function at the expense of the function of control, which, lacking adequate expression in the organs of government, tends to pass outside of them to become part of the inorganic mass of public opinion, confused with popular prejudice and ignorance, operating blindly and spasmodically upon the conduct of government, and exposing it to violent alternations in character and tendency.

Summary of Conclusions Reached

In view of all these considerations, we must conclude that the truly remarkable thing about American institutions of government is not that they work so badly as that they should work so well. Owing to misconceptions which have hardened into political superstition our institutions have been subjected to conditions violating principles of government universally recognized and usually correctly applied except in the administration of public affairs. That with such defective organization a tolerable degree of administrative efficiency has been secured is the strongest possible proof of the great capacity of American character. This opinion is corroborated by the weighty authority of Bagehot, whose writings evince a rare combination of business sagacity and political insight. He remarked: "The Americans now extol their institutions, and so defraud themselves of their due praise; but if they had not a genius for politics, if they had not a moderation in action singularly curious where superficial speech is so violent, if they had not a regard for laws such as no great people have yet evinced, and infinitely surpassing ours, the multiplicity of authorities in the American constitution would long ago have brought it to a bad end."[2] The particular reference is to the organization of the national government, but it applies to all our institutions of government. The chief agency of the moderating influence which makes actual results endurable is that very spirit of commercialism against which sentimentalists are in the habit of inveighing. It establishes connections of interest which enfold the organs of government, and while it imparts to government a plutocratic character it interposes defences against disorder. When our institutions are imitated by countries in which the spirit of commercialism is not sufficiently developed to acquire political ascendency, chronic disorder is the result. In this way our political example has been a source of immense mischief in the politics of Central and South America. For the same reason, municipal institutions of the American type introduced into Porto Rico and the Philippines, where the commercial spirit is not strong and masterful enough to govern by corruption, will tend to generate fraud and violence as their political adjuncts. This may be asserted with the certainty of scientific deduction.

The results of our extended inquiry may be summarized as follows: The bad operation of American municipal government is due not to defect of popular character, but to defect in the organization of government. The organic defect lies in the fact that the executive and legislative departments, in addition to being separately constituted, are also disconnected, and this very disconnection has prevented in practice the degree of separation in their functions which their integrity requires, a

2. *The English Constitution.* Walter Bagehot. Chapter VIII.

consequence precisely what Madison predicted if separate powers are not duly connected in their operation. The remedy is therefore to be found in establishing a proper connection between the executive and the legislative organs of government, so as to make the functions of administration and control coextensive. No arrangement can secure this short of one which gives the executive department complete legislative initiative, and at the same time secures to the legislative department complete supervision over all administrative transactions. If this be accomplished, nominal relations or divisions are unimportant.

Who, or What, Started the Evil?

Lincoln Steffens

SAN FRANCISCO learned nothing from the graft prosecution, nothing but facts—no lessons that were applied either economically or politically. The fighting passion persisted. Francis J. Heney was hated and admired as a fighter and highly respected as a lawyer, but his practice was so damaged by the fear of the prejudice of the courts against him that he had to remove his office to Los Angeles. Fremont Older was punished by business men through his paper. The circulation had gone up and continued to grow as his change of policy from righteous wrath to mercy for the under dog became clear. Its advertising suffered, and his personal standing as an editor was attacked privately by the business men who finally drove the owners to get rid of him. Hearst called Older to his rival evening paper, the *Call*, which immediately began to rise till it passed and finally absorbed the *Bulletin*. William J. Burns had proved himself to the men he called sons of bitches so that when he organized a national detective bureau they joined it as subscribers. Hiram Johnson, as governor, put the railroad out of power for a while; he gave one of the most efficient administrations any State has ever had, was reelected, and then went to the U.S. Senate as the political reform boss of California. But there was no fundamental reform in the city or the State.

Were exposures useless? I could not at that time believe this. I went back to my theory that it was the threat of punishment which, by forcing men to defend themselves, put them in a state of mind where they could not see straight and learn. I wrote an article entitled "An Apology for Graft," showing that our economic system, which held up riches, power and acclaim as prizes to men bold enough and able enough to buy corruptly timber, mines, oil fields, and franchises and "get away with it," was at fault, and that San Francisco's graft trials showed that; and showed that we should change the system and meanwhile let the crooks go, who would confess and tell us the truth. The

Reprinted from The Autobiography of Lincoln Steffens, *pp. 570–574, copyright, 1931, by Harcourt, Brace & World, Inc.; renewed, 1959, by Peter Steffens. Reprinted by permission of the publishers.*

only reaction I got from the article was the wonder of good citizens and liberals whether I had sold out and gone back on reform!

Then it occurred to me to go to Los Angeles to see if that city had learned anything from the sight of San Francisco exposed. No one down there had been threatened with punishment; they had only to look on and see themselves in the fix of the San Franciscans. I called on Dr. John R. Haynes, a rich, very kind veteran reformer, who understands economics and men pretty well. He took me into the swell Jonathan Club, introduced me to some public service corporation men; others that I knew came up, and soon there was a group of "knowing" Los Angeles business leaders deploring the conditions of politics and business in San Francisco. They were cheerful about it. There was a self-congratulatory note in their grief at the shame of San Francisco, poor San Francisco. Los Angeles was, fortunately, not like that. I thought they were joking.

"Wait a minute," I said. "You have been having your sport with me, a San Franciscan. It's my turn now. You know, don't you; I know you know, and you know that I know, that Los Angeles is in the same condition as San Francisco. The only difference is that San Francisco has been, and Los Angeles has not been, shown up."

Silence. Uneasiness, but no denial. I waited for the street railway or gas men to think, and one of them did mutter something about "another difference, San Francisco had a Labor government."

"Labor government!" I exclaimed, and I reminded them that that Labor government had sold out to capital and represented business.

Again no denial, only silence. They knew. They had forgotten. They wished to forget, to ignore what they knew. They had no fear of punishment, but they had learned no more from the experience of San Francisco than the San Franciscans had.

"I'll tell you what I'll do," I said into their silence. "If you will call a closed meeting somewhere soon and invite only yourselves, and your wives, and your associates, fellow directors, managers, attorneys, and— and your priests and their wives, no outsiders at all—I will show you that you yourselves should want, at the least, the public ownership of all public utilities and natural resources."

They laughed; it was partly the laugh of relief. The tension of my accusations had been unclublike. They laughed and we broke up, but they accepted my challenge. They would have a little dinner and eat me up.

Dr. Haynes managed the affair very well. He had the right kind of people there, some hundred or more. No outsiders. Nobody to enjoy and spoil the debate by making us conscious of a contest. It was a conversation. The arrangement was that I was to state my thesis and argument in a short twenty minutes, after which any one of the company might challenge any point of mine, preferably in the form of a question. But I asked leave to answer each question before another spoke. No objections.

I restated my thesis. My argument was a narrative, my own story. I had gone forth, thinking what they thought, that bad men caused bad government, especially politicians. Having to see them for information, I found politicians to be not bad men; they were pretty good fellows. They blamed the bad business men who, they said, bribed them.

Who, then, were those bad business men? They named them, each in his city, and as I saw them they were not bad, but they were always in the same businesses. Regardless of character, education, and station, the people in these businesses were in the corruption of politics and the resistance to reform. This suggested that it was these businesses, not the men in them, that were the cause of our evil. And that's what they told me. They did not like or wish or mean, they said they "had to" do evil. I could not for a long time believe this. It sounded like a weak excuse when a big, powerful captain of industry declared that the bad politicians "held him up" and struck him for a bribe or a contribution to a campaign fund. It was only after going through many cities and States and hearing always the same plea of compulsion that I was persuaded at last that it is true.

"You cannot build or operate a railroad," I said, "or a street railway, gas, water, or power company, develop and operate a mine, or get forests and cut timber on a large scale, or run any privileged business, without corrupting or joining in the corruption of the government. You tell me privately that you must, and here I am telling you semi-publicly that you must. And that is so all over the country. And that means that we have an organization of society in which, for some reason, you and your kind, the ablest, most intelligent, most imaginative, daring, and resourceful leaders of society, are and must be against society and its laws and its all-around growth."

My conclusion was that we all of us, they as well as I—they more than I—should seek to rid all individuals of those things that make them work against the greater, common welfare.

The first question from that company, and the last, was, "Who started the evil?" I reminded them that the question should be what, not who, and that everything they believed would be brought together by the answer. If it was some Thing that hurt us we could be Christians and forgive sinners; we could cease from punishing men and develop an environment in which men would be tempted to be good. No use; those business men wanted me to admit that the politicians made the conditions that business men were subject to. I related how the San Francisco banker, William H. Crocker, had argued that he had to do business under conditions as he found them, and I had reminded him that his father and the rest of the Big Four who built the Central Pacific Railroad were blamed by the politicians for corrupting the State and making the conditions he, the son and successor, "had to" continue.

Somebody mentioned the fear that government operation was always inefficient. I cited Seattle, where a publicly owned power plant was breaking down so often that there was an investigation, and they learned that the private competitors had paid certain political employees to sabotage the city's plant.

Another voice asked if the public operation of utilities would not put them into politics. To answer that, I turned to William Mulholland, the popular, highly respected engineer, who was the manager of the city's water system. He had been the manager when the water company was a private corporation, and it was notorious that he was then a very active and efficient politician. Everybody in that room knew that Mr. Mulholland had said over and over again that the change from private to public operation had got him and the business out of politics. When I passed the question of politics to him he did not have to answer. The whole company burst into laughter.

There were other questions, other arguments against business in politics, which I learned in college. But the ever-recurring question that night was Who? Who started it? Who is to be blamed and—punished? And at last, the Episcopal bishop of that diocese stated it in a form that suggested an answer. I was emphasizing the point that society really offers a prize for evil-doing: money, position, power. "Let's take down the offer of a reward," I said. "Let's abolish—privileges."

The bishop rose and very kindly, very courteously said that he felt that I was not meeting the minds of my hearers. "What we want to know," he said, "is who founded this system, who started it, not only in San Francisco and Los Angeles, in this or the last generation, but back, 'way back, in the beginning."

"Oh, I think I see," I said. "You want to fix the fault at the very start of things. Maybe we can, Bishop. Most people, you know, say it was Adam. But Adam, you remember, he said that it was Eve, the woman; she did it. And Eve said no, no, it wasn't she; it was the serpent. And that's where you clergy have stuck ever since. You blame that serpent, Satan. Now I come and I am trying to show you that it was, it is, the apple."

The bishop sat down. You could hear him sit down. For there was silence, a long moment, and in that silence the meeting adjourned.

The Class Basis
of the Reform Ideal

Jane Addams

IT IS DIFFICULT both to interpret sympathetically the motives and ideals of those who have acquired rules of conduct in experience widely different from our own, and also to take enough care in guarding the gains already made, and in valuing highly enough the imperfect good so painfully acquired and, at the best, so mixed with evil. This wide difference in daily experience exhibits itself in two distinct attitudes toward politics. The well-to-do men of the community think of politics as something off by itself; they may conscientiously recognize political duty as part of good citizenship, but political effort is not the expression of their moral or social life. As a result of this detachment, "reform movements," started by business men and the better element, are almost wholly occupied in the correction of political machinery and with a concern for the better method of administration, rather than with the ultimate purpose of securing the welfare of the people. They fix their attention so exclusively on methods that they fail to consider the final aims of city government. This accounts for the growing tendency to put more and more responsibility upon executive officers and appointed commissions at the expense of curtailing the power of the direct representatives of the voters. Reform movements tend to become negative and to lose their educational value for the mass of the people. The reformers take the role of the opposition. They give themselves largely to criticisms of the present state of affairs, to writing and talking of what the future must be and of certain results which should be obtained. In trying to better matters, however, they have in mind only political achievements which they detach in a curious way from the rest of life, and they speak and write of the purification of politics as of a thing set apart from daily life.

On the other hand, the real leaders of the people are part of the entire life of the community which they control, and so far as they are

Reprinted from Democracy and Social Ethics (*New York: The Macmillan Company, 1902*), *pp. 222–227, 257–260, and 266–271.*

representative at all, are giving a social expression to democracy. They are often politically corrupt, but in spite of this they are proceeding upon a sounder theory. Although they would be totally unable to give it abstract expression, they are really acting upon a formulation made by a shrewd English observer; namely, that, "after the enfranchisement of the masses, social ideals enter into political programmes, and they enter not as something which at best can be indirectly promoted by government, but as something which it is the chief business of government to advance directly."

Men living near to the masses of voters, and knowing them intimately, recognize this and act upon it; they minister directly to life and to social needs. They realize that the people as a whole are clamoring for social results, and they hold their power because they respond to that demand. They are corrupt and often do their work badly; but they at least avoid the mistake of a certain type of business men who are frightened by democracy, and have lost faith in the people. The two standards are similar to those seen at a popular exhibition of pictures where the cultivated people care most for the technique of a given painting, the moving mass for a subject that shall be domestic and human.

This difference may be illustrated by the writer's experience in a certain ward of Chicago, during three campaigns, when efforts were made to dislodge an alderman who had represented the ward for many years. In this ward there are gathered together fifty thousand people, representing a score of nationalities; the newly emigrated Latin, Teuton, Celt, Greek, and Slav who live there have little in common save the basic experiences which come to men in all countries and under all conditions. In order to make fifty thousand people, so heterogeneous in nationality, religion, and customs, agree upon any demand, it must be founded upon universal experiences which are perforce individual and not social.

An instinctive recognition of this on the part of the alderman makes it possible to understand the individualistic basis of his political success, but it remains extremely difficult to ascertain the reasons for the extreme leniency of judgment concerning the political corruption of which he is constantly guilty.

This leniency is only to be explained on the ground that his constituents greatly admire individual virtues, and that they are at the same time unable to perceive social outrages which the alderman may be committing. They thus free the alderman from blame because his corruption is social, and they honestly admire him as a great man and hero, because his individual acts are on the whole kindly and generous.

In certain stages of moral evolution, a man is incapable of action unless the results will benefit himself or some one of his acquaintances, and it is a long step in moral progress to set the good of the many before the interest of the few, and to be concerned for the welfare of a community without hope of an individual return. How far the selfish politician befools his constituents into believing that their interests are identical with his own; how far he presumes upon their inability to distinguish between the individual and social virtues, an inability which he himself shares with them; and how far he dazzles them by the sense of his greatness, and a conviction that they participate therein, it is difficult to determine. . . .

That the alderman has much to do with setting the standard of life and desirable prosperity may be illustrated by the following incident: During one of the campaigns a clever cartoonist drew a poster representing the successful alderman in portraiture drinking champagne at a table loaded with pretentious dishes and surrounded by revellers. In contradistinction was his opponent, a bricklayer, who sat upon a half-finished wall, eating a meagre dinner from a workingman's dinner-pail, and the passer-by was asked which type of representative he preferred, the presumption being that at least in a workingman's district the bricklayer would come out ahead. To the chagrin of the reformers, however, it was gradually discovered that, in the popular mind, a man who laid bricks and wore overalls was not nearly so desirable for an alderman as the man who drank champagne and wore a diamond in his shirt front. The district wished its representative "to stand up with the best of them," and certainly some of the constituents would have been ashamed to have been represented by a bricklayer. It is part of that general desire to appear well, the optimistic and thoroughly American belief, that even if a man is working with his hands to-day, he and his children will quite likely be in a better position in the swift coming to-morrow, and there is no need of being too closely associated with common working people. There is an honest absence of class consciousness, and a naive belief that the kind of occupation quite largely determines social position. This is doubtless exaggerated in a neighborhood of foreign people by the fact that as each nationality becomes more adapted to American conditions, the scale of its occupation rises. Fifty years ago in America "a Dutchman" was used as a term of reproach, meaning a man whose language was not understood, and who performed menial tasks, digging sewers and building railroad embankments. Later the Irish did the same work in the community, but as quickly as possible handed it on to the Italians, to whom the name "dago" is said to cling as a result of the digging which the Irishman resigned to him. The Italian himself is at last waking up to this fact. In a political speech recently made by an Italian padrone, he bitterly reproached the alderman for giving the-four-dollars-a-day "jobs" of sitting in an office to Irishmen and the-dollar-and-a-half-a-day "jobs" of sweeping the streets to the Italians. This general struggle to rise in life, to be at least politically represented by one of the best, as to occupation and social status, has also its negative side. We must remember that the imitative impulse plays an important part in life, and that the loss of social estimation, keenly felt by all of us, is perhaps most dreaded by the humblest, among whom freedom of individual conduct, the power to give only just weight to the opinion of neighbors, is but feebly developed. A form of constraint, gentle, but powerful, is afforded by the simple desire to do what others do, in order to share with them the approval of the community. Of course, the larger the number of people among whom an habitual mode of conduct obtains, the greater the constraint it puts upon the individual will. Thus it is that the political corruption of the city presses most heavily where it can be least resisted, and is most likely to be imitated. . . .

A reformer who really knew the people and their great human needs, who believed that it was the business of government to serve them, and who further recognized the educative power of a sense of responsibility, would possess a clew by which he might analyze the situation. He would find out what needs, which the alderman supplies, are legitimate ones which the city itself could undertake, in counter-distinction to those which pander to the lower instincts of the constituency. A mother who eats her Christmas turkey in a reverent spirit of thankfulness to the alderman who gave it to her, might be gradually brought to a genuine sense of appreciation and gratitude to the city which supplies her little children with a Kindergarten, or, to the Board of Health which properly placarded a case of scarlet fever next door and spared her sleepless nights and wearing anxiety, as well as the money paid with such difficulty to the doctor and the druggist. The man who in his emotional gratitude almost kneels before a political friend who gets his boy out of jail might be made to see the kindness and good sense of the city authorities who provided the boy with a playground and reading room, where he might spend his hours of idleness and restlessness, and through which his temptations to petty crime might be averted. A man who is grateful to the alderman who sees that his gambling and racing are not interfered with, might learn to feel loyal and responsible to the city which supplied him with a gymnasium and swimming tank where manly and well-conducted sports are possible. The voter who is eager to serve the alderman at all times, because the tenure of his job is dependent upon aldermanic favor, might find great relief and pleasure in working for the city in which his place was secured by a well-administered civil service law.

After all, what the corrupt alderman demands from his followers and largely depends upon is a sense of loyalty, a standing-by the man who is good to you, who understands you, and who gets you out of trouble. All the social life of the voter from the time he was a little boy and played "craps" with his "own push," and not with some other "push," has been founded on this sense of loyalty and of standing in with his friends. Now that he is a man, he likes the sense of being inside a political organization, of being trusted with political gossip, of belonging to a set of fellows who understand things, and whose interests are being cared for by a strong friend in the city council itself. All this is perfectly legitimate, and all in the line of the development of a strong civic loyalty, if it were merely socialized and enlarged. . . .

Would it be dangerous to conclude that the corrupt politician himself, because he is democratic in method, is on a more ethical line of social development than the reformer, who believes that the people might be made over by "good citizens" and governed by "experts"? The former at least are engaged in that great moral effort of getting the mass to express itself, and of adding this mass energy and wisdom to the community as a whole.

The wide divergence of experience makes it difficult for the good citizen to understand this point of view, and many things conspire to make it hard for him to act upon it. He is more or less a victim to that curious feeling so often possessed by the good man, that the righteous do not need to be agreeable, that their goodness alone is sufficient, and that they can leave the arts and wiles of securing popular favor to the self-seeking. This results in a certain repellent manner, commonly regarded as the apparel of righteousness, and is further responsible for the fatal mistake of making the surroundings of "good influences" singularly unattractive; a mistake which really deserves a reprimand quite as severe as the equally reprehensible deed of making the surroundings of "evil influences" so beguiling. Both are akin to that state of mind which narrows the entrance into a wider morality to the eye of a needle, and accounts for the fact that new moral movements have ever and again been inaugurated by those who have found themselves in revolt against the conventionalized good.

The Locus of Corruption Has Changed

Edward N. Costikyan

JUST AS OUR IDEAS about good city government are largely the product of confusing a symptom of bad government with its cause, so our defenses against the symptom of bad government—corruption—are the product of the same confusion. In narrow obedience to our tradition, the principal defense against corruption continues to be an attempt to keep political leaders out of the government process. Nothing more is thought necessary to mind the store.

This defense presupposes that political leaders as a group are less honest and more likely to engage in nefarious conduct than other groups such as lawyers, businessmen, and civil servants. The evidence to support this assumption is flimsy at best. I do not have the statistics, but I suspect that the percentage of political leaders convicted of crime is far less than the percentage of political leaders in the population. It is not, for example, unusual to read in the press of businessmen or lawyers or doctors convicted of income-tax evasion or some other crime of corruption. The back pages usually suffice to carry this not unusual news. But let a charge of corruption be even leveled at a political leader and it is front-page news. Even the prominence accorded to such news is not sufficient in itself to justify the assumption that underlies our defenses against government corruption: that the political leaders are the likeliest causes of the disease.

I reject this assumption.

In my experience it is not true.

That is not to say that all political leaders are honest and incorruptible. They are not, and I know they are not, but I reject the popular assumption about the frail honesty of political leaders, even though I acknowledge that they, like all human beings, are corruptible and from time to time are corrupted.

Indeed, the last thing a serious practitioner of the political process can afford is to be naive about the possibility of corruption. There is nothing worse than having your own people stealing behind your back.

If they do steal, the defect, while hardly yours at law, does not make them less your people in the public's eye. And the public—though it may forget and forgive—will not be wrong. They were your people. You put them there. That you called the police, and they were fined and their offices cleaned out as soon as possible, does not quite take the smell out of the air. For his own effectiveness, then, as well as for his own self-respect, the politician may never forget that men and women who can be corrupted are always in sufficient supply.

A serious politician allows his power to be exercised by subordinates only so long as he trusts them. The flow of power to a subordinate responds with the utmost delicacy to the eddies of disquiet which corruption—or the suspicion of it—inevitably sets in motion.

It is not a particular group of people that is the magnet which attracts corrupters. Power, and power alone, attracts. The natural locus of corruption is *always* where the discretionary power resides. It follows that in an era when political leaders exercised basic power over the government officials whom they controlled, the locus of corruption was in the offices of the political bosses—Tweed, Croker, Kelly, and the rest. But as power has shifted from the political leader to the civil servant and the public officeholder, so the locus of corruptibility and of corruption has shifted. The evidence demonstrates this clearly, and yet little attention is paid to the evidence, because the old myths and preconceptions are too strong.

Let us first put aside the few cases that invite public attention because the items involved are so easily understood. For example, an Oriental rug given to a political official is something the ordinary voter comprehends. Many millions of dollars in a Dixon-Yates contract (involving no political leaders) is not. A bathtub given to a political leader is understood. A television-antenna franchise awarded to businessmen is not. A deep-freeze given to a political leader is understood. Stocking a substantial part of a retired general's farm with cattle from wealthy friends is not. But the deep-freezes and the vicuna coats and the bathtubs and the Oriental rugs are not the great danger to honest government. It is the relationship reflected by these gifts that causes the problem.

The question of whether Sherman Adams used his public power to help his friend Bernard Goldfine is more disturbing than the hospitality enjoyed and gifts received by Adams. Indeed, these gifts are neither the stuff with which corruption is accomplished, nor the subject matter of political deals. The real corrupters rarely leave tangible evidence of where they have been and what they have sought.

Those who seek the benefit of licit and illicit government favors are nothing if not perfectly attuned to shifts in power, and they instinctively go where the power is. What needs to be made clear is that the power is no longer in the hands of political leaders. It has been transferred to the hands of public officials and civil servants long since.

So why deal through a political leader when you can go direct to the source of power? Why contribute to the party when you get more consideration by making your contribution to the candidate himself? Why deal with secondary sources when the primary source is an independent, uncontrolled civil servant?

When a parking-meter company's public relations expert sought to create a "bribe plot," in order, as it later developed, to pocket the bribe himself, the person whose name he invoked as the recipient of the bribe was a former career civil servant, then high in the city government, not a political leader. In 1961, one newspaper, intent upon attempting to discredit the Wagner administration, ran a box-score of "scandals" day after day; I remember that it got as high as twenty-one or twenty-two "scandals." With *one* exception, every one of the "scandals" involved civil servants, not political leaders or appointees. By the same token, Republican strategists, in early 1965, before Congressman John Lindsay decided to run for mayor, were reported to be disheartened at the prospects of "fusion" because fusion had never succeeded in the absence of widespread *political* scandals.

Does the absence of political scandal mean there is no corruption? Of course not. It means that corruption has taken new forms and found a new locus.

By "corruption" I mean not only the use of a consideration such as money to persuade government to do something it shouldn't, although that is one form of corruption. There are other forms: The exercise of discretion to award a government privilege to an old friend as against an equally or better qualified applicant is a form of corruption. The tender treatment of a regulated industry by a regulatory commission whose members look to an ultimate future in private industry is a form of it. In short, corruption is the exercise of governmental power to achieve nongovernmental objectives.

From the point of view of the public and competing aspirants, what difference does it make whether the consideration for such an exercise of power is cash, or friendship, or future campaign contributions, or a future job, or nothing?

For example, since World War II a massive government sponsored housing program has been carried on almost continuously in one form or another. The essence of the slum-clearance program has been to encourage private enterprise by almost guaranteeing builders a substantial profit and perhaps a windfall. The essence of the program— "Title I" or "urban renewal"—is for government to acquire slum properties at market value and resell them (or make them available) to private builders or sponsors at a lower cost. The subsidy is supposed to permit the construction of housing that will rent—or in the case of co-operatives, sell—at lower prices than would otherwise obtain.

The rule is that the sponsor is selected through the exercise of discretion among a host of applicants who are for all measurable purposes equally qualified. Why is A selected, instead of B or C, to sponsor or build such a development? There is no public bidding; no objective measure of who ought to be selected is applied.

Under current practices a "project" for a given area is developed by government officials and approved. A "sponsor" of the development, who is in charge of carrying it out and controls it, is then selected by government officials. The sponsor selects a builder, an architect, a lawyer, an accountant, insurance broker, and all of the rest of the retinue needed to build a complex of buildings, hires them through a corporation organized to build the project, secures financing, and sees that the development is created.

The power to designate these participants is a valuable one. The architect, the lawyer, the insurance broker, may be prepared to share their profits with the source of business. The possibilities for profit to the sponsor are substantial. Certainly the builder, the lawyers, the architect, and the insurance broker are all well compensated.

"Title I," urban renewal's predecessor, was administered by Robert Moses, that conspicuous agent of good government. He and his varied Public Authorities, accountable to no one ("since there are no politicians involved, it must be honest, so why should it have to account?") are a monument to the anti-political good-government tradition of "keep the politicians out and it will be okay."

Moses' administration of Title I was so unsatisfactory that the program was killed. If a political leader had made one-tenth of the mistakes Moses made in that program alone, he would have been destroyed, defeated, out of business. Arbitrariness; designation of favored associates for choice patronage, high salaries, limousines, and chauffeurs; and invulnerability to any requirement of public accountability or auditing of accounts are the earmarks of an entrenched machine. Moses' Public Authorities have them all.

Moses' reward for so directing his many enterprises has been continuing editorial adulation, new jobs, constant praise, and finally the opportunity to run the greatest boondoggle of them all, the 1964–65 New York World's Fair—again, because he is politically pure and deemed to be "efficient."

The potential for abuse in such a set-up could not have escaped the attention of those who seek the pleasures of governmental favor. Who would not prefer the favors of an anonymous Public Authority, which is not subject to public accountability, to the friendship of a political boss. (Moses' critics have repeatedly suggested that his authorities should be subjected to methodical public examination. All to no avail.)

Probably the reason is Moses' accepted and undisputed personal honesty in money matters. But this begs the question. Personal honesty is the *first* requirement for public service, not the only one. And, as noted above, corruption as I have used the term does not require cash as a consideration. There are subtler and more utilitarian forms— future support, campaign contributions, honorific appointments, even ill-defined debts and obligations available for later redemption, or merely old friendships—or whim!

The irregularities in the Moses operation of Title I are well documented elsewhere. Their significance, however, as a demonstration of the new locus of corruption has been generally disregarded–except, I suspect, by the corrupters.

What of Title I's successor—urban renewal? Here again a sponsorship is a valuable asset. Anyone schooled in traditional notions about good government would expect to find the politician's heavy hand allocating sponsorships and designating builders, architects, and the like.

There were political leaders involved in the process, but as supplicants for favors, not dispensers of them. My successor as county leader, J. Raymond Jones, a Harlem political leader, was the most notable of these. Jones's dealings in urban renewal projects—he became a sponsor of at least one major project—came to light when he and Congressman Adam Clayton Powell had a falling out about one project, and a lawsuit was started in which Powell claimed that a sponsorship which was to have been awarded to a company in which they were both interested was at the last moment awarded to a company in which Jones was interested but Powell was not.

Decisions on sponsorships of these projects were made on the very highest level of city government—not by any political leaders. The political leaders, except occasionally as supplicants, played no role in the process. But I cannot believe that their absence rendered the projects $99^{44}/_{100}$ percent pure. For the discretionary power to designate sponsors carries with it all the conditions that inevitably lead to "influence" and influence-peddling. If indeed these sponsorships have value, why shouldn't they be *sold* by government to the highest bidder, instead of given away? If an FCC license to operate a television station is of great value, why not have the government *sell* it, instead of giving it to one of half a dozen equally qualified applicants?

The gift of public privileges by government officials on a discretionary basis in the absence of public bidding is the greatest source of corruption, quasi-corruption, influence-peddling, and demeaning of the governmental process in America today. That distribution of public largess is more and more nonpolitical does not make it any better. Indeed, as in so many other cases, the division of power between political leaders and public officeholders might tend to diminish the opportunities for overt corruption in the dispensation of such government favors. But the greatest preventive would be to charge for the value of the government privileges being dispensed.

A classic example of the whole problem is the tale of the television-antenna franchise in New York City, which briefly attracted public attention in the spring of 1965. Six applicants sought the privilege of running master television antennas beneath New York City's streets, and charging residents at stipulated rates for connecting into the master antenna and thus securing first-rate reception. In some areas of the city where high buildings block reception (especially public housing projects), such a service was badly needed.

The proposed charges and rates varied from a $60 connection charge to $19.95, and from $20 a month service fee to $4.50. Some of the applicants had had extensive prior experience in operating such systems and some had not. Lo and behold, the two approved franchisers had the least experience and the highest charges of all the applicants. According to the New York *World-Telegram and Sun*, one of the two successful applicants had some unexplained connection with a former legislative representative and close confidant of the mayor. This mayoral friend had been involved in the process of securing the franchise. The other successful applicant was a firm headed by another old mayoral friend. Both had cut their proposed fees (although they were still well above those of the other applicants). What is more, according to the New York *World-Telegram and Sun*, the cuts had been made by the head of the Bureau of Franchises at the *mayor's* suggestion. No political leaders were involved in any way with the successful applicants (what a departure from the days of Boss Tweed!), so it was okay. One unsuccessful applicant was represented by the law firm to which New York County's former law chairman belonged. And one of my partners—by then I had retired as a political leader—represented another unsuccessful applicant.

If the myths were true, should not the ex-Tammany law chairman's client and the ex-county-leader's partner's client have triumphed—especially since their rates were lowest and their experience greatest?

The point, it seems to me, is clear. The pathway to government preference no longer passes through Tammany Hall or the internal political leader's office. It goes direct to the source. This phenomenon of modern urban government has hardly been noted by the theorists or the specialists in good government. They seem to be so convinced that civil service and growth of the public officeholder's independence have created such impregnable fortresses of rectitude that they have devoted all their attention when discussing corruption to looking for political leaders in the governmental process. Noting their absence, the good-government forces viewing a veritable parade of nude emperors have been satisfied that corruption has disappeared.

Indeed, not long ago this preconception so dominated the thinking of those investigating the city government that they laid a colossal egg. In 1959 the state legislature created a "Little Hoover Commission" to investigate New York City. The commission's activities were supposed to expose enough political corruption to lay the basis for a 1961 fusion movement to defeat Mayor Wagner. The Commission and its staff honestly believed, I think, that New York City was beset by the same conditions of political corruption that had laid the basis for the 1933 election of La Guardia. The staff apparently immersed itself in the literature of corruption, particularly that revealed by the Seabury Commission, which uncovered and documented the shenanigans of the political leaders of the 1930's. They had fixed judges and commissioners, sold contracts, and generally operated the city through the public officeholder nominees they controlled. (When one of their designees, Mayor O'Brien, was asked in 1933 who his police commissioner would be, he replied: "I don't know. They haven't told me yet." And he was telling the truth!) But thirty years later, the pattern wasn't there. The corruption was among civil servants—usually lowly ones—and it was minor nickels-and-dimes stuff, not the classic corruption of the Tweed era.

Yet, obsessed by their preconceptions about what *ought* to be wrong (i.e., crooked politicans, not dishonest civil servants), the investigators never realized that what had been established was a shift in the nature and locus of corruption from the socially despicable politician middleman to the socially acceptable reform product—the civil servant, the career government servant, the elected public official who was free of domination by the machine. What had happened was that the corrupters, like water, had found their own level—underpaid and frustrated civil servants who yearned for a more affluent life, or ambitious public officeholders hoping to make affluent friends upon whom they could call when campaign funds were needed.

The frustrated civil servants do not represent any real threat to government. Their number is low and the graft is comparatively small, and no serious student of government would attribute to this kind of activity the manifold faults of modern urban misgovernment.

Of course, petty corruption remains a heavy burden to the person who must endure it. The construction of buildings in New York, for example, is still reported to involve substantial amounts in ten- and twenty-dollar payments to inspectors. How much of this gets to the inspector and how much is an excuse for the builder to get a little tax-free income ("petty cash" in his books) is anyone's guess.

But several things are clear. First, the supposition that such bribery exists, whether the supposition is true or not, saps popular confidence in government. Second, none of the principal defenses built up to protect government from corruption—the isolation and elimination of the politician from government—have had any success in eliminating the occasional bribery of civil servants.

My own belief is that the amount of such corruption is exaggerated, that the overwhelming bulk of civil servants are honest and that, like politicians, they have about the same percentage of corruptible people as the population at large—or less.

The real threat posed by corruption to good government is the fact that, as the form and locus of corruption has shifted from the middle-man politician to the civil servant or elected official, so has the technique of receiving discretionary governmental largess.

The corrupter seeking to lease the Brooklyn Bridge for a dollar a year in exchange for $100,000 in cash, or engaged in an effort to accomplish such misbehavior, is a political and governmental joke. Nobody pays any attention to him. Moreover, the political graft of the Tweed and post-Tweed eras—liquor, prostitution, police protection and the like—is simply nonexistent (unless it is a direct deal between criminal and civil-servant policemen).

"Graft" today, if it can be called that, is the kind described by George Washington Plunkitt as "honest graft"—only now it is more "honest" by far. In short, the political plums today are nonpolitical: urban-renewal projects, contracts to build schools and public buildings and roads and sewers, franchises to install community television antenna systems, and what have you—all involving government funds or privileges, with contracts given for value received with built-in profit of varying amounts, and all disbursed on a *discretionary* basis.

When the time comes to raise funds for the public officeholder who dispensed that favor, or this sponsorship, he has a ready-made list of potential contributors, just as Charles Murphy and Boss Tweed and their predecessors did—the recipients of discretionary public largess.

Should a portrait be painted and presented to the city? Run down the list! And before you know it a patron has hired a portraitist. The patron, moreover, has a tax-deduction. He is, of course, a public benefactor, not a political wheeler-dealer.

Sometimes the cloak of purity achieved through association with public officeholders instead of dirty political leaders reaches ridiculous proportions. For example, one prominent citizen, who, unlike the late Vice-President Alben Barkley, would far rather "sit at the feet of the mighty" than be a "servant of the Lord" is famed for his ability to move fireplugs on Park Avenue. The basis of his celebrity arises from the desire of Park Avenue building managements to have a "no parking" area near their front doors, so that tenants don't have to crawl between parked cars as they come and go. The best way to achieve this is to have a fire hydrant right next to the awning—that guarantees twelve feet of "no parking" on each side of it.

And so this scion of civic virtue specializes in securing fireplug movements in exchange for long-term retainers. He accomplishes these results (and Park Avenue's fireplugs have seen a fair amount of movement lately) not because of any relation with political leaders, but because of his nonpolitical, good-government status and his close friendships with significant public officeholders.

The locus of corruption is always where unrestrained power exists. The political leaders present function in the scheme of corruption is to be a scapegoat, who shields the self-styled public vindicator of political morality from public scrutiny. After all, so long as the "bosses" exist, their opponents, being saints, should be protected. So long as the political leaders are excluded from the process, why is it necessary to inquire why fire hydrants are moved or how urban-renewal-project sponsorships are allocated?

Of course, I am sufficiently skeptical to be unable to believe that corruption will be eliminated from the conduct of human affairs, either by eliminating the power of political leaders or by restoring their power to what it once was. But I do believe there are ways to minimize the improper exercise of governmental power—ways that would make it more difficult for the corrupter to corrupt and easier to uncover him and his activities.

The first step is to realize that the locus of corruption is where the power is. The second is to destroy the stereotypes that brand the political leader as thief and the public official as saint. The third is to eliminate the discretionary distribution of governmental privileges—Title I housing projects, urban-renewal sponsorships (and construction contracts), public architecture contracts, and so on—without competition for either quality (where the arts are involved) or quantity (where money is involved).

Is there any good reason why every architect who wants to should not submit a design for a school or a courthouse and have the winning design selected on the basis of the merit, utility, and decent cost ratios of the design, and not because of the name attached to it? Why should not an urban-renewal sponsorship, worth a million dollars to the sponsor, be awarded on the basis of price paid to the city, instead of unexplained "discretion"?

The reason why such discretion is granted to public officials—especially the "nonpolitical" ones—is the public supposition that since they are outside the traditional political structure, they, rather than the politician, should have power—and by some magic, rectitude will be achieved.

What has happened is that a new politics has been created, certainly no better and in some ways worse than the politics this "nonpolitical" politics has replaced. It is indeed time to re-examine the post-Tweed-era assumptions which have led to this new form of urban mismanagement.

The ideas I am suggesting seem at first blush to be radical, perhaps half-baked, certainly unusual. But it seems clear to me that in a city where the power is in the bureaucracy, the locus of corruption must also be there. And the discretionary exercise of power by bureaucrats is to be feared and needs to be dealt with at least as much as—probably far more than—the venality of Boss Tweed's successors.

IV

"Good Government"

"GOOD government" is put in quotation marks because for more than a hundred years it has been part of the jargon of the municipal reform movement. (In Lincoln Steffens' day reformers were called "goo-goos" by unregenerate boodlers because they used the words so much.) In the jargon, good government meant government that was honest, impartial, and efficient—the kind of government that would exist (so the reformers thought) once the machines were destroyed, "petty politicians" driven out, and public-spirited citizens like themselves elected to office. Good government in this sense was neither very democratic nor very much concerned with the needs and wishes of the low-income and low-status elements of the community. But whereas to the reformers the machine represented evil, good government represented virtue.

The ideal of "good government" was a class ideal, of course. As Jane Addams explained in a reading in the previous section, there is wide difference in the moral perspective of middle- and of lower-class voters. The lower class thinks of "goodness" in terms of some advantage for the individual or the family, whereas the middle class thinks of it in terms of the community or some larger abstract public. From the standpoint of the middle-class ethic, characteristically that of native Yankee-Protestants and Jews, the task of government is to serve the "community as a whole." Implicit in this idea is the notion that the community is an entity that has ends or purposes different from those of the individuals who comprise it. In this view, the ends of individuals

267

—indeed, of all private, local, or partial interests—should be subordinated to the "community as a whole." Therefore politics, instead of being a competitive struggle among partial interests, ought to be a cooperative search for the implications of communal interests. In this search the expert—one who is both disinterested and possessed of special technical qualifications—should play a leading, and perhaps a decisive, part.

It will be seen that this conception of politics implies an altogether different set of institutional arrangements than does the individualistic, lower-class conception. It implies nonpartisanship (for the interest of a party is less than, and therefore opposed to, that of the "community as a whole"), election at-large rather than on a ward basis, and a strong, independent executive who will ignore special interests and assert his "impartial" conception of the interest of the "community as a whole." The nonpartisan election system and the council-manager form of government are both expressions of these general principles. Proportional representation, which the promoters of the council-manager plan tried for a time to link with it, did not fit this underlying logic, and, as Don K. Price explains, never had the popularity of the other reforms.

The middle-class, Yankee-Protestant belief that government is mainly a matter of honest, impartial, and efficient pursuit of the interest of the "community as a whole" (and not at all one getting petty favors, protection, or advantage for one's family, ethnic group, or ward) leads, of course, to a conception of government as "administration," or the businesslike conduct of service functions, rather than as "politics," or the management of conflict. It is not surprising, therefore, to find a conservative like Andrew D. White (the first president of Cornell University) and a progressive like Brand Whitlock (a novelist who in 1905 became the first nonpartisan mayor of Toledo) both supporting nonpartisanship on the grounds that city affairs should be kept clear of state and national politics. Both of these men, it must be added, saw other advantages in nonpartisanship. White believed it would put affairs out of the reach of the city proletariat. Whitlock thought that, by eliminating the machine, it would make democracy work.

In practice, the nonpartisan system has by no means always kept the parties out of local elections. Robert L. Morlan, a political scientist, describes the actual working of a nonpartisan system in Minneapolis, one of the many cities where the parties, although without any formal standing, do a good deal of prompting and managing from the wings.

The relation of the city manager movement to the general doctrines of "good government" is explained by Don K. Price, now the Dean of the John F. Kennedy School of Government at Harvard. He shows that the main motivation of the reformers was not to overturn the machine (cities that would accept the council-manager plan were likely to be middle-class ones that had no machines) but rather to make government more effective and more democratic. It was a mistake, Price says, to think that the city manager could "administer" policy, leaving the making of it to others. The most influential spokesman for the point of view Price here attacks was the late Professor Leonard D. White, who argued, in a book that did much to establish doctrine about the city manager profession, that a city manager who attempted to furnish the brains, enthusiasm, and leadership to decide policy for his city would risk having his program rejected and his position weakened. Charles R. Adrian brings some facts to bear upon this old dispute. Observations in three cities that have had managers for more than twenty-five years, he says, show that the managers have been leaders in policy matters—indeed, that they could not help being so even when they tried—but that they have preferred to attribute *innovations* in policy to others. That even an able manager may not be able to survive when a mayor (also able) takes the bit in his teeth is shown by Bruce Kovner in his account of the resignation of Elgin Crull of Dallas.

What Harold A. Stone, Don K. Price, and Kathryn H. Stone have to say about the theory of the city manager plan in their "Three Fundamental Principles" applies equally to nonpartisanship and may be taken as a general account of the theory of the "good government" movement. Implicit is the idea that the community has an interest "as a whole," that the main problem of governmental organization is to give effective and consistent expression to this interest, and that this is to be done by preventing "special interests" from asserting themselves while at the same time giving "impartial experts"—especially the city manager—a free hand. Charles A. Beard, the historian, disputes the premises of this theory. Group conflict is inevitable in a major city, he says, and issues are more frequently pretexts than causes of partisanship. His article is somewhat marred by a confusing use of the word "partisan." Apparently Beard thinks of nonpartisanship, not as a system in which state and national parties play no part (the accepted meaning of the term), but as one in which there are no factional groupings at all. This misunderstanding makes it difficult to follow his criticism of nonpartisanship, but it makes his criticism of the fundamentals of the "good government" position all the more pertinent.

Using relatively "hard" data on a sample of 200 cities with populations of 50,000 or more in 1960, Robert L. Lineberry and Edmund P. Fowler show that nonpartisan elections, at-large constituencies, and manager governments have in fact substantially fulfilled the reformers' hopes by insulating policy decisions from political conflict. As they point out, it is impossible to use contemporary census data to explain the *adoption* long ago or reform institutions. Their evidence is of the *impact* these institutions have had.

In the final reading of this section, James E. Reichley, a novelist and political scientist, criticizes "good government" as he observed it in Philadelphia. In his view, the efforts of upper-class Protestant reformers have emptied political life of much of its interest and meaning. This accounts, he says, for the impermanence of reform and for its lack of real accomplishment. He believes that excessive individualism has led the Protestant elite away from politics, one of man's natural interests. The conclusion as to the reason for the Protestant elite's withdrawal is of course incompatible with the line of analysis in this introductory note. In the editor's opinion, the Protestant elite withdrew from city politics because the only kind of politics it thought moral—a politics of community rather than of individual or group interest—was impossible in the institutional and cultural setting of the large American city.

Municipal Affairs
Are Not Political

Andrew D. White

WITHOUT THE SLIGHTEST EXAGGERATION we may assert that, with very few exceptions, the city governments of the United States are the worst in Christendom—the most expensive, the most inefficient, and the most corrupt. No one who has any considerable knowledge of our own country and of other countries can deny this. . . .

What is the cause of the difference between municipalities in the old world and in the new? I do not allow that their populations are better than ours. What accounts, then, for the better municipal development in their case and for the miserable results in our own? My answer is this: we are attempting to govern our cities upon a theory which has never been found to work practically in any part of the world. Various forms of it were tried in the great cities of antiquity and of the middle ages, especially in the mediæval republics of Italy, and without exception they ended in tyranny, confiscation, and bloodshed. The same theory has produced the worst results in various countries of modern Europe, down to a recent period.

What is this evil theory? It is simply that the city is a political body; that its interior affairs have to do with national parties and issues. My fundamental contention is that a city is a corporation; that as a city it has nothing to do with general political interests; that party political names and duties are utterly out of place there. The questions in a city are not political questions. They have reference to the laying

Reprinted from Forum, *December, 1890, where it appeared under the title, "The Government of American Cities."*

out of streets; to the erection of buildings; to sanitary arrangements, sewerage, water supply, gas supply, electrical supply; to the control of franchises and the like; and to provisions for the public health and comfort in parks, boulevards, libraries, and museums. The work of a city being the creation and control of the city property, it should logically be managed as a piece of property by those who have created it, who have a title to it, or a real substantial part in it, and who can therefore feel strongly their duty to it. Under our theory that a city is a political body, a crowd of illiterate peasants, freshly raked in from Irish bogs, or Bohemian mines, or Italian robber nests, may exercise virtual control. How such men govern cities, we know too well; as a rule they are not alive even to their own most direct interests. . . .

The difference between foreign cities and ours, is that all these well-ordered cities in England, France, Germany, Italy, Switzerland, whether in monarchies or republics, accept this principle—that cities are corporations and not political bodies; that they are not concerned with matters of national policy; that national parties as such have nothing whatever to do with city questions. They base their city governments upon ascertained facts regarding human nature, and upon right reason. They try to conduct them upon the principles observed by honest and energetic men in business affairs. We, on the other hand, are putting ourselves upon a basis which has always failed and will always fail— the idea that a city is a political body, and therefore that it is to be ruled, in the long run, by a city proletariat mob, obeying national party cries.

What is our safety? The reader may possibly expect me, in logical consonance with the statement I have just made, to recommend that the city be treated strictly as a corporate body, and governed entirely by those who have a direct pecuniary interest in it. If so, he is mistaken. I am no doctrinaire; politics cannot be bent completely to logic—certainly not all at once. A wise, statesmanlike view would indicate a compromise between the political idea and the corporate idea. I would not break away entirely from the past, but I would build a better future upon what we may preserve from the past.

To this end I would still leave in existence the theory that the city is a political body, as regards the election of the mayor and common council. I would elect the mayor by the votes of the majority of all the citizens, as at present; I would elect the common council by a majority of all the votes of all the citizens; but instead of electing its members from the wards as at present—so that wards largely controlled by thieves and robbers can send thieves and robbers, and so that men who can carry their ward can control the city—I would elect the board of aldermen on a general ticket, just as the mayor is elected now, thus requiring candidates for the board to have a city reputation. So much for retaining the idea of the city as a political body. In addition to this, in consideration of the fact that the city is a corporation, I would have those owning property in it properly recognized. I would leave to them, and to them alone, the election of a board of control, without whose permissin no franchise should be granted and no expenditure should be made. This should be the rule, but to this rule I am inclined to make one exception; I would allow the votes of the board of control, as regards expenditures for primary education, to be overridden by a two-thirds majority of the board of aldermen. I should do this because here alone does the city policy come into direct relations with the general political system of the nation at large. The main argument for the existence of our public schools is that they are an absolute necessity to the existence of our Republic; that without preliminary education a republic simply becomes an illiterate mob; that if illiterate elements control, the destruction of the Republic is sure. On this ground, considering the public-school system as based upon a national political necessity, I would have an exception made regarding the expenditures for it, leaving in this matter a last resort to the political assembly of the people.

A theory resulting in a system virtually like this, has made the cities of Europe, whether in monarchies or republics, what they are, and has made it an honor in many foreign countries for the foremost citizens to serve in the common councils of their cities. Take one example: It has been my good fortune to know well Rudolf Von Gneist, councilor of the German Empire. My acquaintance with him began when it was my official duty to present to him a testimonial, in behalf of the government of the United States, for his services in settling the north-west boundary between the United States and Great Britain. The Emperor William was the nominal umpire; he made Von Gneist the real umpire —that shows Von Gneist's standing. He is also a leading professor of law in the University of Berlin, a member of the Imperial Parliament and of the Prussian Legislature, and the author of famous books, not only upon law, but upon the constitutional history of Germany and of England. This man has been, during a considerable time, a member of what we should call the board of aldermen of the city of Berlin, and he is proud to serve in that position. With him have been associated other men the most honored in various walks of life, and among these some of the greatest business men, renowned in all lands for their enterprise and their probity. Look through the councils of our cities, using any microscope you can find, and tell me how many such men you discern in them. Under the system I propose, it is, humanly speaking, certain that these better men would seek entrance into our city councils. Especially would this be the case if our citizens should, by and by, learn that it is better to have in the common council an honest man, though a Republican, than a scoundrel, though a Democrat; and better to have a man of ability and civic pride, though a Democrat, than a weak, yielding creature, though a Republican.

Some objections will be made. It will be said, first, that wealthy and well-to-do people do not do their duty in city matters; that if they should, they would have better city government. This is true to this extent, that even well-to-do men are in city politics strangely led away from their civic duties by fancied allegiance to national party men and party issues. But in other respects it is untrue; the vote of a single tenement house, managed by a professional politician, will neutralize the vote of an entire street of well-to-do citizens. Men in business soon find this out; they soon find that to work for political improvement under the present system is time and labor and self-respect thrown away. It may be also said that the proposal is impracticable. I ask, why? History does not show it to be impracticable; for we have before us, as I have shown, the practice of all other great civilized nations on earth, and especially of our principal sister republics.

But it will be said that "revolutions do not go backward." They did go backward in the great cities of Europe when these rid themselves of the old bad system that had at bottom the theory under which ours are managed, and when they entered into their new and better system. The same objection, that revolutions do not go backward, was made against any reform in the tenure of office of the governor and of the higher judiciary in the State of New York; and yet the revolution did go backward, that is, it went back out of doctrinaire folly into sound, substantial, common-sense statesmanship. In 1847 the State of New York so broke away from the old conservative moorings as to make all judgeships elective, with short terms, small pay, and wretched accommodations, and the same plan was pursued as regards the governor and other leading officials; but the State, some years since, very wisely went back to much of its former system—in short, made a revolution backward, if any one chooses to call it so—resuming the far better system of giving our governor and higher judges longer terms, larger salaries, better accommodations, and dignified surroundings. We see, then, that it is not true that steps in a wrong direction in a republic cannot be retraced. As they have been retraced in State affairs, so they may be in municipal affairs.

But it will be said that this change in city government involves a long struggle. It may or it may not. If it does, such a struggle is but part of the price which we pay for the maintenance of free institutions in town, State, and nation. For this struggle, I especially urge all men of light and leading to prepare themselves. As to the public at large, what is most needed in regard to municipal affairs, as in regard to public affairs generally, is the quiet, steady evolution of a knowledge of truth and of proper action in view of it. That truth, as regards city government, is simply the truth that municipal affairs are not political; that political parties as such have nothing to do with cities. . . .

The Absurdity of Partisanship

Brand Whitlock

I HAVE SPOKEN of the Independents as though they were an authentic political party, when it was one of their basic principles to be no party at all. They were Republicans and Democrats who, in the revelation of Jones's ["Golden Rule" Jones, reform mayor of Toledo] death, had come to see that it was the partizan that was responsible for the evil political machines in American cities; they saw that by dividing themselves arbitrarily into parties, along national lines, by voting, almost automatically, their party tickets, ratifying nominations made for them they know not how, they were but delivering over their city to the spoiler. As Republicans, proud of the traditions of that party, they had voted under the impression that they were voting for Lincoln; as Democrats they thought they were voting for Jefferson, or at least for Jackson, but they had discovered that they had been voting principally for the street railway company and the privileges allied with it in interest.

And more than all, they saw that in the amazing superstition of party regularity by which the partizan mind in that day was obsessed, they were voting for these interests no matter which ticket they supported, for the machine was not only partizan, it was bi-partizan, and the great conflict they waged at the polls was the most absurd sham battle that ever was fought. It seems almost incredible now that men's minds were ever so clouded, strange that they did not earlier discover how absurd was a system which, in order to enable them the more readily to subjugate themselves, actually printed little woodcuts of birds —roosters and eagles—at the heads of the tickets, so that they might the more easily and readily recognize their masters and deliver their suffrages over to them. It is an absurdity that is pretty well recognized in this country to-day, and the principle of separating municipal politics from national politics is all but established in law. Mr. James Bryce had pointed it out long before, but [former Mayor] Jones seemed to be almost the first among us to recognize it, and he probably had not read from Mr. Bryce; he deduced the principle from his own experience, and from his own consciousness, if not his own conscience. Perhaps he had some intimation of it from the Genius of These States, whose scornful laugh at that and other absurdities his great exemplar Walt Whitman could hear, echoed as from some mountain peak afar in the west. But it was no laughing matter in Toledo in those days. Men were accused of treason and sedition for deserting their parties; it made little difference which party a man belonged to; the insistence was on his belonging to a party; any party would suffice.

I have no intention, however, of discussing that principle now, but it was the point from which we had to start in our first campaign, the point from which all cities will have to start if they wish to be free. The task we faced was relatively greater than that which [former Mayor] Jones had faced; we had a full ticket in the field, a candidate for every city office and a man running for the council in every ward in town. Jones had run alone, and though he succeeded there was always a council and a coterie of municipal officials who represented the other interest in the community. Of course he had made our work possible by the labor he had done, great pioneer that he was. He had been his own platform, as any candidate after all must be, but with our large movement it was necessary to reduce our principles to some form and we tried to do this as simply as we could. We put forth our belief that local affairs should be separate from, and independent of, party politics, and that public officers should be selected on account of their honesty and efficiency, regardless of political affiliations; that the people should be more active in selecting their officials, and should not allow an office-seeker to bring about his own nomination; that the prices charged by public service corporations should be regulated by the council at stated intervals; and that all franchises for public utilities should first be submitted to a vote of the people, that the city should possess the legal right to acquire and maintain any public utility, when authorized so to do by direct vote of its people, that every franchise granted to public service corporations should contain an agreement that the city might purchase and take over its property at a fair price, whenever so voted by the people, and that no street railway franchise should be extended or granted, permitting more than three-cent fares, and unless it includes provisions for universal transfers, satisfactory service, and reasonable compensation for the use of bridges, and we demanded from the legislature home rule, the initiative and referendum and the recall.

Perhaps it was not such a little platform after all, but big indeed, I think, when one comes to consider its potentialities, and if anyone thinks it was easy to put its principles into practice, let him try it and see! It was drawn by that Johnson Thurston of whom I spoke, and by

Oren Dunham and by Elisha B. Southard and others, citizens devoted to their town, and already with a prescience of the city spirit. They succeeded in compressing into those few lines all we know or need to know about municipal government, and ages hence our cities will still be falling short of the ideal they expressed on that little card. There were many who went with us in that first campaign who did not see all the implications of that statement of principles; none of us saw all of them of course. The movement had not only the strength but the weaknesses of all so-called reform movements in their initial stages. Those who were disappointed or disaffected or dissatisfied for personal reasons with the old party machines, no doubt found an opportunity for expression of their not too lofty sentiments, although later on when they saw that it was merely a tendency toward democracy they fell away, not because the movement had deserted its original ideals but because they at last understood them.

As I now look back on that first campaign, on the experience I had so much dreaded, the perspective has worked its magic, and the hardships and difficulties have faded away. . . .

There was no old gray Molly to jog about from one meeting to another, and if there had been, she could not have jogged fast enough for the necessities of that hour; and we established new precedents when Percy Jones, the son of the Golden Rule Mayor, drove me about at furious speed in his big touring car, the "Grey Ghost" the reporters called it, and it streaked through the night, with its siren singing, from place to place until I had spoken at half a dozen meetings. Every day at noon it wheeled up to the entrance of the factories and shops as the men were coming out for their noon hour. And such meetings I believe were never held anywhere; there was an inspiration as the men crowded about the car to hear the speeches; they were not politicians, they were seeking nothing, they were interested in their city; and in their faces, what is far above any of these considerations, there was an eager interest in life, perhaps a certain hunger of life which in so many of them, such were the conditions of their toil, was not satisfied. . . .

The one thing that marred these contacts was not only that one was so powerless to help these men, but that one stood before them in an attitude that somehow suggested to them, inevitably, from long habit and the pretense of men who sought power for themselves, that one needed only to be placed in a certain official relation to them, and to be addressed by a certain title, to be able to help them. It was enough to make one ashamed, almost enough to cause one to prefer that they should vote for someone else, and relieve one from this dreadful self-consciousness, this dreadful responsibility.

And these were the people! These were they who had been so long proscribed and exploited; they had borne a few of the favored of the of that good to come to them which had been promised in the words and phrases by which their very acquiescence and subjugation had so mysteriously been wrought—"Life, liberty, and the pursuit of happiness."

Where? And for them, when? Not through the efforts of those who employed cold phrases about "good" government, and "reform," and "business" administrations, and efficiency methods, and enforcement of the laws, and law and order, and all that sort of thing, and class consciousness, and economic, or any other interpretation of history, or through initiatives, referendums and recalls. What good would any of these cold and precise formulæ do them? Better perhaps the turkey at Thanksgiving, and the goose at Christmas time which the old machine councilman from the ward gave them; of course they themselves paid for them, but they did not know it, and the councilman did not know it; he had bestowed them with the voice of kindness, in the same hearty human spirit in which he came to the wedding or the wake, or got the father a job, or the oldest son a parole from the workhouse, and rendered a thousand other little personal services. Perhaps Bath House John and Hinky Dink were more nearly right after all than the cold and formal and precise gentleman who denounced their records in the council. For they were human, and the great problem is to make the government of a city human.

There were many, of course, even in our own movement, who were not concerned about that; I was strongly rebuked by one of them once in that very first campaign for declaring that we were no better than anyone else, and that all the "good" men of the world could not do the people much good even if they were elected to the city government for life. No, we may have efficient governments in our cities, and honest governments, as we are beginning to have everywhere, and, happily, are more and more to have, but the great emancipations will not come through the formulæ of Independents, Socialists, or single-taxers, nor through Law and Order Leagues, nor Civic Associations. Down in their hearts these are not what the people want. What they want is a life that is fuller, more beautiful, more splendid and, above all, more human. And nobody can prepare it and hand it over to them. They must get it themselves; it must come up through them and out of them, through long and toilsome processes of development; for such is democracy.

The Unorganized Politics
of Minneapolis

Robert L. Morlan

THE STUDENT of municipal politics in the United States today is being given an extremely one-sided picture of political organization and party activity, at least in so far as existing literature is concerned. Most of the writing on this subject seems to assume that, excepting only those cities under 100,000 population, the pattern is essentially that expounded so entertainingly by the immortal *Plunkitt of Tammany Hall* a half century ago.

The picture almost invariably presented is one of tight political hierarchies extending from a boss and the city or county central committee through ward executives, precinct leaders and multitudinous block workers, all welded into a highly efficient 365-day-a-year machine by the magic of patronage, and controlling votes largely through the familiar process of rendering personal service to the voters.

This is not to deny that extremely effective machines continue to flourish in some American cities but rather to challenge the traditional assumption that this is the way it is done everywhere. Operations of bosses and machines have often been sensational and hence have tended to attract the attention of those investigating the facts of local political life. Interesting and useful studies of bossism have resulted from these researches, but the focusing of attention in that direction has meant the virtual ignoring of cities with less spectacular politics.

Authors of general works on municipal government and politics have found their sources of material almost entirely limited to studies of highly organized cities—and have doubtless also been anxious to include in their texts as much colorful matter as possible. As a result, the politically loosely organized city has received either no attention or has been summarily passed off with a statement that in some small cities party organization is less comprehensive.

There is, in fact, a tremendous variation in the comprehensiveness of party organization and in the extent of party activities in city wards.

Reprinted from National Municipal Review, *November 1949, pp. 485–490.*

Machine strength is, of course, normally centered in the poorer wards, while in the more prosperous wards workers rarely engage in much more than a bit of pre-election activity. The minority party frequently maintains little if any organization in wards which are overwhelmingly of the opposite political faith, but it is also true that even the dominant party is often poorly organized in certain wards. The significant fact too commonly overlooked, however, is that there are some large cities as well as many smaller ones in which *neither* party has a strong organization in *any* ward.

It is time to re-examine our traditional concepts of city political organization, to get away from the universalities in which most of the writing in this field has dealt, and to recognize the fact that even in large municipalities political organization and activity vary all the way from highly concentrated control to loose and haphazard operation.

An Unorganized City

Minneapolis, with a population of over half a million and a long history of volatile politics, is an excellent example of a major city loosely organized politically. Its situation may not be widespread, but it is significant as a striking deviation from a presumed norm, and one may speculate that it is not alone.[1]

It is often difficult for persons familiar with the politics of highly organized cities to believe that political activity in Minneapolis can actually be as "free and easy" as it is. The truth is that any interested person can step immediately into political work, that the average party ward meeting is for all practical purposes open to anyone, that in no ward is there a party organization adequately covering every precinct the year around, that many officers of both parties at the city, ward and precinct levels are practically neophytes in politics, and that the party organizations as such play minor roles in the selection and control of candidates and have almost negligible influence with city officials.

The ease with which a political amateur with a sense of direction may succeed in Minneapolis politics is strikingly illustrated by the career of former Mayor, now U.S. Senator, Hubert H. Humphrey. As a young college political science instructor with a "gift of gab," he was expounding his views on local politics one night in a typical campus bull session when someone brought him up short: "Humphrey, why don't you practice what you're always preaching about political participation, and see what you can do in this next city election?"

The upshot was that Hubert Humphrey, with hastily collected and almost wholly amateur support, little money and organization, not only

---

1. The situation in the other of the "Twin Cities," St. Paul, is essentially similar.

survived the nonpartisan primary in 1943 but also lost to the incumbent mayor in the final election by only 5,000 out of 115,000 votes. Gathering liberal and labor support in the interim, but still operating to a large degree with what was in effect his own organization, he came back to win in 1945 by the largest plurality any mayor has ever secured. In 1947 he swept every ward and the following year went on to defeat Senator Joseph H. Ball by a three to two margin. Never did he have behind him a tight ward and precinct organization even approximating the traditional type.

Part of the reason for this wide open situation is found in the fact that Minneapolis—as do all local units in Minnesota—elects its officials on a nonpartisan ballot, although this of course does not mean that the parties take no part in municipal politics. Party organizations would exist for state and national affairs at any rate and, since essentially the same persons are interested in politics at all levels, it is hardly to be expected that they will remain aloof in municipal campaigns.

Pressure Group Government

Campaigns are managed by volunteer committees for individual candidates, but the parties make endorsements instead of nominations, and in most cases they quite openly support their choices. Nevertheless, since the parties do not manage the campaigns of individual candidates and do not finance them except in the form of minor contributions, nonpartisanship in local elections is definitely a factor. It has resulted in government by pressure groups—labor unions, business associations, etc.—rather than by parties at the city level.

A further cause of party weakness is the almost complete absence of local patronage in the sense of jobs for loyal workers. The city merit system, although it has some shortcomings, covers almost all municipal employment and has been little abused in recent years.

Patronage in the sense of special favors in the expectation of future support is extensive, but it is centered almost entirely in the hands of the 26 aldermen and party officials as a rule have practically nothing to do with it. The aldermen, therefore, to that extent play the role which is normally played by party ward and precinct executives. Being relatively independent, they have tended to build up personal blocs of support with little thought for the parties whose support they receive. They consider themselves more dependent upon the support of powerful pressure groups and party organization has suffered as a consequence.

Political leaders say that a strong party organization not only lives upon patronage but cannot exist without it. Experience in Minneapolis lends credence to the argument. Persons with a sincere interest in politics and reasonably strong party convictions can be stirred by a cause long enough to work for brief periods before election, but they cannot be expected to devote themselves constantly to political activity unless the party has some control over them—or unless they are possessed of a Messianic zeal like that of the Communists.

Frank Kent, in his well known but occasionally inaccurate book, *The Great Game of Politics,* says categorically that eight out of ten ward executives are on the public payroll at good salaries. In Minneapolis, of the 26 ward chairmen serving the two major parties, only one is a city employee, and his is a position under the merit system for which he is in no way indebted to the party. Nor is it true that these officials are to any extent in businesses which stand to profit from political pull. Precinct executives in strongly organized cities often hold minor political jobs, yet in Minneapolis scarcely a handful who are public employees can be found.

One of the leading college textbooks on city government opens its discussion of party organization with a statement concerning the hierarchy of political organization, "at the base of which is the precinct committeeman or committee in each of the 130,000 precincts in the United States."[2] This statement is misleading, since it indicates that precinct committeemen actually exist in each of those precincts. Obviously there is nowhere near the full quota.

In Minneapolis alone, except perhaps in the weeks just preceding an important election, roughly 100 of the 634 possible precinct captaincies will be unfilled and not over half the remainder are filled by active party workers who can be depended upon at all times.

Precinct Captains

The precinct executive, we are told, is a person who holds that position because he can control more votes than can any competitor, and who stays in power only so long as he can "deliver the goods." In the highly organized city the precinct executive must presumably devote a major portion of his time to politics. He must have information about virtually every voter in his precinct, know many of them personally and be able to swing enough votes to carry at least his party's primary. Traditionally he has been able to control votes largely by means of giving personal service in the form of jobs, assistance to those in trouble with the police, relief for the poor, etc. Kent insists that the precinct executive functions in this manner in nine-tenths of the precincts in every city.

As many of these services are becoming institutionalized, being handled at least in part by government employment bureaus and social

2.   Charles M. Kneier, *City Government in the United States,* 1947, page 508.

welfare agencies, for example, the role of the precinct executive has become more and more that of a go-between and a cutter of red tape. But in the unorganized city even this type of service is largely unknown. Minneapolis precinct captains lack the necessary political pull to do the job, even if they have the inclination. Few put any time on politics except in pre-election periods, when they distribute campaign literature from door to door, perhaps make a few phone calls on election day to remind persons to vote and assist in providing transportation to the polls. On rare occasions a few of the more earnest ones may do some doorbell ringing.

The average precinct captain has no personal political following and is unlikely to possess even such an elementary tool as a list of the registered voters of his precinct. He is not in the least concerned over the danger of a competitor developing sufficient strength to take over his job, for the job in most cases means nothing to him and he would be happy to be relieved of it.

"Every ward executive," says Frank Kent, "holds his position because he has the strength to hold it and for no other reason." He is, presumably, a little king in his ward. It is he who sits in the inner councils of the central party organization. It is he who wields influence at city hall, who appoints—or controls the election of—precinct executives and supervises their political activity. He has earned his position by hard work and fighting his way to the top.

The average ward executive in Minneapolis will hardly fit these specifications. Lawyers, labor leaders, business men, housewives—they devote only a relatively small portion of their time to politics and as a rule have but limited control over their ward organizations. As for influence at the city hall, they would be in vastly stronger positions as officers of the central labor union or the chamber of commerce. Not only do they have almost nothing to say in the selection of precinct executives but they can also do little more than request their cooperation once in office. That chairman is fortunate who is able to secure the attendance of over 50 per cent of his precinct captains at a meeting of the ward central committee.

Few Ward Contests

Nor have these ward executives for the most part fought their way to the top. In many cases they had no opposition and have simply been asked to serve—in some instances there are minor skirmishes. The only real battles over these positions come when there is a struggle for control of the state or county organization. After all, the ward chairman gets nothing from his job except the satisfaction of serving the party cause although it has occasionally been used as a stepping stone toward running for elective office. Certainly he is probably one of the most politically active persons in his ward but he is only rarely a political power.

Compared to the length of service required for a person to become a ward executive in a tightly organized city, many Minneapolis ward chairmen are virtually beginners in politics. The turnover is rapid and over half the current chairmen are new to the office within the past two years, while the oldest in point of service has been a chairman for twelve years.

The writer came to Minneapolis in the spring of 1946, in a few months became a precinct captain, and in the spring of 1948 was elected ward chairman for the majority party in one of the most active and most evenly divided wards in terms of party votes. The same year he was elected a delegate to both the county and state conventions of the party—altogether a totally inconceivable series of events for a well organized city.

In the highly organized city, meetings of a ward organization are essentially closed affairs, attended only by ward and precinct officers and a few other trusted workers.

Meetings of the ward organizations of both parties in Minneapolis are open to the public. Any interested person may attend and vote on all matters, helping to elect officials or delegates and to determine party policy. To be sure, an unknown person may be questioned about his party allegiance, and known members of an opposing party would not be permitted to participate, but the individual's word on the matter is usually accepted. At most he can merely be required to state either that he voted for a majority of the party's candidates at the last election or that he intends to do so at the next.

The practice in Minneapolis is to send meeting notices to all persons in the ward who have indicated reasonably active interest. Attendance is normally low and the ward and precinct officers are likely to constitute a sizable bloc. The fact is of little significance, however, since they are rarely if ever united upon any specific course of action in advance. A highly controversial issue may and often does bring out larger crowds, when all are given a chance to be heard and to participate in decisions. Groups with prearranged slates or programs of action are, of course, to be expected when anything of importance is at stake, but rarely is such a group made up of ward and precinct officers.

Caucuses Routine Affairs

Biennial ward and precinct caucuses, the vehicle in Minnesota for election of local party officers and selection of delegates to county and state conventions, are subject to the same conditions as are regular ward meetings. Adherence to the party concerned is checked more rigidly, although legally the individual's statement is all that is required. At a time of intense factional strife these caucuses may be heavily attended, as was the case within the Democratic-Farmer-Labor party in 1948 when as many as six hundred persons jammed certain ward caucuses in Minneapolis. Normally, however, they are routine affairs, with few brisk contests.

The writer in the spring of 1948 was an observer at the precinct and ward caucuses of the Republican party in a ward where the vote is fairly evenly divided between the parties. All were held in a school gymnasium, with the ward caucus being convened after the precinct caucuses had completed their business. Out of 28 precincts there were eleven in which no one appeared for the precinct caucus. One person could have come and elected himself both precinct captain and delegate to the county convention—this happened in two other precincts. Moreover, a person with five followers could have controlled any precinct caucus, and this is not the exception but the rule.

Perhaps this loosely organized state of politics in Minneapolis is unique, or perhaps we have too long accepted the situation in a few tightly organized cities as being universal. Surely we have been too ready to accept without adequate investigation the statement that all cities are organized politically in such and such a manner. There are a great variety of local conditions existing within the pattern of certain fairly common structural arrangements. It is time to recognize the fact that there is, in larger cities as well as smaller ones, an unorganized as well as an organized style of municipal politics.

The Promotion of the City Manager Plan

Don K. Price

IT WOULD HAVE BEEN amusing to write the history of the city manager plan in terms of symbols and publicity techniques alone. By looking at only one aspect of the history of the plan, the narrator could show most plausibly how the hand that manipulates the symbols rules the world. For example—

The city manager plan, the form of municipal government under which an elected council appoints and may remove an over-all chief administrator, was invented and most effectively promoted not only by an experienced public official, and not by any seasoned student of political science, but by a young advertising man who, as he remarked years later in a reminiscent mood, had the knack of "simplifying things until they were no longer so." This young man, Mr. Richard S. Childs, started the Short Ballot Organization as a part-time hobby, with the assistance of a gentleman who had written a book on Congressional Government without ever setting foot in the United States Capitol— Mr. Woodrow Wilson. Mr. Childs found the "commission government" movement well under way, and so he proposed the new idea, part of which was borrowed from a small Virginia city, as the most modern version of the commission plan, and perhaps with his tongue in his cheek, stoutly defended the new idea against the charge of unortho-

Reprinted from Public Opinion Quarterly, *5, No. 4 (Winter, 1941), 563–578, by permission of the publisher and the author.*

doxy. At the same time, he fused the symbols of Big Business with those of the New Freedom—"business corporation," "board of directors," "popular government," "political responsibility."

To continue with this factually accurate but completely unbalanced story: Articles signed or ghost-written by Mr. Childs began to appear in leaflets or magazines throughout the country. They made much of the new municipal official whose name itself was a slogan, consciously chosen as such—the city manager. A charter that Mr. Childs had a draftsman prepare for the city of Lockport, New York, although never put into effect, was inserted on *pink* paper in Mr. Charles A. Beard's otherwise colorless *Loose-leaf Digest of Short Ballot Charters*. Newspapers and magazines about the country began to report the city manager plan as if it were actually in operation, and phrases from Mr. Childs' pamphlets found their way into editorials and after-dinner speeches and became a part of the stock-in-trade of the municipal reform movement. And thus hundreds of cities were led to adopt the city manager plan by a man who remained so inconspicuous that no one at the first convention of city managers that he attended had ever heard of him.

But students of public opinion do not need to be told this story, for they know already that symbols and publicity techniques are useful in promotional campaigns. The significant story is another one: how some symbols were in harmony with the essential nature of the plan and therefore furthered its acceptance, while other symbols handicapped the plan, even though they were used by those who sought to promote it, because they were not suited to the plan's original purpose, and those who used them did not believe in that purpose.

The inventor of the city manager plan was, in the current phrase, a manipulator of symbols. He recognized that "any idea that is to be widely spread and remembered must be condensed to a catch-phrase first, even if such reduction means lopping off many of its vital ramifications and making it false in many of its natural applications." But at the same time, he was deeply concerned with the fundamental structure of government and was convinced that the structure itself could do much to facilitate or impede the effectiveness of public opinion.

Mr. Childs' principal contribution was not the invention and popularization of new symbols. Most of the original symbols of the city manager plan had already been used by advocates of commission government. What Mr. Childs did was to add substance to the symbols, by proposing a structural change in conformity with their essential spirit. Commission government, its advocates said, was "just like a corporation with its board of directors." Mr. Childs saw that this "catch phrase has converted whole cities," but remarked that the commission would not be like a board of directors until it would "appoint a manager who in turn would hire the departmental heads, reporting regularly to the commission and submitting to it only broad matters of policy." The city manager or commission-manager plan was Mr. Childs' effort to make the commission do so.

To Make Public Opinion Effective

Mr. Childs intended the city manager plan to make public opinion effective in municipal affairs. He saw two obstacles to the effectiveness of public opinion—first, that the public was trying to choose too many public officials; second, that municipal governments had to work under intricate systems of checks and balances and legalistic procedures, all of which could be used as barricades by those who wished to fight rear-guard actions against government. To overcome the first obstacle he proposed the "short ballot"; to overcome the second, he proposed a brief charter that simply gave a single small council full control of the city government, with all legislative powers and the power to control the administration of its ordinances by hiring and firing its chief administrative official. Public opinion, he thought, would be most effective if the electorate delegated to a governing body the job of enacting policies, and if the governing body delegated to an expert administrator the job of putting those policies into effect.

The two principal symbols of the city manager plan were based on positive ideas. The adoption of these ideas provided more workable methods for the expression of public opinion on the primary questions, those which public opinion was solely qualified to answer, and discouraged the expression of public opinion on matters in which public opinion would be irrelevant, incompetent, and immaterial.

The first symbol was the "business corporation." It was easy to point to the typical, or at any rate the ideal, business corporation, purposeful in its policies, efficient in its administration, and then in contrast show how the municipal corporation was directed without a program and managed without vigor. The proposal to have the municipality run like a private business meant the abolition of the double standard between business and government that had existed so long in American political thought; the city government was no longer to be tied up in legal red tape, with the selection of all its employees and the spending of each of its dollars subject to ratification by either popular vote, or by several committees or independently elected officials. The city government was no longer to be a parochial institution; like modern business, it was to draw on the entire nation for personnel, purchases, and ideas. The city government, in short, was to become a working institution, controlled by a board of directors who would have plenty of power and discretion from election to election.

The second of these symbols was the manager himself. The word "manager" suggested common sense, energy, leadership, and a preoccupation with results rather than forms and procedures. It implied responsibility to an appointing authority and expertness at a task. Above all, it signified general authority and responsibility for the ways in which policies were effected, and for the choice and control of employees.

The Effects of These Symbols

It is unnecessary to review in detail the effect of these symbols. Wherever an organized effort was being made to improve local government, their appeal was felt. The city manager plan became a movement, and, as its originator expected, the superficial aspects of the movement were sometimes adopted without its substance. In one small city, for example, where the public works director was known as the city commissioner, the city council adopted a resolution that ran substantially as follows:

> WHEREAS it is getting to be the fashion for up-to-date cities to have city managers, and WHEREAS it will make . . . city look like an up-to-date city to have a city manager; therefore, be it *Resolved* that the title of the present city commissioner be changed to city manager.

The principal symbols of the city manager plan were in harmony with the idea that government should be strengthened and made capable of rendering service, rather than weakened to prevent it from doing harm. It was therefore appropriate, no matter how illogical it seemed to some of the leaders of the good government movement, that local campaigners for the adoption of the city manager plan usually put their greatest emphasis on the accomplishment of some specific objective—such as the enforcement of moral regulations or the construction of streets and parks—that was quite distinct from the proposal to change the structure of the government.

Few cities cared what their municipal organization charts looked like, and few people in them cared very much whether municipal employees were selected for merit or by patronage. On the other hand, it often became clear to municipal leaders that the community could not achieve its objective—any important objective—if the structure of government did not permit the city to take two steps: first, organize a majority to make a decision; second, enable that majority to protect against the obstructive tactics of the minority those who put the decision into effect.

Lynchburg, Virginia, had a bicameral council elected by wards: on one occasion it had taken ten months of parliamentary maneuvering to get a $500 sidewalk built, although twenty-one of the twenty-four elected representatives had approved the project from the beginning. The leading advocates of a street paving program in Lynchburg wanted the city manager plan for what it would enable them to do; it was perfectly sensible for the community to emphasize its ultimate purpose, rather than its intermediary purpose, in considering the adoption of the city manager plan.

The interest in general policy was closely accompanied by an interest in personalities in most of these campaigns for the adoption of the city manager plan. As the arguments and discussions of the average campaign clearly indicated, the voters wanted to take one group of leaders out of power and put another group in, and were more interested in doing so than in the details of the charter for which they were voting.

This was not true in cities like Lynchburg, which had managed to keep its community leadership on the city council by continuing to attach more prestige to municipal service than to commercial success. But elsewhere it was quite obvious that the community could accomplish nothing unless it not only simplified its municipal structure, but changed its mind about the worth of municipal political leadership and put its most esteemed men and effective leaders into municipal office.

For this purpose, the proposal to make government "nonpolitical" under the city manager plan was a symbol of the greatest importance in those cities where "politics" had been lowest in connotation and in practice. A businessman of importance could not be induced to take part in "politics," but he might be drafted for a position on the municipal council if he were assured that the municipality was to be managed like a business corporation.

How It Worked

In practice, it was not often the business magnate or the large employer who was drafted for councilmanic service, but citizens who were neither employers nor labor—professional men, salaried executives, small businessmen—who as leaders in church, service club, or lodge would undertake community responsibility only if the curse of "politics" were removed. And in common usage, the antithesis of politics was "business."

The antithesis of "business" in some industrial communities was also "labor." Organized labor in most American cities was not especially interested in increasing governmental services during the 1920's. Its members, or at least its leaders, were usually skilled tradesmen, homeowners and taxpayers, who were not at all eager to help pay for public works to gratify the pride of the Chamber of Commerce, or for social services to further the health and welfare of the very poor. The city manager movements made no very positive appeal to trade unions, which sometimes supported the city manager plan, but were more often lukewarm or actually in opposition.

Chambers of commerce appealed in the average towns to the type of local businessman who was willing to work collectively with his fellows and to exchange ideas with other cities. The same type of businessman took to the city manager plan. (My personal hunch is that the interest and influence of the local businessman in municipal affairs have been reduced in many cities by the displacement of the small independent businessman by the branch manager of the national corporation, and by the movement of community leaders into suburbs outside of the limits of the city where they do business; this hunch needs to be proved or disproved by more systematic observation.) The American City Bureau, an institution which trained civic workers and secretaries for chambers of commerce, taught them the superiority of the city manager plan. The United States Chamber of Commerce publicized it, though never taking a formal stand on the matter.

The American Federation of Labor headquarters, although it too has never taken an official stand, has usually answered inquiries about the city manager plan from its locals with rather discouraging advice. It once, for example, referred to the symbol that, by branding as an "alien" the city manager who is not a resident when appointed, has had the greatest adverse effect on the growth of the profession. The manager, it said, "is generally selected from another state and therefore has no conception of the sentiment among the people regarding their desires as to how the city shall be conducted." It is curious that this prejudice against hiring a city manager from out of town should exist, unless it can be explained on the grounds of the belief that the public payroll—except for school superintendents—should be reserved for neighbors of the taxpayer, for there is usually little prejudice against out-of-town ministers or labor union organizers.

In spite of all this, the student of political science, and more especially the student of economics, is likely to read far too great a flavor of industrial dispute into municipal politics. The contest in municipal politics is often one side of the tracks against the other; occasionally it is one nationality or one denomination against another. But even in a town like Jackson, Michigan, which before the first World War had a strong Socialist movement in those wards which were predominantly German, Irish, and Polish, Democratic, Catholic, and "wet," and where the factory owners all lived in wards that were predominantly Republican, Protestant, British in national origin, and prohibitionist, the issue over the city manager plan had nothing to do with the traditional issue between "conservative" and "radical." Time after time in such cities, research on the history of the city manager plan showed, the so-called

"businessmen's" group got a new city manager who introduced new
social services, while the representatives of the "across the tracks" section ridiculed social welfare programs and opposed the idea of expert
administration. At the same time, the title "manager" had probably had
a rather favorable connotation among workingmen, who objected to it
no more than to that of the Sunday School "superintendent." Recognizing that the title "manager" was a plus symbol, the leaders of the
opposition to the city manager plan have always had to call the manager something else—in the old days, "czar," in more recent years,
"dictator."

The connotation of the symbols which connect the city manager
plan with "business" has probably become less favorable during the past
decade. The prestige of the businessman and business ideas in government has been pretty badly battered, but the original symbols are probably still useful except in communities that have seen acute industrial
disputes.

The city manager plan has become snarled in its own symbols
less often because their connotation has changed for the worse than
because many of its supporters have not believed in its original and
fundamental ideas.

What City Government Should Do

Back of the symbol of the business corporation was the idea
that the city government should do an important job and a productive
job rather than confine itself to regulatory functions and ceremonial.
Back of the symbol of the manager there was the idea that the city government should go about its job with a primary emphasis on results
rather than on ritual and procedure. And back of both of these ideas
was the primary approach of the original sponsors of the plan: "Good
government is not our object. The short ballot movement is a contest
for *popular* government." The original advocates of the city manager
plan were not proposing to lower tax rates, to introduce a merit system,
to destroy the influence of national parties in local affairs, to make
administration more efficient—they were proposing primarily to make
city government more democratic, to make "every man a politician."

Instead of advocating the city manager plan as a vehicle for expanding and vitalizing the social services of the municipality, in many
a city its supporters have handicapped it by implying that "business-like
government" would be cheap government, and by making extravagant
promises of reductions in expenditures and tax rates without waiting
to discover whether or not a business-like investigation would show a
need for an increase in capital investment and maintenance expenditures. Such promises had little appeal to begin with, and handicapped

the city manager plan after its installation in two ways. First, many a city manager found himself being attacked as a cold-hearted economizer, a boss with "ice water veins," even if he were actually instituting new social services and persuading a surprised council that it should spend more money rather than less. Second, many a property owner supported the city manager plan to get taxes reduced and withdrew his support when he found that they were not.

Instead of emphasizing the positive virtues of the city manager plan, many of its supporters have made the error of proposing it as a means of abolishing machine or boss rule in cities that never had machines or bosses. The symbol of the boss is an inviting target for the attack of reformers, especially when it is taken straight from the classic mythology of Thomas Nast: fat paunch, checked suit, big cigar, and all. The idea of a machine, although a little less tangible, will do well enough. But it is doubtful strategy to label as a machine the "city hall crowd" that happens to hold office at the moment, regardless of whether it has a continuous and cohesive organization, or to label as a boss an amateur politician who likes to get jobs for his friends or fix their parking tickets. The voter, especially in a small city, is too likely to know the man in question as a deacon in his church who has a fondness for getting about with the boys, and to dismiss the labeller as an officious busybody.

The second fundamental idea on which the manager plan was originally based—the idea of emphasizing first the job to be done and second the discretion to be given the governing board and its appointee in doing that job—has been violated by supporters of the manager plan who have insisted on emphasizing procedure rather than purpose in the arguments that they have presented to the public. They have done so in three ways.

Rule of Political Etiquette

First, they have tried to impose on the city manager a most un-American rule of political etiquette. They have promised that under the city manager plan the city manager would not only refrain from taking part in political campaigns, i.e., contests for public office, but would not be connected in any way with factional disputes and would not undertake to promote policies. Those who did so were following such expert opinions as that of I. G. (now Sir Gwilym) Gibbon, then assistant secretary to the British Ministry of Health, who warned the city managers in 1925 that the future of the whole movement was imperiled by the incursion of city managers into matters of policy, because by becoming identified with questions of policy they risked discharge when policies changed.

Generally speaking, this idea has never taken root in America. In Great Britain, the civil servant, like Jeeves, takes pride in carrying out with discreet reserve the whims of his elected masters, and in offering advice only confidentially on request. But in the United States, Bertie Wooster's Jeeves is not as close to the popular ideal of a servant as is Jack Benny's Rochester. The public admiration of the city manager who is not afraid to disagree with the council that appoints him has been so marked that it has occasionally, I suspect, led certain managers to make an unmannerly show of their "independence." But the council's privilege of discharging the city manager at will has held such tendencies in check pretty effectively.

In city after city where the manager plan was studied, it was clear that the manager was less likely to get fired for advocating a policy than for administering one; less for proposing a bond issue or a health program than for firing somebody's cousin, or collecting somebody's taxes, or refusing someone a building permit. The city managers who held their jobs in the face of early political turmoil were those who, with their council's approval, led their communicities into popular new policies and distinguished themselves as much by their leadership as by their operating efficiency.

It was inevitable that the city manager would become identified with policies and would be unable to observe the principle of anonymity. He had to make recommendations to the council and no one could keep gossip and newspaper reporters from picturing him rather than his superiors, the council members, as responsible for the measures that they adopted. It has therefore been a mistake for advocates of the city manager plan to assure the public in advance that the city manager will not become involved in disputes over policies, and to give the opposition the argument that he ought not to do so.

The City Manager Charter

Second, too many advocates of the city manager plan, because of their interest in "good government," have rejected the original idea of emphasizing purpose and leadership rather than procedures and checks and balances, and have put far too much reliance on the city manager charter. Almost invariably excessive emphasis on charter provisions defining procedures under the city manager plan has led to or been a result of weak councilmanic leadership. It is hard to persuade the public at once to support a political leader and to support provisions that imply a distrust of him.

As a matter of practical strategy, it should be obvious that a charter may be a prerequisite, but it cannot be a guarantee, of city manager government. For the essential theory of the city manager plan, and an effective feature of every city manager charter, is that the city manager shall be continuously responsible to the council and shall serve at its pleasure. The relationship between council and manager is so intimate that it is generally impossible to prove whether the manager is using his own judgment in taking an administrative action or is acting under coercion or threat by the council or some of its members, or whether the council in adopting a policy is following the ideas originated by its members or the advice of the city manager. A manager may be discharged merely for doing his legal duty and the courts will not interfere. Yet in city after city the charter has been set up as the principal symbol of city manager government; indeed in Cincinnati the plan is popularly known as "charter government."

In consequence, a great deal of energy has usually been devoted to talking about the charter, and too little energy and leadership have gone into service on the council. In San Diego, this tendency was carried to its logical conclusion. After four years of expensive and arduous effort at charter drafting, the reform group that got the city manager charter enacted refused to enlist or support candidates for the council, hoping, as its leader explained privately, that "the public may be aroused by the time the campaign is over to a point of a lack of confidence in those [councilmen] elected, and that they will then be in a mood to place their hopes in the city manager."

The reform group then tried to get the councilmen to delegate authority freely to the city manager by acting as a sort of unofficial supreme court, looking on the "city manager formula" in the charter as a municipal constitution; they tried to defend the city manager's control over personnel, for example, primarily in order to keep the council from misusing its influence over appointments.

The reform group discovered by experience what too few cities have been told as they adopted the city manager plan: that it is useful as a system to enable elected representatives to get something done, but it is useless as tactics to keep them from doing the wrong things. In short, it is impossible to enforce the proper confidential relationship between master and servant by publicity, and the city manager is very definitely in the position of servant to the council—as the San Diego council proved to the reform group in question by firing four managers in less than three years and giving none of them a chance to do a job.

The early publicity for the city manager plan made a sharp distinction between the scope of the work that the city council ought to permit the manager to do and the scope of the powers granted him by the charter. The theorists who invented the city manager did not want him to be a mere routine clerk; on the contrary they wanted him to exercise broad discretion in the administration of policies and to help to formulate new policies of social welfare and municipal enterprise. But thinking of the council's ability to discharge the city manager at will—the primary feature of the city manager plan—they wanted to make it clear that the manager would be given administrative powers because the council would want to get a good job done, not at all because the charter said so. And they explicitly insisted that a city manager charter should not restrict the council's authority over administrative matters.

In the early publicity for the plan, the charter was considered mainly as a device to free the council from existing legal restrictions so that it could employ a manager and delegate power to him. The first city persuaded by this publicity adopted a one-sentence "charter," an optional law empowering the council to "employ a male person of sound discretion and of good moral character not of their number of such salary and upon such terms as they may decide, who shall be subject to such rules and regulations as may be provided by said councilmen." And in the state where the city manager plan has made the greatest progress—I am referring to Virginia, where 21 of the 29 cities of more than 5,000 population have adopted the plan—the usual legal procedure has been for a city to adopt the state optional law. This law (which merely states in a few brief paragraphs that the city council shall be the legislative body and the city manager shall be its chief executive officer, holding office at its pleasure, and which otherwise has no effect on the municipality) contains none of the gadgets which have been added to so many "home rule" charters as integral parts of the city manager plan.

In too many cities advocates of the city manager plan, desiring primarily to hamstring the politician, have thought of the essential features of the plan as secondary to such gadgets as election by proportional representation, prohibitions of political activity on the part of employees and of employment for political reasons, or a charter provision forbidding councilmen on penalty of fine, imprisonment, and removal from office, to interfere with the administrative work or appointments of the city manager.

Proportional Representation

But of all these the greatest handicap to the promotion of the city manager plan has been proportional representation. P.R. and the city manager plan have no essential relationship; the city manager plan, indeed, is peculiarly ill-suited to P.R. Under the city manager plan, if there is any political division at all within the council, it is peculiarly necessary to have a consistent majority. For under this plan the council is not only a legislature, but a governing or an executive board, which will not work through its executive officer—the city manager—unless its members, or a majority of them, have confidence in him. If P.R., as its logic intends, brings to the council representatives of all groups, and assures them that they can keep their seats if they maintain minority support, the city manager will be in a most difficult position. If there is no coherent majority, but only shifting alliances of members who are *consciously* group representatives, the manager is likely to antagonize each of them in turn if he attempts in any way to provide administrative leadership.

A "strong mayor" may have enough legal authority and political independence to preserve a degree of administrative integration and order even if his council runs off in different directions after different policies; a city manager, being responsible to the council, can do nothing of the sort. If there are factions in the city so antagonistic that they will not ally themselves during a campaign, it is exceedingly dangerous to assure them seats in the council and expect them to unite in favor of an administrative program after the election. The story of ward elections under the city manager plan shows clearly how easy it is for a minority group—if sure of a seat or two on the council—to disrupt municipal administrations, and to wreck a reform or policies that have majority support.

Regardless of the merits of P.R., however, to connect it with the city manager plan is to check the spread of the city manager plan. The American Proportional Representation League worked for twenty-two years without effect, until it began to concentrate its efforts on cities considering the manager plan. Since then about five hundred cities have adopted the manager plan, but less than a dozen of them—in spite of the virtual consolidation of the city manager and P.R. movements—have been induced to try P.R. The comparative popularity of the two devices leads to the conclusion that the city manager plan is relatively popular, and that it would be accepted much more readily alone than in combination with P.R.

What has been the effect on public opinion of the emphasis on charter detail? The answer to this question cannot be quantitative. It cannot be expressed in terms of number of votes for or against charters, or for and against "reform" councilmen. A statement in such terms, whether accurate or not, would be irrelevant, for two reasons. First, the spread of the city manager plan has been checked most effectively not by defeats in charter elections, but by the failure of state legislatures to empower cities to consider the city manager plan. Second, important changes after the adoption of the city manager charter were not brought about by charter changes, or by the election of the same men who had been thrown out by "reform." Public opinion changed in a different way; it did not decide to go back to the old system, it merely lost interest in the city manager plan as the leading reformers lost their zeal. The leading reformers, in turn, cooled off because their interest had been in the charter and in a pattern prescribed in detail by its provisions, and when they saw that the pattern was not being followed as they had planned, they were inclined to voice their distaste for "politics" and drop the matter. And thus a "drafted" council and its city manager would be left without support, simply holding the charter. And after the next election, the city manager plan, which consists in the willingness and ability of the council to delegate administrative authority rather than in any charter provisions, would be quickly abandoned without the change of so much as a comma in the existing law.

It is customary to talk about an invariable "cycle" of reform and corruption in municipal politics, and to deplore the decline in "citizen interest" and the persistence of "sinister influences" that make the downswing of the cycle inevitable. This point of view is a stock excuse of those who try to sell the public political prayer-wheels, or gadgets that will make sure that the voters will want what the salesman thinks they ought to want. For there is available the story of city after city that for many years has had no municipal political machine, no organized corruption, and a fair degree of community coherence; the evidence suggests strongly that the voters are likely to give sustained support to public-spirited political leaders who are willing to adopt rules for the game of local government that facilitate rather than impede the effectiveness of public opinion.

There is no question that the city manager, like other public officials today, needs to have a weighty sense of responsibility to the ideal of his profession, to the integrity of its purpose, and to the effectiveness of its techniques. This is the responsibility which Professor Friedrich has called "functional responsibility." It is significant that the municipal administrators who as a group have developed the strongest sense of functional responsibility have been those who have been subjected to the most immediate and stringent political responsibility—the city managers.

It was unfortunate for the city manager plan and for American local government in general that in so many cities the promotion of the plan was taken over by those who attached the wrong symbols to it— symbols that were inconsistent with its fundamental structure. For they made it a movement of "reform" and a procedural pattern; they hopelessly confused many persons about the relationship of the city manager to public opinion and the democratic process; and by trying to strengthen the city manager's functional responsibility at the expense of his political responsibility, they damaged both without improving either.

They have not completely succeeded, for the city manager plan has done well in spite of its friends, as the improvements that it has effected in nearly five hundred American cities indicate. City after city has forgotten the catchwords for which it adopted the city manager plan and the disillusion which followed, and has retained that plan as a system of responsible government which encourages the expert executive to make the greatest possible contribution to policy and administration without even monetary immunity from political responsibility.

The Role of the City Manager

Leonard D. White

EVERY GENERATION is swept along the tides of deep-flowing currents, which, unperceived by most men, silently govern the direction of events.. The form and methods of our government—city, state, and national—are ceaselessly modified in a thousand particulars but in a general sequence which reflects the primary drift of the time. To survey the city manager in the large and attempt to grasp the inner significance of his work and position, it is therefore essential to have in mind at least the more obvious of the underlying tendencies of the age.

In any enumeration of these tendencies the steady growth of urban population must be included. The people of the United States are already, and are destined to become in greater measure, city-dwellers— cliff-dwellers of the modern world. The government of the people of the United States is destined to be the government of municipalities. The government of municipalities, especially the larger range, presents in the sharpest form most of the problems of modern democracy and raises insistently the question whether local government can rest on a popular base and hold high standards of operating efficiency.

The course of modern municipal government also reflects the growing conviction of the people of the United States (1) that they must effectively control, and in increasing measure own and operate, the public utilities; and (2) that they can use their government to render service on a scale as yet untouched. This concept of the function of municipal government is crystallizing as rapidly as confidence in the city government is established. The city is understood to be not merely an organization for purposes of construction, to build and maintain pavement, sidewalk, sewers, water pipe, and police stations; it is understood also to exist for the purpose of securing as far as possible the conditions of the good life for its inhabitants. In this larger range of duties co-operate the church, the school, and the municipal government. Education, formal and informal, recreation, reading, the organization of community groups, music, the arts, and loyalty to the general interest of the city are all struggling up into the consciousness of the public

Reprinted from The City Manager *by Leonard D. White (Chicago: The University of Chicago Press, 1927), pp. 292–302, by permission of The University of Chicago Press.*

authorities as subjects with which they must concern themselves if they are to discharge their full duty to the city.

Having become now the dominant type of local government, and faced with a constantly enlarging program of municipal activity, how are the American cities responding to their opportunities? In what way is the structure of municipal institutions being adapted to the greater strain constantly put upon it? The adaptations which the twentieth century has witnessed in the cities are to a considerable extent paralleled by corresponding movements in the state, and even in the national government.

Of these, one of the clearest is the tendency to bring together in the hands of one person the responsibility for the administrative affairs of government. In the United States the director of the Bureau of the Budget is making the president's control of administration effective; in the states, the Illinois Civil Code has led the way in concentrating power in the hands of the governor; in the cities the growth of the strong mayor plan (Boston, New York, Philadelphia) and of the council-manager plan all point in the same direction. The unco-ordinated, disorganized many-headed administrative systems of the states and of the cities seem to be on their way to disappearance.

Parallel with this movement is the tendency to allow the chief executive a relatively free hand in dealing with the business affairs of the government. The American people distrust the business ability of their elected representatives, especially when acting collectively in a political situation. They view with satisfaction a strong executive, who not only takes the leadership of the council or assembly but who insists on being master in his own house.

This point of view coincides with a gradually emerging preference for a non-partisan administration. This preference is hardly to be discovered in some cities and states, but a broad survey of the course of events of the twentieth century can hardly fail to convince one that the spoils system is gradually receding. Higher standards of official integrity, impartiality, and loyalty are reached decade by decade, however great the variation may be from place to place.

These changes are proceeding along with another profound alteration in our public affairs, the decline of the organized political party. The "machine" has all but disappeared in the small- and medium-sized cities. The state "machine" has gone in many of the western commonwealths. The field is open to a new type of political organization in which idea and ideals are stressed, appointments and contracts neglected. This transformation deserves much more careful study than has been given it, for its consequences are likely to be of great importance.

The conditions of life in America are now such that these changes seem almost inevitable. Governmental problems have become intricate and even more insistent. They call for solution with the aid of science, not with the wisdom of a ward politician. The amazing mobility of the American people leaves no community a law unto itself; each and all are responsible for their own good government to the larger whole of which they are a part. What the whole world is witnessing is the emergence of government by experts, by men and women who are trained technicians highly specialized to perform some service by scientific methods. It is indeed a fair question whether we shall not be forced to reinterpret American government as a means for utilizing the services of experts in the performance of ends democratically defined.

The council-manager plan has an intimate relation to these fundamental tendencies. It is the most perfect expression which the American people have yet evolved of the need for combining efficient administration with adequate popular control. The council, elected for a term of two or four years, sometimes by wards and sometimes at large, representing the voters with whatever fulness the voters demand, holds complete and undivided power over the whole city government. It determines the metes and bounds of city policy; it appropriates the necessary funds; it selects the city manager; and it can remove him at will. There is no separation of power, for all power is in the hands of the council, the direct representatives of the voters. To insure effective and continuing popular control, many cities have adopted the recall with respect to the council—and Dayton with respect to the manager. These arrangements give no valid reason for disputing the essential democracy of the council-manager plan.

The voters, however, do not elect directly, nor do they usually have the power to recall directly, the manager. The operating executive is chosen by a delegate body. American experience shows with sufficient clearness that we cannot expect to maintain high standards of administrative ability in an elective office. Waiving the question whether the voters can be depended upon, year in and year out, to select the best administrative ability, it is perfectly certain that the best executive brains will not be interested in an office to secure which requires the embarrassments of a political campaign, and the tenure of which is liable to interruption by the hazards of later campaigns at the intervals of two or four years. It is true that we cannot depend upon a city council always to make the wisest choice, but it seems clear that the likelihood of having high ability to choose from and of a satisfactory choice are greater when this duty is performed by the council rather than by the voters. This is indeed one of the fundamental advantages of the manager plan. Most city managers could not and would not be elected to the office of mayor, but they have no hesitation in accepting the lesser hazards of the manager's office.

By establishing the confidence of the voters in the integrity and efficiency of the city government, the managers are steadily developing new opportunities to serve the people. It appears in an earlier chapter that the managers are not of one mind concerning the extent of their service to the citizens of their community; but as they succeed, and to the measure of their success, they and their councils will be swept along by a growing desire to utilize in greater and greater degree the service of an efficient municipal government.

The office of manager is a typical specimen of the modern conception of integrated consolidated administrative power. The manager has in full measure the administrative power which the reconstruction of our state and national governments is seeking to acquire for the governors and the president.

The professional manager is himself an expert. He understands the need for experts in the conduct of municipal government. He knows the necessity of allowing experts a substantially free hand in carrying on their specialty and leaves them substantial freedom. He is willing to protect the expert from political or other influence. He is not blind to the necessity of opening up freedom of movement for the expert from city to city, for his own future depends on this same freedom. In short, the effective utilization of expert, trained, and professional service is a characteristic sign of the manager-governed cities.

The manager is profiting by the decline of partisanship and is contributing to the elimination of spoils politics and hidden influence. This unrecognized change in municipal life is sweeping at full tide through the manager cities. There has not been an important political campaign in Winnetka, Illinois, since Manager Woolhiser took charge a decade ago. While differences of opinion are inevitable in most communities and will inevitably crystallize in parties, temporary or permanent, bringing about sharp clashes at the elections, the political life of the American city of the future seems likely to be relatively devoid of the unscrupulous personal "politics" of the past. The managers on the whole are pulling in the center of the stream in this respect.

In fact, as one observes the significant tendencies of the twentieth century in public affairs, one feels that the managers are unconsciously perhaps, but none the less truly, marking out the clear pattern to which certainly municipal government, if not county and state, will conform. The manager movement is the product of deep-lying physical and psychological forces which are bound to affect all levels of government, but, although a product of these forces, they are now serving to intensify them. The American people have a deep conviction that their business organizations and methods are uniquely successful, and they readily understand the resemblance between the city manager and the general superintendent. The council-manager plan seems to be the application of American business methods to government, a practical answer to the demand for more business in government.

The council-manager plan has passed beyond the experimental

stage, but it has not, and probably never will, reach the point when problems of great importance and difficulty will not confront it. Some of these problems will be presented by the environment in which manager government finds itself, the character of the town and its principal figures, the quality of its newspapers, chamber of commerce or labor unions; others will be set by the character and quality of the councils; still others by the ability and purposes of the managers themselves. As a student surveys the scene at the end of nearly two decades' experience with the manager plan, he may readily discover present problems of the greatest significance, some of them fraught with the most serious consequences to the manager movement. . . .

The failure of the city council is one of the most startling weaknesses of the council-manager plan. Making exception of the first council elected under the manager plan and of a few residential cities like East Cleveland or Winnetka, the failure of the council to measure up to its responsibilities is widespread. The first council elected under the new régime is likely to be satisfactory; but before many years have passed an insidious process of decline sets in. The old crowd regains its courage and persistently prepares the way to elect one of its representatives to the council, then two, finally a majority. The "business men" meanwhile find that their personal affairs cannot be neglected too long; they insist on being replaced by others; and they seldom display the tenacity or the ingenuity of the professionals who make politics their business.

Manager Carr complained once that the greatest weakness of the manager plan was that there was no organized body back of it. There is usually organized opposition to it, and this opposition rightly understands that control of the council will give absolute control of the city government. In some cities the reaction against "politician government" has been so thorough that it seems unlikely that it can be restored; but, viewing the country at large, it is clearly an unsettled question whether the desire for non-partisan, scientific city government has a commanding position in the minds and hearts of the American voter. In the smaller cities the answer seems fairly clear; but in the larger cities many an engagement will be fought before the ultimate triumph of modern ideals of government is assured.

Apart from the political phase of this situation is another of perhaps equal importance. The decline of the council is not only usually a reversion to politics; it involves also a loss in ability and foresight and capacity for leadership. No organization, however perfect, will function to give good government unless it is manned by men who can breathe into it the will and vision of good government. A council composed of men without a broad vision of the opportunities and needs of city government, lacking the courage to take the initiative, devoid of the will to discharge their duties intelligently, and unable to assume the leadership of their community, can nullify the efforts of the best manager in the country—or drive him to assume their responsibilities. It is unfortunately true that the majorities in many city councils in council-manager cities are composed of such men. There is a continuing danger that the preoccupation of business men with their affairs and the unwillingness of civic leaders to accept the often unpleasant duties of a campaign will hold the level of council ability at far too low a level. The council-manager plan will not show clear-cut superiority as long as it is forced to labor under this handicap; and vice versa, the mayor-council plan will not demonstrate its potential promise until the voters select a different type of representative in the councils.

All this means perhaps no more than to say that the performance of the manager is fundamentally conditioned by the kind of a council with which he has to work; but it should be understood that the first years of the council-manager plan are likely to be the best unless constant effort is made to hold up the level of ability in the council. It is hardly too much to say that the council is the real problem in the manager city.

A second hazard facing the manager movement is to be found in the adventuresome spirit of many managers, especially those new to the game. These aggressive personalities seek not only to give good administration, but also to furnish the brains, enthusiasm, and leadership in deciding what shall be the policy or program of the city. . . . The temptation to follow this path is intensified by the unwillingness or inability of the council to supply effective leadership. This course is one which, if persisted in, will sound the death knell of the manager plan as now conceived, for a manager who undertakes civic leadership stakes his position on the acceptance of his program by the voters. If his program is rejected, and no man can supply effective leadership without openly courting the possibility of rejection, he sacrifices his position as manager. Moreover by entering the area of public opinion and identifying himself with a policy or program, he allies himself with one group of citizens and against another and incurs ill will which is bound to be transferred to the purely administrative phases of his work.

It ought to be possible in this country to separate politics from administration. Sound administration can develop and continue only if this separation can be achieved. For a century they have been confused, with evil results beyond measure. The managers have an unparalleled opportunity and a deep obligation to teach the American people by their precept and conduct that their job is to administer the affairs of the city with integrity and inefficiency and loyalty to the council, without participating in or allowing their work to be affected by contending programs or partisans. Their duties with regard to the policy of the city are properly restricted to recommendations to the council and to supplying information to citizens upon request. They have a duty on their own initiative to keep the city informed on the administrative program and achievements, but can hardly go beyond this to dabble in the public advocacy of an unsettled policy. Mr. I. G. Gibbon, an English authority on local government, was well within the truth when he wrote,

> The manager often becomes not only the initiator but also the public advocate of policy. . . . This indicates the chief danger of the whole system. The manager, if he dabbles in policy, if he becomes to the electorate a prominent, perhaps the most prominent, representative of particular measures, marches beyond his intended beat, and he, and the system of which he is a pattern, may suffer disaster with the particular policy which is advocated.

A third hazard which faces the manager is the inclination of American cities to prefer local men. This is a matter of fundamental importance, the significance of which has been obscured by reason of the rapid expansion of the movement and the momentary creation of a large number of new positions. This frontier is doomed, and probably in the not far-distant future. As the number of manager towns becomes stable, the number of initial appointments will dwindle and eventually disappear. Examination of the figures presented in an earlier chapter demonstrates that as the order of appointment moves from first to second and third and fourth, the proportion of outside appointments declines. But in ten years most of the manager towns will be in their fourth or fifth or sixth appointments. The evidence now available indicates a most unfortunate progressive restriction of the opportunity for a manager to be promoted from city to city.

If this restriction coincides with a persistent attempt of the manager to concern himself with policy, the outcome is almost inevitable. A local manager, who is also a community leader, is the counterpart of the strong mayor; and it would not be long before the people would insist on electing the official who takes the lead in advocating policy. This would mean a reversion to the strong mayor plan of city government.

The City Manager as a Leader

Charles R. Adrian

THIS IS A REPORT on a continuing study of policy leadership in three middle-sized council-manager cities. All three cities are in the 50,000 to 80,000 population range, are in Michigan, and have been council-manager cities for over twenty-five years. The study covers the period of the calendar years 1953 to 1957. The manager in each city had been in office before the beginning of this period and remained in office throughout the period.[1]

None of the cities is within the six counties of the Detroit metropolitan areas. Cities A and B are manufacturing cities with a fairly slow population growth; city C, also predominantly a manufacturing city, has grown somewhat more rapidly. All have nonpartisan elections. Labor is organized in the three cities but has been of little influence in the selection of the council in cities A and B. City C had one AFL and CIO endorsee elected to the council during the period studied; two other councilmen were given limited labor endorsement.

Tentative conclusions reached in this preliminary report indicate that the manager and his administration are the principal sources of policy innovation and leadership in council-manager cities, even though the manager seeks to avoid a public posture of policy leadership; that the manager has resources and techniques that enable him to withstand even strong attempts by some councilmen to take policy leadership away from him; that nonofficial groups provide a greater amount of

1. I wish to extend special thanks to William Cottrell, graduate Falk fellow at Michigan State University, for his able and considerable assistance in the collection of data for this paper. Concerning the research method used: council records and newspaper accounts were examined to determine the issues that were taken up by the city councils during the five-year period; newspaper stories were used to delineate the public roles played by the various individuals involved in the development of public policy toward each issue. Informants in each community helped to clarify the nonpublic roles played by these persons.

Reprinted from Public Administration Review *(American Society for Public Administration, 6042 Kimbark Avenue, Chicago 37), 18, No. 3 (Summer, 1958), 208–213, where it appeared under the title "Leadership and Decision-Making in Manager Cities, a Study of Three Communities," by permission of the publisher and the author.*

leadership in council-manager cities than is allowed for in the theory of the plan; and that this leadership is a result of councilmanic leadership falling short of the idealized role assigned to it by the theory. Councilmen who do seek to lead place their political careers in greater jeopardy than do other councilmen. It is also found that there were few important issues confronting city councils in middle-sized cities and that even some of these were settled with little conflict, particularly those where few solutions seemed to be available.

The Manager Plan

The basic idea of the council-manager plan is well known: an elective council of laymen is to make policy and a professional administration under a chief administrative officer selected by, and responsible to, the council is to carry out policy. It is not necessary to comment here on the fact that this approach to organization seems to imply the acceptance of the dichotomy which was held, some years ago, to exist between policy and administration. Practicing city managers quickly learned that they could not avoid taking leadership in policy-making. (The tempests created in academicians' teapots when the idea was presented that politics and administration cannot be separated were of little or no interest to managers and their subordinates who must have discovered the necessary interrelationship of the two about the time that the first manager was appointed in 1908.) Summarizing some studies which were made about twenty years ago, Stone, Price, and Stone noted that:

> It is generally impossible for a city manager to escape being a leader in matters of policy, for it is an essential part of his administrative job to make recommendations. The most important municipal policy is embodied in the budget, and the city manager, of course, must prepare and propose the budget. The city manager's recommendation on an important policy, even if he makes it in an executive session of the council, is usually a matter of common knowledge.[2]

Thus, while it was recognized no doubt almost at once that the manager would have to be a policy leader, he was also expected to do this in a discreet manner. The codes of ethics of the International City Managers' Association enjoins each manager to further "positive decisions on policy by the council instead of passive acceptance of his recommendations," and to give formal credit for policy decisions to the council. (The code, with some modifications, dates from 1924.)

2. Harold A. Stone, Don K. Price, and Kathryn H. Stone, *City Manager Government in the United States* (Public Administration Service, 1940), p. 243. See also, Steve Matthews, "Types of Managerial Leadership," 39 *Public Management* 50–53 (March, 1957).

Thus, the role of the manager was conceived realistically decades ago and is well described in the study by Stone, Price, and Stone. On the other hand, neither that study nor other writings on the council-manager plan have paid very much attention to the role of other individuals and groups in the municipal policy-making process: the mayor, the council, and interest groups confronting the manager and the council between election campaigns. It is principally to these areas that this paper is addressed.

Scarcity of Issues

A study of the role of various groups and actors in the making of municipal public policy is handicapped to some extent by the relative scarcity of issues that could be classified as important. Most of the work of the council appears to consist of routine approval of recommendations from the city manager or his staff; these actions are routine because they fit within general policy already well established.

Judged on the basis of the amount of controversy engendered, the time required to achieve a policy decision by the council, and the amount of space devoted to the issue by the local press, the number of important issues coming before the councils of the three cities averaged about two per year. There was little variation among the cities on this point. It should be noted, however, that an issue may be divided into a number of parts and take many forms. A major conflict between the manager and one of the councilmen in City C, for example, was raised as a background issue in connection with almost every other councilmanic discussion during the period of the controversy.

The Role of the Manager

In all three cities studied, the manager played the social role expected of him by his professional organizations. In each case, he avoided taking a public role of policy innovator, except at the specific request of the council or in cases involving matters on which he could be considered a technical expert (e.g., on the effect of allowing a bank to install a drive-up window or of a proposed shuffling of administrative agencies).

If we assume, along with Herbert Simon,[3] that major decisions are almost always made through a "composite process" involving many people, so that no single person is wholly responsible for the final product, it becomes advantageous to view the policy-making process as

3. *Administrative Behavior* (2d ed., Macmillan Co., 1957).

one in which individual roles are specialized. Since the leader, according to Simon, is a person "who is able to unite people in pursuit of a goal," alternative goals must first be perceived by someone. This is done through a precedent role of *policy innovation*, by which I mean the development of ideas, plans, or procedures that may be presented as alternative choices to the decision-makers. A decision might be said, for purposes of this article, to refer to the selection of an idea, plan, or procedure from among the perceived choices. Many decisions must be made in the development of a policy. To name only a few, the innovators of policy must decide whether their incipient suggestions are worthy of development and subsequent presentation for consideration by the leaders. Each leader must decide upon a policy from among what may be several proposals coming from a single individual or agency or from more than one agency. Once the manager or other leader has decided upon a proposal, he will seek to secure its acceptance. The governing body must then choose a proposal presented by one leader or must consolidate the proposals of two or more leaders. Final acceptance by the council gives the policy legitimacy. Of course, the council may veto all proposals, which would then force a reconsideration of the earlier decisions by other actors.

In the council-manager cities studied, the manager presented and sometimes strongly defended policy proposals that had originated largely from one of his own agencies (e.g., the police department on parking policies), from an advisory group (e.g., the planning commission which developed urban renewal plans), from study committees of lay citizens (e.g., citizens seeking to prevent the breakdown of public transportation), or private groups (e.g., downtown merchants interested in off-street parking).[4] There appeared to be a psychological advantage to the manager if he could place himself in the position of defending a policy developed by these individuals or groups.[5] He would take a strong stand, but would use the protective coloration of saying, "professional planners tell me. . . ." He would, in other words, take a public position of *leadership* in policy matters, but preferred to attribute policy *innovation* to technical experts or citizens' groups.

Although managers in all cities appeared to exercise considerable skill in avoiding a public appearance of being the tail that wags the dog, in two cities they were accused of seeking to "control" the mayor or

4. In City C, however, the manager was in the position of presenting an off-street parkng plan that was strongly opposed by the downtown merchants and parking lot owners. The opponents were able to delay but not prevent the adoption of the plan developed by the manager and his staff.

5. One manager (not from Cities A, B, or C) pointed out in an interview that his office is one from which "trial balloons" can be sent up. If a proposed policy is greeted with general disfavor, the council can reject "the manager's suggestion"—he takes the blame regardless of where the idea may have originated. If the proposal is well received, councilmen accept it as their own.

council. In City C, the manager had to overcome major opposition which, for a short while, actually held majority control of the council. The manager chose to wait out the opposition, almost succeeded in keeping from being quoted in the newspapers concerning his own views on the conflict, and eventually weaned the mayor from the opposition, thus making his supporters on the council a majority. In City B, two councilmen, elected to office late in the five-year period studied, accused the manager of policy domination and voted against proposals that had his blessing, but there appears to have been no support for the two men from other councilmen. In an election toward the end of the period studied, a little-known candidate, seeking to join them, failed to secure nomination.

The Role of the Mayor

What of the mayor as a leader? In two of the cities studied, the mayor did not play a special leadership role. In one, he was elected by the council; in the other he was directly elected. In the third city, the mayor was the councilman receiving the largest number of votes. An individual of high prestige both among the public and on the council was regularly elected mayor through the period studied. Because of his high status, he appears to have been deferred to by other councilmen and his views were respected. His leadership was rather inconspicuous, however, and he did not play the role of policy innovator, or of a chaperon of legislation through the council.[6]

In the thirty issues of importance during the five-year period, the mayor was a principal leader on only two, both of them in City B. The mayor in this case was an elderly man who had held office for many years. He was chief spokesman on the council for an unsuccessful proposal for a metropolitan area hospital authority, although the plan had first been worked out by a citizen group which strongly supported it. A new city hall for the community was a matter close to his heart, but he was opposed by the chamber of commerce and the taxpayers group which thought the plan extravagant and unnecessary. Although the mayor had the support of the manager and of the planning commission, the council finally accepted the plan of the economy groups.

It is impossible to conclude whether the manner by which the mayor was selected affected his role as a policy leader. In general, there was not much reason to believe that the office of mayor, as such, was prestigious enough to give the incumbent a significant advantage over other potential leaders.

6. In one of the cities, the office of city attorney was elective. The incumbent played a definite policy-making role independent of the manager. In the two cities where the attorney was appointed, his role was much less important.

The Role of the Council

Members of the council did not emerge as either general policy innovators or as general policy leaders. The individual councilman, rather, was likely to assume leadership in connection with a specific issue or function of government. He developed pet interests or came to know one area of municipal activity especially well and concentrated upon that.

There was one exception: a councilman who acted as a leader both in the general development of policy and in seeking support for policies first presented by some other individual or group (Councilman n in City A). To this case might be added another, somewhat similar. In City C, one councilman definitely acted as the leader of the opposition to the manager, regardless of the particular policy issue under discussion. His leadership, with a few exceptions, was of a negative sort, however. Since the conflict over the management began almost at the outset of the period covered by this study, it is impossible to say if this councilman could also have served as a constructive policy leader under other conditions.

While a councilman might concentrate upon a particular aspect of municipal policy, it was found to be dangerous for him to seek to make some specific issue a *cause célèbre*. If he chose to do so, he immediately subjected himself to greater public attention and scrutiny than was the case for the typical councilman, and he risked a defeat on the issue which could in turn have disastrous political consequences for him. There is danger in leadership, relative safety in conformity and anonymity. The study indicated that councilmen were aware of this.

In the five-year period covered, there were two incidents in which councilmen chose to make major controversies out of particular issues, and in each case the councilman was defeated in his try for re-election. In City A, Councilman m, who had served continuously for a quarter of a century and who came from one of the city's high prestige families, chose to take the lead in a full defense of municipal ownership of the light plant. The plant, long owned by the city, competed with a private utility. It served relatively few customers and costs were higher than those of the private company. As a result, patronage was falling and unit cost rising. Shortly after a new councilman took office, he began a campaign for the sale of the light plant to the private utility. His proposal was immediately and vigorously opposed by Councilman m. The issue was carried along at council meetings, through referendums and into court before it was finally settled in favor of sale to the private company. When Councilman m ran for re-election, he was defeated. He lost again two years later. (The referendums on the issue indicated that he was on the unpopular side of the controversy.)

Another case, in City C, involved the leader of a group opposing the city manager and his policies. Councilman y in this case was hostile to the manager at the beginning of the period studied. It took him some time, however, to organize a bloc. After an election, he picked up two new council members. When the mayor joined with him on two important issues, involving the dismissal of two employees and wage and salary policies, Councilman y had a 4-3 majority on the council. The local newspaper speculated on the possible resignation of the manager. The manager apparently decided to wait for further developments and for public opinion to become crystallized. He neither fought back nor made plans for resignation. Later, he became ill and the mayor acted in his stead for a few weeks. Shortly after, the mayor began to support the pro-manager group under Councilman z's leadership. This switch produced a new one-vote majority in support of the administration and talk of the manager's resignation stopped. A hard fought election campaign followed in which the issues included the question of wage and salary policy, support for the principle of the council-manager plan (all groups claimed to support it, but Councilman y was accused of seeking to sabotage it), and support for the incumbent manager. Councilman y was defeated for re-election by one of the city's leading industrialists, a supporter of the manager.

Leadership on Important Issues

Since in both policy innovation and leadership, the role of the councilmen was a relatively modest one, it is necessary to look elsewhere for the actors who played these parts. They were the manager, the members of his administration, and the leaders of interest groups.

Not all issues that were regarded in the community as being important involved intense controversy. In the case of some significant community problems, only one plausible solution was offered. In others, no councilman seemed to see any political advantage in presenting alternative solutions.

When the bus companies came to the councils from time to time asking for fare increases, each councilman would deplore the trend toward higher fares and poorer service, but since the only discernible alternative to refusing the rate increase was a discontinuance of service, almost all councilmen voted in favor of the request. In each of the cities, study committees of lay citizens were appointed to seek solutions to the bus problem. In two cities, they recommended that the city lease the lines and then hire the bus company to run them, thus avoiding certain taxes. In the third city, the committee found another bus company to operate in the city when the existing company sought to withdraw. In each case, the council gratefully, and with little discussion, accepted the proposed solutions. Although the operation of the bus lines was considered vital to each community, a crisis situation was solved in each of them with little or no conflict.

In cases where controversy did exist, as Table 1 indicates, leadership in favor of a proposal was most likely to come from the administration, with outside groups the second most likely source. In fact, nearly all the really significant issues derived their leadership from these two sources. (The cases are too few to attempt to correlate the types of issues with the sources of leadership.) Councilmanic leadership came in annexation proposals, in seeking to make suburbs "pay their own way," and in revolts against the manager. Only in the proposal to sell City A's light plant and in a water supply revenue bond plan in City B did a councilman provide the leadership. In the second case, he had strong administration backing. Issues involving sharp conflict were rarely resolved as the result of leadership coming from the governing body.

In contrast to the leadership *for* proposals, councilmen did lead in opposition to proposals more often than did persons in any other category. Most of the opposition was aimed either against the manager or against expanded services or capital outlay. A good bit of it was non-constructive and perfunctory. The picture of the council, in summary, was one of a largely passive body granting or withholding its approval in the name of the community when presented with proposals from a leadership outside itself.

Nonofficial leadership was important in the case of two types of issues in addition to those that were regarded as "hot potatoes" and so treated gingerly by elected officials. The first type included those submitted by both neighborhood and downtown businessmen seeking municipal assistance in solving their problems. The second included the public transportation problems which, in all three cities, were turned over to citizens committees to bring in recommendations. The first is the kind of interest group activity commonplace before legislative bodies at all levels of government. The second offers something of a puzzle,

TABLE 1   *Leadership on Municipal Issues in Three Michigan Cities*

Source of Leadership	In Favor	Opposed
Administration	15	—
Mayor	2	—
Councilmen	7	15
Outside Groups	10	7

Note: The table covers the 30 important municipal issues discussed during the years 1953–57. Because leadership was shared in several and lacking in others, the totals do not equal 30.

however. It would seem likely that the solution to the bus problem in each city was one that might have been pushed by almost any council-man, and to his political advantage. Yet, this was not the pattern. Possibly councilmen feared that any solution would also involve increased rates or the necessity of the city buying the transportation system—a solution that seemed unpopular in each city. Possibly controversy was anticipated that never materialized.

It might be noted that the important policy and leadership role of the manager, of his administration, and of leaders of nonofficial groups differs from the pattern intended in the original theory of the council-manager plan. That theory assumed that able, respected leaders of the community would be willing to serve on councils and would take responsibility for policy decisions in government as they did in their businesses. While the typical councilman in the three cities studied gave the impression of being a sufficiently competent person, it seems clear enough that he was not willing to assume a public leadership role under circumstances where he might thereby be plunged into controversy. The politician in the council-manager city, though he may be an amateur, thus follows the traditional practice of American politicians and seeks to avoid taking sides in closely matched battles.

Suggested Areas for Further Study

A study covering a span of only five years in three cities is scarcely sufficient to serve as a basis for firm generalizations. It is, however, possible for certain tentative hypotheses to be offered from the work reported on here and these may properly provide a basis for further investigation. The following seven hypotheses appear to be most worthy of further inquiry:

1] There will be relatively few issues coming before the council that will be regarded by councilmen, the manager, or the press as involving important, nonroutine decisions.

2] A manager will avoid taking public positions as a policy innovator on items of major importance, but will serve as a leader in presenting and publicly defending policy recommendations developed within the administrative departments, the advisory boards and commissions, study committees of lay citizens, or private groups.

3] The mayor is not chosen on the basis of leadership ability or willingness to play a leadership role and he is, therefore, no more likely to serve as a policy leader than is any other councilman.

4] A councilman is likely to assume leadership in connection with a specific function of government, but not as a general policy leader.

5] A councilman who chooses to make some specific issue a *cause célèbre* thereby becomes subject to greater public attention and scrutiny than is the case with the typical councilman and, if he fails in his objective, runs serious risk of defeat in the following election.

6]   Important issues, measured by the consequences of failure to act, may involve little controversy if no alternative solutions are perceived, or if no political advantage is seen in the advancement of alternative solutions.

7]   When issues are regarded as being important, but when possible solutions are controversial, or many plausible solutions are discernible, the alternative finally selected is likely to come from the administration or from a group outside of the local government structure.

Further inquiry into these hypotheses should help to expand our areas of knowledge about local government and the characteristics of the public policy-making process.

The Resignation of Elgin Crull

Bruce Kovner

AFTER FOURTEEN YEARS of service, Elgin Crull, the city manager of Dallas, submitted his resignation to the city council on June 6, 1966. He was resigning, the press said, for financial reasons; he was to become an executive of one of the biggest banks in Texas. The council unanimously praised his long service, accepted his resignation, and appointed his assistant his successor. Since in Dallas, as in most other council-manager cities, a manager may not argue his case in public, Crull's resignation appeared to much of the city as another case of a good man going on to a better job. But the events leading to the resignation were largely hidden from public view, and, with examination, they reveal a different story, one with interesting implications for council-manager government.

Crull began his career as a newspaperman covering city hall for the old Dallas *Dispatch-Journal.* It was a job that required a man to learn about and know those who were politically important in the city. When the then city manager found that he needed someone with this kind of political acumen, he persuaded Crull to become his assistant. Six years later, Crull was manager.

In some cities it would have been held against a manager that he had not been trained in engineering or administration and had not followed the normal career line, working his way up from the managership of a small city to that of a medium-sized one and from there to that of a large one. In Dallas, however, being unprofessional was something of an asset. The city preferred a home-grown product, like Crull, to an outsider who might not be sympathetic to the special qualities and values of Dallas life.

Crull's point of view also suited Dallas. He was, a newspaper said, "an impregnable rock against extravagance and waste." City government, he believed, should do only what was clearly essential and it should do that in the most economical way possible. He was not indifferent to the human problems that governments are supposed to

Published for the first time in this book by permission of the author.

solve, but he believed, along with much of Dallas, that the best way to improve matters was to keep government interference and costs at a minimum.

Had his point of view been very different from this, Crull would never have been made manager. His predecessor was a conservative who wanted him not as an "idea man" and still less as someone who could introduce Dallas to the latest thing in social experimentation but as someone who by his knowledge of the ins and outs of Dallas politics could help him (the manager) get his own ideas across. Later on, it was a city council controlled by conservative businessmen that made him manager. No one suspected of wanting to spend money would have had the backing of that council. Crull was someone who could be counted on to run things honestly, efficiently, and cheaply, and that was all the council wanted.

For several years all went well. Eventually, however, the city council's composition and therefore its point of view began to change. Reflecting the changes in the outlook of the business community and probably also of the electorate, the council became less interested in economy and more in projects to improve the city. People began to call Manager Crull not "economical" but "tightfisted."

Even so, Crull might still have been the manager of Dallas if it had not been for the rise on the civic scene of an immensely wealthy and prestigious businessman named J. Erik Jonsson. He had come to Dallas from New Jersey during the Depression and had risen to prominence as chairman of the board of Texas Instruments, one of the country's largest manufacturers of electronics equipment. He had never run for public office, but he had been active in civic affairs and it was known that he wanted to "repay Dallas for all it had done for him" with public service of some kind. When in 1964, the old mayor (who was at the same time a council member) resigned, the city council appointed Jonsson to the council and then chose him as acting mayor.

Although the new mayor and the city manager had both lived in Dallas for many years they were in a sense residents of different worlds. Crull had dealt mainly with Dallas people, and mainly on a personal basis. He did not know or care much about what went on outside of Dallas. Jonsson, by contrast, had always been oriented toward a worldwide network of professionals, government officials, and businessmen, who were in some way a part of his huge company's environment. He was used to dealing impersonally with abstract interests of various kinds; what went on at M.I.T., in Wall Street, or in the far corners of the earth was as real to him as anything in Dallas. He knew the city well, but it was a small part of his world. Following the sociologist Robert K. Merton, one might say that he was a "cosmopolitan," whereas the city manager was a "local."

Crull's experience in government, the goals of which were almost always vague and conflicting and the successes and failures of which could never be measured precisely, had oriented him toward certain outward signs that were generally taken as indicators of good administration—a lean budget was one, absence of corruption another, and freedom from criticism a third. Jonnson's business experience had given him a very different orientation. In the electronics industry the criterion of profit usually provided an unambiguous rule by which to judge success or failure; the important thing was to keep up with—or, better yet, to stay ahead of—technological change. Public relations mattered very little.

To Jonsson, most problems appeared to have technical solutions; there was no point in arguing about them: the intelligent thing was to employ research workers who would find the solutions. To Crull, on the other hand, problems seemed to consist of differences of opinion and conflicts of interest that had to be worked out by patient discussion and compromise, a process that could not be done away with by research, and often did not succeed in spite of everyone's efforts. Whereas Jonsson, looking at things from the perspective of the fast-growing electronics industry, thought of all change as progress and was eager to invest large sums in order to hasten its coming, Crull, from his experience as city manager, knew that change meant trouble.

As Mayor, Jonsson soon found that repaying Dallas for what it had done for him would not be easy. Under the city charter, the powers of his office were almost entirely ceremonial: the mayor presided over council meetings and represented the city on public occasions. That was all. His was a part-time job with no staff and practically no authority. The manager was the one who would run the city government.

This, of course, was the way that it was supposed to be under the council-manager plan. Historically, the plan had been introduced as a reform for the express purpose of transferring control from "politicians" (persons elected to office) to "professionals" and "experts" (persons appointed to office from their special training and knowledge). The mayor had been left without staff for the very purpose of restricting him to matters of "policy" and giving the manager and his staff freedom to manage the city's business without interference.

Jonsson's first four days as mayor were something of a surprise. It had been assumed that since he was such a busy executive and was an appointed rather than an elected mayor he would remain in the background for a while. Far from it. He was front-page news almost every day, visiting the city departments, calling upon the council to prepare for the challenge of the future, appointing an "emergency committee" on traffic safety, and urging the public to make Dallas great. It was not that he did not realize that his office was mainly honorific. When he visited the city departments he went only to those over which the council had direct jurisdiction. In his speeches, he showed an awareness of his restricted role: he did not talk about matters that were in the sphere of "administration" as opposed to "policy." Even Crull was satisfied that the mayor knew the rules of the game and meant to abide by them. Jonsson, he said later, "damn near strangled himself trying to keep out of my way."

It soon appeared, however, that if he were to accomplish anything the mayor would not be able to keep entirely out of the manager's way. This was evident when, soon after taking office, the mayor turned his attention to traffic safety. Dallas had had about a hundred traffic deaths the year before; this was a rather small number for a city of its size, but the mayor was shocked and wanted to do something to save the lives. The regulation of traffic was the responsibility of the police, however, and they were under the jurisdiction of the manager. In order to get anything done, Jonsson would have to persuade, cajole, or bully Crull. This was the way it had to be with everything. Initiating an ambitious program of any kind was out of the question. The best that the mayor could hope for was to convince or force the manager to take an action here and there. Sometimes he could not even do that.

In the spring of 1965 Jonsson ran for the mayor's seat to which he had been temporarily appointed. In his campaign he made much of a proposal called "Goals for Dallas." The idea was that the "best minds" would be brought together to solve the problems of Dallas by the methods of research and analysis that worked so well in big business. Jonsson won overwhelmingly—he got 73 per cent of the vote—and he regarded his victory as a popular mandate to carry out the Goals for Dallas program.

Crull was opposed to Goals for Dallas. He was sure that it would lead to undertakings that would be outside the city government's proper sphere and he doubted the ability of the mayor's experts to find any workable solutions for the problems in question. That Jonsson and some of his business friends had offered to put up most of the money that would be required made him more rather than less skeptical. He who pays the piper, he remarked, usually calls the tune. It may also be that he was apprehensive that Goals for Dallas would result in interference with his management of the city government.

In the manager's opinion, the mayor was not only trying to do things that the city government had no business doing, but was neglecting matters which required his attention. The past practice had been for the manager to put before the mayor and council questions on which he wanted policy advice; as a rule such questions had always been dealt with promptly. Jonsson, however, paid little attention to what he considered the council's "busywork." He felt that he had been chosen mayor because of his talent for dealing with large matters and that voters had given him a mandate to engage in comprehensive planning. It would be a waste of his time to spend it on the petty questions that the manager raised. The manager, for his part, felt that the mayor's preoccupation with "glamorous" subjects interfered with the efficient administration of the city's business. When the mayor said that he needed an administrative assistant, the manager opposed him sharply. What, he asked, did the mayor have to administer? At the same time, he remarked privately that Jonsson just wanted someone "to work with him on his dreams."

The budget was another source of conflict. From a formal standpoint, it was the manager's responsibility to prepare it and the council's to pass upon it. In practice, once the manager made his budget public it was very difficult for the council to change it in any respect. This was partly because the budget was complex and time was short but it was also partly for a political reason: the public was likely to suspect that there were political—i.e., narrowly political—motives behind any amendment that a councilman might propose. The difficulty of amending the budget worked to the advantage of the manager and of his department heads and against that of the councilmen. As the mayor explained to an interviewer,

> The people in the administration are trying to build careers for themselves. It is only natural that they would build up ways of concealing things from the Council or try to get things done their own way. The chief way of doing this is by giving the Council only a very short time to examine the budget.

After the election of 1965, the mayor and manager were on collision courses. The manager was convinced that the mayor's program was not one that he could conscientiously support or carry out. "It's not true that a City Manager can work with any Council," he told an interviewer. "You can't do a good job at what you don't believe in." The mayor, for his part, was determined to carry out the program that he thought was needed and wanted. "The Council must enforce its will," he told the same interviewer. "If the manager won't go along, you get rid of him."

The showdown came on August 9, 1965, at an informal meeting of the council in one of the city's plush private clubs. Prompted by the mayor, the council compelled Crull to raise the tax rate by two cents; this would bring in about $500,000 in new revenue—enough to finance a few projects dear to the mayor's heart. The council's action raised issues that transcended the money, however. From the manager's view, the main issue was one of fiscal integrity. From the mayor's, it was one of control: who was to run Dallas? In the course of conversation at the club the manager was criticized for his unwillingness to appropriate money for new projects or to support services at high enough levels. The manager defended himself against these criticisms on the grounds that the budget and the principle of fiscal integrity placed certain limits on what could be done. According to the recollection of one who was present, Mayor Jonsson was not entirely pleased with the manager's response and so spoke up,

Jonsson: We ought to tell the City Manager what services we want and he'll tell us how much it will cost. If he tells us what the budget is to be, he's making policy. We need to look ahead ten years. We need a ten year cash flow picture for basing a capital improvements program.

Crull: The public doesn't understand long term programs.

Jonsson: Elgin, you are no longer running the old farm. This city is a big business. We are exploring and we need your help. But we find a kind of passive resistance on your part. You're always telling us how *not* to do it.

There was no point in arguing with the man who had recently received 73 percent of the vote, especially as it was evident that most of the other councilmen agreed with him. Crull concluded, in fact, that his usefulness as manager of Dallas had ended and he soon began looking for another job. Characteristically, he wanted one in Dallas, and so he left the city management profession for a job as a Dallas businessman.

It may seem anomalous that the showdown came because the politician, Jonsson, favored long-term planning, capital budgeting, and other standard practices of large-scale organizations, whereas the manager, Crull, opposed them on the political grounds that public opinion was adverse to them. The anomaly may be more apparent than real, however, for in present-day Dallas the prestige of big business and its methods may be such as to make planning, capital budgeting, and all the rest advisable on political as well as other grounds. The conflict was not, as might first appear, between a manager pretending to be a politician (Jonsson) and a politician pretending to be a manager (Crull). Rather it was between two politician-managers, one a "cosmopolitan" and the other a "local." In any case, it is clear that the generally accepted doctrine of the council-manager movement oversimplifies matters considerably, both in asserting that any manager can work successfully with any mayor who is honest and believes in the principle of the council-manager plan, and in implying that the more able, vigorous, and conscientious a mayor and a manager the better for all concerned.

THE THEORY OF "GOOD GOVERNMENT"

Three Fundamental Principles

Harold A. Stone, Don K. Price,
and Kathryn H. Stone

THE LEADING ADVOCATES of the city manager plan in nearly every city had a general purpose in common: to have the city government devote its energies more effectively toward getting work done for the community and toward wasting less of its money and effort on incidental or factional purposes. To achieve their purpose, they proposed three ideas—the three principal political ideas that characterized the city manager movement. Each of these ideas was reflected or embodied in one of the three fundamental principles of the city manager form of government.

First, there was the idea that the most capable and public-spirited citizens should serve on the governing body as representatives of the city at large, to determine policies for the benefit of the community as a whole, rather than for any party, faction, or neighborhood. This idea was embodied in the nonpartisan ballot and in the system of election at large of a small council.

Second, there was the idea that municipal administration should be delegated to a thoroughly competent, trained executive, who should get and hold his job on his executive ability alone and should be given a status and salary comparable to that of an executive in charge of a private corporation. The idea was embodied in the concentration of administrative authority in the city manager.

Third, there was the idea that the voters should hold only the

Reprinted from City Manager Government in the United States (*Chicago: Public Administration Service, 1940*), *pp. 236–242.*

councilmen politically responsible and should give the city manager a status of permanence and neutrality in political controversy. This idea was embodied in the unification of powers in the council as a body comprising the only elected officials in the city government.

No matter how many different immediate objectives characterized the campaigns for city manager government, the city manager movement was motivated by these ideas. In cities that were accustomed to partisan patronage, the advocates of the city manager plan expressed them in terms of a crusading appeal for the elimination of partisan influence in municipal administration and for an increase in the influence of technical experts. In other cities there was no such public appeal; members of the governing body simply decided to get a city manager in order to get their job done better. In other words, the objectives of the city manager movement were pretty much the same in all these cities, although its advocates had to adapt their tactics to different local conditions.

Then why did different cities have such sharply different experiences with the plan? Why did some cities have violent political disagreements over the adoption of the plan and then drag the city manager into political controversy, while other cities adopted the plan quietly and allowed their managers to lead a relatively peaceful existence? It was not—in the main—because one city had a charter that was superior in certain details to that of another or because the leaders of the city manager movement in that city adopted superior tactics. It was because of a great difference between the cities in the political ideas or attitudes of the rank and file of the voters.

Respected community leaders were able to induce the generally uninterested voters in all these cities to support a change to the city manager plan. Then in one city such voters would continue to support the ideas of the city manager plan because those ideas were in harmony with their established habits; in the other city the uninterested voters would follow dissatisfied political leaders in a reaction against the unfamiliar ideas. Thus, the cities in which the city manager plan operated most smoothly were the cities in which its fundamental ideas were accepted without a conflict. . . .

On the other hand, the cities in which the possibilities of the new form of government were not fully realized were those in which the ideas of the city manager movement came into conflict with traditional political ideas. In such cities some of these ideas that contributed to the reaction against the city manager movement were held by leading advocates of the city manager plan. This reaction, which developed several years after the establishment of the plan in most of the so-called Machine-Ridden and Faction-Ridden cities . . . , was by no means caused entirely by the selfish material interests of professional politicians. The reaction was instigated by such politicians in some cities, but not in all of them. Nevertheless, in all cities in these two groups the success of the reaction depended on popular support, which could be organized only where the reaction was in harmony with popular political ideas—ideas which the reader, according to his point of view, may call either ideals or prejudices.

The adoption of the city manager plan brought about improvements in the political leadership of municipalities in two ways. First, it broadened the possibilities of municipal politics. Second, it heightened the prestige of the councilmanic office and thus led men of greater ability and reputation to be willing to serve as councilmen.

The first type of improvement came about in all groups of cities. In a municipal organization that included no administrators of ability and performed none but the minimum routine functions, the political leader at best was a dignified but negative participant; at worst he was a grafter. An effective organization under an expert manager, on the other hand, broadened the political leader's scope; he could promote more positive municipal policies because their effective execution had become a possibility.

This contrast is stated in extreme terms, but the general improvement in administrative machinery under the city manager plan certainly changed the function of the political leader to some extent in nearly every community, no matter what its former political tradition. In Lynchburg the councilmen gave less time to detailed supervision of public works and to parliamentary red tape and were considering city planning and co-operation with the state municipal league; in Austin they forgot the old neighborhood factionalism and promoted housing projects in Mexican districts; in Rochester they paid less attention to patronage and more to transportation facilities and to the industrial development of the city.

In the increase in the prestige of the councilmanic office and in the improvement in the ability and the reputation of councilmen the changes were less uniform. Some cities that adopted the manager plan had long been accustomed to electing the community leaders of the greatest prestige and public spirit to their governing bodies, and the change in the form of government did not affect this habit. In these cities, a councilmanic election was not a contest between factions that were interested either in patronage or in special policies. It was an expression by the community of confidence in its leaders, who served for the prestige of the office and from a sense of civic responsibility rather than from a desire to further the interest of any group. But no one group—economic, religious, or political—maintained a monopoly on municipal affairs. Voters, in choosing councilmen, thought more of the general prestige of candidates in the community than of their membership in any faction. Councilmen, as a result, tended to think more of the community as a whole and less of factional interests in making their decisions.

This was the state of affairs which leaders of the city manager movement wanted to bring about in the other cities that adopted the city manager plan. . . . In these cities politics had not attracted the community leaders of the greatest public spirit and prestige, and members of the governing body had served their factions rather than the community as a whole. Since the subject matter of municipal government was largely routine business, factional competition was based, not on broad policy, but on special favors and patronage.

The leaders in the city manager movement in these cities, seeking to have the affairs of the municipal government administered impartially for the community rather than for the benefit of factional groups, formed a citizens' association and drafted as councilmanic candidates men who were accustomed to taking the lead in other community institutions— churches, schools, service clubs and commercial organizations, labor unions, and other organizations which enlisted upaid leaders. Some candidates were professional men, a few were workingmen, and many were business executives or men engaged in independent commercial enterprises. Their common quality was that they possessed the respect of the community. But in these cities the idea that the community should delegate control of municipal affairs to its most respected citizens and should permit them to direct the administration of the government without giving factional followers special favors was not supported by tradition or by general sentiment. The impartial administration of the government aroused resentment among those who had been accustomed to exceptional treatment, and the resentment was directed at the symbol of the new regime--the city manager.

The Theory of Group Representation on the Council

In the reaction against the city manager plan, which usually produced a conspicuous decline in the prestige of the council, one of the arguments most frequently used was that various groups—geographical, racial, political, social—ought to be represented on the council. The leaders of the political reaction against the first council and the first city manager made the councilmen out to be, not merely respected community leaders, but businessmen who had little regard for the common people. The reactionary leaders argued that a small council consisting mainly of men who were successful community leaders was unrepresentative of the city and therefore undemocratic. By this argument they proposed that the voters should restore to office the traditional political leaders of the city or even that the charter should be amended to enlarge the council and to restore the system of election by wards. This argument was often used by factional leaders who were seeking any stick with which to beat the reformers. Nevertheless, it probably carried considerable weight with the rank and file of the voters, who thought of representation in terms of groups because they were accustomed to pay more attention to factional purposes than to community purposes in municipal politics.

In some cities, of course, leaders in the city manager movements, conforming to local habits, formed factions of their own, and used their control of the local government to keep their friends in office and their enemies out—regardless of the desire of either of them to cooperate for the welfare of the community. The existence of strong political animosities made it difficult for those who wanted to establish impartial administration to be impartial; until a united community spirit developed, every one of their actions was interpreted according to its effect on the factional controversy. Under these conditions an electoral system that would have guaranteed each political faction seats in the city council would have tended to defeat the will of the majority, which had affirmed itself in favor of impartial administration. Different factions did not want representation in order to participate in the discussion of policy which should then be administered impartially; they wanted representation in order to be able to bargain for special favors and to be able to obstruct those who were trying to put into effect the new system of government.

The original advocates of the city manager plan were not in every city the only leaders who could be trusted to operate it properly. On the contrary, the reformers who put it into effect were not always best able to maintain popular support for its principles. As long as they held office, the plan might be identified with them alone and might not be accepted by the city as a whole; the plan might be put on a stable basis only by the election to the council of leaders who had formerly opposed the plan. To have the city government run smoothly, it was sometimes better to have all self-conscious social groups represented on the council —as long as their representation depended on the sanction of the community as a whole and as soon as they thought in city-wide, not ward or factional, terms.

Under election at large all groups could be represented so long as they were willing to cooperate in a program approved by the majority; under a group representation system of election, each faction could retain its councilmanic seats even if it was willfully sabotaging the policies of the administration. The theory of group representation was accepted by a great many advocates of the city manager plan, as well as by its opponents. In practice it was most often embodied in a system of election by wards; in theory, it was embodied in the system of proportional representation, which was recommended by the Model Charter as an alternative that was preferred to election at large and as an improvement on election by districts.

Assumptions Underlying the Theory of Group Representation

The whole idea of group representation depends upon certain assumptions that are not truly applicable to city government and overlooks what is usually the most important issue of municipal politics. It assumes that the policy determined by the council will depend more on what groups or factions the councilmen belong to than on how much public spirit and intelligence the councilmen have. A councilman elected by the votes of a neighborhood of underprivileged citizens, according to this theory, should be more active in promoting that neighborhood's welfare than a councilman elected at large or by some other group of voters. In the cities covered by this survey, however, real changes in municipal policy were rarely brought about by competition among self-interested political groups. The most conspicuous changes were not made by representatives acting on mandates from a group of their constituents that stood to benefit by the new policies; on the contrary, they were made by leaders of the community as a whole, acting out of public spirit on the proposals of a trained administrator. For example, there were the inaugurations of the comprehensive health, recreation, and welfare programs in Dayton, in Austin, and in Janesville. These programs were established on the recommendations of city managers by councilmen, most of whom were well-to-do and important businessmen, in the face of bitter political attacks from the traditional political leaders of the lower-income neighborhoods, the very neighborhoods that needed the new programs most.

The idea that various groups ought to have representatives on the council to look after their interests overlooks what is usually the most important issue of municipal politics. In many cities the greatest issue, and the greatest conflict of interests, was between those who supported a system of partisan patronage and those who demanded impartial administration. The interests of any social or economic group may often be more greatly affected by the quality of administration of noncontroversial municipal policies than by the decision—one way or the other—of the controversial issues. The competition of municipal political factions did little in these cities to bring about democratic control of policies. On the other hand, it did a great deal to destroy the prestige of local government and to subordinate its fundamental purpose of community services to factional interests. The idea of group or neighborhood representation was one of the great handicaps to the election of public-spirited representatives for the city as a whole under the city manager plan.

Group Conflict Is Inevitable in a Major City

Charles A. Beard

IF I WERE to make an excursion into utopian politics and sketch a new "City of the Sun," assigning to political parties their proper place in my dream-made republic, I should start out by saying with the great chief justice, John Marshall, that nothing more debases and pollutes the human mind than partisan politics. When we see men otherwise just and fair in their judgments vilifying, maligning, and slandering their opponents, even in unimportant political campaigns, those of us who are not enamoured of billingsgate are moved to exclaim that political parties have no place at all in a rational society. But this would be a vain flying in the face of the hard and unpleasant facts of life and a vain longing for the impossible.

Viewing the subject from a practical angle we may inquire whether the issues which divide men and women into national parties are issues which have any relation to municipal questions as such. The facile reformer usually answers in the negative. It is true that there seems to be no connection between ship subsidies, tariff, labor legislation, farm loans, and kindred matters and the problems that arise in our great urban centres. Superficially there is none. But I cannot be too emphatic when I say that not a single one of our really serious municipal questions—poverty, high cost of living, overcrowding, unemployment, low standards of life, physical degeneracy—can be solved, can be even approached by municipalities without the co-operation of the state and national government, and the solution of these problems calls for state and national parties. No big vision of this mighty nation as it is to be can exclude from its range an economy which is both urban and rural, one and truly indivisible.

Of course, speaking practically there is no real division between the Republican and the Democrats on municipal issues. The usual

Reprinted from National Municipal Review, *6, No. 2 (March, 1917), 201–206, where it appeared under the title "Political Parties in City Government: A Reconsideration of Old Viewpoints."*

slogans of economy, efficiency, and good management are accepted by both of them. No party is willing to advocate waste, inefficiency, and bad management. The Socialist party is the only party that has a complete program of public economy which includes national and state and city issues. That is a program of collectivism, public ownership and operation of the great utilities or economic processes upon which all depend for a livelihood. We may or may not approve of that program, but we cannot deny that it is a consistent municipal, state, and national program. Neither can we deny that the Socialists are both logical and sound, from their point of view, when they insist upon maintaining a municipal party organization and linking it up with the state and national organization. Insisting that not a single great problem of social economy is purely or even primarily municipal, the Socialists rightly stick to a unified party organization. Up to the present time, however, they have been almost negligible factors in most of our great cities, and as we are not here concerned with prophecy or speculation we may leave them out of account.

I have said above that there is no real division between the Republicans and Democrats on municipal issues, but I do not mean that issues create parties. On the contrary I think the causes of party division lie deeper than superficial paper declarations of party principles. Issues are more frequently pretexts than causes of partisanship. That profound statesmen, Alexander Hamilton, said in the convention that framed the constitution of the United States: "All communities divide themselves into the few and the many. The first are the rich and the well-born, the other the mass of the people." I think we have in that laconic statement more information on the place of political parties in municipal government than in all the literature that has been issued by the reformers since the foundation of this republic. Disparity in the kinds and distribution of property, as the father of our constitution, James Madison, said, is the most fundamental cause of parties and factions in all ages and all places.

Of other cities I have little knowledge, but I know something about the history of parties in the city of New York, from the days of Jefferson to the days of Mitchel. By a long and painstaking study of election returns, ward maps, occupations, and wealth distribution, I arrived at the conclusion that the first great party division in New York city—that between the Federalists and the Jeffersonian Republicans—was a division between "wealth and talents" on the one hand and the masses on the other hand. Anyone interested in the facts will find them on pp. 383–387 of my *Economic Origins of Jeffersonian Democracy*. The studies I made for that work have been carried forward with great skill, accuracy and ingenuity by one of my colleagues, Mr. Dixon R. Fox, who has now completed the maps of the elections by wards down until 1840. He finds that in every great contest the "wealth and talents" were in the main with the Federalists or later the Whigs, while the masses were Democrats. I believe that fundamental division exists to-day in our great northern cities. I do not mean to say that there are not wealth and talents in the Democratic party, but I do contend that the center of gravity of wealth is on the Republican side while the center of gravity of poverty is on the Democratic side. Anyone who wants official confirmation of this view may read President Wilson's *New Freedom.*

Of course in the smaller cities like Des Moines, Iowa, or Dayton, Ohio, where the area of the great industrial proletariat is not large and where distinction of group and class are not marked, the materials for party divisions are not so obvious and so persistent. In the south cities are few and new, and there are special problems. As Plato and Aristotle long ago pointed out where there is similarity and approximate equality of property interests, there unity and stability may take the place of divisions and contests. To anyone really interested in the profound philosophical problem set by the theme of my paper I commend a long and prayerful study of Aristotle's *Politics.* There he will find more genuine information on the subject than in all the books that have ever been written on American government. Speaking, therefore, not as a prophet or an advocate, I should say that parties are inevitable and unavoidable in modern society.

By that I do not mean to say that the corruption and excesses which have characterized political organizations in our great cities will continue unabated. On the contrary, I look forward with confidence to a diminution in corruption, partly on account of the increasing number of independent voters who cannot be counted upon to follow slavishly the dictates of leaders, but mainly on account of the fact that the opportunities for corruption are now materially reduced. There will be no more boards of "forty thieves" in New York disposing of Broadway franchises, not because we are better than our fathers but because the Broadway franchise has been disposed of and made perpetual. With more than 95 per cent of our surface railway franchises granted in perpetuity in New York City we may feel reasonably secure from the attacks of franchise grabbers masked as party organizations.

In other words, to use academic terminology, the law of diminishing returns has set in against municipal corruption in its grosser forms, and so we may expect to see an increasing number of the so-called "interests" becoming good and non-partisan. They are like Great Britain. Having possession of the earth, she is for peace and the *status quo.* Certain financial groups in New York that formerly looked with kindly toleration on Tammany, having "got theirs," are now for efficiency and economy. Providence works in mysterious ways His wonders to perform, and those who are weary of Tweed rings and gas scandals may look forward with confidence and hope. The age of great graft in our cities is over; we have eaten our cake. We shall be bothered with petty graft, but that is not so dangerous to public morals. But we shall have parties for such a long time in the future that we need not make our last will and testament now.

If this analysis is correct then those of us who dwell in large cities must arrange to live and work with parties. Rural villages may experiment with "non-partisanship." From what I can gather from newspapers and gossip with visitors from non-partisanship cities of any size, the abolition of city parties by statutory devices is a delusion. Perhaps some of the delegates from Boston will inform us whether there are any Democrats or Republicans in the city government there. Of course some one will rise up from Dayton and tell us that utopia is there, but some of us skeptics from the east must be pardoned if we do not rewrite our entire political science in the light of three years' experience of an Ohio city, whose population is about equal to the annual increment in the population of New York. I know of nothing more amusing than the report of the first trial of the "new non-partisan election system" in San Francisco, reported by the *National Municipal Review* in its first number. The reporter told us that the results of the same were "generally considered satisfactory," and then proceeded: "A candidate has but to secure ten electors to take the sponsor's oath, to get his name printed on the primary ballot. No candidate succeeded, however, unless he was backed by a large organization. Six such organizations took part in the contest: the municipal conference, the good government league, the Republican, Democratic, Union Labor, and Socialist parties. The first four combined on James Rolph, Jr., a prominent shipowner, as a candidate for mayor and had many other candidates in common. The Union Labor party put forward Mayor McCarthy and a straight ticket. The Socialists named Wm. McDevitt." Surely an Irishman wrote this account of a "genuine, non-partisan" election under a non-partisan law.

In fact, I am prepared to defend the thesis that non-partisanship has not worked, does not work, and will not work in any major city in the United States. We have plenty of non-partisan election laws designed to smash party organizations. We also have direct primary laws designed to take nomination out of the hands of party leaders. I think these laws have in many instances put a wholesome fear in the minds of political leaders, but I do not believe that they have permanently reduced the power of the expert political minority that manages public affairs.

To come right down to practical conclusions, I should make the following summary: (1) that the causes of parties lie deeper than election laws or most so-called issues; (2) that the causes of parties being social and economic, we must expect the continued existence of party organizations in our municipal affairs; (3) that the task before the reformer is not the enactment of non-partisan laws but the development of legislation and public opinion which will makes parties responsible for their conduct of municipal government; (4) that fusion is a temporary process better calculated to frighten and educate party leaders than to develop a unified and well-planned city administration; (5) that the independent, self-directing citizens are relatively few in any community or party but education will widen that number and from them we may expect a check upon the party extravagance which has disgraced so many of our cities; (6) that men who want wise and just government in cities are likely to do as much good by co-operating with parties and insisting upon the establishment of sound party policies and genuine party responsibility as they are by running to the legislature for new non-partisan election laws; (7) that there is a power, not in legislation, that worketh for righteousness.

The Effects of the Reform Ideal on Policy

Robert L. Lincberry
and Edmund P. Fowler

A DECADE AGO, political scientists were deploring the "lost world of municipal government" and calling for systematic studies of municipal life which emphasized the political, rather than the administrative, side of urban political life.[1] In recent years, this demand has been generously answered and urban politics is becoming one of the most richly plowed fields of political research. In terms originally introduced by David Easton,[2] political scientists have long been concerned with inputs, but more recently they have focused their attention on other system variables, particularly the political culture[3] and policy outputs of municipal governments.[4]

The present paper will treat two policy outputs, taxation and expenditure levels of cities, as dependent variables. We will relate these policy choices to socio-economic characteristics of cities and to structural characteristics of their governments. Our central research concern is to examine the impact of political structures, reformed and unreformed, on policy-making in American cities.

1. Lawrence J. R. Herson, "The Lost World of Municipal Government," this REVIEW, 51 (June, 1957), 330–345; Robert T. Daland, "Political Science and the Study of Urbanism," *ibid.*, 491–509.

2. David Easton, "An Approach to the Analysis of Political Systems," *World Politics,* 9 (April, 1957), 383–400.

3. Edward C. Banfield and James Q. Wilson, *City Politics* (Cambridge: Harvard University Press and the MIT Press, 1963); see also James Q. Wilson and Edward C. Banfield, "Public-Regardingness as a Value Premise in Voting Behavior," this REVIEW, 58 (December, 1964), 876–887.

4. See, for example, Thomas R. Dye, "City-Suburban Social Distance and Public Policy," *Social Forces,* 4 (1965), 100–106; Raymond Wolfinger and John Osgood Field, "Political Ethos and the Structure of City Government," this REVIEW, 60 (June, 1966), 306–326; Edgar L. Sherbenou, "Class, Participation, and the Council-Manager Plan," *Public Administration Review,* 21 (Summer, 1961), 131–135; Lewis A. Froman, Jr., "An Analysis of Public Policies in Cities," *Journal of Politics,* 29 (February, 1967), 94–108.

Reprinted from American Political Science Review, *Vol. LXI, No. 3 (September 1967), 701–716, where it appeared under the title "Reformism and Public Policies in American Cities," by permission of the publisher and the authors.*

I. Political Culture, Reformism and Political Institutions

The leaders of the Progressive movement in the United States left an enduring mark on the American political system, particularly at the state and municipal level. In the states, the primary election, the referendum, initiative and recall survive today. The residues of this *Age of Reform*,[5] as Richard Hofstadter called it, persist in municipal politics principally in the form of manager government and at-large and nonpartisan elections. The reformers were, to borrow Banfield and Wilson's phrase, the original embodiment of the "middle class ethos" in American politics. They were, by and large, White Anglo-Saxon Protestants reacting to the politics of the party machine, which operated by exchanging favors for votes.[6]

It is important that we understand the ideology of these reformers if we hope to be able to analyze the institutions which they created and their impact on political decisions. The reformers' goal was to "rationalize" and "democratize" city government by the substitution of "community oriented" leadership. To the reformers, the most pernicious characteristic of the machine was that it capitalized on socio-economic cleavages in the population, playing on class antagonisms and on racial and religious differences. Ernest S. Bradford, an early advocate of commission government with at-large elections, defended his plans for at-large representation on grounds that

> . . . under the ward system of governmental representation, the ward receives the attention, not in proportion to its needs but to the ability of its representatives to 'trade' and arrange 'deals' with fellow members. . . . Nearly every city under the aldermanic system offers flagrant examples of this vicious method of 'part representation.' The commission form changes this to representation of the city as a whole.[7]

The principal tools which the reformers picked to maximize this "representation of the city as a whole" were the commission, and later the manager, form of government, the nonpartisan election and the election at-large. City manager government, it was argued, produced a no-nonsense, efficient and business-like regime, where decisions could be implemented by professional administrators rather than by victors in the battle over spoils. Nonpartisan elections meant to the reformer that state and national parties, whose issues were irrelevant to local politics anyway, would keep their divisive influences out of municipal decision-

---

5. (New York: Alfred A. Knopf, 1955.)
6. John Porter East, *Council Manager Government: The Political Thought of Its Founder, Richard S. Childs* (Chapel Hill: University of North Carolina Press, 1965), p. 18.
7. Ernest S. Bradford, *Commission Government in American Cities* (New York: Macmillan, 1911), p. 165.

making. Nonpartisan elections, especially when combined with elections at-large, would also serve to reduce the impact of socio-economic cleavages and minority voting blocs in local politics. Once established, these institutions would serve as bastions against particularistic interests.

Banfield and Wilson have argued that the "middle class ethos" of the reformers has become a prevalent attitude in much of political life. The middle class stands for "public regarding" virtues rather than for "private regarding" values of the ethnic politics of machines and bosses. The middle class searches for the good of the "community as a whole" rather than for the benefit of particularistic interests.[8] Agger, Goldrich and Swanson, in their study of two western and two southern communities have documented the rise of a group they call the "community conservationists," who "see the values of community life maximized when political leadership is exercised by men representing the public at large, rather than 'special interests.' "[9] Robert Wood has taken up a similar theme in his penetrating analysis of American suburbia. The "no-party politics of suburbia" is characterized by "an outright reaction against partisan activity, a refusal to recognize that there may be persistent cleavages in the electorate and an ethical disapproval of permanent group collaboration as an appropriate means of settling disputes."[10] This ideological opposition to partisanship is a product of a tightly-knit and homogeneous community, for "nonpartisanship reflects a highly integrated community life with a powerful capacity to induce conformity."[11]

Considerable debate has ensued over both the existence and the consequences of these two political ethics in urban communities. Some evidence has supported the view that reformed governments[12] are indeed found in cities with higher incomes, higher levels of education, greater proportions of Protestants and more white-collar job-holders. Schnore and Alford, for example, found that "the popular image of the manager city was verified; it does tend to be the natural habitat of the upper middle class." In addition, manager cities were "inhabited by a younger, more mobile population that is growing rapidly."[13]

8. Banfield and Wilson, *op. cit.*, p. 41.

9. Robert Agger, Daniel Goldrich, and Bert E. Swanson, *The Rulers and the Ruled* (New York: John Wiley and Sons, 1964), p. 21.

10. Robert C. Wood, *Suburbia: Its People and Their Politics* (Boston: Houghton Mifflin Co., 1959), p. 155.

11. *Ibid.*, p. 154.

12. We refer to cities characterized by commission or manager government, nonpartisan elections, and at-large constituencies as "reformed." Our use of the term is historical and no value position on reformism's merits is intended. To refer to reformed cities as "public regarding" or "middle class" is, it seems, to assume what needs to be proved.

13. Leo Schnore and Robert Alford, "Forms of Government and Socio-Economic Characteristics of Suburbs," *Administrative Science Quarterly*, 8 (June, 1963), 1–17. See also the literature cited in Froman, *op. cit.*

More recently, Wolfinger and Field correlated socio-economic variables—particularly ethnicity and region—to political structures. They concluded that "the ethos theory is irrelevant to the South . . . inapplicable to the West . . . fares badly in the Northwest . . ." and that support for the theory in the Midwest was "small and uneven."[14] Region proved to be a more important predictor of both government forms and of policy outputs like urban renewal expenditures than did the socio-economic composition of the population.

In our view, it is premature to carve a headstone for the ethos theory. It is our thesis that governments which are products of the reform movement behave differently from those which have unreformed institutions, even if the socio-economic composition of their population may be similar. Our central purpose is to determine the impact of both socio-economic variables and political institutions (structural variables) on outputs of city governments. By doing this, we hope to shed some additional illumination on the ethos theory.

II. Research Design

Variables

The independent variables used in this analysis, listed in Table 1, consist of relatively "hard" data, mostly drawn from the U.S. census.[15] These variables were selected because they represent a variety of possible social cleavages which divide urban populations—rich vs. poor, Negro vs. White, ethnic vs. native, newcomers vs. old-timers, etc. We

TABLE 1   *Independent Variables*

1. Population, 1960
2. Per cent population increase or decrease, 1950–60
3. Per cent non-white
4. Per cent of native population with foreign born or mixed parentage
5. Median income
6. Per cent of population with incomes below $3000
7. Per cent of population with incomes above $10,000
8. Median school years completed by adult population
9. Per cent high school graduates among adult population
10. Per cent of population in white collar occupations
11. Per cent of elementary school children in private schools
12. Per cent of population in owner-occupied dwelling units

14. Wolfinger and Field, *op. cit.,* pp. 325–326.
15. The source for the first nine variables is *The City and County Data Book* (Washington: United States Bureau of the Census, 1962). For the last three variables, the source is Orin F. Nolting and David S. Arnold (eds.), *The Municipal Yearbook 1965* (Chicago: International City Managers' Association, 1965), pp. 98 ff.

assume that such social and economic characteristics are important determinants of individual and group variations in political preferences. Data on each of these independent variables were gathered for each of the two hundred cities in the sample.[16]

Our principal theoretical concern is with the consequences of variations in the structural characteristics of form of government, type of constituency and partisanship of elections. The variable of government form is unambiguous. Except for a few small New England towns, all American cities have council-manager, mayor-council or commission government. There is, however, somewhat more ambiguity in the classification of election type. By definition, a "nonpartisan election is one in which no candidate is identified on the ballot by party affiliation."[17] The legal definition of nonpartisanship conceals the wide variation between Chicago's and Boston's nominal nonpartisanship and the more genuine variety in Minneapolis, Winnetka and Los Angeles.[18] We will quickly see, though, that formal nonpartisanship is not merely an empty legal nicety, but that there are very real differences in the political behavior of partisan and nonpartisan cities, even though we are defining them in legal terms only.[19]

Our classification of constituency types into only two groups also conceals some variation in the general pattern. While most cities use either the at-large or the ward pattern of constituencies exclusively, a handful use a combination of the two electoral methods. For our purposes, we classified these with district cities.

The dependent variables in this study are two measures of public policy outputs. A growing body of research on local politics has utilized policy measures as dependent variables.[20] The present research is intended to further this study of political outputs by relating socioeconomic variables to expenditure and taxation patterns in cities with varying political structures.

The dependent variables are computed by a simple formula. The between unreformed and reformed cities disappear when controls for

16. We used a random sample of 200 of the 309 American cities with populations of 50,000 or more in 1960. All information on the forms of government and forms of election are drawn from *The Municipal Yearbook, 1965, op. cit.*

17. Banfield and Wilson, *op. cit.*, p. 151.

18. For Minneapolis, see Robert Morlan, "City Politics: Free Style," *National Municipal Review*, 48 (November, 1949), pp. 485–490; Winnetka, Banfield and Wilson, *op. cit.*, p. 140; Los Angeles, Charles G. Mayo, "The 1961 Mayoralty Election in Los Angeles: The Political Party in a Nonpartisan Election," *Western Political Quarterly*, 17 (1964), 325–339.

19. At least one other variable may produce a given institutional form in a city—the legal requirements of a state government, which vary from state to state and may even vary for different kinds of cities within the same state. We have not taken account of this variable because systematic information on comparative state requirements in this area was unavailable to us. However, Wolfinger and Field consulted several experts and eliminated cities which are not given free choice over their institutions. Nevertheless, a comparison of our figures with theirs revealed no important differences.

20. See footnote 4, *supra*.

measure for taxation was computed by dividing the total personal income of the city into the total tax of the city, giving us a tax/income ratio. Similarly, dividing expenditures by the city's aggregate personal income gave us an expenditure/income ratio as the measure for our second dependent variable. These measures, while admittedly imperfect,[21] permit us to ask how much of a city's income it is willing to commit for public taxation and expenditures.

Hypothesis

Much of the research on city politics has treated reformed institutions as dependent variables. Although we shall briefly examine the social and economic differences between reformed and unreformed cities, our principal concern will be to explore the *consequences* for public policy of political institutions. From our earlier discussion of the political culture of cities we hypothesized that:

1] The relationship between socio-economic cleavages and policy outputs is stronger in unreformed than in reformed cities.

This hypothesis focuses on the intention of the reformers to minimize the role of particularistic interests in policy making.

III. Reformed and Unreformed Cities: a Comparison

The economic and social contrasts between reformed and unreformed cities have been the subject of much research,[22] and for our purposes we may be brief in our treatment. We divided the independent variables into three groups, one measuring population size and growth, a second containing social class indicators and a third including three measures of social homogeneity. The means and standard deviations for each variable by institutional category are found in Table 2.

It should initially be noted that population size and growth rate

21. We recognize that these are only rough indicators of city finance policies. Definitions of taxation vary from city to city and what may be financed from taxes in one city may be financed from fees in another. Expenditures present a more complex problem because the types and amounts of state transfer payments vary from state to state according to state laws, the division of governmental labor in a state, the incomes and sizes of cities, not to mention political factors at the state level. We think it important, however, that our independent variables explain a large proportion of the variation in municipal outputs as we measured them. No doubt one could explain an even larger proportion of the variation in measures which specify different functional responsibilities of cities. At least these measures constitute a starting point, and we hope others will improve on them.

The source of our output measures was the *County and City Data Book, op. cit.*

22. See, for example, Robert Alford and Harry Scoble, "Political and Socio-Economic Characteristics of American Cities," *The Municipal Yearbook 1965, op. cit.*, pp. 82–97; Sherbenou, *op. cit.*; John H. Kessel, "Governmental Structure and Political Environment," this REVIEW, 56 (September, 1962), 615–620.

fairly clearly separate the reformed from the unreformed cities. As Alford and Scoble have amply documented,[23] the larger the city, the greater the likelihood of its being unreformed; the faster its growth rate, the more likely a city is to possess manager government, non-partisan and at-large elections. These differences are largely accounted for by the fact that very large cities are most likely to (1) have unreformed institutions and (2) be stable or declining in population. Since neither of these variables emerged as particularly important predictors of our output variables, we relegated them to secondary importance in the rest of the analysis.

The data in Table 2 (on page 340) indicate that reformed cities (at least those over 50,000) do not appear to be "the natural habitat of the upper middle class." While reformed cities have slightly more educated populations and slightly high proportions of white collar workers and home ownership, unreformed cities have generally high incomes. In any case, whatever their direction, the differences are not large. What is striking is not the differences between the cities but the similarities of their class composition.

Homogeneity is easily one of the most ambiguous terms in the ambiguous language of the social sciences. We have followed Alford and Scoble who used three measures of homogeneity: for ethnicity, the per cent of population native born of foreign born or mixed parentage; for race, the per cent nonwhite; and for religious homogeneity, the per cent of elementary school children in private schools. The last measure, while indirect, was the only one available, since data on religious affiliation are not collected by the Census Bureau.

With the exception of race, reformed cities appear somewhat more homogeneous than unreformed cities. While the differences in homogeneity are more clear-cut than class differences, this hardly indicates that reformed cities are the havens of a socially homogeneous population. Although the average nonpartisan city has 16.9 per cent of its children in private schools, this mean conceals a wide range—from 2 to 47 per cent.

Our findings about the insignificance of class differences between reformed and unreformed cities are at some variance with Alford and Scoble's conclusions. There is, however, some support for the argument that reformed cities are more homogeneous. While we used cities with populations of over 50,000, their sample included all cities over 25,000; and varying samples may produce varying conclusions. The only other study to analyze cities over 50,000 was Wolfinger and Field's and our conclusions are generally consistent with theirs. We differ with them, however, on two important questions.

First, Wolfinger and Field argued that what differences there are

---

23. Alford and Scoble, *op. cit.,* The particularly large differences found between the populations of reformed and unreformed cities reflect the fact that New York City and several other urban giants are included in the sample.

region are introduced: "The salient conclusion to be drawn from these data is that one can do a much better job of predicting a city's political form by knowing what part of the country it is in than by knowing anything about the composition of its population."[24] Since regions have had different historical experiences, controls for region are essentially controls for history, and more specifically, historical variation in settlement patterns. The problem with this reasoning, however, is that to

TABLE 2 *Comparison of the Means (and Standard Deviations) of Socio-Economic Characteristics of Reformed and Unreformed Cities*

| Independent Variable | GOVERNMENT TYPE | | | | | |
	Mayor-Council		Manager		Commission	
Population:						
Population (10^3)	282.5	(858.6)	115.7	(108.0)	128.6	(115.2)
% Change, 1950–60	36.4%	(118.8)	64.1%	(130.4)	18.5%	(36.7)
Class:						
Median Income	$6199.	(1005.0)	$6131.	(999.6)	$5425.	(804.4)
% Under $3000	15.3%	(7.0)	17.3%	(6.9)	21.5%	(7.9)
% Over $10,000	16.9%	(7.2)	17.5%	(6.7)	12.5%	(3.7)
% High School Graduates	40.7%	(10.8)	48.1%	(8.9)	41.6%	(10.4)
Median Education (yrs.)	10.7	(1.1)	11.4	(8.9)	11.0	(2.1)
% Owner-Occupied Dwelling Units	54.9%	(15.1)	57.3%	(13.6)	54.6%	(13.7)
% White Collar	44.1%	(9.0)	48.1%	(7.1)	44.2%	(7.6)
Homogeneity:						
% Nonwhite	10.6%	(11.5)	11.6%	(10.8)	16.5%	(14.9)
% Native with Foreign Born or Mixed Parentage	19.7%	(9.9)	12.4%	(8.3)	11.7%	(10.7)
% Private School Attendance	23.5%	(11.9)	15.3%	(11.8)	16.6%	(11.8)
	N = 85		N = 90		N = 25	

| Independent Variable | ELECTION TYPE | | | |
	Partisan		Nonpartisan	
Population:				
Population (10^3)	270.8	(1022.1)	155.8	(198.7)
% Population Increase 1950–1960	17.1	(40.1)	58.3%	(136.1)
Class:				
Median Income	$5996	(904.5)	$6074	(1045.5)
% Under $3000	16.8%	(7.1)	17.2%	(7.2)
% Over $10,000	16.1%	(6.1)	16.7%	(7.0)
% High School Graduates	40.5%	(9.2)	45.3%	(10.6)
Median Education (yrs.)	10.6	(1.1)	11.2	(1.2)
% Owner-Occupied Dwelling Units	51.5%	(14.4)	57.7%	(13.8)
% White Collar	43.5%	(7.5)	46.7%	(8.3)
Homogeneity:				
% Nonwhite	13.0%	(11.9)	11.5%	(11.8)
% Native with Foreign Born or Mixed Parentage	17.5%	(10.7)	14.7%	(9.6)
% Private School Attendance	24.1%	(13.6)	16.9%	(11.3)
	N = 57		N = 143	

24. *Op. cit.*, p. 320.

TABLE 2   (*Continued*)

Independent Variable	CONSTITUENCY TYPE			
	District		At-Large	
Population:				
Population (10^3)	246.9	(909.8)	153.6	(191.2)
% Population Increase 1950–1960	23.1%	(36.4)	59.1%	(143.7)
Class:				
Median Income	$6297	(965.2)	$5942	(1031.9)
% Under $3000	14.7%	(6.5)	18.2%	(7.6)
% Over $10,000	17.7%	(7.1)	16.0%	(6.6)
% High School Graduates	43.6%	(10.9)	44.4%	(10.4)
Median Education (yrs.)	10.9	(1.1)	11.2	(1.2)
% Owner-Occupied Dwelling Units	55.1%	(14.4)	56.9%	(14.5)
% White Collar	45.2%	(9.4)	46.3%	(7.5)
Homogeneity:				
% Nonwhite	9.8%	(10.6)	13.0%	(12.3)
% Native with Foreign Born or Mixed Parentage	18.9%	(9.4)	13.4%	(9.7)
% Private School Attendance	23.2%	(12.5)	16.6%	(11.7)
	N – 73		N = 127	

"control" for "region" is to control not only for history, but for demography as well: to know what region a city is in *is* to know something about the composition of its population. Geographical subdivisions are relevant subjects of political inquiry only because they are differentiated on the basis of attitudinal or socio-economic variables. The South is not a distinctive political region because two surveyors named Mason and Dixon drew a famous line, but because the "composition of its population" differs from the rest of the country.

It is therefore difficult to unravel the meaning of "controlling" for "region" since regions are differentiated on precisely the kinds of demographic variables which we (and Wolfinger and Field) related to reformism. Cities in the Midwest, for example, have a much higher proportion of home ownership (64%) than cities in the Northeast (44%), while northeastern cities have more foreign stock in their population (27%) than the Midwest (16%). Hence, to relate ethnicity to political reformism and then to "control" for "region" is in part to relate ethnicity to reformism and then to control for ethnicity. Consequently, we have grave reservations that the substitution of the gross and unrefined variable of "region" for more refined demographic data adds much to our knowledge of American cities. "Controlling" for "region" is much more than controlling for historical experiences, because region as a variable is an undifferentiated *potpourri* of socio-economic, attitudinal, historical and cultural variations.[25]

25. In statistical parlance, the problem with "region" as an independent variable might be described as treating a complicated background variable as the first variable in a specific developmental sequence. But, as Blalock argues, ". . . *one should avoid complex indicators that are related in unknown ways to a given underlying variable.* Geographical region and certain background variables appear to have such undesirable properties": Hubert M. Blalock, *Causal Inferences in Nonexperimental Research* (Chapel Hill: University of North Carolina Press, 1964), p. 164 (italics in original).

We also differ with Wolfinger and Field in their assertion that their analysis constitutes a test of the ethos theory. As we understand it, Banfield and Wilson's theory posits that particular attitudes are held by persons with varying sociological characteristics (ethnic groups and middle class persons, in particular) and that these attitudes include preferences for one or another kind of political institution. But relating the proportion of middle class persons in a city's population to its form of government says nothing one way or another about middle class preferences. An important part of understanding, of course, is describing and it is certainly useful to know how reformed cities differ from unreformed cities.

In our view, however, such tests as Wolfinger and Field used cannot logically be called explanations, in any causal sense. The most obvious reason is that they violate some important assumptions about time–order: independent variables are measured with contemporary census data, while the dependent variables are results of decisions made ten to fifty years ago. Moreover, this problem is multiplied by the difficulty of inferring configurations of political power from demographic data. Presumably, their assumption is that there is a simple linear relationship between sheer numbers (or proportions) of, say, middle class persons and their political power: the larger the size of a group in the city's population, the easier it can enforce its choice of political forms. At least one prominent urban sociologist, however, has found empirical support for precisely the opposite proposition. Hawley concluded that the smaller the proportion of middle class persons in a city, the greater their power over urban renewal policies.[26] Similarly, it may also be dubious to assume that the size of an ethnic population is an accurate indicator of influence of ethnic groups. Although we recognize the importance of describing the socio-economic correlates of political forms, the logical problems involved suggest the need for a good deal of caution in interpreting these differences as explanations.[27]

In any case, the question of why the city adopts particular structures is of less interest to us than their consequences for public policy. It is to this analysis that we now turn.

IV. Policy Outputs and the Responsiveness of Cities

We are now in a position to take three additional steps. First, we can compare the differences in policy outputs between reformed and unreformed cities. Second, we can assess the cumulative impact of

26. Amos Hawley, "Community Power and Urban Renewal Success," *American Journal of Sociology*, 68 (January, 1963), 422–431.
27. See also the exchange between Banfield and Wilson and Wolfinger and Field in "Communications," this REVIEW, 60 (December, 1966), 998–1000.

socio-economic variables on these policy choices. Finally, we can specify what variables are related in what ways to these output variables. In essence, we can now treat political institutions, not as dependent variables, but as factors which influence the *level* of expenditures and taxation and the *relationship* between cleavage variables and these outputs.

Differences Between Reformed and Unreformed Cities' Outputs

Contrary to Sherbenou's conclusions about Chicago suburbs,[28] our data indicate that reformed cities both spend and tax less than unreformed cities, with the exception of expenditures in partisan and nonpartisan cities. It appears that partisan, mayor-council and ward cities are less willing to commit their resources to public purposes than their reformed counterparts. What is of more importance than the difference in outputs, however, is the relative responsiveness of the two kinds of cities to social cleavages in their population.

The Responsiveness of Cities

We have argued that one principal goal of the reform movement was to reduce the impact of partisan, socio-economic cleavages on governmental decision making, to immunize city governments from "artificial" social cleavages—race, religion, ethnicity, and so on. As Banfield and Wilson put their argument, the reformers "assumed that there existed an interest ('the public interest') that pertained to the city 'as a whole' and that should always prevail over competing, partial (and usually private) interests."[29] The structural reforms of manager government, at-large, and nonpartisan elections would so insulate the business of governing from social cleavages that "private regarding"

TABLE 3 *Mean Values of Tax/Income and Expenditure/Income Ratios, by Structural Characteristics*

Structural Variables	Taxes /Income	Expenditures /Income
Election type:		
Partisan	.032	.050
Nonpartisan	.030	.053
Government type:		
Mayor-Council	.037	.058
Manager	.024	.045
Commission	.031	.057
Constituency type:		
Ward	.036	.057
At-large	.027	.049

28. Sherbenou, *op. cit.,* pp. 133–134.
29. *Op. cit.,* p. 139.

interests would count for little in making up the mind of the body politic. But amid the calls of the reformers for structural reforms to muffle the impact of socio-economic cleavages, a few hardy souls predicted precisely the opposite consequence of reform: instead of eliminating cleavages from political decision-making, the reforms, particularly the elimination of parties, would enhance the conflict. Nathan Matthews, Jr., a turn-of-the-century mayor of Boston, issued just such a warning:

> As a city is a political institution, the people in the end will divide into parties, and it would seem extremely doubtful whether the present system, however illogical its foundation be, does not in fact produce better results, at least in large cities, than if the voters divided into groups, separated by property, social or religious grounds.[30]

Matthews recognized implicitly what political scientists would now call the "interest aggregation" function of political parties.[31] Parties in a democracy manage conflict, structure it, and encapsulate social cleavages under the rubric of two or more broad social cleavages, the parties themselves. "Parties tend to crystallize opinion, they give skeletal articulation to a shapeless and jelly-like mass . . . they cause similar opinions to coagulate . . ."[32] The parties "reduce effectively the number of political opinions to manageable numbers, bring order and focus to the political struggle, simplify issues and frame alternatives, and compromise conflicting interests."[33] Since parties are the agencies of interest aggregation, so the argument goes, their elimination makes for greater, not lesser, impact of social cleavages on political decisions.

Political scientists have recently confirmed Matthews' fears, at least with regard to electoral behavior in partisan and nonpartisan elections. Evidence points to the increased impact of socio-economic cleavages on voting when a nonpartisan ballot is used than when the election is formally partisan. Gerald Pomper studied nonpartisan municipal elections and compared them with partisan elections for the New Jersey State Assembly in Newark. He concluded that the "goal of nonpartisanship is fulfilled, as party identification does not determine the outcome. In place of party, ethnic affiliation is emphasized and the result is 'to enhance the effect of basic social cleavages.' "[34] If (1) this

---

30. Quoted in Banfield and Wilson, *op. cit.*, p. 154.

31. For a discussion of the concept of interest aggregation, see Gabriel Almond, "Introduction: A Functional Approach to Comparative Politics," in Gabriel Almond and James S. Coleman (eds.), *The Politics of Developing Areas* (Princeton: Princeton University Press, 1960), pp. 38–45.

32. Maurice Duverger, *Political Parties* (New York: Science Editions, 1963), p. 378.

33. Frank J. Sorauf, *Political Parties in the American System* (Boston: Little, Brown and Co., 1964), pp. 165–166.

34. Gerald Pomper, "Ethnic and Group Voting in Nonpartisan Municipal Elections," *Public Opinion Quarterly*, 30 (Spring, 1966), p. 90; see also, J. Leiper Freeman, "Local

is typical of other American cities and if (2) electoral cleavages can be translated effectively into demands on the government in the absence of aggregative parties, then we might assume that the reformed institutions would reflect cleavages more, rather than less, closely than unreformed ones.

Essentially, then, there are two contrasting views about the consequences of municipal reform. One, the reformers' ideal, holds that institutional reforms will mitigate the impact of social cleavages on public policy. The other argues that the elimination of political parties and the introduction of other reforms will make social cleavages more, rather than less, important in political decision-making.

DIAGRAM 1   *Proportion of variation explained* (R^2) *in taxation policy with twelve socio-economic variables, by institutional characteristics*[a]

Independent Variables	Structural Variables	Dependent Variable
	Reformed Institution:	
	Government: Commission	62%
	Government: Council-Manager	42%
	Election: Nonpartisan	49%
	Constituency: At-Large	49%
Twelve Socio-Economic Variables		Tax/Income Ratio
	Unreformed Institution:	
	Government: Mayor-Council	52%
	Election: Partisan	71%
	Constituency: Ward/Mixed	59%

[a] In the total sample, the twelve independent variables explained 52% of the variation in taxes.

DIAGRAM 2   *Proportion of variation explained* (R^2) *in expenditure policy with twelve socio-economic variables, by institutional characteristics*[b]

Independent Variables	Structural Variables	Dependent Variable
	Reformed Institution:	
	Government: Commission	59%
	Government: Council-Manager	30%
	Constituency: At-Large	36%
	Elections: Nonpartisan	41%
Twelve Socio-Economic Variables		Expenditure/Income Ratio
	Unreformed Institution:	
	Government: Mayor-Council	42%
	Constituency: Ward/Mixed	49%
	Elections: Partisan	59%

[b] In the total sample, the twelve independent variables explained 36% of the variation in expenditures.

"Party Systems: Theoretical Considerations and a Case Analysis," *American Journal of Sociology*, 64 (1958), 282–289.

The Measurement of Responsiveness

We have hypothesized that socio-economic cleveages will have less impact on the policy choices of reformed than unreformed governments. Thus, one could do a better job of predicting a city's taxation and expenditure policy using socio-economic variables in partisan, mayor and ward cities than in nonpartisan, manager and at-large cities. Operationally, we will test this hypothesis by using multiple correlation coefficients. Squaring these coefficients, called "multiple R's," will give us a summary measure of the total amount of variation in our dependent variables explained by our twelve independent variables.[35] The results of the correlation analysis are summarized in Diagrams 1 and 2.

On the whole, the results of the correlation analysis strikingly support the hypothesis, with the exception of commission cities. Thus, we can say, for example, that our twelve socio-economic variables explain 71 per cent of the variations in taxation policy in partisan cities, and 49 per cent of the variation in nonpartisan cities. In commission cities, however, socio-economic variables predict substantially more variation in both taxes and expenditures than in the unreformed mayor-council cities.[36] The anomaly of commission governments is interesting, for they present, as we will see, marked exceptions to virtually every pattern of relationships we found. The substantial explanatory power of these socio-economic variables is not altered, but confirmed, by examining the variables independently. The rest of the correlations show a consistent pattern: reformed cities are less responsive to cleavages in their population than unreformed cities.

If one of the premises of the "political ethos" argument is that reformed institutions give less weight to the "private regarding" and "artificial" cleavages in the population, that premise receives striking support from our analysis. Our data suggest that when a city adopts reformed structures, it comes to be governed less on the basis of conflict and more on the basis of the rationalistic theory of administration. The making of public policy takes less count of the enduring differences between White and Negro, business and labor, Pole and WASP. The logic of the bureaucratic ethic demands an impersonal, apolitical settlement of issues, rather than the settlement of conflict in the arena of political battle.

35. It is possible that the difference between two correlations may be a function of very different standard deviations of the independent variables. A quick look at Table 2, however, suggests that this is not likely to affect the relationships we find.

36. Wolfinger and Field, *op. cit.*, p. 312, ". . . omit the commission cities from consideration since this form does not figure in the ethos theory." Historically, however, commission government was the earliest of the structures advocated by the Progressives and is quite clearly a product of the reform era. While history tells us that commission cities can not legitimately be excluded from the fold of reformism, they appear to be its black sheep, characterized by low incomes, low population growth and large proportions of nonwhites. In fact, they present a marked contrast to both mayor-council and manager cities.

V. To Spend or Not to Spend

If efforts to expand or contract the scope of government stand at the core of municipal political life,[37] they are nowhere better reflected than in the taxation and expenditure patterns of cities. A generation ago, Charles Beard wrote, "In the purposes for which appropriations are made the policies of the city government are given concrete form— the culture of the city is reflected. Indeed, the history of urban civilization could be written in terms of appropriations, for they show what the citizens think is worth doing and worth paying for."[38] Pressures to expand and contract government regulations and services are almost always reflected one way or another in the municipal budget. Labor, ethnic groups, the poor and the liberal community may press for additional services and these must be paid for; the business community may demand municipal efforts to obtain new industry by paring city costs to create a "favorable business climate"; or business-men may themselves demand municipal services for new or old business. In any case, few political conflicts arise which do not involve some conflict over the budget structure.

Class Variables and Public Policies

Part of the political rhetoric associated with the demand for a decrease in the scope of the national government is the argument that the initiative for policy-making should rest more with the state and local governments. Opposition to high federal spending levels, as V. O. Key has demonstrated, is found more often among persons with middle class occupations than among the blue-collar workers.[39] It is not inconceivable that the middle class argument about state and local responsibility might be more than political rhetoric, and that at the local level, middle class voters are willing to undertake major programs of municipal services requiring large outlays of public capital. Wilson and Banfield have argued that the "public regarding" upper-middle class voters in metropolitan areas are often found voting for public policies at variance with their "self-interest narrowly conceived," and that "the higher the income of a ward or town, the more taste it has for public expenditures of various kinds."[40] Similarly a longitudinal study of voting patterns in metropolitan Cleveland found that an index of social rank was positively correlated with favorable votes on welfare referenda.[41]

37. Agger *et al., op. cit.,* pp. 4–14.

38. Charles A. Beard, *American Government and Politics* (New York: Macmillan, 1924, 4th edition), p. 727.

39. V. O. Key, *Public Opinion and American Democracy* (New York: Alfred A. Knopf, 1961), p. 124.

40. Wilson and Banfield, *op. cit.,* p. 876. Footnote 5 in the same article conveniently summarized research supporting this proposition.

41. Eugene S. Uyeki, "Patterns of Voting in a Metropolitan Area: 1938–1962," *Urban Affairs Quarterly,* 1 (June, 1966), 65–77.

If these data reflect middle class willingness to spend on a local level, they might indicate that the "states' rights" argument was more than ideological camouflage: middle class voters stand foursquare behind public expenditures at the local level even when they oppose those expenditures from the national government. Therefore, we hypothesized that:

2a] The more middle class the city, measured by income, education and occupation, the higher the municipal taxes and expenditures.

In line with our general concern of testing the impact of political structures on municipal policies, we also hypothesized that:

2b] Unreformed cities reflect this relationship more strongly than reformed cities.

With respect to hypothesis 2a, the data in Table 4 on three middle class indicators are unambiguous and indicate a strong rejection of the hypothesis. However we measure social class, whether by income, education or occupation, class measures are negatively related to public taxes and expenditures.

It is possible, however, that income does not have a linear, but rather a curvilinear relationship with municipal outputs. Banfield and Wilson argue that "In the city, it is useful to think in terms of three income groups—low, middle, and high. Surprising as it may seem to Marxists, the conflict is generally between an alliance of low-income and high-income groups on one side and the middle-income groups on the other."[42] If the relationships between income and expenditure is curvilinear, then we should expect to find that proportions of both low and high income groups were positively correlated with outputs. Our data, however, lend no support to this notion of a "pro-expenditure" alliance. Rather, the proportion of the population with incomes below $3000 is positively correlated with expenditures in all city types (although the relationships are small) and the proportion of the population in the above $10,000 bracket is negatively correlated with ex-

TABLE 4 *Correlations Between Middle Class Characteristics and Outputs in Reformed and Unreformed Cities*

| Correlations of | GOVERNMENT TYPE | | | ELECTION TYPE | | CONSTITUENCY TYPE | |
	Mayor-Council	Manager	Com-mission	Partisan	Non-Partisan	Ward	At-large
Taxes with:							
Median Income	−.13	−.24	−.19	.03	−.19	−.17	−.22
White Collar	−.23	−.12	−.62	−.21	−.33	−.30	−.32
Median Education	−.36	−.22	−.08	−.45	−.24	−.48	−.18
Expenditures with:							
Median Income	−.19	−.32	−.43	−.04	−.32	−.23	−.34
White Collar	−.24	−.23	−.58	−.18	−.39	−.32	−.35
Median Education	−.32	−.36	−.26	−.36	−.38	−.44	−.32

42. Banfield and Wilson, *op. cit.,* p. 35.

penditures. Summing the two measures and correlating the combined measure with outputs produced no correlation greater than .15 and the relationships were as likely to be negative as positive. Tests for nonlinearity also suggested that no such coalition exists in the cities in our analysis.

To be sure, aggregate data analysis using whole cities as units of analysis is no substitute for systematic survey data on middle class attitudes, but it is apparent that cities with larger middle class population have lower, not higher expenditures. As we emphasized earlier, the "ethos theory" deals with attitudes and the behavior of individuals, while our data deal with cities and their behavior. The coalition suggested by Banfield and Wilson, however, is not discernible at this level of aggregation in these cities.

Hypothesis 2b is not consistently borne out by the data. In fact, the relationships between middle class variables and outputs are, if anything, stronger in the reformed cities than in their unreformed counterparts. One would not want to make too much of the data, but a large body of literature on city politics, which we discuss below, suggests that reformed institutions maximize the power of the middle class.

We originally assumed that the proportion of owner-occupied dwelling units constituted another measure of middle class composition, but it soon became apparent that it was only weakly related to income, occupation and education measures. Nevertheless, it emerged as the strongest single predictor of both expenditure and taxation policy in our cities. We hypothesized that:

3a] Owner-occupancy and outputs are negatively correlated, and

3b] Unreformed cities reflect this relationship more strongly than reformed cities.

Hypothesis 3a is consistently borne out in the data presented in Table 5. These relationships were only slightly attenuated when we controlled for income, education and occupation. No doubt self-interest (perhaps "private regardingness") on the part of the home owner, whose property is intimately related to the tax structure of most local governments, may account for part of this relationship. Moreover, home ownership is correlated (almost by definition) with lower urban

TABLE 5 *Correlations Between Owner Occupancy and Government Outputs in Reformed and Unreformed Cities*

Correlations of Owner Occupancy with:	GOVERNMENT TYPE			ELECTION TYPE		CONSTITUENCY TYPE	
	Mayor-Council	Manager	Com-mission	Partisan	Non-Partisan	Ward	At-large
Taxes	−.57	−.31	−.73	−.64	−.45	−.56	−.48
Expenditures	−.51	−.23	−.62	−.62	−.40	−.50	−.40

population density. High density, bringing together all manner of men into the classic urban mosaic, may be itself correlated with factors which produce demands for higher expenditures—slums, increased needs for fire and police protection, and so on.

In confirmation of hypothesis 3a, the unmistakable pattern is for unreformed cities to reflect these negative relationships more strongly than the manager, nonpartisan and at-large cities, although commission cities show their usual remarkably high correlations.

Homogeneity Variables and Public Policies

Dawson and Robinson, in their analysis of state welfare expenditures, found strong positive relationships between the ethnicity of a state's population and the level of its welfare expenditures.[43] If this is symptomatic of a generalized association of ethnic and religious minorities with higher expenditures, we might find support for the hypothesis that:

4a] The larger the proportion of religious and ethnic minorities in the population, the higher the city's taxes and expenditures.
And, if our general hypothesis about the impact of political institutions is correct, then:

4b] Unreformed cities reflect this relationship more strongly than reformed cities.

The correlations between ethnicity, religious heterogeneity and outputs (see Table 6) are, with one exception, positive, as predicted by hypothesis 4a. These associations may reflect the substantial participation by ethnic groups in municipal politics long after the tide of immigration has been reduced to a trickle.[44] The relatively intense

TABLE 6 *Correlations between Ethnicity and Religious Heterogeneity and Outputs in Reformed and Unreformed Cities*

| Correlations of | GOVERNMENT TYPE | | | ELECTION TYPE | | CONSTITUENCY TYPE | |
	Mayor-Council	Manager	Com-mission	Partisan	Non-Partisan	Ward	At-large
Taxes with:							
Ethnicity	.49	.26	.57	.61	.43	.56	.40
Private School							
Attendance	.38	.15	.37	.33	.37	.41	.25
Expenditures with:							
Ethnicity	.36	.02	.21	.48	.21	.44	.13
Private School							
Attendance	.34	−.01	.07	.25	.24	.40	.05

43. Richard E. Dawson and James A. Robinson, "The Politics of Welfare," in Herbert Jacob and Kenneth Vines (eds.), *Politics in the American States* (Boston: Little, Brown and Co., 1965), pp. 398–401.

44. Raymond Wolfinger, "The Development and Persistence of Ethnic Voting," this REVIEW, 59 (December, 1965), 896–908.

politicization of ethnic groups at the local level,[45] the appeals to nationality groups through "ticket balancing" and other means, and the resultant higher turnout of ethnic groups than other lower status groups,[46] may produce an influence on city government far out of proportion to their number.

We found when we related all twelve of our independent variables to outputs in various city types that the associations were much weaker in cities we have labeled reformed. The correlations for ethnicity and religious homogeneity show a generally similar pattern, with commission cities exhibiting their usual erratic behavior. The data, then, show fairly clear support for hypothesis 4b.

The third variable of our homogeneity indicators—per cent of population non-white—had almost no relationship to variation in outputs, regardless of city type. We found the same weak correlations for the poverty income variable, which was, of course, strongly related to the racial variable. An easy explanation suggests that this is a consequence of the political impotence of Negroes and the poor, but one should be cautious in inferring a lack of power from the lack of a statistical association.

We have dealt in this section with factors which are positively and negatively related to spending patterns in American cities. While social class variables are associated negatively with outputs, two measures of homogeneity, private school attendance and ethnicity are related to higher taxes and spending. Examining the strengths of these correlations in cities with differing forms, we found some support for our general hypothesis about the political consequences of institutions, especially for the homogeneity variables and the home ownership variable. Interestingly, however, this was not the case with class variables.

VI. Reformism as a Continuous Variable

The central thrust of our argument has been that reformed governments differ from their unreformed counterparts in their responsiveness to socio-economic cleavages in the population. Logically, if the presence of one feature of the "good government" syndrome had the impact of reducing responsiveness, the introduction of additional reformed institutions should have an additive effect and further reduce the impact of cleavages on decision-making. We therefore decided to treat "reformism" as a continuous variable for analytic purposes and hypothesized that:

45. Robert E. Lane, *Political Life* (Glencoe, Ill.: The Free Press, 1959), pp. 236–243.
46. *Ibid.*

5] The higher the level of reformism in a city, the lower its responsiveness to socio-economic cleavages in the population.

We utilized a simple four-point index to test this hypothesis, ranging from the "least reformed" to the "most reformed." The sample cities were categorized as follows:

1] Cities with none of the reformed institutions (i.e., the government is mayor-council, elections are partisan and constituencies are wards).

2] Cities with any one of the reformed institutions.

3] Cities with two of the reformed institutions.

4] Cities with three reformed institutions (i.e., the government is either manager or commission, elections are nonpartisan and constituencies are at-large).

We can not overemphasize the crudity of this index as an operationalization of the complex and abstract concept of "reformism." Nonetheless, we think some of the relationships we found are strongly suggestive that reformism may in reality be a continuous variable.

To test this hypothesis, we took four variables which had moderate-to-strong correlations with our dependent variables and computed simple correlations in each reform category. If our hypothesis is correct, the strength of the correlations in Table 7 should decrease regularly with an increase in reform scores. While there are some clear exceptions to the predicted pattern of relationships, there is some fairly consistent support for the hypothesis. Even when the decreases in the strengths of the correlations are irregular, there is a clear difference between cities which we have labeled "most reformed" and "least reformed."

Again, we would not want to attach too much importance to the results of this rough-and-ready index. But, the patterns support our

TABLE 7 *Correlations between Selected Independent Variables and Output Variables by Four Categories of Reformism*

	REFORM SCORES			
Correlations of	1 (least reformed)	2	3	4 (most reformed)
Taxes with:				
Ethnicity	.62	.41	.50	.34
Private School Attendance	.40	.32	.28	.25
Owner-Occupancy	−.70	.39	−.54	−.44
Median Education	−.55	−.27	−.32	−.13
Expenditures with:				
Ethnicity	.51	.27	.41	.05
Private School Attendance	.46	.23	.16	.08
Owner-Occupancy	−.67	−.30	−.54	−.38
Median Education	−.49	−.19	−.38	−.37

previous argument about the impact of reformism: the more reformed the city, the less responsive it is to socio-economic cleavages in its political decision-making.

VII. A Causal Model and an Interpretation

A Causal Model

The implicit, or at times explicit, causal model in much of the research on municipal reformism has been a simple one: socio-economic cleavages cause the adoption of particular political forms. A more sophisticated model would include political institutions as one of the factors which produce a given output structure in city politics. We hypothesize that a causal model would include four classes of variables: socio-economic cleavages, political variables (including party registration, structure of party systems, patterns of aggregation, strength of interest groups, voter turnout, etc.), political institutions (form of government, type of elections and types of constituencies), and political outputs. Diagram 3 depicts one possible causal model.

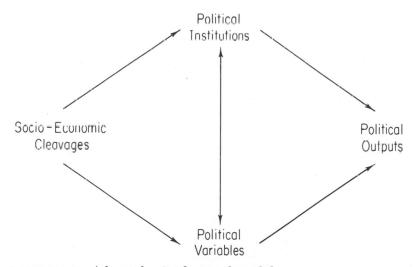

DIAGRAM 3 *A hypothesized causal model*

This study has of necessity been limited to exploring the linkages between socio-economic cleavages, political institutions and political outputs. We found that political institutions "filter" the process of converting inputs into outputs. Some structures, particularly partisan elections, ward constituencies, mayor-council governments and commission governments, operate to maximize the impact of cleavage indicators on public policies. We conclude by discussing some of the reasons why different structures have varying impacts on the conversion process.

An Interpretation

Three principal conclusions may be derived from this analysis.

1. Cities with reformed and unreformed institutions are not markedly different in terms of demographic variables. Indeed, some variables, like income, ran counter to the popular hypothesis that reformed cities are havens of the middle class. Our data lent some support to the notion that reformed cities are more homogeneous in their ethnic and religious populations. Still, it is apparent that reformed cities are by no means free from the impact of these cleavages.

2. The more important difference between the two kinds of cities is in their behavior, rather than their demography. Using multiple correlation-coefficients, we were able to predict municipal outputs more exactly in unreformed than in reformed cities. The translation of social conflicts into public policy and the responsiveness of political systems to class, racial, and religious cleavages differs markedly with the kind of political structure. Thus, political institutions seem to play an important role in the political process—a role substantially independent of a city's demography.

3. Our analysis has also demonstrated that reformism may be viewed as a continuous variable and that the political structures of the reform syndrome have an additive effect: the greater the reformism, the lower the responsiveness.

Through these political institutions, the goal of the reformers has been substantially fulfilled, for nonpartisan elections, at-large constituencies and manager governments are associated with a lessened responsiveness of cities to the enduring conflicts of political life. Or, as Stone, Price and Stone argued in their study of changes produced by the adoption of manager governments, the council after the reform "tended to think more of the community as a whole and less of factional interests in making their decisions."[47]

The responsiveness of a political institution to political conflicts should not be confused with the "responsibility" of a political system as the latter term is used in the great debate over the relative "responsibility" of party systems.[48] In fact, the responsiveness of political forms to social cleavages may stand in sharp contrast to "responsible

47. Harold Stone, Don K. Price and Kathryn Stone, *City Manager Government in the United States* (Chicago: Public Administration Service, 1940), p. 238.

48. The standard argument for party responsibility is found in the works of E. E. Schattschneider, esp., *Party Government* (New York: Farrar and Rinehart, 1942) and in the report of the Committee on Political Parties of the American Political Science Association, *Toward a More Responsible Two-Party System* (New York: Rinehart, 1950).

government" on the British model. Presumably, in American cities, partisan elections, ward constituencies, and mayor-council governments maximize minority rather than majority representation, assuring greater access to decision-makers than the reformed, bureaucratized and "de-politicized" administrations.

Partisan electoral systems, when combined with ward representation, increase the access of two kinds of minority groups: those which are residentially segregated, and which may as a consequence of the electoral system demand and obtain preferential consideration from their councilmen; and groups which constitute identifiable voting blocs to which parties and politicians may be beholden in the next election. The introduction of at-large, nonpartisan elections has at least five consequences for these groups. First, they remove an important cue-giving agency—the party—from the electoral scene, leaving the voter to make decisions less on the policy commitments (however vague) of the party, and more on irrelevancies such as ethnic identification and name familiarity.[49] Second, by removing the party from the ballot, the reforms eliminate the principal agency of interest aggregation from the political system. Hence, interests are articulated less clearly and are aggregated either by some other agency or not at all. Moreover, nonpartisanship has the effect of reducing the turnout in local elections by working class groups,[50] leaving officeholders freer from retaliation by these groups at the polls. Fourth, nonpartisanship may also serve to decrease the salience of "private regarding" demands by increasing the relative political power of "public regarding" agencies like the local press.[51] And when nonpartisanship is combined with election at-large, the impact of residentially segregated groups or groups which obtain their strength from voting as blocs in municipal elections is further reduced.[52] For these reasons, it is clear that political reforms may have a significant impact in minimizing the role which social conflicts play in decision-making. By muting the demands of private-regarding groups, the electoral institutions of reformed governments make public policy less responsive to the demands arising out of social conflicts in the population.

The structure of the government may serve further to modify the strength of minority groups over public policy. It is significant in this respect to note that commission governments, where social cleavages have the greatest impact on policy choices, are the most

49. See Pomper, *op. cit.*; and Freeman, *op. cit.*

50. Robert Salisbury and Gordon Black, "Class and Party in Partisan and Nonpartisan Elections: The Case of Des Moines," this REVIEW, 57 (September, 1963), 584–592.

51. One newspaperman said of nonpartisan politics that "You can't tell the players without a scorecard, and we sell the scorecards": Banfield and Wilson, *op. cit.*, p. 157.

52. Oliver P. Williams and Charles Adrian, *Four Cities* (Philadelphia: University of Pennsylvania Press, 1963), pp. 56–57.

decentralized of the three governmental types and that manager governments are relatively the most centralized.[53] From the point of view of the reformer, commission government is a failure and their number has declined markedly in recent years.[54] This greater decentralization of commission and of mayor-council governments permits a multiplicity of access points for groups wishing to influence decision-makers.[55] It may also increase the possibilities for collaboration between groups and a bureaucratic agency, a relationship which has characterized administrative patterns in the federal government. As a result of this decentralization, group strength in local governments may be maximized.

It is important in any analysis of reformism to distinguish between the factors which produce the *adoption* of reformed institutions and the *impact* of the new political forms once they have been established. We can offer from our data no conclusions about the origins of reformed structures, for it is obviously impossible to impute causation, using contemporary census data, to events which occurred decades ago. Once a city has institutionalized the reformers' ideals, however, a diffused attitude structure may be less helpful in explaining the city's public policy than the characteristics of the institutions themselves. With the introduction of these reforms, a new political pattern may emerge in which disputes are settled outside the political system, or in which they may be settled by the crowd at the civic club at the periphery of the system.[56] If they do enter the political process, an impersonal, "non-political" bureaucracy may take less account of the conflicting interests and pay more attention to the "correct" decision from the point of view of the municipal planner.

These conclusions are generally consistent with the ethos theory developed by Banfield and Wilson. If one of the components of the middle class reformer's ideal was "to seek the good of the community as a whole" and to minimize the impact of social cleavages on political decision-making, then their institutional reforms have served, by and large, to advance that goal.

53. Alford and Scoble, *op. cit.,* p. 84.

54. In our view, the failure of the commission government to achieve the intended reforms is more plausible as an explanation of its demise than its administrative unwieldiness—the conventional explanation.

55. Williams and Adrian, *op. cit.,* pp. 30–31.

56. Carol E. Thometz discusses the role of the "Civic Committee" in decision-making in Dallas: see *The Decision-Makers* (Dallas: Southern Methodist University Press, 1963).

Philadelphia: "Good Government" Leads to Moral Frustration

James Reichley

REFORM, it has been said, is what we have in America in place of ideology. Political participation by those not professionally involved in politics is built around periodic attacks on the alleged corruption in government. Unfortunately, these attacks in most areas turn out to be few and far between, and the reform doctrine does not supply the kind of motivation that would keep the greater part of the population politically activated during the long dry spells between uprisings. What is the reason for this failure of "reform" to produce permanent interest in politics, and is there any possibility that it will in the future perform a function of social integration as well as eliminate the abuses at which it is primarily aimed? To answer these questions it will first be necessary to examine the nature of the reform idea.

Let us begin by turning back to the years immediately following the end of the Second World War when reform politics in Philadelphia was chiefly an exciting brew being passed from lip to lip among a little band of idealists in the city's gentleman's clubs and intellectual associations. A part of the nature of this mixture we have already suggested: Dislocated aristocrats were turning to politics as a means of winning back their own from the managerial class that was displacing them in practical life.

How was this strictly upper-class motivation, and the genuine social idealism that undoubtedly accompanied it, translated into a battle-cry that activated citizens of Philadelphia by the thousands to enlist in the army of reform? In the first place, of course, the reform spirit received its mass base by allying itself with the downtrodden city Democratic organization which had been waiting through almost half of the twentieth century for the logic of urban politics finally to sweep the local offices into the grasp of the party of the working man. But what was the aspect of the reform spirit that the Democratic

Reprinted from The Art of Government *by James Reichley, published by The Center for the Study of Democratic Institutions, 1959, pp. 107–114 and 122–124.*

357

politicians at last accepted, and how was it that this aspect was for a time not only acceptable but actually popular with the henchmen of the minority party organization? A clue to the answer to this question may be found in the story of the actual binding of the Democratic and reform causes.

Early in 1947, Michael Bradley, who was then chairman of the Democratic city committee and a leading proponent of alliance between his party and the reformers, gave consideration to four possible reform candidates for mayor: Walter Phillips, a leisured member of the upper class who had led the city planning crusade; Joseph S. Clark, a dabbler in Democratic politics over the years and anxious to be "rung in on things" since his return from the wars; Richardson Dilworth, a flamboyant war hero hovering on the outskirts of the city's old society; and Lewis Stevens, a starchy Philadelphia lawyer and leading lay figure in the Presbyterian Church of Pennsylvania. Phillips had gained attention through his association with city planning, Clark through advocacy of civil-service reform, Stevens through his religious activities, and Dilworth through his publicly expressed intention to "throw the crooks out of City Hall." With little hesitation, the Democratic city chairman chose Dilworth. Emotional moralizing over the alleged corruption of the opposition, it seems clear, was the element of the reform program that most appealed to the organization Democrats. Had they not for years been threatening to "throw the rascals out?"

Dilworth's campaign in 1947 and virtually every campaign he has waged since that time have been built around the image of himself as prosecutor of the "crooks" whom he has sought to represent as the leaders of the GOP. (A young lawyer, a typical "clean-cut" Republican member of the legal fraternity with no trace of underworld connections, tells of having asked Dilworth in the early Fifties a rather difficult but fair question at one of his street-corner rallies, to which the reformer replied in rasping ones, "Young man, may I ask what numbers bank you represent?") This strategy paid off at the polls, not so much in 1947 as Michael Bradley had hoped it might, but particularly in 1949 and 1951 after the newspapers had exposed the fact that there was indeed a good deal of corruption in the Republican administration of City Hall.

More recently, such an approach has been somewhat undermined by the fact that it has become Dilworth's own Democratic party that controls the city administration, but the reform leader, seeking to maintain his stance as champion of the only aspect of the reform movement that has seemed much to interest him, has pretty broadly suggested, particularly during the Blanc campaign, that even under Democratic rule the City Hall still has its share of crooks and these would be likely to run riot were it not for the vigilant efforts of Richardson Dilworth. "I seem," he says, "to see the same faces in the corridors here that I saw eight years ago."

Unfortunately, the image of crook-catcher has been a little dimmed by the circumstances that Dilworth has in point of fact caught rather few crooks (the numbers racket, for instance, his special target, seems to thrive as much as ever throughout the city), and that his sometimes very courageous stands against the Democratic organization have usually been followed by back-sliding attempts to get back into the good graces of its leaders. The present mayor, it would seem, has been demoralizingly trapped between a desire to avoid Clark's outright defiance of the organization and a wish to be at the same time regarded in the public mind as the organization's reforming nemesis.

The spirit of Clark and of Walter Phillips, which dominated the first reform administration elected in 1951, may be said, in the long run, to have channeled the reform impulse in Philadelphia more successfully than Dilworth's moral preachments against the rascals in City Hall.[1] This spirit, expressing the typical American mid-twentieth century philosophy of "good government," is less moral than institutional and economic. When Clark moved into the mayor's office in 1951, he directed, with the assistance of Phillips and the three governmental technicians who composed his cabinet, a thorough overhaul of the city's financial structure, its system of record, the operation of almost all its departments, and the entire decision-making process within the municipal hierarchy. At the same time, the new administration devoted serious attention to long-range problems like urban renewal and traffic control which had been almost completely neglected by its hand-to-mouth predecessors. Electronic machines appeared in City Hall to perform efficiently the tasks of recording that generations of ward-heelers had carried out with doubtful competence; trained economists brought fiscal sophistication to a budget that previously had been planned on the level of inky-ledgered arithmetic; employees hired under civil service replaced a large number of the party workers who formerly had given irregular service at their nominal jobs; great housing and commercial developments began to spring up in all parts of the city.

So complete were the changes made at this time that it is most unlikely that the return of any conceivable Democratic or Republican machine administration could alter many of the most important of them. It is probably true, as Lennox Moak, who served as first director of finance under Clark and now is director of the Pennsylvania Economy League in Philadelphia, says: "The reforms that will stick

1. The religiously oriented spirit of the fourth proposed reform candidate for mayor in 1947, Lewis Stevens, is perhaps more difficult to find in any of the administrations that were later elected under the reform banner. The absence of any deep emotional content, such as might be produced by a religious basis for political action, may, I shall argue later, be the very thing that is wrong with the reform spirit. Stevens himself served as an excellent city councilman in the Clark administration, and was later appointed by Governor Leader, to the dismay of Bill Green, as State Secretary of Highways. On Green's insistence, he was passed over by Leader for a vacancy on the State Supreme Court in 1958. Green's, and as a result, Leader's choice for this vacancy was the able Judge Curtis Bok.

are the reforms that we made in the city's institutions. I cannot believe that any organization would wilfully put bad policies in place of good policies in areas where its patronage and so forth are not affected. The normal organization, once it gets into power, does things 'as they have always been done.' They will most probably in nine cases out of ten follow the precedents that we laid down for them." The city of Philadelphia will never return to the condition in which Joe Clark found it. With the single vital exception of civil service (ironically, Clark's special concern) the reforms that he and his collaborators made can almost certainly not be undone. And yet, in at least one respect, the Clark-Phillips school of institutional reform has been even less successful than the "throw-the-rascals-out" approach practiced by Richardson Dilworth.

"The problem that we have never solved is the problem of continuity," admitted Joe Clark in the summer of 1958. It is perfectly true that neither he nor Dilworth has constructed the kind of city-wide organization that could give any sort of permanence to the spirit as distinguished from the institutions of reform in city politics. Beyond a handful of activists in City Hall and the ADA, the reform movement appears to have lost all cohesiveness in the city; the Democratic organization, almost universally regarded as a "bunch of political bums," is universally rolling into power. This is due partly to certain biases within the spirit of reform. Before turning to these, however, it will be well to attempt to determine how much of the failure is due to the personalities of the two reform leaders themselves.

Despite their shared upper-class background and their common interest in reform, Richardson Dilworth and Joseph S. Clark are about as unlike as two men in public life can be. Dilworth is the warm, all-too-human, relatively simple extrovert in politics; Clark, in contrast, is reserved, reflective, some say cunning, complex, the thinker as politician. Dilworth seems to require heavy doses of admiration if not adulation from his sizable entourage; Clark, a loner by temperament, is sometimes accused of being difficult to work with. The current mayor, despite his retinue of supporters, runs what is in the last analysis a one-man show; all persons who deal with the city government are used to receiving phone calls from him in which pending problems are often settled in a few minutes of personal negotiation. The former mayor was a man of the staff who operated through his subordinates whenever he could; many of the people who now are consulted by Dilworth several times a month never had a personal conversation with Clark during his four years in office.

Dilworth rather resembles one of those heroes of F. Scott Fitzgerald, who came out of the Middle-Western gentry to be educated and make a name in the patrician East: Like them, he is charming, generous, unstable, not remarkably scrupulous, brave, ambitious, fond of high living, eager to make a splash, and fundamentally innocent. Dilworth, one feels, is forever playing out a role that he has only half understood, concentrating on the show while frequently growing bored with the substance. Like them, too, he seems to be motivated by an odd and not entirely ignoble idealism—the restless yearning to realize "the Platonic ideal of himself." It is harder to find a literary parallel for Clark. He is more tough-minded than the heroes of John Marquand whose background he shares, and he is more ambitious than the philosophic upstate squires created by James Cozzens (the Arthur Winner of Philadelphia is, in some ways, Walter Phillips). The truth is that he is the product of an upper class more deeply rooted in time than those which American novelists have usually got around to describing. To find his model one must probably turn to such European writers as Conrad, Stendhal, or Tolstoy; perhaps, even, it is in that crafty creator of a commonwealth, Shakespeare's King Henry IV, that one discerns his features most clearly.[2]

In attitudes toward government Dilworth seems at first the more conservative, but on further thought one realizes that he is merely the more conventional (T.R. riding forth for another loud and fairly ineffectual crack at the forces of political unrighteousness). Senator Clark, who is frequently accused of being a radical, may on the other hand be "the most conservative leader in American public life today," as a friend of his calls him, but, if so, it is the calculated conservatism of Disraeli rather than the visceral conservatism of Burke. The Senator has given ample evidence for his attachment to such nonradical concepts as class, authority, and tradition, but he appears to believe that these concepts can be preserved in the modern world only with the assent of the mass of ordinary human beings. He has thus become the aristocratic leader of the commons against the "oligarchs" who seek to diminish the formal government so that their wills may be informally absolute in their private baronies.

Were (or are) either or both of these two most fascinating individuals capable of building an organization that might carry on the good-government ideal after they themselves have passed out of public life or at least out of intimate connection with city politics? Certainly they would have had great difficulties—Dilworth perhaps be-

2. A story which illustrates many of Clark's characteristics tells of a visit paid by a friend of his to the preparatory school in which the future statesman received his early education. The friend was shown a wall decorated with plaques carved by all of the school's graduates, and noted that on the plaque bearing the name of Joseph S. Clark was displayed a relief of the American flag. When this evidence of youthful interest in government was later mentioned to the Senator, Clark declared that he had aspired to the upper house of the federal legislature since he was a very small boy. Pausing, he then added: "The truth is, though, that I didn't really carve that plaque. I was never good with my hands, and, since I wanted the carving above my name to be well done, I hired another, more skilful boy to do it for me."

cause he is too much the prima donna anxious to win victories and big headlines rather than to attempt any fundamental restoration of civic life, Clark perhaps because the very ruthlessness and cold intelligence that have made him personally strong tend to alienate him from the camaraderie and fellow-feeling that form the indispensable mortar to any enduring political organization. All the same, both possess great natural talents—an unfeigned fondness for humanity in the case of Dilworth, a lucid understanding of human nature in the case of Clark—which might well have suited them for the gigantic task of creating a permanent reform movement in the city. That both have so signally failed to do so (and with them the somewhat more earnest reformers like Phillips, not to mention the Republican public-relations reformers like Longstreth and Pomeroy) is, I think, partly due to the good-government philosophy itself which all have in one way or another represented.

This philosophy, in both its moral and its economic forms, seems to be oriented toward particular projects rather than toward any broad social image. It promises to perform certain worthwhile tasks of government, whether throwing the crooks out of City Hall or providing a more efficient means of circulating downtown traffic, instead of seeking to understand and to satisfy the fundamental needs of human beings. It takes the needs of human beings as given, and sets out to eliminate obstacles to the relief of these needs which it detects in the framework of society (like crooks) or which have been created by society's own rapid expansion (like street congestion). These objectives, even the moral ones, seem finally to be reducible to an economic view of the nature of man: Crooks are bad because they steal the tax-payers' money; traffic congestion is bad because it is strangling the economic life of the city; city planning is good because it provides an orderly means for the development of metropolitan commerce (though with city planning of the Bacon-Phillips kind, it must be admitted, a humanistic note is often struck).

. . . The economic view, coupled with a prevailing individualism which insists that government must limit itself to removing the obstacles to fulfillment of the economic needs of the population rather than undertake to fulfill them itself, makes difficult if not impossible any sustained, large-scale political effort dedicated to the objective of "reform." The declared purpose of reform is the solution of this or that economic problem; when the problem is solved or when it has turned into a bore, the whole reason for the effort has collapsed. The possibility of "continuity" in the reform movement therefore becomes slim, and before very long it is "the same faces" of the organization politicians or ones very much like them that again begin to appear in the halls of government.

. . . Most Americans do *not* actively participate in politics. The fact is that most Americans, except for occasional bursts of reform spirit, have been willing to permit their governments to be operated in a slovenly and irrational fashion which they would not dream of tolerating in any field in which they considered themselves to be personally concerned. The reason for this, I suspect, is that the case for good government has as a rule been presented in terms too simply economic: If elected, the reformer has generally seemed to be saying, I will save you money and I will rationalize our government so that our city will be a place in which you can make a good living. Well and good, the voter has seemed to think, and has cast his ballot for a Dick Dilworth or a Joe Clark.

But if the motive for political participation is strictly an economic one, then it must take its place within the hierarchy of similar economic motives and concerns. Inevitably, the place that it enjoys there cannot be a very high one. It must rank behind the job which is the direct source of personal income; it must rank behind the nominally social activities that are really instruments for personal advancement; it must rank behind the numerous exercises for self-improvement which can be turned back into the direct economic struggle. Since man does not live by bread alone, it will also probably rank behind the explicitly non-economic activities of leisure time. Unable to gain a high priority among economic motives, it is removed by its economic taint from competition with the activities that are labeled "pleasure." If political activity is really primarily motivated by economic concerns, as many reform politicians have seemed to assume, there is little hope that the greater portion of the population can ever be drawn for long stretches of time into active politics. Luckily, this does not seem to be the case.

Let us look again at the sense of moral frustration that has overcome the reform movement in Philadelphia and that, we have suggested, is a common characteristic of reform campaigns in this country. At first sight the frustration seems somewhat unreasonable. Since the amount of corruption carried on under the Republicans was not really so very great, and since the amount of corruption being carried on now is very likely even less, and since the institutional changes that have been made have been of a worthwhile and permanent nature, the reformers seem to have little cause for the sense of moral dismay that they clearly feel. At the same time, however, we have noted that the reform movement in Philadelphia has suffered one real failure: It has failed to change in any fundamental way the practice of politics in the city.

Let us now suggest that the sense of frustration and the real failure in fact belong together: that the reformers and the voters are frustrated today not so much because a few crooks still loiter about in the corridors of City Hall but because they have failed in extending the opportunity for active political participation to the larger number of ordinary citizens. But why should these citizens feel frustrated over being denied the opportunity for political participation when, as we have argued, the economic motive for political activity is not a very intense one?

This returns us to the question of what the "boys" really mean when they say they "love politics." We have admitted that the quest for status is involved in this motivation, as no doubt it is with the urge that the ordinary citizen may feel toward the political realm. But we have also suggested that status hunger alone cannot explain the satisfaction the "boys" seem to gain from their work, just as it does not explain the clear emotional return experienced by a Joe Clark or a Richardson Dilworth or a Thacher Longstreth. Let us look more closely at the concept, "love politics." What, after all, is politics? Politics, we are told, is who gets what, when, and how. Viewed in one light, no doubt. But if that is politics, then what is economics? Is not economics also who gets what, when, and how? Are politics and economics then identical? Hardly, since there are clearly economic activities–like selling automobiles and buying cucumbers—that are not political activities. Is politics, then, a division within the general class of economics? One thinks not. The feeling of frustration associated with reform, for instance, seems to have little economic basis, and neither does the feeling of camaraderie that is so valued by the "boys." Is not politics more truly defined, all things considered, as the expression of the will of the individual within the society of his fellows, or, more completely, the participation of human beings in the activities of conserving, distributing, and improving the values that are created by a civilized community? In short, is not politics the "art of government"? And if this is true, is not the question of why human beings should "love politics" similar to the question of why men should love women? Is not the answer to both, that is, that it is the nature of the beast? Is it not true, then, that political activity is a normal manifestation of human nature, and the real question is: Why should there be men who do *not* love politics?

With this question in mind, let us return for another look at the Protestant group whose mores have set the dominant pattern in the United States, and whose general lack of political interest has been used as an argument in favor of the theory that politics, insofar as it is not economic, is a "status-conferring" function. Let us suggest now that the general lack of political activity among members of the Protestant middle class is due not so much to the fact that they may be in a secure status position as to the effect of any unduly individualistic philosophy which over-emphasizes the private will at the expense of the social context in which it seeks to operate.

V

The Trend of Urban Politics

THE most significant single fact for the future of urban politics in America is its changing class character. Until recently, our cities have been predominantly working class. Today, they are in most cases predominantly middle class, and soon they will be overwhelmingly so. What has happened, according to Samuel Lubell, is that the sons and daughters, and the grandsons and granddaughters, of the immigrants (the "old underdog elements") have climbed into the middle class. These new elements of the middle class are different from the old middle class in several important respects. Having made their gains during a time of depression and war, they do not share the hostility of the older middle-class generation to Big Government. And whereas the old middle class was preoccupied with the task of creating a nationwide economy, Lubell thinks that the new middle class is ready for an "adventure in social unification." This "new frontier," he says, is the creation of the kind of nationwide social structure required by an industrial civilization. It is, therefore, an "urban frontier."

Lubell overlooks one striking feature of the situation: in spite of the differences in their history and outlook, the new middle classes have accepted the political ethos of the old. They have moved from what Jane Addams called a "personal" to a "social" morality. Most of those who were Catholic in theology before are so still, but they have become Yankee-Protestant in their political ethos. They are avid for ethnic recognition (Lubell points out that in this they differ from the old middle class), but they want a kind of recognition that is flattering by the new standards they have come to accept. To have a surname that marks one as a member of what Mayor Curley of Boston called "the newer races" is a political advantage in any large city, but only when it is accompanied by attributes—not only speech, dress, and manner, but also public virtues: honesty, impartiality, and regard for efficiency— that the public mind associates with the old Yankee-Protestant elite. The "new immigrants" indignantly reject those political ways—above all, the boss and the machine—that remind them of their pre-middle-class past. Thus, as Frank J. Sorauf explains, patronage, an indispensable element in the equilibrium of incentives of the machine, has practically disappeared in most cities. According to Sorauf a party that tries to clean house after an election is likely to encounter public indignation because the middle class respects the "public-spirited citizen" and not the "self-interested party worker," and because it will not excuse the presence of mediocrities in public service in the name of party loyalty. Edward C. Banfield shows how the one remaining powerful big city machine, that of Chicago, is beleaguered by middle-class elements in the outlying neighborhoods and suburbs. To get the necessary support from these elements, the machine must accept one reform after another, and so must eventually reform itself out of existence.

The new style of politics takes its character not only from the political ethos of the mass of voters, but more especially from the mentality of the elite. This elite, which is necessarily small, consists of those who run for office, select candidates, and manage and finance campaigns. About this mentality and its significance for urban politics, Robert C. Wood and Joseph Lyford, tell us a good deal. Although the elites they describe are very differently situated—they are suburbanites in the case of Wood, and Manhattan cliffdwellers in the case of Lyford —it is nevertheless apparent that they share a single mentality. In other words, what is significant is not where they live (whether in the suburbs or the central city), but their class, age, and educational characteristics. Although these new-style political activists are likely to be hi-fi addicts and to wear toreador pants, these readings suggest that their outlook is not essentially different from that of earlier generations of reformers. They feel a lively concern (to use a characteristically Protestant word) for the welfare of the community and a corresponding obligation to participate in its affairs. They believe that disinterested and expert search for the interest of the community "as a whole" is far better than political struggle as a way of solving public problems. They believe, with Steffens and the Progressives, that the popular will, when it expresses itself without distortion by defective institutions or other "external" corrupting elements like the machine or, nowadays, TV or advertising, is always good, right, and wise, and that therefore the cure for the ills of democracy is more democracy. They think that a political party is tolerable only to the extent that it persuades on grounds of public interest, and they regard party discipline based on anything else—above all, on personal material incentives —as a form of corruption. And they conclude that for all practical purposes party is an evil, although perhaps a necessary one, and that the ideal should be nonpartisanship.

Carried to its logical conclusion, this ideal implies government without politics. An executive (whether called mayor, manager, or chairman) would run the government as if it were a business. Presumably he would decide matters strictly on the basis of technical criteria. He would be high-handed, of course, but he would "get things done" and the voters would have the satisfaction of knowing that things were being done honestly, impartially, and efficiently. For all practical purposes his tenure would be permanent—he would be re-elected or reappointed almost automatically—and he would play no part in the partisan politics of the state and nation. In the intervals between the going of one such executive and the coming of another, there would, of course, be flurries of what Robert L. Morlan calls "unorganized" politics. Interest groups and voluntary associations would move to the center of the stage, but the character of their performance would be influenced by that of their audience, which would, for the most part, be dedicated to the cause of "good government." And when another strong executive was found, "unorganized" politics would again dissolve into no politics.

How the Negro population, which is still predominantly working class, will fit into this middle-class style of politics is hard to predict. By 1970 fifteen cities of 100,000 or more population are expected to be at least 40 percent Negro, and four of these—Washington, D.C., Richmond, Va., Compton, Calif., and Gary, Ind.—are expected to have Negro majorities. The presence of large numbers of Negroes in a city does not necessarily mean that they will exercise great influence in its affairs, however. One reason for this, which John Hadley Strange documents heavily with respect to Philadelphia, is that they may choose not to participate in politics very fully. Another, which Lee Sloan, a sociologist, shows in the case of "Lakewood," is that whites may find ways of reducing their influence when they do participate.

The New Middle Class

Samuel Lubell

THE ESSENTIAL DIFFERENCE between the Republican-rooted middle class and the newer Democratically inclined middle class is hardly one of conservatism versus liberalism, in the true meaning of these terms. What really separates these two middle classes is the factor of timing—of when each arrived at the state of middle-class blessedness. Because of the timing of their rise, the newer middle-class elements probably had tougher going during the depression and differ in occupational and business interests. Having achieved their gains in a period of expanding governmental authority, they are not as hostile to "Big Government" as the older middle-class elements. They also are apt to be of different ethnic or religious backgrounds.

The ethnic differences are not crucially important in themselves. What makes them so significant politically is that having come to this country in roughly the same period, the so-called "new" immigrants and their offspring shared common experiences in this country. All have been part of one of the epic population movements in history—of the upsurging out of the slums toward the middle class which has swept our major cities over the last fifty years and which still is going on.

To map the growth of almost any of our larger cities since the turn of the century is to map this upward, outward push of the masses toward the greener suburbs, propelling the older residents before them. And the story of the Democratic party in the big cities is really the story of the social and political revolution which marched along with this exodus from the slums.

The exodus was not accomplished in a single, mass evacuation, but through successive moves, from one neighborhood to the next. Each new neighborhood represented a higher rung on the social and economic ladder. And as they climbed, the masses were transformed. By the time the heights of middle-class status had been scaled, the immigrant generation which had begun the trek had died off or had become grandparents, relegated to the role of baby sitters, and a new native-born generation had come into its own.

A similar clocklike progression through successive frontier zones marked our westward expansion. So alike, in fact, are the dynamics of the two movements that one is justified in asking: Did the frontier ever really pass from American life? True, the supply of free land was virtually gone by 1890. But did the frontier really die with the exhaustion of free lands? Or did it merely sink from sight temporarily, to reappear in a new form in our developing industrial civilization?

The Old Tenement Trail

Possibly because it lacked the excitement of the Indian wars or because it still is so close to us, the saga of this twentieth-century odyssey of America's urban masses has gone unsung. Yet the parallels between the old western frontier and the new urban frontier are striking.

To Frederick Jackson Turner, who made American historians frontier-conscious, the ever-receding frontier was the zone of most rapid and effective Americanization. At the outer edge, "where civilization and savagery met," was where "men of all races were melted down and fused into a new race." Each new zone of frontier settlement was a "beginning all over again" which took Americans ever further away from dependence on Europe's economy and ways.

That holds equally true for the new frontier. For the urban masses each advance into a new neighborhood has also been a "beginning over again," which took them ever further from their European origins in the case of the immigrants, or, with Negroes, from the Plantation South. There has been much pooh-poohing of social climbing, without appreciation of the fact that it is a vital part of the Americanization process. The move to a "nicer" neighborhood would often be celebrated by a shortening or Anglicizing of names. Items of alien garb would be dropped; foreign accents would lighten. There would be more American food in the grocery stores, less orthodoxy in worship, more inter-marriage with other ethnic elements and—as an ironical index of Americanization—more divorce.

The role of the railroads in opening up the Western lands has been duplicated first, by the subway and streetcars, and, currently, by the automobile, in making ever newer housing accessible. The role of the pioneer woman was repeated in the immigrant mother who, with the sieve of drudgery, rescued the savings which enabled the family to climb to higher rental reaches. The immigrant mother was also the guardian of respectability on the urban frontier.

Like the Old West, the ever-changing urban frontier has been more "a form of society" than a geographical area. And as the story of America's social evolution could be read page by page in the successive frontier zones through which the pioneer pushed, so the march of the urban masses can be charted by tracing the neighborhoods through which these groups have climbed.

For example, when the late Arnold Bennett wrote his impressions of the United States in 1911, he closed his narrative with an account of a visit to New York's Lower East Side. The "astounding populousness" of the streets—some of which had more inhabitants per square foot than most crowded areas of Bombay—roused the famous novelist to helpless indignation. On Rivington Street the "very architecture seemed to sweat humanity at every window and door." The thought of the "picturesque, feverish and appalling existences" endured by these "sickly-faced immortal creatures who lie closer than any wild animal would lie" stirred Bennett to protest to his American companions. They retorted, "Well, what are you going to do about it?"

The sequel to Bennett's visit can be read in any of several Old Tenement Trails which had their beginning in the dreary, cold-water flats of the East Side. The northward trail mounted first to Harlem or Yorkville, where hot water and steam heat were at least available, even if one had to bang the pipes before the janitor stoked the furnace. The next jump was out of Manhattan to the East Bronx, where trees stepped out of poems onto the streets; then to the West Bronx, crossing that Great Social Divide—the Grand Concourse—beyond which rolled true middle-class country. West of the Concourse, janitors were called superintendents; apartment houses had lift elevators and parquet floors, which needed no scrubbing. The migration then swept north paralleling the Concourse, the mink coats growing thicker as one mounted to Fordham Road and beyond.

Having run the length of both Manhattan and the Bronx, in recent years the Tenement Trail has swung abruptly eastward to the expensively filled-in marshes of Queens, which is currently the outermost fringe of New York's housing frontier. Here today will be found many of the "sickly-faced immortal creatures" whom Bennett saw. But how they have changed! Because they spent their youth in rootless tenements which knew no community life, they have been buying homes and have become doubly civic-minded in their eagerness to build a community in which their children might escape the deprivations of their own childhood.

From Rivington Street to Forest Hills in Queens is only a few miles. Historically, the spanning of that distance was a social revolution.

This same process of social exploration can be repeated with any of the former minority elements and in all of our larger cities. By going up and down the ladder of neighborhoods through which these different elements have climbed, one can see the progress they have made and the setbacks they have suffered—their clashes and reconciliations with other ethnic elements, and their assimilation into American society generally.

Do you wonder how the manners and habits of Negroes alter when they reach the middle class? In the North Bronx, around Gunhill Road, can be found a group of Negroes, mainly white collar and professional people, who have bought homes in recent years. As if feeling themselves on trial, they are as unlike the Harlem stereotype as imaginable in their habits. Their tastes in clothes and furnishings are sober. They pay cash at the neighborhood stores. At nearby Evander Childs High School their children rate tops scholastically. "Their drive to get an education is terrific," observes Dr. Hyman Alprin, Evander's principal. Oddly, every Negro child in the school takes Latin, as if seeking some mark of culture.

Or, one can follow the trek of the Irish in Boston, from the hilly streets of Charlestown out to Cambridge, on to Arlington and Newton; or of the Czechs in Chicago from South Lawndale, to Cicero and Berwyn. In Detroit the "uptown" upsurge has been eastward toward Grosse Pointe; in Milwaukee it has been northward along Lake Michigan and westward towards Granville.

If land hunger was the propelling force behind the agrarian frontier, the drive behind the urban frontier has been the hunger for social status. The changed nature of present-day political issues is largely a reflection of this contrast between the earlier agrarian frontier and its urban counterpart.

As the pioneers moved westward the obstacles they had to overcome were primarily physical and natural—breaking the sod in the semiarid plains, clearing the wilderness, driving railroad spikes across an untracked continent. Along the urban frontier the obstacles have been primarily manmade. The mountain barriers which have to be scaled are those of rents and restrictive covenants. Unemployment is the drought which could wither one's labors. The swiftly flowing rivers which have to be forded and bridged are those of class and social distinction, none the less treacherous because they are intangible.

The politics of westward expansion were bound to be sectional, since some parts of the country unavoidably lagged behind others and the newer settlements were often indebted, colonial offshoots of the older creditor areas. In contrast, the urban migration was bound to quicken class and social conflict, mirroring the uneven progress toward acceptance by different social groups.

In today's perspective, the Republican-dominated era can be said to have centered around one enormous historical fact: the spanning of the continent and the creation of a nation-wide economy. In the perspective of the future, we may look back upon today's Democratic era as an adventure in social unification, in the creation of the kind of nation-wide social structure which an industrialized civilization requires.

In any case, the reappearance of the frontier in a new urban form has been one of the most important political forces of our time. It explains the divisions between the old and new middle class. It generates the explosive force behind the civil rights issue. . . . It also has been transforming the big-city political machines, dooming the old-style political boss.

For the Democratic machines the spoils of office over the last twenty years have been fat indeed. Yet the reigns of the bosses have been growing progressively shorter. Fewer and fewer are dying with their patronage boots on. Usually this is credited to the fact that a beneficent federal government has replaced the political clubhouse in dispensing relief and other favors. Of equal, if not greater, significance has been the simultaneous coming-of-age of most of the old underdog elements.

As its large families have grown to voting age and as it has developed its own leadership, each minority group has been demanding an ever-increasing share of political recognition. Today, the plight of the Irish Democratic bosses, who managed most of the big-city machines, is not unlike that of the wearied rulers of the British Empire, who are everywhere on the defensive before the rising "nationality" elements they once ruled.

Tammany Hall, once as Irish as St. Patrick, fell to the Italo-Americans in ·1947. A year earlier the Kelly-Nash dynasty in Chicago was superseded by Jacob Arvey, a Jew. In 1949, a coalition of dissident Irish, Italo-Americans and Polish-Americans terminated the thirty-two years, "I am the Law" role of Frank Hague in Jersey City.

Currently, the most dramatic illustration of this trend is the rise of the Italo-Americans. In 1948 eight Italo-Americans were elected to Congress, twice as many as in any previous year. Two of these congressmen were from Newark, which in 1949 named an Italo-American mayor. Hoboken, Passaic and Paterson are among the other larger New Jersey cities which have elected Italo-American mayors since the war's end. Compared with 1936 more than twice as many Italian names are answering the legislative roll calls in Pennsylvania, New Jersey, New York, Connecticut, Rhode Island and Massachusetts—the six states with the heaviest Italo-American concentrations.

The intensifying Irish-Italian feud which has accompanied this rise wracks not only the Democratic party but also the Catholic Church whose hierarchy in this country is mainly Irish. It rocks gangland too. The struggle between James Pendergast and Charles Binnaggio in Kansas City ended in violent murder. Of the gangsters cited by name in the Kefauver Crime Report, almost one half are clearly Italian.

That does not mean that Italians are peculiarly susceptible to criminal activity. The battle to control the nation's rackets now being pressed by Italo-American racketeers is part of the same "coming of age" process[1] which is reflected in the growing frequency of Italian names on big league baseball and college football teams. Until 1929 not a single Italian name was listed on Walter Camp's annual all-star football team. Since then there has been hardly a year in which there wasn't at least one Italian name on the all star list. . . .

Jacob's Ladder

What is often described as "The March of the Masses" is usually thought of as a radical, even insurrectionary development. The very phrase murmurs suggestions of mob rule and political lynching. Yet, with the Italo-Americans we have seen that their political upthrust was sparked not by hard times but by boom times. Their leadership came not from the most oppressed and discontented, but from those with the strongest middle-class drive.

The same pattern holds for other minority elements as well. None were stirred to political uprising when their grievances were heaviest. It was as they emerged from the social cellar and got their first whiffs of the fresher, middle-class air that their political spirits quickened. The key to the political progress of any minority element in this country would seem to lie in just this success in developing its own middle class. Sheer numbers alone are not sufficient for political power—witness the ineffectiveness so far of the Mexican-Americans in the Southwest. To be effective, numbers must be supported by economic, educational and social progress.

The climbing masses can hardly be described as a conservative force. But are they as radical as they appear? Since their emergence stirs class conflict, it is easy to view their rise as confirming Karl Marx's dire prophecies of class warfare. Actually we are witnessing an almost complete refutation of the Marxian thesis. Our class struggle, if it can be called that, arises not from the impoverishment of the masses but from their progress. It is evidence not of the failure of the American dream but of its successes.

Despite all the talk of monopolistic control of American economic life and the supposed end of opportunities, even the most downtrodden elements have been able to climb. And if the urban masses are challenging the *status quo*, their challenge, essentially, is a demand for acceptance into our predominantly middle-class society.

The trends of our times seem to be strengthening this middle-class bias of American politics. Not so long ago political appointees were

1. Both Frank Costello and Joe Adonis have attributed their interest in politics to the desire to gain greater recognition for Italo-Americans.

more often graduates of saloons and street gangs than of universities. Old-timers in the Bronx can remember an amusing pair of local Irish judges who not only knew no law but couldn't even read. One of these judges, after hearing a case, would take down a thick lawbook, pore over it learnedly and announce, "This is a fine point of law, I will reserve decision."

At lunchtime he would hotfoot it to a higher court, get coached on the law, return and announce his verdict.

The second judge, equally unlettered, kept making a spectacle of himself until he decided to imitate his colleague. After hearing one case, he reached up to the nearby shelf, took down a fat volume and thumbed through it. Making quite a show of learned deliberation, he announced, "An exceedingly fine point of law is involved. I think I'll reserve decision." The spectators burst into laughter. The book the judge had consulted so learnedly was the telephone directory.

Today college training or its equivalent is required for an increasing proportion of appointments. To register its political strength a minority group has to have its own lawyers or leaders with equivalent training. In turn, the broader the middle-class base developed by any upclimbing element, the more clamorous become its demands for political recognition.

Patronage is peculiarly important for minority groups, involving much more than the mere spoils of office. Each first appointment given a member of any underdog element is a boost in that element's struggle for social acceptance. It means that another barrier to their advance has been lifted, another shut door has swung open. Whenever Roosevelt nominated a Negro to a white collar post in the federal government, for example, he transmitted a vicarious thrill to every young Negro who thought instinctively, "Maybe there's a place up there for me or my child."

The opening of these new opportunities, in turn, stimulates the political consciousness of the group, encouraging its leaders to eye the next highest post on the patronage ladder.

In most northern cities, the Democrats have actually developed a ladder-like succession of posts, through which the political progress of various minority elements is recognized. Just as one can judge how far any minority has climbed economically from its position on the residential ladder, so one can measure its effective political power by its place on the patronage ladder.

The earliest stirrings of any group usually are appeased by an appointment as assistant district attorney, which entails little more than that some members of the group be educated as lawyers. A county judgeship, on the other hand, requires a candidate who has succeeded in a lower post, a large enough vote to withstand the competing claims of other minority blocs, and the economic backing to finance a campaign. Similarly, with elected posts, the solid vote of an ethnic element may win an aldermanic district or a seat in the legislature or even in Congress. But no minority group can be said to have arrived politically until its members can appeal beyond their own ethnic boundaries, to win a county-wide or city-wide election.

This system of succession obstructs as well as advances minority progress. By compelling each element to serve its apprenticeship in lower posts, the machine bosses have been able to slow and temper the rise of the underdog elements. Largely through this system of seniority and by playing off one ethnic element against the others the Irish have been able to cling to a much larger representation among officeholders than their voting strength would warrant.

The emphasis on hyphenated candidates, or what has come to be known as "League of Nations" politics, is often condemned as "un-American." Yet it is really an integral part of the Americanization process, serving as a means through which minority elements are assimilated into the structure of government. This was true during the Republican era, when the sons of the Norwegian, Swedish and German immigrants banded together to wrest greater recognition from the Yankee bosses who then controlled the Republican party. It holds equally true today.

Another fundamental difference between the Republican and Democratic parties is that they have been the vehicles for the political advancement of quite different ethnic elements. The Republicans, by political necessity, became sensitive to the aspirations of the "old" immigrant elements, who settled so largely on the farms. The Democrats, in turn, have been more alive to the aspirations of the "new" immigrant elements who crowded the teeming cities.

The Silent Revolution in Patronage

Frank J. Sorauf

WITH LITTLE FANFARE and only quiet celebration the movement to install merit systems in place of the older patronage is well on its way to full victory. The federal government has almost completely been conquered by one form or another of merit appointment, while the traditional political machines, long the major consumers of patronage, are everywhere else in hurried retreat. And the scholars and administrators who for so long fought in the vanguard of the movement now savor a triumph in practical affairs of the sort rarely vouchsafed to intellectuals.

The case against patronage, based largely on the need for administrative expertise and professionalism, is overwhelming. But only rarely have the opponents of patronage stopped to worry about the effects on the parties and political system of abolishing it.[1] Some scholars of political parties have argued that patronage is important to the political process, but there has never been an attempt to compare the merit system's contribution to good administration with its supposed weakening of the party system in the total balance of effective government.

Such a comparison may not be necessary, however. Patronage is slowly dying out—more from its own political causes than from the campaigns of civil service reformers. However substantial the need of the parties for patronage fifty or even twenty years ago, the need is

1. One would, however, have to mention three specialists in public administration who have recognized and addressed themselves to the conflicting needs of party and administration. See especially Harvey C. Mansfield's paper on "Political Parties, Patronage, and the Federal Government Service," in the American Assembly volume, *The Federal Government Service: Its Character, Prestige, and Problems* (Columbia University, 1954), pp. 81–112. Also relevant are Richard E. Neustadt's review, "On Patronage, Power and Politics," 15 *Public Administration Review* 108–114 (Spring, 1955) and James R. Watson, "Is Patronage Obsolete?" 18 *Personnel Administration* 3–9 (July, 1955).

Reprinted from Public Administration Review, XX, No. 1 (Winter, 1960), pp. 28–34.

vastly less today. On the one hand, the organization, functions, and style of American politics, and the consequent need for patronage, have changed dramatically in the last generation; on the other hand, the nature and usefulness of patronage itself also have changed.[2]

Uses of Patronage

Patronage is best thought of as an incentive system—a political currency with which to "purchase" political activity and political responses. The chief functions of patronage are:

Maintaining an Active Party Organization

Experienced politicos maintain that the coin of patronage is necessary to reward the countless activities of an active party organization. The promise or actual holding of a political appointment, they report, is necessary to induce the canvassing of neighborhoods, mailing and telephoning, campaigning and electioneering, and other activities of the local party organization. Illustratively, many a city hall or county court rests vacant on election day as its denizens go out to man the party organization.

Promoting Intra-Party Cohesion

In the hands of a skillful party leader, patronage may be an instrument of party cohesion, edging defecting partisans back into the discipline of the party hierarchy and welding the differing blocs within the party into a unified whole. In one sense President Eisenhower's historic agreement with Senator Taft in Morningside Heights represents an attempt to enlist the support of the Taft Republicans in 1952 by promising them consideration in the party's appointments.

Attracting Voters and Supporters

The patronage appointment often may be used to convert the recipient (and a large portion of his family and friends) into life-long and devoted supporters of the appointing party. Gratitude for the job will win his support for the party, it is said, and a desire to retain the job

2. Very few studies exist of the actual operation of patronage systems across the country. Among the few are: David H. Kurtzman, *Methods of Controlling Votes in Philadelphia* (published by author, 1935); Frank J. Sorauf, "State Patronage in a Rural County," 50 *American Political Science Review* 1046–1056 (December, 1956); and H. O. Waldby, *The Patronage System in Oklahoma* (The Transcript Co., 1950). In the absence of specific reports and data, one can only proceed uneasily on a mixture of political folklore, scattered scholarship, professional consensus, and personal judgment.

by keeping the party in power will enforce it. In some urban areas of Pennsylvania, experienced party men calculate that a well-placed appointment should net the party between six and eight voters. The same reasoning, of course, lies behind the appointment of representatives of special blocs of voters, such as ethnic, national, or religious groups.

Financing the Party and Its Candidates

The cruder and more overt forms of this function of patronage have long been known to the fraternity as "macing" the payroll. In the heyday of patronage in American politics, something close to 5 per cent of the appointee's salary was thought a fair return to the party for its benefice. Patronage, always reward for past activity as well as inducement for the future, may also be used to reward a decent contribution to the party coffers.

Procuring Favorable Government Action

Less commonly acknowledged, perhaps for its dubious ethics and legality, is the use of patronage to secure favorable policy or administrative action for the party or its followers. At the local government level it may involve the fixing of a traffic ticket, preference for certain applicants for public assistance, the calculated oversight in a public health inspection, or the use of public equipment to remove snow from private rights-of-way. By exploiting the appointee's dependence on the party, the organization reaps the political advantages of a preferred access to public policy-making.

Creating Party Discipline in Policy-Making

This last function of patronage redounds less to the advantage of political parties than to presidents and governors who use appointments to build support for their programs in legislatures. Franklin Roosevelt's wily use of the dwindling federal patronage, especially his delaying of appointments until after satisfactory congressional performance, scarcely needs more than mention. A number of governors still have at their disposal a vast array of political jobs to use in coordinating executive and legislative policy and in joining the separated powers of government.

But patronage may certainly be misused in ways that adversely affect the parties and political system. It may build up personal machines or followings that parallel and compete with the regular, formal party organization. Poorly administered, it may cause new resentments and hostilities, create more friction within the party than it eases. Also, patronage seldom can perform all of the six purposes at once since to use it for one purpose is to destroy its effectiveness for another. For example, appointments that solidify and activate local party organization may disturb centralized party unity at a higher level and impair party discipline within both party and legislature.[3]

Just how well patronage has performed the six functions for the parties over the years is a matter for considerable conjecture. Partisans usually claim patronage is the "life-blood" of American politics, and yet even among its most devoted and skillful users, many dissent and some are ambivalent. James Farley, for example, has boasted that he could build a major party without patronage, and yet he dissented from the recommendation of the second Hoover Commission that rural postal carriers be taken from the patronage lists.[4] The scholarly studies of patronage and general political folklore indicate that it is fairly effective in maintaining an active organization and, to a lesser extent, in attracting voters and supporters, but that its value in performing the other functions is highly questionable. Political appointees do contribute money to the party treasuries but hardly enough to run a party today. As for the promotion of party cohesion, the intra-party bickering and bitterness occasioned by the division of the spoils is, to this observer, truly staggering.

Decline in Usefulness

Regardless of the effectiveness of patronage in the past, it is today undergoing rapid changes, most obviously in its steady shrinkage. One observer has estimated that the federal patronage available to the Eisenhower Administration has ". . . not exceeded a fraction of one percent of the total federal establishment."[5] A precise estimate of the number of jobs still under patronage in city, county, and state administrations throughout the country would be impossible to come by, but all hands agree it is declining.

There do remain states where merit systems have made few inroads into patronage and where large numbers of positions (about 50,000 in Pennsylvania, for example) remain at least technically available for distribution by the victorious. But even in these instances the parties are using a steadily decreasing percentage of the jobs for political purposes because patronage as a political currency has been devalued. Merit systems make their greatest inroads into patronage in the

3. I have questioned the political usefulness of patronage at greater length in "Patronage and Party," 3 *Midwest Journal of Political Science* 115–126 (May, 1959).

4. The claim is in James A. Farley, *Behind the Ballots* (Harcourt, Brace, and Co., 1938), p. 237, and the dissent in the Commission on Organization of the Executive Branch of the Government, *Report on Personnel and Civil Service* (U.S. Government Printing Office, 1955), p. 91.

5. Mansfield, *op. cit.* note 1 above, p. 94.

well-paid, specialized positions where the call for expertness and training is greatest. The parties are left the less-desirable, poorly-paid positions generally. With continued economic prosperity and high levels of
employment the economic rewards of these jobs, hardly princely in
most cases, are less appealing than formerly. While low pay and chronic
job insecurity plague the patronage jobholders, private employment has
become progressively more attractive with rising wage levels, union
protections and securities, unemployment compensation, pension plans,
and fringe benefits. Viewed by most Americans as a short-term, despera-
tion job alternative, the patronage position has lost considerable value
as a political incentive.

Patronage also is losing its respectability. Its ethic—the naked political *quid pro quo*—no longer seems to many a natural and reasonable
ingredient of politics. Parties often find that the attempt to clean
political house after an election produces public outrage and indignation. The mores of the middle-class and the image of civic virtue in-
stilled by public education extol the unfettered, independent voter
rather than the patronage-seeking party-liner. The public-spirited citizen rather than the self-interested party worker is celebrated. And the
public no longer tolerates the presence of political mediocrities in public
service in the name of party loyalty.

Even the job-seekers themselves no longer accept the political obligations of their appointments as readily as once they did. Briefly,
patronage has fallen into public disfavor for appearing to approach an
outright political payoff, with the result that its usefulness to the parties
has diminished.

Changes in Parties and Politics

The partial passing of the boss and the political machine has
been perhaps the most obvious new development in party behavior. Depending heavily on the motive power of patronage, these machines long
dominated big city politics and some county and state strongholds as
well. They flourished especially in those urban centers inhabited by
large groups of immigrants and minorities—groups not yet integrated
into American life, often poor and insecure and bewildered by the traditions of American politics. The machine spoke to them in the simple
terms of a job, of sympathy in city hall, and of food and fuel to soften
the hardest times.

This is not to suggest that political machines have vanished or even
that they will vanish within the next generation. But the machine, and
the politics of the underprivileged on which it rests, is surely on the
decline. Government and other private agencies have taken over the
social welfare functions these organizations once provided. Further-

more, first and second generation groups, traditional recipients of the attentions of the machine, are disappearing, and their children and grandchildren now luxuriate in the prosperity and conformity of the suburbs, though in many cities their place will be taken for a time by immigrants from rural areas of the United States. In sum, rising levels of prosperity, higher educational levels, declining numbers of unassimilated groups, and greater concern by government for the unfortunate all point to a decline of the boss and machine and of the patronage they relied on.

Furthermore, party conflict since the 1930's has reflected social and economic appeals to a greater extent than in the preceding decades. Even though they do not yet approach the ideological fervor of European campaigns, American politics has become more involved with issues and less with the issueless politics of patronage, favor, and preferment. Campaigning, too, has shifted from the door-to-door canvass, local rallies, and controlled blocs of votes to the mass media and advertising agencies. Great, attractive candidates serve as the focus of these national campaigns. As a result the importance of the national party organization is increased—the center of party power shifting away from the local units just as clearly as the center of government power is shifting from the states and localities to the national government.

The New Party Worker

What is emerging, then, is a system of political organization more compatible with the middle-class values of suburbia than those of the ethnic or racial neighborhood of the urban center. Rather than relying on the organized party hierarchy, it depends more and more on the volunteer and *ad hoc* political groups and personal followings. In some states, such as California and Wisconsin, party leaders are converting this fleeting volunteer activity into more permanent clubs and party organization,[6] but the manpower of these changing parties contrasts sharply with the ward or precinct committeeman of the older machines. The new political men are far more likely than their predecessors to be motivated by belief, by loyalty to an attractive candidate (e.g., the Citizens for Eisenhower movement), by a sense of civic duty, or by a more generalized social and sporting enthusiasm. They view their political activity more as avocation than vocation.

The parties also have found fresh resources in the organized power of the interest group. It recruits voters for the favored party or candidate and provides campaign and financial assistance as well. Many a candi-

6. The literature on the California political clubs is rather extensive, especially the nonacademic journals, but the only general work on the volunteer movement in politics of which I am aware is Stephen A. Mitchell's *Elm Street Politics* (Oceana Publications, 1959).

date today prizes the contacts and communication channels of the local labor union or chamber of commerce more highly than he does the face-to-face campaign. Voters in many corners of the country can testify that candidates rarely knock on their doors any more. Business and labor are major sources of party funds; the contributions of payrollers no longer suffice. Even the "new style" political leader, in contrast with the classic model of the boss, usually has closer ties to interest groups in the community. He may even have been recruited from one.

For these educated, secure, and even prestiged workers and leaders of the new parties, a political appointment holds little fascination. One sophisticated and experienced politician has written that "Men and women are drawn into politics by a combination of motives; these include power, glory, zeal for contention or success, duty, hate, oblivion, hero worship, curiosity, and enjoyment of the work."[7] Today's political worker may more and more find his reward in the satisfaction of a deeply-rooted psychological need, the identification with a purposeful organization or a magnetic leader, the ability to serve an economic or professional interest, the release from the tedium of daily routine, or the triumph of an ideal. His "pay-off," instead of a political job, may be endorsement for elective office, membership on a civic commission, access to new and influential elites, or a reception in the White House gardens.

The New Personnel Needs of the Party

These shifts in organization, functions, and personnel of the parties have meant that the patronage that does remain is not the patronage that the parties might easily use. The parties cry for trained, educated, experienced men of ability and affairs, albeit fewer men than formerly. The vast majority of patronage positions are poorly paid and generally unappealing to the men and women of skills and achievement the parties would like to enlist. Very likely the man placed on a trash collection crew will lack the social and political experience to be useful in today's politics, and his meager pay offers the party scant opportunity for fund-raising. The middle-level job, potentially the most useful to the party in rewarding its more capable partisans, is rarely available for political appointment. These are the specialized, expert positions that are generally the first to be put under a merit system. When they do remain under patronage, their specialized qualifications are the hardest to fill from the rank and file of political job-seekers.

At the top, the party often has highly-placed positions available, at least in small number, to reward its leadership corps. Here, however,

7. Stimson Bullitt, *To Be a Politician* (Doubleday and Co., 1959), p. 42. The reader will, in fact, find all of chapter two a stimulating review of the incentives and motives of politics.

the party often fails to persuade its most capable men to give up, even temporarily, their positions in business and the professions for a political appointment. In turn, the party workers who would find the patronage position an attractive alternative to their private employment, lack the executive and administrative experience for the positions. Paul David and Ross Pollock write of these problems in the national government:

> For positions at the higher levels, the party organization has only rarely been successful in convincing the administration that its nominees were sufficiently qualified. The administration, on its part, has had to go out and hunt, cajole, and persuade in order to recruit the kind of talent it wanted. . . . The supply of persons with the requisite competence and availability is simply not large enough in either political party, and there is little evidence to suggest that the supply is on the increase.[8]

As its usefulness to them declines, patronage imposes hard and worrisome choices on the party hierarchies. Often the parties' appointments to the plenitude of unattractive patronage jobs go to the men and women with no particular record of service to the party and little promise for future service, or whose appointment will do little to integrate the party organization or build party cohesion. Their chief recommendation is their need for a job, and the party, functioning as employment bureau, hopes only for a little gratitude and possible support at the polls. The better paid, more enticing jobs are losing their incentive power for those partisans qualified to hold them, and the party finds itself haunted by the aggressive availability of unqualified job-hunters.

One is forced to conclude that the classic dependence of party on patronage is being undermined on both sides. Forced by the changing nature of American society and by new political problems and values, the parties are shifting to a new mode of operation that relies less than formerly on the incentives of patronage. Patronage, on the other hand, is declining in both quantity and quality, both in the number of jobs available and in their value to the party.

Short-Term Adjustments

Since party changes were not simply adjustments to the gradual demise of patronage, a further reduction in the supply of patronage in those states where the supply remains large will hardly alter the long-run development of the party system. It may, however, accelerate change in party operations or produce short-term side effects.

In the first place, patronage has persisted chiefly at the local levels

8. Paul T. David and Ross Pollock, *Executives for Government* (The Brookings Institution, 1957), pp. 25–27.

and remains the bulwark of local party organization, a faintly anachronistic bulwark, one might add, in an era of centralized party and
government. It is in these state and local party organs, despite their
declining vigor and importance, that one finds the most vocal proponents of patronage—even of the remaining federal patronage, much
of which is channeled through them. This concentration of patronage
in the localities fortifies the local party and permits it to resist discipline
or centralization by organs higher in the party structure.[9] Thus fortified,
these decentralized pockets of political power also fight party cohesion
and responsibility in legislatures and, paradoxically, often nullify the
value of executive patronage in achieving legislative discipline.

Inevitably, these local units, as they lose their vitality and their
part in major policy-making, become primarily dealers in patronage,
converting it from a political tool to a political goal. When patronage
declines there, a major resistance to party centralization and to issue-
centered campaigns and candidates will die with it.

Secondly, restrictions on patronage weaken the Democratic party
more than the Republicans. Patronage appeals more predictably to
lower economic strata, to unskilled and semiskilled workers, to urban
dwellers, and to minority groups—all of the demographic groups which,
studies show, support the Democratic party. Patronage as an incentive
system comports with the economic needs, the understanding of the
relationship between citizen and government, and the somewhat ex-
ploitative view of politics more common among lower social and economic groups than among the American middle class. Furthermore, the
Democratic party also has greater problems in finding substitutes for it.
The personal and financial support of the business community are not
often at its disposal. The formation of a genteel party, dedicated to a
philosophy of government and based on sociability and civic virtue, falls
more easily to the Republicans.

Thirdly, since the appeals of patronage are largely economic, its
political value and usefulness are apt to be greatest in the remaining
pockets of unemployment and economic hardship, for it is there that
private employment fails to provide opportunities superior to patronage
positions. In these areas, and in the country as a whole if widespread
unemployment returns, patronage might enjoy a brief renaissance as a
political incentive.

Finally, patronage has been involved in legislative-executive rivalry.
Presidents of the United States, harassed by congressional attempts to
control patronage through clearance systems and "senatorial courtesy,"
have been more willing to surrender it than has the Congress. State
governors, however, are not so willing to abandon one of the few

9. The classic expression of this view is E. E. Schattschneider, *Party Government*
(Rinehart and Co., 1942).

weapons they have over unruly legislatures.[10] Since the loss of patronage will certainly affect legislative-executive relations in the states more sharply than in the national government, one is justified in supposing that its further loss will make the task of gubernatorial leadership just that much more difficult.

In Conclusion

To expect anything but a further contraction of patronage would be naive. 1. Patronage does not meet the needs of present-day party operations. Activities requiring a large number of party workers—canvassing, mass mailings, rallies—are being replaced by radio and television. Political costs are so high that assessments on public salaries are minuscule beside the party's cost. 2. Patronage no longer is the potent inducement to party activity it once was. Public attitudes are increasingly hostile to patronage and the political style it represents. Employment in the private economy also provides an increasingly attractive alternative to patronage positions. 3. As a result, the incentives once provided by patronage are being replaced in the political system. The persons who can contribute most to campaigns, in skill and funds, seek different payoffs—prestige, power, or personal satisfaction rather than jobs.

Even though the further decline of patronage will certainly not destroy or seriously hamper the parties, it will produce political shocks and pockets of discomfort. It will probably hurt Democrats more than Republicans, will be slower and more crucial in economically distressed areas, and will weaken the influence of governors on legislative action more than the President's influence on Congress.

American political parties have, after all, been getting along without patronage to various extents for some time now, and they have survived. Even many large metropolitan cities, whose patronage needs the scholars emphasize, have managed without it. The political party has its causes and justification deep in the American political process and not in the dispensation of political privileges. Patronage is necessary to a certain type of party operation, but others can be maintained without it. The old machines and local party organizations relied on patronage, but they were rooted in social and economic conditions that are disappearing. As they disappear, so will the parties and patronage they fostered.

Ultimately, the decline of patronage will, among a number of

10. See Duane Lockhard, *New England State Politics* (Princeton University Press, 1959) for reports of the value of patronage to governors in New England. For instance, he describes patronage as "perhaps the most important of these gubernatorial weapons" in Massachusetts (p. 160).

causes, speed the parties to further centralization, to the heightening of their ideological content, to a greater reliance on group participation in politics, to greater nationalization of the candidate image and party campaigning, and to the establishment of some modicum of party discipline.

There is something almost quaint in these days of big parties, big government, and advertising agency politics about a political institution that conjures up images of Boss Tweed, torchlight parades, and ward heelers. As the great day of patronage recedes into history, one is tempted to say that the advancing merit systems will not kill patronage before it withers and dies of its own infirmity and old age.

The Dilemmas of a Metropolitan Machine

Edward C. Banfield

TO UNDERSTAND how the political heads evaluate their opportunities, i.e., how they decide the terms on which they will use influence
or allow it to be used upon them, it is necessary to look at some salient
facts of political geography.

"Downstate" (all of Illinois outside of Cook County) is white,
Protestant, Anglo-Saxon, rural, and normally Republican. It elects the
governor (a Democrat has held the office in only 16 of the last 58
years), and it controls the General Assembly. Under a recent reapportionment, the Senate is safely downstate and Republican; a narrow
majority of the House may be from Cook County, but some of the Cook
County representatives are sure to be Republicans, and some downstate
Democrats are almost sure to vote with the Republicans. Downstate
hates and fears Chicago, which it regards as an alien land.

Chicago is heavily Democratic. The Democratic heartland is the
slums and semi-slums of the inner city; here, in wards which are predominantly Negro, Italian, Polish, Lithuanian, or Irish, and (except for
the Negroes) almost entirely Catholic, the machine gets the hard core
of its support. The lower the average income and the less average education, the more reliably Democratic is the ward.

The vote is less Democratic as one moves outward from the center
of the city. Some of the outlying wards are usually Republican. So are
most of the "country towns" (that part of Cook County which lies outside Chicago); for the most part, the suburbanites of the "country
towns" are white, Protestant, and middle-class. Their affinity is with
downstate rather than the inner city.

The inner city wards are so populous and so heavily Democratic
that they can usually offset the Republican vote of the outlying wards.
In the future, the ascendancy of the inner city wards is likely to be
even more complete. White, middle-class families are moving to the
suburbs, and their places are being taken by Negroes and poor whites

Reprinted from Political Influence (*New York: The Free Press, 1961*), *pp. 244–253.*

from the South. Since the newcomers are almost all Democrats, and since many of those who leave are either Republicans or upward mobile types likely to become Republican, the proportion of Democrats in the inner city is increasing.

One might expect, then, that a mayor of Chicago would make the maintenance of the Democratic machine his most important business. So long as he controls the machine and it controls primary elections in the inner wards, he is invincible. And, of course, the way to maintain the machine is to pass out "gravy" with a generous hand—to give jobs, favors, and opportunities for graft and bribery to those who can deliver votes in the primaries.

This is, in fact, the strategy followed by the bosses of the most powerful machine wards.

It is not, however, the strategy of the mayor. He is normally the chairman of the county Democratic committee and therefore the leading figure in the party in Illinois and one of its leading figures nationally. Consequently, it is not enough for him merely to maintain himself in office in Chicago. He must take a wider view. He must carry the county and, if possible, the state, and he must contribute all that he can to the success and prestige of the party nationally. When the interests of the party on the larger scene conflict with its interests in the inner city of Chicago, the interests of the party in the inner city must usually be sacrificed.

As the table shows, to win a county-wide election a heavy vote in the inner city wards is not enough. There must also be a fairly strong Democratic vote in the outlying wards and in the suburban "country towns." The voters in these places are not in the habit of doing what the precinct captains tell them to do; their incomes are generally high enough, and their positions in society secure enough, to make them indifferent to the petty favors and advantages the machine has to offer. Many of them even seem to have absorbed the idea that "independence," i.e., splitting the ticket, is a mark of middle-class sophistication. To get

Relative Importance in the Cook County Electorate of Inner City Wards of Chicago, Outlying Wards of Chicago, and "Country Towns"

	POPULATION (IN THOUSANDS)		PER CENT CHANGE	PER CENT CONTRIBUTED TO COUNTY DEMOCRATIC VOTE	
	1950	1960[a]		1948	1956
18 Inner City Wards	1,257	1,291	3	37	31
Outlying Wards (Rest of Chicago)	2,364	2,616	11	50	51
"Country Towns" (Suburbs)	888	1,532	73	13	18
Total Cook County	4,509	5,439	20	100	100

[a] Estimate.

the vote it needs from these outlying areas, the Democratic party must appear not as a "machine" but as a "force for clean and progressive government." To do this it must offer "blue-ribbon" candidates, and it must give the city and county the kind of administration that will win the approval of the press and of "good government" forces generally. ("Good government" is some kind of a mixture—the proportions vary greatly from context to context—of the following principal ingredients: (*a*) "reform" of the old-fashioned kind, i.e., the suppression of vice, crime, and political corruption; (*b*) "efficiency" in the sense of doing what public administration "experts" recommend with respect to organization structure and "housekeeping" functions like budgeting and personnel management; (*c*) following "progressive" policies in the fields of housing, planning, race relations, and welfare; and (*d*) executing big projects—airports and exhibition halls, for example—to boost the size, business, and repute of the city.)

The preference of the outlying wards and "country towns" for good government has for a good many years been a force which the inner city machine has had to take into account. Its importance, moreover, is growing every year. In part, this is because the whole population —and especially that of the outlying wards and "country towns"—is becoming more discriminating in its voting behavior. In part, also, it is because the numerical strength of the outlying areas is growing while that of the inner city remains approximately the same.

In this situation, a rational county Democratic leader will be less attentive to the inner city wards, whose vote he can count on, than to the outlying areas, whose independence is a danger. His strategy in dealing with these outlying areas is clear: he must help his party live down its reputation as a "corrupt machine" and establish a new one as the honest and energetic servant of the people. The welfare of the suburbs must be his special concern; he must show the suburbanites that they have nothing to fear and much to hope for from the Democratic organization in the central city.

By the same token, a rational Republican leader will endeavor to keep alive the old image of the "boss-ridden" and "crooked" machine. He will do his best to frighten suburbanites and downstaters with stories of the growth and spread of the machine and of its designs on them.

These strategies are the ones the Democratic and Republican political heads do, in fact, follow. Mayor Daley, whose slogan is "good government is good politics and good politics is good government," has made it clear that he will not tolerate corruption in office and has kept a very tight rein on gambling, prostitution, and other organized crime. At the same time, he has inaugurated many reforms: he established an executive budget, introduced the performance-type budget, passed a performance zoning ordinance and housing code, extended the merit system, established a centralized purchasing system under a respected administrator, took control over contracts from the City Council, and transferred authority to issue zoning variation permits from the City Council to a Zoning Board of Appeals. His policy toward the suburbs has been sympathetic and generous: through James Downs, the highly respected businessman who is his consultant on housing and planning, he has offered them the assistance of the city-planning department and of such other technicians as might help with their transportation, water, drainage, and other problems. In his campaign for re-election in 1958, the Mayor presented himself as an efficient and non-partisan administrator. His principal piece of campaign literature did not so much as mention the Democratic party or the Democratic slate.

The Republicans have also followed a rational strategy. They have tried to paint the Mayor as a "boss" and the Democratic organization as a corrupt and rapacious "machine." In the 1958 election, for example, Daley was dubbed Dictator Dick, and the Republican organizations distributed buttons marked "S.O.S."—"Save Our Suburbs from the Morrison Hotel Gang" (the Morrison Hotel is Democratic headquarters in Chicago). Some buttons showed the Democratic machine as an octopus reaching out to grasp the unprotected suburbs.

These and other antagonisms put adoption of any plan of metropolitan area organization out of the question. Because of their strength in the outlying wards and in the suburbs the Republicans would have a good chance of controlling a metropolitan area government. But in order to avail themselves of the chance, they would have to relinquish their present control of most of the suburbs. For if the whole metropolitan area were, so to speak, put in the same pot, the Democrats might now and then win the whole pot, and even when they could not win it they could offer a troublesome and expensive contest. Therefore, although the bolder Republicans and the Republicans whose interests are mainly metropolitan favor proposals for putting one or more functions on an area-wide basis, the more timid ones and those whose interests are in particular "safe" suburbs are opposed to it. With the Democrats the situation is similar. Mayor Daley would probably be glad to take his chances with the electorate of the metropolitan area. But the leading ward committeemen of Chicago much prefer certain success in the central city to occasional success in the metropolitan area.

The central city–suburban cleavage is the fundamental fact of party politics in the metropolitan area. But the cleavage is not simply a party one. . . . Party differences reflect differences of interest and outlook that are deep-seated and pervasive.

It will be seen that the influence of the mayor depends largely upon his being "boss" of the party in the county and that this in turn depends upon his ability to maintain the inner city machine while attracting support from the "good government" forces in the outlying wards and suburbs. In short, the mayor must bring the machine and the independents into a working alliance.

To become the county boss, one need only have the backing of the principal ward bosses of the inner city. There are 80 members of the county committee, 50 from the central city and 30 from the "country towns," and their votes are weighted according to the number of Democratic votes cast in each district in the previous general election. The inner city wards are therefore in a decided majority. These are grouped into ethnic blocs each of which has its own boss: there is a bloc of Negro wards under the control of Congressman William L. Dawson, a bloc of Italian wards under an Italian leader, a bloc of Polish wards under a Polish leader, and certain mixed wards under Irish leaders. Four or five of the most powerful bloc leaders, together with the president of the County Board, can, by agreeing among themselves, choose the county chairman.

Left to themselves, the bloc bosses would doubtless prefer someone who would not trouble them with reform. They realize, however, that the voters in the outlying areas will not leave them to themselves and that, unless the machine's reputation is improved, it will be swept out of existence altogether. They accept, therefore—although, no doubt, as a necessary evil and probably without fully realizing the extent of the evil—the need of a leader who will make such reforms as will maintain the organization.

In choosing a leader, the bloc bosses look for someone whose identifications are with the inner city wards (he has to be a Catholic, of course, and one whom ward politicians will feel is "their kind"), whose "nationality" will not disturb the balance between the Italians and the Poles (this virtually means that he must be Irish), who knows the workings of the organization from long experience in it and who is felt to have "earned" his promotion, who has backers with money to put up for campaign expenses (for it will be assumed that the county chairman will have himself nominated for office), who is perfectly "clean" and has a creditable record of public service, and who has demonstrated sufficient vigor, force, and shrewdness to maintain the organization and lead it to victory at the polls.

Once he has taken charge of the machine, a new leader need pay very little attention to the ward bosses who selected him. If he can win elections, he is indispensable to them. Moreover, possession of office—of the county chairmanship and the mayoralty—gives him legal powers (patronage, slate-making, and control of city services, including police) which make the ward bosses dependent upon him. Without them to hold the ladder, he could not climb into his position. But once he is in it, they cannot compel him to throw something down to them.

He is likely, therefore, to prove a disappointment to them and a pleasant surprise to the friends of good government. The bloc bosses need him more than he needs them. They want "gravy" to pass out to their henchmen. But he is a county, state, and national leader, and as such his task is to limit or suppress the abuses upon which they fatten.

To win the respect and confidence of the independent voters in the outlying wards and the suburbs, he must do the things that will hurt the bosses most.

The requirements of his role as a leader who must win the support of the independent voters are enough to account for his zeal to show himself honest and public-spirited. But it is likely that another circumstance will be working in the same direction. Ethnic pride may swell strongly in him and make him want to show the skeptics and the snobs that a man from the wrong side of the tracks can be as much a statesman as anyone from an "old family" or an Ivy League college.

The political head is not likely to take a lively interest in the content of policy or to be specially gifted in the development of ideas or in their exposition. If ideas and the content of policy interested him much, or if he were ideologically-minded, he would not have made his career in the machine, for the machine is entirely without interest in such matters. Similarly, he is not likely to be a vivid public personality, to be eloquent, or to have a flair for the direct manipulation of masses. The qualities that make a popular or charismatic leader would tend to prevent a man from rising within the organization. The kind of leader produced by it is likely to be, above all, an executive.

Any mayor of Chicago must "do big things" in order to be counted a success. It is not enough merely to administer honestly and efficiently the routine services of local government—street cleaning, garbage collection, and the like. An administration that did only these would be counted a failure, however well it did them. As a businessman member of the Chicago Plan Commission explained to an interviewer:

> The Mayor—no public official—is worth his salt if he isn't ambitious. That's true of you and everyone else. Now, what's a political person's stock in trade? It's government, of course. For a public official to just sit back and see that the police enforce the laws is not dynamic enough. I don't know that he would reason it out this way, but you have to get something with a little sex in it to get votes. In the old days, there were ward-heelers with a fistful of dollar bills. But that, even in Chicago, is passé.
>
> What makes a guy have a civic pride? A worker in a factory, a cab driver? He gets a sense of pride in taking part in an active community. The Mayor's smart enough to realize it. Today the tendency all over the country is for the public officials to take the lead more than they did a few years ago. . . .

Wanting to do "big things" and not caring very much which ones, the political head will be open to suggestions. (When Mayor Daley took office, he immediately wrote to three or four of the city's most prominent businessmen asking them to list the things they thought needed doing.) He will be receptive, particularly, to proposals from people who are in a position to guarantee that successful action will win a "seal of approval" from some of the "good government" groups. He may be impressed by the intrinsic merit of a proposal—the performance budget, for example—but he will be even more impressed at the prospect of being well regarded by the highly respectable people whose proposal it is. Taking suggestions from the right kind of people will help him get the support he needs in order to win the votes of independents in the outlying wards and suburbs.

For this reason, he will not create a strong staff of policy advisers or a strong planning agency. The preparation of policies and plans will be done mainly within those private organizations having some special stake in the matters involved and by the civic associations. Quite possibly, the political head might, if he wished, assemble a technical staff of first-rate ability and, working closely with it, produce a plan far superior to anything that might be done by the private organizations and the civic associations. But a plan made in this way would have one fatal defect: its makers could not supply the "seal of approval" which is, from the political head's standpoint, its chief reason for being. On the other hand, a plan made by the big business organizations, the civic associations and the newspapers, is sure to be acclaimed. From the political head's standpoint it is sure-fire, for the people who make it and the people who will pass judgment upon it are the same.

Under these circumstances, the city planning department will have two main functions: (*a*) to advise the mayor on the technical aspects of the various alternatives put before him by private groups, and (*b*) to assemble data justifying and supporting the privately-made proposals that the mayor decides to "merchandise," and to prepare maps, charts, perspective drawings, and brochures with which to "sell" the plans to the public. . . .

There are often fundamental differences of opinion among those whose approval the political head wants. Chicago is too big a place, and the interests in it too diverse, for agreement to occur very often. When there is disagreement within the "good government" forces, the rational strategy for the political head usually is to do nothing. Watchful waiting will offend no one, and to be negative when one does not have to be is . . . bad politics. The political head is therefore inclined to let a civic controversy develop in its own way without interference from him, in the expectation that "public opinion" (the opinion of "civic leaders" and newspapers) will "crystallize." Controversies . . . serve the function of forming and preparing opinion; they are the process by which an initial diversity of views and interests is reduced to the point where a political head feels that the "community" is "behind" the project.

The political head, therefore, neither fights for a program of his own making nor endeavors to find a "solution" to the conflicts that are brought before him. Instead, he waits for the community to agree upon a project. When agreement is reached, or when the process of controversy has gone as far as it can, he ratifies the agreement and carries it into effect.

The No-Party Politics of Suburbia

Robert C. Wood

ESPECIALLY at the municipal level, suburban politics appear to differ, at least in degree, and probably in substance, from those of other American communities, both urban and rural. In the end, this difference has important implications for the state and national pattern.

One indication of this difference, which Harris has described, is the relative respectability and restraint of suburban politics at the local level—the yearning to shed the disreputable political habits of the big city. Another bit of evidence, which Whyte and Henderson have discovered on a sample basis, is the strong sense of community consciousness and civic responsibility that impels active participation in local affairs. Deeply concerned with the quality of schools, conscious of their new status, suburbanites are inclined to "care" about local affairs—zoning regulation, recreational plans, garbage collection, school curricula, street paving—in an especially intense way. As the logical converse of their apathy toward strong party affiliations, suburbanites approach the politics of the community on the basis of individual preferences; they are, more and more frequently, nonpartisan, sharply distinguishing their local public preferences from their views of national and state affairs.

Suburban nonpartisanship takes several forms. Sometimes, as in the Washington environs, it is simply a way of interjecting another party on the local scene, an organization closely identified in attitude and outlook with a national party but separately organized to overcome the minority status of its big brother in the area. In these cases nonpartisan groups parallel the earlier efforts of municipal reformers in the large cities to overthrow an established—and in their eyes—unpalatable party machine. Sometimes, as is customary in New York and Connecticut suburbs, nonpartisanship takes the form of the inclusion

Reprinted from Robert C. Wood, Suburbia, Its People and Their Politics (Boston: Houghton Mifflin Company, 1959), pp. 153–158, by permission of and arrangement with Houghton Mifflin Company, the authorized publishers.

of members of the minority party in local councils in a ratio that pre-
serves the majority party's control but that the minority could never
achieve on its own. Finally, and apparently most frequently, local
politics have no association, open or covert, with the established parties
at all. Public affairs are the province of essentially political organizations—civic clubs, social leagues, or improvement organizations—
whose members are loosely tied together and whose announced goals
are "what is best for the community." There are exceptions amid the
variety of suburbs, of course; some remain staunchly and overwhelmingly partisan in outlook. But the general trend is in the other direction
—nonpartisanship is legally recognized in 61 per cent of the suburban
governments reporting in the *Municipal Yearbook*, and for those under
10,000 population, the percentage is probably even higher.

This emphasis on nonpartisanship is, of course, a familiar element
in the local politics of many communities which are not suburban. As
the authors of the Federalist Papers early noted and as V. O. Key has
more presently pointed out, nonpartisanship reflects a highly integrated
community life with a powerful capacity to induce conformity. "Party,
as such, often has no meaning except as a combination to fight the
opposition. It is rather an expression continued from generation to
generation of the consensus of a more or less individual community or
at least of a majority in such overwhelming command that it is unaware
of any challenge to its position. The politics of the locality is a politics
of personality and of administration rather than a politics of issues."
In this broad sense, suburban nonpartisanship does resemble the politics
of all localities, stressing the candidate and not the platform, and
exhibiting a high degree of disorganization.

Yet there is a significant distinction between the no-party pattern
common to suburbia and the one-party localism that Key identifies, just
as there is a distinction between the structured homogeneity of a relatively isolated town, with its banker, lawyer, merchant, farmer, clerk,
and workingman, and the more unified composition of an individual
suburb. In traditional one-party politics, intramural competition among
factions, interest groups, and cliques within the same organization is
accepted as normal at the local level, disruptive as it may sometimes
be for party leadership. This kind of factionalism, prevalent in one-party
states and large cities, is not antagonistic to the idea of partisanship
as such and does not preclude organized group action at higher levels.
On the contrary, party regularity beyond primary or convention fights
is expected and encouraged; the existence of the party srtucture, tightly
or loosely organized, is taken as natural, and the politically minded
work within it.

The no-party politics of so many suburban governments, however,
often exhibits quite different characteristics. There is, first of all, an
outright reaction against partisan activity, a refusal to recognize that

there may be persistent cleavages in the electorate, and an ethical disapproval of permanent group collaboration as an appropriate means
for settling public disputes. "No-partyism" eats away at the idea of
partisanship by outlawing party influence to "outside" elections and by
discouraging outright displays of party allegiance in the community
as indicative of bad taste. The political animal is tamed; as the suburbanite approaches the ballot box in local elections, he is expected to
strive for a consensus with his friends and neighbors, to seek "the right
solution" as distinct from favoring one or another faction of his party.

One explanation for this rise in the number of independents is that
this view of citizenship spills over into national and state campaigns.
The "local political man" dampens proclivities of the party political
man, restrains his condemnation of the Man in the White House or his
suspicion of big business or his conviction that labor racketeers spell
the downfall of the nation. Instead, the nonpartisan is more likely to
believe that the good citizen seeks the best man and the right answer
in every campaign, so that the almost inarticulate loyalties common in
one-party localities are consciously rejected.

Thus, Edward Janosik, after an investigation of politics in 57
suburban counties around the 20 largest metropolitan areas, concluded:
"Many suburbanites in the United States seem to take pleasure in culti-
vating a politically independent state of mind. Some counties normally
designated as suburban have population densities as high, if not higher,
than sections of the core city. Even so, the pattern of political favors
and resultant political obligations characteristic of older urban areas
has never been strongly established in suburban communities."

A second feature of nonpartisanship is the suburbanite's acceptance of an obligation for extensive civic participation on the part of
the lay constituency. So far as general political activity is concerned,
this proclivity shows up in the large proportion of eligible voters who
actually get to the polls in national elections. Janosik estimates that for
these elections the chances are nine to one that the eligible suburban
voter will cast his ballot. On the local level civic interest may express
itself in the citizens' inclination to undertake the supervision of the local
bureaucracy directly, or in his suspicion of the role of the professional
political leader. Here the image of resurrected grassroots democracy
commits the citizen, theoretically at least, to a do-it-yourself brand of
politics, in which as many issues as possible, simple and complex,
require his personal sanction, and the acceptable elected official is the
part-time amateur, taking his term in office just as he once led the
community chest drive.

Finally, and most fundamentally, no-party politics implies some
positive assumptions about political behavior that go beyond simple
antagonism to partisanship. Inescapably, there is a belief that the individual can and should arrive at his political convictions untutored and

unled; an expectation that in the formal process of election and decision-making a consensus will emerge through the process of right reason and by the higher call to the common good. Gone is the notion of partisan groups, leaders and followers, and in its place is the conscious or unconscious assumption that the citizen, on his own, knows best.

This set of convictions, of course, marks the basic distinction between one-party and no-party politics, for it establishes a standard for acceptable political behavior that antedates the party system. As a theory, nonpartisanship harks back to the traditional concept of local government, to Jefferson's high expectations for the rational capacity of the yeoman, and to that strand in American political reasoning that relies on unfettered individualism, and that manifests itself in the agitation for primaries, referendums and recalls. It is in these assumptions that the suburbanite is linked most directly with his small town ancestors, and not in a coincidence in political attitude, which the theory of conversion tried to establish between the two.

This resurrection of conscious nonpartisanship so evident in the suburban brand of politics—as distinct from big city and rural patterns—has some quite specific consequences in the modern world. The antagonism toward party, the obligation for extensive citizen participation, and the expectation that there is likely to be a single right answer to a political problem results in an unwavering commitment to political forms in which direct democracy can be applied. This commitment, in turn, leads to an important redefinition of the relationship between the citizen and the bureaucrat, and an equally important de-emphasis on the role of the politician. Most important, under the cloak of local nonpartisanship, specific patterns of small, informally organized cliques develop which interact against the doctrine of nonpartisanship itself.

The New Hurrah

Joseph P. Lyford

IN 1960, the reformers considered the possibility of running a reform slate for major citywide offices in 1961. But Mayor Wagner agreed to break with Carmine De Sapio and the other Tammany leaders, and thereby won Governor Lehman's support for re-election as mayor. The entry of a reform candidate for the Democratic nomination against Mayor Wagner was made difficult by the fact that Tammany decided to oppose Wagner's renomination and offered its own candidate for mayor, State Controller Arthur Levitt. Governor Lehman, convinced that the entry of a third candidate would split the anti-De Sapio vote and result in Levitt's election, issued an ultimatum to the reformers to support Wagner "or else." There was little anti-Wagner reformers could do but yield.

"It took all the starch out of the reform movement," said one of the ex-officers of the FDR-Woodrow Wilson Club. "Up until we supported Wagner, a lot of people believed we really meant what we said about cleaning up city politics. After that, many people deserted the reform movement, not just on the West Side, but all over the city." Another unhappy club leader described the Lehman-dictated reform support for Wagner as a "death blow" to the reform movement.

Frustrated in its efforts to elect a reform administration, the FDR-Woodrow Wilson Club turned inward. Its position as the official Democratic organization of the Fifth North and its success in re-electing district leaders gave it responsibilities which inhibited the club's original free-wheeling character, yet real power did not accompany these responsibilities. Since the Wolfson victory, there has been a great turnover in membership and leaders, Few of the original founders of the club are still active in its affairs. Membership has declined from sixteen hundred to below eight hundred. Meetings, once regularly attended by several hundred people, now rarely number even a quorum. The club presidency and the district leaderships, once fought over in historic meetings with several candidates in the running, now go almost by default. With

Reprinted from The Airtight Cage *by Joseph P. Lyford, pp. 141–153, by permission of Harper & Row, Publishers. Copyright © 1966 by Joseph P. Lyford.*

one exception, there has not been a contest for either the club presidency or the district leadership in several years. Sometimes the positions have gone to people not considered highly qualified by the membership. "Several people were asked but nobody wanted the job," is the explanation a club official will offer to people who protest belatedly about the club's choices. The club presidency, highly prized at the beginning of the club's history, for a while changed almost as rapidly as captaincies in the 24th Police Precinct.

Much of the fervor of the early crusades against the Dennis Mahon Association, and later for the election of William F. Ryan, who won the district's congressional seat from Congressman Ludwig Teller, has vanished along with the crusaders. In one way, the club's loss of membership has been a paper loss, since, of the sixteen hundred members on its rolls at the highest point, many simply paid their dues to express support in a general way but never attended meetings or were active on committees or in campaigns. Others, known as "bodies," had joined the club to back a friend for some office and lost interest in the club. Still others joined the club solely to qualify for its low-price charter flights to Europe.

The loss of another type of member, however, did seem to have raised complications. Many people had originally joined because they saw the club as a means of involving themselves in community activities. After the club won its battle against Tammany and itself became the regular organization, many of these people became bored or irritated by the less-exciting operational problems of running a club and dropped out.

To some club officers, the loss of the "social service type" seemed unavoidable. Nancy LeBlanc, a former president, says: "Many people who came to the club originally were the type who might have been working in Hull House, except that social service organizations today are so professional there is no longer much of a place for volunteers. It's a social service worker's world now, you know; you can't even work with a teen-age girls' club unless you have professional training. A lot of the people who came to us had no interest in politics. When they understood what a political club was, they were shocked. These people were purists; political action was a compromise. They didn't see that a political club was primarily related to the process of government, not to the community service process.

Theodore Weiss, now a City Councilman, says his new Reform Independent Democratic Club has had a similar dropout of community service people. The RID had hoped to function as a community service as well as a political organization, but the dual personality never seemed to work out. "Community service at the outset was something all our people felt was a vital part of our function as a club. We thought it was a field in which a new political group could demonstrate its superiority over the established club. It is ironic because the old-line Tammany clubs had been very adept at this social service type of thing before the social welfare legislation in the thirties turned this function over to the government—they built themselves up by taking care of people.

"Then government welfare programs began taking over many of these functions. The old clubs didn't know how to react or what their function was, and their world came down around their ears. But as the social problems got bigger and the government agencies lost control of the situation, the community's need for community service returned. It was both an opportunity and a problem for the reformers. We did make an effort to help, but in the end the clubs could not become community service organizations. The important thing was that the political machinery of the city was rotten. This was a political problem that demanded a political cure. It meant we had to take over the political machinery and get to the point where we could put responsible people in at the head of city departments, and this was the way we could help with community problems. The community service people didn't understand that if a political club couldn't demonstrate power on a political level, it couldn't be much help in rebuilding a community."

The loss of the community-service-oriented membership has not disturbed Hedi Piel, a former Fifth A. D. district leader. "We had a real gung-ho membership but many of these people were never really political to start with—this was a bit of a fling they had, then the fling ended. Granted, we have fewer activists in the club today, but I think they are more representative of the community, and many of them are active in community service organizations outside the club."

However, Wolfson, the club's first district leader and the chief proponent of the community service approach, feels that the community-service-oriented people were the very ones who were the most effective in the club's political affairs as well. "During the FDR club's first primary campaign the bulk of the election district captains and other 'political' workers came from the community service group; and it was these people who produced over four hundred votes in our club for Austin Laber's City Council candidacy against a combined vote of three hundred for eight other candidates backed by the so-called 'political' people. As another example take the reform Riverside Democrats, just to the north of us, where community service activities have been more actively pursued. The Riverside Democrats have a larger membership and are more effective politically than any of the other reform clubs on the West Side."

It seems to be commonly agreed that the club has also been damaged by intense personal conflicts among the members. One former officer says, "I don't know what is behind the conflicts—I doubt that it is just neuroticism—but nobody listens to what the other person is saying." A former acting president of the club described the difficulty as a "spirit of chronic insurgency."

Club officials who disagree strongly with each other on many issues are almost unanimous in saying that the membership has been abnormally destructive of its leaders, which accounts partially for the rapid turnover of officers. Some members argue that it would have helped if the club had had some of the benevolent social atmosphere of the Dennis Mahon Association. Members of the association never became upset about ideologies or issues and got along fine as long as the patronage was handled properly. To the reformer, politics is a series of intense emotional conflicts that could make or break friendships, and it seems to gratify all sorts of psychological, even sexual, needs. One club leader asks, "Where else in town could you get a group therapy for six dollars in annual dues?"

A former club leader, Seymour Schwartz, now inactive, thinks that a good percentage of the club's members, especially the women, are so intolerant if not "mildly paranoid" that they are constitutionally unable to cooperate with anyone. "With all our elected officials and all the programs and successes we had early in the reform movement, the leaders—with the exception of Congressman Ryan—who have shown real promise and ability have somehow been ground down. There is something inherent in reform politics that makes this grinding-down inevitable. Why? Because one big reason middle-class types go into reform politics is to assuage their guilts. This means you are going to get unstable and aberrational conduct. You will get a different type of behavior than if you had people in the organization looking for economic gain.

"When you get too many neurotics in any organization, political or religious, they will quickly find reasons to dislike their fellows, be intolerant of them, feel they don't represent the same high principles, ability, dedication, etc. They consider themselves the true carriers of the message. They search out the evil people and form their cabals. Any leader knows that he will always have a militant and suspicious minority working against him, absolutely convinced he is a liar, a crook, a shifty conniver, and that his only objective is to feather his own nest.

"To our club members, everything and everyone quickly became either all black or all white. After enough of this grinding-down of the original leadership, the people who begin to come to the top are those who have never committed themselves too heavily, who can pass from one situation to another without much trouble. These are the gray people who take over leadership positions in the reform movement, and unfortunately they are third- or fourth-echelon people; they lack ability, intellect, and imagination."

This view is spoken by a man who was driven out by his enemies. One of his friends, another leader who has become inactive, expresses a different view. "We should have realized that many people came into our club intrigued and excited, but also sensing an opportunity to earn some social or psychic income. They wanted a feeling of closeness to the center of activity, that they were sharing in the gossip and small talk. We just didn't spend enough time with our own people, although I don't know where we could have found the time to do this along with everything else. Maybe we should have kept the kaffee klatches going even when the campaigns were over."

One of the early club group, Barbara Jeffers, expresses a rather common feeling of pessimism. "Our club has lasted as long as any I have seen, and that's something. But I've concluded that, if you are going to have a good-government organization that means anything, it has to be built out of intelligent, articulate, hard-working, emotionally involved people who completely control, completely run the organization. They sit in the driver's seat and drive the officers; the officers do not drive them. But when you get this driving type of membership you build an organization that in the long run will tend to destroy itself because it is undisciplined. It comes into being to fight an old authority, and it dies because it cannot trust the new authority it has erected for itself."

Latter-day FDR club leaders are always irritated at the dour reflections and criticism of those who have moved to the sidelines. Very often the newer generation is composed of people who were treated rather contemptuously by the earlier leadership. Instead of having been groomed for the succession, they were paid little attention, or regarded as "zombies" or "creeps." They usually obtained club office only as the incumbents quit in disgust, because they could no longer afford to spend the time, or they grew tired of phone calls at all hours of the night. The leadership of the moment will usually speak more hopefully about the club's future—in public. Privately they agree that personal conflicts and factionalism discourage old members and hurt the recruiting of new, active people.

Out of the club's total membership, it is doubtful if more than a dozen people are active enough to spend much time each week helping with the club operations. In the club's early days, the moment anyone suspected that a handful of members was taking too much power unto itself, there would be a protest that a "clique" was taking over and before long mutiny would break out in the ranks. Today, according to Nancy LeBlanc, the fourth of the club's many presidents, the membership refers most decisions to committees or the president.

"As soon as an organization starts leaving everything up to the officers, then they don't care, and if they don't care they don't volunteer, and then where are you?" she comments.

In the past three or four years, the various club committees have slowed down considerably or have gone out of existence. For a time, the club's small but articulate public affairs committee studied state and national issues and passed on suggested policy planks to the executive committee, covering such matters as condemnation of the McCarran Immigration Act, criticism of civil defense programs, and statements on foreign affairs. It also held a few successful forums. The auditorium was packed to the rafters in 1962 when the club debated and voted on a resolution supporting the inclusion of more low- and middle-income units in the West Side urban renewal plan. A public debate on the military budget held in 1963 drew over one hundred people—almost all of them in the middle-class, white professional group typical of the attendance at most club affairs. But, except for a meeting packed with "bodies" in April, 1965, to vote on a district leader contest, there have been no events at the clubhouse to compare with these meetings. At most FDR meetings, says Nancy LeBlanc, "you worry about whether the first three rows will fill up. You just sit there and die, especially if you are new to the reform movement."

In the spring of 1963, the club's executive committee, faced with a shrinkage of its activities, combined its community affairs and public affairs committees. At that time, the club still had a functioning housing committee, but a few months later even the housing committee was out of action, yet it had once been the most energetic in the club, and had been responsible for such projects as a middle-income housing coöp in the urban renewal area, a rat control program, a rent clinic, a program to harass slum landlords, a program to uncover fire hazards in substandard dwellings, a survey to chart attitudes of relocated families, a grading of housing accommodations in blocks adjacent to the urban renewal area, and a comprehensive study of the city's West Side Urban Renewal Plan with carefully thought-out criticisms and recommendations.

One explanation for the club's difficulty in focusing its energies has been the immense variety of demands made upon it. In addition to everything else, it has tried to serve as a forum of debate on what club members consider the basic governmental, social, and moral issues in American life. An old-style Democratic leader would not understand such a political organization.[1] A discussion of Medicare on the agenda of a district political club would strike him as irrelevant, yet the FDR Club members consider that the club should educate the public on such issues, and "take a position."

1. The attitude is illustrated by a comment from John M. Bailey, chairman of the Democratic National Committee, to the author at the time the latter was chairman of the Democratic Town Committee of Westport, Connecticut. The committee, dominated by ex-Volunteers for Stevenson, met often and argued long about education, foreign aid, civil rights, local zoning, tax assessments, etc. "Why do you people hold so many meetings?" Bailey wanted to know. "What is there to talk about?" He then added that the best way to run a political organization was to hold as few meetings as possible, preferably once a year.

Preoccupation with the "big issues," characteristic of many reform clubs, put a heavy tax on the FDR Club's time and energy. The meeting agenda is defenseless against the intrusion, at particularly inappropriate moments, of a resolution calling for the end of the war in Vietnam, or abolition of civil defense drills. Debates on such matters not only sidetrack local issues, but they seem to fan personal animosities which always lie beneath the surface. The protagonists in these intense but transient commotions have very little patience with anything else the club is doing. Once their particular hurricane has blown itself out, they are not seen at meetings again. The extent to which some of the more ideologically canted members narrow their interests is illustrated by the experience of a candidate for district leader who had asked a young couple to vote for her. The husband phoned with one question: "Where do you stand on the recognition of Red China?" Assured that his candidate favored the idea, the man said, "Fine; you've got my vote," and hung up.

Club leaders have ambivalent feelings about the ideologues among them. One ex-president says, "I'm not sure they care anything at all about political reform. They speak the language of reform, but they seem to want to use the club for their own personal desires. They're againsters. They are infiltrators. They are energetic, but their energy doesn't help the club very much. Most of the time we can't get a dozen people to come in and run off a few stencils, but let the executive committee pass a resolution that has to do with, say, something the SANE nuclear policy people are for, and suddenly you get a whole army to run mimeograph machines, and send out nineteen stencils, and type letters to everybody in town telling them about the resolution. Okay, I don't object to people trying to propagandize, but if we passed a resolution tomorrow having to do with discrimination against Negroes not one of these would show up to do any work."

One reason for the frequency and bitterness of the club's internal conflicts may be, ironically, the thorough trouncing the reformers gave the Tammany regulars in 1959. Since that time, the club has had things pretty much its own way in its own district. There has been no threat to its power from any local party sources. In Greenwich Village, the reform Village Independent Democrats—where the internecine warfare is just as intense—have had to call off their civil wars from time to time to repel the efforts of ex-Tammany chieftain Carmine De Sapio to regain the district leadership. No such threats materalize in the Fifth North. The absence of local Republican party strength means no challenge from that source, either. Yet with no other adversaries, and since conflict is vital to many amateur politicians, the FDR Democrats "fracture each other."

A certain kind of inbreeding also contributes to the conflict. The club's predominantly middle-class white membership suffers from the absence of people who speak a different social language and who have different priorities. One might say that the club is culturally deprived. The lack of fresh and contrasting viewpoints encourages repetitive, ingrown discussion, stained with all the guilts and complexes of introverted, middle-class professionals. The FDR club is not the only reform club to have this sort of trouble. Weiss's Reform Independent Democrats have not been able to attract a significant number of Spanish-speaking members, and, while the Riverside Democratic Club has done better in this regard, the situation is not satisfactory there either. The FDR Club has three dozen or so Negro dues payers, but there is little representation of low-income Negroes who could provide new avenues of information and ideas. The Negro members of the club are, by and large, like the white members, professional people, a good number of whom send their children to private schools and who are often afflicted with certain ambivalences of their own. A Negro taxidriver who is an election district captain is an exception.

The scarcity of minority group members in the club is not because the club has tried to discourage their participation, despite allegations to that effect which have been made on occasion by Alberto Gerena-Valentin, president of the Puerto Rican Federation of Home Towns.[2] FDR Club canvassers who have tried to register Negro and Puerto Rican voters in the district and interest them in the club have given up after also total failure.

Many of the club's running arguments are never resolved. Although there have been no recent bouts over the club's position on patronage (especially since the election of a Republican mayor), the subject comes up continually in conversations with club members. Some of them to go further than the official position that reform club officers and district leaders should not hold political jobs in government. They oppose all patronage, a reaction against the old organizational basis of Tammany politics in which patronage was the bait to attract and hold party workers.

Another group argues that the hard line against patronage is not only impractical but that there is a certain amount of hypocrisy among those who are against it. One rather outspoken partisan in behalf of patronage is the recently deposed female district leader, Hedi Piel, who thinks "it is impossible to demand of people that they give unstintingly of their time without any kind of compensation. I question whether the holier-than-thou attitude of many reformers on this matter is even genuine—many of the people who go around attacking the idea of patronage are applying for jobs like mad on the side. I also question whether a club's barring patronage actually benefits the community in the long run. Wouldn't it be better if someone had a

2. These allegations were made many months before the FDR Club endorsed Gerena-Valentin for the Democratic nomination for City Commissioner-at-Large.

patronage job that would give him the time to spend the day at a Board of Estimate or a City Council hearing, where he could represent the community?"

At one full-dress debate on patronage, the classic points pro and con were stated by Jane Mills and Noel Gilmore. Mrs. Mills (who was later appointed to a city job) felt that the club had a responsibility to get people into city government who were responsive to the reform point of view. In response to Mrs. Mills, Miss Gilmore declared: "We are so preoccupied with patronage that we are not doing the things we should do in the community. This club is far more important than all of the patronage jobs we consider. We should be strengthening our club, getting more action out of it; we should not be tearing ourselves apart over patronage matters."

The flare-ups over patronage have subsided because the arguments never seem to get anyplace, also, because patronage is an academic issue as far as the majority of club members is concerned: their sources of financial and emotional support lie elsewhere. As people, generally in the professions, with nonpolitical careers, they have at times felt imposed upon by what they feel is a small group interested in personal political or financial advancement. It should also be said that the club was not overwhelmed by job offers from a Wagner administration quite aware of the club hostility.

The club's loss of vitality is so obvious that there would seem to be no point in denying it even if anyone wanted to—and nobody wants to, particularly a club member like Murray Richmond, a young attorney, who was talked into becoming president of the club in 1964 and then marooned by the people who had urged him to take the job. Although he was one of a group in the club which strongly opposed the early leadership of Wolfson and Cohen, Richmond at times sounds more bitter about the club than his old antagonists. After refusing the club presidency several times he finally agreed to take the job, on one condition.

"I told seven or eight people who wanted me to take the presidency that I would do it if I could count on them to give a lot of their time to the club. I had an objective. I hoped we could get our middle-class people in the club to take a much more active part in the civil rights movement. This meant I would have to have at least a small corps of people who would work very hard, who would be available. I told my friends that I didn't want to end up sweeping out the clubhouse and piling up chairs after meetings. The president was going to quit being a housemaid for the membership. I thought my friends, who had been active in the civil rights movement, would stick by me on this, even though my whole experience in the club argued against any such expectation.

"Well, what happened? I found myself fixing the lights, and

climbing ladders. I had to repair the banister one day. I had to call up the secretary to get out the minutes, and so on. Where did all my supporters go? Most of them seemed to have other things keeping them busy—another campaign to work on. One of them even joined another club. So I resigned."

Richmond does not dwell on the usual complaints—the rivalries, the loss of the community-oriented people, the dissipation of the club's energies over too many areas. He agrees that these developments have damaged the club, but they are symptoms rather than causes of the club's decline.

"The fact is that the club had to fail. It was fated to lose power; it has been a narrow, parochial, middle-class organization. It never understood the Puerto Rican and the Negro. Most important, it lost its determination—if it ever had it—to make a complete break with traditional big-city Democratic politics. Reform could have succeeded only if it had been a truly revolutionary movement in city politics. Reform should have aimed at overthrowing the leadership of the Democratic party in New York. The movement was doomed the moment it abandoned this objective. Reform defeated itself by accommodating itself to tradition. The endorsement of Wagner for mayor in 1961 was a prime cause of disillusionment in the reform movement. But if it hadn't been the Wagner endorsement, something else would have happened to cause the disillusionment."

The early reform movement "was full of promise and idealism. Today it's a sad contrast. The club has no housing committee, no school committee, no rent and social referral committee, no committees at all outside a campaign committee." Richmond says that in the first few years the "contribution of the club was immense. The club was loaded with talent. Leadership played an important role. People strove for leadership. We had many members who worked five days a week until two or even six in the morning. They asked for nothing in return There was an intense zeal in the club to do something in the community. Hopes and expectations pushed people forward. But people can't go along on that sort of dream forever. The disenchantment began, and the people know now the club will never do what it set out to do. The institutions in this city are too great, too strong. They won't give way and now the desire to make them give way is gone."

The trouble was, Richmond says, "we didn't keep the promises we made to ourselves."

The Negro and Philadelphia Politics

John Hadley Strange

PHILADELPHIA, PENNSYLVANIA, is the fourth largest city in the United States and, like most other large cities, is experiencing an enormous growth in its Negro population. Between 1950 and 1960 the Negro population in Philadelphia increased by 156,000 persons. During the same decade the white population declined by 225,000 persons. Nonwhites constituted 26.7 percent of the total population in 1960. Recent unofficial estimates place the Negro percentage of the total population at a still higher level—between 30 and 35 percent.

Despite the increasing Negro population, Negroes have not made correspondingly significant gains in political power or in the rewards and benefits they receive from the local political system. The reasons for this are many, but they include the fact that whites sometimes engage in political actions explicitly designed to limit benefits distributed to Negroes and, secondly, that Negroes do not participate as effectively as they might in local politics. This latter explanation is the central topic of this paper.

Negro Political Participation: Mode

There are many possible ways of examining the complex question of Negro political participation in Philadelphia's politics. One classification which is useful is the distinction between two groups of participants in politics: voters or "indirect participants," and others, more active in politics, here called "direct participants." It is also useful to distinguish between the ways or modes of Negro political participation and the extent of that participation. We shall discuss the former first.

On the basis of an investigation covering Negro political participation in Philadelphia between 1963 and 1966,[1] nine important descriptive statements can be made concerning the modes of Negro political participation.

1. See John H. Strange, "The Negro in Philadelphia Politics: 1963–1965," unpublished Ph.D. dissertation, Princeton University, 1966.

Published for the first time in this book, by permission of the author.

Participation by the "Activists"

First, *Negroes do not participate in politics through a Negro political machine in Philadelphia. There is no Negro political organization in Philadelphia now, and there never has been one.* Only white-controlled Democratic and Republican organizations exist in Philadelphia today; only the Democratic one is important. Negro politicians, successful and aspiring alike, publicly acknowledge that the city organizations determine which Negroes are nominated and elected.

Negroes do, on occasion, suggest Negroes for slating by the white Democratic organization, but it is the City Committee and its Chairman, not the Negroes, who decide when a Negro can have a particular office. An aide to Negro Congressman Nix put it succinctly: "Negroes with political ambitions [should know] two vital facts . . . Fact One: If you're endorsed by Bill Green [then Democratic party boss] for elective office in Philadelphia, you can rear back and say, I'm on my way . . . Fact Two: If you're seeking a federal appointment and can't get Green's endorsement, your chances of succeeding are slimmer than the thread that links the buttons to your coat."

The Democratic City Organization has been quite effective in defeating attempts to create a Negro political organization. One of the most effective methods has been legislative apportionment. Both the Pennsylvania General Assembly and the Senate were reapportioned in 1963. In the Senate redistricting, the percentage of the population which is Negro was reduced in every Philadelphia Senate district, despite the city's exceptionally large increase in the Negro population. The only Senate district with a Negro majority in 1963 was reduced from 81 percent to 69 percent Negro. (A white Senator represents this district.) The number of Assembly districts in Philadelphia with a majority Negro population was decreased from eleven electing thirteen Assemblymen to six electing eight Assemblymen. Before the reapportionment there were nine Negroes in the General Assembly; afterward there were eight.

But the City Democratic Organization is not content with keeping a close check on reapportionment. Moves to replace white ward leaders with Negroes, on those rare occasions when they occur, are met with strong resistance. Patronage is withdrawn, rules are ignored, and the white political machine retains control. For example, in January 1965 the City Committee successfully defeated a plan to elect a Negro, Edgar Campbell, to the vacant ward leadership in the Fifty-second Ward, a ward that was approximately 65 percent Negro. Campbell was the expected (and some claim legal) successor since he was then serving as chairman of the ward committee. But through the open use of its patronage and other threats, the City Committee had Campbell defeated 50–9 even though 41 out of the 71 committeemen eligible to vote for ward leader were Negroes. Herbert Fineman, whose brother Irving Fineman had been ward leader, was elected. Later Campbell lost his job as assistant to City Council Democratic Majority Leader George X. Schwartz. Fred Handy, a Negro committeeman from the Fifty-second ward and one of Campbell's supporters, was also fired from his state job as the only Negro inspector in the Bureau of Weights and Measures. Herbert Fineman is reported to have said. "Ace [Handy] spearheaded that Edgar Campbell drive. Why did Ace do it? I don't understand him."

When Negroes are appointed or elected to political office the decisions to give an office to a Negro are made by whites and the Negroes are selected by whites. There is no Negro political organization in Philadelphia. Negroes work for whites in Philadelphia politics.

Second, *Negroes do not participate in Philadelphia politics as a monolithic bloc.* Not only is there no Negro political organization, but the multitude of Negro groups and individuals interested in politics lustily compete among themselves for the relatively few opportunities to be heard and seen and the decidedly scarce positions of influence.

In general one can identify four major, but not distinct, groups of Negro activists. First, there are the *politicians*, those who hold elective and appointive office. Second, there are the ministers, many of whom hold a political office, aspire to hold a political office, desire to rent their churches to the city for school classrooms, or want to protect their churches from demolition under urban renewal. Third, there are the *civic leaders* who represent Negro civic organizations in appeals before political bodies. Fourth, there are the *civil rights leaders*, who attack the political status quo with the new weapons of the boycott, the picket, and the mass demonstration.

There is great antagonism and competition between and within these groups. They disagree over goals, tactics, personalities, and patronage rights. And there is no hesitation in waging bitter and vituperative attacks upon each other.

Third, *Negroes make no demands for legislation, nor do they propose legislation.* The Philadelphia Fair Employment Practices Law was proposed, sponsored, and successfully lobbied for by the Philadelphia Fellowship Commission, a private interracial nonsectarian organization, run primarily by Jews, advocating their motto, "Let's all live by the Golden Rule," and the American Friends Service Committee. The Pennsylvania Civil Rights Law, covering employment and housing, was a result of the joint efforts of the Philadelphia Fellowship Commission, the American Friends Service Committee, and the Pennsylvania CIO. When the 1963 Philadelphia fair housing law was proposed by the Philadelphia Commission on Human Relations, the major backer was again the Fellowship Commission. The NAACP opposed the law because "we resent a special tribunal being set up to involve problems affecting Negroes. We object to the Human Relations Commission, or any agency, having sole control to determine the validity of something that affects the rights of individual citizens."

There has never been any significant legislation of any kind proposed by a Negro or a Negro organization in Philadelphia, nor has the political activity necessary to pass any legislation been conducted under the direction of a Negro organization. Moreover, legislation is a peripheral concern of Negroes in Philadelphia. Five issues education, housing, general employment, police brutality, and political appointments—dominate the news and editorial columns of Negro newspapers. These are also the concerns of the Negroes interviewed for this study and of the Negroes whose speeches or letters are reported in newspapers and magazines. The actions which have been called for by Negroes concerning these issues have not involved legislation but have rather involved administrative decisions. The School Board is called upon to institute *policies* leading to integrated schools and faculties, equal educational facilities, and the use of buses to end overcrowding and to promote integration. Demands are made that the Bureau of Licenses and Inspectors enforce existing inspection and condemnation statutes and that it relocate Negroes in integrated, safe, sanitary houses. Demonstrations are held to force the mayor to take *administrative action* against construction unions to force employment opportunities in these trades. Legislation is not suggested, but rather the enforcement of existing contract provisions prohibiting discrimination in city building projects is demanded. Economic boycotts are used to force alterations in hiring practices by private employers. Negroes in Philadelphia also call for administrative actions to end police brutality and to punish offending policemen. Political offices and appointments are also sought by Negroes, but not through legislation. Clamorous demands have been made by Negroes for a state Senate seat, magistrate posts, ward leaderships, a city commission seat, or to become poverty program director, school-board members, and police officials.

Fourth, *Negroes in Philadelphia do not want to change the social, economic, and political system in Philadelphia.* Their desire is to succeed on the same terms and in the same system as other Philadelphians; to end discrimination in its most overt forms; and to open new opportunities for advancement within the system. Robert Dahl considers this fact an important element in ethnic politics. He notes in his book, *Who Governs?*, that in New Haven the early ethnic groups did not consider the socioeconomic order illegitimate; but they did so consider discrimination. The evidence in the case of the Negro in Philadelphia, although limited, supports this conclusion.

The Negroes interviewed for this study were unanimous in their support of the present political system. Virtually every Negro directly or indirectly involved in Philadelphia politics had an overwhelming desire, most often *explicitly* mentioned, to hold a political office. In practically every case the office coveted was a seat in the United States Congress. No attacks are made by Negroes in Philadelphia on the nature of the political system; only the distribution of rewards are questioned. There are no significant advocates of radical political or economic change among Negroes in Philadelphia. Every Negro interviewed is convinced that the political system *will* improve his lot; he also implies that this optimistic outlook is applicable to *all* Negroes, or most of them at least, in Philadelphia.

Fifth, *Negroes generally do not make appeals for election based on their race*. Rather they claim they represent the Democratic Party, are for "the working man," or are trying "to help all Americans." One exception to this was the 1964 primary in which Cecil Moore, the caustic, militant former president of the city's NAACP, sponsored five Negro candidates to run as Negroes. Their main campaign appeal was that Negroes should represent Negroes. Four of the opponents of these candidates were Negroes. These opponents were dubbed "so-called Negroes" and "tools of the white power structure" by Moore and the Moore-backed candidates.[2]

Although it is not customary to make racial appeals to Negroes, it is the practice in Philadelphia to demand positions for Negroes from the white political organization. Between 1963 and 1966 the Negro newspaper, *Philadelphia Tribune*, ended every story with a line of type "A Negro [for] State Senator." Cecil Moore, aides of Congressman Nix, Rev. William Gray, Rev. Leon Sullivan, and other influential Negroes in Philadelphia have all made suggestions at various times that a Negro should be slated for the Senate, that Negroes should be appointed as judges, or ward leaders, or that Negroes should be given some particular administrative job. But this appeal for representation *because of race* is infrequently made to the electorate, and when the electorate is appealed to on the basis of race, large numbers of Negroes cry out in opposition.

Sixth, and related to the two previous descriptive statements, *Negroes who hold appointive and elective office do not engage in activities on behalf of the Negro*. Negro officials act as if their primary responsibility is to serve the political organization or reform group, or civic faction that secured their job for them, rather than to pursue goals or interests of large numbers of Negroes. Demands to engage

2.   There is some truth to this charge. One state legislator related to me that upon becoming a member of the legislature (in 1954) it was necessary to sign the pay checks of the other Negroes in the Assembly, since they could neither read nor write. Several of the legislators and former legislators I interviewed were illiterate. One of the seats which Moore's group contested was not sought by the incumbent Negro assemblyman. Moore had threatened to campaign against him because he was an illiterate. Although the city organization did not "slate" Moore's candidate, they did "retire" the incumbent (who ran unsuccessfully as a Republican) and nominated a patronage employee of the Board of Revision of Taxes. Moore, and his candidates, were soundly defeated.

in activities to aid Negroes (which one might expect) are infrequently made. Apparently the fact that *a Negro* holds the position is reward enough, and he is placed under no special obligations to assist his race. Consequently, Negro officials make no special attempts to secure legislation or administrative action to benefit Negroes, nor do they engage in racial appeals to the Negro population.

Seventh, *Negroes in Philadelphia do not contribute to the financing of political and civic organizations.* No Negroes are large contributors to either the Democratic or Republican party. In fact, very few Negroes make even small contributions to political organizations.

Considering the incomes Negroes receive during campaigns, Negroes probably accept more money from political organizations than they contribute. Both of the Philadelphia Negro newspapers benefit from the large amount of political advertising placed in their papers. Forty percent of all the campaign funds expended by the parties is spent for campaign workers and between one-half and two thirds of these expenditures for workers go to Negroes. One Negro public official told me "If you don't have the money for the [Negro] workers on election day—forget it."

Eighth, *Negroes do not organize committees, nor do they have organizations which have permanent staffs that are continuously engaged in collecting information on matters of concern to Negroes.* There are no groups to initiate proposals for governmental action or to lobby for certain goals. The NAACP, the major Negro organization in Philadelphia, operated without an executive director from 1963 to 1966 when it was divided in five chapters. (This action was taken by the national NAACP in order to reduce the influence of Cecil Moore.) Because the Urban League is financed largely through the United Fund, it has avoided becoming involved in local politics. Moreover, the League only elected its first Negro president in 1964. The League has long been dominated by white business and professional men. CORE, a relative newcomer to Philadelphia, has been completely insolvent on several occasions since its inception in Philadelphia in 1962. This lack of organizations is in contrast to the multitude of organizations on behalf of business and other white-dominated groups ranging from the AFL-CIO or the Archdiocese of Pennsylvania to the greater Philadelphia Movement and the Old Philadelphia Development Corporation.

Ninth, *Negroes have, since 1963, engaged in direct protest activities against the city government and its officials.* Although demonstrations, boycotts, and picketing are not new tactics, having been used by labor and other groups for many years, the use of these tactics against local governments is new, with the exception that it has long been the practice in Pennsylvania to gather a large number of persons together to be present at legislative hearings on particular bills of importance. But the demonstrations and protests described here are different. They have taken the form of picketing city officials'

homes, "sit-ins" in public offices, and mass picketing of construction and other sites. The first use of these tactics was by the Congress
of Racial Equality on April 13, 1963. Seven CORE members, led by
CORE Regional Director Louis Smith, picketed Mayor Tate's home
for two hours, carrying placards protesting discrimination in unions
involved in municipal construction projects.

Between April 1960 and June 1965, Negro organizations conducted at least eighty-eight demonstrations, boycotts, and picketing
campaigns. Some campaigns lasted several days. One, the NAACP
picketing of all-white Girard College, began May 1, 1965, and continued
until December 17, 1965. Twenty-four of these campaigns were directed
against local government officials and agencies; six against federal
officials (including two general protests by CORE of conditions in
Mississippi.) The remaining forty-seven protest campaigns were
directed against local business firms except for one incident of picketing
at the offices of the Democratic City Committee.

In addition to the eighty-eight demonstrations actually carried out,
there were forty-two threats of boycotts and demonstrations. Nineteen of these threats were made by the 400 ministers of Philadelphia
(Negro). These ministers led a successful mass boycott of consumer
goods manufactured or processed in the Philadelphia area in 1963 and
1964. The boycotts substantially reduced sales, and the representatives
of the ministers were consequently listened to. Because of the reputation for success which the boycotts attained among Philadelphia
businessmen, over half of the companies approached yielded when the
threat was made, obviating the necessity for a boycott.

Participation by the Electorate

Four major descriptive statements (based on data covering elections from 1947 through 1964) can be made about the participation
of the Negro electorate in Philadelphia politics.

First, *Negroes in Philadelphia vote overwhelmingly for the candidates of the Democratic Party.* In sixteen out of the sixty wards in
Philadelphia in 1964, over half of those registered to vote were Negroes.
Not a single one of these wards had a Democratic vote for President
of less than 75 percent. Ten out of the sixteen returned Democratic
margins of over 90 percent. Using data for election districts rather
than wards (there were 1,647 election districts in Philadelphia in 1964),
the completely Negro areas can be more accurately isolated. In 210 of
these election districts in 1964 at least 90 percent of those persons
registered were Negroes. And 155 of these election districts (74 percent) gave Johnson at least 95 percent of the vote cast. Only seven
had Democratic margins of less than 90 percent, the lowest being 81
percent.

However, 1964 could be considered an unrepresentative year. Yet, none of those wards in which Negroes constitute at least half of those registered has given a majority to the Republican head of the ticket since 1954. At least half of these wards have voted Democratic in every election since 1948. Sixty percent of the time since 1947 these wards have been at least 70 percent Democratic, and in only 12.3 percent of the cases in the last 18 years has the Republican at the head of the ticket won in these wards. This is truly a phenomenal record of Democratic strength in these "Negro wards."

A second descriptive statement is evident from an analysis of similar data: *not only do Negroes vote Democratic but they register Democratic.* Until 1955 Negro wards did not have predominately Democratic registration lists. Since 1958, however, there have been no Negro-majority wards with a majority of those registered calling themselves Republicans.

A third descriptive statement about the way the Negro electorate in Philadelphia votes is that *Negroes, unlike other ethnic groups, do not vote for candidates on the basis of their race.* Take for example the 1964 Democratic primary contest, referred to earlier, in the seventh Senatorial District between Charles R. Weiner, Democratic Minority Leader in the state Senate, and Rev. Marshall Lorenzo Shepard, Jr., son of one of the two Negro city councilmen. Shepard, whose campaign was sponsored and supported by Cecil Moore, campaigned primarily on the theme that a Negro Senatorial District should elect a Negro State Senator. This was the first campaign in Philadelphia in which a Negro candidate attempted to use his race as the primary appeal to the electorate. This type of campaign was possible in this instance because in 1960 the seventh Senatorial District had a population 69.2 percent Negro and in December 1963 a registered electorate 64 percent Negro. Despite the large size of the Negro electorate, however, Shepard received only 23.6 percent of the vote.

That race is not a primary consideration for Philadelphia Negroes when they vote is also evidenced by data which follows in support of the fourth statement about the ways in which Negroes participate in Philadelphia elections. Fourth, *Negro voters in Philadelphia do not effectively split the straight party ticket to support Negro candidates in multicandidate elections.* In Philadelphia all city magistrates, seven city councilmen at large, and three city commissioners are elected on ballots with more than one candidate competing. Voters may vote for, and each party can nominate, two-thirds the number of magistrates to be elected, five city councilmen, and two city commissioners. Consequently the minority party is guaranteed at least one-third of the magistrates offices, two City Council seats at-large, and one City Commission post. This electoral system permits "cutting" procedures whereby one or two of the minority-party candidates are supported at the expense of one or more majority-party candidates. This voting system also permits "bullet voting"; that is, a voter can cast a ballot for only one candidate, thereby avoiding support of potential rivals, even in the same party, since all candidates run against each other. Negroes have been somewhat more successful in securing nominations in these multicandidate contests, especially from the minority party, than in situations where either a Democrat or a Republican wins. In these elections Negroes can be nominated, thereby indicating recognition of the importance of Negro voters, without too great a risk to the white political organization that a Negro might be elected. Negroes come in last among the minority-party candidates. They lose, while the white minority candidates win.

The 1963 race for City Council is a good case to observe the effects of "cutting" and "bullet voting" on Negro candidates, since both the Democrats and the Republicans nominated a Negro for city councilmen-at-large. The Democrats nominated Rev. Marshall Shepard, Sr., an incumbent and long an active Democratic politician. The Republican Negro candidate was Robert Evans, former football star for the University of Pennsylvania and presently a funeral director in North Philadelphia. Seven-at-large council seats were being contested, but each political party was limited to five nominees. The Republicans had little hope of electing all five of their candidates in 1963; the real contest therefore was to see which two Republicans would win. A Republican voter who had one or two Republican favorites would, to maximize his candidate's chances for victory, cast a "bullet vote" for his Republican choices (not over two so as not to vote for the real opponents—the other Republicans) and throw away his other votes. A Democrat, if he wanted to determine which two of the Republicans would be elected, would vote for one or two Republicans and "cut" one or two Democrats—since the likelihood that all the Democrats would be elected anyway was high. Of course, the Democrat might cast a "bullet vote" also. If either of these activities were especially prevalent, then there should be a fairly large difference in the totals for the Republicans with the highest and lowest number of votes. The same would be true among the Democratic candidates. Out of the 120 "contests" (among the Republicans and Democrats in 60 wards) there were 44 instances in which the lowest candidate of a party got less than 95 percent of the number of votes of the leading candidate of his party. These wards can be arbitrarily "cutting wards." In 25 out of these 44 contests, or in 56.8 percent of the cases, it was the Negro candidate who trailed the other candidates of his party. In seven other instances the Negro candidate was next to last. In the twelve remaining cases the Negro candidate led his party. Republican candidate Evans led in eight "cutting wards," all of them being wards in which a majority of those registered to vote were Negroes.

Marshall Shepard, Sr., led in four "cutting wards," but none of these was a Negro ward.

In eight out of the fifteen Negro wards Evans benefited from cutting. In one Negro ward, Ward 13, Evans was the victim of cutting tactics, finishing fifth out of the five Republican candidates. Cutting tactics were used against Evans in fifteen out of forty-five white wards. In three of these wards Evans was cut more than 10 percent. Although a large percentage of Negro wards helped Evans with cutting, more wards used the cutting tactics against Evans than for him.

In the Democratic contests only one Negro ward engaged in cutting tactics to the extent that classified it as a "cutting ward." Marshall Shepard, Sr., the Negro Democratic candidate, was the victim of cutting tactics in this Negro ward as well as in fifteen non-Negro wards.

According to this analysis, whites use cutting tactics against Negroes in minority-party contests. In addition, Negroes use cutting tactics to aid Negro candidates in these contests, but the cutting tactics employed by Negroes are not effective in electing Negro candidates.[3] In majority-party contests, Philadelphia Negroes apparently do not use cutting tactics to support Negro candidates. Yet even in the majority-party contests, whites do cut Negroes. The evidence indicates that whites are both more persistent and more proficient in cutting Negroes than Negroes are in cutting whites.

Negro Political Participation: Extent

It is not enough to look at the way in which Negroes, both activist and voter alike, participate in politics. The magnitude, or the extent, of that participation must also be investigated. Again, with no other intention than to distinguish voters from other, more active participants in political affairs, the following analysis separately examines the extent of political participation in Philadelphia by activist Negroes and by the electorate.

Negro Activist Participation in Politics

There are two ways of observing the extent of political participation by activist Negroes without using sophisticated research tools such as survey analysis: the extent of officeholding and the number of Negro political organizations.

OFFICEHOLDING. Since one of the most effective positions from which to influence politics is a political office, the number of political offices held by a group of people is an important clue to the extent of

---

3. This has been true for all recent elections in Philadelphia, not just the election analyzed.

their political participation. Of course, political decisions can be influenced by people not holding office, and often are. But public office is an important base for political power. In Philadelphia Negroes have held political offices, but they have not held offices in numbers proportionate to their representation in the electorate. The more important and powerful the political office, the smaller the number of Negroes who have held that position.

Of course there has been no Negro mayor of Philadelphia. Negroes have also been excluded from the Pennsylvania Senate, and no Negro has held the post of City Commissioner. Negroes were elected to the City Council as early as 1884, but in modern times Negroes have served as councilmen only since 1936.

State legislative posts were the first political offices opened to Negroes in Philadelphia in any numbers, and they have been the only political offices which the Negroes have held in numbers proportionate to their representation in the electorate. Since 1920, Negroes from Philadelphia have been members of every session.

The extent to which Negroes have participated in public office can be expressed in terms of an Index of Negro Job Opportunity. This index is constructed by taking the percentage of the jobs which are held by Negroes and dividing this figure by the percentage of the electorate (registered voters) who are Negroes. Thus, if 10 percent of the jobholders are Negroes and 10 percent of the registered voters are Negroes, the proportion of Negroes in both cases is the same and the Index of Negro Job Opportunity is 100.00. Another way of putting this is that Negroes would have 100 percent of their quota of the jobs if the jobs were allocated by race, or if they were distributed in such a manner that Negroes had the same chance of holding a political (or other) job as they have of being registered to vote.

Participation by Negroes in the Pennsylvania General Assembly has been quite high. Since 1924 Negroes have held at least half as many seats in the General Assembly as they could expect on the basis of the proportion of the electorate who were Negroes. Since 1936 Negroes have had an Index of Job Opportunity in the General Assembly ranging from 74.8 to 107.2. Negroes have not been successful in capturing other elective positions in Philadelphia. City Council posts, since the city charter revision in 1952, and the County Court judgeships have been the local offices most available to Negroes. The Index of Negro Job Opportunity for councilmanic seats reached a high of 63.2 in 1956 and ten years later was 45. The Index for County Court judges has been over 56 since 1948 and was 76.5 in 1956.

The most political of all elective positions are the Magistrate Court offices. This is the patronage post most coveted by party workers, including ward leaders. Negroes have been especially underrepresented as magistrates since 1948. Their magistrate Job Opportunity Index for that period ranged from a high of 43.8 to a low of 22.2. The hostile attitude of the political organizations toward Negro officeholding is clearly demonstrated by these low indices.

In appointive positions, the story has been the same. Only a handful of Negroes have ever been appointed to a significant city position. Only since 1951 has a Negro headed a city agency, the Department of Records. Most of the boards and commissions in Philadelphia, including the Zoning Board of Adjustment (very important politically), the Department of Public Health, the Department of Welfare, the City Planning Commission, the Recreation Department, and the prestigious Fairmount Park Commission remain totally white.

Negroes have, however, been able to gain appointments to race relations groups such as the Philadelphia Commission on Human Relations and the Mayor's Advisory Committee on Civil Rights, and the city's antipoverty agency. Two Negroes are among the nine members of the city schoolboard.

Turning from elective and appointive positions to positions in the city political organizations, we encounter still further limitations on Negro officeholding. Although figures are unavailable as to the number of Negro district committeemen (there are 1,640 districts in Philadelphia; each has two Republican and two Democratic committeemen), it is quite likely that they hold this unimportant post in a number roughly proportionate to the size of the Negro electorate. It is obvious, however, that Negroes do not find it so easy to become ward leaders in Philadelphia. In fact, both the Democratic and Republican organizations take specific actions to limit the number of Negro ward leaders, as the fight over the Democratic ward leadership in Ward 52, discussed above, clearly demonstrates. Between 1937 and 1943, neither party had any Negro ward leaders. Since 1944, however, both the Republican and Democratic parties have had at least one Negro ward leader. By 1964 eleven, or 9.2 percent, of the 120 war leaders in Philadelphia were Negroes. The Index of Negro Job Opportunity for ward leaders was a low 35.0.

PARTICIPATION THROUGH ORGANIZATIONS. Negro participation in politics through organizations, directly or indirectly active in politics, is, like officeholding, very minimal. Henry Klein, in a study of Philadelphia's voluntary civic, educational, and social welfare organizations, found 4,410 board positions occupied by 3,010 different people. Only five Negroes were among the seventy-nine men who were members of five or more boards. There were at least three additional Negroes among the eighty-one persons serving on four or more boards. Although these board memberships may not be a source of *political* power, the lack of Negroes among the most active board members is indicative, at least, of the lack of participation by Negroes in organizational activities. This is made even clearer when it is recognized that there are only a very few Negro-dominated organizations active in political affairs in Philadelphia; yet the number of white-run organizations, such as the Greater Philadelphia Movement, AFL, CIO, Americans for Democratic Action, Archdiocese of Philadelphia, Philadelphia Fellowship Commission, Chamber of Commerce, University Science Center Corporation, Old Philadelphia Development Corporation, Bureau of Municipal Research, Pennsylvania Economy League, Citizens for a Modern Constitution, and a number of others, is seemingly infinite.

Participation by Negro Voters

The above evidence demonstrates that there are proportionately fewer Negroes among the politically active in Philadelphia than there are Negroes among the Philadelphia electorate. Moreover, these Negro activists do not hold the important political positions in Philadelphia. Is there a correspondingly low rate of participation by Negroes among those citizens whose major political act is voting? Although a complete answer is impossible without conducting a sample survey, *it is obvious from an analysis of rates of registration and rates of turnout that Negroes are less active than whites in performing these two political acts.*

Let us examine registration rates first.[4] Between 1950 and 1960 the difference between white and Negro registration rates had grown. In 1950 Negroes had higher registration rates than whites in eighteen wards and lower registration rates than whites in thirty-four wards. In 1960 Negroes had lower registration rates than whites in fifty-five out of fifty-nine wards. In 1950 the percentage of the white population registered to vote exceeded the percentage of the Negro population registered to vote by at least ten percentage points in fourteen wards. The percentage of Negroes registered exceeded the percentage of whites registered by the same margin in nine wards. In 1960 whites led Negroes in registration by ten or more percentage points in thirty-seven wards, and had registration rates lower than Negroes by the same margin in only one ward.

The increasing difference between the registration rates of Negroes and whites is even clearer when we examine the city as a whole. Between 1950 and 1960 the percentage of the Negro population in Philadelphia registered to vote *declined* from 44.4 percent to 41 percent while the registration rate of whites *increased* from 52 percent to 54.4 percent. For the third straight decade the registration rate of Negroes declined, and for the fourth straight decade the margin of the white registration rate over the Negro registration increased.

The increase in the white registration margin deserves closer ex-

4. Data on registration are kept by race in Philadelphia. Consequently, these can be dealt with directly.

amination. If we look at those wards in which at least half of those registered are whites we find that the white registration margin increased from 5.9 points to 17.5 points. In Negro wards the white registration margin declined very slightly from 5.3 points to 2.5 points. Yet a higher proportion of whites registered to vote than did Negroes, even though these wards were Negro wards, and the increase in white registration in the white wards, an increase of over 11.5 points, can truly be called phenomenal.

Whites not only register in greater proportions than Negroes, they also vote in greater proportions than Negroes. If we examine the percentage of those persons registered who actually vote, that is, the turnout rate, in white wards and Negro wards, we find that turnouts are consistently higher in the white wards. This is true for every election, for every major office in Philadelphia since 1947.

This is the manner in which Negroes participated in politics in Philadelphia, Pennsylvania, between 1963 and 1966. I suggested earlier that more effective participation by Negroes in politics might change the extent of rewards and benefits they receive. But other, less modifiable variables, such as governmental structure, the formal rules of the political system, unawareness on the part of whites of the difficulties facing Negroes, and explicit anti-Negro actions by whites tend to limit the gains made by Negroes. Do these conditions make change impossible or very slow? Can these conditions lead to frustration with politics and the political system by Negroes? Is this perhaps the explanation for the apparent decrease in voting by Negroes noted above? Will new forms of political activity develop to replace those described here? These are the important questions which remain unanswered.[5]

5. These questions are more fully explored in John H. Strange, "Racial Segregation in the Metropolis," in Michael A. Danielson, *Metropolitan Politics* (Boston: Little, Brown & Co., 1966).

The "Black Beater"

Lee Sloan

FOR TWENTY-THREE YEARS Lakeland,[1] a Michigan industrial city of 85,000, elected its city commissioners in nonpartisan, ward-based elections. Under this system District 1, which is 90 percent Negro, elected its own version of Adam Clayton Powell. Charles Washburn, a fiery ultramilitant Negro leader, used his commission seat as a forum from which he criticized community leadership and the unfairness with which it treated the Negro subcommunity. Rank-and-file Negro citizens identified with their commissioner in his struggles against the "white power structure." With Washburn, as with Powell, style was more important than goal attainment. He was most appreciated not for what he accomplished, which was relatively little, but rather for how he went about it.

But if Washburn's style made him popular among Lakeland's Negroes, it made him a nuisance and an irritant to the city's influential whites. To get rid of him and to make more difficult the election of other bothersome candidates, a change in the electoral system was proposed and adopted in a 1962 city-wide referendum.

The new system provides for a primary in which the voters of each district nominate two candidates who subsequently oppose one another in the general election. In the general election, voters cast seven votes, one for a candidate from each of the city's seven districts. Essentially, the idea is to give the city-wide electorate a choice between the candidates proposed by each district.

White voters could have made elections totally at-large. This is the procedure in most United States cities, and in Lakeland it would have made the election of *any* Negro all but impossible. Instead, a less common, less exclusive system was chosen. In 1966, only fifty-six cities with populations over 5,000 used such a system.

What are the effects of Lakeland's modified at-large system on the Negro subcommunity? While it does not automatically exclude all

1. The name of the city is fictitious, as are the names of all persons mentioned.

Published for the first time in this book, by permission of the author.

Negroes from city government, it does mean that Negroes will be elected only from those districts in which they constitute an overwhelming majority. Whereas District 1 (approximately 90 percent Negro) customarily elects a Negro commissioner, District 7 (approximately 60 percent Negro) has never elected a Negro candidate. Furthermore, since the Negro candidate must face a city-wide electorate without benefit of a party label, he will need newspaper and associational support if he is to be successful. This means that the Negro candidate hopeful of winning must be acceptable to middle-class whites (i.e., he must be conservative on racial issues), though he *need not* have strong support in his home district. Indeed, the evidence suggests that strong support in his home district would be the political kiss of death. For the primary serves to "key" the white electorate as to the "acceptable" Negro candidate—the rule is to vote for the candidate with the poorest primary showing.

Thus, white citizens of Lakeland can prevent the election of *militant* Negro leaders. At the same time, they can co-opt a *conservative* Negro leader. The Negro community will not be without representation —but in the eyes of many Negroes, their representative will be unwilling to protect or advance their interests.

In the 1964 and 1966 general elections the two Negro districts were unable to elect the candidates of their choice. Merritt Reed, a conservative Negro leader, won in both elections, despite his inability to carry his own District 1.

In District 7 in the 1964 election, a white candidate who had missed being nominated in the primary by one vote was nonetheless elected on a write-in campaign. He was elected despite the fact that he polled less than 30 percent of the votes in his home district and less than 2 percent in the other "Negro" district in this general election. The candidate preferred by the voters of Districts 1 and 7 in this election was the (white) incumbent mayor. Even when District 7's preferred candidate was white, then, the city-wide electorate rejected him.

For the two elections in these two predominantly Negro districts, the city-wide electorate rejected the district's preferred candidate four times out of four. In the other five districts, this happened in only one instance out of ten.

We may learn still more of the consequences of the Lakeland system by taking a closer look at the 1966 elections. In the District 1 primary, James Corbin, a militant, and Merritt Reed, a conservative, were nominated to run against one another in the general election. In the primary, Corbin polled 703 votes to Reed's 443. Reed was the incumbent commissioner, having won Washburn's seat in the 1964 election. In that election, Reed had demonstrated his voter appeal in the white districts of the city. His image among Negroes was conservative, though moderate among whites. Corbin, on the other hand, was president of the NAACP and was known as a Negro realtor who had played a large role in integrating a residential area within the city. His image was definitely militant. In the general election Reed beat Corbin with 60 percent of the city-wide vote, although he had lost 30 to 70 percent to Corbin in his home district.

Not surprisingly, many Negroes in Lakeland consider themselves to be disfranchised under the new electoral system. They are now denied the "right" to choose "their" representatives. In effect, the white electorate of Lakeland selects representatives for them, a pattern which characterized the accommodating leadership of the Old South. The fact that democratic procedures were used to take from them a "right" which was theirs under the old ward system leads many Negroes in Lakeland to view democratic government as but another form of white hypocrisy. The new system is referred to as the "Black Beater," and a great deal of time is given over to strategies to beat it.

The strategy which appears most obvious is that of running two moderate or militant Negro candidates in the primary. Numerous persons have asked Charles Washburn to run in the primary in the hopes that he and another militant or moderate would win and face one another in the general election. The hope then would be that white voters would vote *against* Washburn and *for* the other "more preferable" candidate. Since the electoral system was changed, however, Washburn has refused to run. (As a matter of fact, Washburn has almost completely withdrawn from Lakeland; he is now a leading nationalist or separatist leader in Detroit and on the national level.) It is doubtful that this strategy would work. In the primary, each voter casts but one vote. If two militants or moderates are to win nomination in a primary, it would be necessary to split the vote in such a fashion that both would poll more votes than a conservative candidate likely to poll the white vote in the general election. This would require more effective political organization than exists at this time in the Negro subcommunity.

Even assuming that two militants or moderates were to be nominated in the primary, there is still the possibility of a white-supported write-in campaign such as that which succeeded in District 7 in 1964. Most Negro militants are certain that this would be the result if they were to succeed in nominating two Negro candidates considered unacceptable to white voters.

Some moderate Negro leaders in Lakeland have given thought to the possibility of legal recourse. Most of these have been reluctant to challenge the constitutionality of the amendment, fearing that if they won, the city would adopt a regular at-large system under which *no* Negro could win. Many of these moderate leaders also are convinced that legal action would lead to a serious racial cleavage in Lakeland, and they are anxious to avoid that.

Some conservative and moderate leaders actually prefer the present arrangement. Some like the idea of having a Negro commissioner who represents "all the people." And some were always unhappy with Washburn and consider Reed and the system by which he was elected the lesser of two evils. These people will not go to any trouble to change the present system.

Disunity and the general lack of political knowledge and sophistication on the part of Lakeland's Negroes have prevented the development of an effective strategy to cope with the new electoral system. But one may argue that Negroes are not the only ones disadvantaged by it. Although the whites of Lakeland adopted the new system in order to control the quality of Negro representation on the commission, the system has other effects. It operates to the advantage of those candidates who can finance a city-wide campaign, and those who can count on newspaper support. Thus it appears to make it easier than ever before for economic elites to control city politics. The resultant conservatism of the commission often operates to the disadvantage not only of Lakeland's Negroes, but to the disadvantage of the entire working class.

VI

Influence
and Leadership

IT is characteristic of the American political system that persons who
have no office nevertheless participate actively in the conduct of affairs
and sometimes exercise more influence than elected and appointed officials. In part, this is no doubt a consequence of the extreme decentralization of the system. Officials must collaborate with private interests in
order to bring together the scattered pieces of power that are needed to
get anything done. In part, too, it is a consequence of our conception of
democracy, according to which everyone must be allowed, and indeed
encouraged, to take an active part in the business of governing. The
fact remains that by looking only at the activities of people who hold
office, one can get an impression of the American political system so
incomplete and distorted as to be downright wrong.

The first six readings in this Section are descriptive accounts of
interests that figure largely in urban government. Floyd Hunter, a sociologist, asserts that in Regional City (Atlanta), decisions in community affairs are made by a few "power leaders" who are at the apex
of a stable, hierarchical "power structure." These leaders, most of whom
are heads of large corporations, pass directions on to second, third, and
fourth rate personnel (the "under-structure" of power); public officials,
it is interesting to note, are among the second and third rate personnel.
The first two ratings are said to "set the line of policy"; the other two

"hold the line." If an understructure man is presumptuous enough to question a decision made by the top leaders, he may lose his job or be otherwise punished. Robert A. Dahl finds nothing like this in New Haven. There the Economic Notables, as he calls them, are only one among many groups "out of which individuals emerge" to exert influence; like other groups in the community (Negroes and schoolteachers, for example), the Economic Notables sometimes have their way and sometimes do not.

It may be asked why Hunter's findings differ so greatly from those of Dahl. One explanation may be that Hunter's research method, which involved asking people active in civic affairs to rate others according to their relative power, tended to produce the kind of answers that were expected, whereas Dahl's method, which was based mainly on observation of events rather than of opinions or attitudes, did not. Nelson W. Polsby compares Hunter's "stratification" method with Dahl's "pluralist" one to the advantage of the latter; researchers, he concludes, should study "the outcomes of actual decisions." But Peter Bachrach and Morton S. Baratz point out that the pluralist approach also makes assumptions which may predetermine findings. They criticize the idea of studying "actual" and "key" decisions on the ground that "nonissues" (that is, issues that do not come up for decision because powerful interests prevent them from doing so) may be more important. There is, they insist, more to community power than meets the eye.

The remaining readings have to do with influence in a variety of concrete settings. Basing his observations largely on interviews that he conducted in Boston and Cleveland, Norton E. Long says that, although the idea of a "power elite" may be comforting, there is little in reality that corresponds with it. Instead, there is undirected cooperation of particular social structures, each seeking particular goals (for example, the newspaper, which seeks prestige, readership, and advertising) and, in so doing, meshing with the goals of others. He concludes that although this meshing makes possible cooperative action on projects, it is very far from constituting a structured government. Paul H. Weaver's article is very apposite to this argument. He shows how in changing its "style" a newspaper may also change—in ways that it may not intend— the amount and kind of its influence. Since the newspaper in question is *The New York Times*, the metropolitan coverage of which helps to create the stereotypes about urban America, his discussion of this is of special significance. Another "particular social structure" is the labor union; as Edward C. Banfield and James Q. Wilson emphasize, the goals of unions in local politics range from almost everything to almost nothing. For other studies of influence and leadership at work the reader is referred to Section VIII of this book.

The Power Structure of Regional City

Floyd Hunter

ONE OF THE FIRST INTERVIEWS had in Regional City was with James Treat of the Southern Yarn Company. He gave a great deal of information concerning power relations in the community. Among other things, he supplied a clue to certain existing clique relationships and considerable information about them which was later verified. Several times in his conversation he had used the term "crowds" in describing how certain men acted in relation to each other on community projects, and he was asked to explain the term. His reply ran in this vein:

"I simply mean that there are 'crowds' in Regional City—several of them—that pretty well make the big decisions. There is the crowd I belong to (the Homer Chemical crowd); then there is the First State Bank crowd—the Regional Gas Heat crowd—the Mercantile crowd— the Growers Bank crowd—and the like."

Mr. Treat was asked to give the names of some of the men who were active in each crowd, and he said:

"Sure! The biggest man in our crowd is Charles Homer. I belong to his crowd along with John Webster, Bert Tidwell, Ray Moster, Harold Jones, James Finer, Larry Stroup, and Harold Farmer. There are others, but they would be on the edges of this crowd. These would be the ones to be brought in on anything.

"In the State Bank crowd there would be Herman Schmidt, Harvey Aiken, Mark Parks, and Joseph Hardy. Schmidt used to be the biggest man in that crowd, but young Hardy is coming up fast over there.

"In the Regional Gas Heat crowd there is Fargo Dunham, Elsworth Mines, Gilbert Smith, and Percy Latham maybe. George Delbert might be said to belong to that crowd, but he is a pretty independent fellow. He moves around [from crowd to crowd] quite a bit.

"The Mercantile crowd is made up of Harry Parker, Jack Williams, Luke Street, Adam Graves, Cary Stokes, and Epworth Simpson.

"The Growers Bank crowd would be Ralph Spade, Arthur Tarbell,

Reprinted from Community Power Structure, A Study of Decision Makers *(Chapel Hill: University of North Carolina Press, 1953), pp. 77–81 and 108–112, by permission of the publisher.*

and Edward Stokes. They are kind of a weak outfit, but they come in on a lot of things. Spade is probably the most aggressive of the lot, but he's not too much at that!"

With this information given, Mr. Treat was asked to tell how these crowds would operate in relation to one another on a community-wide project, and he outlined the procedure very clearly. This type of action will be given in fuller detail in connection with the techniques of power wielding, but it may be said here that representatives from each crowd are drawn into any discussion relative to a major community decision. Each man mentioned as belonging to a crowd also belongs to a major business enterprise within the community—at least the clique leader does. His position within the bureaucratic structure of his business almost automatically makes him a community leader, if he wishes to become one. The test for admission to this circle of decision-makers is almost wholly a man's position in the business community in Regional City. The larger business enterprises represent pyramids of power in their own right, as work units within the community, and the leaders within these concerns gather around them some of the top personnel within their own organization. They then augment this nucleus of leadership by a coterie of selected friends from other establishments to form knots of interest called "crowds" by Mr. Treat. The outer edges of any crowd may pick up such men as Percy Latham, the dentist, who in turn picks up others in relation to any specific activity in which the crowd may be interested. The top men in any crowd tend to act together, and they depend upon men below them to serve as intermediaries in relation to the general community.

The crowds described by Mr. Treat were also mentioned by numerous other informants. These crowds did not, however, exhaust the possibilities of clique relations within the larger group of policy leaders. Twenty-one distinct groupings were picked up within the forty persons on the list, as the study proceeded, but the crowds mentioned by Treat seemed to be the most generally recognized groupings. Several of the top leaders within the crowds would "clear with each other" informally on many matters. The older men, as mentioned earlier, tended to get their heads together on most matters, as did the younger group, but such relationships were not completely stable. Each man at the top of a "crowd pyramid" depended upon those close to him in business to carry out decisions when made. An older man, for example, could not command another older man to do something, but within his own crowd there would be a hierarchy he could put to work. In most instances decision-making tended to be channeled through the older men at some point in the process of formulation, but many things may be done on the initiative of any combination of several powerful leaders in the crowds named. None of the leaders indicated that he could work alone on any big project, nor did any feel that there was any man in the community with such power. The individual power leader is dependent on others in Regional City in contrast to mill or mining company towns where one man or one family may dominate the community actions which take place.

Society prestige and deference to wealth are not among the primary criteria for admission to the upper ranks of the decision-makers according to the study of Regional City. The persons who were included in the listing of forty top leaders purely on the basis of their wealth or society connections did not, with three or four exceptions, make the top listing of persons who might be called upon to "put across a community project." As has been mentioned before, a distinction is made between persons of wealth and social prestige who engage in work and those who do not. The persons of wealth are perhaps important in the social structure of the community as symbolic persons. They may be followed in matters of fashion and in their general manner of living. Their money may be important in financing a given project, but they are not of themselves doers. They may only be called decisive in the sense that they can withhold or give money through others to change the course of action of any given project. Gloria Stevens spends large sums of money on Regional City projects, but the expenditures are made through her lawyer, Ray Moster. She does not interact with any of the top leaders whom we interviewed, other than Moster, so far as could be ascertained. Hetty Fairly, another woman of wealth, spends her charitable monies through a foundation handled by a lawyer not on the list of leaders. The lawyers may be vigilant in serving the interests of their clients in both instances, and a part of the vigilance exercised is in keeping abreast of possible tax incursions on the "frozen wealth" of the foundations. In this there may be some connection with power, but it is rather obscure in terms of the definition of power as being the ability of persons to move goods and services toward defined goals. If there is power in the charitable foundation structures, it resides in the lawyers who operate them, rather than in the donors who are largely inactive in the affairs of the foundations.

Political eminence cannot be said to be a sole criterion for entry into the policy echelons of Regional City's life, generally speaking. The two exceptions to this statement are embodied in Mayor Barner and County Treasurer Truman Worth. Both Barner and Worth were successful businessmen before becoming involved in local politics to the point of seeking public office. Their interests may be said to be primarily business in the strict sense of the word. Both have a popular following that has kept them in office, but their close associates are businessmen. Mayor Barner had only one picture in his office—that of Charles Homer, the biggest businessman in the community. Both Barner and Worth look to businessmen constantly for advice before they make a move on any project concerning the whole community. Furthermore, they do not ordinarily "move out front" on any project themselves, but rather follow the lead of men like Delbert, Graves, or any one of the other leaders of particular crowds. . . .

The channels of interaction are established in Regional City to conserve the time of the men of power. Even with the channels that are opened, there is still considerable burden of responsibility placed upon these men. In discussing this point with George Delbert, the question was asked, "With so few men in policy positions, isn't there a tendency to choke off many projects which may be of equal merit with those being given consideration?" He thought the question over for a moment and replied, "Yes, I suppose that may be true; but there's only so much time in a year, and we can only handle a certain number of things. Then there's not money enough to go around for everything that comes up. There is always anywhere from one to two million being raised in this community for one purpose or another. It takes time to get around to everything!"

The power leaders do get around with considerable facility in the area of economic activity. When a new corporation is started, as for example a new television company, or a multimillion dollar apartment building project recently established in the city, one or more of the leaders were observed to "find time" to be identified with such developments. Certainly, the top leaders would appear to have time for policy considerations of such economic projects, if one takes into account the reports in the business section of the local press. The day-to-day working arrangements of the corporations are put into the hands of trusted under-structure administrative personnel. The pattern of power implicit in the situation matches that of civic enterprises in formation and development.

"If two institutions," says Hughes, "draw upon the same people . . . they may compete in some measure, for people have but a limited amount of time and money to expend."[1] The leaders of Regional City tend to protect themselves from too many demands by channeling policy execution through an under-structure on matters of policy. This under-structure is not a rigid bureaucracy, as has been pointed out, but is a flexible system. It has elements of stability and tends to operate by level. The men at each level are spoken of as first, second, third and fourth rate by the power leaders, who operate primarily in conjunction with individuals of the first two ratings. The types of personnel which may be found in each rating by a sample classification are as follows:

Examples of Personnel from First to Fourth Rate in Regional City

FIRST RATE: Industrial, commercial, financial owners and top executives of large enterprises.

SECOND RATE: Operations officials, bank vice-presidents, public-relations

1. Everett C. Hughes, "Ecological Aspects of Institutions," *American Sociological Review,* I (April 1936), 186.

men, small businessmen (owners), top-ranking public officials, corporation attorneys, contractors.

THIRD RATE: Civic organization personnel, civic agency board personnel,
newspaper columnists, radio commentators, petty public officials,
selected organization executives.

FOURTH RATE: Professionals such as ministers, teachers, social workers,
personnel directors, and such persons as small business managers,
higher paid accountants, and the like.

These ratings might be expanded. They are given simply to indicate a suggested ranking of selected personnel who operate below the
policy-making leaders in Regional City. The first two ratings are personnel who are said to "set the line of policy," while the latter two
groups "hold the line." The ratings are very real to the under-structure
professional personnel. One of these men said: "I know that the top
boys get together on things. This community is divided into tiers. You
can't get the first-tier men to work on anything originating in the
second- and third-tier level. The top ones may put their names on
second- and third-tier projects, but you cannot get them to work for
you. They will not attend your meetings, but you know they are attending their own meetings all the time." The top leaders are conserving
their time and energies for the primary role they play—policy-determi-
nation. They are also interested in holding a balance of power in the
community.

In discussing the men in the lower group of the top leadership
hierarchy, one of the informants said: "When you see one of the little
fellows move, you know he is not moving on his own. Somebody is
moving him, and it is the bigger fellow who is moving him that you
need to watch, if you want to know what is going on.

"My father, who was a farmer, used to chop wood with me. He'd
say, 'Son, when you see a chip in the woodpile move, look under the
chip. You probably will find something interesting under it.' I've always
remembered that. I've always looked to see what makes the 'chips'
move."

The "little fellows" are continually moved to perform their proper
tasks by those above them. The roles defined for the under-structure of
power personnel are carefully defined in keeping with the larger interests. Their movements are carefully stimulated and watched at all times
to see that their various functions are properly performed.

Stability of relationships is highly desirable in maintaining social
control, and keeping men "in their places" is a vital part of the structuring of community power. Andrew Carnegie expressed the idea of every
man in his place in this manner: "It is the business of the preacher to
preach, of the physician to practice, of the poet to write, the business of
the college professor to teach. . . ."[2] Each of these professions also has a
role to play in the community activities consistent with its economic or

2. *The Empire of Business* (New York: Doubleday, Page and Company, 1902), p. 189.

professional role. Such roles do not ordinarily include policy-making. If one of these under-structure men should be presumptuous enough to question policy decisions, he would be immediately considered insubordinate and "punished," first by a threat to his job security, followed possibly by expulsion from his job if his insubordination continued. To quote Homans:

> A social system is in a moving equilibrium and authority exists when the state of the elements that enter the system and the relations between them, including the behavior of the leader(s), is such that disobedience to the orders of the leader(s) will be followed by changes in the other elements tending to bring the system back to the state the leader(s) would have wished to reach if the disobedience had not occurred.[3]

There may be isolated dissatisfactions with policy decisions in Regional City, but mainly there is unanimity. The controversial is avoided, partly by the policy-making group's not allowing a proposal to get too far along if it meets stiff criticism at any point in decision-making. A careful watch is kept for what "will go" and for what "will not go." Luke Street says, "Most of the carping comes from people who are envious of some of the bigger crowds. When there is such envy, the crowds are talked about and criticized." Such criticism usually is not open. When criticism is open it is generally directed toward some of the under-structure men who are fronting for the larger interests. If criticism is directed toward the top leaders, the critic is liable to job dismissal in extreme cases or more subtle pressures in less flagrant cases. The omnipresent threat of power sanctions used against recalcitrant underlings is recognized by lower echelons of power, and they generally go along with most decisions, grumbling in private with close associates, if at all. Most of these third- or fourth-rate leaders rationalize their behavior—particularly when upper decisions are in conflict with their professional or private value systems.

3. *The Human Group* (New York: Harcourt, Brace & Co., 1950), p. 422.

The Economic Notables
of New Haven

Robert A. Dahl

THE HYPOTHESIS that an economic elite of bankers and businessmen dominates New Haven, dramatic and satisfying as it may be to many people, is false. The temptation to fly from one falsehood to another at the opposite extreme is unfortunately one of the commonplaces of human existence; and hence one might easily interpret the evidence as showing that the Economic Notables[1] are virtually powerless: a conclusion surely as unwarranted as the other. Nor does it get us much closer to the truth if we simply offer the vacuous evasion that the truth lies somewhere between the two extremes; for this is merely to reduce a social complexity to a loose and misleading metaphor.

The most impressive evidence against the hypothesis that the Economic Notables or their delegates completely dominate New Haven consists of a detailed examination of eight major decisions on redevelopment, eight on public education, and all nominations for elective office, but most importantly for mayor, in both political parties for seven elections from 1945–1957. These decisions have been reconstructed from records, newspaper files, and interviews with leading participants.

---

1. The group of Economic Notables, numbering some 238 persons, includes any person in one of the following categories:

The president or chairman of the board of a corporation with property in New Haven assessed in any of the five years 1953–1957 at a value placing it among the fifty highest assessments in the city.

Any individual or groups of individuals with property in the city assessed in the years 1956–1957 at a value of $250,000 or more.

President or chairman of the board of all banks and public utilities in the city.

Any individual who was a director of three or more of the following:

A firm with assessed valuation of $250,000 or more.

A manufacturing firm with fifty or more employees.

A retailing firm with twenty-five or more employees.

Any bank.

All directors of New Haven banks.

Reprinted, somewhat revised, from Who Governs? *(New Haven: Yale University Press, 1961), by permission of the publisher and the author.*

To reconstruct these decisions is to leave no doubt, I think, of the fact that the Economic Notables, far from being a ruling group, are simply one of the many groups out of which individuals sporadically emerge to influence the policies and acts of city officials. Almost anything one might say about the influence of the Economic Notables could be said with equal justice about a half dozen other groups in the New Haven community. What these other groups are and what can be said about *their* influence will develop as we proceed.

If the quantitative indications of the relative influence of the Economic Notables belied the overwhelming testimony provided by the qualitative inspection of these decisions, one might quite properly, I believe, reject the quantitative rather than the qualitative interpretation of the evidence. But in this case each kind of evidence supports the other.

Of the forty-eight Economic Notables participating officially in urban redevelopment plus any additional ones who may have been participating unofficially, only seven seem to have exerted any leadership. . . . Of these, only one, a banker who was the first chairman of the Citizens Action Commission, was among the top five; at least two and probably three others in the top five exerted considerably more influence over the actual course of decisions than he did. There were . . . no Economic Notables among the higher offices in public education; and none were turned up as covert leaders. Only one Economic Notable was a leader in either of the two political parties; and he was something of an anomaly. It will be worth our time to examine this case in some detail.

Politician or Notable?

This unique individual was Mr. John Golden, a Democratic party leader for a generation and a man whom few people in New Haven, if they happened to know his name, would have considered as other than the boss of the Democratic Party.

Golden was, in some ways, a representative of an earlier era. As a political boss he was in the old tradition of urban politics. As a businessman he had this much in common with the entrepreneurs of the late nineteenth century: he had come a long way from modest beginnings.

He was born not far from New Haven in Old Saybrook, where his father was a station agent for the New Haven railroad. Of Irish Catholic stock, descended from a father and a grandfather who had both been Democrats, the boy quite naturally became a Democrat too. About the time of the First World War Golden went to work in the Greist Manufacturing Company and there he rose to the rank of superintendent.

But he was evidently more interested in politics than in manufacturing; he became Democratic chairman in his ward in 1924 (a post he still held a quarter-century later) and in 1931 he ran for public office as Democratic candidate for Registrar of Voters. In the great depression-born surge to the Democrats, he won. But the newly elected mayor, who like Golden was an Irishman and a Democrat, offered him a city post as Director of Public Works; Golden thereupon resigned his job in the manufacturing plant and took the new one. Not wishing to be dependent on the modest income from his city job, he now started an insurance and bonding business; and as he rose in politics his business became highly lucrative. The connection was perhaps not accidental. In due course he was made a director of the General Industrial Bank, a small commercial bank that had been established by Jewish families in New Haven as a result of the systematic exclusion of Jews by other banks; it was probably the only bank in New Haven since Andrew Jackson's day that might be called a "Democratic" bank rather than a "Republican" one. It is by virtue of this directorship that Golden, under the generous conception of economic notability outlined earlier, falls into our present group. But he rightly belongs there, for he is reputed to be a well-to-do man by New Haven standards.

By the time the Democratic mayor under whom Golden served had been defeated in his last try for office in 1945, Golden was the real head of the Democratic organization. His rule was occasionally challenged; but the challengers were regularly defeated. It was Golden who saw possibilities in a young member of the Board of Aldermen, Richard Lee, who ultimately was elected mayor in 1953 with Golden's strong support. As Lee's prestige, confidence, and authority grew, Golden's own control over the organization waned. By the end of the decade it was no longer possible to say which of the two would win in a showdown over control of the organization. But neither man stood to gain by a contest, neither sought one, and except for a brief conflict over charter reform their coalition remained intact.

One could draw a pretty picture of the Economic Notables controlling Golden, and Golden in turn controlling the Democratic Party. But whatever else one might conclude about Golden's role in politics, it has been impossible to turn up any evidence to warrant the conclusion that he was an "agent" of the Notables. Like most successful politicians, particularly Democratic ones, he was not known to entertain a profound respect for the abilities or attainments of successful businessmen, and his style of life, outlook, and interests were those of the old-fashioned urban political leader rather than the man of business. For its part, the business community looked upon Golden with no little suspicion as an organization politician. (Because of their contacts with him on the Citizens Action Commission in recent years, some of the

Economic Notables finally developed a grudging respect for his shrewd-ness and judgment.) Moreover most of the Economic Notables were Republicans who had supported Republican candidates and opposed the Democratic ones supported by Golden.

It might be thought that the Economic Notables had no need to "control" Golden since as a successful insurance executive and bank director his views on policy questions would surely coincide with theirs. There is not only a profound truth in this observation but also an im-portant distortion. If one searches for a massive divergence in opinion between Golden and New Haven business leaders, one will not find it. But if one looks for massive divergencies between Golden and almost any other group in the community, one will not find that either. For like the United States, New Haven is usually governed by "consensus poli-tics" rather than by "conflict politics." This is a matter we shall return to many times, but perhaps it is enough to say now that in the present period there are in New Haven no profound, persistent, invariant, and community-wide cleavages of a "fundamental" kind—e.g., of the kind that divide orthodox Communists and orthodox Catholics in Italy. If Golden's policies could be said to coincide substantially with those of the Economic Notables (in so far as the Notables even agree among them-selves), they could be said to coincide in the same sense with the policies of union leaders, school teachers, and factory hands. In short, in New Haven, as in the United States generally, the search for political conflict is likely to turn up differences that will seem small measured by European standards or considered in the perspective of a revolutionary ideology (whether of the Left or Right), but which nonetheless may be thought of by the participants as quite great.

From the moon, viewed with the naked eye, the Rocky Mountains would seem little different from the plains; but the closer one draws to the Rockies the greater the difference would become. So too in politics, differences shrink with distance. Many observers have viewed American local or even national politics as if they were standing on the moon looking at politics for signs of brutal class conflict and permanent cleavages. Finding only scattered and unsatisfactory evidence, they nonetheless take these as proof that the rich and wellborn have in devious and mysterious ways imposed their policies on all the rest.

The Economic Notables and Public Policies

Like many other groups in the community, from Negroes on Dixwell Avenue to teachers in the public schools, sometimes the Eco-nomic Notables have their way and sometimes they do not. As with other groups, the likelihood of getting their way is a complex function of many factors: the relevance to political influence of the resources at their disposal; the extent to which they agree; their application, persistence, and skill; the amount and kinds of opposition they generate; the degree to which their objectives are viewed as consistent with the political aims of elected leaders; and the agreement of their aims with the fundamental political consensus of the community.

In many areas of public policy, the Economic Notables can hardly be said to have any direct influence at all, either because they do not agree or because they simply never enter the arena of policy. Their direct influence on public education and on political nominations, for example, is virtually nil.

Even on urban redevelopment, their record is a curious one. Few aspects of local policy could be more important to the Notables than efforts to "save" downtown New Haven. Yet the record reveals that the Economic Notables were able neither to agree on nor to put through a program of urban redevelopment, even under a Republican mayor who was as anxious as any mayor can be to please the Notables. When redevelopment came to New Haven the leadership for it came not from the Notables but from a Democratic mayor, whom most of them originally opposed and who as mayor had to wheedle, cajole, recruit, organize, plan, negotiate, bargain, threaten, reward, and maneuver endlessly to get the support and participation needed from the Notables, the small businessmen, the developers (who came principally from outside New Haven), the federal authorities, and the electorate.

Normally, outside of redevelopment and concern over the diminishing prosperity of the city's heart, the main cutting edge of policy to the Economic Notables in their roles as businessmen and property owners is the tax on their property. The individual and particular interests of the Economic Notables can in this case, as in many others, conflict somewhat with their collective interests. Like anyone else a Notable can keep his taxes down by means of a relatively low tax rate, or a relatively low assessment, or both. Uniformly low taxes for the Notables require either that the general tax rate on real property must be reduced, or that the gains of the Notables from reduced assessments must be offset by relatively higher assessments for the other property owners. To an elected mayor—that is, to a politician uninterested in committing political suicide in order to win the gratitude and respect of his beneficiaries among the Notables—the possible advantages of favoritism to the Notables at the expense of other groups are minor compared with the possible costs; for the Notables cast a pitifully small fraction of the total vote at election time. And small property owners, who vastly outnumber the Notables, are no less sensitive to their assessments.

The greater numbers and equal sensitivity to taxes of small property owners help account for the fact that they are underassessed in New Haven as compared with large property owners or with owners of business and nonresidential property. In recent years small single-family dwellings have been assessed at somewhat less than 40 per cent of their market values (as indicated by sales prices for comparable dwellings), whereas large single-family dwellings have been assessed at nearly 60 per cent, and nonresidential properties at 60 to 80 per cent of their sales values. If, in short, there has been any shifting of the tax burden via assessments, it has been from the poor to the wealthy rather than the other way around. Hence if a Notable acting in his own personal or corporate interest succeeds in having his assessment reduced, the effect is mainly to pass the bill to another Notable.

Even this tactic is not always successful; for success varies, depending on how hard up the city administration is for money and how much of a *quid pro quo* it can foresee in campaign contributions. The political mores of the community and the dangers of public scandal forbid anything so crass and brutal as an explicit deal. But there are certain tacit understandings in the local political culture that sophisticated participants might hope to rely on. If a firm protests its assessment and threatens to appeal to the courts, the city attorneys may conclude that the reasonable course—particularly in view of genuine uncertainty as to whether the city's claims will hold up in court—is to reduce the assessment. Later, the firm's executives may contribute funds generously to the campaign of the incumbent administration. (Possibly they may then even recoup their contribution by awarding themselves a larger bonus out of gratitude for their labors on behalf of the corporation.)

An administration running close to the wind, however, may prefer a court fight to the loss in tax income from a settlement out of court; for in the case of a large firm a reduction sizable enough to make it worth while for the firm to engage in a court fight may also be big enough to throw the city's revenues out of whack. (In 1957, the ten largest owners of real estate in New Haven paid almost one-fifth of the total taxes levied by the city, and their taxes financed one-eighth of the city's total expenditures for that year.) Consequently, the city administration may prefer to contest the appeal. Thus the Lee administration, hard pressed for city funds and fearful of the political consequences of a tax increase, refused to settle with the National Folding Box Company on its 1954–1956 assessment, which was the fourth largest in the city. In court, the city lost the case—and $130,000 in taxes.

Moreover, the game of assessments can be played roughly by both sides. A city administration typically lives in dread of raising the tax rate. But a general increase in assessments, particularly on large firms, may do the trick instead. Under the Lee administration, current city expenditures rose by 45 per cent in five years with no increase in the tax rate; a policy of vigorous reassessment paid off in tax returns high enough to cover the increase in expenditures.

Because manipulating assessments is a game of beggar-thy-neighbor, the collective as distinct from the purely individual interests of the Economic Notables might seem to dictate a common strategy of keeping expenditures and taxes down. To a very great extent, however, this collective interest is highly abstract, for the impact of taxes and city outlays on the Notables varies with the extent to which their incomes are affected directly or indirectly by taxes and city services, their perspectives on policy questions and ideological matters, their loyalties and identifications, and other complex factors. To many corporations the local property taxes are such a small proportion of costs that corporate executives can scarcely be expected to give them more than marginal attention. Four of the twelve largest real property owners in New Haven are public utilities; because local property taxes are considered as costs in computing their rates, the taxes can be passed on to consumers. Mr. John Day Jackson, the nonagenarian owner and publisher of New Haven's two newspapers, one of the fifty largest property owners in the city, and a firm believer in the pure essence of Herbert Spencer, for many years carried on an unremitting campaign against every proposed expansion of governmental activity, local, state, or federal, on the grounds that it would cost money and raise taxes. Yet almost without exception the business and financial leaders we interviewed in New Haven looked upon Mr. Jackson's editorial policies with a mixture of amusement, disdain, and irritation; he was thought by them to be shortsighted, penny-pinching, and eccentric.

Despite all these qualifications, however, the main policy thrust of the Economic Notables is to oppose tax increases and hence expenditures for other than the minimal traditional city services. In this effort their two most effective weapons have probably been the mayor and the Board of Finance. Since the members of the Board of Finance, aside from the mayor himself and one alderman, are appointed by the mayor, the influence of the Notables on the budget is sharply reduced if the mayor exerts strong leadership and has policies that differ from those of the Notables. Consequently, the policies of the Notables are most easily achieved when they have a strong mayor on their side or, under a weak mayor, if they have the support of the Board of Finance.

Historically, the relative number of businessmen of all kinds—the heads of large firms, small independents, and managers—on the two main legislative boards, the Board of Aldermen and the Board of Finance, has declined enormously since the high period of business eminence in the last half of the nineteenth century. But on the Board of Finance itself, businessmen have continued to play a predominant role; indeed, the heads of firms all but took over that Board in the twenties and even now comprise a large proportion of the Board's appointive members. The contrast with the position of the clerical and working class groups is striking. During the first half of the nineteenth century no one from these groups sat on either of the two boards; but at midcentury their numbers began to increase, and in the twentieth century they have averaged around 40 per cent of the membership of the two boards. This increase in clerical and working class participation, however, has taken place almost entirely on the Board of Aldermen; their relative numbers increased only slightly on the Board of Finance.

It seems reasonable to conclude that the steady pressure of the Notables against the expansion of public services and taxes has some effect. It is impossible to say, however, just what the magnitude of that effect has been. Had their demands for public economy been in opposition to the demands of a large proportion of the citizenry, the natural incentive of politicians to secure their own election would doubtless have resulted in policies designed to appeal to numbers rather than wealth.

But it would be wrong to suppose that Economic Notables and businessmen were in conflict with other significant groups over the policy of keeping taxes and expenditures low, or that they always succeeded. Their essential strategy was a familiar aspect of American politics: to gain services and benefits from government and, so far as possible, to displace the costs from themselves to others. In the context of American ideology and perspectives, contests over taxes and services were evidently seen less as grand conflicts among social classes over relative shares in the public pie than as struggles by individuals or small constellations of individuals: a family, a grocery store, a business firm, a neighborhood, or an ethnic or religious group. Even workers shared this view. In the depths of the Great Depression a sociologist interviewing workers in New Haven concluded that "no abstract ideal nor current issue matters very much to the politically minded wage earner. He cannot afford to be concerned over such matters, because he looks upon the political party as a source of help in time of need, to get a job, to get one of his boys out of a court scrape, to show him how to fill out forms."[2]

Thus the policies of the Economic Notables precipitated factional rather than class battles—if, indeed, they caused any conflict at all. For it must be remembered that throughout much of this century, Democratic and Republican mayors alike sought to outdo one another in their reputations for "economy." Until the New Deal, the national leaders of the Democratic Party, though less worshipful toward business than the general run of Republican spokesmen, were no less keen on economy and budget balancing. In Connecticut, even the Socialists were economy-minded; their "business-like" administration in Bridgeport drew the admiration and political support of conservative Republican businessmen. During the Depression the Democratic mayor of New Haven was a union official, the only person of nominally working-class

2. John W. McConnell, *Evolution of Social Classes* (Washington, D.C.: American Council on Public Affairs, 1942), p. 156.

status at the time of his election ever to hold the office of mayor in New Haven; yet his policy was one of such strict economy on public outlays that his defeat by a Republican in 1945 after fourteen years in office was widely attributed to general discontent with the shabby state of public services in New Haven, particularly with the semistarved condition of the public school system.

The fact was, then, that the Economic Notables operated within that vague political consensus, the prevailing system of beliefs, to which all the major groups in the communuity subscribed. Even the rather limited influence the Notables possessed over the level of taxes depended upon the extent to which their aims fitted within the dominant system of beliefs of the community. Within limits, they could influence the content of that belief-system; but they could not determine it wholly. As a belief system it contained elements of both rigidity and great flexibility; it had precise injunctions and vague mandates; and it was chock-full of inconsistencies. Skilled leaders, exploiting these various elements in the belief system (yet always imprisoned within its constraints), could manipulate the flow of local costs and benefits in different ways; some of these would be inconsistent with the dominant concern of the Economic Notables over low taxes.

Even a Republican mayor, elected in 1945 on a campaign to improve the public schools and city services in general after a long period of starvation, had to increase taxes; and his Democratic successor, as we have seen, had to raise assessments. Over the decade from 1947–1957, total city expenditures more than doubled, while income from taxes rose by more than 70 per cent as a result of increases both in the rate and in assessments. During this same period, the total assessments of the ten largest real property owners in New Haven rose by nearly 85 per cent.

Thus the influence of the Notables, though not feeble, is spotty and limited. To be sure, under certain circumstances they could exercise more influence in more areas of policy than they now do. But this is also true of every other significant group in New Haven.

How to Study Community Power

Nelson W. Polsby

POLITICAL SCIENTISTS ARE BEGINNING TO VIEW certain major contributions to the study of community politics less favorably than one would have expected after hearing the fanfare surrounding the original acceptance of these works.[1] Often billed as studies of "community power structure," these works have been produced mostly by sociologists, whose orientation has been to study the politics of American communities as a subsidiary aspect of social structure.[2] "The political organization of Jonesville," writes one such scholar, "fits the

1. For indications that disenchantment is setting in among political scientists, see the following: Robert A. Dahl, "A Critique of the Ruling Elite Model," *American Political Science Review*, 52 (June, 1958), 463–469; Herbert Kaufman and Victor Jones, "The Mystery of Power," *Public Administration Review*, 14 (Summer, 1954), 205–212; Norton E. Long, "The Local Community as an Ecology of Games," *American Journal of Sociology*, 64 (November, 1958), 251–261; Nelson W. Polsby, "The Sociology of Community Power: A Reassessment," *Social Forces*, 37 (March, 1959), 232–236 and "Three Problems in the Analysis of Community Power," *American Sociological Review*, 24 (December, 1959), 796–803; Raymond E. Wolfinger, "Reputation and Reality in the Study of 'Community Power'," *American Sociological Review*, 25 (December, 1960), in press. Sociologists also seem to be re-examining studies of community power: Reinhard Bendix and Seymour M. Lipset, "Political Sociology," *Current Sociology*, 6 (1957), 79–99; Peter H. Rossi, "Community Decision-Making," *Administrative Science Quarterly*, 1 (March, 1957), 415–443. Writings praising community power studies are quite extensive, and include the following: Gordon Blackwell, "Community Analysis," in Roland Young (ed.), *Approaches to the Study of Politics* (Evanston, 1958), 305–317; William J. Gore and Fred S. Silander, "A Bibliographical Essay on Decision-Making," *Administrative Science Quarterly*, 4 (June, 1959), 106–121; Lawrence J. R. Herson, "The Lost World of Municipal Government," *American Political Science Review*, 51 (June, 1957), 330–345.

2. For example, Robert S. Lynd and Helen M. Lynd, *Middletown* (New York, 1929) and *Middletown in Transition* (New York, 1937); Floyd Hunter, *Community Power Structure* (Chapel Hill, 1953); August B. Hollingshead, *Elmtown's Youth* (New York, 1949); W. Lloyd Warner et al., *Democracy in Jonesville* (New York, 1949); C. Wright Mills, the Middle Classes in the Middle-Sized Cities," *American Sociological Review*, 11 (October, 1946), 520–529; Robert O. Schulze, "Economic Dominants and Community Power Structure," *American Sociological Review*, 23 (February, 1958), 3–9; Roland Pellegrin and Charles H. Coates, "Absentee-Owned Corporations and Community Power Structure," *American Journal of Sociology*, 61 (March, 1956), 413–419; Delbert C. Miller, "Industry and Community Power Structure," *American Sociological Review*,

Reprinted from Journal of Politics, *Vol. XXII (August 1960), pp. 474–484, where it appeared under the title "How to Study Community Power: the Pluralist Alternative."*

rest of the social structure . . . curving or bulging with the class outlines of the body politic."[3]

The faults which critics have found with studies following this
general conception of politics as an epiphenomenon of social stratification are many, varied and serious. They include the charges that this
conception encourages research designs which generate self-fulfilling
prophecies,[4] and that it leads to the systematic misreporting of facts[5]
and to the formulation of ambiguous and unprovable assertions about
community power.[6] It would be gratuitous for me to re-explore these
criticisms here. It would be more profitable, instead, to describe some
of the ways in which students have evaded—apparently with success
—the various disabilities of the stratification approach to the study
of community power. With judicious unoriginality, I shall call the
alternative research strategy to be outlined here the "pluralist" approach. Old, familiar pluralistic presumptions[7] about the nature of
American politics seem to have given researchers strategies for the
study of community power which are both feasible to execute and
comparatively faithful to conditions in the real world.[8] What follows is
an attempt to explain why this seems to be the case for pluralist studies,
but not for stratification studies.

The first, and perhaps most basic presupposition of the pluralist
approach, is that nothing categorical can be assumed about power in
any community. It rejects the stratification thesis that *some* group
necessarily dominates a community.[9] If anything, there seems to be
an unspoken notion among pluralist researchers that at bottom *nobody*

23 (February, 1958), 9–15 and "Decision-Making Cliques in Community Power Structure," *American Journal of Sociology*, 64 (November, 1958), 299–310.

  3. Warner *et al., op. cit.*, p. xviii.

  4. See, *e.g.*, Kaufman and Jones, *op. cit.*

  5. See Polsby, *op. cit.*

  6. See *ibid.*, Dahl, *op. cit.*, and Kaufman and Jones, *op. cit.*

  7. I am well aware that for other purposes the "pluralist" approach can be divided
into several schools of thought. However, all variations of pluralist theory contrast
effectively with stratification theory. Pluralist presumptions can be found, for example,
in the writings of de Tocqueville and Madison, and in Arthur Bentley, *The Process of
Government* (Chicago, 1908); E. Pendleton Herring, *The Politics of Democracy* (New
York, 1940); David B. Truman, *The Governmental Process* (New York, 1953); V. O.
Key, Jr., *Politics, Parties and Pressure Groups* (New York, 4th ed., 1959).

  8. Among the researchers who have found pluralist presumptions about the nature
of the political system useful are Robert A. Dahl ("The New Haven Community
Leadership Study," Working Paper Number 1, December, 1957, mimeo); Harry Scoble
("Yankeetown: Leadership in Three Decision-Making Processes," presented at the
meeting of the American Political Science Association, 1956); and George Belknap and
Norton E. Long. See Long, *op. cit.*; Long and Belknap, "A Research Program on
Leadership and Decision-Making in Metropolitan Areas" (New York, Governmental
Affairs Institute, 1956), mimeo; Belknap and John H. Bunzel, "The Trade Union in the
Political Community," *PROD*, 2 (September, 1958), 3–6; Belknap, "A Plan for Research
on the Socio-Political Dynamics of Metropolitan Areas" (presented before a seminar
on urban leadership of the Social Science Research Council, New York, August, 1957).
See also a paper presented to this same seminar by Peter H. Rossi, "The Study of
Decision-Making in the Local Community."

  9. I present some of the characteristics of a stratification theory of community

dominates in a town, so that their first question to a local informant is not likely to be, "Who runs this community?," but rather, "Does anyone at all run this community?" It is instructive to examine the range of possible answers to each of these questions. The first query is somewhat like, "Have you stopped beating your wife?," in that virtually any response short of total unwillingness to answer will supply the researchers with a "power élite" along the lines presupposed by the stratification theory.[10] On the other hand, the second question is capable of eliciting a response which *could* lead to the discovery of a power élite (*i.e.,* "Yes"), or any of an infinite number of stable, but non-élitist patterns of decision-making (*i.e.,* "No, but . . ."; "Yes, but . . ."), or total fragmentation, or disorganization (*i.e.,* "No").

What sort of question is likely to follow "Who runs the community?" in a questionnaire? Obviously, something like "*How* do the people named in the above response run the community?" This entirely probable pattern of investigation begs the question of whether or not those said to rule actually do rule. In the pluralist approach, on the other hand, an attempt is made to study specific outcomes, in order to determine who actually prevails in community decision-making. Consonant with the desire to study actual outcomes, which requires arduous and expensive field work, outcomes in a few (but, for reasons of expense, usually only a few) issue-areas are studied closely. More than a single issue-area is always chosen, however, because of the presumption among pluralist researchers that the same pattern of decision-making is highly unlikely to reproduce itself in more than one issue-area. In this expectation, pluralist researchers have seldom been disappointed.[11] They recognize, however, the possibility that the same pattern *could* reproduce itself in more than one issue-area. Since actual behavior is observed, or reconstructed from documents, witnesses, and so on, it is possible to determine empirically whether or not the same group rules two or more issue-areas. The presumption that the existence of a power élite is unlikely does not, in other words, prevent the finding of such an élite if the data so indicate.

A superficially persuasive objection to this approach might be phrased as follows: "Suppose research in a community discloses different patterns of decision-making in each of these issue-areas. This does not rule out the possibility that all other issue-areas in the community are dominated by a single power élite." How can pluralists meet this objection? First, it is necessary to acknowledge the *possibility* that this is the case. However, pluralists can (and do) protect themselves in part

---

power in other papers, *e.g.,* "Power in Middletown: Fact and Value in Community Research" (March, 1960), mimeo.; "Power as a Variable of Social Stratification" (November, 1959), mimeo.

10. See Kaufman and Jones, *op. cit.*

11. Wolfinger, *op. cit.,* has summarized findings on this point, pp. 7*ff.*

by studying significant issues. In the New Haven study, for example, of which this paper is an outgrowth, we studied (1) nominations by the two political parties, which determine which persons hold public offices; (2) the New Haven Redevelopment program, which is the largest in the country (measured by past and present outlay per capita); (3) public education, which is the most costly item in the city's budget; and (4) a campaign to revise the city charter.[12] In Bennington, Scoble studied political nominations and elections, the issue of consolidation of various municipal governments, the formation of a union high-school district, and the construction of a new high-school building.[13] A pilot study, by Long and Belknap, of a large eastern city embraced the problems of transportation, race relations, traffic, urban redevelopment and recreation,[14] while in the San Francisco Bay area, Belknap studied the issues of urban redevelopment, transportation and race relations.[15] None of these issues was trivial; they probably were, in fact, the most important issues before these communities during the time these studies were being carried out. What sort of a power élite is it—it may appropriately be asked—which asserts itself in relatively trivial matters, but is inactive or ineffective in the most significant areas of community policy-making?

Stratification theory holds that power élites fail to prevail only on trivial issues.[16] By pre-selecting as issues for study those which are generally agreed to be significant, pluralist researchers can test stratification theory without searching endlessly in one issue-area after another, in order to discover some semblance of a power élite. After all, it cannot be reasonably required of researchers that they validate someone else's preconceived notions of community power distributions. If the researcher's design is such that any power distribution has an equal chance of appearing in his result, his result may not properly be criticized on the grounds that it did not conform to expectations. The burden of proof is clearly on the challenger in such a case to make good his assertion that power is actually distributed otherwise.[17]

Another presumption of the pluralist approach runs directly counter to stratification theory's presumption that power distributions are a more or less permanent aspect of social structure. Pluralists hold that power may be tied to issues, and issues can be fleeting or persistent, provoking coalitions among interested groups and citizens ranging in their duration from momentary to semipermanent. There is a clear gain in descriptive accuracy involved in formulating power distributions so

12. See Dahl, "The New Haven . . . ," *op. cit.*, Polsby, *op. cit.*, and Wolfinger, *op. cit.*, and forthcoming publications of the New Haven Community Leadership Study.
13. Scoble, *op. cit.*
14. Long and Belknap, *op. cit.*
15. Belknap, *op. cit.*
16. See, for example, Pellegrin and Coates, *op. cit.*, and Lynd and Lynd, *Middletown in Transition, op. cit.*, p. 89.
17. See Dahl, "Critique . . . ," *op. cit.*

as to take account of the dimension of time, as pluralists do,[18] since it is easily demonstrated that coalitions *do* vary in their permanency. To presume that the set of coalitions which exists in the community at any given time is a timelessly stable aspect of social structure is to introduce systematic inaccuracies into one's description of social reality.

Why do pluralists reject the idea that *some* group necessarily dominates every community? The presumption that communities are likely to be less rather than more permanent in their patterns of decision-making is no doubt part of the answer, but another part is an even more fundamental conception of human behavior as governed in large part by inertia. This view leads pluralists to put a high value on overt activity as indicative of involvement in issues and to look upon the collection of "reputations" for leadership as a much less desirable research procedure.[19]

Pluralists consider as arbitrary the inclusion of certain groups as being "implicated" in decisions when these groups themselves reject such involvement.[20] For pluralists, "false class consciousness" does not exist, because it implies that the values of analysts are imposed on groups in the community. They reject the idea that there is any particular issue or any particular point in the determination of an issue where a group must assert itself in order to follow its expressed values. Rather, the pluralist assumes that there are many issues and many

18. See, for example, Belknap, *op. cit.*, for an explicit discussion of this point. One stratification writer who has attempted to take account of the time factor is Jerome K. Myers, "Assimilation in the Political Community," *Sociology and Social Research,* 35 (January–February, 1951), 175–182. Myers plots a secular trend which indicates slow increases in the number of Italians and Italian-descended persons employed by New Haven municipal government over a fifty year period ending in 1940. Myers claims to have discovered "discrimination" against Italians, because they did not participate in city government jobs to an extent proportional with their representation in the total population of the city. His conclusion was that "the early or quick assimilation of New Haven Italians in the political system does not seem very probable. . . . All indications are that political assimilation is inevitable, although it is at least several generations away."

By taking account of shorter-term cyclical movements within the allegedly "basic" structure, we may be able to explain the delay in the political assimilation of Italians. First, New Haven Italo-Americans were and are predominantly Republicans in local politics, because in New Haven the Republican organization early and energetically courted the Italo-American vote. From 1920 to 1940, years in which that ethnic group would "normally" have been expected to come into their own as a politically significant minority group, the city government was in Democratic hands two-thirds of the time. It might be expected, therefore, that Italo-Americans would be less well represented among officeholders than if these circumstances were reversed. Second, in 1945, a Republican of Italian descent was elected Mayor, whereupon Italian-Americans invaded the top echelons of city government to such an extent that the Mayor pleaded in vain with one who was a candidate for President of the City Council to withdraw in favor of a Yankee Republican, on the grounds that there were "too many Italians" in City Hall, and that the Yankee members of the Republican coalition should have some recognition.

19. See, especially, Wolfinger, *op. cit.*

20. See C. Wright Mills, "The Middle Classes . . . ," *op. cit.*, and my "The Sociology of Community Power," *op. cit.*, on this point.

points at which group values can be realized. Further, pluralists presume that there are certain costs in taking any action at all. This refers not simply to the possibility of losing, of making political enemies, and so on, but also to the costs in personal time and effort involved in political mobilization, in becoming informed, in lobbying or campaigning and in taking the trouble to vote.[21]

It is a demonstrated fact that public activity of all sorts is a habit more characteristic of the middle and upper classes than of the lower classes.[22] Vidich and Bensman, for the first time in a community study, depicted the life of the lowest-class groups in the community sufficiently well so that the personally functional aspects of withdrawal from the community were revealed.[23] The presumption of inertia permits the researcher to regard the public sector of activity as but one facet of behavior capable of giving people satisfaction, and discourages the inappropriate and arbitrary assignment of upper and middle-class values to all actors in the community.

The presumption of inertia also helps put economic and social notables into perspective. If a man's major life work is banking, the pluralist presumes he will spend his time at the bank, and not in manipulating community decisions. This presumption holds until the banker's activities and participations indicate otherwise. Once again, it is very important to make the point that this assumption is not scientifically equivalent to its opposite. If we presume that the banker is "really" engaged in running the community, there is practically no way of disconfirming this notion, even if it is totally erroneous. On the other hand, it is easy to spot the banker who really *does* run community affairs when we presume he does not, because his activities will make this fact apparent. In the absence of the requisite activities, we have no grounds for asserting that the banker, in fact, does run the community.[24]

The pluralist emphasis on the time-bounded nature of coalitions and on the voluntary aspect of political participation leads to a further

21. See Anthony Downs, *An Economic Theory of Democracy* (New York, 1957); Robert E. Lane, *Political Life: How People Get Involved in Politics* (Glencoe, 1959); Samuel Stouffer, *Communism, Conformity and Civil Liberties* (New York, 1955), pp. 58*ff*.

22. Lane, *op. cit.*, pp. 220–234.

23. Arthur J. Vidich and Joseph Bensman, *Small Town in Mass Society* (Princeton, 1958), pp. 69–70, 290–291. Studies of social status have been hampered by a similar problem of upper-class-centeredness. See the criticism of Warner on this point by Seymour M. Lipset and Reinhard Bendix, "Social Status and Social Structure," *British Journal of Sociology*, 2 (June, 1951), esp. pp. 163*ff*.

24. See Bentley, *op. cit.*, pp. 175–222. Note, at p. 202: "If we can get our social life stated in terms of activity, and of nothing else, we have not indeed succeeded in measuring it, but we have at least reached a foundation upon which a coherent system of measurements can be built up. . . . We shall cease to be blocked by the intervention of unmeasurable elements, which claim to be themselves the real causes of all that is happening, and which by their spook-like arbitrariness make impossible any progress toward dependable knowledge."

contrast with stratification theory, since pluralists hold that the "interest group" and the "public" are the social collectives most relevant to the analysis of political processes. In the sociologist's patois, politically important groups would be called phenomena of "collective behavior" rather than of "social structure."[25] Social classes in stratification theory are populations differentially ranked according to economic or status criteria, which embrace the entire community. Everyone in a community is a member of at least one but no more than one class at any given moment, and no one in the community falls outside the system. This is a legitimate heuristic construction; however, it is a mistake to impute to the apparently inescapable fact of class membership any sort of class consciousness. This sociologists have long recognized.[26] But they seem less willing to grant that it is equally incorrect to presume that those sharing similar market or status positions are also equidistant to all the bases of political power, or in fact share class interests. American society has never been noted for its inter-class warfare, a fact often reported with a great show of surprise in stratification studies of American communities.[27]

Pluralists, who see American society as fractured into a congeries of hundreds of small "special interest" groups, with incompletely overlapping memberships, widely differing power bases, and a multitude of techniques for exercising influence on decisions salient to them,[28] are not surprised at the low priority which Americans give to their class membership as bases of social action. In the decision-making of fragmented government—and American national, state and local governments are nothing if not fragmented—the claims of small, intense minorities are usually attended to.[29] Hence it is not only inefficient but usually unnecessary for entire classes to mobilize when the preferences of class-members are pressed and often satisfied in a piecemeal fashion. The empirical evidence supporting this pluralist doctrine is overwhelming,[30] however much stratification theorists may have missed its sig-

25. Only one sociologist seems to have realized what this implies for the methods and conclusions of political analysis. See Rudolf Heberle, *Social Movements* (New York, 1951). The relevant theory is compactly expounded by Herbert Blumer in "Collective Behavior," in Alfred M. Lee (ed.), *Principles of Sociology* (New York, 1953), pp. 167–220.

26. Indeed, Max Weber, the most important "founding father" of modern stratification analysis, makes just this point. See Weber's "Class, Status, Party," in H. H. Gerth and C. W. Mills (eds.), *From Max Weber: Essays in Sociology* (New York, 1946), pp. 180–195, esp. p. 184.

27. See, for example, Lynd and Lynd, *Middletown in Transition, op. cit.,* pp. 454–455, 509; Alfred W. Jones, *Life, Liberty and Property* (Philadelphia, 1941), pp. 336–354; Warner *et al., op. cit.,* p. 27; C. Wright Mills, "The Middle Classes," *op. cit.* Compare also Richard Centers, *The Psychology of Social Classes* (Princeton, 1948), and note the extent to which his conclusions outrun his data.

28. See, for example, Truman, *op. cit., passim.* Alexis de Tocqueville, *Democracy In America* (New York, 1954), esp. Vol. I, pp. 181–205, 281–342, Vol. II, pp. 114–135.

29. See Robert A. Dahl, *A Preface to Democratic Theory* (Chicago, 1956).

30. Truman, *op. cit.,* summarizes a tremendous amount of this material.

nificance for them, namely, that the fragmentation of American governmental decision-making and of American society makes class consciousness inefficient, and, in most cases, makes the political interests of members of the same class different.

Pluralist research is not interested in ascertaining an actor's ranking in a system presumed to operate hierarchically. Rather, pluralists want to find out about leadership *roles*, which are presumed to be diverse and fluid, both within a single issue-area over time, and as between issue-areas. Long and Belknap, for example, identify the following leadership roles in community decision-making: Initiation, Staffing and Planning, Communication and Publicity, Intra-élite Organizing, Financing and Public Sanctioning.[31]

By describing and specifying leadership roles in concrete situations, pluralists are in a position to determine the extent to which power structure exists. If there exist high degrees of overlap among issue-areas in decision-making personnel, or of institutionalization in the bases of power in specified issue-areas, or of regularity in the procedures of decision-making, then the empirical conclusion is justified that some sort of a "power structure" exists. By specifying leadership roles and activities, the pluralist research strategy makes it possible for an empirical determination of the bounds and durability of a community "power structure"—if one exists—to be described, and the stratification theory presumption that community power is necessarily general and relatively immutable can be discarded as arbitrary.

The final contrast I want to make between the pluralist and stratification methods has to do with their differing conceptions of what is meant by "power." I have already noted that stratification theorists emphasize the cataloguing of power bases, meaning the resources available to actors for the exercise of power.[32] Pluralists, on the other hand, concentrate on power exercise itself. This leads to two subsidiary discoveries. First, there are a great many different kinds of resources which can be turned to use in the process of community decision-making—many more resources, in fact, than stratification theorists customarily take account of. One list, for example, includes: money and credit; control over jobs; control over the information of others; social standing; knowledge and expertness; popularity, esteem and charisma; legality, constitutionality and officiality; ethnic solidarity; and the right to vote.[33]

The second product of the pluralist emphasis on power exercise

31. Long and Belknap, *op. cit.*, pp. 9–11. See Polsby, "The Sociology of Community Power," *op. cit.*, and Edward C. Banfield, "The Concept 'Leadership' in Community Research" (delivered at the meeting of the American Political Science Association, 1958), for similar lists.

32. In papers cited in note 9 above.

33. Robert A. Dahl, "The Analysis of Influence in Local Communities" (May, 1959), mimeo., p. 10.

is the discovery that resources are employed only with variations in degree of skill. The elaboration of the ways in which resources are employed enables the pluralist researcher to pay attention to what practical politicians customarily see as the heart of their own craft: the processes of bargaining, negotiation, salesmanship and brokerage, and of leadership in mobilizing resources of all kinds. This approach also makes possible a more realistic evaluation of the actual disposable resources of actors. A corporation may be worth millions of dollars, but its policies and liquidity position may be such that it cannot possibly bring those monetary resources into play in order to influence the outcome of a community decision—even one in which the corporation is vitally interested. And interest itself, as noted above, is differentially distributed in a pattern which pluralists assume is rational for most actors, most of the time. For example, Long and Belknap observe:

> Just as business organizations may be disinterested in community affairs because of the national scope of its (sic) operations, individual businessmen who move or are shifted from city to city may have little opportunity or incentive to participate in community affairs. Some businesses have strong pressures on them to give attention to community and metropolitan problems. Large department stores are particularly tied up with the destiny of the city and must decide whether to keep to the central city or decentralize in suburban shopping centers. Businessmen with a "metropolitan view" would thus be expected to be found here rather than in the branch office of a national corporation.[34]

What practical recommendations emerge from this comparison of stratification and pluralist approaches to the study of community power?[35] First, the researcher should pick issue-areas as the focus of his study of community power. Second, he should be able to defend these issue-areas as being very important in the life of the community. Third, he should study actual behavior, either at first hand, or by reconstructing behavior from documents, informants, newspapers and other appropriate sources. There is no harm in starting with a list of people whose behavior the researcher wishes to study *vis-à-vis* any issue-area. The harm comes, rather, in attributing some mystical significance to such a list so that the examination of activity and of actual participation in decision-making becomes superfluous. This recommendation is not meant to discourage the researcher from collecting information about the reputation of actors, or their intentions with respect to community issues, or their evaluations about the "meanings" of community incidents. All of these kinds of data are of immeasurable value in tracing patterns of decision-making. However, these cultural data

34. Long and Belknap, *op. cit.*, pp. 13-14. This corresponds to the findings—but not the interpretations—of Schulze, *op. cit.*, and of Pellegrin and Coates, *op. cit.*

35. This presumes that the researcher wants to make some generalizations about the "normal" distributions of power in community decision-making.

must be accompanied by information about behavior so that the researcher has some way of distinguishing between myths and facts.

The final recommendation is of the same order: researchers should study the outcomes of actual decisions within the community. It is important, but insufficient, to know what leaders want to do, what they intend to do, and what they think they can do. The researcher still has to decide on the basis of his own examination of the facts what actually emerges from these various intentions, and not conclude prematurely that the combination of intentions and resources inflexibly predetermines outcomes.

Power as Non-Decision-Making

Peter Bachrach and
Morton S. Baratz

THE CONCEPT of power remains elusive despite the recent and prolific outpourings of case studies on community power.[1] Its elusiveness is dramatically demonstrated by the regularity of disagreement as to the locus of community power between the sociologists and the political scientists. Sociologically oriented researchers have consistently found that power is highly centralized, while scholars trained in political science have just as regularly concluded that in "their" communities power is widely diffused.[2] Presumably, this explains why the latter group styles itself "pluralist," its counterpart "elitist."

There seems no room for doubt that the sharply divergent findings of the two groups are the product, not of sheer coincidence, but of fundamental differences in both their underlying assumptions and research methodology. The political scientists have contended that these differences in findings can be explained by the faulty approach and presuppositions of the sociologists. We contend in this paper that the pluralists themselves have not grasped the whole truth of the matter; that while their criticisms of the elitists are sound, they, like the elitists, utilize an approach and assumptions which predetermine their con-

1. This paper is an outgrowth of a seminar in Problems of Power in Contemporary Society, conducted jointly by the authors for graduate students and undergraduate majors in political science and economics.

2. Compare, for example, the sociological studies of Floyd Hunter, *Community Power Structure* (Chapel Hill, 1953); Roland Pellegrini and Charles H. Coates, "Absentee-Owned Corporations and Community Power Structure," *American Journal of Sociology*, Vol. 61 (March 1956), pp. 413–19; and Robert O. Schulze, "Economic Dominants and Community Power Structure," *American Sociological Review*, Vol. 23 (February 1958), pp. 3–9; with political science studies of Wallace S. Sayre and Herbert Kaufman, *Governing New York City* (New York, 1960); Robert A. Dahl, *Who Governs?* (New Haven, 1961); and Norton E. Long and George Belknap, "A Research Program on Leadership and Decision-Making in Metropolitan Areas" (New York, Governmental Affairs Institute, 1956). See also Nelson W. Polsby, "How to Study Community Power: The Pluralist Alternative," *Journal of Politics*, Vol. 22 (August, 1960), pp. 474–84.

Reprinted from The American Political Science Review, *December, 1962, pp. 947–952, where it appeared under the title "Two Faces of Power," by permission of the publisher and the authors.*

clusions. Our argument is cast within the frame of our central thesis: that there are two faces of power, neither of which the sociologists see and only one of which the political scientists see.

I

Against the elitist approach to power several criticisms may be, and have been levelled.[3] One has to do with its basic premise that in every human institution there is an ordered system of power, a "power structure" which is an integral part and the mirror image of the organization's stratification. This postulate the pluralists emphatically—and, to our mind, correctly—reject, on the ground that

> nothing categorical can be assumed about power in any community. . . . If anything, there seems to be an unspoken notion among pluralist researchers that at bottom *nobody* dominates in a town, so that their first question is not likely to be, "Who runs this community?," but rather, "Does anyone at all run this community?" The first query is somewhat like, "Have you stopped beating your wife?," in that virtually any response short of total unwillingness with a "power elite" along the lines presupposed by the stratification theory.[4]

Equally objectionable to the pluralists—and to us—is the sociologists' hypothesis that the power structure tends to be stable over time.

> Pluralists hold that power may be tied to issues, and issues can be fleeting or persistent, provoking coalitions among interested groups and citizens, ranging in their duration from momentary to semi-permanent. . . . To presume that the set of coalitions which exists in the community at any given time is a timelessly stable aspect of social structure is to introduce systematic inaccuracies into one's description of social reality.[5]

A third criticism of the elitist model is that it wrongly equates reputed with actual power:

> If a man's major life work is banking, the pluralist presumes he will spend his time at the bank, and not in manipulating community decisions. This presumption holds until the banker's activities and participations indicate otherwise. . . . If we presume that the banker is "really" engaged in running the community, there is practically no way of disconfirming this notion, even if it is totally erroneous. On the other hand, it is easy to spot the banker who really *does* run community affairs when we presume he does not, because his activities will make this fact apparent.[6]

3. See especially N. W. Polsby, *op. cit.,* p. 475f.
4. *Ibid.,* pp. 476.
5. *Ibid.,* pp. 478–79.
6. *Ibid.,* pp. 480–81.

This is not an exhaustive bill of particulars; there are flaws other than these in the sociological model and methodology[7]—including some which the pluralists themselves have not noticed. But to go into this would not materially serve our current purposes. Suffice it simply to observe that whatever the merits of their own approach to power, the pluralists have effectively exposed the main weaknesses of the elitist model.

As the foregoing quotations make clear, the pluralists concentrate their attention, not upon the sources of power, but its exercise. Power to them means "participation in decision-making"[8] and can be analyzed only after "careful examination of a series of concrete decisions."[9] As a result, the pluralist researcher is uninterested in the reputedly powerful. His concerns instead are to (a) select for study a number of "key" as opposed to "routine" political decisions, (b) identify the people who took an active part in the decision-making process, (c) obtain a full account of their actual behavior while the policy conflict was being resolved, and (d) determine and analyze the specific outcome of the conflict.

The advantages of this approach, relative to the elitist alternative, need no further exposition. The same may not be said, however, about its defects—two of which seem to us to be of fundamental importance. One is that the model takes no account of the fact that power may be, and often is, exercised by confining the scope of decision-making to relatively "safe" issues. The other is that the model provides no *objective* criteria for distinguishing between "important" and "unimportant" issues arising in the political arena.

II

There is no gainsaying that an analysis grounded entirely upon what is specific and visible to the outside observer is more "scientific" than one based upon pure speculation. To put it another way,

> If we can get our social life stated in terms of activity, and of nothing else, we have not indeed succeeded in measuring it, but we have at least reached a foundation upon which a coherent system of measurements can be built up. . . . We shall cease to be blocked by the intervention of unmeasurable elements, which claim to be themselves the real causes of

7. See especially Robert A. Dahl, "A Critique of the Ruling-Elite Model," this REVIEW, Vol. 52 (June 1958), pp. 463–69; and Lawrence J. R. Herson, "In the Footsteps of Community Power," this REVIEW, Vol. 55 (December 1961), pp. 817–31.

8. This definition originated with Harold D. Lasswell and Abraham Kaplan, *Power and Society* (New Haven, 1950), p. 75.

9. Robert A. Dahl, "A Critique of the Ruling-Elite Model," *loc. cit.*, p. 466.

all that is happening, and which by their spook-like arbitrariness make impossible any progress toward dependable knowledge.[10]

The question is, however, how can one be certain in any given situation that the "unmeasurable elements" are inconsequential, are not of decisive importance? Cast in slightly different terms, can a sound concept of power be predicated on the assumption that power is totally embodied and fully reflected in "concrete decisions" or in activity bearing directly upon their making?

We think not. Of course power is exercised when A participates in the making of decisions that affect B. But power is also exercised when A devotes his energies to creating or reinforcing social and political values and institutional practices that limit the scope of the political process to public consideration of only those issues which are comparatively innocuous to A. To the extent that A succeeds in doing this, B is prevented, for all practical purposes, from bringing to the fore any issues that might in their resolution be seriously detrimental to A's set of preferences.[11]

Situations of this kind are common. Consider, for example, the case—surely not unfamiliar to this audience—of the discontented faculty member in an academic institution headed by a tradition-bound executive. Aggrieved about a long-standing policy around which a strong vested interest has developed, the professor resolves in the privacy of his office to launch an attack upon the policy at the next faculty meeting. But, when the moment of truth is at hand, he sits frozen in silence. Why? Among the many possible reasons, one or more of these could have been of crucial importance: (a) the professor was fearful that his intended action would be interpreted as an expression of his disloyalty to the institution; or (b) he decided that, given the beliefs and attitudes of his colleagues on the faculty, he would almost certainly constitute on this issue a minority of one; or (c) he concluded that, given the nature of the law-making process in the institution, his proposed remedies would be pigeonholed permanently. But whatever the case, the central point to be made is the same: to the extent that a person or group—consciously or unconsciously—creates or reinforces barriers to the public airing of policy conflicts, that person or group has power. Or, as Professor Schattschneider has so admirably put it:

10. Arthur Bentley, *The Process of Government* (Chicago, 1908), p. 202, quoted in Polsby, *op. cit.,* p. 481n.

11. As is perhaps self-evident, there are similarities in both faces of power. In each, A participates in decisions and thereby adversely affects B. But there is an important difference between the two: in the one case, A openly participates; in the other, he participates only in the sense that he works to sustain those values and rules of procedure that help him keep certain issues out of the public domain. True enough, participation of the second kind may at times be overt; that is the case, for instance, in cloture fights in the Congress. But the point is that it need not be. In fact, when the maneuver is most successfully executed, it neither involves nor can be identified with decisions arrived at on specific issues.

> All forms of political organization have a bias in favor of the exploitation of some kinds of conflict and the suppression of others because *organization is the mobilization of bias.* Some issues are organized into politics while others are organized out.[12]

Is such bias not relevant to the study of power? Should not the student be continuously alert to its possible existence in the human institution that he studies, and be ever prepared to examine the forces which brought it into being and sustain it? Can he safely ignore the possibility, for instance, that an individual or group in a community participates more vigorously in supporting the *nondecision-making* process than in participating in actual decisions within the process? Stated differently, can the researcher overlook the chance that some person or association could limit decision-making to relatively non-controversial matters, by influencing community values and political procedures and rituals, notwithstanding that there are in the community serious but latent power conflicts?[13] To do so is, in our judgment, to overlook the less apparent, but nonetheless extremely important, face of power.

III

In his critique of the "ruling-elite model," Professor Dahl argues that "the hypothesis of the existence of a ruling elite can be strictly tested only if . . . [t] here is a fair sample of cases involving key political decisions in which the preferences of the hypothetical ruling elite run counter to those of any other likely group that might be suggested."[14] With this assertion we have two complaints. One we have already discussed, viz., in erroneously assuming that power is solely reflected in concrete decisions, Dahl thereby excludes the possibility that in the community in question there is a group capable of preventing contests from arising on issues of importance to it. Beyond that, however, by ignoring the less apparent face of power Dahl and those who accept his pluralist approach are unable adequately to differentiate between a "key" and a "routine" political decision.

12. E. E. Schattschneider, *The Semi-Sovereign People* (New York, 1960), p. 71.

13. Dahl *partially* concedes this point when he observes ("A Critique of the Ruling-Elite Model," pp. 468–69) that "one could argue that even in a society like ours a ruling elite might be so influential over ideas, attitudes, and opinions that a kind of false consensus will exist—not the phony consensus of a terroristic totalitarian dictatorship but the manipulated and superficially self-imposed adherence to the norms and goals of the elite by broad sections of a community. . . . This objection points to the need to be circumspect in interpreting the evidence." But that he largely misses our point is clear from the succeeding sentence: "Yet here, too, it seems to me that the hypothesis cannot be satisfactorily confirmed without something equivalent to the test I have proposed," and that is "by an examination of a series of concrete *cases* where key decisions are made. . . ."

14. *Op. cit.,* p. 466.

Nelson Polsby, for example, proposes that "by pre-selecting as issues for study those which are generally agreed to be significant, pluralist researchers can test stratification theory."[15] He is silent, however, on how the researcher is to determine *what* issues are "generally agreed to be significant," and on how the researcher is to appraise the reliability of the agreement. In fact, Polsby is guilty here of the same fault he himself has found with elitist methodology: by presupposing that in any community there are significant issues in the political arena, he takes for granted the very question which is in doubt. He accepts as issues what are reputed to be issues. As a result, his findings are foreordained. For even if there is no "truly" significant issue in the community under study, there is every likelihood that Polsby (or any like-minded researcher) will find one or some and, after careful study, reach the appropriate pluralistic conclusions.[16]

Dahl's definition of "key political issues" in his essay on the ruling-elite model is open to the same criticism. He states that it is "a necessary although possibly not a sufficient condition that the [key] issue should involve actual disagreement in preferences among two or more groups."[17] In our view, this is an inadequate characterization of a "key political issue," simply because groups can have disagreements in preferences on unimportant as well as on important issues. Elite preferences which border on the indifferent are certainly not significant in determining whether a monolithic or polylithic distribution of power prevails in a given community. Using Dahl's definition of "key political issues," the researcher would have little difficulty in finding such in practically any community; and it would not be surprising then if he ultimately concluded that power in the community was widely diffused.

The distinction between important and unimportant issues, we believe, cannot be made intelligently in the absence of an analysis of the "mobilization of bias" in the community; of the dominant values and the political myths, rituals, and institutions which tend to favor the vested interests of one or more groups, relative to others. Armed with this knowledge, one could conclude that any challenge to the predominant values or to the established "rules of the game" would constitute an "important" issue; all else, unimportant. To be sure, judgments of this kind cannot be entirely objective. But to avoid making them in a study of power is both to neglect a highly significant aspect of power and thereby to undermine the only sound basis for discriminating between "key" and "routine" decisions. In effect, we contend, the pluralists have made each of these mistakes; that is to say, they have done just that for which Kaufman and Jones so severely taxed Floyd Hunter:

15. *Op. cit.*, p. 478.
16. As he points out, the expectation of the pluralist researchers "have seldom been disappointed." (*Ibid.*, p. 477).
17. *Op. cit.*, p. 467.

they have begun "their structure at the mezzanine without showing us a lobby or foundation,"[18] *i.e.*, they have begun by studying the issues rather than the values and biases that are built into the political system and that, for the student of power, give real meaning to those issues which do enter the political arena.

IV

There is no better fulcrum for our critique of the pluralist model than Dahl's recent study of power in New Haven.[19]

At the outset it may be observed that Dahl does not attempt in this work to define his concept, "key political decision." In asking whether the "Notables" of New Haven are "influential overtly or covertly in the making of government decisions," he simply states that he will examine "three different 'issue-areas' in which important public decisions are made: nominations by the two political parties, urban redevelopment, and public education." These choices are justified on the grounds that "nominations determine which persons will hold public office. The New Haven redevelopment program measured by its cost— present and potential—is the largest in the country. Public education, aside from its intrinsic importance, is the costliest item in the city's budget." Therefore, Dahl concludes, "It is reasonable to expect . . . that the relative influence over public officials wielded by the . . . Notables would be revealed by an examination of their participation in these three areas of activity."[20]

The difficulty with this latter statement is that it is evident from Dahl's own account that the Notables are in fact uninterested in two of the three "key" decisions he has chosen. In regard to the public school issue, for example, Dahl points out that many of the Notables live in the suburbs and that those who do live in New Haven choose in the main to send their children to private schools. "As a consequence," he writes, "their interest in the public schools is ordinarily rather slight."[21] Nominations by the two political parties as an important "issue-area," is somewhat analogous to the public schools, in that the apparent lack of interest among the Notables in this issue is partially accounted for by their suburban residence—because of which they are disqualified from holding public office in New Haven. Indeed, Dahl himself concedes that with respect to both these issues the Notables are largely indifferent: "Business leaders might ignore the public schools

18. Herbert Kaufman and Victor Jones, "The Mystery of Power," *Public Administration Review*, Vol. 14 (Summer 1954), p. 207.

19. Robert A. Dahl, *Who Governs?* (New Haven, 1961).

20. *Ibid.*, p. 64.

21. *Ibid.*, p. 70.

or the political parties without any sharp awareness that their indifference would hurt their pocketbooks . . ." He goes on, however, to say that

> the prospect of profound changes [as a result of the urban-redevelopment program] in ownership, physical layout, and usage of property in the downtown area and the effects of these changes on the commercial and industrial prosperity of New Haven were all related in an obvious way to the daily concerns of businessmen.[22]

Thus, if one believes—as Professor Dahl did when he wrote his critique of the ruling-elite model—that an issue, to be considered as important, "should involve actual disagreement in preferences among two or more groups,"[23] then clearly he has now for all practical purposes written off public education and party nominations as key "issue-areas." But this point aside, it appears somewhat dubious at best that "the relative influence over public officials wielded by the Social Notables" can be revealed by an examination of their nonparticipation in areas in which they were not interested.

Furthermore, we would not rule out the possibility that even on those issues to which they appear indifferent, the Notables may have a significant degree of *indirect* influence. We would suggest, for example, that although they send their children to private schools, the Notables do recognize that public school expenditures have a direct bearing upon their own tax liabilities. This being so, and given their strong representation on the New Haven Board of Finance,[24] the expectation must be that it is in their direct interest to play an active role in fiscal policy-making, in the establishment of the educational budget in particular. But as to this, Dahl is silent: he inquires not at all into either the decisions made by the Board of Finance with respect to education nor into their impact upon the public schools.[25] Let it be understood clearly that in making these points we are not attempting to refute Dahl's contention that the Notables lack power in New Haven. What we *are* saying, however, is that this conclusion is not adequately supported by his analysis of the "issue-areas" of public education and party nominations.

The same may not be said of redevelopment. This issue is by any

22. *Ibid.,* p. 71.
23. *Op. cit.,* p. 467.
24. *Who Governs?,* p. 82. Dahl points out that "the main policy thrust of the Economic Notables is to oppose tax increases; this leads them to oppose expenditures for anything more than minimal traditional city services. In this effort their two most effective weapons ordinarily are the mayor and the Board of Finance. The policies of the Notables are most easily achieved under a strong mayor if his policies coincide with theirs or under a weak mayor if they have the support of the Board of Finance. . . . New Haven mayors have continued to find it expedient to create confidence in their financial policies among businessmen by appointing them to the Board." (pp. 81-2).
25. Dahl does discuss in general terms (pp. 79-84) changes in the level of tax rates and assessments in past years, but not actual decisions of the Board of Finance or their effects on the public school system.

reasonable standard important for purposes of determining whether New Haven is ruled by "the hidden hand of an economic elite."[26] For the Economic Notables have taken an active interest in the program and, beyond that, the socio-economic implications of it are not necessarily in harmony with the basic interests and values of businesses and businessmen.

In an effort to assure that the redevelopment program would be acceptable to what he dubbed "the biggest muscles" in New Haven, Mayor Lee created the Citizens Action Commission (CAC) and appointed to it primarily representatives of the economic elite. It was given the function of overseeing the work of the mayor and other officials involved in redevelopment, and, as well, the responsibility for organizing and encouraging citizens' participation in the program through an extensive committee system.

In order to weigh the relative influence of the mayor, other key officials, and the members of the CAC, Dahl reconstructs "all the *important* decisions on redevelopment and renewal between 1950–58 . . . [to] determine which individuals most often initiated the proposals that were finally adopted or most often successfully vetoed the proposals of the others."[27] The results of this test indicate that the mayor and his development administrator were by far the most influential, and that the "muscles" on the Commission, excepting in a few trivial instances, "never directly initiated, opposed, vetoed, or altered any proposal brought before them. . . ."[28]

This finding is, in our view, unreliable, not so much because Dahl was compelled to make a subjective selection of what constituted *important* decisions within what he felt to be an *important* "issue-area," as because the finding was based upon an excessively narrow test of influence. To measure relative influence solely in terms of the ability to initiate and veto proposals is to ignore the possible exercise of influence or power in limiting the scope of initiation. How, that is to say, can a judgment be made as to the relative influence of Mayor Lee and the CAC without knowing (through prior study of the political and social views of all concerned) the proposals that Lee did *not* make because he anticipated that they would provoke strenuous opposition and, perhaps, sanctions on the part of the CAC?[29]

In sum, since he does not recognize *both* faces of power, Dahl is in

26. *Ibid.*, p. 124.

27. *Ibid.* "A rough test of a person's overt or covert influence," Dahl states in the first section of the book, "is the frequency with which he successfully initiates an important policy over the opposition of others, or vetoes policies initiated by others, or initiates a policy where no opposition appears." (*Ibid.*, p. 66)

28. *Ibid.*, p. 131.

29. Dahl is, of course, aware of the "law of anticipated reactions." In the case of the mayor's relationship with the CAC, Dahl notes that Lee was "particularly skillful in estimating what the CAC could be expected to support or reject." (p. 137). However, Dahl was not interested in analyzing or appraising to what extent the CAC limited

no position to evaluate the relative influence or power of the initiator and decision-maker, on the one hand, and of those persons, on the other, who may have been indirectly instrumental in preventing potentially dangerous issues from being raised.[30] As a result, he unduly emphasizes the importance of initiating, deciding and vetoing, and in the process casts the pluralist conclusions of his study into serious doubt.

V

We have contended in this paper that a fresh approach to the study of power is called for, an approach based upon a recognition of the two faces of power. Under this approach the researcher would begin—not, as does the sociologist who asks, "Who rules?" nor as does the pluralist who asks, "Does anyone have power?"—but by investigating the particular "mobilization of bias" in the institution under scrutiny. Then, having analyzed the dominant values, the myths and the established political procedures and rules of the game, he would make a careful inquiry into which persons or groups, if any, gain from the existing bias and which, if any, are handicapped by it. Next, he would investigate the dynamics of *non-decision-making;* that is, he would examine the extent to which and the manner in which the *status quo* oriented persons and groups influence those community values and those political institutions (as, *e.g.*, the unanimity "rule" of New York City's Board of Estimate[31]) which tend to limit the scope of actual decision-making to "safe" issues. Finally, using his knowledge of the

Lee's freedom of action. Because of his restricted concept of power, Dahl did not consider that the CAC might in this respect have exercised power. That the CAC did not initiate or veto actual proposals by the mayor was to Dahl evidence enough that the CAC was virtually powerless; it might as plausibly be evidenced that the CAC was (in itself or in what it represented) so powerful that Lee ventured nothing it would find worth quarreling with.

30. The fact that the initiator of decisions also refrains—because he anticipates adverse reactions—from initiating other proposals does not obviously lessen the power of the agent who limited his initiative powers. Dahl missed this point. "It is," he writes, "all the more improbable, then, that a secret cabal of Notables dominates the public life of New Haven through means so clandestine that not one of the fifty prominent citizens interviewed in the course of this study—citizens who had participated extensively in various decisions—hinted at the existence of such a cabal . . ." (p. 185).

In conceiving of elite domination exclusively in the form of a conscious cabal exercising the power of decision-making and vetoing, he overlooks a more subtle form of domination; one in which those who actually dominate are not conscious of it themselves, simply because their position of dominance has never seriously been challenged.

31. Sayre and Kaufman, *op. cit.*, p. 640. For perceptive study of the "mobilization of bias" in a rural American community, see Arthur Vidich and Joseph Bensman, *Small Town in Mass Society* (Princeton, 1958).

restrictive face of power as a foundation for analysis and as a standard for distinguishing between "key" and "routine" political decisions, the researcher would, after the manner of the pluralists, analyze participation in decision-making of concrete issues.

We reject in advance as unimpressive the possible criticism that this approach to the study of power is likely to prove fruitless because it goes beyond an investigation of what is objectively measurable. In reacting against the subjective aspects of the sociological model of power, the pluralists have, we believe, made the mistake of discarding "unmeasurable elements" as unreal. It is ironical that, by so doing, they have exposed themselves to the same fundamental criticism they have so forcefully levelled against the elitists: their approach to and assumptions about power predetermine their findings and conclusions.

The Local Community as an Ecology of Games

Norton E. Long

THE LOCAL COMMUNITY whether viewed as a polity, an economy, or a society presents itself as an order in which expectations are
met and functions performed. In some cases, as in a new, company-
planned mining town, the order is the willed product of centralized
control, but for the most part the order is the product of a history rather
than the imposed effect of any central nervous system of the community. For historic reasons we readily conceive the massive task of
feeding New York to be achieved through the unplanned, historically
developed co-operation of thousands of actors largely unconscious of
their collaboration to this individually unsought end. The efficiency of
this system is attested to by the extraordinary difficulties of the War
Production Board and Service of Supply in accomplishing similar logisti-
cal objectives through an explicit system of orders and directives. Insofar as conscious rationality plays a role, it is a function of the parts
rather than the whole. Particular structures working for their own ends
within the whole may provide their members with goals, strategies, and
roles that support rational action. The results of the interaction of the
rational strivings after particular ends are in part collectively functional if unplanned. All this is the well-worn doctrine of Adam Smith,
though one need accept no more of the doctrine of beneficence than
that an unplanned economy can function.

While such a view is accepted for the economy, it is generally
rejected for the polity. Without a sovereign, Leviathan is generally
supposed to disintegrate and fall apart. Even if Locke's more hopeful
view of the naturalness of the social order is taken, the polity seems
more of a contrived artifact than the economy. Furthermore, there is
both the hangover of Austinian sovereignty and the Greek view of

Reprinted from American Journal of Sociology, *64, No. 3 (November, 1958), 251–
261, by permission of The University of Chicago Press.*

*This paper is largely based on a year of field study in the Boston Metro-
politan area made possible by grants from the Stern Family Foundation and the
Social Science Research Council. The opinions and conclusion expressed are
those of the author alone.*

ethical primacy to make political institutions seem different in kind and ultimately inclusive in purpose and for this reason to give them an over-all social directive end. To see political institutions as the same kind of thing as other institutions in society rather than as different, superior, and inclusive (both in the sense of being sovereign and ethically more significant) is a form of relativistic pluralism that is difficult to enter-tain. At the local level, however, it is easier to look at the municipal government, its departments, and the agencies of state and national government as so many institutions, resembling banks, newspapers, trade unions, chambers of commerce, churches, etc., occupying a ter-ritorial field and interacting with one another. This interaction can be conceptualized as a system without reducing the interacting institutions and individuals to membership in any single comprehensive group. It is psychologically tempting to envision the local territorial system as a group with a governing "they." This is certainly an existential possibility and one to be investigated. However, frequently, it seems likely, systems are confused with groups, and our primitive need to explain thunder with a theology or a demonology results in the hypostatizing of an angelic or demonic hierarchy. The executive committee of the bour-geoisie and the power elite make the world more comfortable for modern social scientists as the Olympians did for the ancients. At least the latter-day hypothesis, being terrestrial, is in principle researchable, though in practice its metaphysical statement may render it equally immune to mundane inquiry.

Observation of certain local communities makes it appear that inclusive over-all organization for many general purposes is weak or non-existent. Much of what occurs seems to just happen with accidental trends becoming cumulative over time and producing results intended by nobody. A great deal of the communities' activities consist of un-directed co-operation of particular social structures, each seeking par-ticular goals and, in doing so, meshing with others. While much of this might be explained in Adam Smith's terms, much of it could not be explained with a rational, atomistic model of calculating individuals. For certain purposes the individual is a useful way of looking at people; for many others the role-playing member of a particular group is more helpful. Here we deal with the essence of predictability in social affairs. If we know the game being played is baseball and that X is a third base-man, by knowing his position and the game being played we can tell more about X's activities on the field than we could if we examined X as a psychologist or a psychiatrist. If such were not the case, X would belong in the mental ward rather than in a ball park. The behavior of X is not some disembodied rationality but, rather, behavior within an organized group activity that has goals, norms, strategies, and roles that give the very field and ground for rationality. Baseball structures the situation.

It is the contention of this paper that the structured group activities that coexist in a particular territorial system can be looked at as games. These games provide the players with a set of goals that give them a sense of success or failure. They provide them determinate roles and calculable strategies and tactics. In addition, they provide the players with an elite and general public that is in varying degrees able to tell the score. There is a good deal of evidence to be found in common parlance that many participants in contemporary group structures regard their occupations as at least analogous to games. And, at least in the American culture, and not only since Eisenhower, the conception of being on a "team" has been fairly widespread.

Unfortunately, the effectiveness of the term "game" for the purposes of this paper is vitiated by, first, the general sense that games are trivial occupations and, second, by the pre-emption of the term for the application of a calculus of probability to choice or decision in a determinate game situation. Far from regarding games as trivial, the writer's position would be that man is both a game-playing and a game-creating animal, that his capacity to create and play games and take them deadly seriously is of the essence, and that it is through games or activities analogous to game-playing that he achieves a satisfactory sense of significance and a meaningful role.

While the calculability of the game situation is important, of equal or greater importance is the capacity of the game to provide a sense of purpose and a role. The organizations of society and polity produce satisfactions with both their products and their processes. The two are not unrelated, but, while the production of the product may in the larger sense enable players and onlookers to keep score, the satisfaction in the process is the satisfaction of playing the game and the sense in which any activity can be grasped as a game.

Looked at this way, in the territorial system there is a political game, a banking game, a contracting game, a newspaper game, a civic organization game, an ecclesiastical game, and many others. Within each game there is a well-established set of goals whose achievement indicates success or failure for the participants, a set of socialized roles making participant behavior highly predictable, a set of strategies and tactics handed down through experience and occasionally subject to improvement and change, an elite public whose approbation is appreciated, and, finally, a general public which has some appreciation for the standing of the players. Within the game the players can be rational in the varying degrees that the structure permits. At the very least, they know how to behave, and they know the score.

Individuals may play in a number of games, but, for the most part, their major preoccupation is with one, and their sense of major achievement is through success in one. Transfer from one game to another is, of course, possible, and the simultaneous playing of roles in two or more games is an important manner of linking separate games.

Sharing a common territorial field and collaborating for different and particular ends in the achievement of over-all social functions, the players in one game make use of the players in another and are, in turn, made use of by them. Thus the banker makes use of the newspaperman, the politician, the contractor, the ecclesiastic, the labor leader, the civic leader—all to further his success in the banking game—but, reciprocally, he is used to further the others' success in the newspaper, political, contracting, ecclesiastical, labor, and civic games. Each is a piece in the chess game of the other, sometimes a willing piece, but, to the extent that the games are different, with a different end in view.

Thus a particular highway grid may be the result of a bureaucratic department of public works game in which are combined, though separate, a professional highway engineer game with its purposes and critical elite onlookers; a departmental bureaucracy; a set of contending politicians seeking to use the highways for political capital, patronage, and the like; a banking game concerned with bonds, taxes, and the effect of the highways on real estate; newspapermen interested in headlines, scoops, and the effect of highways on the papers' circulation; contractors eager to make money by building roads; ecclesiastics concerned with the effect of highways on their parishes and on the fortunes of the contractors who support their churchly ambitions; labor leaders interested in union contracts and their status as community influentials with a right to be consulted; and civic leaders who must justify the contributions of their bureaus of municipal research or chambers of commerce to the social activity. Each game is in play in the complicated pulling and hauling of siting and constructing the highway grid. A wide variety of purposes is subserved by the activity, and no single over-all directive authority controls it. However, the interrelation of the groups in constructing a highway has been developed over time, and there are general expectations as to the interaction. There are also generalized expectations as to how politicians, contractors, newspapermen, bankers, and the like will utilize the highway situation in playing their particular games. In fact, the knowledge that a banker will play like a banker and a newspaperman like a newspaperman is an important part of what makes the situation calculable and permits the players to estimate its possibilities for their own action in their particular game.

While it might seem that the engineers of the department of public works were the appropriate protagonists for the highway grid, as a general activity it presents opportunities and threats to a wide range of other players who see in the situation consequences and possibilities undreamed of by the engineers. Some general public expectation of the limits of the conduct of the players and of a desirable outcome does provide bounds to the scramble. This public expectation is, of course, made active through the interested solicitation of newspapers, politicians, civic leaders, and others who see in it material for ac-complishing their particular purposes and whose structured roles in fact require the mobilization of broad publics. In a sense the group struggle that Arthur Bentley described in his *Process of Government* is a drama that local publics have been taught to view with a not uncritical taste. The instruction of this taste has been the vocation and business of some of the contending parties. The existence of some kind of over-all public puts general restraints on gamesmanship beyond the norms of the particular games. However, for the players these are to all intents as much a part of the "facts of life" of the game as the sun and the wind.

It is perhaps the existence of some kind of a general public, how-ever rudimentary, that most clearly differentiates the local territorial system from a natural ecology. The five-acre woodlot in which the owls and the field mice, the oaks and the acorns, and other flora and fauna have evolved a balanced system has no public opinion, however rudi-mentary. The co-operation is an unconscious affair. For much of what goes on in the local territorial system co-operation is equally uncon-scious and perhaps, but for the occasional social scientist, unnoticed. This unconscious co-operation, however, like that of the five-acre wood-lot, produces results. The ecology of games in the local territorial system accomplishes unplanned but largely functional results. The games and their players mesh in their particular pursuits to bring about overall results; the territorial system is fed and ordered. Its inhabitants are rational within limited areas and, pursuing the ends of these areas, accomplish socially functional ends.

While the historical development of largely unconscious co-opera-tion between the special games in the territorial system gets certain routine, overall functions performed, the problem of novelty and break-down must be dealt with. Here it would seem that, as in the natural ecology, random adjustment and piecemeal innovation are the normal methods of response. The need or cramp in the system presents itself to the players of the games as an opportunity for them to exploit or a menace to be overcome. Thus a transportation crisis in, say, the threat-ened abandonment of commuter trains by a railroad will bring forth the players of a wide range of games who will see in the situation opportunity for gain or loss in the outcome. While over-all considera-tions will appear in the discussion, the frame of reference and the interpretation of the event will be largely determined by the game the interested parties are principally involved in. Thus a telephone execu-tive who is president of the local chamber of commerce will be playing a civic association, general business game with concern for the prin-cipal dues-payers of the chamber but with a constant awareness of how his handling of this crisis will advance him in his particular league. The politicians, who might be expected to be protagonists of the general interest, may indeed be so, but the sphere of their activity and the glasses through which they see the problem will be determined in great part by the way they see the issue affecting their political game. The generality of this game is to a great extent that of the politician's calculus of votes and interests important to his and his side's success. To be sure, some of what Walter Lippmann has called "the public philosophy" affects both politicians and other game-players. This indicates the existence of roles and norms of a larger, vaguer game with a relevant audience that has some sense of cricket. This potentially mobilizable audience is not utterly without importance, but it provides no sure or adequate basis for support in the particular game that the politician or anyone else is playing. Instead of a set of norms to structure enduring role-playing, this audience provides a cross-pressure for momentary aberrancy from gamesmanship or constitutes just another hazard to be calculated in one's play.

In many cases the territorial system is impressive in the degree of intensity of its particular games, its banks, its newspapers, its downtown stores, its manufacturing companies, its contractors, its churches, its politicians, and its other differentiated, structured, goal-oriented activities. Games go on within the territory, occasionally extending beyond it, though centered in it. But, while the particular games show clarity of goals and intensity, few, if any, treat the territory as their proper object. The protagonists of things in particular are well organized and know what they are about; the protagonists of things in general are few, vague, and weak. Immense staff work will go into the development of a Lincoln Square project, but the twenty-two counties of metropolitan New York have few spokesmen for their over-all common interest and not enough staff to give these spokesmen more substance than that required for a "do-gooding" newspaper editorial. The Port of New York Authority exhibits a disciplined self-interest and a vigorous drive along the lines of its developed historic role. However, the attitude of the Port Authority toward the general problems of the metropolitan area is scarcely different than that of any private corporation. It confines its corporate good citizenship to the contribution of funds for surveys and studies and avoids acceptance of broader responsibility. In fact, spokesmen for the Port vigorously reject the need for any superior level of structured representation of metropolitan interests. The common interest, if such there be, is to be realized through institutional interactions rather than through the self-conscious rationality of a determinate group charged with its formulation and attainment. Apart from the newspaper editorial, the occasional politician, and a few civic leaders the general business of the metropolitan area is scarcely anybody's business, and, except for a few, those who concern themselves with the general problems are pursuing hobbies and causes rather than their own business.

The lack of over-all institutions in the territorial system and the weakness of those that exist insure that co-ordination is largely ecological rather than a matter of conscious rational contriving. In the metropolitan area in most cases there are no over-all economic or social institutions. People are playing particular games, and their playgrounds are less or more than the metropolitan area. But even in a city where the municipal corporation provides an apparent over-all government, the appearance is deceptive. The politicians who hold the offices do not regard themselves as governors of the municipal territory but largely as mediators or players in a particular game that makes use of the other inhabitants. Their roles, as they conceive them, do not approach those of the directors of a TVA developing a territory. The ideology of local government is a highly limited affair in which the officeholders respond to demands and mediate conflicts. They play politics, and politics is vastly different from government if the latter is conceived as the rational, responsible ordering of the community. In part, this is due to the general belief that little government is necessary or that government is a congery of services only different from others because it is paid for by taxes and provided for by civil servants. In part, the separation of economics from politics eviscerates the formal theory of government of most of the substance of social action. Intervention in the really important economic order is by way of piecemeal exception and in deviation from the supposed norm of the separation of politics and economics. This ideal of separation has blocked the development of a theory of significant government action and reduced the politician to the role of registerer of pressure rather than responsible governor of a local political economy. The politics of the community becomes a different affair from its government, and its government is so structured as to provide the effective actors in it neither a sense of general responsibility nor the roles calling for such behavior.

The community vaguely senses that there ought to be a government. This is evidenced in the nomination by newspapers and others of particular individuals as members of a top leadership, a "they" who are periodically called upon to solve community problems and meet community crises. Significantly, the "they" usually are made up of people holding private, not public, office. The pluralism of the society has separated political, ecclesiastical, economic, and social hierarchies from one another so that the ancient union of lords spiritual and temporal is disrupted. In consequence, there is a marked distinction between the status of the holders of political office and the status of the "they" of the newspapers and the power elite of a C. Wright Mills or a Floyd Hunter. The politicians have the formal governmental office that might give them responsible governing roles. However, their lack of status makes it both absurd and presumptuous that they should take themselves so seriously. Who are they to act as lords of creation? Public expectation neither empowers nor demands that they should assume any such confident pose as top community leaders. The latter position is reserved for a rather varying group (in some communities well defined and clear-cut, in others vague and amorphous) of holders for the most part of positions of private power, economic, social, and ecclesiastical. This group, regarded as the top leadership of the community, and analogous to the top management of a corporation, provides both a sense that there are gods in the heavens whose will, if they exercise it, will take care of the community's problems and a set of demons whose misrule accounts for the evil in the world. The "they" fill an office left vacant by the dethronement of absolutism and aristocracy. Unlike the politicians in that "they" are only partially visible and of untested powers, the top leadership provides a convenient rationale for explaining what goes on or does not go on in the community. It is comforting to think that the executive committee of the bourgoisie is exploiting the community or that the beneficent social and economic leaders are wearying themselves and their digestions with civic luncheons in order to bring parking to a congested city.

Usually the question is raised as to whether *de facto* there is a set of informal power-holders running things. A related question is whether community folklore holds that there is, that there should be, and what these informal power-holders should do. Certainly, most newspapermen and other professional "inside dopesters" hold that there is a "they." In fact, these people operate largely as court chroniclers of the doings of the "they." The "they," because they are "they," are newsworthy and fit into a ready-made theory of social causation that is vulgarized widely. However, the same newspaperman who could knowingly open his "bird book" and give you a rundown on the local "Who's Who" would probably with equal and blasphemous candor tell you that "they" were not doing a thing about the city and that "they" were greatly to be blamed for sitting around talking instead of getting things done. Thus, as with most primitive tribes, the idols are both worshiped and beaten, at least verbally. Public and reporters alike are relieved to believe both that there is a "they" to make civic life explicable and also to be held responsible for what occurs. This belief in part creates the role of top leadership and demands that it somehow be filled. It seems likely that there is a social-psychological table of organization of a community that must be filled in order to remove anxieties. Gordon Childe has remarked that man seems to need as much to adjust to an unseen, socially created spiritual environment as to the matter-of-fact world of the senses.

The community needs to believe that there are spiritual fathers, bad or good, who can deal with the dark: in the Middle Ages the peasants combated a plague of locusts by a high Mass and a procession of the clergy who damned the grasshoppers with bell, book, and candle.

The Hopi Indians do a rain dance to overcome a drought. The harassed citizens of the American city mobilize their influentials at a civic luncheon to perform the equivalent and exorcise slums, smog, or unemployment. We smile at the medievals and the Hopi, but our own practices may be equally magical. It is interesting to ask under what circumstances one resorts to DDT and irrigation and why. To some extent it is clear that the ancient and modern practice of civic magic ritual is functional—functional in the same sense as the medicinal placebo. Much of human illness is benign; if the sufferer will bide his time, it will pass. Much of civic ills also cure themselves if only people can be kept from tearing each other apart in the stress of their anxieties. The locusts and the drought will pass. They almost always have.

While ritual activities are tranquilizing anxieties, the process of experimentation and adaptation in the social ecology goes on. The piece-meal responses of the players and the games to the challenges presented by crises provide the social counterpart to the process of evolution and natural selection. However, unlike the random mutation of the animal kingdom, much of the behavior of the players responding within the perspectives of their games is self-conscious and rational, given their ends in view. It is from the over-all perspective of the unintended contribution of their actions to the forming of a new or the restoration of the old ecological balance of the social system that their actions appear almost as random and lacking in purposive plan as the adaptive behavior of the natural ecology.

Within the general area of unplanned, unconscious social process technological areas emerge that are so structured as to promote rational, goal-oriented behavior and meaningful experience rather than mere happen-stance. In these areas group activity may result in cumulative knowledge and self-corrective behavior. Thus problem-solving in the field of public health and sanitation may be at a stage far removed from the older dependence on piecemeal adjustment and random functional innovation. In this sense there are areas in which society, as Julian Huxley suggests in his *The Meaning of Evolution*, has gone beyond evolution. However, these are as yet isolated areas in a world still swayed by magic and, for the most part, carried forward by the logic of unplanned, undirected historical process.

It is not surprising that the members of the "top leadership" of the territorial system should seem to be largely confined to ritual and ceremonial roles. "Top leadership" is usually conceived in terms of status position rather than specifiable roles in social action. The role of a top leader is ill defined and to a large degree unstructured. It is in most cases a secondary role derived from a primary role as corporation executive, wealthy man, powerful ecclesiastic, holder of high social position, and the like. The top-leadership role is derivative from the other and is in most cases a result rather than a cause of status. The primary job is bank president, or president of Standard Oil; as such, one is naturally picked, nominated, and recognized as a member of the top leadership. One seldom forgets that one's primary role, obligation, and source of rational conduct is in terms of one's business. In fact, while one is on the whole pleased at the recognition that membership in the top leadership implies—much as one's wife would be pleased to be included among the ten best-dressed women—he is somewhat concerned about just what the role requires in the expenditure of time and funds. Furthermore, one has a suspicion that he may not know how to dance and could make a fool of himself before known elite and unknown, more general publics. All things considered, however, it it probably a good thing for the business, the contacts are important, and the recognition will be helpful back home, in both senses. In any event, if one's committee service or whatever concrete activity "top leadership" implies proves wearing or unsatisfactory, or if it interferes with business, one can always withdraw.

A fair gauge of the significance of top-leadership roles is the time put into them by the players and the institutionalized support represented by staff. Again and again the interviewer is told that the president of such-and-such an organization is doing a terrific job and literally knocking himself out for such-and-such a program. On investigation a "terrific job" turns out to be a few telephone calls and, possibly, three luncheons a month. The standard of "terrific job" obviously varies widely from what would be required in the business role.

In the matter of staffing, while the corporation, the church, and the government are often equipped in depth, the top-leadership job of port promotion may have little more than a secretary and an agile newspaperman equipped to ghost-write speeches for the boss. While there are cases where people in top-leadership positions make use of staff from their own businesses and from the legal mill with which they do business, this seems largely confined to those top-leadership undertakings that have a direct connection with their business. In general, top-leadership roles seem to involve minor investments of time, staff, and money by territorial elites. The absence of staff and the emphasis on publicity limit the capacity of top leadership for sustained rational action.

Where top leaderships have become well staffed, the process seems as much or more the result of external pressures than of its own volition. Of all the functions of top leadership, that of welfare is best staffed. Much of this is the result of the pressure of the professional social worker to organize a concentration of economic and social power sufficient to permit him to do a job. It is true, of course, that the price of organizing top leadership and making it manageable by the social workers facilitated a reverse control of themselves—a control of whose galling nature Hunter gives evidence. An amusing sidelight on the organization of the "executive committee of the bourgeoisie" is the case of the Cleveland Fifty Club. This club, supposedly, is made up of the fifty most important men in Cleveland. Most middling and even upper executives long for the prestige recognition that membership confers. Reputedly, the Fifty Club was organized by Brooks Emery, while he was director of the Cleveland Council on World Affairs, to facilitate the taxation of business to support that organization. The lead time required to get the august members of the Fifty Club together and their incohesiveness have severely limited its possibilities as a power elite. Members who have tried to turn it to such a purpose report fairly consistent failure.

The example of the Cleveland Fifty Club, while somewhat extreme, points to the need on the part of certain activities in the territorial system for a top leadership under whose auspices they can function. A wide variety of civic undertakings need to organize top prestige support both to finance and to legitimate their activities. The staff man of a bureau of municipal research or the Red Feather Agency cannot proceed on his own; he must have the legitimatizing sponsorship of top influentials. His task may be self-assigned, his perception of the problem and its solution may be his own, but he cannot gain acceptance without mobilizing the influentials. For the success of his game he must assist in creating the game of top leadership. The staff man in the civic field is the typical protagonist of things in general—a kind of entrepreneur of ideas. He fulfils the same role in his area as the stock promoter of the twenties or the Zeckendorfs of urban redevelopment. Lacking both status and a confining organizational basis, he has a socially valuable mobility between the specialized games and hierarchies in the territorial system. His success in the negotiation of a port authority not only provides a plus for his taxpayers federation or his world trade council but may provide a secure and lucrative job for himself.

Civic staff men, ranging from chamber of commerce personnel to college professors and newspapermen, are in varying degrees interchangeable and provide an important network of communication. The staff men in the civic agencies play similar roles to the Cohens and Corcorans in Washington. In each case a set of telephone numbers provides special information and an effective lower-echelon interaction. Consensus among interested professionals at the lower level can result in action programs from below that are bucked up to the prestige level of legitimization. As the Cohens and Corcorans played perhaps the most general and inclusive game in the Washington bureaucracy, so their counterparts in the local territorial system are engaged in the most general action game in their area. Just as the Cohens and Corcorans had to mobilize an effective concentration of top brass to move a program into the action stage, so their counterparts have to mobilize concentrations of power sufficient for their purposes on the local scene.

In this connection it is interesting to note that foundation grants are being used to hire displaced New Deal bureaucrats and college professors in an attempt to organize the influentials of metropolitan areas into self-conscious governing groups. Professional chamber of commerce executives, immobilized by their orthodox ideology, are aghast to see their members study under the planners and heretics from the dogmas of free-enterprise fundamentalism. The attempt to transform the metropolitan appearance of disorder into a tidy territory is a built-in predisposition for the self-constituted staff of the embryonic top metropolitan management. The major disorder that has to be overcome before all others is the lack of order and organization among the "power elite." As in the case of the social workers, there is a thrust from below to organize a "power elite" as a necessary instrument to accomplish the purposes of civic staff men. This is in many ways nothing but a part of the general groping after a territorial government capable of dealing with a range of problems that the existing feudal disintegration of power cannot. The nomination of a top leadership by newspapers and public and the attempt to create such a leadership in fact by civic technicians are due to a recognition that there is a need for a leadership with the status, capacity, and role to attend to the general problems of the territory and give substance to a public philosophy. This involves major changes in the script of the top leadership game and the self-image of its participants. In fact, the insecurity and the situational limitations of their positions in corporations or other institutions that provide the primary roles for top leaders make it difficult to give more substance to what has been a secondary role. Many members of present top leaderships are genuinely reluctant, fearful, and even morally shocked at their positions' becoming that of a recognized territorial government. While there is a general supposition that power is almost instinctively craved, there seems considerable evidence that at least in many of our territorial cultures responsibility is not. Machiavellian *virtu* is an even scarcer commodity among the merchant princes of the present than among their Renaissance predecessors. In addition, the educational systems of school and business do not provide top leaders with the inspiration or the know-how to do more than raise funds and man committees. Politics is frequently regarded with the same disgust as military service by the ancient educated Chinese.

It is possible to translate a check pretty directly into effective power in a chamber of commerce or a welfare agency. However, to translate economic power into more general social or political power, there must be an organized purchasable structure. Where such structures exist, they may be controlled or, as in the case of *condottieri*, gangsters, and politicians, their hire may be uncertain, and the hired force retains its independence. Where businessmen are unwilling or unable to organize their own political machines, they must pay those who do. Sometimes the paymaster rules; at other times he bargains with equals or superiors.

A major protagonist of things in general in the territorial system is the newspaper. Along with the welfare worker, museum director, civic technician, etc., the newspaper has an interest in terms of its broad reading public in agitating general issues and projects. As the chronicler of the great, both in its general news columns and in its special features devoted to society and business, it provides an organizing medium for elites in the territory and provides them with most of their information about things in general and not a little of inside tidbits about how individual elite members are doing. In a sense, the newspaper is the prime mover in setting the territorial agenda. It has a great part in determining what most people will be talking about, what most people will think the facts are, and what most people will regard as the way problems are to be dealt with. While the conventions of how a newspaper is to be run, and the compelling force of some events limit the complete freedom of a paper to select what events and what people its public will attend to, it has great leeway. However, the newspaper is a business and a specialized game even when its reporters are idealists and its publisher rejoices in the title "Mr. Cleveland." The paper does not accept the responsibility of a governing role in its territory. It is a power but only a partially responsible one. The span of attention of its audience and the conventions of what constitute a story give it a crusading role at most for particular projects. Nonetheless, to a large extent it sets the civic agenda.

The story is told of the mayor of a large eastern metropolis who, having visited the three capital cities of his constituents—Rome, Dublin, and Tel Aviv—had proceeded home via Paris and Le Havre. Since his staff had neglected to meet the boat before the press, he was badgered by reporters to say what he had learned on his trip. The unfortunate mayor could not say that he had been on a junket for a good time. Luckily, he remembered that in Paris they had been having an antinoise campaign. Off the hook at last, he told the press that he thought this campaign was a good thing. This gave the newsmen something to write about. The mayor hoped this was the end of it. But a major paper felt in need of a crusade to sponsor and began to harass the mayor about the start of the local antinoise campaign. Other newspapers took up the cry, and the mayor told his staff they were for it—there had to be an antinoise campaign. In short order, businessmen's committees, psychiatrists, and college professors were mobilized to press forward on a broad front the suppression of needless noise. In vindication of administrative rationality it appeared that an antinoise campaign was on a staff list of possibilities for the mayor's agenda but had been discarded by him as politically unfeasible.

The civic technicians and the newspapers have somewhat the same relationship as congressional committee staff and the press. Many members of congressional committee staffs complain bitterly that their professional consciences are seared by the insistent pressure to seek publicity. But they contend that their committee sponsors are only impressed with research that is newsworthy. Congressional committee members point out that committees that do not get publicity are likely to go out of business or funds. The civic agency head all too frequently communicates most effectively with his board through his success in getting newspaper publicity. Many a civic ghost-writer has found his top leader converted to the cause by reading the ghosted speech he delivered at the civic luncheon reported with photographs and editorials in the press. This is even the case where the story appears in the top leader's own paper. The need of the reporters for news and of the civic technicians for publicity brings the participants of these two games together. As in the case of the congressional committee, there is a tendency to equate accomplishment with publicity. For top influentials on civic boards the news clips are an important way of keeping score. This symbiotic relation of newsmen and civic staff helps explain the heavy emphasis on ritual luncheons, committees, and news releases. The nature of the newspapers' concern with a story about people and the working of marvels and miracles puts a heavy pressure for the kind of story that the press likes to carry. It is not surprising that civic staff men should begin to equate accomplishment with their score measured in newspaper victories or that they should succumb to the temptation to impress their sponsors with publicity, salting it to their taste by flattering newspaper tributes to the sponsors themselves. Despite the built-in incapacity of newspapers to exercise a serious governing responsibility in their territories, they are for the most part the only institutions wtih a long-term general territorial interest. In default of a territorial political party or other institution that accepts responsibility for the formulation of a general civic agenda the newspaper is the one game that by virtue of its public and its conventions partly fills the vacuum.

A final game that does in a significant way integrate all the games in the territorial system is the social game. Success in each of the games can in varying degrees be cashed in for social acceptance. The custodians of the symbols of top social standing provide goals that in a sense give all the individual games some common denominator of achievement. While the holders of top social prestige do not necessarily hold either top political or economic power, they do provide meaningful goals for the rest. One of the most serious criticisms of a Yankee aristocracy made by a Catholic bishop was that, in losing faith in their own social values, they were undermining the faith in the whole system of final clubs. It would be a cruel joke if, just as the hard-working upwardly mobile had worked their way to entrance, the progeny of the founders lost interest. The decay of the Union League Club in *By Love Possessed* is a tragedy for more than its members. A common game shared even by the excluded spectators gave a purpose that was functional in its time and must be replaced—hopefully, by a better one. A major motivation for seeking membership in and playing the top-leadership game is the value of the status it confers as a counter in the social game.

Neither the civic leadership game nor the social game makes the territorial ecology over into a structured government. They do, however, provide important ways of linking the individual games and make possible cooperative action on projects. Finally, the social game, in Ruth Benedict's sense, in a general way patterns the culture of the territorial ecology and gives all the players a set of vaguely shared aspirations and common goals.

"Hard" Reporting on
THE NEW YORK TIMES

Paul H. Weaver

EVERY NEWSPAPER arrives at a style (approach, method, and manner) of searching out and reporting the news. Its style is always to some degree, and often primarily, the product of a process of "muddling through," and once a newspaper settles into a style it rarely tries to change it very much. Newspapers avoid major change for good reasons: it can alienate readers; it almost always disrupts the news staff; and many editors, being traditionalists, see little need for it. In the case to be considered here, however, the executives of *The New York Times* made a deliberate and far-reaching effort to introduce a new style of metropolitan reporting. One outcome of this effort was, as planned, to improve the "readability" of local news coverage and to broaden its scope. But another outcome, unintended and largely unforeseen, was a seeming reduction in accuracy and neutrality and therefore in the influence the *Times* itself exerts. Was this, on balance, a good bargain, or did the costs of change exceed the benefits? Inescapably, this issue confronts each of the many newspapers which, like the *Times*, have joined the general trend of the fifties and sixties toward "interpretive" journalism.

The *Times* began this change in 1963, shortly after Arthur Ochs Sulzberger, as president and publisher, assumed responsibility for the management of the newspaper. His immediate predecessors, Orville E. Dryfoos (a brother-in-law) and Arthur Hays Sulzberger (his father), had overseen a decade's gradual alteration of the *Times*'s style of foreign and Washington coverage. For several reasons, however, the metropolitan staff had been more or less exempt from these efforts to increase readability, breadth, and depth. But in 1963, A. M. Rosenthal, who had a distinguished record as a "new-style" foreign correspondent, was chosen as the man to liven up and otherwise improve the *Times*'s metropolitan news.

As metropolitan editor, Rosenthal had some 200 employees under

This article appears for the first time in this book, by permission of the author.

his jurisdiction; of these, about 110 were reporters and 40 were editors and copyreaders. Most of the editors and roughly a third of the reporters looked after specialized subject matter (society, religion, education, real estate, aerospace, and so on), and once hired or assigned, they required comparatively little attention from him. Almost 50 reporters were on general assignment, which meant that they reported news of any kind. (Some of them were kept available, as firemen are, just in case of emergencies; in between "fires" they did odd jobs like following out leads on possible stories and pulling together material for future obituaries, but their real function was to prevent the *Times* from ever being shorthanded.) The other major element of the metropolitan staff was its public-affairs section. Before 1963, there were fewer than ten public-affairs reporters: two or three of them usually reported state politics in Albany, and the rest covered city hall, the political parties and clubs, and (on a less routine basis) the major departments of city government. During his first two years, Rosenthal doubled the number of reporters assigned to New York City politics and government. The city, he thought, needed more and deeper coverage anyway; and the new administration of Mayor John V. Lindsay, which seemed to him to be of special importance not only to New York but also to urban America in general, deserved particularly close scrutiny from the *Times*.

It was with the work of the public-affairs and general-assignment reporters that Rosenthal was most concerned. He was determined to alter their reportorial style by introducing what he called "hard" reporting. Most newspapermen termed this kind of writing "interpretive," but Rosenthal preferred "hard." The word was perhaps more apt than he realized.

In the pre-Rosenthal days the metropolitan staff gathered and reported news in the same way that newspapers generally do. It scrutinized the flood of information that came to the newsroom from outside sources—wire services, press releases, books and articles, even anonymous tipsters—and when something of interest turned up it was usually given to a general-assignment reporter for rewriting or exploration. The primary reliance, however, was on reporters who "covered beats." As an editor of those days once explained, "News breaks through definite channels; it cannot do otherwise. Cover these channels and you catch the news—much like casting a net across a salmon stream."[1] Naturally the structure of the search process to a large extent determined what was found and considered news. And naturally, too, what was considered news to a large extent determined the way facts were selected, organized, and presented to the reader. Tacitly the *Times* defined news as what happened on a reporter's beat during a twenty-four-hour period.

1. Edwin L. James, "The Organization of a Newspaper," *The New York Times; The Newspaper: Its Making and Its Meaning* (New York: Charles Scribner's Sons, 1945), p. 103.

A well-written story was regarded as one which set forth the facts about a happening in order of their descriptive importance and in the most sober, neutral way possible. What good reporting mainly required, therefore, was respect for facts and an instinct for the newsworthy happening. The best reporter was the one who missed the fewest happenings, gathered the most facts, made the fewest errors, and showed the least bias. Usually a reporter served a long apprenticeship before being allowed to report political news on his own. This was not because the *Times* wanted to give him the time to develop a deep understanding of some subject matter: on the contrary, it was held that a capable reporter did not need any special study or substantive knowledge to write an adequate story about almost anything. The long apprenticeship was necessary because the *Times* felt that a record of reliable performance in getting and presenting facts was the best indicator of a reporter's ability. It also gave a reporter time to learn the "territory" —who was who, and what was really new. As one might expect, the best stories were generally given to the senior reporters. These men might not have been the liveliest writers—in fact, they tended to be the dullest—but they had proven their ability to get the facts and to treat them with respect, and that, in those days, was what really mattered.

For this traditional conception of news and news-gathering, Rosenthal substituted "hard" reporting. This, he said,

> is not taking things at their surface value. You try to find the genesis of the thing, the why. What motivates the people involved? Basically, hard reporting is a style of inquiry, an approach to reporting. It has nothing to do with subject matter.

The terminology was somewhat confusing. Newspapermen had generally used the term "hard news" to refer to a story which was about a bona fide happening and accordingly had a news value that did not depend upon mere opinion, certainly not the caprice of an editor or the cunning of a public relations counselor. (At the opposite extreme was the "puff," something passed off as news when it was not, or something manufactured to look like news.) Rosenthal used the word *hard* in an entirely new sense: for him, "hardness" had to do not with an event's claim to being news but rather with the manner in which an event was reported.

For the *Times* metropolitan reporter, the changes "hard" reporting entailed were clear enough. He could no longer confine his attention simply to digging out facts and setting them down. He had to do more than just describe an event: now he had to discuss its significance as well—tell what its causes were, what its effects might be, and how it could bear on the private citizen's concerns—and do so in terms the reader could understand. In order to do this the reporter would have to think and analyze, weigh evidence, and make judgments. In what he wrote he would have to set forth a reasoned argument in support of his conclusions, and he would have to do this in a way that would engage the attention and interest of the reader. Needless to say, a competent "hard" reporter would have to have a very unusual set of qualities. He would have to have a deep understanding of every subject matter on which he reported, the ability to analyze and synthesize, and extraordinary skill as a writer.

More obscure, perhaps, but no less important were the changes "hard" reporting demanded in the structure of the news-gathering process. Because the "hard" reporter had to look beyond the mere happening to the "broad issues and trends" it symbolized, the *Times*' conception of news itself became more inclusive. News could therefore be found in places where it had not been found before, and the beat system accordingly changed. A reporter was still assigned to cover the police department, for example, but he no longer reported "crime"; instead, he concentrated on "the big issues" in law enforcement and the administration of justice—the relationship between mayor and police department, brutality, discrimination, defendants' rights, civilian review, and so on. (The *Times* kept staffers at the various police headquarters to inform the metropolitan desk of criminal happenings, but these were rarely reported in the paper.) Moreover, Rosenthal created several new beats: for the first time, a reporter was assigned to the city departments having responsibility for maintaining the quality of the urban environment—sanitation, parks, air pollution, city planning, and water. Another reporter was assigned to health and hospitals. "Hard" reporting was one reason why the size of the public-affairs staff was doubled. It also accounted for the rehabilitation of the general-assignment reporter, who now began to write stories about topics in urban sociology and anthropology and other aspects of the city which, because they rarely crystallized into a happening, had formerly received little notice in the *Times*.

If "hard" reporting required more reporters, it also required a different kind of reporter. Since news was not only "what happened" on a beat but also anything of "significance," whether expressed by a happening or not, the *Times* reporter needed a broader "news sense" than before. Since more things were potential news, he had to make more judgments about what to report and what to ignore, but his criteria for deciding were less clear-cut and unambiguous. This was true as well of the reporter's judgments concerning what to say in a story and how to say it. Moreover, there was more pressure on reporters in making these decisions, for under Rosenthal what counted was how imaginatively a story was developed and how interestingly it was written. Many of the senior reporters found it difficult and uncongenial to adapt to the demands of "hard" reporting, and Rosenthal relied on them less and less. He also broke tradition by reassigning the aerospace editor as chief political reporter. As older reporters left the paper—which they did in greater numbers than normal—Rosenthal hired many young men with more and better college degrees. These relatively inexperienced reporters began to get many of the best assignments because they were better able to produce "hard" stories and they were more responsive to Rosenthal's purpose.

The role of the metropolitan editor underwent an equivalent change. Previously, his principal job had been to see that beats were properly covered. Rosenthal's conception of news required that he do more than this, for if a "hard" reporter had to make judgments about the meaning of the news, then a "hard" editor had to make judgments about those judgments, and to do this he had to be personally in touch with the scene that was being reported. Rosenthal therefore established a network of personal contacts in the city, just as he had as a foreign correspondent. As metropolitan editor, he told an interviewer,

> I would want to know all the important people involved in making the news. So when I got to New York, I set out to know the mayors, judges, lawyers, theatrical people, and all other important figures in the news. I did this because it's interesting, and I did it because you get stories by knowing these people. I don't see how an editor can judge what is a good story, what isn't, without knowing the people involved. My assistant and I try all the time to think of stories—and the only reason we can do it is that we know the people.

Nor was Rosenthal reluctant to make use of this knowledge. If his predecessors had adopted a laissez-faire attitude toward reporters, he actively involved himself in the process of searching for, making judgments about, and writing the news.

These changes were not without their disadvantages. The *Times*, for example, had always been scrupulously careful not to "boost" political candidates in its news columns. "Hard" reporting put this longstanding practice under strain. Since the news included "big issues" and what was typical (as opposed to the atypical and discrete happening), reporters and editors had to make choices that they had not had to make when news was only what happened on a beat. This meant that there was a better chance that political figures would receive more publicity than their political importance warranted. Thus when Rosenthal decided to do a story on how a neophyte politician campaigns for the Democratic nomination for assemblyman, a by-product was the unexpected nomination of the candidate whom the reporter on the story chose to write about. (The reporter and candidate, incidentally, were old college friends.) To Timesmen brought up in the old tradition, it looked as if the man had been "boosted," as it did to political professionals around town. Rosenthal's view, of ocurse, was that the *Times* had merely taken a look at a typical but neglected aspect of the political process.

In general, "hard" reporting found it difficult to be neutral. Like most serious newspapers, the *Times* had always been reluctant to make explicit assessments of the meaning of the news itself. But making such assessments was one of the defining characteristics of "hard" reporting, and under Rosenthal interpretive statements began to appear "high up" in stories, sometimes even in the lead paragraph or headline. Since there was often room for differences of opinion about what interpretation was the proper one, the *Times* occasionally was in the position of taking sides in its news columns. Sometimes it was suspected of doing so for partisan reasons. Many Democrats, for example, concluded that it "slanted" the news to support Mayor Lindsay. To Rosenthal, who rejected the notion of biased reporting as emphatically as the most traditionalistic Timesman, there was a big difference between "slanting" the news and interpreting it. That he was in personal contact with figures like Lindsay was bound, some thought, to affect his judgment and make him less neutral. But it was, of course, precisely in order to have his judgment affected—that is, to gain a perspective on the big issues as well as on the little facts—that he had established these contacts in the first place.

Perhaps the most important effect of "hard" reporting was its impact on the attitudes and values of reporters. As the ability to write interestingly and to interpret gained in importance, the old values of accuracy, completeness, and neutrality were of necessity cherished somewhat less. This change could be seen in the contrast between the older and younger reporters on the metropolitan staff. The younger ones, most of whom Rosenthal had hired, were better educated than their seniors and seemingly more intelligent. Certainly, as a group, they have proven themselves better writers. But one senses—it is, of course, impossible to provide any objective measure of this—that they are not as deeply attached to the *Times* and do not feel the same fervor for facts.

There can be little doubt that the *Times*'s metropolitan stories are written in a livelier style and are better organized than they used to be. Whether they explain things any better, however, is open to question. Even the "hard" reporter gets almost all his information from the people involved in the events and institutions he covers. His interpretation, far from being an original conclusion that he himself draws, is almost invariably an amalgam of *their* views. Thus the "hard" reporter's interpretation rarely goes beyond the conventional wisdom on the subject under consideration. There are several reasons why a reporter's interpretation cannot be really serious (perhaps one should say really "hard" as opposed to merely brittle). First, no newspaper, not even the lavishly staffed *Times*, can afford a reporter the large amount of time and assistance required for a really serious report. Second, even if the reporter were given the necessary time and assistance, he would not in most cases have the special knowledge and talents needed to produce something really serious. Indeed, even the most highly educated academic experts rarely have the information, understanding, judgment, and expository skill that the ideal of "hard" reporting presupposes. And in any event, the reporter—even the "good" reporter—demonstrates little inclination for serious reading or thinking. Third, even if he had the time and ability, the reporter would not for long be permitted to offer really "hard" reportage: no newspaper, not even the *Times*, could suffer the consequences of trying its readers' patience with stories that go very far beneath the surface.

If "hard" reporting has not done more than increase somewhat the "readability" of the *Times*, it may have done even this at a price higher than anyone would have wanted to pay. Most longtime observers of New York politics agree that there has been some loss of accuracy and neutrality in *Times* metropolitan affairs coverage. Some might well say that even if the loss is small it is too high a price to pay for any gain in readability. But this loss may not be the full price. A further, indirect consequence may be a decline in the influence of the *Times*. An editor spoke frankly of this to an interviewer:

> What has kept the *Times* what it is, what has made it able to survive all the mergers, is that it was always authoritative and correct, even at the expense, sometimes, of readability. You were forming the opinions of the people in the power structure. . . . By losing authoritativeness, you lose influence in the power structure but gain popular influence. So the changes going on in the *Times* today mean that we're losing the one thing that separates the *Times* from all other newspapers. I'll be interested to find out what you learn from the politicians. If they don't like the *Times* as it is today, we've done a very, very bad thing. Our attempt is most certainly not to oversimplify and distort but only to add readability. It is not impossible to be readable and accurate at the same time, but it is very hard.

In fact, many politicians in New York do think that the *Times* is not as accurate as it used to be. No one can say, of course, whether there has been a gain in "popular influence" sufficient to compensate for whatever loss there may have been in "influence in the power structure." On the whole, however, it seems unlikely that the *Times*'s bargain will prove to be a particularly good one, either for it or for New York. Ultimately the influence of a newspaper arises from the respect people feel for it, and readability, one would think, cannot inspire as much respect as reliability.

Organized Labor in City Politics

Edward C. Banfield and
James Q. Wilson

PERHAPS the most striking thing about the part played by organized labor in city politics is its variety. Some unions want nothing more from city government than assurance that the police will not interfere with pickets during strikes. Others aspire to take possession of the city government and to run it as an adjunct of the union. Between these extreme positions there are many intermediate ones. Which position a union takes depends upon many factors, including its organizational structure, the ideological bent of its leaders, the nature of the industry and of the local economy, and structure of party competition within the city.

The Interest of the Union in Local Affairs

The range of interests that unions have in local affairs is suggested by the findings of Joel Seidman and his associates in their study of six locals in and near Chicago.[1] All six of the locals wanted friendly treatment from police, courts, and city officials, especially in the event of a strike. Beyond that, their goals differed considerably. For example, one local of the United Mine Workers paid practically no attention to local politics; it was in a community consisting entirely of miners who could be depended upon to elect fellow miners to office. Although the leaders of this local were very much interested in politics in the state capital and in Washington—where crucial safety and work regulations were framed—they ignored city and county politics.

At the opposite extreme, locals of the United Steelworkers of America and the United Auto Workers (UAW) felt keenly the need for organized political action at the local level. The Steelworkers were engaged in collective bargaining with a powerful firm under conditions

1. Joel Seidman et al., The Worker Views His Union (Chicago: University of Chicago Press, 1958), pp. 227–236.

Reprinted from City Politics (Cambridge: Harvard University Press, 1965), pp. 277–292, by permission of the publisher.

of mutual hostility and suspicion, and were therefore particularly anxious to retain political support from the local Democratic machine in order to ensure its sympathy or at least neutrality. Many local Steelworkers leaders disliked the machine politicians but felt they could not defeat them or dare to risk alienating them. The UAW, on the other hand, did not need political reinforcement of its collective bargaining position because contracts were not negotiated locally, but nationally. At the same time, however, the UAW leaders desired broader political involvement for what were essentially reasons of ideology rather than union security. Since the motivation was ideological, the choice of party tended to be made on ideological grounds, without reference to what party or what party faction controlled local government.

A local of the plumbers' union, one of the nineteen craft unions associated with the building and construction trades department of the AFL-CIO, was vitally concerned with city political matters. Entry into, and rewards of, the plumbing profession were crucially dependent upon the licensing regulations which control the apprenticeship program and upon building and housing codes. Plumbers, like other building trade unions, must work with whatever party or faction happens to be in power locally in order to get favorable codes and the appointment of sympathetic building and plumbing inspectors. Not infrequently the union approves city inspectors or even nominates them from its own ranks. Furthermore, the city and county government is a prime source of construction contracts. The building trades unions have in common with contractors an interest in seeing that these contracts are large and frequent and that the work is done by private industry rather than by municipal or county employees.

These studies and others lend general support to the familiar observation that with respect to political involvement there is a sharp difference between industrial and craft unions. Industrial unions, with a large membership of unskilled or semiskilled workers in nation-wide industries, are concerned about industry-wide or national wage contracts and with the state and federal welfare measures which redistribute income in favor of lower-income groups. Craft unions, with a membership of well-paid skilled workers in competitive local markets, are concerned about access to the local bureaucracy, sympathetic treatment from local police, and local wages and hours.[2] The industrial union finds itself drawn into national political alliances, in particular with that party which seems most favorable to certain welfare measures; craft unions can and must resist such alignments, for they must not allow ideology to prevent them from working with whatever party or faction is in power locally.

Differences in markets create other differences among union lead-

2. See Richard Baisden, "Labor Unions in Los Angeles Politics," unpublished dissertation, Department of Political Science, University of Chicago, 1958.

ers. The heads of the state and national federations of unions involved in local markets (e.g., building trades unions) have few direct links with rank-and-file members. The local leaders negotiate contracts and service the members; the state and national leaders can maintain their position only by persuading union members that they have common interests which only state or national leaders can service. Legislative campaigns waged in Washington, D.C., are thus often dictated not so much by the felt needs of the rank-and-file worker as by the maintenance needs of high-echelon officials who lack any other relationship with the members.

Unions dealing with national markets, by contrast, are apt to vest a much higher degree of influence in state and national leaders. Industry-wide and nation-wide contract negotiations give national union officials considerable authority over the locals. This bargaining pattern, together with the importance of federal legislation for nation-wide and industry-wide markets, imbues the entire organization with a more "political" or even "ideological" tone. As a result, even the local officials of, for example, the United Auto Workers may have more comprehensive political goals than the national leaders of a building trades union.

Given these differences, however, it is nontheless true that local union leaders are generally less ideological than national ones. Where the leader's contact with the members is direct, ideology is typically of minor importance. If the industry is still unorganized, the leaders will be absorbed in establishing themselves as the bargaining agents of the workers and in arranging for the security of the union. Once the industry and the city are organized, however, other activities must be found for local unions. In the case of many craft unions, these other activities consist largely in enforcing agreements and supervising work conditions and job assignments—particularly when, as with the building trades, work is done on widely scattered sites by small groups of workers hired on a contract basis by small, highly competitive contractors. In the case of industrial unions,[3] the leaders must devise other services.

These other services, while something more than a concern for wages and hours, are usually a good deal less than an active involvement in local politics. Where industry-wide contracts have eliminated local wage negotiations, the development of local welfare services becomes even more important.[4] These day-to-day services—often of crucial importance in ensuring the re-election of local officers—include handling individual grievances, providing free legal advice, filling out

3. Seidman, *et al., Worker Views His Union,* pp. 42–47.
4. See the account of the UAW in Windsor, Ontario, in C. W. M. Hart, "Industrial Relations Research and Social Theory," *Canadian Journal of Economics and Political Science,* February 1949, esp. pp. 60–63. Community involvement also emerged as a substitute for collective bargaining among the unions in Lorain, Ohio; see James B. McKee, "Status and Power in the Industrial Community: A Comment on Drucker's Thesis," *American Journal of Sociology,* January 1953, p. 367.

workmen's compensation applications, dealing with eviction notices or medical needs, helping to get loans, interceding with the police, and arranging social events and beer supplies. Many of these activities, not unexpectedly, are of precisely the same kind as a political ward leader spends his time on.

Nonetheless, some unions do engage in a significant amount of direct political action. In most large cities, the AFL-CIO council has a Committee on Political Education (COPE) which participates in party conventions and in primary and general elections. Individual unions may also contribute money and manpower outside the framework of COPE. Normally these tasks are undertaken by a relatively small number of activists who are involved because of personal ties to some candidate. Even in the heavily "political" Detroit UAW, no more than 6 to 10 percent of a random sample of union members when interviewed recalled having participated in any way in the 1952 Presidential campaign.[5]

In many locals it would appear that the pressure for active local political involvement arises, not from the expectations of the membership as a whole, but from the requirements of the union activists from whose ranks officers are drawn and by whose standards those officers are judged. On the extent to which rank-and-file members approve of union political activity, the evidence is conflicting. One study of the UAW in Detroit showed that a clear majority of the members supported such activity.[6] A study of the International Association of Machinists in an Illinois area found that slightly more than half the members believed that the "union should take an active part in politics" although they were not so sure that politics should be discussed at union meetings and were quite opposed to the union's telling members whom to vote for.[7] The Teamsters in St. Louis were in favor of union political action so long as it did not involve telling members how to vote.[8] In the study of six locals by Seidman and others, however, a clear majority of the members of five of the six unions rejected union political-activity organizations, and most of them opposed such organizations when they were explained to them.[9]

Even among the union activists who share a belief in political action of some sort, the precise strategy to employ is often in dispute be-

5. Arthur Kornhauser *et al., When Labor Votes* (New York: University Books, 1956), pp. 124–126.

6. *Ibid.,* pp. 100, 104, 105. The same results appeared in a 1956 survey: Harold L. Sheppard and Nicholas A. Masters, "The Political Attitudes and Preferences of Union Members: The Case of the Detroit Auto Workers," *American Political Science Review,* June 1959, pp. 440–443.

7. Hjalmar Rosen and R. A. Rosen, *The Union Member Speaks* (New York: Prentice-Hall, 1955), pp. 36–42.

8. Arnold Rose, *Union Solidarity* (Minneapolis: University of Minnesota Press, 1952), pp. 83–84.

9. Seidman *et al., Worker Views His Union,* pp. 230–233.

cause of the conflicting roles of the union *lobbyist* and the union *campaign director*.

The lobbyist sees political action in terms of getting concessions from elected officials, particularly legislators. He works alone in attempting to influence a fairly small group of men whose primary concern is with getting re-elected. Often he needs the votes of men from both political parties; thus, he dare not risk aligning himself entirely with one party or faction. Ideally, he would like to be free to commit his union to whoever has helped him the most; this sometimes means supporting—or at least not opposing—a conservative politician not normally friendly to labor. He avoids making allies if by so doing he must take on his ally's causes—"don't get stuck with the other fellow's fights." He chooses his issues carefully and concentrates on specific goals.

The union's campaign director, on the other hand, sees the requirements of political action in entirely different terms. He desires to elect a slate of local candidates. To do so he must create an organization of volunteers. Because of their political convictions, these volunteers often insist on working entirely within one party—usually the Democratic. The campaign director must, therefore, reject "deals" with Republicans and he must avoid endorsing conservative candidates who are not likely to arouse volunteer enthusiasm. He is inevitably restless with prior union commitments for they deprive the volunteers of a sense of participating in making decisions about endorsements. He must seek out allies from other liberal groups; this means he must make their causes his.

This tension means that the unions with the most to gain from local lobbying (like the building trades unions) will tend to reject political campaigns, while those with the least to gain by local lobbying (such as the UAW) will emphasize such campaigning. Between these extremes there are unions which are not infrequently split between the two strategies. Even within the normally "political" industrial unions formerly of the CIO, campaigning has often been undertaken half-heartedly.[10]

The Union as an Agency of Civic Leadership

Leaders of organized labor do not appear as frequently as businessmen among the ranks of reputed civic leaders or on the rosters of important civic or governmental organizations.[11] It is customary to find in most large cities one or two "labor representatives" appointed to

10. For an account of the difficulties experienced in political campaigning in Chicago by certain CIO unions, see James Q. Wilson, *Negro Politics* (Glencoe, Ill.: Free Press, 1960), pp. 125–127, and Fay Calkins, *The CIO and the Democratic Party* (Chicago: University of Chicago Press, 1952), pp. 70, 77, 81–84.

11. See the tables in William H. Form and Delbert C. Miller, *Industry, Labor, and Community* (New York: Harper, 1960), p. 43.

the board of education, the board of the Community Chest, and various public commissions. However, when the members of, say, the board of education are elected rather than appointed, and when—as in most nonpartisan cities—there is no powerful political organization which can draw up and elect a "balanced ticket" to such boards, labor is likely to be unrepresented. This seems to be the case in Detroit and Los Angeles, for example.

Furthermore, there appears to be a crucial difference between business and union membership on such bodies. Organized labor— even if it includes in its ranks the majority of all the adult citizens in the community—is generally regarded as a "special interest" which must be "represented"; businessmen, on the other hand, are often regarded, not as "representing business" as a "special interest," but as serving the community as a whole. Businessmen, in Peter Clark's term, often are viewed as "symbols of civic legitimacy." Labor leaders rarely have this symbolic quality, but must contend with whatever stigma attaches to being from a lower-class background and associated with a special-interest group.[12]

This bias in favor of business and professional occupations among governmental agencies and civic associations does not necessarily mean that such organizations always serve "business ends" to the detriment of labor. Given the many opportunities for private intervention in public decisions, labor, like all other politically involved organizations, may find that it can attain its ends (or prevent others from attaining theirs) with minimal or even no representation on such bodies. Underrepresentation in the politics of large American cities probably does not prevent groups such as labor from blocking civic actions. But this underrepresentation, and the lack of civic status it implies, probably does make it more difficult for labor goals to be placed near the top of the civic agenda. To put it another way, organized labor probably has less influence than businessmen *collectively* over *what kind* of issues are taken seriously in the city.

Labor is handicapped not only by having imputed to it less civic virtue but also by a shortage of money and organizational skills. Unions at the local level often can donate relatively little money to civic projects. Craft unions particularly are likely to have a very small staff, and sometimes a staff which—because its recruitment and tenure are closely tied to the fortunes of particular officers in the annual union elections —is not as competent as it might be if the job were sufficiently secure to attract able men.[13] Large industrial unions, on the other hand, may have a sizable permanent staff at the district or regional level.

---

12. One measure of this difference in civic roles is found in the underrepresentation of labor leaders among those given certain kinds of public honors, including citation in *Who's Who*. See Orme W. Phelps, "Community Recognition of Union Leaders," *Industrial and Labor Relations Review,* April 1954, pp. 417–433.

13. Hart, "Industrial Relations Research and Social Theory," p. 70.

Nonetheless, certain public bodies and civic associations have—particularly in recent years—gone out of their way to enlist union leaders, if only to co-opt potential opponents and increase the agency's resources. William Form and Delbert Miller note the rise of labor representation on the board of the Community Chest in Lansing, Michigan. There were only representatives of "company unions" in 1933 but six union men (on a 36-man board) by 1953. Labor obtained this recognition after having won its organizing fights in the auto plants and after the Chest realized the fund drives among workers would benefit if conducted by the unions (labor now contributes 40 per cent of all Chest funds). In an attempt to increase further its representation in community welfare agencies, labor once threatened to boycott an important fund drive.[14]

A similar increase in labor representation on the Chest was reported in a study of Lorain, Ohio. The invitation to join was extended in order to increase the contributions from workers. Paradoxically, however, the unions made no substantive demands once they were accorded representation. In this city, and probably in many others, labor's demand to be included in civic and welfare associations reflects not so much a desire to attain certain political goals as simply a desire to participate in a status-conferring civic venture. This desire, in turn, probably is based on labor's attempt to acquire the kind of civic legitimacy heretofore reserved for businessmen. "The CIO in Lorain," James McKee wrote, "wants to be regarded as concerned with the welfare of the whole community, not merely with the interests of labor, and views its participation in the Community Chest as demonstrating this concern."[15]

Labor's preoccupation with strictly labor goals and its concern for general civic legitimacy have combined to produce in many cities an antipathy between union leaders and municipal reformers. Although there are cases such as Detroit where the UAW and liberal and reform Democrats have joined forces, the more common pattern is that of New York, Chicago, Los Angeles, and other cities where reform efforts have had to deal with the indifference or active hostility of most unions.[16] To the extent labor is concerned with strictly union objectives —wages and hours, workmen's compensation, unemployment benefits, union security guarantees—it finds the programs of civic reformers largely irrelevant. To the extent labor is concerned with acquiring influence in the local political parties and legislature, it regards the reformers as a rival. And to the extent labor is anxious about its civic reputation, it often sees the liberal reformers as the source of extreme and politically damaging ideology.

14. See Form and Miller, *Industry, Labor, and Community,* pp. 673–674. In San Diego—which is not a pro-labor city—a prominent union official was chairman of the 1961 Community Chest drive.

15. McKee, "Status and Power in the Industrial Community," pp. 368–369.

16. The discussion of unions and reform follows Wilson, *The Amateur Democrat: Club Politics in Three Cities* (Chicago: University of Chicago Press, 1962), pp. 273–277.

Thus, the Los Angeles County Federation of Labor passed a resolution in 1961 opposing the right of the liberal California Democratic Council to make pre-primary endorsements in state and local contests. The New York Central Labor Council in 1961 was largely indifferent to the anti-Tammany campaign then being waged by the reformers in the New York Committee for Democratic Voters, although it joined with the reformers in backing Robert Wagner, the anti-Tammany candidate. In Chicago, with some minor exceptions, union leaders have publicly supported the candidates of the Democratic machine, not those of the reform-minded Independent Voters of Illinois. The Liberal Party in New York, largely backed by unions in the garment industry, has remained independent of the various reform movements in the city.

In those few cases in which there has been a labor-reform alliance (as in Chicago's Fifth Senatorial District in 1950[17]), the union involved has typically been the United Auto Workers. But even the UAW cannot always act independently, for it must consider the costs of political isolation from other unions in the city and from state federations as well as from the local Democratic party. The desirability of playing politics in city affairs must be measured against the necessity of playing politics within labor affairs. It probably takes an energetic and persuasive labor leader to make the advantages of independent civic action more attractive than its costs.

Unions in Urban Political Parties

The common view that "labor is tied to the Democratic party" requires much modification before it is accurate, particularly with regard to local politics. Unions have many different relations with local parties. In a very few cases unions (mostly the UAW) have attempted to take over the leadership of the Democratic party; with the help of allies, they succeeded in this in Detroit, in Gary, Indiana, and in Rockford, Illinois.[18] Or they may act in coalition with party leaders, as in the Democratic Farmer-Labor party in Minneapolis and St. Paul. They may stay aloof from local politics, as in Houston. They may confine themselves to seeking favors from local party organizations, as in Chicago. They may form independent parties to win votes and thereby bargaining power, as in New York City. They may, as do most CIO unions, carry over into city politics their national attachment to the Democrats; or they may, as do many AFL unions, support local politicians with little reference to national party labels. Where the city is nonpartisan, unions may—as they have in the past in St. Paul—endorse and elect a slate of candidates. Or they may—as in Los Angeles—instinctively oppose, with meager resources, whatever candidate the *Los Angeles Times* sup-

17. See Calkins, *CIO and Democratic Party*, pp. 59–85.
18. *Ibid.*, chaps. v and vi.

ports. (Labor-*Times* agreement in backing Mayor Norris Poulson in 1961 was an exception. And he lost anyway.)

Some representative cases of labor involvement in party politics follow.

I.
The Unions Capture a Party: The Case of Detroit

Beginning in 1948, the Wayne County CIO Political Action Committee (PAC), then made up almost entirely of UAW members, began, in alliance with certain liberal Democrats, an effort to take control of the state leadership of the Michigan Democratic party. State law required that precinct captains be elected directly by the voters. The PAC-liberal coalition elected 720 captains in Wayne County in 1948, about one third of the total. This was enough to give them control of the Democratic conventions in five of the six Wayne County Congressional districts; control of these, in turn, was enough to give the liberal coalition control of the state Democratic convention. After a bitter struggle with the party's Old Guard, this victory was repeated in 1950, and since then the liberals—dominated by the UAW—have controlled the state party.[19]

In the city of Detroit, however, elections are nonpartisan. Here labor's Committee on Political Education (the successor to the PAC since the AFL-CIO merger) functions directly as a political party.[20] The AFL-CIO Council, acting on COPE recommendations, endorses candidates and operates the strongest precinct organization in the city. Although the UAW has only slightly more than half of all union members in the city, it provides almost all of the key COPE officials. In some cases, COPE is open to nonlabor Democrats, and some liberals from business and professional backgrounds participate. Most nonlabor liberals, however, work directly through the Democratic party rather than through COPE. About 40 percent of all precinct captains are COPE members; alliances with non-COPE but liberal captains give COPE clear control of the county and thus of the state party. In city elections, these same captains work on behalf of nonpartisan labor endorsees.

The Detroit COPE has had imparted to it by the UAW a militant attitude toward political action. Kenneth Gray and David Greenstone offer several reasons to explain this militancy:

> First, the union was organized and led for some time by radicals . . . who fought violently among themselves but who agreed on the crucial importance of programmatic political action. Second, a bitter and violent

19. *Ibid.*, pp. 112–146.

20. This account follows Kenneth E. Gray and David Greenstone, "Organized Labor in City Politics," in Banfield (ed.), *Urban Government* (New York: Free Press of Glencoe, 1961), pp. 368–373.

struggle for recognition left the UAW with a deep hostility toward management. This hostility was manifested in political action. . . . Third, the union sought to ease a serious problem of ethnic and racial hostilities among its own members by emphasizing class solidarity of workers against management. This emphasis on the members' interest as a class strongly implied broad political goals rather than an exclusive concern with collective bargaining. . . . Fourth, the automobile workers have a tradition of rank-and-file participation, which contributes to the intensity of their activity in COPE.[21]

Militancy may have contributed to the state-wide successes of the Democrats, but it has not produced comparable successes in Detroit. Between 1946 and 1955, CIO-PAC endorsees won 67.5 percent of all primary and 91.2 percent of all general elections for partisan offices at the state, Congressional, and county level, but less than 38 percent of all contests for nonpartisan municipal offices.[22] As observed in an earlier chapter, union members have not hesitated to desert labor nominees in nonpartisan local elections—if, indeed, these members have even known who the labor candidates were. The CIO failed three times (1943, 1945, and 1949) to elect a mayor of Detroit after bitter contests in which labor's political arm emphasized "liberal issues"—Negro rights, public housing, urban redevelopment, and the right of public employees to strike. In 1953, labor regarded opposition to the incumbent as hopeless and made no endorsement. By 1957 a new strategy was emerging: play down ideological issues, back a sure winner, and hope for favors if he is elected. That year COPE joined with business and newspaper groups in supporting the man who won. Pleased with their success, labor leaders tried again in 1961, only to have the noncontroversial incumbent, despite almost unanimous business, labor, newspaper, and civic support, lose to an unknown who had strong support from Negroes.

Despite the 1961 setback, it is unlikely that COPE will revert to the militancy of the 1940's. First, Detroit city government has begun to be responsive to the demands of lower-class and Negro voters even without labor control of the city government. Second, labor has learned "to conform to the peculiar rules of the nonpartisan game" which require that it refrain from overly aggressive political behavior, that it stress the most widely shared community sentiments, and that it avoid the appearance of seeking to "take over" city government.[23]

Not all cases of labor dominance in local affairs are confined to industrial unions, however. For many years, the AFL unions associated with the "Labor Temple" in St. Paul (now the St. Paul AFL-CIO Trades

21. *Ibid.,* p. 370.
22. Nicholas A. Masters, "The Politics of Union Endorsement of Candidates in the Detroit Area," *Midwest Journal of Political Science,* August 1957, p. 149.
23. Gray and Greenstone, "Organized Labor in City Politics," p. 373.

and Labor Assembly) were continually successful in electing their candidates to office in that nonpartisan city. These labor leaders were conservative in temper, but eventually their influence was undermined by the rise of an aggressive coalition of CIO leaders and intellectuals which made up the Democratic Farmer-Labor Party (DFL) that emerged in 1948. After much controversy, an uneasy alliance between the DFL and the Labor Temple developed.[24]

In Minneapolis too the AFL craft unions were powerful. Between 1941 and 1957, they made the Central Labor Union (CLU) the most important political force in that nonpartisan city.[25] With the advent of the DFL, the CLU remained the dominant partner; no liberal candidate felt he could win without labor support. The terms of the DFL-CLU alliance allowed the DFL to nominate candidates for state and national office (where the liberal ideologies of the DFL intellectuals were engaged anyway) while the CLU elected candidates for city posts. After the defeat of labor candidates in 1957 (owing to scandals, indiscretions, and poor tactics), CLU strength began to decline.

2.
Unions Defer to the Party: The Case of New York and Chicago

In large, industrially diversified cities such as New York and Chicago, where political parties have (or have had) power independent of the support of other organized groups, labor has had to be content either with bargaining with elective officials (usually after, rather than before, the election) from a position of relative weakness, or with forming third parties to strengthen that bargaining position. In contrast with Detroit, unions have not attempted to take over party posts, and in contrast with Minneapolis they have not been able to make themselves senior partners in a labor-liberal coalition. Only very rarely have a few unions challenged the regular party leadership (the Democrats, of course) in primary contests.

In Chicago, labor needs the politicians more than the politicians need labor. Both sides know this, and a kind of half-hearted good fellowship results. The craft unions typically remain close to the party and attempt to share in the patronage, particularly in the licensing and building-inspection departments. The industrial unions—notably the steel, auto, and meatpacking workers—usually support regular party candidates. But occasionally they assert their independence in what they know in advance is a lost cause; for example, certain unions backed an insurgent candidate for the Democratic nomination for governor in

24. Alan Altshuler, *A Report on Politics in St. Paul* (Cambridge, Mass.: Joint Center for Urban Studies, 1959, mimeo) pp. II–3 to II–10.

25. Alan Altshuler, *A Report on Politics in Minneapolis* (Cambridge, Mass.: Joint Center for Urban Studies, 1959, mimeo), pp. II–8 to II–9 and V–5 to V–7.

1960. He lost, but the result of the challenge was to increase somewhat the vigor with which the regular candidate attempted to meet union demands in order to arouse their enthusiasm for the general election contest with the Republican. Indeed, labor leaders can probably wield greatest influence by endeavoring to control rather precisely the ardor with which they help Democrats mobilize voters in the closely contested county and state elections. The few union leaders who have been successful at this and at the same time have stayed clear of charges of "left wing" leanings have become important forces in local politics. In case of a showdown with the party, however, there is not much doubt as to who would win.

New York's Democratic party has in recent years been much weaker than its counterpart in Chicago, and therefore labor has probably been more influential. First with the American Labor party and then (after 1944) with the Liberal party, certain New York unions— mostly those Jewish-led unions in the garment industry—have endeavored to act as a third force in city and state politics. The ALP was in 1937 and 1941 a crucial source of votes for Fiorello H. La Guardia. After it was destroyed by the struggle between Communist and anti-Communist factions, the Liberal party continued the strategy of always endorsing Democrats nationally but of playing one side against the other locally. It has always polled a substantial vote, and in 1951 it managed to elect, on its own, a city council president.

Most New York unions, however, have never had any association with either the ALP or the Liberal party. The AFL unions, organized into the Central Trades and Labor Council, followed an almost unvarying policy of supporting regular Democrats in city elections and expecting in return to be given certain assurances about police attitudes toward strikers and certain concessions on local codes, licenses, inspections, and prevailing wage rates on city construction work. The very size of the New York labor movement—the Council had over three quarters of a million members—made it exceptionally difficult for it to speak with one voice on even crucial matters, much less on the secondary issues of political participation. The building trades unions and the Teamsters had their own councils which were part of the larger Council, and union autonomy was jealously guarded.[26]

In 1959, the CIO and AFL unions in New York merged into a Central Labor Council, with a total membership of a million and a half workers. Such an organization, even if it did nothing in politics, would be a force to be reckoned with because of the vast audience it could provide politicians fortunate enough to enjoy access to it. Union meetings are one way politicians have of dealing with the perennial and insoluble problem of how to reach the people.

But the new organization set out to be something more than just an

26. This account follows Wallace S. Sayre and Herbert Kaufman, *Governing New York City* (New York: Russell Sage Foundation, 1960), pp. 508–510.

audience. Its first president, Harry Van Arsdale, was a vigorous exponent of union education and political action. In 1961, he persuaded the Central Labor Council to support Mayor Robert Wagner for reelection even though the mayor had broken with the regular party leaders, and to organize a new political force, the "Brotherhood party," which would do for unions generally what the Liberal party had done for the needle trades. At the time this new party was created, it was widely believed that Wagner would not win the Democratic primary and thus he would need such third parties as the Brotherhood to enable him to run as an independent in the general election. Instead, Wagner won easily in the primary and the immediate need for the Brotherhood party vanished. Though the party had a strong start, organizing political units in most assembly districts in the city, its future became uncertain.

3.
The Dormant Unions: The Case of the Southwest

In the large cities of the Southwest, where strong political parties do not exist and where population and industry are rapidly expanding, labor has been a recent and still minor civic actor. An aggressive union may be able to convert a one-industry town into a one-party town, as in Detroit. And unions may extract concessions from professional politicians in the old, stable cities of the Northeast and Midwest, such as New York and Chicago. But in such booming cities as Houston, Dallas, San Diego, and Los Angeles, where rapid growth is occurring, business (and, more generally, middle-class) influence is often such that organized labor (which, in most of these communities, is only a recent arrival) is lacking in either legitimacy or power.

Businessmen often dominate the politics of these cities (sometimes

TABLE 15   *Cities over 500,000 population ranked by the percentage of employed persons in white-collar occupations, 1960*

Rank	City	Percent white-collar	Rank	City	Percent white-collar
1	Seattle	47.8	12	Boston	35.5
2	Dallas	45.9	13	Pittsburgh	35.2
3	Los Angeles	45.0	14	Philadelphia	35.1
4	San Diego	44.8	15	Baltimore	34.2
5	San Francisco	43.0	16	Chicago	33.4
6	New York City	42.8	17	Detroit	32.1
7	Washington	42.7	18	Milwaukee	31.5
8	Houston	41.6	19	Buffalo	30.4
9	New Orleans	39.0	20	St. Louis	30.2
10	San Antonio	38.1	21	Cleveland	24.8
11	Cincinnati	36.8			

Note: "White-collar" refers to professional, technical, official, managerial, sales, and clerical occupations.
Source: 1960 Census of Population.

by default) so long as they can agree among themselves. Furthermore, business and conservative values are widely shared. Business leadership is not an imposition; it is generally accepted. In Houston and Los Angeles, strong anti-union feelings are still widespread among citizens. The absence of a mass production heavy industry (such as an auto plant) means the absence of a large pool of easily organized unskilled workers. The largest CIO unions are often found in the aircraft plants where there is a high proportion of skilled workers. In San Diego, for example, the largest local industrial union is the International Association of Machinists. As Table 15 shows, these are the cities with the largest percentages of white-collar workers in the labor force, and such workers are extremely difficult—often impossible—to organize.

Despite such constraints, labor in these cities may be a major participant in at least state and national politics. In Houston and San Diego, for example, some labor unions are principal partners in a liberal-labor coalition which contests Democratic primaries. The very absence of a strong party organization, the result in part of nonpartisan, business-dominated city politics, often gives rise to intraparty factional warfare at the county and state level in which labor, albeit weak, is strong enough to play an important role.

VII

Problems
of Management

THE mayor of today's large city occupies a position his predecessors would in some ways have envied. At last most legislatures have ceased to be meddlesome, and the cities in general have a degree of home rule that is adequate for most of their purposes. The authority of the mayor has been vastly strengthened. There are still many independent and quasi-independent offices and bodies, but these are fewer than before. In the city government proper the mayor is now very strong indeed. he appoints department heads, who are accountable directly to him, he makes up the budget, which the council does little more than approve; and he has the advantage of a large, competent, professional staff. The voters—most of them—want and expect government that is honest, impartial, and efficient, and the mayor knows that he will generally be applauded if he resists unreasonable demands from special interests and condemned if he does not.

These very improvements in the mayor's situation have created their own characteristic difficulties, however. For one thing, committed to good government and with no patronage or other "gravy" to dispense, the present-day mayor cannot exercise power as informally as the old-fashioned boss could. What he cannot do by an exercise of formal authority or by salesmanship, he cannot do at all. Thus, despite gains in his formal authority, his net influence position may in some matters be weaker than before. Moreover, since the mayor is supposed to be impartial and even nonpartisan (this is often expected of him even when he is elected on a partisan basis), he cannot let narrowly political criteria guide him in making policy decisions. The interest of the community "as a whole," which his good government supporters tell him should replace "politics," turns out, however, to have no concrete meaning in important and controversial matters. Thus, although not permitted to employ criteria that are frankly political, he generally cannot find others that are appropriate.

One gets a sense both of the improvements in the mayor's situation and of the difficulties that these entail from the report Nat Hentoff, a journalist and novelist, gives of his interview with New York's Mayor John V. Lindsay. "Sometimes," the Mayor tells him, "I feel I'm pushing my shoulder against a mountain. My feet are churning away and the mountain won't budge." Except for the size of the mountain, all mayors are in about the same situation. There are two main problems of "top management": (1) how to organize the executive branch so that the mayor can maintain control over it and make it an effective instrument for carrying out a comprehensive program of action on matters of fundamental importance, and (2) how to use the technical knowledge of planners and other professionals to frame a comprehensive program that represents the interest of the community "as a whole."

The first of these is examined in a wide perspective by Charles R. Adrian. He discusses three types of large-city administrative structure—council-manager government, the management cabinet, and the chief administrative officer—and concludes that the third, which is a sort of cross between the council-manager and strong-mayor forms of government, is most likely to spread; however, he warns, its success will depend to a large extent upon the personality of the mayor and upon his willingness to delegate authority. This conclusion recalls Bruce Kovner's account of "The Resignation of Elgin Crull" which appears in the section on the city manager. Another reading that deals specifically with the problem of organizing the executive branch consists of advice that the late V. O. Key gave to a commission which was trying to decide how to fit a planning body into the structure of a government. The government was that of a state, but Key's remarks are no less to the point when, as has been done here, *mayor* is substituted for *governor* and *city* for *state*. The crux of the problem in both cases is how to bring the planner close to the seat of power without bringing him *too* close to it.

The other main problem of "top management" is treated here in what amounts to a symposium. Alan Altshuler opens the discussion with a critique of the planner's traditional ideal, that of comprehensive (or master) planning. The ideal, he says, is of little or no help because it presupposes the existence of something which in fact does not exist—namely, a complete and consistent set of community goals. Paul

Davidoff, a professor of city planning, agreeing that the people of a city have diverse goals, objects to leaving it to the city planning department to prepare *the* comprehensive plan. It would be more democratic, he says, to consider *"alternatives strongly supported by their proponents"* (the emphasis is his); accordingly he calls for a "plural" as opposed to a "unitary" planning process. In an ideal situation, he says, local political parties would offer platforms containing master plans, as would neighborhoods, including poor ones. Lisa Peattie, an anthropologist, has worked as an "advocate planner" for a low-income section of Boston, and in her article she ponders this experience. Some of her conclusions about advocacy planning for a neighborhood resemble Altshuler's about comprehensive planning for a city. In the neighborhood, she says, the issues are "miniaturized" but their basic structure remains. "Even at the neighborhood level there is no simple aggregation of people's wants and needs into a plan." The problem Altshuler points to is raised also by the late William H. Brown, an economist, and Charles E. Gilbert, a political scientist, in their article about planning for capital expenditures in Philadelphia. The main difficulties the planners encounter, they say, are not political but intellectual: no procedure exists for establishing a set of goals (criteria) such as is required by the ideal of the comprehensive (master) plan. This being the case, about the best that the planning agency can do is to provide information, encourage popular consultation, and make such consultation more meaningful by supplying perspectives on benefits and costs.

The last three readings of the section offer ideas about the direction planning will or should take in the future. Martin Meyerson, a professor of city planning when his article was written, says that what is needed is a type of planning that will give the politicians an enlarged view of the context in which they are acting and yet not be beyond the intellectual and other resources of the planners. He amplifies this "middle-range" conception of planning in terms of five more or less separate functions, one of which is not altogether unlike the traditional view of comprehensive planning. Anthony Downs, an economist and businessman, predicts a revolution in city planning. He agrees with Meyerson and others that the idea of a single "best" plan is passé and that the planner of the future will emphasize quantitative studies of *several* alternative programs. In the final reading, Edward C. Banfield asserts that the trend is toward making a wider range of decisions on technical (or allegedly technical) grounds; professionalism in decision-making will entail, he thinks, application of three concepts: economizing, decentralization, and welfare. It will be seen that he agrees with Downs's prediction that "city planners will become general advisers to key politicians concerning nearly all city government activities and resource uses."

An Interview with Mayor Lindsay

Nat Hentoff

SOMEWHAT to my surprise, Mayor John V. Lindsay was not in his office one morning last fall when I arrived in the west wing of City Hall at eight-thirty to keep an appointment I had made with him. But a few minutes later he came striding down the corridor that leads to his office, handed his secretary a list of things to do, and waved me ahead of him into his office. "I was in the car, out front, getting some paperwork done," he said. "That time in the car first thing in the morning—if there's no one with me—is very useful."

When I had last been to the Mayor's office for a talk with him, in February, just a few weeks after he was sworn in, he had struck me as being under considerable stress, and I asked him if his schedule had eased up any.

"The hours are about as long," he said. "I've been averaging five hours of sleep a night, but on Saturday or Sunday I try to get seven or eight. It's funny, but the few times these past months when I could have got to bed earlier—like when I was away for a short time this summer—I wasn't able to. One thing always leads to another. I watch the late news, read the papers, get a beer, and before I know it it's one-thirty."

The Mayor seemed to me to have changed somewhat since I had seen him in February, and even since the last time I had watched him in action at one of the many public meetings and ceremonies he appeared at during the spring and summer of his first year in office. It was, I decided, a difference in confidence. He now had a more noticeable air of command and of enjoying command. I told him so.

"Yes, I think I've got a grip on the monster now," he said, leaning back in his chair. "I'm much more certain now about how the structure should be changed, and I think I'm staffing the government as best I can. That's terribly important. I still spend a lot of time on it. It won't make any difference how sound the structure gets to be, or even how much money we get, if there aren't pros to run it. There's a rare beast known as an urbanist, and because these beasts are so rare there's intense competition for them among the cities. I've been getting most of the people I go after, except for some from other areas in the country who are anchored. I mean a wife is anchored to a white picket fence and the man is anchored to a bloody pension system. I run into that a lot. I've been trying for three months to get a guy out of the federal government, but so far he can't get unsnarled without a big loss of pension. Senator Muskie, of Maine, has submitted a very good bill that would make it possible for a man to go from the federal to local government without this problem. Pension systems have to be made more mobile."

Turning from the subject of staffing, I asked Lindsay how his money problems in general were coming along. Earlier that summer, when Lindsay testified during Senator Ribicoff's hearing on the problems of the cities, he had said that New York City alone would need fifty billion dollars more in federal aid during the next ten years, but Senator Robert Kennedy, among others, had criticized Lindsay for being totally unrealistic in expecting that kind of money.

The Mayor smiled, "I remember reading in Justice Holmes' memoirs of his years on the bench a line that's stayed with me—'I do expect a rough equation between isness and oughtness.' In testifying before the Ribicoff committee, though, I wasn't requested to use that equation. I was focussing on 'oughtness.' But I'd accept a rough equation. Nobody can put an exact figure on what we need, but I do know that if I'd said ten billion for the next ten years I'd have been in error. If I'd said twenty-five billion, I might have been in the area of the rough equation. What I was trying to do, however, was to lead Congress, which is just beginning to recognize what's happening in the cities, and therefore I had to give them the shock treatment. They especially needed it insofar as New York is concerned. The only budget larger than New York City's in the whole country is the federal budget. The city's population is larger than that of sixty-six of the hundred and eighteen members of the United Nations. And yet, with all our problems—like a welfare budget of seven hundred million dollars, which Mitch Ginsberg, the Welfare Commissioner, says we have to increase to eight hundred and sixty-seven million for the next fiscal year—we contribute something like fifteen billion dollars a year to the federal government in personal and corporate income taxes. Do you realize that represents more than ten per cent of all federal income taxes, even though it doesn't include revenues from Westchester and the Connecticut and New Jersey areas that are part of Greater New York? But in any one year New York City has never got back as much as a billion dollars in direct or indirect federal assistance. This year, we'll get about eight hundred and twenty million, or less than six per cent of this area's contributions in income taxes alone. But New York is accused of asking for a disproportionate share of federal aid.

"We're in a fiscal crisis, and so are the other big cities. And without a vastly increased commitment of federal resources it's going to get worse. We've got to wake up Congress. There are thirty-six standing congressional committees, and not one—not one—represents the needs of the cities. That's why I keep speaking up for the creation of committees on urban affairs in both the Senate and the House. And that's why I keep saying the federal government has to reëxamine its priorities. Instead of making cuts in appropriations for the cities, it ought to see what cuts can be made in all those funds pouring into Vietnam. What it comes down to is which is the more important in the long run— funds for Southeast Asia or funds for Brownsville? I'm for Brownsville."

The Mayor's secretary came in with some papers for him to sign. When she left, I asked him whether, considering all the time he had to spend on city affairs, he had been able to keep up the strong interest in foreign affairs that he had developed during his years in the House of Representatives.

"I try to," he said. "I seem to find out best what I want to know from the *Economist*—even about America. Its American Survey is frighteningly accurate. And my friends send me articles. Some of them in the State Department with whom I've worked on Atlantic affairs, for instance, send me things they've been writing. My reading still covers a very wide area. I try not to miss the *Congressional Record*. In a way, it's like reading the Sears, Roebuck catalogue, but it's so entertaining. God, it's wonderful!"

"When do you get time to do all this reading?" I asked.

"Mostly at night. There's a nice chaise longue in our bedroom where I sit and listen to the radio or TV and read. I've taught myself to read very fast. And, travelling around the city, if I'm not dictating or if there's not a conference going on in the car, all I do is read things. This moving around is important. I don't mean only the walks I take in the ghetto neighborhoods. I've been involved in an educational program in the business community. There have been meetings after meetings of groups of fifteen to twenty or thirty people. I must have talked to a couple of thousand businessmen by now, trying to persuade them not only to keep but to expand their investment in the city. Some are afraid that New York is being strangled by the poor and their needs, but I explain to them that, with the increasing industrialization of the South and of Puerto Rico, in-migration has lessened considerably, and, by contrast with other cities in the North, we've stabilized the problems we do have in that area. Chicago, for example, has never really coped with its welfare problems. It has a bad plan. In fact, other cities are now sending teams to our Department of Welfare to learn how the job should be done. And I tell these people that a lot of us have lost sight of the fact that in some of the so-called ghetto neighborhoods a solid middle class is developing. There's more black ownership on a Hundred and

Twenty-fifth Street, for instance, all the time. I tell them there's a whole world of exploration and development possible in those areas. And as for the city as a whole, I remind them of the immense labor pool we have. Blue-collar, white-collar—all kinds. I think these talks are making a dent, are making businessmen realize what the city's potential is.

"And, for the first time, I think there's an awakening among some of the labor leaders to *their* responsibility to be more flexible. That's a big step—a very big step. We've still got problems with the municipal unions, though, particularly with regard to our right to move men around, which is an essential right. Take the Fire Department. I was struck with luck in appointing Bob Lowery as Fire Commissioner, incidentally. He turned out to be a brilliant administrator. Furthermore, he knows when to roll with a punch and when not to. And he's very sensitive to what the pros call the high-hazard areas for fires. However, over the years fire companies have put down deep roots in certain neighborhoods. For a long time, the men were given limited privileges to moonlight in neighborhoods where they were stationed, and those part-time jobs have made for even deeper roots. Until Bob, no Fire Commissioner had moved them, even when more men were needed in the high-hazard areas. Since he *is* doing that, he's anathema to the heads of their unions. When Bob took men who weren't needed after dark in lower Manhattan and put them in Bedford-Stuyvesant, where there are twelve fires a night, Gerald Ryan, the president of the Uniformed Firemen's Association, was appalled. I said to him, 'Gerry, isn't it logical we do this shifting around?' 'Well, no, not exactly,' he said. 'These people are part of that neighborhood. They have their cars there. They have to get those cars washed at a certain hour—that kind of thing.' It hasn't been easy, and Lowery, while skillful, *is* a Negro dealing with a largely white organization. So sometimes he needs reassurance, and that's why I spend a good deal of time with him. I told him, 'If it gets to that point, crack Ryan over the head publicly, and I'll support you.'"

With some relish, as if at the prospect of more head-cracking to come, the Mayor continued, "This business of trying to get the separate parts of the administration working at maximum efficiency leads to all kinds of resistance. For example, in the Human Resources Administration, under our reorganization plan, there'll be a major division advising me on public-education policy. The Board of Education resisted the idea, but we told them it wouldn't kill them. I've finally got the Police Department responsive to the Mayor, and now the Board of Education and its empire cannot continue to travel in *its* orbit. Education has to be made an integral part of community development, and therefore it has to be subject to a good deal of guidance from City Hall. No matter how many asbestos walls are put between me and the Board of Education, at the end I get the blame if there's trouble, and so I bloody well ought to have something to say about what's going on.

"God, they're slow in that empire! You remember when Freeport, on Long Island, refused a federal program based on teaching machines? The government was going to supply not only the money but bodies to go with it. You couldn't get a better package. We read about it in the paper, and I asked the Board for an immediate decision on whether we should take it over. No, they said, they needed a month to decide. Bernard Donovan, the Superintendent of Schools, was in Europe, and someone else was away. I told them they had twelve hours. You never saw such a crisis and so many telephone calls. But they came to a decision within those twelve hours, and we got the program.

"Then, there was the time the people filming 'Up the Down Staircase' wanted the use of a school building. The Board said it would take months to come to a decision, and that, besides, the picture might present a poor image of our school system. The filming was to take place during the summer, mind you. The schools were empty. So what if they showed a brick going through a window? At least, that would indicate a little activity. Anyway, I called Moe Iushewitz, a labor official who's on the Board. 'Do you realize that you're losing a million dollars in jobs by taking this stuffy attitude?' I asked him. 'How would you like to see *that* in the paper, Moe?' I signed him up, and he delivered the rest of the Board."

Lindsay broke into laugher. "I've got a new slogan—'Wasp Power!' Thought of it the other day. Someone was teasing me about the number of Jews in the administration, and I said, 'We Wasps may have only eleven per cent of the vote in this city, but one day we're going to rise.' "

A phone call was put through. The Mayor, striking his desk with a pencil, listened for a while, and then he said, "Well, do what you have to do. I'll back you up." He hung up and turned back to me. "The things you have to deal with!" he said. "We had a very interesting one a few weeks ago. We got word that the Ku Klux Klan in Baltimore planned to march through Harlem. Howard Leary, the Police Commissioner, sent a couple of smart guys to talk to them—to tell them they were damn fools and they'd get their skulls split open. I thought they'd been convinced, but two weeks later Leary got a telegram signed by the big Grand Wizard saying they were coming by way of the George Washington Bridge in full regalia, and since it was to be a peaceful march, they demanded police protection. Leary called me. 'Well, chief, what do I do now?' he said. 'What are the rights and liberties on this one?' Lee Rankin, the Corporation Counsel, was in transit somewhere and couldn't be reached. But I happened to be talking to Bruce Bromley. He's a former Court of Appeals judge who's now a partner in Cravath, Swaine & Moore. He volunteered to research this one himself. The next day, he called me up in triumph. He'd found an old statute that goes back about a thousand years. 'Does Rankin know,' he said, 'that it's illegal to walk through New York City with something on your head other than a hat?'

Well, we didn't actually use that statute. Leary sent the Wizard a tele-gram that said, 'You are coming to New York only to incite racial disturbance. Don't come. If you do, we'll lock you up.' That settled it. And here I'd had visions of a great scene on the George Washington Bridge. Before we were sure they wouldn't come, by the way, Leary asked me what to do if they did come. 'Surround them with Negro cops,' I told him, 'and you and I will go up to the roof of a tenement and throw bottles at them.' " Lindsay roared with laughter.

"What have been your really roughest times so far?" I asked him.

"Those last days and nights in Albany when we were trying to get an agreement on the city-income-tax program. It was a brutal, bloody show, with little groups in different rooms caucusing and caucusing. That was a rough three days."

"You've been criticized," I said, "for having been too aggressive when you first proposed your tax program, thereby unnecessarily irritat-ing the legislature."

The Mayor looked skeptical. He thought a moment, and then said, "Some say I wasn't aggressive enough. It probably *was* a tactical error for me to say I'd go into the constituency of each guy who didn't go along with us on taxes and campaign against him. It doesn't work to *say* that. It may be a good idea, under certain circumstances, to *do* it, but it's not effective to announce your intentions along that line. And I suppose my charge of legislative cowardice did inflame some of them. On the other hand, all that aggressiveness—if that's the word—may really have helped. It got a lot of people behind us. The non-white com-munity, especially, supported us all the way. Joseph Zaretzki, the minority leader in the Senate, told me he'd never before seen a Mayor come up to Albany asking for more taxes with real backing from his people. That made it look as if Albany, if it didn't give us more taxes, would be *denying* the community. I'll tell you, the taxes we did get—and especially the fact that a graduated income tax was involved—were the subject of a lot of conversation at the conference of mayors I attended in Dallas not long ago. All the cities need new ways of taxing, and perhaps what we achieved encouraged some of the other mayors."

I had been in the Mayor's office for nearly an hour, and, as in February, I had been feeling the pressure rise—on him, and on me as an obstacle to the furthering of city affairs. The lights on the Mayor's phone had been flashing almost continually, and frequently the door would open and a head would pop in, look at me reprovingly, I thought—and pop out. But I did want to find out in the time I had left how much progress, if any, there had been in making certain that new policies, once adopted by the Mayor, were actually being carried through on the lower levels of the administration.

When I asked about this, the Mayor sighed. "Sometimes I feel I'm pushing my shoulder against a mountain," he said. "My feet are churning away and the mountain won't budge. But I'm determined to blast things through. Every week, I tell the commissioners at the cabinet meeting to get out of their offices into the streets and find out what their departments are doing with *people*. I'm always on them to *act*, and to follow through on the action. I'd rather they made three errors out of ten decisions, as long as they made decisions and got them into operation. I know it's tough, and sometimes the bottlenecks have nothing to do with the people in the lower echelons. I've walked by those rattrap buildings in East New York—the ones with rubble and beer cans inside, and, at night, a few guys mainlining it. They've been abandoned by owners we can't find. All the city can do is board them up. Three days later, the boards are down. The logical thing to do would be to tear down those buildings, blacktop the area, and put a basketball or handball court there. Or a place to get cars off the street. But by law you can't pull the mess down without going to court over the damn thing. But I did see one terrible block in East New York and I told the Buildings Commissioner to just pull down the buildings. Sometimes that's the way you have to operate. I learned that in the Navy during the war. Before I became gunnery officer on my destroyer, I was in charge of damage control. I was the housekeeper. My job was to get the necessary repairs done, get the guns we needed, get the ship painted, and get out to sea. You stole from the next guy, you borrowed from somebody else, but you got it done. Cumshawing, we called it. If you'd waited for the paperwork to get to you from this agency and that agency in Washington, you would never have got out to sea again." Lindsay suddenly looked glum. "Of course, you had a great advantage in the Navy. You could shove off. Nobody could do anything to you once you were in the middle of the Pacific." His spirits seemed to rise again. "But the thing is to keep moving and to keep others moving," he said. "We'll break through. And that's one of the reasons I go out into the streets as often as I can—to show movement, to show concern."

"What if you're just raising hopes in the ghettos when you're out in the streets—hopes that will turn into even deeper frustration if movement doesn't lead to visible change?" I asked.

The Mayor frowned. "I've done a lot of thinking about that, but I honestly believe people are reasonable. They don't expect miracles. They do expect some understanding and knowledge of their troubles. And when I'm around they do see some signs of visible change on some level. I was in a Bronx neighborhood where a kid got killed because their was no traffic light. When I left there, I called Henry Barnes, the Traffic Commissioner, and made sure it wouldn't take the usual four months to get a light where the people wanted it. I will *not* walk out of a situation like that without being able to assure the people in the neighborhood that there'll be immediate action." Lindsay grinned. "Sometimes there's even action before I get there. The Sanitation Department, for instance, has a real information system. If they find out I'm going to be in a certain neighborhood, they'll clean it up before I come. That's what they've always done with Mayors. But I don't always tell them where I'll be. Sometimes I don't tell *anyone* where I'm going. And then, when I get there and see they haven't been moving their butts, I yell and scream to get the trucks into that neighborhood. And I go back, or send someone back, to see if they've followed through. Also, going out on those streets is of immense value to *me*. It's the one way I can really find out what people are sweating about, what they care about. I wouldn't have had those houses in East New York torn down if seeing them hadn't hit me in the guts. You see so much grief on those streets."

Harvey Rothenberg, the Mayor's assistant for appointments, came in. "You're all backed up," he said to the Mayor.

I rose. "One more question," I said. "When you see all that grief, and when you read and hear about what's happening in the hospitals, for example, isn't it an enormous burden to have the responsibility you have? I should think the pain and frustration would be constant."

He looked at me, ran a hand through his hair, and said, "My wife's good at handling that. She's tough. Mary reminds me whenever I get very upset that I'm only here for a visit and I can't change the world."

Recent Concepts in Large City Administration

Charles R. Adrian

THERE ARE a variety of historical reasons for the slowness with which concepts for the government of our largest cities have developed. Until recent years, most of these cities were dominated by political machines little interested in governmental structure and even less interested in professional administration. The reformers of the efficiency and economy movement, when they were inspired to action, spent most of their time in the essentially negative activity of fighting the machines. Even when they concerned themselves with positive activity, their almost religious devotion to the council-manager plan kept them from examining concepts. The administrative reform air became charged with emotion, and skepticism concerning any part of the council-manager plan was regarded as heresy that could not be tolerated or discussed on its merits.

The efficiency and economy movement contributed much to the modern management of America's small and moderate-sized cities. But it was of little help to our largest cities, perhaps chiefly because the reformers' two basic assumptions—that politics and politicians are evil and untrustworthy, and that city government is almost entirely a matter of applying the principles of efficient business management—could not be reconciled with the political realities of the large city.

Thus we find that there was little administrative reorganization of large cities between the beginning of the century and the advent of World War II. Some changes took place, to be sure. The very great pressure of demands for complex and technical services in itself produced some modernization of the municipal civil service. Some large cities that matured after the heyday of machine politics—notably Detroit and Los Angeles—developed structures that were integrated to a considerable degree, with administrations that were honest (by middle-class standards) most of the time, and with political atmos-

Published for the first time in the first edition of this book, by permission of the author.

pheres that allowed reformers an opportunity to operate to some degree. Two large cities—Cincinnati and Kansas City—and ten cities of over one-quarter of a million people have adopted the manager plan.

But it was not until after World War II that attention came to be sharply focused on the large city administrative structure. To some extent, this organizational soul-searching has come about because of the decline of the boss and machine, a change that decades of bombardment by reformers have helped bring about but which is largely the result of a basic change in the social environment, which had formerly supported this institution.[1] In part, also, it is probably a reaction to the pressing problems of the core city, which have resulted from the move to the suburbs,[2] and to the increasing technical complexity of governmental services.

In looking at this postwar trend toward the formulation of a set of concepts for the management of large cities, we might consider three areas of activity: council-manager government, the management cabinet, and the chief administrative officer (CAO).

Council-Manager Government in Large Cities

From the second decade of this century to the present, reformers have urged the adoption of the council-manager plan regardless of the size of a city. They have urged—with little empirical basis for their assertions—that size is an irrelevant, or at best insignificant, factor in determining the type of structure to be used.

Habitual iconoclasts, on the other hand, have sought to make light of the semideified manager plan and have insisted that it cannot work in large cities for a variety of reasons, but especially because it does not provide for political leadership in complex situations. Effective government, those on middle ground note, has been achieved in two large cities that have tried the council-manager plan: in Cincinnati from the beginning and in Kansas City after the ousting of the Pendergast machine. They point out that nineteen of the twenty-two California cities with populations of between 50,000 and 500,000 use some version of the manager plan. But only San Antonio of our larger cities has adopted and retained the plan since the years of the Great Depression.

Why have the large cities not turned toward the council-manager form? Does a failure to make adequate provision for political leadership and policy development render it unsuitable? Has the tendency of persons in large cities to look to the mayor rather than the council for

1. For background, see any number of sources, including my *Governing Urban America* (2nd. ed., 1961), Chaps. 3, 6, and 8.
2. *Ibid.,* Chap. 2; and Robert C. Wood, *Suburbia* (1959).

leadership in problem solving been a principal factor in the avoidance of the manager plan in such cities? Just why does the public perceive this role of the mayor differently in large cities as against medium-sized cities? Or does it? Do political leaders fear the plan as much as is often claimed? If so, how can their views be reconciled with those of Thomas Pendergast, who could have junked the plan in Kansas City but did not? These questions, and others, lend themselves to empirical research and need testing.

There are other questions involving matters of fact that can be partially answered through the conventional techniques of historical research. Why have study commissions in large cities so often failed to recommend the council-manager plan even when many reform-oriented persons are members? Why, for example, did the study commission appointed by Governor Thomas E. Dewey and the General Assembly recommend the CAO plan rather than the manager plan for the city of New York even before it began public hearings? The reports of study commissions are consistently inadequate in describing the conceptual schemes of commission members who reject the manager plan.

Some clues as to why the manager plan has been rejected exist, but these merely suggest the need for further study. In 1931, Lent D. Upson recommended the creation of an administrative assistantship to the mayor of Detroit, rather than adoption of the manager plan, because he felt that Detroit's government was at "too high a level" of competence to justify a drastic shift to another plan.[3] Is this a plausible reason in other cities, too—or at any rate, a more important practical consideration than some of the others often mentioned?

In 1926, a committee sponsored by the San Francisco Bureau of Governmental Research considered a manager plan for their city, and at the same time the *San Francisco News* advocated the plan. But a large majority of the 1930 charter revision commission membership opposed the manager plan and rejected it by a decisive vote.[4] Why? Was the size of the city a principal factor in this rejection? In Los Angeles, the CAO plan was thought to be "an improvement over the ordinary city manager proposal—tailored to fit the practical requirements of our great city."[5] What impracticalities did these commission members think they saw in the manager plan? Mayor Fletcher Bowron said he thought a manager plan would never work in Los Angeles because of the "size and complexity" of the city. Did he have reasons for thinking so?

In Philadelphia, the Home Rule Charter Commission felt that the manager plan would not be suitable for local needs because of "the size of the city, its nature, its traditions, its election laws and the patterns of

3. Cited in *American City*, 44 (June, 1931), 93.
4. John C. Bollens, *Appointed Executive Local Government* (1952), p. 12.
5. *Ibid.*, p. 46.

its political life."[6] Yet laws can be amended, and traditions are violated and patterns of political life are modified whenever any city adopts the manager plan.

What is it about large cities that convinces members of study and charter commissions that the manager plan "cannot work" in a large city? The existence of many cultural subgroups with consensus on few matters of consequence, the hostility of political chieftains, the fact that greater public attention is focused on the mayor, and the fact that there is greater inertia working against radical structural changes—all these may well be important factors in preventing the adoption of the manager plan in large cities. But we need to know if these are the real factors, or if there are others, and we would like to know the degree to which each is important.

The Management Cabinet

There is a popular illusion in the United States that the President settles the most vital issues of national policy in meetings with the cabinet and that members of that body are necessarily the principal administrators and top policy advisers in the government. In reality, the cabinet may be highly unimportant, as was the case under Franklin D. Roosevelt, or relatively near the popular image, as was true under Dwight D. Eisenhower. Some of its members are top political advisers, others definitely are not. The fact of the matter is that the President's top political advisers often are not department heads at all, but members of his personal staff. Of particular importance are the assistant to the President and the press secretary. This is significant and is relative to an understanding of recent municipal developments.

The President's cabinet grew out of British practices and developed in the days before the chief executive had a clearly defined personal staff. The attempt to make department heads perform functions more effectively handled by staff personnel has long limited the value of a cabinet whose officers are chosen for reasons independent of their ability to serve as close and confidential advisers to the chief executive.

Although remnants of the old pattern of a cabinet made up of line organization members are still to be found, the trend today is toward the informal operation of an advisory cabinet made up of persons close to the chief executive and consisting largely of his personal staff. The full blossoming of a professional staff for the mayor is in itself a new development and its rise may help account for acceptance of the CAO idea.

We see the beginnings of a management cabinet for large cities in Philadelphia (under the charter) and in New York (by action of Mayor

6. *American City,* 66 (April, 1951), 118.

Robert F. Wagner, Jr.). In Philadelphia, cabinet members are directly selected by the mayor (though council approval is required). The body consists of the Managing Director (CAO), the Director of Finance, the City Solicitor and the City Representative (a new post for handling ceremonial functions and the all-important area of public relations). These are the mayor's top aides, excepting for his personal staff.

In New York, a similar cabinet was established in 1954. The group includes the Deputy Mayor, the City Administrator (CAO), the Director of the Budget, the Director of Planning, the Director of Personnel, the chief legal officer of the city and the mayor's principal personal staff members, including his public relations officer.

Some semblance of a management cabinet probably already exists in quite a number of large cities on a very informal basis. It is likely that such a group, gathering at the call of the chief executive, could be most effective as an informal organization whose membership is determined by the desires of the chief executive, and which is not limited by restrictive requirements established in a charter. Its principal function would logically be found in the threshing out of problems connected with policy development and with political strategy. These were the functions attributed to the traditional cabinet. Large city governments need such a group to allow for frank discussions which permit the ironing out of "bugs" in proposed policy and strategy in governmental situations where complex problems exist.

The New York cabinet has not been especially successful. Members responsible for overhead agencies (such as planning and budgeting) have tended to protect their independence and themselves from criticism by withholding matters from discussion, and there have been other difficulties. To be most effective, an advisory group (perhaps called a cabinet in deference to American tradition) should probably not include persons who have to defend the perimeters of personal empires. The New York and Philadelphia experiments may thus eventually prove to be as unsatisfactory as a cabinet of department heads. Personal staff members seem to be the best sources of advice for the large city chief executive.

The Emerging Post of Chief Administrative Officer

Background

The establishment of a top personal aide to the mayor who serves as the CAO is a postwar development. Whether it represents a new form of city government is an unimportant question. Clearly, it is a special outgrowth of the mayor-council plan. By examining the literature prepared in various cities that have adopted the plan, we find that the CAO's post seems to have been established largely for two reasons: (1) As a compromise between the manager plan and government by a strong mayor; and (2) as a means of providing for professional administration without eliminating the mayor as the symbolic head and chief policy maker of the city.

In the years before World War II, there was little discussion of a post such as CAO. Reformers were generally so bent on ending "politics" in city government—and therefore on removing the powers of the elective mayor—that they failed to recognize that a political chief executive, responsible to the voters, is capable of choosing able underlings. (Reformers have long labored under the strange illusion that a politician's friends and acquaintances and persons recommended to him for appointment are necessarily incompetent, if not downright dishonest.)

We find, for example, no mention of a professional administrator as a possible top executive aide in A. C. Hanford's review of municipal problems in the mid-twenties.[7] Of course, this may partly be the result of the fact that the strong mayor plan, though it dates from the 1880's, was not fully accepted, despite the approval of reformers, until fairly recently. As late as 1929, Chester C. Maxey saw in the choice of a strong mayor "a municipal Mussolini to run the whole works."[8] Persons with such a viewpoint were unlikely to look with favor upon plans designed to strengthen the mayor by adding a professional administrator to superintend the principal departments and thus complement the "dictator's" powers.

During the Great Depression, when municipalities were in serious financial difficulties, E. S. Griffith, musing over the question of improved structural forms, noted that "it is still possible that in the future the American city will continue to evolve new types. None are in sight now."[9]

Actually, two hints of a new type had appeared by then, though one could excuse even the sharpest observer for not having seen them. In fact, their existence was scarcely noticeable for the next decade and a half. The CAO plan first took form in a suggestion from Lent D. Upson and in a provision of a new city charter for San Francisco.

In Detroit, Upson suggseted that the office of administrative assistant to the mayor be created.[10] His view was that such a person could handle much administrative detail, that an incoming mayor would have an experienced person upon whom to rely, that programs would have continuity of administration and that the mayor would be freed for policy development and promotion.

The influence of the efficiency and economy movement was strong

7. A. C. Hanford, *Problem in Municipal Government* (1926).
8. C. C. Maxey, *Urban Democracy* (1929), p. 118.
9. E. S. Griffith, *Current Municipal Problems* (1933), p. 185.
10. *American City*, 44 (June, 1931), 93.

in Upson's thinking. His idea emphasized the value of experienced personnel, continuity in office, and independence from "political influence." He suggested that the assistant, rather than serving at the pleasure of the mayor, should be appointed by the mayor in accord with minimum qualifications described in the charter and from a list of the three or four highest names on a roster established by the civil service commission after examination. The assistant would be dismissable after a hearing on preferred charges. Upson even saw this system being extended to other top administrative officers, so that periodic dismissals and resignations could be curtailed—a reflection of the reformer's belief that the goal was to establish government on a "businesslike" basis.

The CAO provision in the San Francisco charter of 1931 grew out of agitation for the manager plan.[11] A movement for the manager plan had begun in 1926 with support from the Bureau of Governmental Research and the *San Francisco News*. The research subcommittee of the 1930 charter revision commission was generally favorable to the manager plan. Some members of the commission, on the other hand, made statements sharply favoring the strong mayor plan. Finally, "the hearings indicated the necessity for a compromise between a strong mayor and a manager form." As a result, the post of CAO (as it was called) was created, but powers were assigned in a piecemeal fashion, with each proposed function being subject to a vote of the charter commission members.

Thus, the first position of CAO was established in a typically American pattern of expediency and compromise. In accord with the reformer's distrust of politicians, the CAO was made appointive by the mayor, but could be removed only by recall or by hearing followed by two-thirds vote of the board of supervisors.

The San Francisco CAO was given authority over a number of departments, but he has never been given the full powers that his title implies. He is powerless so far as overhead (staff) functions are concerned.

Criticism of the proposed plan in San Francisco ran along the usual lines to be found when the manager plan is proposed. Opponents said it provided for a "dictator" and Jacksonian sensibilities were shocked when it was found that the CAO need not be a resident of the city when hired.[12] On the other hand, one contemporary proponent viewed the CAO provision as "one of the outstanding features of the charter,"[13] and another thought that "this will make for improved coordination and more efficient business administration."[14] A political

13. William H. Nanry, "San Francisco Adopts a New Charter," *National Municipal Review*, 20 (May, 1931), 259–263.

11. Bollens, *op. cit.*, pp. 12–13; J. M. Selig, "The San Francisco Idea," *National Municipal Review*, 46 (June 1957), 290–295.

12. Bollens, *op. cit.*, p. 45.

14. *American City*, 44 (April, 1931), 5.

scientist, noting that something new had arrived on the scene, commented that "the 'chief administrator' is not a manager in the usual understanding of the term. He is entirely restricted in his powers by the mayor."[15]

Local reformers in other cities did not rush to take up the new mechanical gadget for better government, and no John M. Patterson came along with cash and a propaganda machine to support it. In fact, seventeen years were to pass before the next municipal CAO came into being. (In 1941, however, a St. Louis study recommended consideration of the desirability of an administrative assistant to the mayor. Such an official, it was thought, would "keep the mayor informed on the operations of the city government, and would follow up on the carrying out of his instructions to officials."[16])

In 1948, Charles P. Farnsley, mayor of Louisville, appointed a "consultant" at a salary of $15,000—higher than that of any city officer.[17] Farnsley was an advocate of reform and of administrative efficiency. (He had majored in political science in college.) His idea proved attractive; the new post was later adopted by ordinance and it was retained by Farnsley's successor.

Even the Louisville adoption was not decisive, however, and it was not until 1951 that a trend toward the use of the CAO plan could be said to have become established. In that year, Philadelphia and Los Angeles adopted versions of the plan, the former much stronger than the latter. They were followed the next year by New Orleans and Hoboken. In 1953, New York, Boston, and Newark were added. A 1954 staff report by the Chicago Charter Revision Commission recommended the adoption of the CAO plan, but Mayor Richard J. Daley refused to give his support. Others have adopted the CAO plan since.

The Functions of the Chief Administrative Officer

There has been a great deal of controversy over the question of what powers the CAO ought or ought not have—whether he is to perform essentially staff or line functions and whether or not he is "practically a city manager."[18] There has also been considerable variation in the amount of study given the plan before adoption.

In Los Angeles, the CAO plan was considered superior to the

15. E. A. Cottrell, "Three California Charters," *National Municipal Review*, 20 (April, 1931), 242.

16. Mayor's Advisory Committee on City Survey and Audit, *The Government of the City of St. Louis* (1941), pp. 16–17.

17. George Kent, "Mayor Charlie Cuts Corners," *National Municipal Review*, 38 (October, 1949), 433–436.

18. For detailed comparisons among various CAO plans, powers assigned, and methods of appointment and removal, see W. S. Sayre, "The General Manager Idea for Large Cities," *Public Administration Review*, 14 (Autumn, 1954), 253–258.

manager plan because it was tailored to fit the "particular requirements" of the city.[19] The charter amendment was submitted with little advance study (the major department heads had urged the plan two years earlier). Newspapers strongly supported this move toward "efficiency." Opponents—some labor and civic groups, and the League of Women Voters—felt that further study was needed. Others thought there would be conflict between departmental boards and the CAO; still others wanted the manager plan.

In Philadelphia the Home Rule Charter Commission did an especially careful job of checking into the plans adopted or being studied in other cities, and it held public hearings. The reform-minded *Philadephia Inquirer*, thinking of decades of machine mayors, could not believe that a strong chief executive would allow the managing director (CAO) much actual power.[20]

The Hoboken Charter Commission chose one of the options under the Faulkner Act which provided for the CAO. Under this plan, "the business manager would be somewhat akin to a city manager," but the manager plan itself was avoided lest an antireform group secure a majority on the council and appoint an "unqualified" manager.[21] For some reason, it was assumed that such a group would not be able to dominate the mayor and CAO.

The philosophy of the efficiency and economy movement was most strongly reflected in Boston, where the administrative services department was established as a staff agency under a board, principally as a means of increasing "administrative efficiency." The board, under the chairmanship of the director of administrative services, consists of the personnel officer, the purchasing agent, the auditor, the treasurer, the budget officer, and the assessor. The directorship is only a feeble first step toward a chief administrative officer, however. The narrow scope of the office is indicated in the first annual report, which said that "our experience in this new field of government management . . . has given us the incentive to lay the groundwork for an organizational setup that we trust in the future will be a pattern to be followed by other large cities throughout the country for efficiency and businesslike methods in the daily operation of city government."[22] The department reported that it had busied itself with such things as the establishment of a performance budget, a survey of typewriter use by line departments, the renumbering of offices in the city hall, and a survey of the use of city telephones for private calls.

19. Bollens, *op. cit.*, p. 46.

20. *National Municipal Review*, 40 (March, 1951), 150.

21. *New York Times*, July 15, 1952.

22. City of Boston, *Annual Report of the Administrative Services Department* (1954), p. 14.

The New York Testing Ground

Since the San Francisco charter and Upson era, the general trend has been toward the creation of a CAO responsible only to the mayor and serving at his pleasure. In New York, however, where Tammany is not yet a ghost, reformers have expressed skepticism concerning the current theory that administrative expertise and mayoralty politics can be bedpartners—at least they do not see municipal bliss as a result.

The City Manager Study Committee of the Citizens Union wanted to have the CAO appointed after selection by the mayor, a public hearing, and approval by the Board of Estimate. Removal would be similarly cumbersome. The Committee thought that independence for the CAO would "make the position more attractive to a high-grade man."[23] (Later, when the post of city administrator was created with responsibility to the mayor, Luther Gulick, than whom no higher grade could be found, was the first appointee to the post.)

There has been considerable conflict over what role the CAO should play in New York. This has been reflected in editorials, statements by the mayor, and interagency feuds. An editorial in the *National Municipal Review* expressed the hope that New York would be the first city where the CAO would be given management tools—especially over personnel and finance.[24] But it has developed that it was precisely lack of control over these agencies that at first threatened to relegate the city administrator to the role of advisor on management efficiency. This, despite the fact that the Mayor's Committee thought the CAO "would be virtually a general manager for the city" who would assist the mayor "in the general coordination of all departmental activities."[25]

The complex administrative structure proposed by Mayor Wagner when he took office in 1954 made necessary a general briefing session for department heads on who was to report to whom.[26] After the meeting was over, many department heads complained that they still did not know whether they reported to the Mayor through the Deputy Mayor or through the City Administrator. There was evidence that the Mayor was a bit confused, too. He gamely tried to explain the role of the new CAO, saying that he would be an important advisor on "managerial matters" and would be neither a city manager nor a narrow coordinator. Rather, the CAO would be "executive vice president in charge of operations," acting as general manager in dealing with the administrative agencies.

The question of whether a position of any real consequence had been created was quickly raised in connection with an open dispute that

23. *National Municipal Review*, 42 (March, 1953), 134.
24. *Ibid.*, 43 (January, 1954), 4.
25. Mayor's Committee on Management Survey, *Modern Management for the City of New York* (1953), I, 31. On postwar management trends in the nation's largest city, see Wallace S. Sayre and Herbert Kaufman, *Governing New York City* (1960).
26. *New York Times*, January 6, 1954.

arose shortly after the Wagner administration got under way.[27] The adversaries were the City Administrator and the Budget Director.

The new arrangement provided for the Budget Director to report directly to the Mayor. It also happened that proposals for administrative improvements by the CAO had to be referred to the Budget Bureau's division of analysis, which then investigated them and made recommendations to the Budget Director, whose recommendations to the Board of Estimate were normally decisive. This phenomenon had the practical result of placing the CAO, for many purposes, under the Budget Director.

In the struggle that ensued, most reformers sided with the CAO. (In his first annual report the City Administrator claimed that "management savings" accomplished by his agency had trimmed $25 million from the city budget.[28]) Wagner tried to steer a middle course which, for some time, seemed to indicate a lack of understanding of the fundamental problem involved. In April, the proposed budget left the Budget Director with his powers unchanged, but two months later the Board of Estimate, on the Mayor's motion, transferred the controversial division of analysis to the City Administrator.

The New York experiment thus survived a vital early test. If it had failed at this juncture, the whole pattern of development might have changed sharply. If the City Administrator had become merely an individual heading a small office that recommended management economies to the Budget Bureau, the healthy development of the CAO plan might have been dealt a very serious blow.

But such was not the case. By 1960, according to Wallace S. Sayre and Herbert Kaufman, the CAO and his office staff had become "the most fully realized assets of the Mayor's office . . . the Mayor's most active problem-solvers, especially in matters requiring interdepartmental agreements or departmental reorganizations." The office of Managing Director, in Philadelphia, had "contributed both to strong, productive political leadership in the office of mayor and to high-quality professional administration in most departments of Philadelphia's city government."[29]

The Coming Pattern

The future prospects for a further spread of the plan look favorable. Middle-sized cities are beginning to provide for a CAO in reference to a manager when reforms are attempted. St. Cloud, Minnesota, did so in a new charter in 1954, followed by Duluth and Lansing in 1956 and

27. See *New York Times,* April 4, April 14, May 19, and June 14, 1955.
28. Cited in *ibid.,* May 19, 1954.
29. Sayre and Kaufman, *op. cit.,* pp. 665–666; J. C. Phillips, *Municipal Government and Administration in America,* (1960), p. 327.

by other cities since then. In Duluth, the CAO was given sweeping powers over all line departments except the city attorney, while in Lansing the post was conceived of principally as an assistant to the mayor.

It seems likely that we can expect a further spread of the plan into middle-sized cities, if for no other reason than that the adoption of a CAO charter provision is a much less radical break with the past and is therefore politically more feasible than the adoption of the manager plan.

Conclusions

It may be, as Wallace Sayre has said, that the CAO plan reflects "the judgment in the larger cities that the council manager plan represents an unnecessary surrender of the value of leadership and accountability found in the instrument of the elected chief executive."[30] It may be, on the other hand, that the plan represents the only practicable administrative modification available to large cities where, for some reason or reasons, new charters and radical reforms encounter greater inertia or overt resistance than is the case in smaller cities. The factors accounting for the current pattern require more empirical study before they can be stated with conviction.

The officer I have called the CAO has a great variety of powers. In some cities, especially in Philadelphia, in New Orleans, and in New Jersey cities of over 250,000 under the CAO option, he has many of the line and staff powers of a manager. In other cities, such as San Francisco, he presides principally over some line functions; in still others, he is viewed mostly as a staff aide to, or agent of, the mayor; and in Boston, he is interested chiefly in the economies of management reorganization. This narrower concept of the CAO, which is in the tradition of the efficiency and economy movement, hardly establishes a city government organization that maximizes the use of the skills of a first-rate professional administrator.

In each case, regardless of the powers given the CAO, we have seen a movement away from the idea of a professional administrator independent of the mayor and toward the idea of a competent top leadership in the executive office responsible to the mayor, who in turn is accountable to the voters for administration as well as for policy. The desire of the mayor to make a good record for himself rather than the older reform notion of some mechanical device is counted on to keep the officer in line.

The degree to which the CAO plan will operate successfully probably depends as much on the personality of the chief executive involved

30. Sayre, "The General Manager Idea," p. 253.

as upon anything else. The problem today is no longer that of finding "honest" public officials. For the most part, we have them. Nor is the problem any longer one of securing the adoption of the manager plan, for the CAO plan seems to make this sharp change of course unnecessary in large cities. (In smaller cities, where the mayor is a part-time official and much less in the spotlight, the relationship of mayor to professional administrator is not the same and the CAO plan may be less appropriate.) The problem is no longer one of trying to find a mayor with unusual administrative ability. The problem today for large cities is rather one of finding a mayor who is willing to delegate responsibility for administrative detail to a CAO and of finding a CAO who can secure the confidence of the mayor.

It is too early to predict with confidence that the CAO plan will become a permanent instrument for municipal government. It is certainly possible that too much depends upon the personality of the mayor and upon his willingness to delegate appropriate authority. It is also possible that not enough power will be assigned to the CAO to permit full use of his capabilities. It is possible that department heads cannot be persuaded to report to the CAO rather than to the mayor, or that the mayor will not deal with department heads through the CAO. But if such dangers as these do not prove to be insurmountable barriers, it may be that the long-standing problem of finding an appropriate form of government for our largest cities has been resolved.

The Mayor and the Planning Agency

V. O. Key

THE OPERATION of an effective [city] planning agency is a task radically different from that of managing a department of health or a department of welfare or any other such agency that conducts extensive dealings directly with the public. The peculiar aspects of the administration of the planning agency come in part from the fact that its dealings must be principally with other elements of the [city] government. It must make a success of meddling into what other officials are likely to regard as their own business. The problems of operation of a planning agency thus become problems of conduct of relations with other departments of government; those are problems that are in part matters of skill in negotiation and in part matters of bringing either superior technical knowledge to bear on a question or of bringing at least the superiority of an outside and objective view. Given the nature of their operations, the workings of planning agencies are not apt to be improved even by the most extensive and thoughtful statutory prescription. The route to improvement is rather in the main sustained and ingenious application to problems of administration. The principal question is that of the appropriate relation between the mayor and the planning agency. One view is that the planning agency should be an "arm of the [mayor]." By its critics this phrase is interpreted to mean that the Planning Commission would become a "rubber stamp" for the [mayor] who, these interpreters of the theory seem to hold, is invariably a malevolent gentleman with determined but wrong-headed views on even the most minute questions within the purview of the Commission. Some of the advocates of the arm-of-the-[mayor] theory seem to regard the management of the [city] government as about the same sort of problem as the supervision of an automobile assembly plant. That is, the scheduling or planning department should be across the hall from the boss and should work up for him the detailed instructions to the operating units of the plant, so that the required numbers of the ap-

From a report made by the late V. O. Key to the Maryland State Planning Commission and published by it in mimeographed form in November 1958. The words mayor *and* city *have been substituted for* governor *and* state *throughout, brackets being used to remind the reader of the changes.*

propriate models would roll off the line by the end of the day. Whether for good or ill, [mayors] have less control over their domains than do the superintendents of assembly plants; nor is a [city] administration ever so closely articulated as are the elements of an assembly operation. Nor do superintendents of assembly plants have to worry about [city councils].

Perhaps the major aspect of administrative reality overlooked in advocacy of the arm-of-the-[mayor] position is the fact that the planning agency must in large degree establish and earn its own position in relation to the operating departments of the government without benefit of the [mayor's] authority. Thus, the Commission could develop a policy and induce the [mayor] to issue it as an order to the operating departments. Yet the policy might not stick unless (1) virtual agreement of the affected departments had been obtained beforehand, or (2) the Commission had contrived a rule so rational and so adapted to the realities that the operating departments would not dare challenge it. The orthodox administrative theory would prescribe that this procedure of executive approval or order be followed, but the operational practice would necessarily be one of the negotiation of a rational principle more or less acceptable to all concerned. Thus, agencies with functions such as those of the Planning Commission depend in the main for their effectiveness on their skill and sense in building a network of relationships with the operating departments rather than on their capacity to induce the [mayor] to put his signature to their recommendations. And this may be especially true where the heads of operating departments enjoy more than a little independence from the [mayor]. The development of the kinds of administrative relations that are implicit in the arm-of-the-[mayor] theory is apt to occur gradually over a long period of time, if it occurs at all. Moreover, the situation in the short run is certain to vary enormously with the occupant of the [mayor's office].

Another position on the issue runs to the effect that the Planning Commission should be entirely independent of the [mayor] and should occupy itself with the courageous and virtuous application of the scientific criteria of planning uninfluenced by the political winds of the moment. The truth of the matter is, of course, that no statutory gimmick can put the Commission beyond the control of the [mayor], if he is disposed to control it. Further, although a painstaking and skilled study of the questions the Commission must decide yields far better results than off-the-cuff determinations, its major decisions and recommendations must by their nature be policy decisions. To the extent that it is effective, the Commission is inevitably involved in the politics of policy, if not in the politics of who holds office.

Perhaps creation of the most appropriate working relationships between [mayor] and planning commission would be promoted if all concerned could forget the arm-of-the-[mayor] theory as well as the vision of the independent and insulated ivory tower and consider the concrete relationships that would be conducive to the performance of the planning function. As such relationships develop, let it be left to the processes of institutional evolution to christen them.

Some of the major types of relationships that could improve the effectiveness of the planning process may be set out. These categories are built up on the assumption that the Planning Commission will come to have wider concerns and more initiative than it has in the past. A principal assumption underlying the observations that follow is that the danger for the Planning Commission is not so much that the [mayor] will dominate the Commission as that he will ignore it.

1. It seems clear enough that the Commission (or its director) should not be within range of buzzer summons from the [mayor's] desk. The involvement of Commission staff in the day-to-day work of the [mayor's] office is not compatible with the analyses in breadth and depth that the Commission should conduct.

2. Generally a systematic liaison should be maintained between the [mayor] and the Commission. The chairman of the Commission customarily reviews the annual capital improvement program with the [mayor] before its submission to the Department of Budget and Procurement. Certain other types of consultation with the [mayor] should also become customary with the Commission to the extent that such is not already the practice.

3. Major new planning studies should be cleared with the [mayor] prior to their initiation. If the Commission is to do the job open to it, it will conduct inquiries of which the [mayor] should at least be forewarned and perhaps his endorsement solicited. This procedure also has a most practical import in that the Commission will often need special funds to do such studies. Moreover, the [mayor] should be informed of the findings and recommendations of major studies prior to their public release.

4. The Commission should conduct such planning studies as the [mayor] may direct. The odds are that over the years [mayors] will not often have broad ideas to put to the Commission for examination and recommendation. Yet to make explicit the situation as it is already in fact, it is suggested that a section be added to the planning statute: "The Commission shall conduct such planning studies as the [mayor] may direct." The most probable mode of operation under such a clause is that the Commission would identify a problem deserving of examination, outline what it proposed to do, sell the [mayor] on the idea, and present to him for signature a draft of a letter instructing the Commission to work on the problem. Or, far less frequently, the initiative might rest with the [mayor], in which case, in some instances, the Commission might find it advisable to suggest to the [mayor] that he had asked the wrong question and negotiate a workable plan for the

study of the right question. It scarcely need be said that it would be improper for the [mayor] to indicate to the Commission what the answer to the question should be.

5. The Commission should call the attention of the [mayor] to [city] departments that are singularly ineffective or inactive in departmental planning.

6. A critical question arises when the [mayor] asks the Commission to include in the program of capital improvements a project dear to his heart but, in the view of the Commission, not well considered. [Mayors] in situations of pressure may commit themselves to actions of whose ramifications they are not aware. The practice over the life of the capital improvement program has been for the Commission to include most of these projects albeit with reluctance. Yet the uniform testimony is also that as the capital improvement procedure has developed [mayors] have come more and more to support the Commission by insisting that proponents of projects put their requests through the Commission procedure.

Yet it is a safe prediction that from time to time the Commission will be confronted with the question of what to do about such requests. On occasion these episodes can be used by the Commission to suggest the initiation of a broad survey of the general problem raised by the [mayor's] particular project. The Commission will also need to educate successive [mayors] to the advantages of parrying some pressures by referral of proposals to the Commission for extended analysis. That analysis could result in the development of a broad program that would do political credit to the [mayor] or to the burial of the embarrassing question of the moment. In any case, as the statutes now stand the [mayor] is free to include in his budget recommendations any project he wishes even though it has not received the blessings of the Planning Commission. The Commission in turn is free, if it wishes, to withhold its blessings from any such proposal and to leave its advocacy clearly a responsibility of the [mayor] alone.

Some of the problems that arise from projects that are inspirations of the [mayoral] moment would disappear with better long-range planning. An imaginative planning agency, buttressed by solid planning in the operating departments, ought to have on hand an ample stock of well-considered undertakings from which any [mayor] could pick up attractive items to advocate both to his own glory and to the advancement of the public weal.

7. Apart from such individual matters a broader and more difficult problem of policy arises in the capital improvement program. Certainly most of the items in the capital improvement program will be the same whoever the [mayor] is; they are determined, in effect, by the immediate necessities of the going situation with respect to settled policies. Nevertheless, one [mayor] may be strongly committed to the needs of certain

minority groups; another to the improvement, say, of institutions and policies affecting the aged; and another may have another sort of policy inclination. These matters of policy preference—beyond the questions settled by technical and operating necessities—should be adequately cared for by the representation of the mayor's outlook by his appointees on the Commission. Even so, [mayors] should be aware that their problem in impressing such broad policy views on the [city] government is in larger measure one of dealing with the operating departments than of managing the outlook of the Planning Commission. If projects desired by the [mayor] on policy grounds arrive at the Planning Commission weakly presented and ranked low in priority by the operating departments, the Planning Commission, even if it is a rubber stamp, cannot well do what should have been done elsewhere.

8. Whether the [city] debt shall be increased; if so, by how much; whether some capital improvements should be financed from current revenues are, of course, basic issues of [city] fiscal policy. The burden of advocacy and of responsibility on these matters rests in large measure with the [mayor]. Some [mayors] are "builders"; others "economizers"; others fall in between these extremes. Whatever their position, even if it is one of silence, they tend to bear the burden of responsibility. The procedure should bring the issues to the [mayor] or focus operating views upon him in such a manner as to facilitate his decision on these broad questions of fiscal (including debt) policy. One possibility is for the [mayor], during the period of the preparation of the annual operating and capital budget, to make a rough and tentative policy determination which, among other things, would fix an overall limit on the dollar volume of capital improvements to be recommended by the Planning Commission. Thus, in his fiscal planning the [mayor] would fix the size of the pie and the Planning Commission would allocate it among the departments.

Comprehensive Planning,
An Impossible Ideal

Alan Altshuler

THOSE who consider themselves comprehensive planners typically claim that their most important functions are: one, to create a master plan which can guide the deliberations of specialist planners, two, to evaluate the proposals of specialist planners in the light of the master plan, and three, to coordinate the planning of specialist agencies so as to ensure that their proposals reinforce each other to further the public interest. Each of these functions requires for ideal performance that the comprehensive planners understand the overall public interest, at least in connection with the subject matter (which may be partial) of their plans; and that they possess causal knowledge which enables them to gauge the approximate net effect of proposed actions on the public interest.

Introduction

This paper is concerned with some ways in which city planners have approached the first of these two requirements; that is, that they understand the public interest. Contrary to most students of planning, I consider it the more interesting one. If comprehensive planners deal with a great many more areas of public policy than specialists, their factual and causal knowledge in each area is bound to appear shallow by comparison with the specialists in it. Their claims to comprehensiveness, therefore, if they are to be persuasive, must refer primarily to a special knowledge of the public interest.

Every government planner, no matter how specialized, must be guided by *some* conception of the public interest. Since plans are proposals of concerted action to achieve goals, each must express his conception as a goal or series of goals for his community. He will probably

Reprinted by permission of The Journal of the American Institute of Planners, *Vol. XXXI, No. 3 (August 1965) and of the author.*

conceive these goals as constantly shifting rather than highly stable, as always intermediate rather than final, and as more in the nature of criteria than of concrete destinations. Community goal conceptions are likely to have these characteristics because of the limitations on collective human foresight and imagination. Nonetheless, it is impossible to plan without some sense of community goals, call them what you will. Moreover, for the planning process in any community to be democratic, and I assume in these pages that it should be, the goals must win approval from a democratic political process.

The *comprehensive* planner must assume that his community's various collective goals can somehow be measured at least roughly as to importance and welded into a single hierarchy of community objectives. In addition, he must argue that technicians like himself can prescribe courses of action to achieve these objectives without great distortion or harmful side effects of a magnitude sufficient to outweigh the gains achieved through planning. We may conceive a continuum of faith in the feasibility and desirability of comprehensive planning. The "ideal type" defender of comprehensive planning would contend that a serious effort should be made to plan the future evolution of all important economic and social patterns in detail. Other defenders would limit their support to the planning in general outline of change in particular strategic variables.

Certainly few sophisticated American defenders of planning believe that planners can achieve a total comprehensiveness of perspective on any issue. Many do believe, however, that professional planners can come closer to achieving it on numerous vital issues than other participants in the urban decision process. The primary purpose of this paper is to explore some of the foundations of this belief.

It should be noted that the explicit claims of practicing planners often suggest that a fair approximation of genuine comprehensiveness is currently attainable. By way of illustration, some case studies I wrote several years ago[1] provide evidence. They were conducted in two midwestern cities whose programs had especially good reputations among planners consulted. Let us label these cities A and B. Both had non-partisan forms of government, weak political party organizations, and strong civil service merit systems. City A had a commission form of government; City B had a strong council-weak mayor system. City A had a population of roughly 300,000; City B, 500,000.

One case study involved the evolution of a land use plan for City A. The planning director's conception of the plan's function is described in his published introduction to it:

1. These case studies will shortly appear as chapters 2–5 of my book, *The City Planning Process* (Ithaca: Cornell University Press, probably late 1965). Versions of three of them have already been published separately by the Inter-University Program as "The Ancker Hospital Site Controversy," "A Land-Use Plan for St. Paul," and "Locating the Intercity Freeway."

> The total city planning process, of which land use planning is but one part, involves a continuing program of deriving, organizing, and presenting a comprehensive plan for the development and renewal of [the city] . . . The plans must be economically feasible, and must promote the common good, and at the same time [must] preserve the rights and interests of the individual.

Long discussions with every planner involved in the plan's preparation persuaded me that these words were meant literally. City planning was comprehensive and for the common good, not for any lesser objectives. Several members of the planning staff had vigorously criticized the previous planning director for offering advice freely to operating agencies without first developing, or even trying to develop, a comprehensive plan. The predecessor himself, however, had justified his recommendations in terms of their overall "effect on community life." For example, he had written in a publication on the city's proposed freeway system that, while others had considered the cost of the freeways and their effect on traffic, the City Planning Board had "special responsibilities posed by virtue of its function and status as an advisory representative citizens' group concerned with the development of all facets of the community's life."

A second case study concerned the location of a new city-county hospital in City A. In the course of a prolonged controversy, politicians turned finally to city planners to interpret the overall public interest. The City Planning Board shied from this challenge out of political prudence, but the planning staff of the city's Housing and Redevelopment Authority accepted it eagerly. Both groups of planners stated confidently in interviews that they were better equipped to recommend a wise decision than the city's consultant hospital architect, whose primary concern was how best to build a hospital. They believed that because their perspective was broader, their recommendation was very likely to be more rational.[2]

A third case study described the evolution of a central area plan for City B. The plan's primary author, with the full support of his planning director, cast its arguments in the broadest possible terms. Its operational goal was clearly a limited one: economic growth. The planner felt, however, that he had to justify the goal itself. He stressed the functions of downtown as bearer of culture, disseminator of news and

---

2. The words "rational" and "wise" are often used interchangeably in evaluating public choices. This is in accord with the usage of natural law philosophers, but not with that of contemporary economic and social theorists. For the latter, the term "rational" refers to the efficiency of means where ends are known. "Wisdom" refers to deep understanding and the ability to make what are considered "good" judgments on complex human issues, when goals and efficient means are not generally known.

Consequently, the planners' use of the word "rational" in the classic sense to defend their distinctly modern "expert" recommendations makes for confusion of thought. This confusion has a poltical function, however. It conveys the impression that expert logic or technique can produce "good" decisions on complex human issues.

ideas, haven for unique activities, supplier of taxes to support all public services, and so on. When interviewed, he emphasized that his concern was to enrich the lives of all citizens, not to line the pockets of downtown businessmen. It was merely fortuitous, he believed, that in this case the interests of property owners and those of society coincided. He admitted freely, as did all the planners in both cities, that no plan or evaluation could be entirely comprehensive. His (and their) disclaimer was perfunctory, however, as if only a minor detail were at stake. He wrote, for example, that the central area plan could not truly be termed comprehensive because: "there are and always will be elements—new aspects—yet to be studied and yet to be decided upon." He thus rejected a conception of comprehensiveness that I have termed useless; that is, that the comprehensive plan should deal with everything. In short, he admitted that the object of any decision is necessarily limited, at very least in time, but he preserved the implications that the planner's approach—that is, his goal orientation—to the object may be comprehensive.

Planners generally agree that the method of discovery of community goals can in the final analysis only be public discussion. Planners may propose alternative articulations, but goal statements can have no claim to represent community thought unless the community or its "legitimate" representatives ratifies them after serious discussion and deliberation. The primary problem in theory, then, should be to guide the vigorous discussion and to decide when it has gone on long enough. The primary problem in practice, it developed in the two cities studied, was to get any sort of discussion going at all, and then to keep it going.

The planners of City A hoped, for example, that vigorous discussion would follow publication of their land use plan. No one showed any interest in discussing it, however. The reason seemed to be that the plan's stated goals were too general. No one knew how their application would affect him in practice. Those who were not completely uninterested in the plan had learned long ago to be suspicious of "utopian" generalities. As a result, nonplanners decided with uncoordinated unanimity to ignore the plan until someone proposed specific applications of it. Only at this point, they felt, would there be anything comprehensible—whether or not comprehensive—to argue about.

The planners of City B argued that the City A planners' premises were wrong, and would have been wrong even if discussion of their plan had developed. For a discussion truly to influence the planning process, they said, it had to begin before detailed planning got under way. In their view, no one could effectively interpolate changes into a plan after it was complete without upsetting its internal harmony. If one of the goals of a plan were changed, then in theory every specific recommendation should be altered to some extent. No one had the time or intellectual energy, however, to do this when a plan had already taken definite shape. The crucial phase in the evolution of any plan, then, was the development of its first draft. Goals should be determined before this phase moved far along. They themselves tried to obtain approval for planning goals before developing their central area plan. They decided at the start that they needed a goal statement which would be both "operational" and acceptable to all "reasonable" citizens of the city. By "operational," they meant that progress toward the goal could be objectively measured, and that the broad costs, both tangible and spiritual, of striving toward it could be foreseen. Comprehensive goals, they judged, could not be operational. Therefore, reasonable men could not pass on them intelligently. It followed that goals could win intelligent public approval only if they were partial. The question was: *how* partial? Perhaps it was possible to articulate, and plan to achieve, highly general goals even if not truly comprehensive ones.

They endeavored to bring about a public discussion of essential goal options before preparing the detailed plan. Planners had applied themselves to downtown economic problems in recent years, and had developed a fairly integrated theory explaining characteristic downtown problems. Consequently, City B's planners were able to present their preferred goals with tightly reasoned arguments behind them. The parts were related and mutually reinforcing. The man of affairs with a limited amount of time could quickly grasp the objectives and the main lines of reasoning on which the recommendations were based. The most general operational goal that the planners proposed was "the economic growth of downtown." They recognized that this goal was itself deceptive, however, in that it sounded noncontroversial but the measures necessary to its accomplishment could not be. In their publications on downtown planning goals, therefore, they chose to emphasize what they termed "design goals." These were in fact *types* of projects that had been tried in other cities. The planners explained the relationship between these types of proposals and the economic problems facing urban downtowns in the current period. It was possible to discuss the types of dislocation that might be expected, and so on, without bringing in specific project proposals. The discussion was a model of comprehensible argument in favor of middle range (that is, operational but still general) planning goals. It is doubtful that existing theory was (or is) sufficiently developed to support comparable justifications of goal recommendations at any other range of city planning activity.[3]

Even in this area, however, the specific financial costs and unintended side effects that would arise on application in City B were difficult to foresee. Any intelligent discussion of planning goals had to take

3.   A major reason for this, of course, is that in no urban sections but downtown do simple economic goals seem entirely adequate. Outside the United States, planners often consider them inadequate even for downtown. See, for example, the British Town and Country Planning Association's analysis of central London problems: "The Paper Economy" (London: Town and Country Planning Association, 1962).

these (or their unpredictability) into account. For the discussion to be fully useful, the planners judged, its participants had to be willing to inform themselves about planning detail at some significant expenditure of time and effort. The discussion had to continue throughout the planning process, which itself would have peaks of activity but no final termination. Since the overall goal was partial, the discussants had to be urged to consider the full complexity of its side effects. This they could not do if they confined themselves to examination of the central economic reasoning behind the "design goals."

The first problem was how to find appropriate discussants. The comprehensive planner's search is more complicated than that of any specialist. He cannot be satisfied to consult a narrow constituency. Presumably he should understand every important goal of each of society's members. If he must deal in practice with groups rather than individuals, he should not limit himself to constellations of interest that maintain permanent formal organizations. But the planners knew of no way to approach the city's "potential" groups. These would not become actual groups unless some immediate threats activated their potential members; some potential groupings of interest that the observer might identify would not become actual even then. Even those theoretically capable of being activated, however, currently had no leaders to speak for them. The abstract discussion of goals could seldom seem sufficiently immediate to spur them to organize and choose representatives. It seemed that in no other public endeavor than general goal determination was the disproportion greater between the number of groups that might reasonably become involved and the number that would.

The planners soon found that they could carry on a continuing discussion only with men whose jobs required them to spend time on the study and discussion of civic affairs. Only a few organizations in the city had such men on their payrolls. All of these fit into a few categories. Most were large downtown business firms or organizations of businessmen. A few good government groups (supported mainly by the contributions of businesses or businessmen) had representatives who took an interest in city planning, but for the most part they were in the same position as planners; they could talk abstractly about the public interest but they could not claim any special ability to represent particular interests. The other permanent organizations in the city did not have representatives spending the bulk of their time observing civic affairs. Each had a few continuing interests (racial issues, taxes, city hiring policy, and so forth) and became politically active only when immediate threats to these arose.

Making the best of this situation, the planners tried to carry on a discussion of goals with the professional "civic affairs" representatives of downtown business. These professional discussants, however, lacked the power to commit their firms to anything. Consequently, as the discussion became more specific they became more and more noncommittal. The businessmen who had the power to commit their firms to specific courses of action had neither the time nor interest to engage in long discussions with the city planners. In a short while, even the professional discussants found that they had no time to study each tentative planning formulation with care. Thus, a major difficulty was revealed (as it probably would have been in most cities). Even had the planners been able to handle all the complexity of life, they would not have found laymen willing or able to evaluate their work.

If it is so difficult to spur well-informed discussion even of such limited goals as those of the central area plan, the following question necessarily demands attention: what should be considered an adequate discussion of planning goals? Was the discussion in this case adequate even though the only participants were businessmen who took only mild interest in the discussion and were concerned only with direct economic costs and consequences? One might say that it was, because other groups could have entered the discussion to raise additional points had they wished. I was not able to find any elected officials in City B, however, who accepted this reasoning. Most were rather inarticulate about their objectives, but some were able to state their views quite precisely. Their central line of reasoning may be summarized briefly. Downtown businesses are "organizations in being." They are accustomed to watching the civic scene and searching for issues likely to affect their interests. They enter the discussion of any proposal at a very early stage and understand its potential impact on their interests relatively early. Other members of the public, however, tend to reach awareness that something is in issue and conceptualize their interests much more slowly. After the perception begins to clarify most take quite some time to organize. There is an enormous range in the amount of time, and in the degree of immediacy of a threat or opportunity, that it takes to move different groups of people with potential interest in a proposal to the threshold of organizational expression. Government never moves slowly enough or poses issues clearly enough to give everyone his say. It is fair to say that only when government moves at a snail's pace and deals with issues of rather direct and immediate impact can a significant proportion of the great multitude of interests express themselves. Therefore, democratic planning of a highly general nature is virtually impossible. No legislature or committee of interest group leaders can rationally evaluate a statement of general goals. Its members cannot, in the absence of specific project proposals and citizen reactions to them, predict how the countless measures needed to accomplish the goals will affect the overall quality of community life or the interests of their own constituents and organizations. Consequently, they are likely to prefer operating on levels where comprehension and prediction are more feasible, even if this means fragmenting policy choices rather than integrating them. In practice, this means that they will rarely commit themselves to let general and long-range goal statements guide their consideration of lower-level alternatives.

There are, no doubt, many American local politicians who would not find the preceding argument a compelling one. In localities lacking a coehrent "power elite" firmly committed to a plan, however, it has a high degree of plausibility as a prescription for political survival. Its specific dictates are bound to be, at a minimum, a "project" rather than a "general planning" orientation and a disinclination to deal with controversial issues.

Basis for Authority

The point was made in the previous section that truly comprehensive goals tend not to provide any basis for evaluating concrete alternatives. It is thus difficult to stir political interest in them and impossible to plan rationally in their service. Recognizing this, many contemporary planners claim to practice middle-range planning—planning for the achievement of goals that are general, but still operational.

The middle-range planning ideal clearly has much to recommend it. It permits the promise of meaningful political discussion and approval of planning goals, even if (as we have seen) the achievement may be highly elusive. From the viewpoint of the general planner, however, it has one crucial flaw. It provides no basis for the planner to claim to understand the overall public interest. Men who plan to achieve operational—even though relatively general—goals are specialists, not comprehensive planners. Consequently, they have no *obvious* theoretical basis for claiming to know better than other specialists how far each specialist goal should be pursued, and with what priority.

The case for efforts at genuinely comprehensive planning has generally rested heavily on the thought that planners can resolve conflicts among goals in expert fashion. If they cannot, if they can only articulate specialist goals, then elected officials would seem required to act as the comprehensive arbiters of conflict. If it is assumed that arbiters operate most successfully when all important considerations are presented vigorously to them, one may argue reasonably that each important cluster of operational goals should be defended by a separate agency. Philip Selznick, for instance, has contended that leaders who wish to maximize their influence should structure their organizations so that the lines of jurisdiction-dividing sub-units are those along which important issues are likely to arise. His reasoning is that if issues arise within sub-units, they are likely to be decided by the sub-unit head, without the chief executive becoming aware of them. It is when sub-units themselves come into conflict that arbiters at the next higher levels are most likely to learn of issues.[4] Delegation of overall authority to arbitrate, in this view, even within the framework of highly general goal statements, is bound to transfer the substance of power from the delegator to the delegatee. If the delegator retains appellate jurisdiction he may dilute this effect. The more that he is committed to uphold the comprehensive policy vision of the delegatee, however, the less will he feel free to do so. In trying to persuade politicians to commit themselves to the policy visions of planners, defenders of comprehensive planning must contend that the politicians will benefit their constituents by doing so. To the extent that the planners themselves lack comprehensive perspectives, however, this contention becomes less and less plausible.

Beyond this, even in pursuit of their own specialist goals, planners operate in a world of whole objects, not analytical aspects. They cannot conceive means that will further the operational goals of primary interest to them without also affecting innumerable others in uncontrolled fashion. Many planners recognize this, and try not to serve their stated operational goals exclusively. The operational goal of City B's central area plan, for example, was downtown economic growth. Its authors realized, however, that they could not reasonably ignore other goals. They wrote and spoke as though the cultural, political, spiritual, recreational and other functions of downtown could never conflict with each other or with the economic function. In practice, they were saved by their common sense; they did not press their pursuit of economic goals sufficiently far to spur public awareness of potentially serious conflicts. Conceivably, they might have listed all the significant operational goals they hoped to serve, but they would still have been left with the problem of balancing them. In short, every concrete object of planner attention is a miniature of the whole. The important analytical problems that arise in planning for an entire urban area arise also in planning any section of it.[5] Perhaps the only solution is frankly to adopt a specialist orientation, even while remaining willing to adjust specific proposals as highly distasteful side effects become apparent. It may still be plausible to maintain, however, that planners are custodians of values that somehow deserve to take precedence over the values propounded by other specialists. Let us consider the most persuasive lines of reasoning frequently advanced in support of this view.

One of the most straightforward was stated by Allison Dunham in a well-known article several years ago.[6] He claimed to have found after

4. Philip Selznick, *Leadership in Administration* (Evanston: Row, Peterson and Company, 1957).

5. The more limted objects (e.g., neighborhoods instead of whole cities) do present somewhat different, if not lesser, problems to the comprehensive planner. Cause and effect are easier to trace on the small scene, and important differences of interest are likely to be fewer. On the other hand, if planners emphasize the common interests of each homogeneous unit, they may well accentuate the differences between units.

6. Allison Dunham, "A Legal and Economic Basis for City Planning," *Columbia Law Review*, LVIII (May, 1958), pp. 650–71.

a survey of the planning literature that planners almost invariably believed that, at the very least, they were the officials best qualified to evaluate site proposals for every kind of facility. They based their position on the premise that planners were experts in the impact of land uses on each other. The argument, in other words, was not that planners were "wiser" than operating agency officials, but that on certain types of issues their specialty deserved first place in the hierarchy of specialties.

On this point two queries come to mind. First, are the impacts of uses on each other regularly more important in site decisions than the intended purposes of each use? Second, can locational problems be separated meaningfully from all other problems? Let me illustrate by referring to the controversy (mentioned previously) about where in City A to locate the new city-county hospital. One powerful group was anxious to locate the hospital between the city's two largest private hospitals (which in turn were one block apart) in the downtown area. They argued that the three hospitals combined could support a great deal of expensive equipment, could attract outstanding internes and residents more easily than any one alone, and might provide the base within a few years for development of a medical school in the city. The city's planners favored a site just outside the downtown area, emphasizing the traffic congestion that would result from locating the new hospital in the immediate vicinity of the two old ones. Each side advanced other arguments as well, but these were the main ones, and for my purpose it is not necessary to judge the overall merit of either position. It is only necessary to consider the general issues which were posed: first, how much cost in traffic congestion should be accepted to obtain how much benefit to health? and second, is traffic congestion more a locational problem than building a medical center? The proponents of the three-hospital medical center argued that its benefits could be obtained only by building on the site they proposed. No others in the immediate vicinity were available. They considered the site favored by the city planners to be wholly unacceptable. The only way to argue that planners should normally be given the benefit of the doubt in disputes of this kind is to say, as Dunham did, that specialists think of the needs of their constituents, while planners think of the impact of specialist proposals on others. In this case, the constituents were sick people and hospital staff personnel, while the "others" included many of the same people, but in their other capacities: as drivers and investors, for instance. The key question is whether the "others" should have had any more presumptive right to prevail than the recognized constituents.

Another objection to this definition of planner competence is that it provides only the haziest indication of the legitimate jurisdiction of planners and of government. Just what is a locational decision? It is hardly enough to say, as planners generally have, that locational decisions are those that have an impact on surrounding property or people. Almost anything I do to my property affects my neighbor in some way. For instance, if I rent out rooms in my single-family home, I have changed the use of my land and therefore made a locational decision, by a common planning definition. Should government therefore control everything, as it already controls my right to rent out rooms? Planners deny that it should, but they have rarely asked where the cutoff point should be. They have generally been satisfied to say that government should intervene only in cases of "substantial" harm, and that common sense will prevail in interpreting the word "substantial." They may be right, but this formulation gives the citizen no theoretical guidance as to whose common sense should prevail in cases of disagreement between other decision-makers and planners.

A second persuasive line of reasoning to support the view that planners should generally prevail in such disputes is that they alone among city officials analyze city problems from an overall point of view. Operating agency officials cannot rise above their day-to-day administrative chores, and in any event their perspectives are conditioned by the narrow responsibilities of their departments. Even politicians typically devote most of their time to maintaining contacts with, and to performing errand boy services for, their constituents. In dealing with legislative proposals, they generally focus on details of immediate interest to vocal groups rather than on the overall picture. In most cities, moreover, councilmen are elected from wards; in many they work only part time at their jobs; and in some each councilman heads a city department. Only planners can devote all their time to thought about city problems at the most general level.

The most obvious criticism of this position is that freedom from operating responsibility may not be the best condition in which to make high-level decisions. Some prominent decision-makers have argued that it is a poor one. Winston Churchill, for example, has written that Stafford Cripps became restive and hypercritical of his colleagues while serving as parliamentary whip during World War II. What he needed, according to Churchill's diagnosis, was responsibility which would absorb his energies and give him a sense of the concrete issues. Those who are free from operating responsibility, concluded Churchill, tend to develop an unhelpful watchdog mentality. It is unhelpful because they usually think too abstractly to be cogent critics of complex choices among policies.[7] Similarly, Chester Barnard has written that study and

7. Winston Churchill, *The Second World War,* Vol. IV: *The Hinge of Fate* (Boston: Houghton-Mifflin Co., 1950), p. 560.
    Churchill was not arguing against the making of large decisions by generalists, of course. He himself was Prime Minister. Nor was he criticizing the British practice of concentrating authority within the civil service in the hands of generalists. Several points may be noted. The generalists in a British ministry exercise all formal power of decision not exercised by the minister himself. They bear responsibility as well for

reflectiveness without operating responsibility tend to lead to the treatment of things by aspects rather than wholes, to a disregard of factors which cannot be expressed precisely, and to an underestimation of the need for artistry in making concrete decisions. Because so many crucial factors cannot find expression in words, Barnard concluded, the interdependencies of social life can only be grasped intuitively. Only men of long and responsible experience are likely to acquire very much of this intuitive grasp, and therefore only such men—who will also grasp the supreme difficulty of planning in this "world of unknowns"—are qualified to plan.[8] This is unquestionably a rather mystical position, but it is no less for that a respectable and forceful one.

Barnard and Churchill agree, then, that freedom from responsibility for operating decisions is anything but fit training for planning.[9] Those who accept their view are likely to believe that any one of a number of city officials may qualify better than the planning director to serve as the wise chief advisor of politicians on broad policy issues. In cities A and B, the city councils consistently acted on this belief. To the extent that they desired coordination of public works, they normally relied on their city engineers to achieve it. When the City Council of B decided to separate capital budgeting from ordinary budgeting, it set up a committee composed of politicians and civic leaders. The committee was given a small staff headed by a former city councilman. Planners were shut out of the capital budgeting process entirely. When the City Council of A decided that it needed a special advisor on the interstate freeway program, it appointed the incumbent city engineer, who had been about to retire. When the city engineer of B left the city

---

deciding which issues, and which specialists' analyses of them, are important enough for the minister to consider. The elite corps of the generalists, the Administrative Class, are expected on entry only to think, write, and speak clearly, and to have done well in their subject of undergraduate concentration. Any subject will do, although subjects fit for "gentlemen" (i.e., men devoted to culture rather than making a living), notably the classics, have traditionally predominated. British administrators have no formal technical training for their work at all. They are platonic rather than functional leaders, but matured on responsibility rather than study. Those at the higher levels are notably unsympathetic to the ideal of general planning. They take well-known pride in deciding "each case on its merits."

Parenthetically, where city planners are employed in British ministries, they are considered technicians, capable of contributing useful advice on specialized aspects of issues, but not of being entrusted with the power to make decisions.

8. Chester Barnard, *Organization and Management* (Cambridge: Harvard University Press, 1948), ch. 4.

9. It should be clear that when I speak of "planning" in this article, I mean the work of determining overall policy guidelines for public activity, and means of implementing them. No single individual or agency makes such determinations alone in an American community. The recommendations of some, however, are bound to carry more weight than those of others. The crucial questions at issue in this section are (1) whether the views of planning agencies on controversial policy issues should normally be granted presumptive validity in the absence of strong evidence discrediting them; and (2) whether the training and career patterns of professional city planners equip them well for planning at the higher levels.

government for private employ, his successor provided inadequate (in the City Council's view) for the unofficial task of coordinating city public works. Within a year, the Council lured him back into government, giving him the title of Development Coordinator. The city's planners believed that they should have been given the job, but they could offer no strong arguments to support their view that the engineer was less able to take the overview than they. The politician most responsible for bringing him back told me that the planners thought too abstractly and with insufficient regard to cost; whereas the engineer, though less articulate, understood the infinite, inexpressible complexity of governmental choice. In fairness to the planners, it should be added that the engineer had made his entire career in City B, looking to the City Council for his raises, perquisites, and promotions. He had risen primarily because of his technical competence, to be sure, but also because the councilmen felt confident that he would not embarrass them politically and that his overriding loyalty was to themselves. The Planning Director, by contrast, had been chosen after a national search by a citizens' committee (advised by a nationally known planning consultant), had been on the local scene for two years, and had his primary base of political support outside the city government entirely. It should be mentioned that the last factor was not due to simple ineptitude on the Planning Director's part. He had chosen his strategy consciously and deliberately, judging that the city government would support effective general planning only if—and, even then, only perhaps—pressured by outside groups to do so.

A third defense that planners frequently make of their aspiration to be more than "mere" specialists is that governmental efficiency is served by having one agency keep track of everything that every city agency does, calling attention to conflicts and to means of coordinating effort for the benefit of all. The distinction between coordination and planning, however, is of practical importance only so long as planners have no power. Without power, they can as coordinators simply try to persuade groups of specialists that their respective interests will be served by improved coordination. As soon as planners begin to impose solutions or advise politicians to impose them, however, they have entered the substantive planning field. That is, they have set their perception of the public interest on substantive matters against those of the specialists who have rejected their advice. Similarly, when planners request authority to prepare a city's capital budget, they cannot justify the request on grounds of "simple efficiency," which would have to be established by the criteria of all the specialists' own goals. They must assert, at least implicitly, that they have some means of choosing among the values entrusted to each operating agency. In other words, they must claim to have goals. And the coordination of action in pursuit of substantive goals is, if it is anything, substantive planning.

One might say that the planner needs coordinative power only because some specialists stupidly or obstinately refuse to cooperate with others in the interests of "simple efficiency," even though no significant values are threatened. The specialists' answer is that no one can determine that this is the case in any particular controversy without examining it in detail. Philip Selznick has illustrated this point clearly in his analysis of the history of the Communist party.[10] The party refused to cooperate with other leftist parties in the decade before the Popular Front, despite the obvious threat of fascism. Yet this period of isolation, Selznick contends, made the party a much more valuable tool to its masters during and after the Popular Front period. During the isolation period, the "character" of the party developed and became incorruptible. This extreme example illustrates a simple point: that cooperation and isolation in themselves have important effects on organizations. If an agency head claims that a measure advanced in the name of efficiency actually threatens important values—and any agency head who refuses the advice of the planning director will say this—no outsider can refute him until he examines the bases of his arguments in detail. If we assume that most agency heads are men of good conscience, we can likewise assume that they will have some reasons that seem genuinely sufficient to them, and that will seem so as well to at least some reasonable outsiders. In the end, no act of coordination is without its effect on other values than efficiency.

Closing

The purpose here is not to disparage the ideal of comprehensive planning, but rather to challenge the planning profession to reinforce its most fundamental theoretical arsenal.[11] Some of the issues raised may seem overly theoretical, and in the immediate sense perhaps they are—though to me they appeared quite close to the surface in the two cities I studied. In the long run, however, comprehensive planning and evaluation will have little effect on American cities unless their goal premises can be established in sufficiently compelling fashion (both politically and intellectually) to make politicians take notice.

10. Philip Selznick, *The Organizational Weapon* (Glencoe: The Free Press, 1960).
11. I have made a beginning effort at reinforcement in my article, "Reason and Influence in the Public Service," which is scheduled to appear in a forthcoming issue of the *Public Administration Review* and as chapter 7 of my book, *The City Planning Process*.

The Planner as Advocate

Paul Davidoff

IF THE PLANNING PROCESS is to encourage democratic urban government then it must operate so as to include rather than exclude citizens from participating in the process. "Inclusion" means not only permitting the citizen to be heard. It also means that he be able to become well informed about the underlying reasons for planning proposals, and be able to respond to them in the technical language of professional planners.

A practice that has discouraged full participation by citizens in plan making in the past has been based on what might be called the *"unitary plan."* This is the idea that only one agency in a community should prepare a comprehensive plan; that agency is the city planning commission or department. Why is it that no other organization within a community prepares a plan? Why is only one agency concerned with establishing both general and specific goals for community development, and with proposing the strategies and costs required to effect the goals? Why are there not plural plans?

If the social, economic, and political ramifications of a plan are politically contentious, then why is it that those in opposition to the agency plan do not prepare one of their own? It is interesting to observe that "rational" theories of planning have called for consideration of alternative courses of action by planning agencies. As a matter of rationality it has been argued that all of the alternative choices open as means to the ends sought be examined.[1] But those, including myself, who have recommended agency consideration of alternatives have placed upon the agency planner the burden of inventing "a few repre-

1. See, for example, Martin Meyerson and Edward Banfield, *Politics, Planning and the Public Interest* (Glencoe: The Free Press, 1955) p. 314 ff. The authors state "By a *rational* decision, we mean one made in the following manner: 1. the decision-maker considers all of the alternatives (courses of action) open to him; . . . 2. he identifies and evaluates all of the consequences which would follow from the adoption of each alternative; . . . 3. he selects that alternative the probable consequences of which would be preferable in terms of his most valued ends."

Reprinted by permission of the Journal of the American Institute of Planners, *Vol. XXXI, No. 4 (December 1965) and of the author.*

sentative alternatives."[2] The agency planner has been given the duty of constructing a model of the political spectrum, and charged with sorting out what he conceives to be worthy alternatives. This duty has placed too great a burden on the agency planner, and has failed to provide for the formulation of alternatives by the interest groups who will eventually be affected by the completed plans.

Whereas in a large part of our national and local political practice contention is viewed as healthy, in city planning where a large proportion of the professionals are public employees, contentious criticism has not always been viewed as legitimate. Further, where only government prepares plans, and no minority plans are developed, pressure is often applied to bring all professionals to work for the ends espoused by a public agency. For example, last year a Federal official complained to a meeting of planning professors that the academic planners were not giving enough support to Federal programs. He assumed that every planner should be on the side of the Federal renewal program. Of course government administrators will seek to gain the support of professionals outside of government, but such support should not be expected as a matter of loyalty. In a democratic system opposition to a public agency should be just as normal and appropriate as support. The agency, despite the fact that it is concerned with planning, may be serving undesired ends.

In presenting a plea for plural planning I do not mean to minimize the importance of the obligation of the public planning agency. It must decide upon appropriate future courses of action for the community. But being isolated as the only plan maker in the community, public agencies as well as the public itself may have suffered from incomplete and shallow analysis of potential directions. Lively political dispute aided by plural plans could do much to improve the level of rationality in the process of preparing the public plan.

The advocacy of alternative plans by interest groups outside of government would stimulate city planning in a number of ways. First, it would serve as a means of better informing the public of the alternative choices open, *alternatives strongly supported by their proponents.* In current practice those few agencies which have portrayed alternatives have not been equally enthusiastic about each.[3] A standard reaction to rationalists' prescription for consideration of alternative courses of action has been "it can't be done; how can you expect planners to present alternatives which they don't approve?" The appropriate answer to that question has been that planners like lawyers may have a professional obligation to defend positions they oppose. However, in a system of plural planning, the public agency would be relieved of at least some

2. Davidoff and Reiner, *Op. cit.*

3. National Capital Planning Commission, *The Nation's Capital; a Policies Plan for the Year 2000* (Washington, D.C.: The Commission, 1961).

of the burden of presenting alternatives. In plural planning the alternatives would be presented by interest groups differing with the public agency's plan. Such alternatives would represent the deep-seated convictions of their proponents and not just the mental exercises of rational planners seeking to portray the range of choice.

A second way in which advocacy and plural planning would improve planning practice would be in forcing the public agency to compete with other planning groups to win political support. In the absence of opposition or alternative plans presented by interest groups the public agencies have had little incentive to improve the quality of their work or the rate of production of plans. The political consumer has been offered a yes-no ballot in regard to the comprehensive plan; either the public agency's plan was to be adopted or no plan would be adopted.

A third improvement in planning practice which might follow from plural planning would be to force those who have been critical of "establishment" plans to produce superior plans, rather than only to carry out the very essential obligation of criticizing plans deemed improper.

The Planner as Advocate

Where plural planning is practiced, advocacy becomes the means of professional support for competing claims about how the community should develop. Pluralism in support of political contention describes the process; advocacy describes the role performed by the professional in the process. Where unitary planning prevails, advocacy is not of paramount importance, for there is little or no competition for the plan prepared by the public agency. The concept of advocacy as taken from legal practice implies the opposition of at least two contending viewpoints in an adversary proceeding.

The legal advocate must plead for his own and his client's sense of legal propriety or justice. The planner as advocate would plead for his own and his client's view of the good society. The advocate planner would be more than a provider of information, an analyst of current trends, a simulator of future conditions, and a detailer of means. In addition to carrying out these necessary parts of planning, he would be a *proponent* of specific substantive solutions.

The advocate planner would be responsible to his client and would seek to express his client's views. This does not mean that the planner could not seek to persuade his client. In some situations persuasion might not be necessary, for the planner would have sought out an employer with whom he shared common views about desired social conditions and the means toward them. In fact one of the benefits of advocate planning is the possibility it creates for a planner to find employment with agencies holding values close to his own. Today the agency planner may be dismayed by the positions affirmed by his agency, but there may be no alternative employer.

The advocate planner would be above all a planner. He would be responsible to his client for preparing plans and for all of the other elements comprising the planning process. Whether working for the public agency or for some private organization, the planner would have to prepare plans that take account of the arguments made in other plans. Thus the advocate's plan might have some of the characteristics of a legal brief. It would be a document presenting the facts and reasons for supporting one set of proposals, and facts and reasons indicating the inferiority of counter-proposals. The adversary nature of plural planning might, then, have the beneficial effect of upsetting the tradition of writing plan proposals in terminology which makes them appear self-evident.

A troublesome issue in contemporary planning is that of finding techniques for evaluating alternative plans. Technical devices such as cost-benefit analysis by themselves are of little assistance without the use of means for appraising the values underlying plans. Advocate planning, by making more apparent the values underlying plans, and by making definitions of social costs and benefits more explicit, should greatly assist the process of plan evaluation. Further, it would become clear (as it is not at present) that there are no neutral grounds for evaluating a plan; there are as many evaluative systems as there are value systems.

The adversary nature of plural planning might also have a good effect on the uses of information and research in planning. One of the tasks of the advocate planner in discussing the plans prepared in opposition to his would be to point out the nature of the bias underlying information presented in other plans. In this way, as critic of opposition plans, he would be performing a task similar to the legal technique of cross-examination. While painful to the planner whose bias is exposed (and no planner can be entirely free of bias) the net effect of confrontation between advocates of alternative plans would be more careful and precise research.

Not all the work of an advocate planner would be of an adversary nature. Much of it would be educational. The advocate would have the job of informing other groups, including public agencies, of the conditions, problems, and outlook of the group he represented. Another major educational job would be that of informing his clients of their rights under planning and renewal laws, about the general operations of city government, and of particular programs likely to affect them.

The advocate planner would devote much attention to assisting the client organization to clarify its ideas and to give expression to them. In order to make his client more powerful politically the advocate might also become engaged in expanding the size and scope of his client organization. But the advocate's most important function would be to carry out the planning process for the organization and to argue persuasively in favor of its planning proposals.

Advocacy in planning has already begun to emerge as planning and renewal affect the lives of more and more people. The critics of urban renewal[4] have forced response from the renewal agencies, and the ongoing debate[5] has stimulated needed self-evaluation by public agencies. Much work along the lines of advocate planning has already taken place, but little of it by professional planners. More often the work has been conducted by trained community organizers or by student groups. In at least one instance, however, a planner's professional aid led to the development of an alternative renewal approach, one which will result in the dislocation of far fewer families than originally contemplated.[6]

Pluralism and advocacy are means for stimulating consideration of future conditions by all groups in society. But there is one social group which at present is particularly in need of the assistance of planners. This group includes organizations representing low-income families. At a time when concern for the condition of the poor finds institutionalization in community action programs, it would be appropriate for planners concerned with such groups to find means to plan with them. The plans prepared for these groups would seek to combat poverty and would propose programs affording new and better opportunities to the members of the organization and to families similarly situated.[7]

The difficulty in providing adequate planning assistance to organizations representing low-income families may in part be overcome by funds allocated to local anti-poverty councils. But these councils are not the only representatives of the poor; other organizations exist and

4. The most important critical studies are: Jane Jacobs, *The Life and Death of Great American Cities* (New York: Random House, 1961); Martin Anderson, *The Federal Bulldozer* (Cambridge: M.I.T. Press, 1964); Herbert J. Gans, "The Human Implications of Current Redevelopment and Relocation Planning," *Journal of the American Institute of Planners,* XXV (February 1959) 15–26.

5. A recent example of heated debate appears in the following set of articles: Herbert J. Gans, "The Failure of Urban Renewal," *Commentary* 39 (April 1965) p. 29; George Raymond "Controversy," *Commentary* 40 (July 1965) p. 72; and Herbert J. Gans, "Controversy," *Commentary* 40 (July 1965) p. 77.

6. Walter Thabit, *An Alternate Plan for Cooper Square,* (New York: Walter Thabit, July 1961).

7. The first conscious effort to employ the advocacy method was carried out by a graduate student of city planning as an independent research project. The author acted as both a participant and an observer of a local housing organization. See Linda Davidoff, "The Bluffs: Advocate Planning," *Comment,* Dept. of City Planning, University of Pennsylvania, (Spring 1965), p. 59.

seek help. How can this type of assistance be financed? This question will be examined below, when attention is turned to the means for institutionalizing plural planning.

The Structure of Planning

Planning by Special Interest Groups

The local planning process typically includes one or more "citizens" organizations concerned with the nature of planning in the community. The Workable Program requirement for "citizen participation"[8] has enforced this tradition and brought it to most large communities. The difficulty with current citizen participation programs is that citizens are more often *reacting* to agency programs than *proposing* their concepts of appropriate goals and future action.

The fact that citizens' organizations have not played a positive role in formulating plans is to some extent a result of both the enlarged role in society played by government bureaucracies and the historic weakness of municipal party politics. There is something very shameful to our society in the necessity to have organized "citizen participation." Such participation should be the norm in an enlightened democracy. The formalization of citizen participation as a required practice in localities is similar in many respects to totalitarian shows of loyalty to the state by citizen parades.

Will a private group interested in preparing a recommendation for community development be required to carry out its own survey and analysis of the community? The answer would depend upon the quality of the work prepared by the public agency, work which should be public information. In some instances the public agency may not have surveyed or analyzed aspects the private group thinks important; or the public agency's work may reveal strong biases unacceptable to the private group. In any event, the production of a useful plan proposal will require much information concerning the present and predicted conditions in the community. There will be some costs associated with gathering that information, even if it is taken from the public agency. The major cost involved in the preparation of a plan by a private agency would probably be the employment of one or more professional planners.

What organizations might be expected to engage in the plural planning process? The first type that comes to mind are the political parties; but this is clearly an aspirational thought. There is very little evidence that local political organizations have the interest, ability, or

8. See Section 101 (c) of the United States Housing Act of 1949, as amended.

concern to establish well developed programs for their communities. Not all the fault, though, should be placed upon the professional politicians, for the registered members of political parties have not demanded very much, if anything, from them as agents.

Despite the unreality of the wish, the desirability for active participation in the process of planning by the political parties is strong. In an ideal situation local parties would establish political platforms which would contain master plans for community growth and both the majority and minority parties in the legislative branch of government would use such plans as one basis for appraising individual legislative proposals. Further, the local administration would use its planning agency to carry out the plans it proposed to the electorate. This dream will not turn to reality for a long time. In the interim other interest groups must be sought to fill the gap caused by the present inability of political organizations.

The second set of organizations which might be interested in preparing plans for community development are those that represent special interest groups having established views in regard to proper public policy. Such organizations as chambers of commerce, real estate boards, labor organizations, pro- and anti-civil rights groups, and anti-poverty councils come to mind. Groups of this nature have often played parts in the development of community plans, but only in a very few instances have they proposed their own plans.

It must be recognized that there is strong reason operating against commitment to a plan by these organizations. In fact it is the same reason that in part limits the interests of politicians and which limits the potential for planning in our society. The expressed commitment to a particular plan may make it difficult for groups to find means for accommodating their various interests. In other terms, it may be simpler for professionals, politicians, or lobbyists to make deals if they have not laid their cards on the table.

There is a third set of organizations that might be looked to as proponents of plans and to whom the foregoing comments might not apply. These are the ad hoc protest associations which may form in opposition to some proposed policy. An example of such a group is a neighborhood association formed to combat a renewal plan, a zoning change, or the proposed location of a public facility. Such organizations may seek to develop alternative plans, plans which would, if effected, better serve their interests.

From the point of view of effective and rational planning it might be desirable to commence plural planning at the level of city-wide organizations, but a more realistic view is that it will start at the neighborhood level. Certain advantages of this outcome should be noted. Mention was made earlier of tension in government between centralizing and decentralizing forces. The contention aroused by conflict between the central planning agency and the neighborhood organization may indeed be healthy, leading to clearer definition of welfare policies and their relation to the rights of individuals or minority groups.

Who will pay for plural planning? Some organizations have the resources to sponsor the development of a plan. Many groups lack the means. The plight of the relatively indigent association seeking to propose a plan might be analogous to that of the indigent client in search of legal aid. If the idea of plural planning makes sense, then support may be found from foundations or from government. In the beginning it is more likely that some foundation might be willing to experiment with plural planning as a means of making city planning more effective and more democratic. Or the Federal Government might see plural planning, if carried out by local anti-poverty councils, as a strong means of generating local interest in community affairs.

Federal sponsorship of plural planning might be seen as a more effective tool for stimulating involvement of the citizen in the future of his community than are the present types of citizen participation programs. Federal support could only be expected if plural planning were seen, not as a means of combating renewal plans, but as an incentive to local renewal agencies to prepare better plans.

The Public Planning Agency

A major drawback to effective democratic planning practice is the continuation of that non-responsible vestigial institution, the planning commission. If it is agreed that the establishment of both general policies and implementation policies are questions affecting the public interest and that public interest questions should be decided in accord with established democratic practices for decision making, then it is indeed difficult to find convincing reasons for continuing to permit independent commissions to make planning decisions. At an earlier stage in planning the strong arguments of John T. Howard[9] and others in support of commissions may have been persuasive. But it is now more than a decade since Howard made his defense against Robert Walker's position favoring planning as a staff function under the mayor. With the increasing effect planning decisions have upon the lives of citizens the Walker proposal assumes great urgency.[10]

9. John T. Howard, "In Defense of Planning Commissions," *Journal of the American Institute of Planners,* XVII (Spring 1951).

10. Robert Walker, *The Planning Function in Urban Government;* Second Edition (Chicago: University of Chicago Press, 1950). Walker drew the following conclusions from his examination of planning and planning commissions. "Another conclusion to be drawn from the existing composition of city planning boards is that they are not representative of the population as a whole." p. 153. "In summary the writer is of the opinion that the claim that planning commissions are more objective than elected officials must be rejected." p. 155. "From his observations the writer feels justified in saying that very seldom does a majority of any commission have any well-

Aside from important questions regarding the propriety of independent agencies which are far removed from public control determining public policy, the failure to place planning decision choices in the hands of elected officials has weakened the ability of professional planners to have their proposals effected. Separating planning from local politics has made it difficult for independent commissions to garner influential political support. The commissions are not responsible directly to the electorate and in turn the electorate is, at best, often indifferent to the planning commission.

During the last decade in many cities power to alter community development has slipped out of the hands of city planning commissions, assuming they ever held it, and has been transferred to development coordinators. This has weakened the professional planner. Perhaps planners unknowingly contributed to this by their refusal to take concerted action in opposition to the perpetuation of commissions.

Planning commissions are products of the conservative reform movement of the early part of this century. The movement was essentially anti-populist and pro-aristocracy. Politics was viewed as dirty business. The commissions are relics of a not-too-distant past when it was believed that if men of good will discussed a problem thoroughly, certainly the right solution would be forthcoming. We know today, and perhaps it was always known, that there are no right solutions. Proper policy is that which the decision-making unit declares to be proper.

Planning commissions are responsible to no constituency. The members of the commissions, except for their chairman, are seldom known to the public. In general the individual members fail to expose their personal views about policy and prefer to immerse them in group decision. If the members wrote concurring and dissenting opinions, then at least the commissions might stimulate thought about planning issues. It is difficult to comprehend why this aristocratic and undemocratic form of decision making should be continued. The public planning function should be carried out in the executive or legislative office and perhaps in both. There has been some question about which of these branches of government would provide the best home, but there is much reason to believe that both branches would be made more cognizant of planning issues if they were each informed by their own

rounded understanding of the purposes and ramificatons of planning." p. 157. "In summary, then, it was found that the average commission member does not comprehend planning nor is he particularly interested even in the range of customary physical planning." p. 158. "Looking at the planning commission at the present time, however, one is forced to conclude that, despite some examples of successful operations, the unpaid board is not proving satisfactory as a planning agency," p. 165. ". . . (it) is believed that the most fruitful line of development for the future would be replacement of these commissions by a department or bureau attached to the office of mayor or city manager. This department might be headed by a board or by a single director, but the members or the director would in any case hold office at the pleasure of the executive on the same basis as other department heads." p. 177.

planning staffs. To carry this division further, it would probably be advisable to establish minority and majority planning staffs in the legislative branch.

At the root of my last suggestion is the belief that there is or should be a Republican and Democratic way of viewing city development; that there should be conservative and liberal plans, plans to support the private market and plans to support greater government control. There are many possible roads for a community to travel and many plans should show them. Explication is required of many alternative futures presented by those sympathetic to the construction of each such future. As indicated earlier, such alternatives are not presented to the public now. Those few reports which do include alternative futures do not speak in terms of interest to the average citizen. They are filled with professional jargon and present sham alternatives. These plans have expressed technical land use alternatives rather than social, economic, or political value alternatives. Both the traditional unitary plans and the new ones that present technical alternatives have limited the public's exposure to the future states that might be achieved. Instead of arousing healthy political contention as diverse comprehensive plans might, these plans have deflated interest.

The independent planning commission and unitary plan practice certainly should not co-exist. Separately they dull the possibility for enlightened political debate; in combination they have made it yet more difficult. But when still another hoary concept of city planning is added to them, such debate becomes practically impossible. This third of a trinity of worn-out notions is that city planning should focus only upon the physical aspects of city development.

An Inclusive Definition of the Scope of Planning

The view that equates physical planning with city planning is myopic. It may have had some historic justification, but it is clearly out of place at a time when it is necessary to integrate knowledge and techniques in order to wrestle effectively with the myriad of problems afflicting urban populations.

The city planning profession's historic concern with the physical environment has warped its ability to see physical structures and land as servants to those who use them.[11] Physical relations and conditions

11. An excellent and complete study of the bias resulting from reliance upon physical or land use criteria appears in David Farbman, *A Description, Analysis and Critique of the Master Plan,* an unpublished mimeographed study prepared for the Univ. of Pennsylvania's Institute for Urban Studies, 1959–1960. After studying more than 100 master plans Farbman wrote:

have no meaning or quality apart from the way they serve their users. But this is forgotten every time a physical condition is described as good or bad without relation to a specified group of users. High density, low density, green belts, mixed uses, cluster developments, centralized or decentralized business centers are per se neither good nor bad. They describe physical relations or conditions, but take on value only when seen in terms of their social, economic, psychological, physiological, or aesthetic effects upon different users.

The profession's experience with renewal over the past decade has shown the high costs of exclusive concern with physical conditions. It has been found that the allocation of funds for removal of physical blight may not necessarily improve the over-all physical condition of a community and may engender such harsh social repercussions as to severely damage both social and economic institutions. Another example of the deficiencies of the physical bias is the assumption of city planners that they could deal with the capital budget as if the physical attributes of a facility could be understood apart from the philosophy and practice of the service conducted within the physical structure. This assumption is open to question. The size, shape, and location of a facility greatly interact with the purpose of the activity the facility houses. Clear examples of this can be seen in public education and in the provision of low cost housing. The racial and other socio-economic consequences of "physical decisions" such as location of schools and housing projects have been immense, but city planners, while acknowledging the existence of such consequences, have not sought or trained themselves to understand socio-economic problems, their causes or solutions.

The city planning profession's limited scope has tended to bias strongly many of its recommendations toward perpetuation of existing social and economic practices. Here I am not opposing the outcomes, but the way in which they are developed. Relative ignorance of social

---

"As a result of the predominantly physical orientation of the planning profession many planners have fallen victims to a malaise which I suggest calling the "Physical Bias." This bias is not the physical orientation of the planner itself but is the result of it. . . . "The physical bias is an attitude on the part of the planner which leads him to conceive of the principles and techniques of *his profession* as the key factors in determining the particular recommendations to be embodied in his plans. . . .

"The physically biased planner plans on the assumption (conviction) that the physical problems of a city can be solved within the framework of physical desiderata; in other words, that physical problems can be adequately stated, solved and remedied according to physical criteria and expertise. The physical bias produces both an inability and an unwillingness on the part of the planner to 'get behind' the physical recommendations of the plan, to isolate, examine or discuss more basic criteria. . . ."

". . . There is room, then, in plan thinking for physical principles, i.e., theories of structural inter-relationships of the physical city; but this is only a part of the story, for the structural impacts of the plan are only a part of the total impact. This total impact must be conceived as a web of physical, economic and social causes and effects." pp. 22–26.

and economic methods of analysis have caused planners to propose solutions in the absence of sufficient knowledge of the costs and benefits of proposals upon different sections of the population.

Large expenditures have been made on planning studies of regional transportation needs, for example, but these studies have been conducted in a manner suggesting that different social and economic classes of the population did not have different needs and different abilities to meet them. In the field of housing, to take another example, planners have been hesitant to question the consequences of locating public housing in slum areas. In the field of industrial development, planners have seldom examined the types of jobs the community needed; it has been assumed that one job was about as useful as another. But this may not be the case where a significant sector of the population finds it difficult to get employment.

"Who gets what, when, where, why, and how" are the basic political questions which need to be raised about every allocation of public resources. The questions cannot be answered adequately if land use criteria are the sole or major standards for judgment.

The need to see an element of city development, land use, in broad perspective applies equally well to every other element, such as health, welfare, and recreation. The governing of a city requires an adequate plan for its future. Such a plan loses guiding force and rational basis to the degree that it deals with less than the whole that is of concern to the public.

The implications of the foregoing comments for the practice of city planning are these. First, state planning enabling legislation should be amended to permit planning departments to study and to prepare plans related to any area of public concern. Second, planning education must be redirected so as to provide channels of specialization in different parts of public planning and a core focussed upon the planning process. Third, the professional planning association should enlarge its scope so as to not exclude city planners not specializing in physical planning. . . .

Author's Note:

The author wishes to thank Melvin H. Webber for his insightful criticism and Linda Davidoff for her many helpful suggestions and for her analysis of advocate planning. Special acknowledgment is made of the penetrating and brilliant social insights offered by the eminent legal scholar and practitioner, Michael Brodie, of the Philadelphia Bar.

Reflections of an Advocate Planner

Lisa Peattie

THE CONCEPT of "advocacy planning" can only be understood in the context of the management technology of modern American cities. The ancient cities were ones in which planning was primarily a function of individuals and of relatively small groups—families, guilds, and the like. The "squatter settlements" which surround the cities of the developing countries suggest the degree to which, in these cities, public policy and official planning still control only a relatively limited part of urban life, leaving considerable areas for action by private groups and individuals. Our cities, in contrast, are more and more publicly managed environments. Private actions take place within a generally narrowing network of public intervention, public policy, and public planning.

One aspect of this transformation has been the recasting of questions of public policy as problems for technical solution. "Much of the history of social progress in the twentieth century," says Harvey Brooks, "can be described in terms of the transfer of wider and wider areas of public policy from politics to expertise."[1] The increasing complexity of the management apparatus has made it difficult for ordinary voters to make judgments and develop choices relevant to its exercise.

This casting of policy problems in a context of technical analysis too abstract for the ordinary citizen to comprehend clearly has a strong basis in the range and complex interrelationships of our urban technology. But it also has a political function. The number of public policy decisions, and the numbers and varieties of persons affected by each, would probably make our public apparatus unworkable if each of these decisions were to be handled within the traditional framework of political debate.

But we pay a price for this growth of public policy, and for the transfer from politics to expertise. One cost seems to be a sense of

1. Harvey Brooks, "Scientific Concepts and Cultural Change," *Daedalus*, Winter, 1965.

Reprinted by permission of the Journal of the American Institute of Planners, *Vol. XXXIV, No. 2 (March 1968) and of the author.*

being overwhelmed by our own technical apparatus. Our technological civilization in this sense seems to include not merely the changes in goods—new ways of transportation, communication, and the like, which are transforming our lives—but the very man-made institutions which provide the ground rules of our existence. People may respond to this sense of being overwhelmed by political apathy and disengagement. Or they may protest. It is interesting to see the way in which the polemical literature against urban renewal and that against fluoridation of drinking water meet in their angry suspicion of having something "put over" on ordinary people by the experts. In Boston, at least, one sees on an urban renewal picket line an odd alliance of the John Birchers and the Students for a Democratic Society, both in their diverse ways speaking for a resurgence of individualism against "The System." I suspect that the "hippies" represent another manifestation of a more generally distributed sense of being overwhelmed by the social apparatus.

The shift from politics to expertise also changes the rules of the game for exercising power, and in this, changes the structure of effective power. This may be not only a change, but also a cost in equity. The change, it may well be argued, disadvantages especially the people at the bottom of the system—those who are, through lack of education and of technical sophistication, particularly ill-prepared to deal with the presentation of issues in a technical framework. Such groups tend to be disadvantaged in the traditional political framework, but still more so when it comes to dealing with those who speak the language of maps, diagrams, and statistical tables. Advocacy planning has its origins initially in the perception that such groups need planners to make *their* case, to express their interests, within that technical framework which we call planning. It thus represents a search by planners for new kinds of clientele.

But it also represents, it will be seen, a repoliticization of the planning framework. The advocate planners in effect reject both the notion of a single "best" solution, and the notion of a general welfare which such a solution might serve. They take the view that any plan is the embodiment of particular group interests, and they therefore see it as important that any group which has interests at stake in the planning process should have those interests articulated in the form of a plan. Planning in this view becomes pluralistic, and partisan, in a word, overtly political.

There now exist in several cities "advocacy planning" groups which propose to serve the general function of helping people, especially the people of low-income communities, which seem to be underrepresented in the planning process, to make their interests felt in it. The present writer has been a member of such a group in Cambridge, Massachusetts, Urban Planning Aid (UPA), incorporated as a nonprofit institution in

June, 1966 to ". . . review and evaluate specific planning proposals which affect low-income communities; to develop planning strategies, physical designs and implementation programs for these communities" and "to act as planning advocate for these communities in order to make public plans reflect their needs. . . ."[2]

In its first year, UPA, besides short-term consulting relationships with a number of sorts of community groups, has had several major projects differing quite radically in scale. They have included a continuing consulting relationship to a small group representing the residents of a neighborhood in the Boston ghetto where a new high school is to be the central focus of an urban renewal project, and support of opposition to the routing of a major loop highway through the cities of Cambridge and Boston. It has so far failed to find any kind of solid financial base for its activities, and has thus had to struggle to develop techniques for working in a new way while at the same time operating in a context of volunteer help and evening and weekend staff work. That many problems have appeared goes without saying. I should like to comment on some of the problems which would appear to be inherent in the nature of advocacy planning.

Who Should Be Represented?

Urban Planning Aid defined its functions in terms of technical assistance to "low-income communities." A low-income community may be operationally defined as a specific urban area the inhabitants of which have a low average income. But when it comes to identifying the needs of such communities and of establishing a consultant-client relationship, certain difficulties in operationalizing at once appear. How do you identify and define the client, and how do you establish a working relationship with this client?

Planners, and sociologists too, speak readily of "neighborhoods," but the fact seems to be that while city dwellers live in areas with varying physical and social characteristics, the networks of social relationships in which any person takes part rarely cluster together neatly in any local "neighborhood." Some city dwellers are extremely reluctant to move from the territory to which they are accustomed, where many of the individuals and institutions to which they have ties are found, and to which they may be emotionally attached. But even such locality-rooted people do not usually seem to have a clear sense of belonging to a neighborhood with distinct boundaries. Herbert Gans writes of the Boston Italians in the West End as "urban villagers" with a clear sense of being a people, but notes that even in this case "the concept of the West End as a single neighborhood was foreign to the West Enders

2. *Articles of Organization* under General Law 180, June 6, 1966.

themselves. . . . Until the coming of redevelopment, only outsiders were likely to think of the West End as a single neighborhood. After the redevelopment was announced, the residents were drawn together by the common danger, but even so, the West End never became a cohesive neighborhood."[3] Observers since Brooks have noted that the urban slum lacks institutions by which it might represent itself as an entity. As in the instance studied by Gans, "community organizations" tend to appear in such neighborhoods as a response to a threat: "the neighborhood" or "the community" comes to be articulated as that area about to be affected by some public policy, as an urban renewal program. It is the organizations which appear to "represent" such "communities" which are likely to be the natural clients for the advocate planner.

What is the test of such a group's being adequately "representative?" This question arose at once when UPA began to work with an organization called the Lower Roxbury Community Council in the area of a projected campus high school in Boston. It was readily apparent —and the appearance was not lost on the Boston Redevelopment Authority (BRA), UPA's adversary in negotiations—that the active members of the organization were few, did not include members of the most economically deprived social levels in the area, and were not in communication with a sizable proportion of the local residents.

UPA, of course, was committed to supporting all possible efforts by the existing community group to widen its base of representation. One of UPA's first project activities was to assist the local group in designing and carrying out a survey of the area's residents as to their wants and needs in housing and community improvement; the survey project was thought of both as an information-gathering or sounding-out function and as a way of drawing residents into contact with the organization. A number of residents were drawn into the activities of the organization, and several mass meetings called by it drew sizable crowds. But it was at no time possible to describe it as having the active support of the majority of persons living in the area it intended to represent. Many, we can be sure, have to this day not heard of the Lower Roxbury Community Council—in this respect paralleling the situation as to voter knowledge/ignorance of American foreign policy.

Consideration of this situation, and some discussions centering around the question of whether "community groups" in some other parts of the city which had asked UPA for help were sufficiently "representative" to deserve it, led the members of UPA to try to develop a position on what amount of "representativeness" would be "adequate." No mathematical formula seemed possible. The expression of some previously unrepresented interest must necessarily take the form of a small organizational beginning which, with time, with an intent to

3. Herbert Gans, *The Urban Villagers: Group and Class in the Life of Italian-Americans* (New York: The Free Press, 1965), p. 11.

broaden its base, and with some success which makes participation appear rewarding, tends to pick up participation as it goes. It is just this kind of process which advocacy planning is intended to support. The people at the bottom are likely to be the slowest to become organized. Therefore, a preference for groups which are more "representative" in the sense of having more members or a higher ratio of members to potential members, might well mean aiding mainly middle-class groups. The only working position which it seemed possible to adopt was that of seeking to collaborate with organizations which seemed likely to progress in the direction of building representation for people previously unrepresented, and to try to help the organization in that process.

Still more critical difficulties are likely to appear when it comes to identifying the community interests which the advocacy planner is to embody in a community plan. As already noted, cities are such that any specified area in the city, particularly in the central city, is likely to contain people of strikingly different social characteristics, interests, and needs: even in Herbert Gans's "urban village," Italians constituted less than half the population. Also in the area were remnants of earlier waves of settlement—Jews, Poles, Irish, Albanians, Ukranians, and Greeks, and a number of other sorts of people who found the area convenient because of its location and/or because of the low rents. These may include gypsies, families on AFDC, middle-class professionals and students, hospital workers, artists, and families and individuals in various sorts of semi-incapacitating personal troubles.[4] The area in Boston represented by the Lower Roxbury Community Council contained people with a wide variety of kinds of commitment to it—from white and Negro homeowners deploring the "decline of the neighborhood" and "that class of people" presently moving in, but anxious to hang on to their homes and help the neighborhood "come up" again, to families on AFDC and gypsies living in storefronts, with little long-term commitment to the particular area, but dependent on the low rents in a housing market progressively stacked against them.

At one of the meetings with the community group, the BRA representative referred to the evident incohesiveness of the area, and comparing it to the "Chinese community," with which the BRA had previously signed an agreement, suggested that an area which was so little a "real community" as this one could hardly expect the same degree of consideration. At this a resident of the area, as it happened a Ceylonese lady who runs a rather interesting Buddhist nursery school rose and made a little speech. She said that here was a neighborhood in which many different kinds of people lived amicably together; that this was something which public policy should respect and support, rather than depreciating their heterogeneity.

4. Gans, *op. cit.*, pp. 8–10.

The point appeared to me well taken, but the usual heterogeneity of urban neighborhoods makes problems for the advocate planner. Those different sorts of people may turn out to have very different interests when it comes to the countdown. In the Lower Roxbury case the demand for housing to be built on land around the new school was one on which everyone could agree, even if not everyone was equally interested in it. But one may see community groups struggling with the potentially explosive issue of neighborhood improvements which will raise property values (and rents) to the benefit of home-owners and the injury of tenants. In Boston's Washington Park Renewal Project poor tenants were in effect improved right out of the area by an alliance between the public agency and a "community group" dominated by middle-class property owners. It has been the community representatives, not the public agency, which in Boston's South End have opposed locating in the area a treatment center for the alcoholics of the local Skid Row. One might suggest that a consequence of giving every neighborhood in a city its advocate planner might be a general closing up of the city against the poor, especially the sorts of "problematic poor" represented by gypsies and families on AFDC. When poor tenants, particularly those seen to constitute "social problems" coexist in the same neighborhood with better-off property owners, there are natural conflicts of interest which the coexistence in the "same community" only intensifies. One may either say, then, that "the community" —taken as everyone living in a specific area—has no single interest, or that the neighborhood contains several communities. In effect, advocacy planning for the local community miniaturizes, but does not eliminate, the problems of conflicting interest which inhere in the planning activities of city-wide agencies.

Representation or Manipulation

Whether the scale is city-wide or local neighborhood, all sources agree that the people at the bottom of the social structure are very much harder to draw into the planning framework than the members of the middle class. Interpretations of this situation vary. A wide variety of writers have treated this nonparticipation as an aspect of life style; the poor are described, at the least as nonjoiners, more drastically as isolated or anomic. But, one may also say that the poor are often intimidated by people in positions of authority—and with some reason, for the disparity in power resources is clear on both sides.

One view of this phenomenon is that offered by James Q. Wilson, who sees the difference between middle class and lower class in the situation as one of breadth of vision, as "public-regarding" versus "private-regarding" behavior. "Upper and upper middle-class people are more likely to think in terms of general plans, the neighborhood or community as a whole, and long-term benefits (even when they might involve immediate costs to themselves); lower and lower middle-class people are more likely to see such matters in terms of specific threats and short-term costs."[5]

An alternative view is possible. "The generally favorable middle-class response to urban renewal, apparently not based on any unique perceptive powers of that income group, may be partly and more plausibly explained by the dominant role played by the middle class in shaping societal values."[6] As things work, the institutions with which people may collaborate or negotiate are responding particularly to the pressure of middle-class interests, and are (not oddly) more relevant to those interests than they are to those of the people at the bottom. Programs and institutions which have to do primarily with the buildings in which people live are more relevant to people who have some long-term stake in those pieces of property. Joseph Lyford tells an illuminating story of a woman who rose at the beginning of a neighborhood block improvement meeting on New York's West Side to express her wants from the community improvement effort. "She said she had no job and wanted to work and that she had to work because there was no other way for her to live." She talked on, until finally someone managed to tell her, "Pinky Mae, be quiet; this meeting is not a place to ask about jobs." But other people like Pinky Mae asked such questions for which there was no place on the agenda. Nothing could be done with those questions. "Finally the chairman had to ask the strangers to stop talking so that the meeting could proceed with the agenda. As the talk about schools, and housing, and neighborhood improvement got under way, the Negroes left the meeting quietly, one or two at a time. By the end of the meeting only Pinky Mae and the man in the front row who had admonished her were still there, and then they went out too, and never again were any of these people seen at another meeting any place."[7]

Since it is so hard to draw the poor into the planning, why should not the planners go out to them—gather data, take a poll, do interviews—and on this basis draw up an advocacy plan? This they can do, and in fact, this was one of the strategies used by UPA in its Lower Roxbury project. But this kind of sounding-out is not a substitute for genuine participation for several reasons. In the first place, since people (very sensibly) tend to focus their wants on what they conceive they could get, any first round of opinion collecting will produce only a

5. James Q. Wilson, "The Citizen in the Renewal Process," *Journal of Housing,* 1963.

6. "Citizen Participation in Urban Renewal," *Columbia Law Review,* Vol. 66, (March 1966), p. 599.

7. Joseph P. Lyford, *The Airtight Cage* (New York: Harper & Row, 1966), pp. 133–134.

collection of beefs about garbage pickup and street lighting. Only a long process of discussion of possible alternatives which opens new alternatives and makes their consequences articulate will make a meaningful set of opinions possible. The opening up of options must go along with the opening up of opinions.

This is one way of saying which we of UPA took a little while to grasp: that the technical and the political are interconnected at all levels. They are connected because if organization is to bear on issues, people must constitute a relevant interest group; they must be organized around these issues. They are connected because people will not organize to attain something which looks impossible, and to organize around an issue involves some sense that the objective is both a practical and a political possibility. Thus they are connected also because the existence of an interest group in back of an objective helps to make the objective more attainable.

We thought of the situation in Lower Roxbury as one in which the members of the community could become organized around some .fairly finely delineated issues as to the future of their area. It was innocent of us to imagine that this could be done in the way we thought of its being done, with the "community organizers" from the local community centers doing the organizing, and UPA providing the technical assistance, helping the members of the organization to articulate, clarify, resolve issues. This was a naive view, of course. We could only have drawn more of the residents into the organization by raising possibilities relevant to all those kinds of people, and bringing them to their attention. The organizers could not be expected to have the technical know-how to do that. Nor, it turns out, will they particularly want to do so. The organizer is working toward a confrontation, and for that he needs a small group of people who can work together around some central issue, and enough backup interest in the community so that when the time for confrontation comes, those others will come to the meeting and sign the petition. More differentiated, sophisticated, and widespread discussion of the issues is, from this point of view, at least an extra, and probably a political liability. Alinsky is accused of oversimplifying, but there is evidence that he knows his business.

We of UPA had another interesting surprise in Lower Roxbury. We found that we, too, could be looked on as manipulators of the community. This was a surprise because we thought of ourselves as those who were defending the interests of the local people against the manipulating institutions like the BRA. But when, at a meeting of the Lower Roxbury group at which were present BRA representatives, representatives of UPA, and several community organizers, the question was raised as to whether the community group should not be discussing its strategy toward BRA without having members of that group present, the community group put all the outsiders into the hall—the BRA members, the community organizers, and the members of UPA. We were all manipulators.

This was, of course, correct. Even without administrative power, the advocate planner is a manipulator. The power to conceptualize is a power to manipulate. The planner may not be the first to identify "problems" of an urban area, but he puts them on the agenda, and plays a large part in defining the terms in which the problems will be thought about—and those terms in effect play a large part in determining the solution.

He is not and can never be a simple channel through which flow the "interests of the community." Those interests become translated as they pass into the planner's technical framework. And, we noticed of ourselves, the advocate planner, like the establishment planner, finds it easier to deal with some issues—like housing—than with others, which might be more salient to some people in the area.

The agenda which he has such a large part in setting for the community is in turn largely set for him by the action opportunity structure. The items for the agenda are presented by the available programs and institutions and their priority must reflect the necessity of dealing first with actions being taken which affect the group. The advocacy plan thus tends to be more of a reaction to, than an enactment of.

UPA's work with the little community council in Lower Roxbury thus seemed to raise many of the same issues of the relationship of "planning" to "people" which are raised in city-wide planning and redevelopment programs. They are miniaturized, but their basic structure remains. Even at the neighborhood level there is no simple aggregation of people's wants and needs into a plan. Even at the neighborhood level, there is a tendency for the planning process to give greater weight to the people at the top of the social structure than to those at the bottom.

"A New Kind of Politics"

Other issues, or perhaps more accurately, other views of the same issues, were presented by Urban Planning Aid's part in opposing the Inner Belt highway, a large, limited-access loop highway planned for Boston and its inner suburbs under the federal highway program. At first UPA's involvement appeared in the same context as its involvement in Lower Roxbury; it was defending the interests of a "low-income community," in this case, that part of Cambridge, a typical "soft area," which was the designated route of the highway. But this time the controversy soon developed rather another form. The construction of a road is a classic instance of the principle that at times social life may demand that some persons be inconvenienced or disadvantaged in order to execute a project which benefits many people. UPA, in taking up the issue of the Inner Belt, in effect could hardly make a case simply in terms of the interests of the people in Cambridge whose homes were to be taken. It found itself escalating the issue into one of the procedures and criteria used in planning the highway and others like it. UPA members produced a report on metropolitan transportation planning in Boston which argued that the planning of the Inner Belt was not only based on outmoded and inadequate data, and failed to satisfy federal guidelines, but that the procedures used were generally of a character such as to favor the interests of highway users as against those of users of mass transit. At this point, UPA was no longer speaking in the name of a specific low-income community, but appealing to planners' standards of technical adequacy, raising issues of due process in decision-making, and making a claim, in effect, that a certain public policy-making system had a bias against low-income groups.

In defining the issue in these terms, UPA did not lack for supporters, drawn especially from the academic community. But who was now its client? In speaking for those people in cities who would have benefited from a different pattern of public expenditure as between highways and mass transit, and a transportation system which counted the social costs of a reduction in the housing stock and the cutting up of residential communities by highways, UPA was speaking for people widely dispersed geographically, unaware of themselves as constituting an interest group, and unaggregated in any particular social unit or institution. UPA now had neither a clearly defined client nor a clearly defined opponent. It was speaking for institutional restructuring, and its apposite model now appeared not so much that of the lawyer defending an indigent client as the radical political action group.

Indeed, the Inner Belt issue clearly reveals a number of ways in which the analogy between "advocacy planning" and legal representation breaks down. The lawyer takes a client; there is nothing in planner ethics to prevent his starting with an issue and looking for a clientele whose interest is involved. Further, the experience of UPA shows that many issues, if raised at all, will be raised only in this way. What client will raise the issue of the distribution of public resources as between highways and mass transit? It clearly shows also how the advocate planner has no such clear forum and procedures for adjudication as does the lawyer. His issues are adjudicated in the forum of politics, where opposing forces come to a power confrontation. So UPA, in opposing the Inner Belt, found itself working with petitions, meeting with Senators, abetting protest marches. In the Lower Roxbury case, although there was a long period of negotiation between two quite clearly defined groups, again decision would have to rest in the end in a show of power in the City Council voting. Advocacy planning here appears as a new kind of politics.

It seems to be, on the one hand, a way in which localized urban interests can be expressed in a political system from which ward politics has all but disappeared. In this respect, it falls in with a number of other current efforts to decentralize the work of government— ranging from Carl Linn's small community-built parks, to the local planning entities of the War on Poverty.

But it has another potential political function which, as in those community planning projects which raise conflicts between home-owners and tenants, may compete with the local community interest function. It can also appear as a way of dealing with issues which are not at all particular to any single local community—issues of race and class, and of particular interest groups as these emerge in the context of the technical and managerial apparatus with which our kind of society runs. The slogan which calls urban renewal "Negro Removal" is an expression of this sort of interest—in this case, localized through racial segregation and the project boundary. Other interests, like those of the groups dependent on mass transit, or on very low-cost housing, are more widely dispersed and concomitantly harder to articulate politically.

Finally, advocacy planning may be one of the channels of action through which people may try to humanize their technical apparatus, to make society less "one-dimensional," to prevent the exercise of bureaucratic power from leading to a new, diffuse despotism, in which power appears in the image of technical necessity. Perhaps in advocacy planning we are seeing one way in which we work toward a kind of politics suitable for a time which has seen the end of ideology, but which finds social management institutions more and more the determinant of human possibility.

It may well be argued that the politicization of our management apparatus will mean its incapacity to act: that if every group affected by planning is permitted to argue for its interests, no projects for the common good can ever be carried out. The danger is, I suppose, a real one. But at the same time, to the efficiency argument the remarks of the Cahns on coordinated community-wide structures for the provision of social services seem apposite: "Monopolies are characterized by tendencies to expand, to perpetuate themselves and to operate at less than optimal efficiency. These tendencies do not disappear when the market monopolized is the market for social services or when the product is social change. In such a market monopoly power presents special hazards because it can be used to achieve insulation from the democratic market place, to secure relative immunity from criticism and evaluation, and to obviate genuine responsiveness to consumer demand."[8]

I would suggest that the weight of the evidence so far, in looking at the effects of "citizen participation" and of raw citizen protest on the urban renewal program indicates that the very considerable short-term inefficiencies and exasperations of advocacy are paid for by the pressure which they generate for a social policy more sensitive and adaptive to social reality.

At the same time, the experience summarized briefly here should be enough to suggest how far we have to go and how difficult is the way in developing social policies which effectively articulate the interests of the people at the bottom of the system. Our policies are always approximations; we can hope only to work toward making them better approximations.

8. Edgar S. Cahn and Jean Kamper Cahn, "The War on Poverty: A Civilian Perspective," 73 *Yale Law Journal,* 1317 (1964).

Capital Programming in Philadelphia

William H. Brown, Jr., and
Charles E. Gilbert

I

MUCH, THOUGH SURELY NOT ALL, of city planning today is directly related to capital programming. This is especially so in *large* cities for at least three major reasons: basic physical plant and utilities are often run down or obsolescent for a complex of historical reasons; many routine programs are "capital-intensive" and are becoming more so under the impact of new technology and professional standards; and urban renewal has entailed an increasingly entrepreneurial approach to land-use planning. Capital programming itself is a process of separate budgetary decision on capital items, however defined.[1] The rationale for the separate decision process values "planning" highly and emphasizes *fiscal* planning of outlaying that is loan-financed and *physical* planning of projects distinguished by "lumpiness" and/or longevity. It follows from these considerations that the planning and programming of physical improvements cannot be sharply separated from the remainder of municipal policy. City planning as applied to capital programming has to do not only with land use but with most functional programs and with fiscal policy.

While some long-range municipal planning will probably take place in the line departments, the focal point of planning is likely to be the review and assembly of the over-all capital program, at which point fiscal, programmatic and land-use planning all come into play even if the principal competence and concern of the planning agency is in land-use planning. The planning agency can be conceived as performing any or all of the four roles of *research, integration, allocation,* and provisions of the *long view.* While conceptually distinguish-

---

1. An excellent treatment, with references to the not voluminous literature, is Jesse Burkhead, *Government Budgeting* (New York, 1956), ch. 8.

Reprinted from American Political Science Review, *October, 1960, pp. 659–668, by permission of the publisher and of the authors.*

able, these roles tend to merge in the practice of capital program review. Thus planning research tends to support a longer view of policy and facilities through the anticipation of trends and the gradual adumbration or articulation of goals, perhaps in a master plan. Integration of projects for the effective fulfillment of program goals and the avoidance of land-use conflicts or premature project obsolescence tends to slide into inter-agency capital budgetary allocations as priorities are attached to project requests.

Students of municipal affairs have differed as to the proper role or balance of roles of the planning agency in capital programming. Some have argued that over-all efficiency of the city's programs and physical plant will best be served if the planning agency in effect confines itself to research and integration; others have maintained that these same ends require more-or-less authoritative capital budgetary allocations by the planner based upon more-or-less definitive determinations of city goals.[2] Much, though not all, of the literature of city planning has been tending to expansiveness about the role of the planner and the comprehensive plan in capital programming and in municipal policy generally.[3] Yet the recent literature of public administration has increasingly emphasized constraints and limitations upon "rationality" and thus, by implication, upon long-range and comprehensive planning.[4] The arguments most relevant here have been those of economists who for a combination of institutional and intellectual reasons have been skeptical of the "efficiency" implied in the "classical" or "neo-classical" organization theory and in central and comprehensive decisions, and who have questioned whether administration—especially in a pluralistic political context—can possibly or profitably operate in a logical and long-range optimizing fashion.[5]

Capital programming should provide a good test of these conflicting views of the intellectual and institutional role of planning in city

2. For the first view, see Allison Dunham, "A Legal and Economic Basis for City Planning," *Columbia Law Review*, Vol. 58 (1958), pp. 650–671. For a thoroughgoing statement of the second view, see Rexford G. Tugwell, "Implementing the Public Interest," *Public Administration Review*, Vol. 1 (1940), pp. 32–49.

3. See, *e.g.*, Harvey S. Perloff, "Education of City Planners: Past, Present and Future," *Journal of the American Institute of Planners*, Vol. 22 (1956), pp. 186–217; and the rejoinder by James M. Lee, "The Role of the Planner in the Present," *ibid.*, Vol. 24 (1958), pp. 151–157. See also Henry Fagin, "Organizing and Carrying Out Planning Activities within Urban Government," *ibid.*, Vol. 25 (1959), pp. 109–114, which appeared after completion of our study and while this article was in a draft.

4. Though "rationality" is among the slipperiest of terms, we use it here to imply clear-cut and central decisions about goals (usually based upon research into alternatives and consequences) and the more-or-less rigorous "suboptimization" of such decisions at lower administrative levels. The term embodies meanings often given to "coordination" and "efficiency," and emphasizes long-range perspectives. On "efficiency," see Herbert Simon, *Administrative Behavior*, 2d ed. (New York, 1957), ch. 9.

5. See C. E. Lindblom, "Policy Analysis," *American Economic Review*, Vol. 48 (1958), pp. 298–312, "Tinbergen on Policy-making," *Journal of Political Economy*, Vol. 66 (1958), pp. 531–538, and "The Science of 'Muddling Through,'" *Public Administration Review*, Vol. 19 (1959), pp. 79–88; and Roland N. McKean, *Efficiency in Government through Systems Analysis* (New York, 1957), Part II.

administration (though our treatment is largely confined to its institutional role). Both recommended and ultimate decisions and eventual accomplishments are clear, more-or-less quantified, and recorded. Agencies of planning, administration, and politics are involved at various points in the decision process and so is the entire spectrum of municipal policy in its physical, fiscal, and functional aspects.

The Philadelphia experience should provide an especially critical test for reasons that can only be briefly listed here. Capital programming in that city has attained a reasonable maturity: the process of decision and of ultimate appropriation and executive was mandated in the Home Rule Charter of 1951 and has since been conscientiously implemented by two "reform" administrations. Some say that capital programming is now further developed in Philadelphia than in any other American jurisdiction.[6]

The *political setting* of capital programming is one in which public expectations (as manifest in citizen organizations and the press) appear to support "planning" and "rationality" in city decisions. There is active and organized citizen support for city planning and public improvements, extending from what is loosely termed the "grass roots" to what can equally loosely be termed the "power structure." While providing support for the process of capital programming, however, the various citizen groups differ over the substance and extent of improvements.[7] The city's "organization" politics offers few obstacles to long-range planning, in our observation, and might on balance be classified as a stabilizing factor.[8]

The *governmental setting* seems equally appropriate to a test of planning. Philadelphia is decidedly a strong-mayor city. The small (17-member) Council is partially elected at large and its role in budgeting and personnel policy is sharply limited by the charter. The mayor is

6.   We are not aware of any written statement to this effect, but several students of municipal government have expressed this view to us. For treatments of the Philadelphia experience, see Aaron Levine, "Philadelphia Story: A New Look," *New York Times Magazine,* July 14, 1957, p. 8 ff.; and Edmund N. Bacon, "Capital Programming and Public Policy," *Journal of the American Institute of Planners,* Vol. 22 (1956), pp. 35–38. The authors are executive directors of, respectively, the Citizens' Council on City Planning and the Philadelphia City Planning Commission.

7.   The principal city-wide groups concerned with capital programming are: The Citizens' Council on City Planning; the Philadelphia Housing Association; the Health and Welfare Council; the Chamber of Commerce; the Bureau of Municipal Research-Pennsylvania Economy League; and the Greater Philadelphia Movement (and its auxiliary, the Citizens' Budget Committee). Some idea of the concerns of these groups can be gained from their titles. The last-named (GPM) is a prestigeful and primarily businessmen's organization which has conceived and strongly supported a number of policy and capital improvements; its subsidiary (CBC) is primarily a fiscal watchdog agency. The leading interests of the other organizations broadly include: tax-consciousness, government organizations and reform, welfare and social service, urban renewal and housing, industrial promotion and renewal, and citizen involvement in planning. Some of these agencies reach into the neighborhoods directly or through affiliates.

8.   For a recent study see James Reichley, *The Art of Government: Reform and Organization Politics in Philadelphia* (New York, The Fund for the Republic, 1959).

served at the top level by a Managing Director who heads the principal line departments, a Commerce Director in charge of major transportation *termini* and promotional and commercial facilities, and a Finance Director under whom most financial functions are centralized. These three officials are *ex officio* members of the quasi-independent Planning Commission. The small number of departments and the Planning Commission are highly professionalized. Urban renewal and transportation policy alone cut athwart the remainder of the administration, and these functions are served by coordinators in the mayor's office.[9] In summary, government in Philadelphia generally conforms to the conventional canons of "sound" city organization. A more favorable setting for long-range planning in a still highly pluralistic society would seem hard to find.

Our study of capital programming in Philadelphia began with an examination of its "stability"—that is, of the extent to which projects and allocations in the later years of six-year programs actually move forward on their original schedule to budgeting and execution. Taken in this sense stability should provide a good (though not literally sufficient) index of the effectiveness of long-range planning. Our unequivocal finding was that the process was characterized by a marked lack of stability as here defined, even allowing for the vicissitudes of intergovernmental grants, "forced" deferred maintenance, and acts of God.[10] This led us to an analysis of the main institutional processes bearing upon stability and instability. The characteristic roles of public agencies (though not, by and large, of private parties) are discussed in the remainder of this paper.

II

Since 1952 capital programming decisions in Philadelphia have tended to gravitate from the Planning Commission to the administrative line. While the literature of public administration would suggest such a development, expectations surrounding capital pro-

9. See Lenox L. Moak, "Background and Principal Features of the Philadelphia Charter," Appendix 1-A of Leverett S. Lyon, ed., *Modernizing a City Government* (Chicago, 1954); and Joseph S. Clark, Jr., "Experience with Philadelphia's New Charter," *ibid.*, Appendix 1-B.

10. Space precludes extensive documentation of the point here, though we have made a number of measurements in terms of funds and projects. Many changes are made between the second year of any capital program and the year following when it becomes a capital budget; and changes measured from the more remote years of capital programs are even more numerous and sizeable even though the most remote years are "filled up" to the $25 million ceiling on annual tax-supported city funds. In the 1959 capital budget no department's appropriation differed (up or down) by less than 13%; 6 departments showed changes of more than 30% and one department of more than 100%. Eleven departments are included, and the net dollar changes tend to hide a number of project changes. *Most* projects and appropriations, moreover, are amended during the executory period of capital budgets.

gramming in Philadelphia appear to point rather to a definitive (though penultimate) allocative (as well as integrative) role for the Planning Commission.[11] Though its intent was somewhat obscured by the *ex officio* device, the charter evidently envisaged such a role for the Planning Commission, and the Commission evidently performed a more decisive role in adjudicating among agencies and allocating funds in the early years than it has more recently.

Capital budget and program requests usually originate with the departments and are revised and assembled in the capital program and budget by the Planning Commission. The recommendations of the Commission go to the Mayor for review and eventual transmittal to Council, which must adopt a capital budget as an actual appropriation for the year ahead and a capital program as a six-year guide. Neither budget nor program can be amended without requesting the advice of the Planning Commission. Not all of the capital program receives the same treatment in the initial and reviewing stages. Some items—they are usually "lumpy" and exigent—are matters of top administrative policy and receive their impetus or their argument from the Mayor and his cabinet. The remainder of the program is finally settled at the level of the staff principals and deputies in the Planning Commission, the Managing Director's office, the Finance Director's office, and the office of the Director of Commerce. For the most part these decisions result from a collective, constant, cooperative, and consultative process which, however, is not without administrative bargaining at departmental and cabinet levels. In this process it now appears that the point of most influence is the Managing Director's office.

The principal factors in line predominance appear to be the following:

1. The importance of being on the spot and active in day-to-day operations is considerable; policies (or projects) tend to emerge from ongoing operations or immediate necessities.

2. There has been an improvement in long-range planning in the departments stimulated, in fact, by the role of the Planning Commission in programming the demand for better project justifications. Progress has varied among departments because of substantive difficulties and factors of leadership and bargaining power. Such plans as there are fall

11. For a representative statement in the literature of public administration, see Herbert A. Simon, Donald W. Smithburg, and Victor A. Thompson, *Public Administration* (New York, 1950), ch. 20, esp. pp. 442–447. The prevailing Philadelphia view is expressed in the following editorial comment on an issue between City Council and Planning Commission: ". . . the Planning Commission is only doing its job when it reshuffles priorities. Its purpose is to consider the City as a whole, and to balance desirable capital spending ideas against each other, and against the amount of money which may be spent. Without over-all planning, the Commission would have no function. City building would then descend to pork-barrel tactics. . . ." *The Evening Bulletin* (Philadelphia) 27 October 1958.

into three main types: (a) efforts at broad definitions of public responsibilities in certain fields (*e.g.*, medical care for the needy) which have been produced by broadly representative committees; (b) essays at standards for services and facilities (*e.g.*, recreation space standards) embodying in varying degree existing professional standards; and (c) attempts simply to schedule facilities, modernizations or improvements, generally but not always on the basis of some data on age or cost (*e.g.*, the replacement of water mains). Actually, few detailed, written departmental plans are in existence.

3. The Managing Director is formally charged with coordination of most departments. The City's Managing Directors have been able and vigorous, and have believed that the principal responsibility for all aspects of forward planning save over-all physical planning should rest with the departments rather than with the Planning Commission.

4. The Managing Director's office has kept a rather tight grip on the departments through central staff work in reviewing their operating and capital budgets. It has instituted an initial screening of departmental capital project requests both at their inception and on an over-all basis before their submission to the Planning Commission. The rigor of this preliminary screening has varied among departments but has increased in recent years. It has reflected the Managing Director's view of a reasonable capital allocation among agencies and his judgment of projects' chances of survival later in the reviewing process. The Planning Commission, for its part, has often cut departments financially, leaving to them the decisions as to which projects are to be eliminated or deferred (save for those projects that raise problems of integration with one another or with the Commission's developing land-use projections and policies). Not infrequently the Managing Director intervenes at this stage also.

5. Recently the administrative screening process has been extended and formalized by creation of a cabinet subcommittee charged with reviewing the "big" projects of large displacement that are the troublemakers in capital programming.[12] Naturally, this means scanning the capital program as a whole to see what projects can be deferred or displaced. The subcommittee does not finally decide these points; it reports to the Cabinet which then decides and communicates its decision to the Planning Commission. While the Commission staff may not follow the policy of the Cabinet, it will know that the *ex officio* Commission members will be following that line in Planning Commission meetings.

6. The *ex officio* device has all along given substantial weight to the administration members of the Commission, but it has left to the Commission a function of arbitrating or adjudicating those cases in

12. Members of the subcommittee are the Managing Director, Finance Director, Director of Commerce, and Development Coordinator.

which the *ex officio* members were unable to reach prior agreement. Such cases were not infrequent in the past, but the cabinet subcommittee appears to have reduced their number.

7. The ability of the Planning Commission to cope with its *ex officio* members has depended upon the information and interest of the Commissioners respecting the capital program. While these appear to have been considerable in the early years, there is much testimony to the effect that they have declined. Chairmen excepted, many Commissioners have attended hearings and meetings on the capital program less frequently in recent years and have tended to concentrate on a few pet projects. The role of the Commission's staff *vis à vis* the Commission appears to have grown, and it may be that some commission "marasmus" has set in where capital programming is concerned.[13]

8. Two staff divisions of the Planning Commission are involved in capital program review and assembly; these are the Projects Division and the Comprehensive Planning Division. The latter has entered the picture only in recent years, reviewing departmental requests for conformance with the City's projected comprehensive plan. This review has not had much influence to date—despite the imminence of the comprehensive plan—because that plan has been tentative and has provided broad standards, projections and goals rather than concrete criteria for fund and project allocations.[14] The Projects Division is formally in charge of assembling the capital budget and program and, on the testimony of those most closely involved, the decisions result from informed judgment rather than explicit criteria. The leading members of the Division are long-time City servants (not trained planners) who know intimately the departments and attendant political pressures. They consciously and continuously supplement desk and drawing board decisions with the gleanings of sidewalk and corridor conversations. They have been prone to recognize that the range of choice for the Commission is limited by continuing programs, administrative and Councilmanic attitudes, top-level policies and popular demands for some projects working their way forward in the program. Their decisions thus rest substantially upon (a) their knowledge of the projects' etiology in the departments and their assessment of departmental planning and appraisal of "need," and (b) the "law of anticipated

13. These observations apply only to the Commission's work in capital programming. Some informants have argued that, as the outline and specific requests of capital programs have matured and become familiar, less detailed Commission consideration is necessary to control of the program. This argument would not, however, appear to affect our conclusions about the Commission's role in relation to its *ex officio* members and its staff, and several informants who are very close to the Commission agree with our conclusions.

14. This conclusion rests upon testimony of some staff members of the Division and of other Divisions, and upon our own comparisons of the recommendations of the Comprehensive Planning Division with the Planning Commission's final capital program document.

reactions" with reference to administration and Council. Integrative and long-term considerations are far from being ignored but the Projects Division lacks explicit criteria. The nature and sources of its information and the personal background of its members probably cause it to act to some extent as a buffer between administrators and planners.[15]

The Commission's role remains a significant one. Its vigorous Chairmen have prevailed in numerous policy decisions; generally they have been consulted in such decisions. Its prestige has given weight to its occasional protests over projects or scheduling. It has been conceded a genuine role of an integrative sort in the prevention of future diseconomies through conflicting projects or land uses or (from the City-wide view) inefficient scheduling. Increasingly the administration has been attending to some of these aspects itself, thus restraining the integrative role of the Planning Commission from becoming one of thoroughgoing allocation, but the Commission will clearly continue to play a role in identifying and shaping long-range goals and in integrating the scheduling of projects over the shorter run.

III

Philadelphia's capital budgets and programs are, in the first instance, shaped by processes of planning and administration designed to maximize integration and the long view, and the City Charter seeks to maximize administrative initiative *vis à vis* Council. Capital programs are bulky and complex and the annual capital budgets carry more than a hundred line items, thus complicating Council's role in long-range planning. In general, it is clear that the administration has the initiative, but Council is nonetheless active in capital programming —largely through shifts in scheduling of projects rather than through their initiation, or the broad review of policies. Its effect is felt in three main ways, which may be briefly reviewed.

1. Council tends to exert pressure for regional parity in the distribution of projects, for four apparent reasons. One is the structure of Council, in which ten of the seventeen Councilmen are elected from districts.[16] Councilmen agree that district and at-large members have

15. Though perhaps peculiar to Philadelphia, it may be worth noting that there are differences in orientation toward capital programming within the Planning Commission relating to function and background. Thus, the projects Division relies upon administrative contacts and "informed judgment"; the Comprehensive Planning Division is interested in more abstract and categorical analysis; the executive director relies a good deal upon personal identification with the city and upon esthetic and fluid rather than categorical and abstract approaches; and the Commissioners' approaches appear to be quite individual.

16. The Charter provides that each district shall contain approximately 10% of the population by the decennial census, and the districts are, in fact, fairly equal in population. The total voting population of the city is about 1 million, so the districts are quite populous.

characteristically different orientations to capital programming.[17] A second distributive tendency probably lies in the legislative process of decision, which is said to lend itself more to trading and logrolling than does hierarchical organization. Philadelphia's Council, dominated by one party, takes its capital program decisions in the closed caucus of that party, and the decision is reportedly characterized by a good deal of trading in which the party leadership is careful to see that everyone gets something to show his district, though no one gets all he wants. A third factor doubtless tending toward regional parity, and accentuating Council's concern for this value in comparison with the administration's, is the fact that most Councilmen are members of the dominant Democratic "organization," while the Mayor is not and is frequently at odds with it. A frequent generalization about big-city political organization runs to the effect that, while it is capable of achieving some centralization and overview, its most basic virtues are sectional responsiveness and flexibility.[18] The following news item is illustrative:

> Democratic Ward leaders in the Northeast will ask that $250,000 which was stricken from the capital program for acquisition of land for recreation purposes be restored, it was announced today.
>
> The leaders met Monday with City Council leaders to discuss with them the needs of the Northeast area. . . .
>
> This item was knocked from the program by the City Planning Commission (Councilman) McDevitt said. "All of the Northeast Democratic leaders are pledged to have this item reinstated. The Councilmen who met with us indicated agreement with this and have agreed to have this item added to the 1959–64 Capital Program."[19]

Finally, government and city-wide citizen organizations in Philadelphia have actively encouraged and created citizen organizations in the neighborhoods. The political party is far from being the only method of voicing or creating local demands. Administrative agencies, as well as district Councilmen, work closely with the neighborhood groups, which are alert to capital program decisions and mark the progress of relevant items in the printed Capital Program. Thus, the news account just quoted had its origin in a review of the Planning Commission's capital program recommendations by the Philadelphia Health and Welfare Council, which notified its Northeast Area Committee, which put "heat" on the Democratic organization and on a Councilman who was already faced with a difficult primary fight.

City informants agree that Council is more solicitous of regional

17. One Democratic Councilman-at-large, who lives in a district now represented by a Republican, told us that he is under constant pressure from his party leadership to "represent" that district, and that he takes great care to avoid being labeled as the Councilman from that district in order to preserve his independence and breadth of view.

18. For a recent discussion, see Martin Meyerson and Edward Banfield, *Politics, Planning and the Public Interest* (Glencoe, Ill., 1955), chs. 3, 9–11.

19. *The Evening Bulletin* (Philadelphia) 12 November 1958, p. 24.

parity than either the administration or Planning Commission; but, to the extent that the other parties endeavor to anticipate Council, the tendency toward parity spreads beyond Council. Council's regional distributive bent shows up chiefly in annual scheduling decisions. While the administration is likely to attempt a measure of geographical distributions in the six-year program as a whole, Council tends to make this an annual goal.[20]

2. Council exhibits a marked tendency toward financial conservatism. It has strongly supported the existing 25 million ceiling on tax-supported City funds in capital budgets and has usually cut the budget somewhat below this figure, accomplishing still further reductions during the execution of the budget. The relative tight-fistedness of Council challenges explanation, since city councils might be expected to approximate more closely than other governmental bodies the model of Anthony Downs, in which governments spend up to the point at which the financing of projects outweighs in adverse votes the votes gained from the projects themselves; and because the chief pressures upon councils might be expected to be spending rather than retrenching pressures.[21]

We think there are two explanations of Council's fiscal conservatism, and that both are about equally important. One relates to the representative structure of Council and the distribution of organized attitudes and interests in the city. The small Council, partially elected at-large, with a strong leadership based in an entrenched party organization, appears to respond to the several city-wide citizen organizations that serve as fiscal watchdogs.[22] Significantly, the fiscal conservatism of Council is centered in its leadership rather than in the rank-and-file, and serves as something of a counterweight to the pressures for regional distribution discussed above. A second explanation relates Council's fiscal conservatism to its governmental, rather than its political, role. On this view, Council's economizing tactics can be seen as an aspect of legislative-administrative rivalry, as a reaction to the administrative budgetary initiatives provided in the strong-mayor Charter, as a means of publicly demonstrating some form of budgetary participation and control, and—in the absence of more formal criteria for investment

20. Space precludes a detailed discussion; but examination of Council's decisions, and a comparison of them with those of the Planning Commission and administration, bears out the thesis put forward here.

21. Anthony Downs, *An Economic Theory of Democracy* (New York, 1957). Downs' simplified theoretical model does not include separated governmental powers, however; and it appears to deal mainly with operating expenditures, or, at least, reasonably divisible expenditures.

22. *Cf.* the discussion in Leverett Lyon, *op. cit.*, ch. 4. There Gilbert Y. Steiner, discussing the advantages of election at-large *versus* election by districts, suggests that the "city-wide" interests that are alleged to prevail over "local" interests in councils elected at-large are chiefly interests in tax reduction, whereas the "local" interests tend to favor projects. Three citizen organizations in Philadelphia are primarily based upon tax and fiscal concerns; Council's leading fiscal monitor is elected at-large.

decisions—of forcing detailed project justifications from departments and administration.

3. Council's orientation to capital programming tends to be immediate and concrete rather than long-run and abstract. It is more interested in capital budgets than in the program as a whole, and displays little interest at all in the remote years of capital programs. Its principal point of assertion is in the scheduling of projects rather than in over-all allocations or the initiation of projects, though a few projects are conceived or introduced by Councilmen and scheduling changes in capital budgets of course produce changes in programs. Councilmen argue that *they* are the "experts" on scheduling since they know what the people want at the moment.

Such abstract investment criteria as professional standards for service levels and facilities, or land use prescriptions, do not weigh heavily with Council, but it is difficult to show that the legislative body consistently favors certain types of projects at the expense of others. It is commonly said that Council prefers "visible" projects (*e.g.*, health centers over storm sewers), by which is really meant "politically popular," and *most* projects command popularity in *some* quarters. It is clear that recreation centers, health centers, and fire stations have been especially popular in Council and that libraries have had an indifferent reception; but there are two qualifications on any order of preferences. One is that projects of all types have been deferred in Council to make room for exigent items at administrative urging (recreation centers lend themselves to this treatment because they are numerous and individually inexpensive); the other is that Councilmanic attitudes (particularly among the leadership) seem to be undergoing some change. More receptivity to "economic base" projects at some cost to "welfare" projects is in evidence today than was the case three or four years ago—a change that may reflect recent progress and a widely acknowledged "catching up" in some welfare fields, together with the fiscal conservatism of Council's leadership and of other influential groups. But the political appeal of "welfare" projects remains strong, as election campaigns indicate.

Two general comments are in order respecting Council's participation in capital programming. One is that there are conflicting tendencies and orientations within Council itself—*e.g.*, between regional or neighborhood parity and fiscal conservatism—and that these tendencies marginally distinguish the leadership from the rank-and-file with respect to political pressures and tactics. The other comment is that, despite the complexity of capital programming and the administrative initiative it entails, Council's activity in scheduling indicates a continuing legislative role in relating "planning" to popular tastes and utilities. Capital programs, unlike operating budgets, closely approach the "alternative budget" conception in giving Council a cafeteria of projects to choose among. Given the official promises in printed capital programs, popular interest in the projects, and organized reactions and importunities, Council is likely to amend the judgments of professionals and planners by applying its own political conclusions respecting the people's wants.[23] It should be added, however, that amendments by Council account directly for only a small proportion of the "instability" noted above in Philadelphia's capital programming; *most* deviations from the capital program result from decisions in the administration and Planning Commission, and from delays and amendments during execution of the capital budget.

IV

Generally speaking, the time horizons of the planners outrun those of the administrators; administrators take a somewhat longer view than the mayor's; and the time horizons of Council are the shortest of all. For many planners, of course, such a statement simply amounts to an implicit definition of "planning," "administration," and "politics."[24] The use of the comprehensive plan as a guide to capital budgeting, or the emphasis upon spending today for site acquisition rather than on immediate improvements, are both commonplace evidences of the planner's concern with the long-run.

Administrators might be expected to be less firmly committed to the future, more committed to flexibility in decision and action. The administrator is skeptical about the ability of anyone to predict accurately the circumstances under which he will be operating in two or three years, let alone six or twenty. His attitude may reflect in part the importance he attaches to administrative detail as a determinant of decision and action; in part it may be a reflex bow to the political environment. In any event, some of Philadelphia's top overhead administrators evince some feeling that even six-year capital programming tends to hamper administrative initiatives and action, and that a better procedure might be one in which departmental plans were only roughly blocked out in capital programs for, say, a three-year period, thus reserving funds but reserving, too, the right to change course when necessary and to determine details at a later date. Although long-range planning in the departments has increased in recent years, such plans fall far short of definite commitments in most cases and leave ample room for adjustment. Administrators are inclined to defend flexibility

23. On the "alternative budget" proposal see Verne B. Lewis, "Toward a Theory of Budgeting," *Public Administration Review*, Vol. 12 (1952), p. 42 ff.

24. For a classical statement in the planning literature that planning means (1) applying the factor of adjustment and coordination among competing ideas, specialties and pressures, (2) supplying the long-range view and counteracting the pressures of the moment, and (3) research and data-gathering free from the pressures of the moment, see Alfred Bettman, *City and Regional Planning Papers* (Cambridge, 1946), ch. 5.

in capital budget execution—a process that has to date been quite unpredictable. Though it is now general practice to schedule funds for project planning and site acquisition for the first year of the project, with the larger construction funds following later, capital budgets are still amended freely in the executory period. This period (the capital budget "fiscal year") consists of eighteen months, but several top administrators have argued for its extension.

The mayor actively intervenes in capital programming only in the case of major policy decisions and implications. Informants in the City government generally agree that neither of Philadelphia's mayors since 1952 has had a capital program, though each has pressed certain pet projects, programs or general but imprecisely defined emphases respecting the direction of city development. Both mayors have characteristically reserved major capital policy decisions until as late as possible; though both have on occasion attempted to take leadership for certain projects and, on a few occasions, have retreated in the face of opposition. To the extent that firm investment decisions were made for the long-run the mayor's freedom to respond to or manipulate the pressures on his office would probably be reduced and his political risks would probably be enhanced. Generally, then, and with some exceptions, it would *a priori* seem to be to the mayor's advantage to postpone decisions; the exceptions relate to the testing of public reactions or the heading off of developing opposition. In Philadelphia a large proportion of the major policy items (which tend to be "lumpy" items) enter the capital budget late in the game and have often not appeared at all in the capital program.

The short time horizon of Council has already been discussed. The mayor, due to his city-wide constituency and his administrative protection, is probably not as exposed as Council to a broad range of immediate pressures. While the hypothesis of a kind of hierarchy of perspectives of the sort discussed here is widely current, its illustration in this instance may be worthwhile because of its implications for long-range planning and central decision. Much of the "instability" of capital program decisions probably results from the differing time horizons of participants in the decisions, and these differences in perspective seem embedded in institutional activities, interests, and pressures.

V

Until quite recently there has been little interest in or employment of explicit or formal criteria in departmental programming or central review and allocation.[25] One key official in the process aptly

25. There have been continuing overhead efforts to sharpen project cost estimates

describes it as "more like peeling an apple than slicing a pie." Sophisticated economic analyses or professional standards are difficult to develop and apply because of measurement problems and frequently arbitrary assumptions, and a few City officials have hoped that the long-awaited comprehensive plan (which is mandated by the City Charter) would provide scheduling criteria. Others probably hope it will never arrive, distrusting its inflexibility; still others doubt that the plan will greatly change or govern capital programming. But there are other reasons for reliance upon "informed judgment" besides these.

One is a complex of administrative factors. Philadelphia, like many cities, emerged from the years of depression and World War II with its physical plant run down to the point where a number of "under-developed area" analogies applied, and it lacked a vigorous administration until 1952. When thorough-going capital programming began under the Charter of 1951, large allocations went for deferred maintenance and were simply "forced."[26] While substantial "forced" allocations are probably a thing of the past, each capital budget contains a number of lines of "continuing programs" or recurring expenditures—some of them simply deferred maintenance.[27] The fact that roughly one quarter of the tax-supported segment of capital budgets consists in such programs and that nearly one-half is comprised of projects only secondarily related to land-use planning probably tends to reinforce administrative initiatives, judgment and flexibility in capital programming and to narrow the area of explicit decision open to planners in the field of their principal and traditional expertise.[28] Intergovernmental aids in selected fields appear to narrow reviewing discretion somewhat further and to lend leverage to particular departments. Thus, the Planning Commission's Projects Division finds that, within the $25 million tax-supported limit, there is annually only $10 to $13 million to manipulate, once allowance has been made for administrative "givens" and political pressures (sometimes building on the prescriptive prior appearance of

relative to both capital and operating budgets, but these efforts are of a different order from formal criteria for decision, though they might facilitate their use.

26. A striking example occurred as late as 1955 when, as a result of State and City inspections, some 24 bridges were declared unsafe, facing the administration with a choice between closing down important parts of the City's circulation system or repairing the bridges immediately at a large sacrifice to the rest of the capital program. The second alternative was chosen and the current capital budget and capital program were drastically revised to accommodate the deferred maintenance. Ultimately, some of the bridges were simply posted with weight limits and remain to be repaired.

27. For example, such programs for the Streets Department total about $3.5 million annually within the $25 million limit, and have deviated by more than $25,000 from that total in no year save 1955 (on which see the previous note). The programs are: grading and new paving; street openings; street lighting; unallocated engineering services; traffic signals; road construction and paving in Fairmount Park; construction of traffic islands.

28. For an argument, on this basis, for narrowing the content of capital programs in New York City to primarily land-use-related items, see Frederick C. Mosher, "Fiscal Planning and Budgeting in New York City," in *Report* of the New York State-New York City Fiscal Relations Committee (New York, 1956), pp. 65–84 at pp. 80–81.

projects in capital programs). Finally, the emphasis of the Clark and Dilworth administrations upon energizing and professionalizing the departments has probably encouraged "flexibility" and "informed judgment" at the expense of formal standards and criteria in departmental programming.

A complex of political factors has seemingly served as a second discouragement to the adoption of formal criteria. The 1951 election overturned an administration of many years' incumbency and was fought by the victors with emphasis on specific reforms as well as general City redemption. It could be argued from the tenor of the campaign and the drama of the victory that the new administration had a mandate for large-scale development that would support its leadership and judgment on issues upon which campaign promises or emphases provided no guidance. On the assumption that the City was badly run down and "behind," it could further be argued that political demands should not be discounted nor administrative responsiveness discouraged; that expressed demands reflected real needs and that large (if intangible) returns would accrue to projects that commanded political support. We are not aware that such arguments received explicit statement during the Clark administration (1952–1956); we simply suggest that they provide a rationale for the fact that the use of informal political and professional judgments was generally accepted without debate in the early period of capital programming.

VI

Nonetheless, as the City catches up to what are by publics and professionals considered more satisfactory levels of service, and as the comprehensive plan approaches completion (it is expected in 1960), the pressures for more complete and sophisticated project justifications are likely to mount.[29] Such pressures will probably be resisted by those departments that are politically and administratively in a good bargaining position (e.g., the Streets Department), but political necessity as well as professional pride may foster more long-range planning in other departments. Such plans have now appeared in a very few departments; but, for the most part, they constitute adumbrations of department responsibilities rather than the articulation of standards from which the programming of facilities might in turn be derived.

This experience in part reflects intellectual as well as institutional difficulties in the formulation of formal criteria for capital program-

29. The comprehensive plan did appear in 1960. It is too early to assess its effect on capital programs, but it may be noted that its statements as to goals and levels of service tend to be broad ones.

ming. Without taking the space to argue the point here, it may be said that: derivation of service "standards" from broad statements of "responsibilities" or goals is often a logically loose enterprise; that most existing professional standards, on the contrary, imply goals without making them explicit, lack inter-agency comparability, and often tend only to rationalize pressure group claims; that insofar as city planners' comprehensive plans simply embody such standards elsewhere than in land-use fields they are unlikely to afford a basis for capital program allocations; and that techniques of economic analysis (such as benefit-cost or rate-of-return) are limited today to a few fields. At the same time, comprehensive plans, while affording a basis for the *integration* of projects, are unlikely to afford a basis for firm *allocations* unless they embody a more specific articulation of goals than the political agencies or the publics of Philadelphia have yet provided or seem likely to provide, on the findings presented above.

Thus the institutional and intellectual constraints upon long-range planning appear mutually reinforcing and in the political and administrative pluralism of the metropolis there is probably a more-or-less irreducible minimum of both. Philadelphia, we think, is close to the institutional minimum, and the intellectual problems of planning and "suboptimization" remain to be solved. Our findings on the lack of "stability" in capital programming and its institutional bases, together with the intellectual difficulties with comprehensive planning as a basis for central capital allocations, lead us to conclude that the comprehensive plan is as likely to follow from the process and substance of capital programming as *vice versa*. If this is so, attention should then be centered upon the *process* of capital programming for the procedural desiderata that it may serve.

Four principal conclusions can be derived from the foregoing. (1) Political and administrative forces, working together, induce instability (*i.e.*, limit long-range planning) as well as stability. There are conflicting tendencies, but the institutional constraints upon long-range planning are real. (2) On this interpretation, the probable role of the planning agency in capital programming is basically one of *research* and project *integration;* though to some extent research may gravitate toward the definition of goals, and integration may approach allocation through temporal scheduling decisions and deferrals. (3) To some extent the constraints upon long-range planning result from a perhaps inevitable diffusion of responsibility in the process; yet the machinery described above is probably as centralized as that of any American municipal government.[30] It seems doubtful that a reorganization of planning would have much effect upon stability, though it might

30. Compare the discussion of the effectiveness of "comprehensive" planning and its relation to governmental organization in Meyerson and Banfield, *op. cit.,* pp. 273–275.

adversely affect other desiderata.[31] (4) Several other ends are served by the process. Administrative initiative, energy, and competence are encouraged. It provides a "rational" context for popular consultation through the pre-provision of alternatives and of temporal and regional perspectives on benefits and costs. It encourages the contributions of city planning in the land-use fields of its traditional competence and provides a broader field for planning research. These are important accomplishments by which Philadelphia has been well served and, in the light of them, the tentative nature of long-range planning may be unimportant. Expectations of stable or predictable long-range planning are likely to be disappointed; they are also likely to conflict with other ends.

31. On the organization of planning see, *e.g.,* Robert A. Walker, *The Planning Function in Urban Government,* 2d ed. (Chicago, 1951); Henry C. Fagin, *op. cit.;* and Fagin and C. McKim Norton, "Physical and Fiscal Planning," in New York State-New York City Fiscal Relations Committee, *Report* (New York, 1956), pp. 85–94. The last is most expressly aimed at capital programming.

Five Functions for Planning

Martin Meyerson

WHEN DE TOCQUEVILLE visited here well over a hundred years ago, he commented that whenever two Americans got together, they formed an organization. In recent years, it has become fashionable for European observers to laugh about our tendency to elaborate on organization—now, these observers say, whenever two Americans doing the same sort of work get together, they form a profession.

Professionalization

The social scientists have also focussed on this tendency to professionalize. They have analyzed certain general procedures followed by all emerging professional groups. Their analyses amount to a recital of the natural history of professionalization. First, persons of imagination and vision, and a profound dissatisfaction with the world as they see it, outline the scope of new problems and propose new approaches to these problems. These are persons trained in other disciplines, often diverse disciplines; they are people of broad interests and an ability to dramatize problems and inspire others. Whatever literature is produced is polemic, general, devoted to portrayal of problems, and clamors for the attention of a citizenry already perplexed and vexed by other matters.

As more and more recognition is given to the importance of the newly discovered problems, limited funds are made available for exploring or solving these problems. More people are attracted as lay enthusiasts or as practitioners in the field; organizations are set up; conferences are held. Schools are established to give specialized training; the course of instruction grows longer and longer. A unique vocabulary is developed; nonprofessionals cannot talk it. A literature geared to specific problems emerges; nonprofessionals find it complex and dull. Soom people begin to think in terms of "careers" as well as

Reprinted by permission of the Journal of the American Institute of Planners, *Spring 1956, and of the author.*

in terms of solving problems. Salaries, job classifications, personnel qualifications, specialization within the field become important. Attempts are made to broaden functions and responsibilities, to grow bigger and bigger, to be imperialistic in scope and numbers. More and more efforts are made to make the activity expert, technical, scientific—and beyond the ken of nonprofessionals. This culminates in licensing or registration to keep out pretenders. By this time, the profession has "institutionalized"; its members acquire the power of reproduction—that is, it is the present professionals not the market situation who determine what standards must be met by new entrants.

Despite the gibes of some European observers and despite the implied gibes of the social scientists, I think our American tendency to professionalize on the whole is a good one. By being self-conscious about our work activities we do try to develop our methods and body of knowledge and to improve our competence. The danger lies in the stage when we become too rigid, when we are no longer capable of absorbing new ideas or going in new directions, or willing to discuss our problems with people in other fields. However, planning is too new an activity to be that institutionalized. We are in the expansionist, imperialistic stage, and who am I to go counter to the natural history of our emerging profession?

Therefore, I want to speak today as an imperialist for city planning. I want to speak today about expansion—about increasing our numbers, multiplying our budgets, strengthening our effectiveness, expanding our functions, and, of course, raising our salaries.

Expanding Functions

I shall focus on expanded city planning functions and responsibilities which if not performed by planning agencies may very well be performed by other agencies of local government. However, I believe planning agencies are not only best equipped to perform these functions, but their own effectiveness will be enormously increased by doing so.

However, we might well ask if increasing our scope of operations will not be done by sacrificing preparation of long-range plans. Do not the administration of zoning and subdivision control already rob us of time and energy to devote to long-range planning? Of course they do. Yet they are also ways in which planning is translated effectively into daily changes of urban development.

For background to some of the additional functions I want to discuss, let me wear two hats. One is my hat at ACTION—the American Council to Improve Our Neighborhoods. The other is my hat as city planning professor. Wearing ACTION's hat, my responsibilities during the past year and more have required me to travel to many parts of the country, and to talk with many of the people who made the key decisions which shape our cities and towns. These are the mayors, the city managers, the heads of operating municipal departments, the homebuilders, the merchants and industrialists, the civic leaders. Their decisions are the decisions that set the stage for the decisions of the everyday citizen—his choices on where he lives, his kind of work, the activities he and his family will have an opportunity to participate in. And I was struck by the fact that the mayor and the merchant, the head of the renewal agency and the homebuilders are at a loss to find the specific framework to provide them with the kinds of guidance they need to make rational decisions.

As I talked with these people, it was very encouraging to me to find the respect in which they hold the city planner and to recognize it as a tribute to the responsible growth of our profession. However, their respect is rarely derived from an awareness of the importance of long-range comprehensive planning. Rather their respect is based on the project-planning accomplishments of the city planner and related officials. They speak their admiration for the highway extensions, the new zoning districts, the design of a group of public buildings, the development of a park preserve or a new terminal improvement. Partly, of course, it is because so much of our attention has necessarily gone to project-planning that little effort has been left for long-range comprehensive planning, and thus little opportunity for it to be understood, let alone for it to be vigorously supported.

Yet the framework required by the people who make some of the key decisions for both private and public community development is not provided by project-planning. Nor is the urgency of these decisions met by the kind of long-range comprehensive planning we usually do. I have concluded that a middle ground is needed. An intermediate set of planning functions must be performed on a sustained, on-going basis to provide the framework for the homebuilder who must decide how many units he should, as well as can, build next year; for the government official who must decide whether the signs of unemployment in the locality require special public action; for the appointed commissioner who has no sense of whether a particular policy which his agency might follow and obtain bonds to execute will fit in with other current city policies; for the industrialist who wants to know what specific land use changes will be made in an area within the next few years before he commits his corporation's resources; for the redevelopment agency which has no knowledge as to what the effects of previous slum-clearance projects have been and the lessons that can be learned from them.

Now changing my hat, as a professor of city planning, one of my major concerns is that we train students for the responsible posts they will hold not only this year but ten years from now. An apprenticeship might be a far superior way to a university curriculum if our main object were to prepare people for specific present jobs. What kind of a job will the planner be expected to do ten years from now? I have been trying to get some sense of this and thus of needed educational programs. I am of course talking primarily about city planning, although I believe what I am saying applies to resources planning and other kinds of planning as well. I also recognize that most city planners in the future may not work for what we regard as city planning agencies. This does not mean that they should not be trained as city planners.

Now, wearing both my hats at the same time, I wonder very much whether the impressions I have got for the need and importance of a middle-ground planning activity may not be a clue to some of the crucial functions of the profession in the years ahead, and thus a clue to planning education in the years ahead as well. The additional functions I propose are suggested not to detract from long-range planning but to make it more meaningful.

I propose that we consider whether the following middle-ground community planning functions are appropriate to our province:

1] *A Central Intelligence Function* to facilitate market operations for housing, commerce, industry and other community activities through the regular issuance of market analyses.

2] *A Pulse-Taking Function* to alert the community through quarterly or other periodic reports to danger signs in blight formation, in economic changes, population movements and other shifts.

3] *A Policy Clarification Function* to help frame and regularly revise development objectives of local government.

4] *A Detailed Development Plan Function* to phase specific private and public programs as part of a comprehensive course of action covering not more than 10 years.

5] *A Feed-Back Review Function* to analyze through careful research the consequences of programs and projects activities as a guide to future action.

These are interrelated functions. The intelligence, pulse-taking and review functions roughly parallel the types of measures we are learning to utilize nationally, for example through the Council of Economic Advisers, to encourage equilibrium and new growth in employment and investment. On the community level, we would not want to restrict ourselves to just economic concerns. But nationally we have developed during the last twenty years a type of sensitivity to changes in the economy which permit adjustments when the economy gets markedly out of balance. We have developed a whole series of statistics and indices such as building starts, prices of hogs, consumer credit, a type of periodic information which we never had before. Then, if there are maladjustments in the economy revealed through periodic checks, we may adjust the mortgage rate, place governmental orders in areas where there is unemployment and try to take other measures to bring about equilibrium.

The five functions I want to discuss envisage a similar role for the city planning agency—a role which brings planning and policy closer together. They are functions which city planning agencies to some extent fulfill already. However, they are not part of the routine view of appropriate city planning activity.

What do these five functions mean for municipal planning?

1. THE CENTRAL INTELLIGENCE FUNCTION: The planning agency as the local G2 to aid the operations of the market.

The market place—the mechanism which brings together producer and consumer, supply and demand—is the primary method under democratic capitalism by which land and other resources are allocated to those activities by which people live, work, play and raise their families.

Market decisions are more important than governmental ones in giving substance to the design and structure of our urban communities. In our cities, for example, we see that people who desire housing accommodations are more and more choosing to live in the suburbs. These represent individual choices to satisfy individual values and fit individual circumstances. But these individual choices add up to a major shift in urban patterns not only in housing, but in shopping and many other facilities as well. The changes in urban patterns due to market selection are so decisive and have such widespread and interlocking consequences that they almost appear as though someone had directed them. (Perhaps this is the invisible hand of the market to which Adam Smith refers.)

However, the local businessman, the industrialist and the consumer rarely have the kind of accurate information to make rational decisions. Currently, builders, investors, business and industrial firms have such vast unknown factors with which to deal that the risks involved either operate as brakes on activity or inflate the costs of production or financing. The consumer has to act on conjecture rather than real knowledge of choices open to him.

The city planning agency in most communities is the local unit of government best equipped to provide a market analysis function. Data would have to be obtained and analyzed continuously. Regular market reports would be issued by the planning agency. Depending on the urgency of the market decisions, some of the reports could be issued monthly, some quarterly, some semiannually, some annually. There could be special reports on the new home building market, on investment in plant, on consumer income and spending, on land and building costs. The planning agency is an appropriate one for this function, not only because it has a nucleus of people dealing with these community characteristics but also because this kind of regular and constant market analysis is crucial to the achievement of present functions of planning and some of the other ones I am discussing today.

Detailed market analysis for the city, for the metropolitan area and for subregions in this area would enable both the producer and the consumer to make more intelligent choices in respect to the location, investment, building and land utilization for industry, commerce, housing and other main facilities and activities. The political philosophy of the country rests on the market as the key means to allocate resources. If the city planning agency regularly checks and interprets the local market situation as I suggest here, it can lubricate the process of urban development and achieve many of the main objectives of city planning by facilitating intelligent individual actions.

2. THE PULSE-TAKING FUNCTION: The planning agency as the watchdog for community danger signs.

It is true that most community development decisions are made through market mechanisms rather than through governmental planning mechanisms. However, one of the reasons why planning has become an accepted governmental activity is that the market has frequently exhibited such frictions and even malfunctioning that desired community ends have not been achieved. For example, a main impetus to planning came from the fact that the market was not allocating land uses in such a way as to preserve residential values during the useful life of the property. Planning was expected, through land use and other controls, to compensate for the problems—the failures—of the market.

However, planning has too often been in the position of correcting mistakes after they have happened rather than in the position of detecting and removing trouble spots before they lead to major mistakes. I therefore recommend that the planning agency submit a quarterly or other periodic report to the local chief executive alerting the community danger signs. Which neighborhoods are showing blight factors at an increased pace? Are certain transit routes losing most of their passengers? Are there signs that certain industries are about to either come in or leave the area? The planning agency should thus perpetually scan the community for indications of maladjustment. Failures of firms, increased congestion, incipient changes in land use, new demands for services might thus be detected before they gather a momentum almost impossible to stop.

To be effective the planning agency's pulse-taking report must not only alert the community to trouble spots, but must also point to remedial action. Inevitably this means a policy focus.

3. THE POLICY CLARIFICATION FUNCTION: The planning agency as an aid in framing and regularly revising development objectives of local government.

I have just suggested that the planning agency be alerted to detect any trends potentially harmful to the community. This implies that policies would be devised to halt undesirable changes and promote desired ones in the community, and that the planning agency would take some initiative in indicating the most suitable policy measures. Specific inducements to encourage private actions as well as direct public measures would be needed.

Much of the determination of community policy will evolve through the political process. In a pluralistic society such as ours, there are many conflicting values and there is, as a result, competition among goals. The competition will be expressed and settled largely through politics.

The planning agency, however, can analyze alternative policies. It can help determine what benefits can be achieved as against what costs will be incurred by different specific policies.

Politicians could be given detailed information on the advantages and disadvantages of alternative courses of action to achieve desired goals. Planners should be prepared to say to politicians—if you wish to do such and such, then such and such consequences are likely to result. The planning agency would not be usurping the task of political decision-making but it would be making clear what the implications of alternative policy decisions are, so that more meaningful policy choices can be made. The planning agency, furthermore, can serve as the instrument for making known the policy choices once they are made. The planning agency, by suggesting revisions to policymakers on the basis of changed condition, can encourage periodic presentations of community development policy. Probably a coherent development policy statement should be consciously revealed each year through the mass media of communication.

4. THE DETAILED DEVELOPMENT PLAN FUNCTION: The planning agency as the preparer of a short-range comprehensive plan spelling out specific actions to be taken.

The gap between the developmental policies of government discussed above and a long-range master plan for the future community can be bridged by the preparation of short-run plans, of five to 10 years in time span. The development plan would link measures to deal with current problems with long-range proposals to attain community goals.

For many politicians and businessmen the master plan is too generalized and too remote to seem real. For planners, on the other hand, ameliorative measures which attack symptoms rather than basic problems are too piecemeal, too hastily considered to seem worthwhile. I suggest the short-run development plan as that compromise between immediate problems and future expectations which will permit coherent policy effectuation. This type of plan preparation will require detailed, timed and localized programming of governmental policies for private as well as for public actions. Detailed cost estimates of private as well as public development, and specific administrative and legal measures to carry out the programs will have to be worked out.

Long-range comprehensive plans commonly reveal a desired state of affairs. They rarely specify the detailed courses of action needed to achieve that desired state. By their long-range nature they cannot do so. The development plan, in contrast, will indicate the specific changes in land use programmed for each year, the rate of new growth, the public facilities to be built, the structures to be removed, the private investment required, the extent and sources of public funds to be raised, the tax and other local incentives to encourage private behavior requisite to the plan. The development plan—which incidentally in a more limited form is required by law in England—would have to be acted upon each year and made an official act for the subsequent year, much as a capital budget is put into law. Revised yearly it would become the central guide to land use control, to public budgeting and to appropriate private actions to achieve directed community improvement.

5.   THE FEED-BACK REVIEW FUNCTION: The planning agency as analyzer of the consequences of program and project activities in order to guide future action.

Currently, we in planning agencies have no systematic means of analyzing the effect of planning measures or programs of action. It is astonishing, for example, that we have never analyzed the effects of zoning. We have never studied what the effects of this interference in the land market have been on the monopoly position of different kinds of businesses, on the costs of land, on the encouragement or discouragement of certain types of development.

I suggest that we maintain a constant feed-back of information on the intended and the unintended consequences of programs that are adopted locally. For example, if a new area is developed in the central business district with new office buildings, shopping facilities, and cultural activities, we ought to assess the unintended effects as well as the intended ones of just what happens to the older, existing sections of the central business district and to the surrounding area. Does the new development serve as catalyst and stimulator of further improvements or does it drain off activities from the remainder of the district? These kinds of questions must be asked and answered so that we can learn from our experiences and can adjust our future programming and planning.

The more such a review function is performed, the more readily it can be performed. As a body of review knowledge is built up on the parking effects of highways, on the use made of playgrounds, on whether public housing and redevelopment projects achieve their objectives, on the impacts of off-street loading ordinances, the more simply can new measures be gauged.

Implications of These Functions for Planning Agencies

This may sound like a formidable range of new or at least much enlarged functions. Whether such proposals are practical depends on the situation in particular cities.

I have made a plea that we consider adding certain functions intermediate between ad hoc decisions on a subdivision plot, for example, and long-range comprehensive planning. The capital budget and program in current city planning practice comes closest to this intermediate position. Of course I believe that the functions I have suggested are ones that would be of great benefit to local government and to community development. However, the functions I mentioned could be lodged in various existing or possible municipal agencies. Assuming these functions have merit, I am convinced that the planning agency should be the appropriate niche for them. This is for us in the A.I.P. to decide, or it may be decided for us. We will not have a great deal of time in which to decide. Two cities, a large one and a moderate-sized one, both known in recent years for their good government, are establishing posts called "development coordinator." Should this responsibility not have been delegated to or assumed by city planning? It is too early to say that this is prophetic of a trend. It is not too early, however, to say that planners have the opportunity to take on the development coordination function, to extend their range from the generalized plan on the one hand and the day-to-day demands on the other to the intermediate type of sustained on-going planning activities I have suggested.

But a planning agency capable of achieving some of the functions I have suggested today will require far greater specialization than we have ever had in municipal planning. It is true also that more planners will be required by specialized agencies in transportation, housing and other fields. They will be required especially in such agencies if the functions I suggest above develop. However, the specialization will be required mostly by the planning agencies themselves to prepare detailed development plans, perpetual inventories of market characteristics and the other tasks demanded. It will require personnel with joint specialization, or more properly, people who are specialists in a particular field and generalists in planning. Joint designer-planners, statistician-planners, highway expert-planners, real property lawyer-planners, utility engineer-planners and other dually trained personnel will be necessary. Incentives will have to be provided to enable people willingly to acquire such dual background—in other words, we will have to pay them as well as offer intellectual satisfactions and the satisfactions which come from socially useful work.

But if we do extend our planning functions—and even if we

merely try to fulfill our present tasks as we see them—we need a level of budget for local planning of a kind we have never seen before. The planner currently is responsible for advising on expenditures running into hundreds of millions of dollars and on programs intimately affecting the lives of thousands, or in some cases, millions, of people. Decisions of such far-reaching consequences should not be financed through substandard salaries, blighted budgets and penny-pinched research. It is true that planning costs our local communities in the United States between 7½ and 10 million dollars annually. But this is insignificant when a single mile of an expressway in a single city may cost twice that much. It is unnecessary for me to point out that the total annual expenditure on city planning in the United States is less than the cost of a single public building or a fraction of the budget of my own and other academic institutions or that some of the efficiencies which can be derived from city planning in even a single city could pay for the entire cost of city planning in the country.

I do not know how much the additional functions I have suggested would cost. Costs would vary, of course, with the thoroughness of performing each function and with the size of the community. (I have completely side-stepped the issue of whether the planning agency should also attempt to administer or to oversee the short-range development plans, and if so, to what degree.) However, such planning will clearly be very costly.

My own basic premise is that good staff is essential to the performance of planning functions and good staff is expensive staff. I agree completely with the statement in the Schuster report of Great Britain that "more than ever before the planning authorities need to recruit people with first-class intellectual qualities and first-class educational attainments. Everything else that we have to say is secondary in importance to this."

It is to the credit of planning that we have been able to attract people so far through the challenge of the field rather than the remuneration offered them. However, we must recognize that just as our universities and colleges cannot well exist from the subsidy of low salaries, so planning and other governmental activities cannot sustain high quality work through the subsidy of underpaid labor. Beardsley Ruml recently advocated paying professors as much as $30,000 a year. We should hardly be expected to feel that the top jobs in planning should pay less than that.

I prefaced my comments with a thumbnail sketch of the natural history of all professions. Each attempts to get for itself a bigger share of the pie of responsibility, of status, of resources and of income. Just within this last week a colleague, a neighbor, and a third person whom I did not know, made the following claims in the press: The race relations expert said discrimination was America's Number One problem.

The criminologist said the rising wave of juvenile crime was America's Number One problem. The third person—the psychiatric administrator —said mental health was America's Number One problem.

But these claims are not true. Naturally, you and I as city planners are convinced the Number One problem of America is the development of America's cities, their housing, their transportation and all the other elements that make them viable.

In conclusion, as an imperialist for the profession I have computed that about one-half of one per cent of municipal expenditures in the United States could result in an expenditure for planning of almost ten times what it is now. Such an expenditure I feel sure would clearly enable us to do our day-to-day jobs, to do long-range planning, and to add major substance to our work through the on-going middle-range type of comprehensive planning I have described. Since Chicago 50 years ago, we have urged others to make no little plans. Let's make no little plans for the development of our own profession in terms of re-sources, in terms of public support, in terms of education, and in terms of laying claim to emerging new functions.

The Coming Revolution in City Planning

Anthony Downs

I. Introduction

DURING the next two decades, there will be a revolution in city planning in most large American cities.[1] This revolution will involve drastic changes in the nature of city planning, the type of people who carry it out, and its role in the urban government process. As a result, city planning will become both more difficult and more important to our society than ever before.

These changes will really be only one part of a general "revolution" which is already underway in the United States. It involves radically new administrative techniques in all large organizations, shifts in the geographic and social distribution of political and economic power, and new roles for government in society. Since all the basic causes of the changes I predict have been at work for some time, some people may consider those changes as *evolutionary* rather than *revolutionary*. Nevertheless, insofar as city planning is concerned, I believe that both the degree and rate of change will be great enough to justify my use of the more dramatic term.

II. The Four Causes of the Revolution

There are four major causes of the forthcoming revolution in city planning. *The first is the broadening of city planning to include a great many variables other than those connected with physical design and layout.* In recent years, city planners have devoted more and more of their attention to economic, political, social, cultural, and other factors affecting the urban environment. This has resulted from their

1. Throughout this article, the term *city planning* is used as equivalent to the more precisely correct but less familiar term *urban planning*.

Published for the first time in this book, by permission of the author.

growing realization that the physical structure of every city is largely a resultant of nonphysical factors.

Two examples illustrate this trend. The first is the gradual evolution in the type of cure for "the urban problem" embodied in federal legislation. In the thirties, public housing legislation focused upon physically improving each family's dwelling unit and its immediate environs. However, experience showed that this approach did not eliminate the social ills plaguing urban low-income families. Therefore, postwar urban renewal legislation was designed to improve entire neighborhoods. But this approach has also proved disappointing as a panacea for underprivileged people. Therefore, current emphasis has shifted to the social and cultural factors stressed in the antipoverty, aid-to-education, and civil rights programs.

This gradual widening of the variables considered as causes of "the urban problem" has been reflected in city plans too. A remarkable example is the recent Basic Policies Plan published by the Chicago Department of City Planning in August 1964. In some respects, this document reads more like Aristotle or Plato than like traditional city plans. Thus, it states that the basic objective of city planning is "to improve the quality of living for every resident."[2] Such an extremely general objective necessarily shifts planners' attention to a fantastic variety of forces and factors within the city. For example, one of the main goals expressed in this plan is encouraging middle-income families with children to live in the city. Clearly, if city planning is going to concern itself with such nonphysical objectives, city planners will have to become well-versed in analyzing and manipulating a great many variables outside their traditional sphere of interest.

This broadening of attention has two crucial impacts upon city planning. First, it makes the whole planning process infinitely more complicated and difficult. We are still embarrassingly ignorant about the nature of cities. Moreover, merely taking into account so many different variables is extraordinarily taxing to the limited capacity of the human mind. The other impact is that city planners—or at least some of them—will have to become expert in many subjects other than those traditionally associated with their profession.

The second major cause of the revolution in city planning is a shift of the focus of planning from a product-oriented activity to a process-and-program-oriented one. Many city planners believe that their primary objective is to produce an object called *"the* city plan." This object can be a report, or an annotated map, or a book combining both of these things. In any case, it is the embodiment of what the planner believes the city should ultimately be like, an idealized city design.

However, recent changes in the way planners are organizationally

2. Department of City Planning, City of Chicago, *Basic Policies for the Comprehensive Plan of Chicago,* August 1964, p. 13.

related to government decision-makers have contributed to a new emphasis in city planning. In organization theory, there is a general principle that the farther away an official is from the day-to-day decision-making process, the more attention he is likely to devote to long-run planning. Conversely, the closer he is to decision-makers "on the firing line," the more his attention will be dominated by short-run "crises."[3] In many cities, planning was originally conducted under the auspices of semiautonomous citizens' commissions. This structure encouraged planners to concentrate upon future-oriented urban designs without much regard for the practical problems of putting those designs into effect. But, in recent years, there has been a marked shift toward more closely integrating city planners with other urban governmental processes. For example, in many cities, planners now form a department reporting directly to the mayor. This shift forces planners to concern themselves—perhaps excessively—with helping the mayor "fight fires." Hence they no longer concentrate solely upon "the big picture."

As a result, many planners have become involved in such daily affairs as making zoning decisions, helping coordinate capital improvement budgets, and even giving advice on the effects of various political reapportionment schemes. Thus they are thinking more than ever before about *how to achieve* short-run goals. Moreover, they have entered into a continuous give-and-take decision-making process with plenty of feedback between their own ideas and those of other people. These changes have produced reorientation of planning from a product-oriented activity to a process-or-program-oriented one.[4]

This shift in emphasis does not imply that city planning no longer creates any products at all. Planning still requires some definite specification of objectives to be attained. However, the revolution implies that these objectives will concern a great many nonphysical aspects of the city as well as its appearance and layout, and will include specified programs of action for arriving at the desired outcomes.

The third major underlying cause of the coming revolution in city planning is the likely future influence of the national government upon urban activities.[5] In recent years, the federal government has supported a wide variety of different local programs in both large and small cities.

---

3. This principle has been called "Gresham's law of planning" by March and Simon, who state it as follows: "Daily routine drives out planning." See James G. March and Herbert A. Simon, *Organizations* (New York: John Wiley & Sons, Inc., 1958), p. 185.

4. My emphasis upon planning as a process follows a precedent set by earlier writers on this subject. For example, see Martin Meyerson, "Building the Middle Range Bridge for Comprehensive Planning," *Journal of the American Institute of Planners,* Spring 1958; Melvin M. Webber, "The Prospects of Policies Planning," in Leonard Duhl, ed., *The Urban Condition* (New York: Basic Books, Inc., 1963); and Marshall Kaplan, "The Planner, General Planning, and the City," *Land Economics,* Vol. XL, No. 3 (August 1964), pp. 295–302.

5. This point was suggested by Professor Lloyd Rodwin of M.I.T.

These include public housing, urban renewal, planning assistance grants, community facilities assistance grants, federal highway programs, FHA mortgage programs, and—more recently—federal aid-to-education and antipoverty programs.

In part, these programs are disguised means of providing federal government financing for hard-pressed urban governments, particularly in large central cities. They tend to redistribute income from wealthier suburban and central city areas where the federal government collects much of its income taxes to poorer central city areas where the major urban problems lie.

These federally assisted programs have had two divergent impacts upon city planning at the local level. First, both the total quantity and the quality of city planning has been markedly increased by the expansion of federal urban assistance programs. Second, there has been a proliferation of relatively uncoordinated planning efforts. This occurs because federal programs are administered by many federal agencies with different objectives, varying attitudes toward planning, and different planning criteria. Such lack of coordination is naturally furthered by the fragmentalization of governmental power among many political bodies in a single metropolitan area, and even among many departments within a single large municipality. The resulting lack of planning coordination is particularly acute in cities which do not have strongly centralized power structures (such as New York City and Los Angeles).

In the last few years, the federal government has made a greater effort to provide incentives for more coordinated planning among local agencies. For example, the Urban Renewal Administration has been promoting Community Renewal Programs, in which a conscious effort must be made to develop a long-run renewal strategy based on coordination of various city activities. The recent emphasis upon federally financed metropolitan transportation studies also attempts to bring "big picture" thinking to knotty problems involving many modes of travel. Lately, the antipoverty program has pushed another coordinated approach to the activities of various welfare agencies within major metropolitan areas.

Now that a federal Department of Housing and Urban Development has been created, the promotion of such broadened planning activities—probably incorporating entire metropolitan areas as well as multiple functions—will undoubtedly be encouraged. As a result, national government activities will surely provide a strong future impetus toward increasing the scope of city planning both geographically and functionally.

The fourth factor which will cause dramatic changes in city planning is the development of new techniques of analyzing extremely complicated policy-formulation problems. The most glamorous and widely publicized of these new techniques involve computers. However, I believe that the development of systems analysis will have a greater impact upon city planning in the long run. The now-popular term "systems analysis" is used to denote a wide variety of different analytic techniques. However, I am referring to a specific method of analyzing extremely complicated and uncertain situations in order to develop "optimal action programs" aimed at achieving definite goals. Hence this type of systems analysis is a method of organizing thinking about complex problems, rather than any abstruse mathematical formulations concerning those problems.

Systems analysis has been refined into a relatively sophisticated tool by technicians working on two different types of defense-oriented problems. The first type consists of theoretically comparing the merits of competing weapons systems or defense strategies, as is often done at the RAND Corporation.[6] The second type consists of coordinating incredibly complicated weapons development and construction processes, such as those involved in creating the Polaris and Atlas missiles. Thus, this kind of systems analysis combines methods of analyzing problems under conditions of uncertainty, and methods of coordinating complicated action and development programs.

The main differences between this kind of systems analysis and the types of thinking formerly done in most city planning are as follows:

1] Systems analysis almost always involves the evaluation of several alternative approaches to a problem, rather than the elaboration of "one best way."

2] Systems analysis uses explicit cost-benefit calculations in order to evaluate alternatives. In contrast, traditional city planning concentrates primarily upon "needs" or benefits (that is, what courses of action might be desirable) and tends to play down costs, or ignore them altogether.

3] In systems analysis, *quantification* of important variables— however approximate—is attempted wherever possible. Such quantification is a crucial part of discovering the marginal "trade-offs" which can be obtained by partially sacrificing attainment of one objective in order to increase attainment of another. In contrast, traditional city planning stresses the *direction* of desirable change, but not the *amounts* thereof. Hence traditional city planning usually ignores trade-offs by assuming that *all* objectives can be attained simultaneously.

4] Systems analysis has a definite *programmatic* orientation. It specifies *how* to achieve certain objectives, and develops *relative priorities* among objectives and action programs. Although traditional city planning has been moving in the direction of discussing how to attain

6. The RAND approach is described in E. S. Quade, ed., *Anaylsis for Military Decisions* (Santa Monica: RAND, R-387-PR, November 1964), and Roland N. McKean, *Efficiency in Government Through Systems Analysis* (New York: John Wiley & Sons, Inc., 1958).

objectives, it still tends to present its programs in the form of what I call "wish lists." These are enumerations of "requirements" (that is, desirable outcomes such as more jobs, improved education, a new expressway along a certain route, or building new parks according to certain plans) without any quantification of their costs and benefits which could lead to assessing their relative importance.

5] In systems analysis, uncertainty is handled by evaluating multiple outcomes (such as the worst and the best foreseeable) and comparing their differences, rather than by selecting the most likely outcome on the basis of probabilities and evaluating only that outcome.

6] Proper systems analysis not only proposes action programs, but also links them to definite time periods and resource costs.

These differences illustrate that *systems analysis provides city planners with greatly expanded capabilities for coping with the extremely difficult analytical problems they face.* One major reason why city planners have traditionally shied away from dealing with many nonphysical variables and developing program priorities is the extraordinary difficulty of these tasks. It was impossible to handle the welter of variables and relationships involved effectively, even though many planners certainly realized that doing so would be desirable. Now systems analysis gives them tools with which to enter this conceptual and empirical jungle with more confidence that they can carve on effective path through it. Certainly difficult problems of analysis and measurement remain, for systems analysis is no panacea. Recent attempts to build even simplified mathematical models of cities indicate that analyzing their formidable complexities will never be easy. Nearly all of these attempts have fallen far short of the sometimes extravagant claims of their promoters. Systems analysis will undoubtedly experience some failures too. Nevertheless, I believe that it represents a significant technical advance of profound importance to the future of all planning—including that of cities and urban affairs.

III. The Effects of the Revolution

Even though none of the four causal factors described above is really new, their interaction will nevertheless produce dramatic changes in the character of city planning in the next decade. These changes will not occur in all parts of the country at the same time or to the same degree. However, to illustrate the *direction* of the coming revolution, I will briefly describe the form which each of its most significant elements will take when it occurs to the *maximum* degree.

1] *City planners will become general advisers to key politicians concerning nearly all city government activities and resource uses.* This change will have two profound impacts. First, city planners will become involved in the entire municipal government budget process. The door has already been opened to this shift in some cities where capital improvement budgeting has been placed under city planning departments. Second, since alternative city action programs have crucial political impacts, city planners will begin advising elected officials in more detail about possible *political* effects of various programs. Such "politicalization" of city planning will simultaneously increase the power of planners, involve them in greater conflicts with former political advisers, and make them more vulnerable to changes in city administration.

2] *City planning will involve development of coordinated operating programs for many city departments—hence it will become a group activity.* City planning policies will be developed by committees of department heads within various governments. This will occur because it is necessary to involve the men who actually carry out programs in the planning process itself. Otherwise, planned programs will never be brought to fruition. Moreover, coordination of all city departments is too complicated for any one person to plan without direct assistance from experts representing each department.

3] *The idea of developing a single "best" plan for the city will be replaced by the idea of planning as a continuous process.* This shift has long been advocated by such planning theorists as Martin Meyerson, and has already begun in some cities.[7] The resulting process will include specification of goals, development of major strategies for accomplishing those goals, recurrent production of detailed plans within the broader framework of those strategies, and constant adjustment of all these items in response to feedback from the communities affected and the major political and economic interest groups therein. Any planning requires concrete conceptions of the objectives of action. Therefore, city planners will still continue to produce visually oriented plans. However, the idea of developing a single such visually oriented plan for the entire city will be abandoned. Instead, the comprehensive framework for planning will be a *verbal* specification of basic government policy objectives. This specification will be translated into specific action programs for all government departments. These programs will in turn be developed by means of overall city planning strategies, expressed in both graphic and verbal terms. Hence the specific *physical* designs involved in city planning will cover only those relatively narrow geographic areas capable of being actively changed within short time horizons.

4] *There will be a greater emphasis upon quantitative studies of costs and benefits, including the specific evaluation of alternative programs.* This emphasis will spring from increased capabilities for conducting quantitative analysis, and greater pressure from politicians for

7. See footnote 4.

practical advice on how to spend tax and other monies. The need for such practical advice will also focus planners' attention upon evaluating *several* alternative programs as a means of settling political controversies and providing effective guidance to mayors and city managers.

5] *City planning staffs will contain economists, sociologists, geographers, systems analysts, and political scientists, as well as designers and architects.* This "infiltration" has already started. Moreover, the top officials of such staffs are increasingly likely to be systems analysts or economists rather than design specialists. Urban design will still be a very important component of the city planning process. But it will tend to become more of a specialized segment of that process rather than the dominant theme thereof. Clearly, this change in emphasis has great implications for the type of training which city planners ought to receive in the future. It is already reflected in the curricula of leading planning schools.

6] *City planning will make extensive use of data-coordinating and data-processing systems for quantifying the information developed by virtually all city operating departments.* The governments of our major cities generate enormous amounts of information in widely dispersed offices. For the first time, modern equipment has created the possibility of quickly gathering these data together in a centralized spot and analyzing the relationships between them. This could provide key decision-makers with greatly improved information for their day-to-day choices. The city planning department is one of several logical places for coordinating this information—which is now 90 percent unutilized. Even if we make no advances whatever in the *analysis* of such data, merely gathering all the data cities are now producing into one spot and placing them in usable form should have an enormous impact encouraging better coordination—and therefore increased power in the hands of the coordinators. In fact, such improved data collection is an essential prerequisite to effective urban systems analysis.

7] *City planning departments will become coordinators and supervisors of "floating research teams" utilized by all operating departments.* Nearly all major urban decisions are underresearched. Much city government activity in particular could be substantially improved in quality if more advanced analysis were done by operating departments. This fact will gradually gain greater recognition by city governments themselves. However, the need for such additional research will vary from time to time and from department to department. Hence, the most efficient way for cities to increase their investment in research without undue rigidity is to develop "floating research teams" which can focus their efforts upon those problems which are the most important at any given moment.

Each of the above impacts will not only be important in itself, but also will tend to reinforce one or more of the others. For example, data processing systems will improve the advice which city planners can offer politicians, and will therefore cause the latter to rely upon the former for broader advice than formerly.

IV. Why "The Powers That Be" Will Encourage the Revolution

The changes described in the preceding section amount to a significant realignment of power within city governments. Members of city planning departments will gain broader responsibilities and more authority, while other officials will lose some of their existing power. Since city planners have long been notorious for their *lack* of political strength, it is not obvious why "the powers that be" will permit such shifts of authority. However, I believe that powerful forces will favor and encourage this revolution for the following reasons:

1] *There will be an ever-stronger "fiscal squeeze" on city governments* as local citizens demand more and better services but resist paying any higher local taxes. This squeeze will pressure mayors and city managers to develop better coordination among their various departments so as to save money without reducing service levels. Hence they will increasingly seek advice from their technical staffs about how to improve such coordination.

This squeeze will be particularly painful in older central cities for several reasons. First, they will contain a rising number and proportion of low-income and deprived citizens. This will both increase their costs and reduce their taxable wealth. Second, the citizenry will become better educated and demand higher-quality services, as is already occurring regarding schools. Third, the demand for certain nonmarket services not now performed by any governments will rise sharply because the need for such services will become painfully obvious. Last summer's smog crisis in Los Angeles, and the constantly worsening traffic congestion in New York are examples. Though most such problems cannot be handled by individual cities acting alone, attacking them will create a need for more planning, even if federal money is used to finance it.

2] *Federal government funds will be increasingly tied to the coordinated planning of many city functions*, especially now that the Department of Housing and Urban Development has been created. Since national government planning funds form a very significant part of all expenditures on urban planning in this country and elsewhere, the pressure of requirements for greater coordination from the national government will strongly favor the planning revolution.

3] *As city planners become better educated themselves, they will perceive their problems more broadly*, and will wish to use the latest techniques in solving them. City planners seek advancement not so much through promotion *within* organizations they belong to, but more through "jumping" from one city to another and gaining status in the process. In such a milieu, the *profession* of city planning itself and the standards it creates have a strong influence upon the behavior of individual planners. Hence, as they become more aware of the interdependence of physical design with other variables, they will generate pressure to create the revolution I have described.

4] *Mayors and other key urban politicians will also become better educated and more sophisticated.* Hence many will begin to demand improved planning services along the lines mentioned above. Moreover, President Johnson's insistence that *all* federal agencies use the cost-effectiveness approach developed under Defense Secretary McNamara will bring this approach to the attention of mayors much faster than would otherwise have occurred. The resulting prestige of systems analysis may create a certain "band-wagon" effect which will further the city planning revolution.

V. Obstacles and Problems

The city planning revolution will not occur in all American cities at the same speed. The change-inducing forces described previously will encounter overwhelming obstacles in some areas, severe but surmountable ones in other areas, and little resistance in still other places. Many of these obstacles are rooted in the particular constitutional structure and the particular preferences of the local electorate in each community. Hence the degree to which they obstruct the revolution will depend in part upon those specific elements in each city.

In essence, three of the five main obstacles to the coming revolution are decentralizing forces. Analyzing them emphasizes that *the revolution we have described will tend to centralize decision-making power within the city government.* This centralization involves two shifts of power. The first will occur within the city government administration from operating departments to the mayor (or some other political chief). The second will occur within the community as a whole from fragmentalized sections of the electorate to the majority which supports city government itself—or even to the government from the electorate. The significance of these remarks will be illustrated by further analysis of the following three major obstacles:

1] *The revolution in city planning cannot take place where there is no strong power center within the city government itself.* Better coordination of city government programs implies that a single power center exercises authority over all city departments. But in some cities, governmental power is so decentralized and fragmentalized that no single politician or group of politicians can play this coordinating role. For example, some observers contend that New York City is virtually ungovernable in this sense.[8] Also, the perennial conflict between the mayor and the City Council in Los Angeles, plus the nature of that city's charter and the extremely mobile character of its population, tend to prevent the kind of coordinated decision-making implied by the revolution we have described.

Such extreme fragmentalization is incompatible with the systems analysis approach, which requires formulation of a consistent set of objectives before action programs can be designed. However, if power is fragmentalized among groups or individuals with different goals, no internally consistent set of objectives can be formulated. As a result, it becomes impossible to evaluate the costs and benefits of any given program.

This situation makes it virtually impossible to use systems analysis to devise acceptable solutions to problems involving entire metropolitan areas. The solutions are *technically* possible—even easy—once the interests involved can agree upon a single consistent set of goals. However, the incentives for the many government bodies in a metropolitan area to reach such agreement have so far not been very strong (though they will probably become stronger in the future because of greater federal emphasis on metropolitan-area planning and worsening air-pollution and transportation-congestion conditions).

2] *Future changes in the nature and composition of central-city electorates may make it more difficult for politicians to formulate unified goals broadly acceptable to their constituents.* There are some indications that the voters in many of our larger central cities are becoming increasingly polarized around conflicting sets of goals. On the one hand, lower-income and lower-middle-income groups—especially Negroes—are becoming more interested than ever before in the substantive content of city policies regarding schools, employment, police activity, housing segregation, and other crucial matters. They want policies which will improve their own economic and social status. Moreover, their growing relative and absolute size in central cities, and their newly awakened awareness of their own potential power, will certainly increase their future influence upon public policy in such cities. On the other hand, middle-income households are also becoming more issue-conscious as their educational and income levels rise. Many such households—especially among whites—want policies which will protect and improve the status they have already achieved. In some cases, their policy desires directly conflict with those of lower-income minority groups. Under these conditions, many central-city politicians will be caught in a dilemma which will make it extremely difficult for them to

8. See Richard J. Whalen, *A City Destroying Itself* (New York: William Morrow & Co., 1965).

formulate a single consistent set of goals acceptable to a preponderant majority of both groups. Yet systems analysis cannot be effectively employed in city planning unless key politicians have a reasonably consistent set of goals.

3] *A trend toward greater direct citizen participation in city planning may similarly weaken the applicability of systems analysis by reducing unity of goals.* Experience in some cities where the government has encouraged neighborhood groups to interact with planners shows that the interests of such groups tend to be focused primarily upon local problems rather than city-wide matters. But neighborhoods within a city often have strikingly different inhabitants. Therefore, a shift of effective power from governing officials to neighborhood associations or other citizen participation groups may result in greater disunity of goals regarding overall government action programs. This fragmentalization of power would reduce the utility of systems analysis in the same way as the fragmentalization of power *within* the government described above.[9] Moreover, insofar as a city's electorate becomes increasingly polarized concerning basic economic, social, or ethnic issues, giving it a greater voice in policy formation will make development of consistent goals even more difficult.

This conclusion should not be construed as an attack on increasing citizen participation in the planning process. I merely wish to point out that, insofar as such participation leads to greater disunity of goals, development of *any* coordinated policies becomes more difficult.

In addition to the above decentralizing obstacles to the coming revolution in city planning, the following forces will also tend to retard its arrival:

4] *All the persons likely to lose power because of the changes in city planning described earlier will fight to prevent those changes from occurring.* Two groups in particular will battle the revolution ferociously: heads of city government departments who now operate almost autonomous empires, and political advisers to mayors who have survived because of the very imprecision of their forecasts (and everyone else's). These people will naturally resist yielding power to systems analysis "eggheads," just as the heads of the Armed Services have fought Secretary McNamara's civilian "whiz kids." Hence old-style political advisers will ridicule attempts to introduce computerized data processing and other sophisticated tools into actual government decision-making. In contrast, city department heads are more likely to fight for their own independent data processing systems.

Even within the city planning profession itself, some groups will oppose the trends I have described. Specialists in urban design will

9. See James Q. Wilson, "Planning and Politics: Citizen Participation in Urban Renewal," *Journal of the American Institute of Planners,* Vol. XXIX, No. 4 (November 1963), pp. 242–249.

understandably resent the rising significance of "new-style" planners equipped with greater knowledge of economics, sociology, statistics, and systems analysis. And many city planners who believe they should "stay out of politics" will shy away from providing elected officials with quantified estimates of the political impacts of alternative programs.

5] *Other city government departments may take the lead in developing systems analysis and computerized data processing as methods of coordinating all city activities, thereby "capturing" this function.* City planners will have no monopoly on these new techniques. In fact, the way some city governments are structured, other departments will seem to be more "organizationally logical" locations for these activities. Examples are the city comptroller and the administrative staff of the mayor or city manager. However, as Robert Moses has demonstrated in New York City, the personalities and abilities of key officials are likely to be more important in determining who performs these functions than any formal organization charts. The official who first realizes the potentialities of this approach and develops the capability of carrying it out within his own department will tend to dominate this function. Therefore, the accidents of personnel juxtapositions within each city government will have a crucial impact upon the nature of the revolution in city planning in that city.

6] *All politicians and many professional planners have very important goals which they do not wish to state publicly; hence these goals cannot be overtly and systematically incorporated into systems analyses.* For example, most elected officials have a strong desire to be reelected. They normally accord this goal a very high priority. Yet no politician would authorize a city planner to develop a systems analysis for various government action programs aimed explicitly at getting him reelected (unless he thought it could be kept 100 percent secret, which is virtually impossible in municipal government).

Similarly, many city planners regard their current assignments as "stepping stones" in their overall career. Hence they may privately seek to develop a city plan which embodies a glamorous "technical breakthrough" or fancy new illustration techniques. Yet they, too, would not dream of explicitly stating such objectives as part of the goals to be "maximized."

Hence whenever city planners use systems analysis, they will have to shape their programs in conformance with important unexpressed goals, as well as with the goals they specifically set forth. Moreover, if key politicians fear that their planners will be incapable of skillfully carrying out such modifications, they may choose to eschew systems analysis altogether.[10]

10. I do not mean to imply that such behavior is necessarily unethical. Everyone has personal aims logically unrelated to his social functions which influences the way he performs those functions. Moreover, everyone would be embarrassed if *all* the

7] *Competent systems analyses tend to reveal things which some politicians may prefer to keep concealed.* For example, the assignment of specific priorities to future programs may reveal that some parts of the city will not receive often-promised improvements for many years to come. Such revelations frequently crystallize and aggravate opposition which might have remained relatively ineffective if fobbed off with vague promises and continued inaction. Since systems analysis has precisely the effect of clarifying such situations in quantitative terms, it may cause heightened tension within the community if its results are made public.

In this respect, systems analysis raises certain issues about public accountability which are critical in all government decision-making. The President need not reveal what happens in Cabinet meetings because he must have the freedom to discuss alternatives he later rejects without having to explain either why he considered them at all or why he rejected them. However, it is extremely difficult to keep city planning affairs secret, since there are no legal penalties for publicizing them (as there are for publicizing military secrets). Hence key politicians may prefer to prevent the use of systems analysis in certain sensitive areas rather than trying to keep its preliminary results confidential.

VI. How Fast Will the Revolution Occur?

The foregoing catalog of obstacles to the coming revolution in city planning may seem to preclude its ever arriving. However, in this age of stunningly rapid technological and social change, it would be foolish to forecast that the forces supporting the status quo will triumph over those supporting changes that are already underway. Hence we can be certain that the revolution is going to come—and probably soon.

Furthermore, the analysis presented herein can be used to make predictions about the relative speed with which this revolution will occur in different cities. It will take place most rapidly and to the greatest extent in cities exhibiting three characteristics: the city government is accorded broad authority by its constitutional structure and its electorate; power within that government is relatively highly centralized; and the city planning agency is headed by a strong personality with a favorable attitude toward systems analysis. Conversely, the revolution will occur slowly and to the least extent where power is fragmentalized both within the government and between the government and the electorate, and the city planning agency is run by a relatively

---

workings of such motivations were exposed to public view. Hence politicians who seek to conceal part of their motivation may be merely behaving like everyone else.

weak personality or one hostile to the trends described herein. Nevertheless, at least some aspects of the revolution in city planning which we have described will undoubtedly have taken place in every metropolitan area in the United States by 1975. Many cities will have experienced nearly all these aspects by that date.

Moreover, the revolution may occur even faster in other parts of the world. This is particularly likely in underdeveloped nations because their national governments are relatively much more powerful than in the United States. They not only have a stronger voice in the policies of local governments, but also control more of the economy through state-owned economic activities operated under national economic plans. Thus, they exert great influence on both the *supply* of local government services, and the *demand* for such services. Furthermore, in both roles, it is in their interest to coordinate local planning with national planning so as to conserve their limited capital and managerial resources. Finally, because there is almost no city planning of any kind in many underdeveloped countries, no entrenched group of traditional planners exists to impede adoption of the systems analysis approach.

True, one tremendous obstacle in such countries is the acute shortage of trained personnel. But many of these nations are sending at least some young planners to urban planning schools like those at M.I.T. and Berkeley. These schools are incorporating the revolutionary changes I have described into their curricula much faster than local governments are incorporating them into their behavior. Hence the practice of sending foreign planners to American schools may produce a more accelerated revolution in the limited amount of urban planning done in these countries than in this country.

VII. Conclusion

The individual causes of the revolution I have forecast have been at work for some time; so many city planners are aware that significant changes are about to occur in their profession. This awareness is reflected in the comparative ferment and uncertainty recently exhibited in professional planning literature and at this year's meeting of the American Institute of Planners in St. Louis. Naturally, the prospect of such dramatic change is causing a great deal of conflict, uncertainty, insecurity, and even anxiety in the profession—as in many other types of governmental service. Yet for those planners who are willing to look ahead and to adapt themselves to the rapidly altering nature of their profession—in a word, to plan for their own futures—the challenge of "riding out" the revolution and taking advantage of its many opportunities should make the next decade an exciting and rewarding one.

Three Concepts for Planners

Edward C. Banfield

IN THE LAST COUPLE of decades there has been a conspicuous increase in the range and importance of the matters that local (and for that matter other) government officials are expected to decide on grounds that are "nonpolitical" and "in the public interest." This is not the place for me to speculate on the nature of the forces that are tending in this direction or to discuss whether, assuming such a thing to be possible at all, it is on the whole good to have important decisions made "nonpolitically." I start from the assumption that, whether it is good or not, administrative, technical, and professional personnel (as well as a good many elected officials whose outlook is like that of these others or who find it expedient to pretend that it is) will be making ever more decisions on grounds that are technical or allegedly technical. The pressure of this growing professionalism will be toward the adoption of concepts, methods, and modes of thought different from the ones now current in government. In this paper I shall describe briefly three closely related sets of ideas which seem likely to pervade the professionalism of the future and thus to affect deeply the way government is organized and governmental affairs conducted. I am far from asserting that these ideas will ever prevail or even gain wide acceptance outside of professional circles. Professionalism is not, after all, the only force at work in determining the character of government. Nor are all professionals likely to be united on these ideas or any others. I do believe, however, that such influence as professionals have in the future is likely to be largely along the lines I shall describe.

The three sets of concepts, or ideas, relate to (1) the "economizing" approach, which in its more formalized and technical versions is often called "systems analysis"; (2) the theory and practice of decentralization, and (3) conceptions of "welfare" and of the institutional arrangements that will promote it under various circumstances. All three of these matters are relevant to all parts of government. However, I think they are peculiarly relevant to a city planning body.

Published for the first time in this book.

The Economizing Approach—Systems Analysis

The economizing approach is a decision-making procedure which starts from the premise that nothing is free—that any gain in terms of some ends always involves a loss in terms of others. Starting from this premise, the decision-maker is on the alert to search out and measure as accurately as he can both the losses and the gains that will follow from actions that he may take. He tries to identify the course of action that will yield the largest net gain.

This may appear to be the obvious way to approach a problem. It is not, however, the way in which problems are usually approached in government. The usual procedure, sometimes called the "requirements" approach, is to lay out a course of action that is expected to lead to the attainment of the end or ends sought and then to present in the form of a budget request an itemized list of the means ("requirements") that are needed. There would be nothing the matter with this approach if resources were unlimited. Since they are not unlimited, it is wasteful. It is not enough to achieve the end or ends that are sought. The real problem is to achieve them with a minimum use of resources or, depending on the situation, to use a fixed stock of resources so as to maximize the attainment of the ends.

This is what the economizing approach does. Instead of proposing one course of action which will "achieve the end" it studies a variety of courses of action to find the one that will achieve it "most efficiently." If, for example, the end is to increase the city's water supply by a certain number of gallons, the requirements approach would imply a proposal (say) to build an additional reservoir. The economizing approach, by contrast, would "cost out" all of the plausible ways of getting the additional water—e.g., repairing leakages in street mains, installing meters to prevent waste, and purifying water from a nearby river—in order to find the one that was cheapest.

Usually different ways of doing something do not yield exactly the same "mix" in terms of the various ends that are sought. This complicates the problem of choice. It is necessary to measure the amounts of the different benefits, as well as costs, that are associated with each course of action. In doing this, the economizer assumes that substitutions (or "trade-offs") may be made among benefits as well as between benefits and costs. (For example, consumers would be willing to trade some amount of dependability in their water supply for some amount of purity; similarly, they would be willing to trade some amount of both dependability and purity for some saving in money cost). The economizer's task, therefore, is to find that combination of benefits and costs which is optimal; it is, in other words, to make such trade-offs as will maximize net benefits. In making his calculations of benefit and costs he must be careful to take into account the effects on third parties as well as those on the persons primarily involved. If the action will have an incidental ("side") effect on third parties, this must be counted as a benefit or cost even though the persons so affected may be themselves unaware of it or even if the precise individuals affected are unspecifiable (e.g., if they are "the public at large"). Things that appear "free" may not turn out to be so at all when the whole system of relations involved in the action is taken into account. (For example, if we regard only the welfare of the inmates of the city jails, it may be advantageous for the city to employ abler physicians to treat them. But if we remember that paying abler physicians to treat people in jail amounts to paying them not to serve people not in jail—the number of able physicians being limited and their time being fully employed—it is obvious, regarding the system of activity in its entirety, that net benefit may be decreased rather than increased by moving the able physicians from one set of patients to another.) It is characteristic of the economizing approach that it measures benefits and costs in terms of entire systems of relations, hence the term "systems analysis."[1]

As a further illustration of the difference between the requirements and the economizing approaches, consider how a school superintendent might act if his budget were raised to permit him to improve the education of his pupils. If he adopted the requirements approach, he would (let us say) hire more teachers because he knows that a higher ratio of teachers to children improves teaching. On the other hand, if he adopted the economizing or systems analysis approach, he would break the end "to improve education" into component ends (e.g., to improve the reading ability of handicapped children, to improve the math of college-bound ones, etc.) and then decide the terms on which he would trade off a marginal unit of benefit in terms of one end for a marginal unit of benefit in terms of another. At the same time he would be examining all the plausible ways of achieving the various ends that he seeks. He would carry on research to find out the marginal rate of return (in terms of his various ends) of investment in (say): (1) additional teachers, (2) raising teachers' salaries, (3) employing television and "teaching machines," and (4) buying additional laboratory equipment. He would take into account as benefits and costs any side effects that could be anticipated (e.g., the influence this or that action might have on the morale of the parents of handicapped children). In the end he might well conclude that no course of action was best by all relevant criteria (in this case he would have to toss a coin or make a "political" decision). In reaching this conclusion, however, he would probably have discarded some highly plausible courses of action on the grounds that they were worse than others by *all* relevant criteria. This

---

1. See Roland McKean, *Efficiency in Government Through Systems Analysis,* Wiley, 1958; also, J. A. Kershaw and R. N. McKean, "Systems Analysis and Education," RAND Corporation monograph RM-2473-FF (1959).

in itself would have prevented him from making the most serious errors.

As the influence of professionalism increases in local government I should expect to see the economizing mode of thought more generally employed. I should expect, also, to see specialized systems analysis units created within police departments, water departments, boards of education, port authorities, and all the rest. City planning departments may be expected to facilitate this development, perhaps by establishing training schools to which operating departments and agencies can send their personnel for instruction in the techniques of systems analysis or by maintaining pools of analysts from which the departments and agencies may draw consultants. The city planning department's main function, however, will be the analysis of systems that cut across departmental and agency lines or transcend them all. The question of how to make a city more beautiful, for example, is not one that architects and physical planners, using the requirements approach, can best answer; it is one which calls for comparison of a very wide assortment of means, each with its own distribution of benefits and costs.

Decentralization

Another impetus of professionalism will be toward decentralization of administration. The search for efficiency is bound to lead in this direction. I am not asserting that local, state, and federal jurisdictions will shrink; they will doubtless be enlarged. But within the jurisdictions the distribution of decision-making will move to lower levels. The tendency of professionalism will be to economize on executive judgment and on the assembly of information of the kind relevant to judgment, both of which are expensive, and to make the most of the principle of specialization and division of labor.

The general theoretical principle that will be employed is that of "suboptimization."[2] According to this, problems that are independent of each other (or as nearly so as possible) are identified and an organization set up to solve each one. The managers of these separate organizations have a stock of resources assigned to them by a central budget-maker and are told to do the best they can within this constraint. If they have been provided with a complete set of criteria of choice to start with and if their operations do not interact (i.e., impose costs or benefits on each other as side effects), the managers by maximizing the attainment of their separate outputs also maximize the total output. Where interactions appear or criteria of choice are lacking, a coordinator adjusts matters from "above" so as to assure the maximization of total output. He may do this by reallocating budget amounts (if organization

2. See A. C. Enthoven and H. S. Rowan, "Defense Planning and Organization," in ed.? *Public Finances: Needs, Sources, and Utilization* (Princeton: Princeton University Press), 1961, esp. 394–405.

A is conferring benefits on organization B, the budget allocation to B may have to be reduced in order to maximize total output) or by changing the design of the operations. Each manager, of course, "factors out" independent subproblems and creates suborganizations under submanagers who are instructed to suboptimize. The manager's task is to make a correct initial budget allocation and then to function as a coordinator to the extent required.

This schema has been applied to the city planning function by Professor Allison Dunham.[3] He believes that operating departments should be left free to decide matters like the size and location of parks and the width of streets. Assuming that the initial budget allocation is correct and that adequate criteria of choice have been given to the departments, there is reason to believe that their decisions will be better than any that could be made for them from above. The task of the central planning body, according to Dunham, is to keep track of the side effects that the departmental operations give rise to—that is, to identify and measure the costs and benefits that are incidentally being imposed on other departments and on third parties of all sorts. The central planning body, in other words, is a coordinator, whose task is to so arrange the situation that the managers (operating departments, business firms, etc.) in maximizing their separate outputs will also maximize total output ("the public interest"). To say the same thing in other terms, it is engaged in systems analysis where the "system" is a constellation of subsystems.

Dunham's account of how the city planning body ought to function may be taken as a paradigm of the proper functioning of managerial bodies at every level, local, state, and federal. For example, the hundreds of local governmental units within a large metropolitan area may be thought of as suboptimizing. The task of a coordinator is to distribute resources among them properly (e.g., by grants in aid) and to make adjustments in the design of their operations (e.g., by giving or withholding permission to discharge wastes into a river used by more than one city) so that when the benefits and costs accruing throughout the governmental system are fully taken into account the net output will be at a maximum. The redesign of operations might often involve changing municipal or other boundaries so as to reduce or eliminate the imposing of costs by some units on others; the coordinator would consider, for example, what costs are imposed upon the people of the central city by the zoning practices of the suburbs. Where serious interdependencies were found to exist the coordinator would consolidate the interdependent units, for where constant appeal must be made to a higher authority the higher authority may as well dispense with managers and run the interdependent operations directly.

3. Allison Dunham, "City Planning: An Analysis of the Content of the Master Plan," *Journal of Law and Economics* Vol. I (Oct. 1958).

Whereas in the past the tendency has been to deal with problems by setting up organizations to build physical structures and to exert direct, consciously felt control over the behavior of large numbers of people, in the future it will be to deal with them by arranging the situation so that individuals, in seeking to maximize the attainment of their own ends, do not impose so many costs upon each other. One of the simplest ways of relieving downtown traffic congestion would be to stagger working hours, for the problem is almost entirely one of peak loads. When it arranges work hours so as to reduce peak loads a planning agency designs the operations of a large set of "organizations" (in this instance, persons who travel) so that the "manager" of each (the traveler) can be left to maximize the attainment of his organization's ends (to go his own way) without any instructions from a coordinator and without imposing unacceptable costs (congestion) on others.

Welfare

Officials who must make decisions on grounds that are not political must find some way of deciding whose ends and which ends should be served. Is there a "public interest" in the situation? If so, what is its content? Or is the problem, perhaps, to serve the preferences of the individual citizen-consumer as he himself defines them? If it is this, how is the official to get accurate knowledge of these preferences? And when the preferences of different persons are incompatible, as they normally are, how is he to decide whose preferences are to prevail or on what terms a compromise is to be made?

Probably the normal thing in such situations is for officials to "decide" without "choosing." They are likely to continue more or less habitually in whatever direction they were pointed by the political forces that were operating at some earlier time. In other words, if an agency does not receive continuing political direction its course of action tends to be an extrapolation from the past, although perhaps one that is "bent" by the (nonpolitical) necessities of organizational maintenance. For example, a municipal zoo established a century or so ago when the city was run by a Protestant elite that was entranced with natural history (almost the only science then existing) and with the bizarre animals of the newly opening continents and that wanted to stimulate the poor immigrant masses to self-improvement continues today along very much the same lines although natural history is no longer regarded as a suitable introduction to science and the poor would rather go to baseball games or watch TV.

Very often officials evade the problem of deciding whose ends and what ends should be served by falling back on "standards" that are promulgated by some authoritative professional body. Libraries, parks, hospitals, and police and fire departments, for example, may discover from the publications of a national association what is deemed an adequate level of service for a city the size of theirs. Needless to say, no such association can possibly decide by looking at one item alone (e.g., libraries, apart from hospitals, police departments, and all the rest) what allocation will maximize the attainment of "public purposes" or, if these be the relevant quantity, consumer tastes. All such standards are based on premises (hidden, of course) that are in some sense political. The enthusiasm of the specialist for his speciality is one ingredient of such standards; his awareness of the limits of what the public will stand for is another.

The impetus of professionalism, I believe, is away from institutional habit and from standards and toward taking the satisfaction of the citizen-consumer as the ultimate goal of policy, i.e., as "welfare." This implies a new respect for the competitive market and for private as against public enterprise. If the only object is to give people what they prefer, by all odds the best way to go about it is to let the zoo compete on an equal basis with the circus, Disneyland, TV, opera, the supermarket, and all else. If this is the way things are to be done, there is no advantage—in fact a good deal of disadvantage—in keeping the zoo a public institution.

The individualistic conception of welfare does not, however, imply the complete dismantling of government. The demand for certain goods and services must be set by the government. One category includes goods and services (e.g., air pollution control) which by their nature cannot be sold to individuals. Another category includes goods and services which, because of the benefits and costs their consumption confers on third parties, must in order to maximize total welfare be consumed in greater quantity (e.g., education) or in lesser quantity (e.g., narcotics) than individuals, taking account only of themselves, would consume them. In other words, with regard to the first category decentralization is impossible and with regard to the second its operation must be regulated by a coordinator.

That the government must fix the demand in such cases does not mean that it must also organize the production and distribution of the goods or services in question, however. In principle, at least, it is possible for most of that to be done under private auspices (i.e., to be decentralized). The Defense Department sets the demand for missiles but it does not manufacture them itself. Similarly, a public school system sets the demand for textbooks, but it does not write them or manufacture them.

The tendency of professionalism will be to divest the government of activities which can be carried on as well or better under private auspices (i.e., with respect to which the government need neither set the demand nor organize production and distribution). This is a much wider range of activities than one might think. (If the public school board need not write or manufacture textbooks, why must it do the teaching?)

Where for one reason or another the government does organize the production and distribution of a good or service, the impetus of professionalism will be toward employing the price mechanism and market-like devices to the greatest extent feasible. User-charges will be favored by professionals not so much on grounds of equity (although as a general rule there is something to be said for making those who receive the benefits bear the costs) as because such changes afford a means of giving people what they really want. The amount that people are willing to pay to enter a zoo, for example, would indicate to the manager whether its facilities should be expanded or contracted. In effect, user-charges are a device for rationing scarce resources in accordance with people's preferences. If the subway is overloaded at peak hours the price of a ride at the peak hour should be raised; those who could as well travel at another time would then have an incentive to do so. Similarly, if there is a shortage of water, the price of it should be raised to eliminate such use of it as is of little or no value to anyone.

To the extent that this view of welfare prevails, we may expect government agencies in general and city planning bodies in particular to become more and more occupied with the following functions: (1) setting the demand for those goods and services which cannot be, or should not be, left to individual choice; where it is asserted that a higher (or lower) level of consumption of a particular commodity (e.g., zoos or public libraries) would confer benefits (or costs) on third parties, the special task of the agency will be to identify and measure the alleged benefits (or costs) and by the methods of systems analysis to establish how they may be secured at least cost; (2) creating and maintaining "rules of the game" and institutional arrangements (e.g., a competitive market or a para-market of some kind) which would tend to give citizen-consumers as wide a range of choices as possible; this would imply government efforts to stimulate the private market to offer needed goods and services; it would also imply "rigging the market" to secure side effect benefits for third parties and to prevent the imposition of side effect costs on third parties; and (3) maintaining a correct (which is not necessarily an equal) income distribution so that in the operation of the price mechanism the preferences of the relatively well-off will not be overweighted in comparison with those of the poor.

VIII

The Formation
of Policy

THIS last section deals with the process of policy formation and with the concrete content of policy in several fields of particular interest. The readings have been chosen for what they tell about the matrix out of which policy emerges (especially the "givens" that constrain policy-makers, the interests and groups that shape policy, the nature of the interaction among these interests and groups, and the terms on which differences of interest are adjusted or balanced) and about the major alternatives that are open to decision-makers—not only politicians and administrators, but also ordinary citizens.

The first reading of this section, Harold Kaplan's account of Metro Toronto, deals with a policy formation process that goes on at two levels. At the substantive level decisions are made about transportation, water supply, sewage disposal, revenue collection, and so on; at another level, which with some risk of confusion will be called the constitutional, decisions are made about the process of (substantive) decision-making; and between the two levels, substantive and constitutional, there is interaction, one kind of decision influencing the other. Since Kaplan is writing about policy formation in the *Canadian* political system, his article is particularly useful here because it points by implication to what is different and special in the American system as revealed in the other readings. It is a constitutional question in the

American context that Robert H. Salisbury discusses in the next reading. The public schools, he points out, have always had a high degree of formal autonomy and most people have felt that they should be kept "out of politics." This has left the schools without much support in state and national capitals and naked against community pressures. On the whole it might be better, he thinks, if the schools were under a greater degree of control by the mayor. But he adds that the justification for any solution to the problem cannot be found in its effect upon education considered apart from the other issues and problems of the metropolis. In other words, the proper policy formation process for education is the one that will contribute most to the solution of the whole complex of urban problems. The public library, according to Edward C. Banfield, is the product of a policy formation process which proceeds on assumptions that badly need to be reexamined. The goals of the library may have been appropriate in the last century and the early part of the present one, he argues, but conditions have changed in ways that make them inappropriate now. His discussion of the library illustrates the application of principles of policy-making developed by economists in the field of public finance. In the next reading, James Q. Wilson looks at the administrator's contribution to the policy formation process. The police administrator (chief, superintendent, commissioner, captain) like the administrator of most public agencies, has no satisfactory way of assessing the effectiveness of his organization's performance; lack of information both about what the organization is achieving and about what it would achieve if it did things differently is a principal constraint on the administrator as policy-maker. Another is the difficulty, amounting often to an impossibility, of laying down general rules adequate to guide a patrolman in dealing with particular cases. The nature of the patrolman's task, Wilson says, necessitates his being a policy-maker too. In the next reading, Richard A. Cloward, a sociologist, and Frances Fox Piven, a political scientist, write about another bureaucrat who exercises a great deal of discretion: the welfare professional. Policy in welfare, they say, is largely made by and for the welfare professionals and their organizations; since it is to their interest to keep the low-income client dependent upon them, government programs for the poor are likely to diminish rather than increase the political vitality of the poor. In the final reading, H. R. Wilde shows to what extent the policy of a city may be formed on the basis of stereotypes reaching it through the mass media. Milwaukee's perception of its 1967 "riot" was, he thinks, formed largely in New York and Washington and conveyed to Milwaukee by the television networks, *The New York Times*, and in general the national arbiters of "good government" and "sound" opinion. The tendency of the new style of city politics, he believes, is to bring the city more publicity, more money, and more bitterness.

Metro Toronto: Forming a Policy-Formation Process

Harold Kaplan

ONE OF THE PROPOSALS often mentioned in discussions of municipal reorganization is the metropolitan federation plan. This scheme attempts to meet the regional problems of a metropolitan area not by consolidating municipal units but by interjecting a regional government between the municipalities and higher levels of government. Variations of this regional federalism have been adopted in the Miami, Nashville, and Winnipeg metropolitan areas. The first of these federations was the Municipality of Metropolitan Toronto, which has now been in operation for over fifteen years. The Toronto experience, then, should be of interest to those readers concerned with problems of metropolitan reform, particularly those who wish to reach some evaluative conclusion on the idea of metropolitan federation. This essay attempts to summarize some major findings of a study the author recently conducted on the first fourteen years of the Metro Toronto political system.[1] Particular attention will be paid to the reform and policy implications of these findings.

The postwar development of the Toronto metropolitan area followed the usual North American pattern: an aging central city losing population to rapidly growing suburbs; the proliferation of suburban governmental units; and the appearance of serious, region-wide problems, which the municipalities, by themselves, could not solve. A group of the suburban municipalities decided to apply to the province of Ontario for the creation of a joint-service area. The city of Toronto countered with a request to annex most of the inlying suburbs, leaving the newer, relatively uncompleted suburbs outside this expanded city. In 1953, the province rejected both requests in favor of a metropolitan federal system. This plan appealed to provincial politicians because it

1. See Harold Kaplan, *Urban Political Systems. A Functional Analysis of Metro Toronto* (New York: Columbia University Press, 1967). The policy implications of the Toronto experience are suggested in this book but are spelled out more explicitly in the present essay.

Published for the first time in this book, by permission of the author.

did not greatly disturb interests and structures at the municipal level. A new level of government would be added, but municipal boundaries and governmental structure would be left undisturbed.

This solution was imposed on the area by provincial order. Because the nineteenth-century crusade for local home rule was less significant in Canada than in the United States, Canadian provinces exert a far tighter and more pervasive control over their municipalities than do American states. Canadian provinces, although certainly sensitive to the demands of municipalities, are prepared to rearrange municipal boundaries, policies, and governmental structure in a much freer fashion than any American state would contemplate. In approving the Metro plan, Ontario officials did not insist on a popular referendum in the area and did not give municipal officials a veto over the proposed reform. If either test had been applied, the Metro plan probably would have been defeated. Municipal officials were almost unanimous in their opposition to Metro, the suburbs because the plan went too far in the direction of centralized authority, the city of Toronto because the plan did not go far enough. Among the public, there appeared to be widespread indifference and ignorance of what a federal system would mean. The key to Metro's success in 1953 was not a popular groundswell in favor of reform but the Canadian tradition on provincial-municipal relations. For that reason, the way in which federation was achieved in the Toronto area does not hold many lessons for American reformers interested in duplicating the feat.

According to the terms of the Metro Act, decisions at the Metro level were to be made by a 25-member Metro Council, composed of one delegate from each of the twelve suburbs, twelve delegates from the city of Toronto, and a Metro Council chairman. Provincial officials decided that the Council would consist of elected municipal officials serving *ex officio* rather than directly elected Metro councilors. In this way, it was felt, quarrels between Metro and the municipalities would be minimized and municipal support for Metro maximized. The Metro chairman, named by the province initially but elected by the Council in subsequent years, was to preside over Council meetings and cast a deciding vote in case of a tie. Aside from this vote, the formal powers of the chairman were insignificant. The province was eager to demonstrate to the municipalities that Metro would be a loosely knit, intermunicipal conference rather than a municipal government and that the chairman would be a presiding official rather than a mayor.

In allocating powers, the Metro Act left welfare, health, police, fire, licensing, and libraries at the municipal level. (Police and licensing were later shifted to the Metro level.) Only public transit was made a wholly metropolitan program. The other programs were shared by both Metro and the municipalities. In these shared programs, the Metro government generally provided funds and guidelines, while the municipalities retained much of their control over detailed policy.

The accomplishments of the Metro system came early and in a dramatic fashion. Ambitious programs were undertaken to build a regional network of highways, to greatly expand the area's modest subway network, and to help the outlying suburbs meet their need for new schools, roads, and water and sewer facilities. Substantial though less dramatic progress was made in the construction of public housing and homes for the aged, the execution of a regional plan for parks and recreational areas, and the extension of bus service into the outer suburban areas. The Metro Act stipulated that the Metro government would do all the capital borrowing for the area and would apportion capital funds among the municipalities. Before 1953, the outlying suburbs had found it increasingly difficult to borrow. For these suburbs, involvement in the Metro plan meant a reopening of the bond market and a resumption of municipal construction projects.

One should not hastily conclude that the federal form of government produced these achievements. Federation was a necessary but not sufficient cause. Any explanation of these policy achievements must include a statement on the structure and culture of politics in the Toronto area, along with some recognition of the important role played by particular personalities.

At the Metro level, a highly centralized, informal structure was created. In law the chairman was an insignificant figure; in fact he became the most powerful person in Council and the pivot of the entire Metro scheme. These developments are largely attributable to Frederick Gardiner, who served as chairman from the beginning of Metro until his retirement in 1961. The tradition of a strong chairman was carried on by his successor, William Allen.

Gardiner was convinced that the Metro Act had not made sufficient provision for leadership at the Metro level. He insisted that Metro could not carry on significant programs while retaining the structure of an intermunicipal conference. Gardiner stepped into the breach by informally assuming the powers of chief administrator, legislative floor leader, and link between legislature and administration. Within the Council, he secured agreement on a plan to greatly centralize power in an Executive Committee, consisting of three city delegates, three suburbanites and the Metro chairman. In subsequent years, Gardiner usually secured approval of his proposals by the Executive Committee and, since Committee proposals were difficult to overturn, by the entire Metro Council as well. In the administrative branch Gardiner created all the trappings of a cabinet system. He met regularly with the heads of the departments and secured agreement among them on proposals going before the Council. Local newspapers began to speak of "Gardiner's Administration" and of "the cabinet's policy." Typically the cabinet initiated a policy proposal and the chairman then decided whether a majority in Council could be secured for that proposal, when the proposal should be brought forward, and whether any substantive changes would have to be made in the proposal to improve its chances of legislative approval. Gardiner became the crucial middleman. The Metro councilors rarely interacted directly with the cabinet; Gardiner, alone, interacted with both.

Metro's policy achievements are to be explained not only by the emergence of this informal leadership structure but also by the broader pattern of Toronto area politics. The Metro area has a sedate, low-pressure brand of politics. Interest groups were weakly involved in Metro issues. They frequently took no stand on major questions facing Metro Council and almost never exerted pressure on behalf of their viewpoints. If there were significant demands and tensions in the community at large, they were not being translated into political issues or transmitted to the political system. In Metro the interest-articulation function was poorly performed. The Metro councilor, far from viewing himself as an interest-group spokesman or as a mediator of group demands, often was unaware of what the groups wanted. Thus, Metro avoided the stalemate and inaction that seem to result from the interplay of competing interest groups in many large American cities. But the price Metro paid for this ability to move ahead quickly with important decisions was the weak interrelation of politics and the larger community.

The Metro Council, like the municipal councils, was unstructured by any factions or parties. The area's electoral politics were highly personal, unstructured, and issueless. Turnout and voter interest were very low. Incumbents were very rarely defeated. Elections, then, did not produce mandates or stable divisions in Council. With respect to attitudes on policy, one Metro Council was very much like another.

There was a tendency for suburban and city delegates to vote on opposite sides of issues. In that sense Council voting contained hints of a stable bifactionalism. But the great majority of issues coming before Council was settled by near-unanimous votes, in which most members of both blocs voted on the same side. Even when the issue was a factional one, pitting the two blocs against each other, the unity of the two blocs was weak. Neither bloc could prevent a large number of mavericks from "crossing the aisle." The initial fears that the Council would be constantly deadlocked and that the chairman frequently would have to break tie votes proved unfounded. By providing a regional legislative arena, metropolitan federation did seem to encourage give-and-take or pragmatic bargaining, which otherwise would have been absent from intermunicipal relations.

Much of the placidity of Metro area politics is attributable to the prevalence of middle-class politicians and middle-class values. The newer groups, mainly Catholics from eastern and southern Europe, were underrepresented in the ranks of the area's political decision makers. This fact helps explain why Metro politics appeared at times to be a family quarrel, restricted almost entirely to the middleclass and to people who advocated conservative, good-government, reform values.

The relative lack of conflict and political pressure, and the ability to move quickly on certain policy matters, is also due to the nature of Canadian political culture, particularly its emphasis on deference to persons in positions of authority. This deference to leadership could be seen in the Metro councilors' attitude toward the chairman and in the interest groups' reluctance to exert pressure. In the Canadian view, persons in positions of authority, proceeding mainly *in camera* and free of political pressures, search out the public interest. Canadians are less willing than Americans to accept the idea that the public interest will emerge through the open agitation of issues and the open clash of opposing groups in a free political marketplace.

In explaining Metro's achievements, one must also mention the willingness of the members of Metro Council to go along with the chairman on most policy matters, a willingness that was partly but not wholly attributable to Canadian political culture. The councilors devoted most of their time and energies to municipal matters, mainly because it seemed to them that their electoral futures depended on their handling of municipal rather than Metro issues. These councilors were weakly committed to the Metro system and weakly involved in Metro issues. They did feel strongly about issues that impinged upon "municipal prerogatives" and did insist that an overall regional parity be maintained in the distribution of construction projects. But aside from these issues, the councilor was prepared to follow the chairman's lead. If councilors did raise objections, the chairman, who alone was intensely involved in these issues, usually had the facts at command and easily outdebated the objecting councilor. Paradoxically, the councilors' weak interest in the Metro government helped account for its policy achievements.

All of the above factors made it easier to get things done in the Metro area than is the case in many large American cities. Given these other factors, one hesitates to say that metropolitan federation would lead to the same dramatic policy achievements in other metropolitan areas.

Some of the liabilities of metropolitan federation in the Toronto area should also be mentioned. After the initial achievements, Metro's policy output began to drop off rather sharply. Having solved a set of problems, Metro seemed capable of administering those solutions but incapable of grappling with new problems. Clearly, Metro's initial successes were partly due to the popularity of the capital-works programs that dominated Metro's early activities, although the existence of regional government was a necessary cause of these achievements. The construction programs were not only popular but relatively simple. The outlaying suburbs desperately needed road, sewer, water, and school facilities; the answer obviously was to build the necessary facilities. By comparison, most of the city's problems—like welfare, urban renewal, and all the social problems resulting from the assimilation of a large immigrant population—were less tangible, more subtle, and more difficult to solve.

In other words, Metro tackled the easy problems first. When the Council turned from the popular, construction programs to questions of air-pollution control, health and welfare, public-transit service, urban renewal, and licensing, its achievements were far less significant. Contrary to Gardiner's expectations, there was no spillover of goodwill or agreement from the construction programs to the welfare, service, and regulatory programs. On these latter issues, municipal officials were more often at odds with each other, were generally less enthusiastic about the program, and were less committed to resolving their differences. Bringing municipal officials together in a regional legislature did not alter those basic political facts.

Emphasis on construction mainly benefitted the outlying suburbs, whose major needs were in this area. The next result of Metro's policy was to eliminate obstacles to further suburban expansion and to help speed the process of metropolitan sprawl. The perennial problems of the central city were hardly scratched.

Some reformers see metropolitan federation as an opening wedge which might generate a metropolitan-wide commitment among local officials and might pave the way for a more centralized form of metropolitan government. It now is apparent that this was Gardiner's long-range stategy. On this score, the record of Metro Toronto is disappointing. Municipal officials tolerated Metro but never actually supported it. The members of Metro Council saw themselves as municipal delegates to an intermunicipal conference, primarily responsible for protecting the prerogatives of their municipalities from the imperialistic tendencies of the Metro giant. Prolonged participation in Metro Council did not alter this view. There was no more municipal support for Metro after fifteen years than there had been at the outset. Without provincial constraint, Metro could not have survived—in either 1953 or 1968. To use Gardiner's phrase, "Metro-mindedness" did not emerge.

Indicative of this limited commitment to Metro was the persistent refusal of the Metro Council to expand its powers at the expense of the municipalities. For the most part, powers left with the municipalities in 1953 remained there, unless the province ordered a change.

Metro Council also proved totally incapable of undertaking any structural reorganization. All questions relating to the form of Metro government produced a stalemate in the Council and had to be referred to the province. The Council, for example, was unable to reapportion its seats, even though it recognized the glaring inequities produced by the meteoric growth of outlying suburbs and even though it debated the question for almost ten years. The crux of the problem was that the councilors were more interested in demonstrating how Metro had abused the municipalities than in making Metro more workable or enhancing its effectiveness.

Much of the stalemate evident in recent Metro politics is due not to metropolitan federation per se but to the requirement that members of Metro Council be local officials serving ex officio. The Metro councilor, then, stands or falls in a municipal election, generally run on municipal issues. Campaign platforms almost invariably take a pro-municipal, anti-Metro line. In Metro Winnipeg, on the other hand, Metro councilors are directly elected from constituencies that cut across municipal boundaries. This arrangement produces councilors who are committed to Metro, but also produces constant warfare between Metro councilors and municipal politicians. The strength of the Winnipeg plan is the sweeping actions that can be taken at the Metro level; its weakness is the gap it leaves between the Metro and municipal levels of government. The Metro Toronto plan closes this gap and minimizes conflict between Metro and the municipalities, but only at the price of limited Metro achievements.

The 1966 reforms in Metro Toronto government are unlikely to alter the basic pattern or to produce any new surge of policy achievements. The number of suburban municipalities was reduced from twelve to five and the size of the Metro Council was expanded; but the essential features of the 1953 plan were retained.

In conclusion, two favorable statements might be made about metropolitan federation. The Metro Toronto plan clearly made it possible for the area to meet regional problems—mainly in the public works field—which the municipalities separately could not have solved. Beyond this the Metro Toronto plan has one very important political asset: it is the solution that divides politicians least. It is the plan that most politicians can live with, perhaps more comfortably than with any other single solution. Federation is not the first choice of many politicians at the provincial or municipal level, but it seems to be everyone's second choice. Perhaps this aspect of the federation scheme will commend it to other metropolitan areas as well.

Autonomy vs. "Political Control" of Schools

Robert H. Salisbury

AFTER DECADES of silence, both social scientists and educators are at last explicitly examining and re-examining all the options regarding the relationship between the political system and the schools. Descriptive analysis has greatly enriched our understanding of how alternative structures operate. A full menu of recipes for changing the structures has been developed and here and there implemented. And while we are far from realizing closure on our uncertainties, the art of social engineering with respect to school-community relations is finally getting an underpinning of evidence and systematic analysis.[1]

Broadly, there seem to be three themes running through this new wave of literature. One is primarily descriptive: How are educational decisions made, and what variables are relevant for explaining alternative outcomes? A second theme merges this descriptive task with a special concern: What accounts for variations in the money available to the schools, and implicitly, how might more money be made available? The third theme is a bit different. It raises a more complex question, and answers depend not only upon careful descriptive analysis but also upon performance criteria that are very difficult to work out: How may the school system do a more effective job in the total context of community life?

It is apparent that the "context of community life" is a concept fraught with snares and difficulties. I propose to look at it mainly with reference to the problems of the core city; there, it encompasses major facets of the problems of race, of poverty, of physical decay and renewal,

1. I have chosen not to try to provide a full array of bibliographical citation to the relevant literature. Partly, this decision is based on my desire to present an argument which raises questions for public examination and debate rather than to assert that some things are so and others not. Partly, however, this particular body of literature is growing so rapidly that reference footnotes would be incomplete virtually as soon as they were written.

Reprinted from "Schools and Politics in the Big City," Harvard Educational Review, *37:3 (Summer 1967), pp. 408–424. Copyright © 1967 President and Fellows of Harvard College.*

of perennial fiscal trauma, indeed most of those troubles we label "urban problems" in contemporary American society. The issue I wish to ruminate about here is whether one type of political system–school system relationship might be more effective than another in attacking these dilemmas of urban life. Specifically, I propose to consider the thesis that direct political-system control of the schools (historically anathema to educators) might have significant virtues in making the schools more effective instruments of social change and development.[2]

We know that many big-city school systems operate with substantial formal autonomy. They are not run by the political or administrative leaders of the city, but are insulated from those leaders and the interests they represent. In part this autonomy is a consequence of various formal features of local government which give to the schools the authority to run their affairs with little or no reference to the demands of other city officials. Perhaps in larger part, however, the insulation of the schools may be a function of the ideology, propagated by schoolmen but widely shared by the larger public, that schools should be free from "politics," i.e., the influence of non-school officials. Insofar as this view is shared, it has made formal independence a less relevant variable, and most of what evidence we have suggests that the formal structure of school-city relations does not matter very much: the schools are largely autonomous anyway.

It has been argued that autonomy for the schools means that professional educators would be free to carry out educational policies which they, as professionals, deem most effective without the intrusion of conflicting and educationally deleterious demands from nonprofessionals. But autonomy and insulation may also result in other things. Autonomous schools may be unresponsive to important groups in the community whose interests are not effectively served by the dominant values of professional schoolmen. Autonomy may mean a fragmenting of efforts aimed at solving community problems because of inadequate coordination and planning. And autonomy may also bring vulnerability as well as insulation. If the schools are separated from the rest of the community's political system, they may be more easily exposed to the protests or demands of groups which are disaffected from that system, unable to work their will within its often labyrinthine structures, but able to organize direct popular support. And if they attempt direct protest action, they can make life most difficult for schoolmen who are unable to retreat into positions of mutual support among city officials with many programs and agencies and client groups. Unable to trade off one group against another, the schools may be and often are the targets of protest which may well have its roots in other facets of the city's

2. I have explored some facets of this question in briefer compass in my essay, "Urban Politics and Education," in Sam Bass Warner, Jr., *Planning for a Nation of Cities* (Cambridge, Mass.: MIT Press, 1966), pp. 268–84.

life, but are directed against the schools precisely because they are autonomous and vulnerable.

The argument that the costs of "political control" far exceed the costs of autonomy needs re-examination. I have been struck by the frequent reference in that argument to the allegedly baleful effects of Big Bill Thompson's 1927 campaign for election as mayor of Chicago in which he concentrated much of his flamboyant oratory on the issue of control of the public schools. Big Bill promised to sack the superintendent who was, said Thompson, a lackey of King George and the British. Educators have ever since been agreed that a mayoral campaign subjecting the schools to this kind of educationally irrelevant attack was ample evidence of the need for protection from big city politics. Thompson's rhetoric was, of course, so blatantly demagogic that he makes an easy object lesson, but behind the rhetoric the issue has other features which make its moral much less clear.

In a most interesting book, called *School and Society in Chicago*,[3] George S. Counts examined the 1927 election soon after it happened. Counts' assessment is one of considerable ambivalence. On the one hand, he has no sympathy for Thompson's tactics of catering to his anti-British constituents by threatening to "punch King George in the snoot." Yet Thompson, in denouncing Superintendent McAndrew, was exploiting a very real conflict within the schools which had already engaged socio-economic sectors in the community.

William McAndrew had come to Chicago in 1924 in the wake of a series of political scandals and convictions affecting members of the school board. McAndrew was looked to as a reformer who would use his office more vigorously than had his predecessors. Particularly, he was expected, apparently by all the most interested parties, to establish the superintendency as the center from which the schools would thereafter be run. Professional educational criteria were to prevail. No more politics!

McAndrew interpreted this mandate to mean that *he* would select the criteria; the classroom teachers would not. He believed that *professional* educators should embrace teachers and administrators in the same organizational units, so he effectively discouraged the previously vigorous teachers councils in the Chicago schools. Chicago had a strong and long-standing set of teacher organizations including units of the American Federation of Teachers, and McAndrew's unsympathetic view of their status led to abiding tension. Counts reports that the teachers' groups provided effective support for Thompson's election.

In addition, McAndrew had alienated organized labor in general. Not only had he rejected the propriety of the teachers' unions. He had introduced the junior high school. Chicago labor spokesmen construed

3. New York: Harcourt, Brace and Co., 1928.

this to be a step toward separate vocational training for working-class children. They viewed the junior high as an early breakaway from an equalitarian curriculum and this, they feared, was aimed at producing a docile, cheap labor force. Finally, McAndrew was a champion of the platoon system, or, as it was generally referred to, the Gary Plan. He favored the alleged efficiencies of the Plan and justified them quite frankly in a business-oriented way. Moreover, he actively and often consulted with representatives of the Chicago Association of Commerce; never with spokesmen of labor.

The result was a fairly considerable class conflict over McAndrew and his policies, both inside the school system and in the community. William Hale Thompson exploited these tensions and, in a way, helped resolve them. At least, after Thompson won, McAndrew was fired.

The important morals of this story seem to me to be the following: First, McAndrew provoked a severe conflict among the schoolmen themselves. The alleged intrusion of "politics" into the schools was really more the widening of a breach that already existed. Breaches among the schoolmen have been rather exceptional, from McAndrew's time until very nearly the present. Educators have proclaimed their fundamental unity of purpose and interest; and to a remarkable degree, they have lived up to it. But as teachers' unions grow strong and make demands and, occasionally, strike, and as community-wide controversies develop over the location, programs, and financing of the schools, the myths and practices which lead educators to maintain a united front in facing the outside, nonprofessional, world cannot survive. And, if there are conflicts, they will be exploited. The only question is, "By whom?"

The second lesson of the Chicago case of 1927 relates to the ultimate problem-solving machinery. McAndrew and the schools became a central issue in a partisan political race. Was this an appropriate mechanism for resolving a virtual class conflict involving the largest category of public expenditure? If it was not, then what is the regular political process for? Why are educational issues not properly determined in this arena? Why not indeed, except, perhaps, that Big Bill made the final determination. This dramatic fact has been enough to cinch the argument whenever some hardy soul could be found to play devil's advocate.

Later in this paper I shall explore further the two features I have drawn from the Chicago case; the political significance of unity among the schoolmen, and the possible consequences of determining school questions within the regular political processes of the community. Before I do, however, I would like to consider further what seems to me an important element of the context of school politics, in Chicago and every other city, then and now. This is what I shall call *the myth of the unitary community.*

George Counts concludes his analysis of the McAndrew affair by calling for "the frank recognition of the pluralistic quality of the modern city. Such recognition would involve the extension of a direct voice in the control of education to the more powerful interests and the more significant points of view."[4] The recommendation troubled Counts. He believed that it would really only "regularize practices already in existence," since these groups were already actively engaged in the struggle for influence over the schools. Still Counts recognized that he was making a "radical" proposal. It went directly counter to an historic perspective which has long pervaded the thinking of educators: namely, that the city is a unity for purposes of the school program. That is, regardless of ethnic, racial, religious, economic, or political differences and group conflicts in other arenas of urban life, education need not, and should not if it could, recognize or legitimize those differences. Education is a process that must not be differentiated according to section or class. Learning is the same phenomenon, or should be, in every neighborhood. Physical facilities and personnel should be allocated without regard to whatever group conflicts might exist in the community.

Schools have not always been run this way in reality. In the nineteenth century, some concessions were made to such prominent ethnic groups as the Germans by providing special classes in the German language; but in St. Louis, these were discontinued in 1888, or just about the time that ethnic heterogeneity really blossomed in the city. In recent years, a good many departures from the norm can be observed. In many cities, ethnic representation on the school board has been accepted as a hostage to the times, though the tendency is generally to deplore the necessity of special group recognition. Representatives of labor, of Negroes, and of Catholics hold big-city board memberships today and their constituents would complain if they did not. But the prevailing doctrines have not altered as much as the practice, I suspect, and the perspective which denies the legitimacy of group conflicts over school policy is certainly still widely held.

Surely an important element of this view of the city was the egalitarian democracy espoused by a large portion of professional education's intellectuals. The common school, later the high school, and now the community college have been urged and supported as mechanisms for equalizing the life chances of everyone in the community. To introduce programs for one group that were not available to another; or to build different kinds of school buildings for different neighborhoods, would cultivate group and class differences in the twig-bending stage which would lead to deeper socio-economic cleavages in the adult community. Most people, it seemed, never considered the

4. *Ibid.,* p. 357.

possibility that the have-not groups might receive *more* and *better* education than the middle class.

It looked like the poor could only get short-changed in a system of differentiated education and a caste system would result. This was the position not only of educators but probably of most actively concerned lay citizens too. It was an operative theory to guide education policy, and it was linked to a view of the community beyond the school system. For a consensual, integrated, organic community was and is an abiding standard for many American intellectuals. A proper city should manifest no deep-seated social or economic cleavages. Groups and classes with opposing interests are considered dangerous to the continued tranquillity of the polity. When they exist, as they increasingly did in the industrial city of turn-of-the-century America, it became necessary to adopt programs, such as universal education, and institutions, such as nonpartisan local government or at-large elections, that overcome the threatening heterogeneity.

But burgeoning immigration, the rise of the urban political machine, the emergence of corporate economic interests, and the enormous increases in scale of the urban community were parallel and closely connected phenomena of the 1880–1910 era. The metropolis which emerged threatened to erupt in group conflicts that would engulf the schools unless defenses could be found. The unitary-community perspective, more or less accurate as description a generation before and still serviceable for many smaller communities outside the metropolis, from that time on has been primarily a myth for the big city.

Still, it is a useful myth, and its uses were and are many. First, it served as a sharp contrast to the "political" world. Urban politics in the muckraker era was plainly a politics of group conflict and accommodation. The boss was a broker of social and economic tensions, and part of his brokerage fee to the community was the heightening of group consciousness. Ethnic identity for many Europeans was first achieved through the processes of American ward politics. Irish, Italian, or Czech nationalisms, for example, were much promoted in the cities of this era, as candidates and parties sought ways to secure the loyalties of the urban electorate.

With the political arena patently corrupt and marked by the conflicts of a myriad of "special" interests, the unitary-community perspective of education could justify the institutional separation of the schools from the rest of the political community. Independence from "politics" would keep out the selfish aims and corrupt tactics of the politician.

Independent school systems were not new of course. Institutional separation had always been a prevailing pattern. But in the larger cities, until the end of the nineteenth century, the structure of the independent school systems had been highly political.[5] Many school boards were chosen by wards. Some were selected by the city council, some by direct and frequent election. Ward representation was not originally viewed as a way of representing diverse group interests in the city as much as it was a means of keeping the board in close touch with the electorate. It resulted, however, in highly "politicized" school boards, sensitive to neighborhood pressures, particularly in the area of school-building. The ward system promoted log-rolling among sections of the city over many components of the school program. Neighborhoods sometimes traded off advantages, thereby probably facilitating rapid construction in many cities. Wards might also block one another, however, and thus retard the whole system.

The development of the professional educator to fill the newly created position of superintendent of schools inaugurated a different approach to education in which lay control would operate in increasing tension with the professional expert. With ward representation, this tension might well have been unbearable, at least to the professional educator. But parallel to the rise of the superintendency came the elimination of the ward system, and at-large election systems were rapidly adopted for the selection of school-board members.

The unitary myth was and is of great use in justifying an at-large school board. If the community is an organic whole with a single public interest in education, the board member should be protected against local, "selfish," interests by giving him a city-wide constituency. Moreover, since there are no legitimate "special" group interests in education, any responsible citizen can serve on the board, and there is no reason to give particular groups in the community a seat. To give a seat to labor, for example, would be wrong because it would constitute recognition of a special-group perspective on educational policy. Indeed, in a unitary community, there is really no such thing as representation on the school board, since there are no interests to represent. If, as George Counts and others found, urban school-board members were drawn predominantly from middle class, WASP, business-oriented strata of the community, it was a fact without significance in a unitary community.[6] In a recent study of school desegregation in eight northern

5. See the discussion in Thomas McDowell Gilland, *The Origin and Development of the Power and Duties of the City School Superintendent* (Chicago: University of Chicago Press, 1935), esp. Ch. vi.

6. George S. Counts, "The Social Composition of Boards of Education: A Study in the Social Control of Public Education," *Supplementary Educational Monographs*, Vol. XXX, July 1927, p. 83. See also the more recent findings of Roy Coughran, "The School Board Member Today." *The American School Board Journal*, No. 6 (December, 1956), pp. 25–6, reprinted in August Kerber and Wilfred R. Smith, eds., *Educational Issues in a Changing Society*, rev. ed. (Detroit: Wayne State University Press, 1964), pp. 284–7. W. W. Charters argues cogently that whatever the political significance of middle-class membership on school boards may have been, there is little empirical basis for concluding that membership really has meant policy control anyway. See his "Social Class Analysis and the Control of Public Education," *Harvard Educational Review*, Vol. XXIII (Fall, 1953), pp. 268–83.

cities, Robert Crain found that business and professional persons who serve on the school board, do so as individuals, not as class or elite spokesmen, and that such "nonrepresentative" individuals have been more acquiescent to integration than Board members elected by party or ethnic constituencies.[7]

The myth has thus been important in underwriting equalitarian educational programs, in separating the school systems from the main political process of the city, and in validating middle-class control of the schools. In addition, it was a useful adjunct to the emergence of professional expertise in education and school administration. Expertise rested on the assumption that valid ways and means to run the schools existed and were independent of the particular interests and values of particular groups. A good school system is good for everyone, not just a portion of the community. Experts, those people with professional training in the field, are qualified by their specialized training to tell good from bad, and laymen, if they are sensible, should defer to this expertise. If the unitary assumption is undermined, however, then no one, however well trained, can identify or administer a "good" school system. One may then ask only, "Good for whom? For which groups?"

Apart from a social scientist's perverse interest in exploring the myths we live by, is there any point to this discussion of the unitary-community myth? I believe the answer is "Emphatically, yes!" When educators treat the community as a unitary phenomenon, they are less able to offer programs and facilities which are differentiated to serve the diverse needs and values of particular subgroups in the city. It is an indictment of educational political theory that head-start projects for the urban poor only began on a large scale in 1965. Not that schoolmen did not often recognize the differential needs of slum children and sometimes tailor programs to fit those special needs. Rather, they had to do it in an inarticulate, often *sub rosa*, fashion since such programs went counter to the main stream of schoolmen's thinking. And so the programs were generally ineffective in meeting a problem of such magnitude.

The unitary-community idea was not simply for the guidance of educators. As we have seen, it helped protect the independence of the schools from the community's political processes. Or did it? Raymond E. Callahan has argued that the independent urban schoolmen were, in the period from about 1910 to 1930, extremely vulnerable; not, perhaps, to partisan political pressure, but to the dominant socioeconomic interests of the community.[8] In this period, business was pretty generally dominant, and Callahan attributes the rise of the "cult

7. Reported in "Educational Decision-Making and the Distribution of Influence in Cities" (paper presented to the American Political Science Association, September 7, 1966).

8. *Education and the Cult of Efficiency* (Chicago: University of Chicago Press, 1962).

of efficiency" in educational administration to the desire of vulnerable schoolmen to please the influential businessmen. In a way, Counts's story of Chicago confirms this point; during the relatively "nonpolitical" period when McAndrew was exercising full authority, the Association of Commerce occupied a very influential place while labor was excluded from school affairs. The "intrusion of politics" under Thompson meant the return of the teachers' and other nonbusiness interests to active and influential positions.

Independent schools, operating according to the myth of the unitary community, were and are rather feeble instruments for seeking public support, and this weakness is one key to the business domination Callahan has described. School-tax rates and bond issues and, in some states, the annual school budget, may require specific voter approval in a referendum. How are the schoolmen to persuade the electorate to say yes? They have relatively little of what in urban politics is sometimes called "clout." They have no network of support from groups and interests for whom the educators have done favors in the past and who now can be asked to reciprocate. They may sometimes get the teachers and the parents and the children to ring doorbells, but such efforts are often ineffectual compared to the canvassing a strong party organization might do. Since approval of a school referendum invariably costs the taxpayers money immediately—there is no intervening lapse of time as there is between the election of a candidate to a city office and the possible future increase in taxes—a sizable negative vote may normally be assumed. Where is the positive vote coming from? Educators have gone on the assumption, quite probably correct, that the benevolent patronage of the business leadership was necessary if they were to have a chance of referendum success.

Today, in the big city, the structure of the situation has not changed. Only the interests which effectively make demands upon the schools have changed. Negroes, the poor, middle-class intellectuals, and teachers have partially, perhaps largely, displaced the businessmen. The unitary-community myth is still used as a defense of the schools. In order to persuade predominantly Catholic, lower-middle-class voters of Irish or Polish descent to support higher taxes for public schools, it is very important to emphasize the undivided benefits which all residents receive from an undifferentiated educational program. The difficulty is that today the pitch is no longer believed. It is evident, for example, that Negroes do not buy the myth that the community is unitary. They know better. Moreover, even though a school board with a unitary-community perspective may permit integration, Negroes demand a differentiated school program with compensatory facilities to help them fight prejudice and poverty, to help them reach a high enough level so that equal educational programs will no longer leave them behind. Meanwhile, those ethnic groups whom Wilson and Banfield have shown to be comparatively unwilling to vote for public expenditures for *any* purpose are especially unenthusiastic about putting high-cost programs into Negro slum schools.[9] Unions are anxious about job competition from the products of improved vocational programs. And although property taxes for schools may be only a minor problem for large corporate business, they are often severe in their effect on smaller business and on small householders. The latter groups, especially, are potential city dropouts; that is, they may move to suburbia if taxes go up, and the result may be to depreciate further the city's tax base while its educational needs increase. The unitary-community myth no longer serves to quiet the demonstrations or to pass the tax increase. It has largely outlived its usefulness. Yet it is still frequently articulated by schoolmen and lay supporters of the schools, perhaps because, as the inveterate gambler said in explaining his continued patronage of the crooked card game, "It's the only one in town."

There is another dimension in which unity has been emphasized with respect to schools. Educators have tried very hard to achieve and maintain consensus among all those engaged in the educational enterprise. Unity is a prerequisite to a reputation for expertise, and it thus adds to the bargaining power of schoolmen as they seek public support. Unity inside the school helps justify independence from "politics." In the Chicago case of 1927 and again today, in Chicago and elsewhere, the vulnerability of the schools to group pressures from the community depends heavily on the extent to which the board, the superintendent and his administrative associates, and the teaching staff remain as professional allies rather than splitting into conflicting camps.

The consensus among school interests is equally sought after at the state level, and as my colleagues and I have suggested in our study of state politics and the schools,[10] a number of devices have been developed to help achieve and preserve unity, even at some cost in terms of goal achievements—dollar volume of state aid, or teacher tenure law protection, for example. The point I wish to make here, however, is that unity among schoolmen is frequently a considerable handicap for big-city school interests, particularly in their efforts to get increased state aid.

Let me illustrate my point with a discussion that leans heavily on experience in Missouri. There, a moderately malapportioned legislature for many years exhibited great fiscal prudence. They spend more than they used to, but the state still ranks much lower in comparison to other states in expenditures than in income. Education is no excep-

9. James Q. Wilson and Edward C. Banfield, "Public-Regardingness as a Value Premise in Voting Behavior," *American Political Science Review,* Vol. LVIII (December, 1964), pp. 876–88.

10. Nicholas A. Masters, Robert H. Salisbury, and Thomas H. Eliot, *State Politics and the Public Schools* (New York: Alfred Knopf, 1964).

tion, but, thanks largely to the skillful efforts of the Missouri State Teachers Association, both district consolidation and equalization grants under a foundation program have steadily improved the financial condition of most *rural* schools. But these programs are of much less benefit to schools in the large cities.

St. Louis and Kansas City schools receive state aid, to be sure, but on a somewhat different basis from other districts. State aid is legally less assured in the large cities, and it gets a smaller portion of the job done. The city of today has high-cost educational needs as compared to noncity areas. The core-city wealth, which is effectively taxable by local action, is comparatively less great than it used to be. State-aid programs which aim at providing minimum per-pupil expenditure do not solve big-city needs, and the states have not been receptive to extra demands of urban educators any more than they have responded to other urban interests.

When the city-school interests go to the state capital to press their special claims, they carry with them the norms of their professional colleagues everywhere, the norms of unity. All educators are united in favor of education, one and indivisible, to be provided equally for all. Yet this same delegation comes to ask special treatment from the state, either in the form of additional state money or additional authority to act for themselves. Moreover, the statewide education interests normally take no stand on the requests of the city-school interests. The statewide groups are interested in equalization, not special programs for the cities. They might even oppose urban-oriented school legislation since it would either compete for monies desired for equalization or, at the least, serve the needs of "the city," a symbol which noncity school leaders look on with suspicion. And these school leaders occupy the state department of education and dominate the state teachers association. From the point of view of the city schools, the best thing, and the usual thing, is to have the state groups stay out.

The urban school forces, assuming they have at least the neutrality of the state educational groups, confront another unity norm when they arrive at the state capital. This is the unwritten rule of the state legislature for dealing with all "local" issues, and the school needs of a city like St. Louis are treated within the same system of legislative practice as a proposed salary increase for the sheriff. They are all local issues. The rule provides that the legislators will approve a request from a local community provided that the state representatives from that community are substantially united in their support of the request.

One might suppose that, since the school groups all strive for internal unity, the legislators' prerequisite would be easy to fulfill. Such is not the case, and much of the reason lies in the separation of the schools from the political system of the city. The problem lies in the relationship, or rather the lack thereof, between the spokesmen for the schools and the city delegation in the legislature. City legislators are not interested in the schools. They avoid service on education committees, take little part in debate on school issues, and generally are thought by other legislators who are concerned about state school policy to contribute very little. Urban legislators are likely indeed to be profoundly uninterested in the concerns of *any* groups which successfully keep themselves apart from the political system of the city. They, after all, are products of that system and their points of reference are mainly contained within it. The school representatives cannot eschew politics and still make meaningful contact with the legislature.

Although most state legislators would be merely indifferent to the schools' plea for state help, some may actively, though covertly, oppose the requests. In the St. Louis case, a number of influential city legislators identify themselves with the "state" as a fiscal entity apart from the "city," and resist increased state expenditures of any kind for the city. Others may reflect a Catholic constituency and say, for instance, that unless money is provided for transportation to parochial schools they will oppose extra funds for public education in the city. Still others have been known to be engaged in various kinds of alliances, for instance with school-building and maintenance crews, and hope to gain benefits for their allies by helping to block the school board's requests in the legislature. Most of the city-based legislative opposition will be behind the scenes. In a roll call vote it would seldom show up. Nevertheless it may effectively block passage of the program.

The key to the problem is in the fact that the schoolmen have no way to reach the pivotal legislators where it counts. There is no network of mutual obligation and support connecting the two groupings. The school board can cash no influence checks in payment for past or future favors done for legislators. There are a few favors the school can do for a highly political legislator, but every element in professional education training and ideology contributes to the refusal to think in these terms. Parenthetically, it might be noted here that lay board members seem to get more righteously indignant than professional superintendents at the suggestion that they do a little trading if they want their program passed. Political naiveté, especially at the level of articulated ideology, helps reinforce the incapacity of urban school interests (though not necessarily in rural areas where schoolmen are often highly skilled in the arts of "forks of the creek" politics) to get what they want from the state. Not only the congenital opposition of educators to these elemental political tactics, but the widespread misconception of the source of their opposition further confounds them. Newspapers and other "spectator elites" such as academics have assumed that it was the rural interests that were doing in the urban claims. The inability to understand that urban legislators were often unresponsive, not only regarding school problems but on many other desires of some city-based interests, has led to invalid inferences about what to do next. One of these has been simply to reassert the evils of politics and the importance of insulating the schools against their bitter breath. The second is to await with confidence the coming of reapportionment. "Give us an urban majority and our urban programs will pass," is the assumption underlying this optimism. But an urban state legislative majority may still not care much about the schools; and, without more political savvy than they have displayed in the past, the spokesmen for city school interests will continue to get unsatisfactory treatment.

There is, obviously, the now genuinely optimistic prospect of federal funding, especially rich for urban schools serving slum populations. I shall not explore this dimension in detail, but I want to note an important point: urban interests have for years done much better at the federal level than in the state capitol. The reasons are complex and not very well understood, but among them is the strong, warm, and skillfully administered relationship between city political leaders and federal officials. Federal officials in all the relevant branches and agencies have come to be responsive to political leaders and politically skillful administrators in the cities. Mayors, urban-renewal directors, and local poverty-program administrators are especially skilled, individually and through their national associations, at bringing their points of view to the sympathetic attention of Washington. The newspaper accounts of the federal treatment of the Chicago schools in 1965 suggest to me that, as Mayor Daley salvaged Superintendent Willis's federal school money from the fire, so the help of political leaders in other cities may be necessary to maintain satisfactory relationships with this newly opened source of major financial assistance to big-city schools. Indeed, the requirement, which Washington officials seem to be taking seriously, that poverty programs and the new educational programs be closely coordinated may, in turn, force the schools into closer relationship with many other agencies of city government and thus, inevitably, into the mainstream of urban politics.

Earlier I raised the question of the significance of deciding the McAndrew affair within a partisan electoral process. Let us return to that dimension of our general problem. I have suggested that autonomy and isolation have serious disadvantages for urban schools. What is to be said on the other side? What would it be like if the schools were a more integral part of the urban political system; if, for example, they were made a regular line department of the city government with a director appointed by the mayor to serve at his pleasure? How would such a process work? What would be the substantive effects on educational policy and on the city generally?

To examine this issue directly, we need to be clear about how city political systems actually function. No single formulation will do justice to the complexities of the question but at least three points seem especially pertinent. First, political scientists generally have found that in large cities, and some of the smaller ones too, influence is rather widely dispersed, specialized, and exercised in a discontinuous fashion. That is, one person or group will be active and influential on one set of issues while quite a different array dominates the next set. This tendency is perhaps accentuated when a specialized set of issues, such as education, is determined within a specialized institutional framework. But the institutional framework is primarily reinforcing, not by itself determining. A second, related, finding of political scientists' examinations of the urban community is that great pressure is generally exercised in questions of substantive policy program (though not so much on elections or top level personnel appointments or tax rates) by the program's professional and administrative experts. In urban renewal or public health and hospitals, to take two examples from regular city government, the professional personnel run the programs about as completely as schoolmen run the schools; perhaps, more so.

A third finding is rather different from the first two, however. In many cities, though by no means in all of them, a critical and continuing role of substantial import is played by the mayor. He is the chief organizer of the dominant coalition of interests and the chief broker among them. He is the chief negotiator in balancing not only the disparate and often conflicting groups in the city but also in representing city needs to state and especially to federal agencies. More than that the mayor is the single most important problem-solver. He is committed, out of sheer re-election necessity if for no other reason, to rebuilding the slums, attracting new business, renovating downtown, implementing equal rights and opportunity and, as federal money is at last making it possible, improving the life chances of the urban poor. Not all mayors face the same circumstances, of course. Some are weak in formal authority to control even their governmental environment; many are lacking in the fiscal and human resources to get the necessary leverage on the social and economic environment. Nevertheless, there is a substantial similarity in the orientation and role of big-city mayors, and this convergence has been especially pronounced during the past decade. In style or substance, mayors of today have little in common with Big Bill Thompson. Actually, mayors might not relish taking more direct responsibility for the schools. Why should they take on another large problem area when they too can fall back on the argument that the schools should be nonpolitical? If they were to accept a more active role, it might be because they really want to resolve the complicated difficulties of urban life, and solutions *must* include effective use of the schools.

These three generalizations are all relevant to my question but in somewhat different ways. They suggest that if the school were integrated with the urban governmental system, the educators would continue to make most of the technical and administrative decisions but the mayor and his coalition of community support would play a major role in giving over-all program and fiscal direction. The schools would compete more directly than now with other city programs for available money. Their programs might be more differentiated among different segments of the community, as the mayor tried at once to solve problems and ease tensions and to please the major elements of the coalition that elected him. Their top administrative personnel might be more vulnerable to the vicissitudes of electoral fortune, though mayors might be only slightly more effective in breaking through the defenses of the educators' bureaucracy to choose (or fire) their own men than are independent school boards now. Educators might find themselves and their programs more often subordinated to other agencies and programs than is presently the case, but this subordination might be more a difference in perception than reality; an independent school system already must compete for money and support, but in an indirect and segmented manner. It is not clear that mayor-directed schools would be more generously financed from the local community but neither is it inevitable that they would be poorer.

In my judgment, the principal difference between the existing arrangements for the government of urban public education and this hypothetical control by the mayor would be in the schools' relationship with the increasingly pluralistic and tension-filled community. An independent school system asks for community support directly, unprotected by any of the confusions of mandate that attend the election of political officials. The schools are naked against community pressures except as their unitary-community ideology and whatever rational citizen demand there may be for their services may shield them. I have argued, and so do the protest demonstrations and the negative votes in referenda, that these are not sufficient protection if the urban schools are to perform the extraordinarily difficult, high cost, tasks of educating the urban poor. It is not coincidence, I think, that recently the schools have been so often the target of the alienated and disaffected elements of society. Whether protesting against *de facto* segregation, double taxation of Catholics, or alleged Communist infiltration, the pickets know that the schools are vulnerable to direct assault. No other programs or interests get in the way. No other issues or loyalties intrude.

But the processes involved in electing a mayor and a council, especially on a partisan ticket, but also in a large, heterogeneous city with nonpartisan government, do mute these kinds of pressures. Mandates *are* vague; constraints on the specific policy choices which the officials will subsequently make are loose. And the protection afforded to the professionals is considerable. They may administer their programs while someone else takes the heat, and diffuses it.

There is evidence that in the controversies over fluoridation those communities in which the voters decided the question in a referendum were often in the process racked by deep social conflict. In those cities where a mayor played a strong role, on the other hand, fluoridating the city water supply by administrative order, there was little untoward excitement.[11] The schools have far more substantive impact on urban life than fluoridation, of course; the latter seems to be mainly symbolic. But educational issues are laden with affect, and they may come more and more to resemble fluoridation as a focus for the manifold discontents of the city. The broader political process might help to protect the schools against becoming the urban community's battlefield.

In all that I have said thus far, my principal points appear to be as follows: (1) more direct and effective political (mayoral) control of the schools will be difficult to engineer because of the resistance of schoolmen, regardless of formal governmental structure, to "nonprofessional" direction; and (2) big-city school interests might get a more receptive hearing in state and national capitals and be partially screened from local direct action protests if they merge their interests more fully with the over-all city administration. But would this type of result lead to more effective education? This, in my judgment, is precisely the *wrong* question. In the urban center, there is no education which is separate from the issues of race, poverty, housing, crime, and the other human problems of the metropolis. The issue we need to face is whether greater mayoral control would lead to changes in school policy (e.g., better coordination and cooperation with urban renewal, recreation, and poverty programs) which would make the educational program more effective in solving the larger complex of community problems. In a simpler era, one could argue that Big Bill Thompson may well have done just this in Chicago. And, forty years later, one might well feel that, in the same city, Mayor Daley might have achieved more effective integration than Superintendent Willis seemed disposed to provide had the mayor chosen to violate the educators' code of independence and exert more direct control of the situation.

At the same time, there should be no mistake about the fact that greater administrative integration of schools with city would, in many cases, mean subordination of the schools to the city government. Moreover, such subordination might often mean that the schools were being used as instruments to achieve policy goals which extended well beyond more narrowly defined educational objectives. To some extent, of course, this is happening anyway, and indeed it has always been so. But the issue of political control forces us to be explicit about the question

11. See Elihu Katz, Robert Crain, Donald Rosenthal, and Aaron J. Spector, *The Fluoridation Decision: Community Structure and Innovation* (Mss, March, 1965). The processes by which an affect-laden issue like education may ignite previously latent community tensions have been inadequately explored. James S. Coleman's highly suggestive synthesis of the then existing materials. *Community Conflict* (Glencoe, Illinois: The Free Press, 1957), has not been followed by much further empirical work.

of how the many goals we wish to achieve in the city can best be approached. If it turned out that education was not at the head of the list, educators would be compelled to acknowledge that fact in a situation where they had to bargain for their share of the local resources against the direct competition of other programs as well as against the fiscal prudence of the electorate.

Direct competition for local money; subordination of educators to other public officials with other interests and programs; the self-conscious use of the schools as instruments to fight poverty, improve housing conditions, or fight city-suburb separation: these have been virtually unthinkable heresies to devoted schoolmen. Yet, are they much more than an explicit statement of steps and tendencies already being taken or implicit in present practices? I think not; we are already moving this way, to some extent we always have been doing so, and the real question to be faced is: How might we do these things better? A greater measure of local political leadership in education and coordination of the schools with other portions of the community might well contribute to this end.

Some Alternatives for the Public Library

Edward C. Banfield

THE PUBLIC LIBRARY has more users and more money today than ever before, but it lacks a purpose.[1] It is trying to do some things that it probably cannot do, and it is doing others that it probably should not do. At the same time, it is neglecting what may be its real opportunities. What the library needs is, first, a purpose that is both in accord with the realities of present-day city life and implied by some general principles, and, second, a program that is imaginatively designed to carry its purpose into effect.

This paper will begin with a brief look at the principles justifying *public* action. (Why should a public body distribute reading matter and not, say, shoes?) In the light of these principles, it will then consider what the public library has been, what it is now, and what it ought to be.

Some General Principles

Economists offer several justifications for governmental intervention to set the demand for a commodity or good (in this case library service).[2] One justification exists when the good is of such a nature that it cannot be supplied to some consumers without at the same time being supplied to all—examples are national defense and air pollution

---

1. For evidence see the report of the eighty-fourth annual conference of the American Library Association, *New York Times,* July 4, 1966, p. 40. The theme of the conference was "Libraries for a Great Society" and the president of the association announced that an inventory of public and school library needs made by the U.S. Office of Education and the association revealed that $3.1 billion would have to be spent to bring the nation's libraries to the level of "adequacy" and operating budgets would have to be raised $1.2 billion a year to keep them there. "These are enormous figures, of course," he said, "but our wealthy nation can easily contribute all that is called for and then some." With regard to the library's purpose, he seems to have said nothing.

2. *See* Richard Musgrave, *The Theory of Public Finance* (New York: McGraw-Hill Book Company, 1959), Chapter 1.

Reprinted, slightly revised, from The Public Library and the City, *edited by Ralph W. Conant (Cambridge, Mass.: M.I.T. Press, 1965), pp. 102–113, by permission of the publishers.*

control; in such cases, it is impossible for the distributor of the good to charge a price for it, since he cannot withhold it from anyone who refuses to pay the price. Therefore (apart from philanthropists) only the government, which through its tax power can coerce everyone into paying, is in a position to offer the service. Clearly this justification has no application to libraries.

Another justification—and one which presumably *does* apply to the library—exists when the public will benefit in some way if the consumer consumes more (or less) of the good than he would if the government did not concern itself in the matter. If my consumption of a good —my immunizing myself against disease or my sending my children to school, for example—confers benefits of some kind upon the community at large, the government ought, in the community's interest if not in mine, to see to it that I consume a proper amount of it. In order to encourage consumption of such "merit goods" (to use an economist's term), the government may employ subsidies.

That consumption of certain goods confers benefits upon the community does not automatically justify government subsidies, however. No doubt it is a good thing from a public standpoint that I eat well, have a safe roof over my head, and go to the doctor when I am sick. But if I am compos mentis and not indigent the chances are that I will look after these matters without any encouragement from the government. The public does not have to pay me to eat; I will do so both because I must in order to stay alive and because I enjoy eating.

Public intervention to set the demand does not necessarily involve public production or distribution of the good. The school board sets the demand for school books, but it does not hire authors to write them and it does not operate its own printing press. The Air Force sets the demand for planes but it does not manufacture them.

By the same token, that a good is produced or distributed under public auspices does not imply the necessity of a public subsidy for the people who consume it. The function of the government may in some instances be merely to make up for a deficiency in the private market by offering consumers a good which from the standpoint of the community they ought to have and which for some reason no private enterprise offers. If no one saw fit to go into the shoe business, the government would have to. But if it went into the shoe business it would not have to give shoes away, or sell them for less than the cost of manufacture.

The Nineteenth-Century Purpose

Let us now look at the public library of the past in the light of these principles. In the very beginning, libraries were private associations for the joint use of a facility that was too expensive for any but the well-off to own individually. Some state legislatures conferred on the associations certain corporate powers, including the power to tax their members provided that a two-thirds majority concurred. They did this on the grounds that benefits to the community at large would ensue—i.e., that library service satisfied a "merit want." "These libraries," Franklin remarks in his autobiography, "have improved the general conversation of Americans, made the common tradesmen and farmers as intelligent as most gentlemen from other countries, and perhaps have contributed in some degree to the stand so generally made throughout the colonies in defense of their privileges." Early in the nineteenth century charitable societies were formed in the larger cities "to furnish wholesome religious, moral, and improving reading of all kinds to the poor, cheaper than they now get fanatical or depraved reading." There were complaints that the books circulated were not improving enough (a director of the Astor Library in New York wrote that "the young fry . . . employ all the hours they are out of school in reading the trashy, as Scott, Cooper, Dickens, Punch, and the 'Illustrated News'") to which the reply was made that "if people will not come to your library you may as well establish none." No one, however, would have justified a charitable library on the grounds that it provided entertainment.[3]

Later on the corporations thus created were made public and were supported in part by taxation of the whole public. This was about the middle of the last century, when bright and ambitious farm boys who had mastered the 3 R's but not much else were flocking to the cities to seek their fortunes. "Mechanics libraries" were established to afford these Alger characters opportunities to pick up by home study the small amount of technical knowledge that then existed. Such libraries were not supported in full by the public—philanthropists provided most of the support—but they were tax exempt and they enjoyed other advantages. There were good reasons for giving them these advantages: anything that encouraged self-improvement on the part of the "respectable poor" tended to increase the productivity and wealth of the community. Besides, to the Anglo-Saxon Protestant elite that ran the cities, self-improvement appeared good in and of itself.

It was not until near the turn of the century, however, that most sizable cities had public libraries in the present-day sense. There was no doubt about the public purpose of these libraries. They were to facilitate the assimilation of European immigrants to the urban, middle-class, American style of life.

The immigrants—many of them—were highly receptive to what the library offered. They came—many of them—from cultures that respected books and learning; with few exceptions they were eager to learn the language and customs of their new country and to get ahead

3. David B. Tyack, *George Tichnor and the Boston Brahmins* (Cambridge, Mass.: Harvard University Press, 1967), pp. 208–211.

in a material way. There was, accordingly, a high degree of harmony between the public purposes being sought through the library and the motives and aspirations of its potential clientele.

Times Have Changed

Today the situation is entirely different. The Horatio Alger characters and the immigrants have long since passed from the scene. There are, to be sure, more poor people in the large cities than ever (they are not as poor in absolute terms, however, and they constitute a smaller proportion of the metropolitan area's population), and the movement of the poor from backward rural areas of the South and Puerto Rico is likely to continue for some time to come. The present-day poor, however, represent a new and different problem. Their poverty consists not so much of a lack of income (although they lack that) as of a lack of the cultural standards and of the motivations, including the desire for self-improvement and for "getting ahead," that would make them more productive and hence better-paid. "The culturally deprived of today's cities are not on the bottom of a ladder; they do not even know that one exists," the editor of a bulletin for librarians has written in an article extremely apposite to the present discussion.[4] Many of the poor are "functionally illiterate," some though they have gone to, or even graduated from, high school. Giving them access to books will not accomplish anything.

Assimilating the lower class into the working and the middle classes may be a public purpose of the highest urgency. (Some people, of course, assert that lower class values—certain of them, at any rate— are as worthy of respect as any others.) But however compelling the case for assimilation is thought to be, the question has to be faced whether the library is a fit instrument for the purpose.

Certainly no one believes that the library is now of any service to the lower class. By and large, libraries are of the middle class and for the middle class. With rare exceptions, librarians have the wrong skin color, the wrong style of dress and make-up, the wrong manner of speech, and the wrong values (among other things, they think that people should be quiet in the library!) to be acceptable to the lower class. The feeling is mutual, moreover, for most librarians are probably no freer of class and race prejudice than are other middle-class whites. The consequence is that the lower class is repelled by the library, or would be if it ever got near it.

A few library boards have tried to change this, but without much

4. Kathleen Molz, "The Public Library: The People's University?" *The American Scholar*, Vol. 34, No. 1 (Winter 1964–1965), p. 100. The writer wishes to express his appreciation of Miss Molz' criticism of an earlier draft of this paper.

success. Some will say that their methods have not been sufficiently ingenious: they should establish store-front libraries and staff them with lower-class librarians, preferably radical ones; they should employ supersalesmen to go from door to door selling cheap reprints, and so on.

If one believes that lower-class adults can be enticed to read, there is much to be said for making this a primary purpose of the library and for trying any approach that offers the least promise. It may be, however, that the educational level of the lower class is so low and its demoralization so great that no efforts on the part of the library will have much effect. Something much more fundamental than library service may be needed—for example, compulsory nursery school attendance from the age of two or three.

Not being able or willing (or both) to serve the lower class, the public library has tended to make itself an adjunct of the school, especially of the middle-class school. Children have always been an important class of library users, but in recent years they have become the principal clientele of the public library in many places. Children sent by teachers to use books in connection with course assignments crowd some libraries after school hours to such an extent that adult users have to leave. (In certain Los Angeles schools, teachers require each pupil to borrow at least one book a week from the public library!) Here and there libraries have been forced by the sheer weight of the children's numbers to place limits on service to them.

One reason for this invasion is that, thanks to the "baby boom" of a few years ago (which, of course, is still continuing), there are more children than ever. Another is that the schools do not have adequate libraries of their own. (Two-thirds of all elementary schools have *no* central library, and those with central libraries have only five books per pupil in them on the average.) Still another reason is that it has become fashionable among teachers to require "research" papers (in some places third-graders swarm into the public library to do "research") and to assign, not a single textbook, but a list of readings, some in very short supply, selected by the teacher from a variety of sources.

Public libraries were not designed for large numbers of children and are usually not staffed to handle them. The wear and tear on books, librarians, and innocent bystanders is therefore very great. In Brooklyn, it was recently reported, book losses—not all of them caused by children—run to 10 per cent of the library budget. In some places rowdyism is a serious problem.

In fairness to both the children and the adults, the schools ought to have adequate libraries of their own; presumably they will have them if the aid-to-education legislation now pending in Congress is passed. Children should not be excluded from public libraries, however —it is a good thing for them to go now and then to a place the atmosphere of which is decidedly adult—but they should not be sent there to do assignments; they should go to the public library on their own initiative to find books that please them and in the expectation of entering a world that is not juvenile.

The Light Reader

Apart from school children, the most numerous class of library users consists of light readers, especially middle-class house-wives. The books these readers borrow are not *all* light, of course, and even the ones that are light are not the very lightest; public librarians do not buy out-and-out trash. Nevertheless, a considerable part of the circulation is of romantic novels, westerns, detective stories, and books on how to repair leaky faucets, take off excess fat, and make money playing the stock market. About two-thirds of the books public libraries lend to adults are fiction, and most of these are probably light fiction. (Unfortunately, libraries do not use more relevant categories than "fiction" and "nonfiction" in their record keeping.)

It is hard to see how encouraging light reading can be regarded as a public purpose. That the housewife finds it convenient to get her detective story from a public rather than a rental library is certainly not a justification for the public library. Her neighbor, who may not care to borrow books and whose income may be less than hers, will be coerced into paying taxes to support a facility that is for her convenience. Why should he be? Whether she gets to sleep by reading a novel, by watching the late show, or by taking a sleeping pill—indeed, whether she gets to sleep at all—is a matter of indifference to him and to the community at large.

If it could be shown that light reading leads to serious reading, a justification for public action would exist. In the case of uneducated people who are introduced to books by the library, such a showing might possibly be made. But it is highly unlikely that it can be made in the case of the middle-class readers who constitute most of the adult library users. For the most part, light reading leads to nothing except more light reading.

Unless reason can be found for believing that light reading confers some benefit upon the community, the public library should leave the light reader to the rental library, the drugstore, and the supermarket. If for some reason these readers *must* be served by the public library, they should be charged the full cost of the service, including, of course, a fair share of the rental value of the library building and site. Charging the full cost of service would soon put the public library out of the light-reading business, but this would prove to be a benefit even from the standpoint of the light reader. He would find that when the public library stopped competing with rental libraries by giving its service free, they and other profit-making enterprises (the paperback counters of the drugstore and supermarket, for example) would fill the gap and give him better service than he got before. If there is a demand for thirty copies of *Peyton Place,* the rental library makes haste to put that many on its shelves. The public library, not being under the stimulus of the profit motive and (let us hope) feeling itself under some obligation to serve more important purposes, buys only one or two copies of such a book if it buys any at all. This, of course, accounts for the more than 3,500 rental libraries (not to mention the drugstore and supermarket counters) that are competing successfully with the tax-supported libraries.

The Serious Reader

The proper business of the public library is with the *serious* reader and—assuming that the library cannot be an effective instrument for educating the lower class—with him alone. "Serious" reading is any that improves one's stock of knowledge, enlarges one's horizons, or improves one's values. Reasonable men will disagree as to where the boundary should be drawn between light and serious reading; that does not render the distinction invalid or useless, however, although it will lead to some practical difficulties.

The common-sense assumption is that all serious reading confers some benefit upon the community. This would be hard to demonstrate in a rigorous way (imagine trying to specify the amounts and kinds of benefits conferred upon various sectors of the community by, say, so many man-years of novel reading, so many of historical reading, and so on); but the difficulty, or impossibility, of demonstrating it does not mean that the assumption is wrong.

That an activity confers benefits upon the community does not, however (as was remarked above), constitute a sufficient justification for publicly supporting it. Perhaps those who read serious books would read as many of them if public libraries did not exist. (Indeed, conceivably they might read more of them, for if an existing institution did not stand in the way, a new and more effective one, public or private, might come into existence. Any foreigner who has observed the operation of the government salt and tobacco monopoly in Italy will agree that other and better ways of distributing these commodities are possible. To the Italian who has never been abroad, however, the idea of putting the government out of the salt and tobacco business might seem preposterous. "How then," he might ask, "could one possibly obtain these indispensable articles?") Most serious readers have adequate or more than adequate family incomes; it seems likely that if they had to pay the full cost of their reading they would not read less. If this is so, there is no reason for the public to subsidize their reading.

The relatively few serious readers who are poor—so poor that to pay for library service would entail a sacrifice of something else that is necessary to an adequate standard of living—present a problem. They would of course be given service at reduced rates or free. This is widely done by colleges, and there is no reason why there should not be "library scholarships" for all who need them. If such an arrangement involved use of an objectionable means test (would it be objectionable to give service free to all families with incomes of less than $5,000 if the user's statement that he belonged to that category were accepted without question?) or if the costs of record keeping were unduly high, the sensible thing would be to make the service—the standard service, not necessarily special services—free to all.

If it is decided that serious reading must be subsidized in order to secure for the community all of the benefits that it wants, it need not follow that the best thing for the library board to do is to own and circulate a collection of books. There may be much better ways of accomplishing the purpose. Perhaps, for example, those who have responsibility for allocating the library fund—let us now call it the "fund to encourage serious reading"—would get a greater return on the investment by inducing the local supermarket to display a big stock of quality paperbacks and to have one-cent sales of them now and then. Or, again, perhaps the fund would best be used to subsidize the rent of a dealer in used books who, because of the ravages of urban renewal or for other reasons, could not otherwise stay in business.

Some Illustrative Ideas

Assuming, however, that such radical innovations are out of the question and that the practical problem is to make some minor changes in the existing institution, what might be done?

Here are a few suggestions.

1. Provide soundproofed cubicles that readers may rent by the week or month and in which they may keep under lock and key books (subject to call, of course), a typewriter (rented, if that is what they want), and manuscripts. Nowadays few people have space at home for a study. Many libraries have reading rooms, but there are no places where one can read, let alone write, in privacy and comfort. (An habitual smoker, for example, cannot read if he is not permitted to smoke.) The New York Public Library at 42nd Street is probably the only public library with cubicles (they are supported by an endowment); there is a long waiting list for them.

2. Offer the services of a "personal shopper" to take orders by

phone and to arrange home deliveries and pickups. Many readers are too busy to go to the library, especially when there is no more than an off-chance that the book they want is in. The personal shopper could also arrange fast interlibrary loans and for the photo-copying of hard-to-get, out-of-print books. (Publishers naturally object to the copying of copyrighted material. But perhaps they could be persuaded to give libraries a general permission to make one copy per library of works that are not available for sale.) A fair number of the larger libraries have had "readers' advisers" ever since WPA days; the advisers' time is usually entirely taken up by children, however; in any case, only handicapped persons are assisted *in absentia.*

3. Buy a large enough stock of *serious* books so that no reader will have to wait more than, say, two weeks for a copy. Bentham's remark about justice can be paraphrased here: "Reading delayed is reading denied."

4. Display prominently, and review in library newsletters, those current books that are not widely reviewed by "middle-brow" journals. Many people suppose that all worthwhile books are listed, if not actually reviewed by the better newspapers and magazines. This is not the case. Scholarly books are ignored as often as not; some of them are unknown to most serious readers. The natural tendency of the library is to make a fuss about the very books that the ordinary reader would be most likely to hear of anyway. It should try instead to make up for the deficiencies of the commercial institutions by calling attention to the less-well-advertised books.

5. Maintain up-to-date, annotated bibliographies of the sort that would help introduce a layman to a specialized field. A physician, let us suppose, wants to know what social science has to say that is relevant to problems of medical organization. What books and journals should he look at first? If the library had a file of reading lists, course outlines, and syllabi used in colleges and universities, together with bibliographical notes and articles from academic journals, he could be assisted to make his way into the subject. A good many of the better libraries have materials of this sort—more materials, probably, than most of their serious readers realize. Even so, there is probably a good deal of room for improvement both in the quality of the materials that are collected and in the methods by which they are made known to library users.

6. Offer tutorial service for readers who want instruction or special assistance. Perhaps the physician would like to discuss his questions with a social scientist. The library might have a social scientist on its staff or it might bring one as a consultant from a nearby college or university. The tutor would be available for an hour's discussion or, at the other extreme, to give a short course.

7. Have a mail-order counter supplied with a directory of all books in print, a list of available government publications, and the catalogues

of some dealers in used and hard-to-find books. A librarian should be on hand to help buyers find what they want. In the many towns and small cities that are without proper bookstores, this kind of service might go a long way toward making up for the lack.

The Library's Failure Is Typical

The library is by no means the only public institution that with passage of time has ceased to serve its original purpose and has not acquired a new one that can be justified on any general principles. Very likely it could be shown: (1) that the professionals most involved, and a fortiori everyone else, have given little serious thought to the nature of the purposes which presumably justify not only public libraries but also public parks, museums, schools, and renewal projects (to mention only a few activities of the sort that are in question): (2) that such purposes as might plausibly be advanced to justify such activities are ill-served, or not served at all, by the activities as presently conducted; (3) that these purposes could usually be better served by the market (rigged perhaps by public authorities) than by public ownership and operation; (4) that in most cases using the market would result in greater consumption of the good and in less waste in the supplying of it (public institutions tend to offer too much of those goods that are in light demand and not enough of those that are in heavy demand); and (5) that certain goods not offered by private institutions are not offered by public ones either, and this even though increased consumption of these goods would confer relatively large benefits upon the community at large.

To find the reasons for this state of affairs, one must look deep into the nature of our institutions and of our political culture. Organizations tend to perpetuate themselves and therefore to embrace whatever opportunities come along, however unrelated these may be to any previously-stated purposes. Public organizations, moreover, often exist as much to symbolize something as to accomplish something. These are only two of many considerations that doubtless should be taken into account.

The Police Administrator as a Policymaker

James Q. Wilson

THE POLICE ADMINISTRATOR—variously called chief, superintendent, commissioner, or captain—has in common with all other executives, especially those of governmental organizations, responsibility for the policies of his agency. In principle, he is supposed to "set policy" and, having set it, to obtain resources (money, manpower, public support) from the community in order to carry it out. Ideally, performing this function requires that the administrator have sufficient knowledge about and control over the rank-and-file members of his organization— especially the patrolmen—so that he can show what the police are doing and how well they are doing it, alter more or less precisely their behavior to accord with such policies as the community may agree to, and evaluate a particular officer's actions in the light of a specific citizen complaint. With respect to some members of his organization, and with respect to some aspects of the work of all members, the administrator does have knowledge and control. He knows, or can find out, whether his officers are tolerating the operation of a brothel and how many traffic tickets they are issuing. But with respect to how well they are preventing crime, catching criminals, and maintaining order, he has very little information.

The police share with most other public agencies—the schools, foreign ministries, anti-poverty organizations—an inability to assess accurately the effectiveness of their operations. Indeed, some writers, such as Anthony Downs, have made the absence of an output which can be priced on a market (or otherwise given an objective, continuous evaluation) a defining characteristic of bureaucracy.[1] However they choose to interpret such measures, automobile dealers know how many cars their salesmen have sold, television producers know what audience ratings their programs have earned, and baseball managers know their

1. Anthony Downs, *Inside Bureaucracy* (Boston: Little, Brown & Co., 1967), Chap. III.

Published for the first time in this book, by permission of the author.

clubs' standing and the batting averages of their players. But just as the school superintendent has only the most approximate measures of how well his schools are educating children (partly because "education" is so hard to define and measure, partly because the school's contribution to education however measured is so hard to estimate),[2] so also the police chief has only the most rudimentary knowledge of how well his patrolmen are preventing crime, apprehending criminals, and maintaining order. No police department, however competently led or organized, can know how much crime and disorder a community produces, or how much would be produced if the police functioned differently (or not at all).

Most crime becomes known to the police through citizen reports, but the citizens are likely to underreport many kinds of crime for reasons of self-interest which the police and the community cannot easily change. The true rates for rape, robbery, assault, burglary, and larceny are many times higher than the reported rates; though some of the difference is due to police error or malpractice, most of it is due to the failure of citizens to notify the police. A third to a half of the assaults in one survey went unreported; because most assaults occur among people known, or even related, to each other, it is not surprising that half the victims who did not report these offenses gave as their reason that they felt "it was a private matter" or that they did not want to get the offender into trouble.[3] Between 40 and 60 percent of all thefts and cases of malicious mischief were unreported; because these are largely crimes of stealth, they are rarely solved by the police. Thus, it is not surprising that well over half the victims who did not report them gave as their reason that the police could not do anything. The two crimes most accurately reported are murder (presumably because it is so serious and because most murderers *are* caught) and auto theft (presumably because insurance companies require such a report and because most stolen cars are recovered by the police).

If the self-interest of the citizen causes him to underreport certain crimes, it may cause him to overreport others. A false report of a theft may be filed in order to make an insurance claim; disorderly conduct may be charged against a neighbor with whom one has a grudge to settle or against teen-age boys whose rowdy (but noncriminal) behavior one wants curbed. And ignorance may cause other distortions—a stolen purse may be presumed lost, an unmarried couple caught in a motel may be thought of as having violated a moral but not a legal code.

Even when the police have accurate information, it is often difficult or impossible to devise a strategy that would make the occurrence of a

2. James S. Coleman, *et al., Equality of Opportunity in Education,* Chap. III.
3. President's Commission on Law Enforcement and Administration of Justice, *Report,* pp. 21–22.

crime less likely. Many serious crimes—murder, forcible rape—are of this character: though they are often reported with minimum distortion or delay, they occur, in many cases, in private places, among people who know each other, and in the heat of an emotional moment. A police department may assign an officer to each street corner, but inside the buildings on those corners, a drunken husband may still maul or murder his wife's lover as though the police were a hundred miles away.

Crimes that occur in public places are more easily suppressed by police patrol, but the police can never know whether a crime suppressed in one neighborhood reappears in another, less closely patrolled neighborhood, or in another community served by a different police department, or within the same neighborhood but in a different form. Stealing cars parked along the curb may be reduced by intensive patrol, but car thieves may then go elsewhere to steal or, abandoning the streets to the police, burglarize stores by entering them from the alley.

The rate of certain crimes is determined to a significant but unknown degree by factors over which the police have little control. Street crimes are affected by the weather, crimes against property by the prevailing economic conditions, crimes against the person by the racial and class composition of the community, delinquency by the nature and strength of family and peer group controls. The police know these things—or think they know them—but they cannot estimate the magnitude of such factors, or distinguish their effect from that of police tactics, or bring these factors under police control.[4]

Though he may talk publicly a good deal about crime rates, the police administrator knows or senses that he cannot get really reliable figures and that if he could get them he would not be able to show that police work makes a visibly dramatic difference in them. He will tell a visitor that "the police don't cause crime" and the "police alone can't stop it," and of course he is right. If the apparent crime rate goes down, he will not object if the newspapers give him credit; if it goes up, he will point (perhaps with ample justification) to reasons over which the police have no control.

4. In addition, of course, police departments vary considerably in the accuracy with which they report such crimes as are known to them. See Ronald H. Beattie, *Journal of Criminal Law, Criminology, and Police Science*, XLVI (July–August 1955), pp. 178–186; Marvin E. Wolfgang, "Uniform Crime Reports: A Critical Appraisal," *University of Pennsylvania Law Review*, CXI (April 1963), pp. 708–738; President's Commission, *Report*, pp. 25–27; James E. Price, "A Test of the Accuracy of Crime Statistics," *Social Problems*, XIV (Fall 1966), pp. 214–221; James Q. Wilson, "Crime in the Streets," *The Public Interest* (Fall 1966), pp. 26–35. The President's Commission found that crime reports are significantly affected by local police reporting systems. For eleven large cities which recently changed their system, the increase in major (so-called "Index") offenses *in one year* ranged from 26.6 percent in Miami to 202.0 percent in Kansas City, Mo. The cities that have made such significant changes in their reporting systems since 1959 account for *nearly 25 percent* of all reported index crimes against the person committed in the United States.

As a result, few police administrators show much interest in "planning" the deployment of their manpower and equipment. There is no information—and in the nature of the case, can never be sufficient information—on the effects of alternative police strategies on the several kinds of crime. Some problems could be dealt with by rational analysis, however. The Task Force of Science and Technology of the President's Commission on Law Enforcement and Administration of Justice showed that the probability of apprehending a suspect increased as the response time of the police decreased.[5] Operations research techniques are available to show how response time can be reduced most economically in a given department. Controlled experiments could be performed to assess the effect on citizen reports of crime by systematically altering the number of patrolmen and the frequency of patrol in an area.[6]

But few police administrators take even those steps that might lead to modest gains in optimal resource allocation. No department visited for this study, for example, tried systematically to measure response time and the consequences of its variations. Some departments have experimented with varying the forces assigned to particular beats, or even the dimensions of these beats, in accordance with reported crimes and calls for service, but they are the exception.[7] It is even rare for a department to keep careful and long-term records on the effect of "saturation patrol" (by a tactical squad or the like) in one or more neighborhoods.

Adequate information, of course, is not all that would be needed for a "rational" allocation of police protection. Even if the administrator had perfect knowledge of the outcome of various police deployment strategies, he would also have to have a decision rule that would tell him which outcome to prefer. There are at least two such rules and they are in conflict. One is the "crime minimization" criterion: allocate patrolmen so that the last one assigned would deter an equal amount of crime no matter where in the city he was placed. This criterion would produce the smallest total amount of crime in the city, but since the deterrence value of a patrolman varies by type of neighborhood, some neighborhoods would have more crime than others. The other rule is

5. President's Commission, *Science and Technology,* pp. 92–93.
6. Such experiments are likely to have two weaknesses, however. One is that it is often difficult to know the effect of altering patrol practices on crime reports in parts of the city outside the experimental area. The other is the "Hawthorne effect"—citizens may report more crimes in experimental areas because they see more policemen about, or because they are aware they are part of an experiment, even though the actual rate of crimes has not changed; conversely, they may report fewer because they feel more secure.
7. The procedures used to allocate patrol forces in Los Angeles, Oakland, and Cincinnati are described in Frank E. Walton, "Selective Distribution of Police Patrol Force," *Journal of Criminal Law, Criminology, and Police Science,* XLIX (1958), pp. 165–171. The few such efforts as are made to allocate patrol forces rationally are critically evaluated in "Program Budgeting for Police Departments," *Yale Law Journal,* LXXVI (March 1967), pp. 822–838.

the "crime equalization" one: allocate patrolmen so that the probability of being victimized is the same in all parts of the city. This might well leave the total amount of crime high in the city as a whole—equalizing victimization rates may be achieved by concentrating police in the most crime-prone areas to drive down those rates while allowing the rates in relatively crime-free areas to rise. In short, the police administrator— like all administrators—must make decisions about equity as well as about efficiency.[8]

Even if he had a decision rule, a police administrator would rarely have the funds, the information, the extra manpower, or the professionally competent assistants to make its systematic application possible. But most police administrators show little interest in such projects—partly perhaps because they have not been trained to think in these terms, but partly because they see these things as largely irrelevant. The administrator does not believe he and his organization are judged by the public in these terms, nor does he believe they should be: no statistics can be devised that would fairly measure what the police and the public take to be the true worth (or failure) of police work. Repeatedly, interviewers for this study were told that "you can't go by the statistics" or "you have to use judgment and you've either got it or you don't." Even those departments with the most modern technologies—including IBM machines, punched cards, computer tabulations, and the like—were administered by men who by and large used the numbers thus produced merely to compile annual reports, satisfy the FBI's need for data, and keep track of payrolls and operating expenses. Most departments gather data the way the telephone company gathers phone numbers—individual by individual, to be filed alphabetically and consulted only when somebody needs to "look something up."

The police administrator must nevertheless deal from time to time with a public hue and cry about "rising crime rates" or the "lack of police protection." If he knew how to prevent crime, of course he would, but he is in the unhappy position of being responsible for an organization which lacks a proven technology for achieving its purpose. (In this, he is somewhat like the superintendent of a mental hospital: he too must deal with a problem of great importance for which there is no generally effective cure.) What he can do about rising crime rates, of course, is to hire more men (although the productivity of the marginal officer is impossible to measure, it is generally assumed that more men will not make matters worse and may make them better) and to use the ones he has "more aggressively." "Aggressive" police practice means gathering more information about people who may be about to commit, or recently have committed, a crime. Since he cannot, except by due process of law, put people in private places under sur-

8. Carl S. Shoup, "Standards for Distributing a Free Governmental Service: Crime Prevention," *Public Finance,* Vol. XIX, No. 4 (1964), pp. 383–392.

veillance (and the opportunities for eavesdropping or wiretapping are being restricted by court decision to the point where *any* surveillance in a private place may soon be impossible), he must gather the information in public places by stopping and questioning "suspicious" persons, checking cars, searching (where possible) people and vehicles for contraband, and keeping an eye on those locales—street corners or taverns in rowdy neighborhoods, for example—where criminal acts often occur.

In short, "doing something" about rising crime rates mean putting more patrolmen on the street and ordering them to be more alert. This, of course, increases the likelihood of the patrolmen coming into an adversary relationship with citizens—innocent people (to say nothing of guilty ones) usually do not like being stopped, questioned, or frisked. Furthermore, the patrolman cannot stop everyone, and in deciding who "ought" to be stopped he will rely on whatever clues he can. Persons who appear to be lower class are more likely than others to commit crimes; Negroes are more likely than whites to commit the crimes of violence about which the public is most concerned; young men are more likely than older ones to steal automobiles. Intensifying surveillance will be experienced by people in these categories as "harassment"; failure to intensify surveillance will be regarded by people not in these categories as being "soft" on crime.[9]

Even assuming that there are substantial benefits from aggressive patrol (as there may be), these may be offset by increased citizen irritation. Today, more citizens are aware of their rights, more organizations are prepared to articulate and defend those rights, and the local political system is more vulnerable to (that is, finds it harder to ignore) complaints about the violation of rights. Those people who are most likely to believe, rightly or wrongly, that they are being "harassed"— Negroes, young adults, lower-income persons—are increasing as a proportion of many cities' population, and thus it will be more difficult than ever for the police administrator to carry out a crime prevention program based on aggressive patrol.

Managing Discretion

For these and other reasons, the administrator will have difficulty specifying in advance the circumstances under which a patrolman should intervene. To get the patrolman to do "the right thing" when he is making "street stops" in order to question persons, the administrator must first be able to tell him what the right thing is. This is seldom

9. In 1967, the liberal mayor of Detroit, Jerome P. Cavanagh, faced a campaign led by certain white groups to recall him from office on the grounds that he had not done enough to halt the growing crime rate. He had first been elected mayor in part by Negro voters who felt they were being "harassed" by a police crackdown on crime led by the previous administration. *New York Times,* May 7, 1967, p. 66.

possible. It is difficult to describe what constitutes a "suspicious person" or a "suspicious circumstance," and some things that might have to enter into such a description cannot safely be put in writing or made official. A poorly dressed Negro alone at night in a wealthy white neighborhood may be a suspicious person in a suspicious circumstance, but one can imagine what reaction a police administrator would get from various civic groups (to say nothing of the courts) if he instructed his men to stop all such persons and question them. One list that was made of persons who should be subject to "field interrogations" yields plenty of illustrations of the problem. Some of its items were reasonable enough ("person who fits description of wanted suspect," "narcotics users," "persons who loiter about places where children play") but most of them either gave the officer very little guidance or else made almost anybody subject to interrogation ("person wearing a coat on a hot day," the driver of a "car with mismatched hub caps," persons who are "visibly rattled when near the policeman," "unescorted women or young girls in public places," and so on).[10]

With respect to his preventive patrol function, the patrolman can be given a clear statement about *how* to intervene even if not about *whether* to intervene. He can be taught how to approach a suspect, what to say, what kind of identification to ask for, what other questions to put, and how to check the name by radio to see if the person is wanted.

But with respect to his order maintenance function, guidance on *how* to intervene is especially lacking. Some rules, of course, can be formulated, particularly ones stating what *not* to do (don't use a racial epithet, don't hit a man except in self-defense, don't arrest without a warrant unless you have seen the misdemeanor), but no very useful—certainly no complete—set of instructions can be devised as to what the officer *should* do with, say, quarreling lovers. Defining a policy in such matters is difficult, not because the police have not given much thought to the matters or because they do not know how they should be handled, but because so much depends on the particular circumstances of time, place, event, and personality. Psychiatrists do not use "how to do it" manuals, and they have the advantage of dealing with people at leisure, over protracted periods of time, and in periods of relative calm.

Law-enforcement situations, once the intervention has occurred, can often be handled by rule; order maintenance situations usually cannot. Some rules may be prescribed for order maintenance situations but they will be either *ambiguous* (i.e., open to various interpretations and, especially, failing to specify the circumstances under which they are operative) or *equivocal* (i.e., combining inconsistent or competing values, presumably because the rule-maker cannot decide which value he prefers).

10. Thomas F. Adams, "Field Interrogation," *Police* (March–April 1963), p. 28, quoted in Skolnick, p. 46.

If the police administrator persists in formulating ambiguous or equivocal policies, the patrolman is likely to perceive them as "unrealistic" or irrelevant. "You can't go by what the book says" is one of the remarks an interviewer most often hears from a patrolman and that a rookie patrolman most often hears from the "old hands."[11] In this respect, too, the police administrator is in the same position as the school superintendent, the hospital director, or the secretary of state. But unlike these others, he must deal with the problem of wide discretion being exercised by subprofessionals who work alone (and thus cannot be constrained by professional norms) and in situations where because both the stakes are high and the environment apprehensive or hostile the potential for conflict and violence is great.

In response to this state of affairs, the police administrator tries to define his organization's mission as much as possible as one of law enforcement rather than of order maintenance (except for the special case of large public disorders, such as riots or demonstrations). For several reasons, he deals with the community at large in terms of the "crime problem," not the "order problem." First, crime, especially the crime which the FBI tabulates in its annual "Crime Index," is thought by the public to be "more serious" than disorder. In this, of course, the public may be quite mistaken. Many of the most serious crimes (murder, for example) cannot be prevented by the police no matter what they do and in any case the kind of killing that is most frightening—a respectable person being killed by a stranger—is relatively rare.[12] Also, many of the more common "Index" crimes (larceny or burglary) are less serious than some of the consequences of family quarrels or juvenile disturbances. Second, "enforcing the law" is less controversial than "maintaining order," though certain methods of enforcing laws against street crime (aggressive patrol, for example) are quite controversial. Third and most important, when "enforcing the law" the police can act within the legal fiction, as ministerial agents applying unambiguous, unequivocal rules to clear-cut cases.[13]

11. Arthur Niederhofer, *Behind the Shield* (Garden City: Doubleday & Co., 1967), pp. 44, 60.

12. For example, there were 205 homicides in Philadelphia in 1965, for a rate of about 10 per 100,000 population. Wolfgang's study of murder in that city (the findings of which are generally supported by FBI and other data) showed that between 1948 and 1952, only 12.2 percent of all murders were committed by a stranger; the rest were committed by relatives or acquaintances. (Marvin E. Wolfgang, *Patterns of Criminal Homicide* [Philadelphia: University of Pennsylvania Press, 1958]). This means that only slightly more than one person in every hundred thousand was murdered by a stranger and, since many of these were lower-income persons, the chances of a middle-class person being the victim of a homicidal stranger were even lower. For other crimes of violence, especially robbery, the chances of being victimized are much higher (in Philadelphia, perhaps 140 times greater) but, again, the great majority of victims are lower-income persons.

13. Except with respect to "unpopular" laws governing private conduct among consenting parties. Both police and public recognize that discretion is exercised with respect to "friendly" gambling, seduction, adultery, or the like.

Many a patrolman wishes his job could be in fact what it is in theory—enforcing the law. After answering a series of calls that require him to fill out forms, provide non-law-enforcement services, or handle domestic disturbances, a patrolman will frequently tell an interviewer that "this isn't *real* police work" and he will grumble about all the "dull" or "messy" jobs he is given. To him, "real" police work is catching "real" criminals—making a "good pinch" on a felon, preferably while the felony is in progress. But good pinches are rare, and when the patrolman uncovers a felony from which the suspect has fled, the case is turned over to the detectives who, if they find the culprit, get all the credit.[14] The patrolman may believe that if he were left alone to handle things his own way, he could improve on the law enforcement record of the department. On his own, he might spend his time watching a liquor store where there have been several armed robberies, questioning certain people in an area where a known criminal is believed to be hiding, keeping an eye on a car that doesn't belong in the neighborhood, or picking up information by casual conversation with people hanging around on street corners.

But to do these things the patrolman requires time, freedom, and the right to assert his authority. Time is scarce because so much of it is consumed by "service" or "information" calls that "don't amount to anything" and by whatever demands his superiors put on him to issue traffic tickets or pick up drunks. Freedom is limited by supervisors (sergeants, lieutenants, detectives) who arrive on the scene whenever anything "big" develops. And authority is hard to assert because, in the patrolman's eyes, so many citizens have lost their respect for the police, refuse to cooperate with them, and complain to the department about the least little thing.

Because of the law enforcement orientation of the administrator (or because of what he believes to be the orientation of the public), the department will be organized around law enforcement rather than order maintenance specialties. If order were the central mission of the department, there might be a "family disturbance squad," a "drunk and derelict squad," a "riot control squad," and a "juvenile squad"; law enforcement matters would be left to a "felony squad." Instead, there is a detective division organized (in the larger departments) into units specializing in homicide, burglary, auto theft, narcotics, vice, robbery, and the like. The undifferentiated patrol division gets everything else. Only juveniles tend to be treated by specialized units under both schemes, and this is partly because the law requires or encourages such specialization. The law enforcement orientation of most departments means that new specialized units are created for every offense about which the public expresses concern or for which some special technology is required. The patrolman, who once had a chance to perform

14. Niederhofer, p. 58.

some detective functions, sees his scope of activity steadily narrowed by specialization until what remains for him is clerical work, service work, and (of course) order maintenance.

Because most crimes cannot be solved and because a comprehensive policy for order maintenance is impossible to develop, the police administrator acquires, in addition to his law enforcement orientation, a *particularistic* concern for the behavior of his men. That is to say, what preoccupies him—other than the overall level of crime—is not how patrolmen *generally* behave but how they behave in a *particular case*. Police chiefs do not as a rule lose their jobs because crime rates go up; indeed, rising crime rates may make it easier for them to get more money and manpower from city councils. But they often get into trouble and sometimes lose their jobs because a particular officer takes a bribe, steals from a store, associates with a gangster, or abuses a citizen who is capable of doing something about it.

The administrator becomes attuned to complaints. What constitutes a "significant" citizen demand will of course vary from city to city. In some places, a political party will tell the police whom to take seriously and whom to ignore; in other places, organized community groups will amplify some demands and drown out others; in still other places, the police themselves will have to decide whose voices to heed and how to heed them. Whatever the filtering mechanism, the police administrator ignores at his peril those demands that are passed through. The typical demand is for *more* police protection—a patrolman to stand on a particular corner, a car to stop speeding on a certain street, a "crackdown" to curb teen-age rowdies or drunks sleeping on steps or thieves preying on liquor stores. Other demands are for services not strictly "police" in nature—taking people to the hospital, for example. Every department studied had more or less elaborate ways of making sure that the chief would not have to admit that, in response to a citizen call, nothing was done. Incoming telephone messages and outgoing radio dispatches are logged; in many larger departments, they are also tape recorded automatically. Each patrolman must keep a daily log or a memo book and, in important matters, file a report. Most such cases end inconclusively—there is little the police can do. The reporting system is not designed to insure that the problem will be solved (often it cannot be) but to protect the department against a charge that it "did nothing."

One police administrator was asked how he allocated patrolmen to the various beats. He said there were two systems: one called for leaving the same man in the same beat for a long period in order that he might become familiar with the neighborhood and its people; the other for rotating men around so as to minimize the time it would take the police to respond to a given call. Under the latter system, if one officer is busy with a call, another from an adjoining beat would fill in for him; on a busy night, the entire city may become one large beat, with everybody covering everywhere. Good arguments could be made for both systems, he said, but only the latter was used.

> If you want to develop a knowledge of the area, you would delay a call, unless it's an emergency, until the beat man concerned is free. [But] if you look around the country . . . you would find, I would guess, that 99 per cent of [the departments] are geared to response time because it's response time . . . that produces citizen complaints . . . Developing knowledge of your beat may in the long run be a better objective, but it's hard to measure and it's not reinforced by citizen complaints.

Welfare for Whom?

*Richard A. Cloward and
Frances Fox Piven*

THE GROWTH of the bureaucracies of the welfare state has meant the diminished influence of low-income people in public spheres. This has come about in two ways: first, the bureaucracies have intruded upon and altered processes of public decision so that low-income groups have fewer occasions for exercising influence and fewer effective means of doing so; and second, the bureaucracies have come to exert powerful and inhibiting controls on the low-income people who are their clients.

In response to the critics who point to these propensities of the public bureaucracies, several recent federal programs have made special provisions for citizen participation. It is our contention that such measures fail to offset the conditions which permit bureaucratic usurpation of power. Not only is citizen participation by and large a ritual conducted at the discretion of the public agencies, but it tends to become another vehicle for the extension of bureaucratic control.

Political leaders obviously must strive to accommodate groups that will provide them with the votes to win elections. To this extent, the flow of influence is upward. Programs for public benefits, however, are not simple electoral decisions to be made and reconsidered by a new polling of electoral sentiments. They are ensconced in bureaucratic complexes which are the domain of experts and professionals, masters of the special knowledge and techniques considered necessary to run the public agencies and administer the public benefits. Whole spheres of decision are made within these agencies, or in deference to their advice. The professional bureaucracies represent a new system of public action, only occasionally subject to electoral control.

The bureaucracies are exposed to direct control by broad constituencies only at periodic formal junctures: elections, budget hearings, or public referenda on appropriations. And at those points at which they are vulnerable, public agencies are themselves able to exert powerful counter-influence in electoral decisions. They bring to bear on

Reprinted from The Role of Government in Promoting Social Change: Proceedings of a Conference (*Murray Silberman, ed.; New York: Columbia School of Social Work, 1965*), *by permission of the authors.*

their own behalf the weight of their acknowledged (but obscure) expertise and their great organizational capability, as well as a host of supportive liaisons formed with political leaders and other organizations in the public and private sectors.

The low-income clientele whom the bureaucracies are charged to serve, to placate, and to contain are a special source of sensitivity to them. Any disruption or assertiveness on the part of clients, to the extent that it is visible, will put in jeopardy the support of groups and organizations that watch over the public agencies. The bureaucracies therefore manipulate the benefits and services on which their clients come to depend in such a way as to control their behavior. In this way, governmental benefit systems have become a powerful source of control over low-income people, used to ensure the conforming client behaviors which the bureaucracies require both for internal stability and in order to maintain electoral support. Through these processes, the bureaucracies come to serve as the filter of power, selectively accommodating the alert, the organized, and the influential, but containing the low-income groups which, by depending on public benefits, fall under bureaucratic control.

Our central proposition is that the public bureaucracies strive chiefly to maintain the conditions necessary for their stability and expansion. They are essentially neutral, aligned with neither class nor party, except as such alignments serve jurisdictional claims or determine the availability of necessary resources. They distribute public benefits in response to organizational requirements, adjusting the distribution to maintain and enlarge the flow of organizational resources. The influence of any group upon them ultimately depends on its role in this process—either contributing resources and supporting jurisdictional claims, or threatening the attainment of these objectives. Public agencies strive to maintain themselves with the least possible internal stress and change and therefore try to use their organizational capacity to limit both the occasion and the extent of their vulnerability to outside groups. Organizational equilibrium and enhancement are, in short, the compelling forces in bureaucratic action.

In this paper we will discuss three sets of tactics by which the bureaucracies pursue these goals: tactics of organizational consolidation and coalition; tactics of political accommodation; and tactics of low-income client control.

Tactics of Organizational Consolidation and Coalition

When by legislative mandate we establish an agency and charge it with the distribution of some public benefit, we vest in it powerful resources by which to influence electoral decisions, other organizations, and its own clientele. These resources consist of the technical expertise with which the agency is credited, the benefits it is charged with distributing, and control of its own elaborate organizational structures and processes. These resources are employed by the public agency and extend its jurisdiction in the following ways.[1]

Acknowledgment of expertise is a component of the political mandate initially granted to the public agency. It is inherent in political acceptance of technical definitions of problems and solutions, and also in political reliance on complex bureaucratic structures to carry out these solutions.

The expertise that is initially acknowledged by political mandate is itself used by public agencies to extend and consolidate the need for expertise. To acknowledge expertise in a given area is to grant authority. By its nature, expertise is obscure and its appropriate boundaries cannot easily be judged by the non-expert. It is therefore difficult to contain the propensities of expert-bureaucrats to elaborate still further the specialized knowledge and technique required in the recognition and solution of problems.

There seems to be a tendency, moreover, toward the coalition of expertise, both within and among organizations. Problems are interpreted not only as highly technical but as multifaceted; thus they require the application of a variety of expert skills. Consequently, the public bureaucracies come increasingly to be staffed by coalitions made up of experts from a variety of professions. A non-expert trying to appraise the claims of the professional bureaucrats has virtually no recourse once the importance of expertise is acknowledged, but to turn to other experts. A competitive pluralism among organizations and professions provides some counter to bureaucratic influence, not only by fostering alternative programs but by fostering alternative experts whose opinions may be a basis for evaluating and controlling given programs. Coalitions of experts, by contrast, constitute monopolies on expertise which foreclose alternative appraisals, confronting electoral leaders, the general public, special-interest constituents and competing organizations with a virtually impenetrable professional phalanx.

The Consolidation of Benefits

The professional bureaucracies are vested with control over the distribution of various benefits, presumably to serve some public purpose. Benefits are also inducements or sanctions and therefore are a resource for influence which the agencies control. We have referred to

1. We use "jurisdiction" to include the various ways in which an agency's operations are limited by legislative or administrative mandate. There are obviously any number of dimensions according to which jurisdiction can be defined: area, population (or "target group"), duration of operation, and a host of criteria limiting the kind of benefits or expertise allowed the agency and the manner or occasion of application.

the bureaucratic capacity to distribute benefits which, by serving the purposes of electoral leaders, may procure political support for the bureaucracies. We will subsequently show how the use of benefits as inducements or sanctions also ensures client behaviors which are consonant with the agency's larger political concerns.

In seeking to extend and entrench their jurisdictions, professional bureaucracies reveal a tendency to expand organizational control to a variety of benefits. The emphasis on "multifaceted" problems leads not only to the formation of coalitions of experts under one organizational structure but to the consolidation of a range of benefits within the same structure. The "multiproblem" family is thus said to require a variety of both experts and benefits; thus the web of experts and benefits becomes more intricate with the "saturation" and "comprehensive" approaches to a social problem.

This tendency is everywhere discernible in social welfare services. The schools include a variety of guidance counselors, psychologists, and physicians in their coalition of experts and they dispense the benefits over which these experts have jurisdiction. Public housing authorities sponsor a host of special programs and services involving many different professionals and many diverse facilities.[2] With each repeated discovery of the persistence of problems in service, the professionals make their bid for more experts and benefits, co-opting new and different varieties along the way.

The Joining of Benefits and Expertise

A third tactic of the professional bureaucracies is to link expertise to benefits so that benefits are conditional on the use of expertise. In this way the importance of benefits tends to accrue to expertise and conversely, the discretion inherent in expertise is employed in the distribution of benefits. We are told that public housing is of little value without social service; that welfare cash assistance must be accompanied by "rehabilitation" programs; that education requires therapeutic and guidance specialists.

The legislation of a benefit ordinarily implies political acknowledgment of a collective problem which the new benefit is intended to ameliorate. Distribution of the benefit is therefore important to the political collectivity. When that distribution is defined as requiring expert skills, expertise gains importance, and experts acquire influence

2. Most commentators see such expansion as reform. Writing about housing, Wolf Von Eckhardt notes approvingly that "Mrs. Marie C. McGuire, head of the public housing agencies, reports that there are 19,000 community service programs—such as scouting, health care, homemaking, arts and crafts, and literacy training—concentrated in public housing projects throughout the nation. These programs attract 2.6 million people a month . . . they are on the side of good community design, social awareness and social integration" ("The Department of Headaches," *New Republic*, November 6, 1965, p. 20).

in confrontations with electoral leaders and public groups. And, as will be shown later, a similar use is made of benefits in dealings with clients, for whom benefits are especially critical.

The linkage of expertise and benefits extends the discretion of the professional bureaucracies. Discretion is inherent in expertise; the mystique of esoteric knowledge and technique shields the bureaucratic management of benefits from easy review by political leaders or public groups and from the assertions of client claimants. In this connection, it is interesting to note that those now ensconced in the government bureaucracies—educators, social workers, vocational counselors—are members of the less authoritative and prestigeful professions. Bureaucratic control over benefits and bureaucratic obfuscation of practice lend these professions a complement of authority and prestige. They are thus able to claim critical functions in the public sector in their bid for full professional recognition.

. . .

These are some of the tactics by which professional bureaucracies extend and consolidate the resources with which they are initially endowed by public mandate. Concretely these tactics can be recognized in the characteristic efforts of the bureaucracies to "coordinate" different organizational and professional activities, to form "comprehensive" programs, and to unify organizational jurisdictions—always under the banner of increased effectiveness and efficiency.

Once they are charged with the distribution of a class of benefits, and once their technical and organizational capabilities are acknowledged, the bureaucracies employ these assets in subsequent confrontations with political leaders, electoral groups, and other organizations. Their control of technical and organizational expertise permits public agencies to remove themselves from scrutiny and at the same time to form for public view all-embracing but esoteric legitimations of their operations. Ultimately they succeed in these tactics, of course, only because the functions they perform by distributing benefits have come to be regarded as essential to the society.

Tactics of Political Accommodation

For their initial public mandate and for subsequent public allocations, the bureaucracies depend on political decisions. They require the support of political leaders. They also require at least the tacit support of those organized forces in the community that are able to watch over governmental policies and to threaten intervention in political decisions. The agencies must therefore bring their distinctive capabilities to bear in inducing supportive responses and discouraging action which might subvert agency jurisdiction.

Political Leaders

New welfare programs are typically legislated when political leaders are confronted with mounting concern among their electoral constituencies, often in response to some form of social disruption. With newspapers and civic groups in the lead, there is a call for action on some issue which has come to be defined as a public problem. The politician looks for a solution which will placate public concern without jostling any groups on whose support he relies. He tries to find a solution which will appear to be forceful and yet will avoid controversy. The general electorate should feel unduly offended in neither their purses nor their sentiments. Nor should the solution activate and engage any new groups in the fray by threatening their particular interests.

The task in any political proposal is to find that course of public action which minimizes conflict and reflects the broadest possible agreement among those alterted by the issue. Welfare problems bring into public focus the poor, the minorities, or the deviants, groups which are not themselves part of the middle-class political consensus and whose cause is as likely to arouse the wrath of some as it is the pity of others. To invent a solution to a welfare problem is not easy. It is vastly facilitated, however, by the professional bureaucracies.

What to the politician is a disturbance in his constituency and a threat to his majority becomes for the professional bureaucrat an opportunity to extend his public mandate, his resources, and his jurisdiction. The agencies are ready for liaison with the political leader. They bring to that liaison the capacity to convert political problems into technical problems. Issues which are rooted in group conflict, which have been framed as "who gets what," are transmuted into issues of method and framed in terms of a technology. That the technology is obscure is largely an advantage; the germinal political issue of "who gets what" is thereby also obscured. Moreover, the authority and prestige of expertise, and the faith in science and progress which it calls forth, are added to the political equation and made still more compelling by the complexity of the proposal. Indeed, the ultimate public action may be a program of research and demonstration to devise or advance the necessary technology.

Once a new program is initiated, the public agencies and their political allies continue in close symbiotic relationship. Politicians rely on professionals for information and recommendations regarding policies which are increasingly esoteric and complex. The bureaucracies, in filling this function, are in turn closely responsive to the concerns of their political patrons.

In this kind of partnership between political leaders and the public agencies, there is clearly gain to be had for both sides. The politicans are able to offer to their constituencies programs which inspire confidence and assuage conflict by their very technicism. The bureaucracies, for their part, are extended and made more powerful. This, too, is an advantage for politicians, for when public action is contained within bureaucratic spheres, it is less likely to produce politically disruptive change.

Peer Organizations

Government and private spheres have experienced a parallel growth of large, rationalized organizations. The bureaucracies are vulnerable to these organizational peers which have the resources to maintain a steady watch over the complex activities of public agencies, to decipher the implications of these activities, and to threaten to exercise comparable influence in electoral processes.

Large, rationalized organizations are able to keep abreast of the maze of actual and proposed legislation and procedures, and exploit many formal and informal occasions for negotiations and bargaining. They have the ability to generate public issues; they have access to the press and the political parties and can call on other organizations with whom they have regular liaisons. In addition, the technical capability of other organizations and their programatic cooperation are often valuable assets to the publice agencies.

Consequently, public agencies strive to form liaisons with organizational peers, public and private, accommodating them in ways designed to ensure their support or at least to avoid attack. A planning commission deals with other municipal agencies and with organizations of realtors and homeowners; a board of education deals with teachers' unions and parents' associations; and social welfare agencies deal with each other, with professional societies and philanthropic federations.

Tactics to Control Clients

The bureaucracies employ their distinctive capabilities to make certain of client acquiescence in agency actions, and to prevent any public display of assertiveness by low-income clients which may reflect on the agency and put in jeopardy the support of other community groups. As a consequence, the political influence of low-income people has been diminished by their involvement as clients of the agencies of the welfare state. Benefits are formed and distributed in ways which inhibit the development of client groups capable of collective action, which in turn limit the capacity of low-income people to exert influence in the electoral system. Ordinarily a group gains influence because it organizes for the collective application of its resources, whether the tactics it employs are negotiation, block voting, or disruption. The working classes were organized through the political machines in the residential areas where they lived and through the unions in the factories where they worked. They were able to improve their position in part by political influence through which they secured governmental regulation of economic institutions. Today's poor, by contrast, not only have little leverage as workers in economic spheres but have few organizational resources for influencing government and they are increasingly cast into a relationship with the institutions of the welfare state which entrenches and reinforces their powerlessness.

Benefits Which Discourage Interaction

Public benefits to the contemporary poor inhibit the emergence of collective low-income power in two ways. First, benefits are of a kind which isolate low-income people from major social roles, particularly occupational roles. Second, benefits are designed as individual benefits and the manner in which they are distributed discourages the aggregation of clients.

ISOLATIVE BENEFITS. In general, group interests are expressed politically by organizations developed around the major roles which people perform, and principally around economic roles. Regular participation in an institutional role makes possible the tacit organization of people—or rather of their contributions—as a concomitant of role performance. Thus political interest groups are typically associations of tradesmen or professionals or homeowners. Less obviously, civic associations seem to prosper when they are closely linked to economic roles.

Similarly, the power of organized labor depends on the role of workers in economic institutions, and on the factory as a context for building regular and stable union organization. As a consequence, most of the social welfare innovations of the last few decades have reinforced the occupational role, ensuring economic stability and a higher standard of living for people employed in preferred occupations. The welfare state has come to be the bulwark against downward mobility from the working class for the temporarily unemployed, the survivors of deceased workers, and the old. Through organization in occupational roles workers not only gained leverage in private enterprise but came, through the unions, to exert influence in securing various government benefits for the working classes.

The client categories by which public bureaucracies define eligibility for benefits, however, are not coterminous with regular role categories in the social structure. Rather, these categories define people by "non roles": clients are school dropouts, broken families, or unemployables. Eligibility for benefits is thus established by inability to gain access to or to maintain educational roles, occupational roles, family roles, and the like. Consequently, people receiving benefits cannot associate with their status as clients any set of common rights and obligations derived from other major social roles. Nor are people likely to form groups as clients when to do so is to collectively acknowledge and label themselves by the role failure which the client status represents. Finally, and perhaps most important, benefits of this kind, by isolating people from major social roles, also isolate them from major institutional spheres, from the mainstream of social and economic life. Clients do not gain the influence which can be derived from regular participation in major institutions. They remain separated from the leverage inherent in regular role performance and without the opportunity for organizing that leverage which an institutional context provides.

INDIVIDUAL BENEFITS.   Another important characteristic of benefits to the poor is that they apply to individuals rather than to groups and so constitute no inducement for the formation of groups. Nor does the manner in which benefits are distributed tend to aggregate people, a means by which latent incentives for organization might be activated. The right to bargain collectively, for example, was a benefit *to an organization* and therefore an inducement to organize, provided by legislation to those workers who were not yet unionized. No comparable inducement flows out of the benefits provided to the contemporary poor.

At least embryonic organizations must exist before influence can be directed to secure benefits which nurture organizations. The emerging labor movement produced a leadership that was in a position to recognize organizational concerns and to press management and government for the benefits which enhanced the unions as organizations. By contrast, the contemporary poor are disorganized. What influence they have in electoral processes is not exerted for organizing benefits. The working classes were already partially unionized when they pressed for legislation giving them the right to bargain collectively; so were the Negroes of the South when they demanded legislation empowering them to vote. For the most part, today's poor are atomized. Aggregate action, when it occurs, takes form as waves of unrest and disruption—as in the recent uprisings in the ghettos of the North—from which no leadership comes forth. The poor are placated with individual benefits and, by receiving them, remain unorganized.

Tactics to Counter Collective Action

Low-income groups occasionally emerge in the context of public benefit systems. In some instances benefits simply cannot be managed by individualized distribution (e.g., education and large-scale housing); in other instances bureaucratic action unites people who are already loosely affiliated by imposing on them a common deprivation, uncompensated by benefits (e.g., slum clearance). Such low-income groups are not likely to join the ranks of organized constituents with whom the bureaucracies form accommodating relations. Bureaucratic responsiveness to low-income groups incurs the risk of arousing hostile forces in the community and of eventually undermining electoral support for the bureaucracies. This risk has to do not only with the substance of these responses to the low-income groups but with the very fact of engaging in reciprocal relations with the poor.[3] Low-income groups can themselves offer the bureaucracies little significant support in a wider community context. Moreover, the bureaucracies have certain capabilities for containing and directing such groups which provide an alternative to accommodation.

Containment and direction are in fact, the strategy which the bureaucracies typically employ in response to low-income groups which impinge upon them. For this strategy they are uniquely equipped by their capacity to manipulate information and benefits. First, the bureaucracies can withhold or dispense information about their own procedures which low-income groups require in order to formulate any challenge to bureaucratic action. This is in part a consequence of the highly complex and technical maze of bureaucratic regulation and practice. It also has to do with the fact that most bureaucratic activity is not visible from the vantage point of clients, and even less so from the vantage point of low-income protest groups, which are outside the system entirely. Complexity and obscurity are, as we have noted, an asset in many contests in which bureaucracies strive for influence. Bureaucrats are not likely to take the initiative in so structuring and advertising their actions as to encourage surveillance by anyone, and especially not by low-income groups whose claims will generate controversy or strain their supportive liaisons.

The second major tactic which bureaucracies employ in controlling and directing low-income groups is the manipulation of benefits. When such groups are formed among clients, the bureaucracies are able to offer peripheral benefits as incentives for conformity and to threaten the withdrawal or curtailment of essential benefits as punishment for dissent.

Thus, housing programs seem occasionally to provide a context for the formation of groups among low-income people. In the public housing program, for example, low-income people were necessarily aggregated in the course of receiving benefits simply because housing was provided in large projects. The project structure was dictated by other considerations having to do with administrative efficiency and political acceptability (Note the recent alarm over the rent-supplement proposal, which might have subsidized low-income tenants to live

3. See Georg Simmel's essay on "The Poor" (*Social Problems,* Fall 1965, pp. 118–140) for a dilineation of the sociological bases for the exclusion of the poor from participation in the administration of public assistance.

in middle-class areas). Not long after World War II, and rather early in its bureaucratic life, the New York Public Housing Authority was confronted with militant tenant groups in several of its projects. Not only were these groups taking active positions on public-housing matters, but they appeared to have a politically radical character of some notoriety. The Housing Authority reacted by prohibiting the use of project facilities by tenant organizations.

Not only the withdrawal of benefits, but also the proffering of benefits can work to weaken low-income groups. This is, of course, a more likely tactic when the bureaucracies confront groups of people who are not yet beneficiaries. When tenants in some of the slum buildings of New York organized "no heat, no hot water" protests, the housing agencies responded by selectively redressing only the most vigorous tenant complaints. With much publicity, the agencies seemed to bring to bear their total armory of legal enforcement and rehabilitation aids, but only on a few star buildings. Tenant leadership was turned aside and the protests were deflated, but the grievances of most slum dwellers remained unanswered.

Public action in urban renewal has occasioned some of the most stubborn and aggressive low-income group protests of recent years. These groups were composed of residents in areas scheduled for renewal. Confronted with the stress of upheaval, the loss of neighborhood, and the prospect of greatly increased rentals,[4] these people were the hardest hit by the costs of renewal but were not to receive the benefits provided by the new developments. They were people already together in neighborhoods, united by a common deprivation or threat of deprivation to the neighborhood, and in no significant way appeased by any benefits. The new developments included chiefly high-rental housing; slum clearance was no boon to slum dwellers for whom it meant mainly dislocation.

The adamancy of these local protest groups often threatened to disrupt urban-renewal projects. The agencies countered with programs for "community participation," consisting largely in the careful advertisement of renewal plans to resident groups and the active initiation of local leaders at an early stage in order to "educate" and win them to the plans. Thus programs for directed community participation were developed to offset the spontaneous, but disruptive, participation of local protest groups. At the same time, many of the facts of renewal (e.g., the numbers to be displaced and the relocation alternatives available) continued to be concealed and sometimes appeared to be simply fabricated.

4. For review of problems in relocation see Chester Hartman, "The Housing of Relocated Families," *Journal of the American Institute of Planners,* November 1964, pp. 266–286.

Tactics of Political Socialization

Governmental benefit systems are also structures for political socialization.[5] Low-income people are drawn into these systems as recipients. They are attracted by the promise of benefits, and once in the system, they remain tied to it by the benefits they receive. These benefits are typically not vested by law or conferred as a matter of unambiguous right; they are profferred at the discretion of the professional bureaucracy. They can be employed as threats and rewards to influence client attitudes and ensure conforming client behavior. Access to resources which people require—money, housing, education— is made conditional on acceptable behavior, including often acquiescence to professional counseling or therapy. The threatened denial of essential benefits is a powerful sanction to control client behavior.

CONDITIONAL BENEFITS. All public bureaucracies require some measure of discretion in the distribution of benefits, for no mandates can be so precise and inclusive as to provide firm guidelines for all the varied circumstances presented for decisions. All bureaucracies tend to expand that discretion by elaborating technical expertise and organizational complexity. When recipients of a program are primarily low-income people, several circumstances combine to support the further enlargement of bureaucratic discretion.

The initial establishment of a public agency is a consequence of a collective political decision in which low-income people are not likely to have been very forceful, and surely not forceful as organized political actors. The framing of statutes establishing public benefits for low-income people typically reflects the attitudes of other groups which *are* effective political proponents. These include the middle-class groups whose attitudes dominate political consensus, the bureaucracies, and the professional associations linked to the bureaucracies. Such proponents prefer to vest discretion in the public functionaries who deal with the poor rather than to establish these benefits as a right, to which the poor are entitled.[6]

The dominant view of the poor among the American middle class is that they are defective, morally as well as in other ways, and are likely to take advantage of public beneficence. And public agency personnel feel themselves constrained by the constant threat of arousing powerful community forces to employ criteria in defining eligibility

5. For a general discussion of the political power inherent in public benefits see Charles Reich, "The New Property," *Yale Law Review*, Vol. 73, No. 5, April 1964.

6. The New York City Public Housing Authority, for example, is not governed by formulated regulations in selecting tenants. Nor have successive reforms impelled by professional and civic organizations moved in this direction. Instead, a maze of criteria establishing priorities and ineligibility has been developed, to be applied largely at the discretion of the agency functionaries.

for benefits which go beyond objective economic need and take account of widely held invidious definitions of the poor. The New York City Welfare Department, for example, enjoins its investigators to discourage malingering, reminding them in its manual that "the denial or withdrawal of assistance is as constructive a factor as the granting of assistance, both to the client and to the community."

The threat of community opposition is real, as attested by the recurrent attacks upon welfare departments and public housing authorities for allegedly fostering immorality and degeneracy among their clients. Accordingly, the administrators of these agencies employ the discretion allowed to them in an array of investigatory and policing practices intended to ensure that the recipients or potential recipients of benefits will be publicly regarded as "worthy" of the sums and services dispensed to them. Public housing functionaries maintain surveillance over the morals of their tenants, employing their own police forces and their own quasi-judicial procedures, made potent by the threat of eviction and virtually unrestrained by laws or regulations protecting the rights of tenants. In New York City, the project managers have even developed a system of tenant "fines" which are imposed for all manner of behavior which the manager regards as bad tenancy. Similarly, public welfare departments invest enormous organizational energy in the initial determination of a client's worthiness and eligibility for the dole. Once approved, the recipient is the object of constant surveillance to make sure he continues to meet these conditions. The most striking example of such practice is the "post-mid-night raid" to which mothers receiving ADC grants are subjected in order to catch by surprise a man who may be on the premises.

The ambiguity surrounding the nature of client rights pertains also to procedures for appeal from agency decisions. It is not clear with many benefits whether an aggrieved person has the right to do anything more than complain. By and large, appeals procedures are not defined in legislation. With appeals, as with the initial dispensing of benefits, bureaucratic discretion over low-income clients is supported because it permits practices which accommodate to the invidious attitudes toward the poor held by dominant groups in the community.

The professionals who staff the bureaucracies are a second factor in reinforcing bureaucratic discretion over clients. Professionals generally tend to view the problems of low-income people as resulting from defects in socialization. Remedies for these defects are said to require exposure to professional services, and the discretion inherent in professional services is often employed to make judgments about the dispensing of benefits on which low-income people depend.

The third circumstance which expands bureaucratic discretion in dealing with clients is the general tendency of the bureaucracies to coordinate and consolidate their functions. In an earlier era of private charity, the poor could solicit cash relief or other benefits from one or another private agency, never entirely and finally subject to the judgment of any one. Now they confront one comprehensive welfare bureaucracy from whose decision they have no recourse. Even private agencies have developed mechanisms for maintaining broad supervision of their clientele. The Social Service Exchange, for example, is a device for comprehensive surveillance, designed in part to identify low-income people who shop around for services.

Proposals for bureaucratic reform seem inevitably to involve reorganization to establish more comprehensive jurisdiction over one category of clients or another, and to call for extension of the professionalization of staff and services. Through years of controversy regarding housing-code enforcement practices in New York City, reformers have repeatedly recommended consolidation of all housing agencies. Whether consolidation will in fact improve the condition of the low-income plaintiff remains questionable. Conflicting and overlapping jurisdictions may be administratively inefficient, but they give the low-income tenant some alternative course of action when, as has frequently been the case, his complaint is not heeded by a given agency. Similarly, the improvement of bureaucratic services means greater professionalization of staff and the extension of professional services and discretion. For example, in reform of criminal practices it is argued that probation officers should be social workers, surveillance should be therapeutic, and therapeutic evaluations should be the basis for criminal sentencing.

That the discretion derived from systems of conditional benefits is a source of enormous power over low-income people is self-evident. For people on public welfare, their very livelihood, however meager, is at stake; for the public-housing tenant it may be his only chance for a decent dwelling; to the family of the child confronted with the possibility of school suspension it is the only chance to give their offspring an education and indeed a future livelihood. There are few institutionalized safeguards against the exercise of discretion by government agencies which distribute conditional benefits to the poor. The laws which establish these benefits are vague and administrative procedures are complex and ambiguous.

POLITICAL DESOCIALIZATION.   Exposure to bureaucratic discretion leads to political desocialization. First, bureaucratic procedures reflect the premise that the poor have few rights. Recipients of benefits are not apprized of procedures but are continually confronted with apparently arbitrary actions. Bureaucratic procedures are also punitive, reflecting the premise that the poor are unworthy and the constant fear that the client will lapse into sloth and chicanery. Such procedures in fact make people into what they are already said to be, for when their rights are ignored, men do indeed live by their wits, evading what is capricious and arbitrary or lapsing into apathy. Thus the clients of the welfare state come to live in fear, moving to control their fate not by political action, but by evasion and ultimately by acquiescence. In this way, welfare programs debilitate and demoralize; the attitudes and ways of life into which clients are forced inhibit their effective participation in even ordinary social roles and surely inhibit political activism.

Secondly, clients are often socialized to particular forms of political participation through the exposure to professional services which receiving benefits entails. Professional service is an opportunity for educating clients in political beliefs and modes of political participation that are consonant with the views of the middle-class majority.[7]

For example, public-housing tenants who use recreational facilities are required to submit to supervision by agents of the housing authority and recreation becomes an occasion for political education. In the case described earlier, the New York Public Housing Authority continued to suffer publicly after eliminating tenant organizations, not so much for the radicalism of tenants as for their ostensibly antisocial behavior. The right-wing press launched periodic exposes of crime, delinquency, and abuse of property in the projects. In time, the Authority developed a more sophisticated strategy than simple fiat for the containment of tenants: it undertook to form its own tenant organizations, linking these to various community services and dominating them through staff organizers. Tenants were encouraged to participate in recreational and self-help programs such as project beautification, consumer education, and household skills,[8] and were steered away from actions troublesome to the Authority.

Whether the professional bureaucrat is a caseworker, a guidance counselor, an educator, a recreational expert, or a community organizer, and whether the program is a youth employment agency or a "Headstart" operation, the professional is the agent of socialization, and the program is the vehicle for socialization, as to the legitimacy of existing political arrangements and the propriety of middle-class political styles. The consequences of this socialization are clear. Established institutional arrangements are endorsed, their democratic character is asserted, and middle-class styles of formalized participation and negotiation are inculcated. These beliefs leave no role for the conflict and protest which often characterize lower-class activism; indeed, they even make conflict and protest immoral. But today's unorganized poor have few

7. The use of professional service as a means of control is by no means limited to government bureaucracies. The industrial counseling profession, for example, seems to owe its genesis to the functions it serves for management in allaying worker discontent, a use of counseling first made evident in the Mayo studies.

8. One of the most notorious public-housing projects in the country, the Pruitt-Igoe project in St. Louis, is now undergoing major rehabilitation and reform. In this, the Housing Authority, "aware that fiscal rehabilitation may only provide 'something else to break' has a series of programs underway to involve the tenant in the process" (James Bailey, "The Case History of a Failure," *Architectural Forum*, December 1965).

of the resources needed for middle-class styles of participation and negotiation. They have little to bargain with and so are partners to no one's negotiations. And by becoming educated in the beliefs and strategies of action appropriate only for groups in higher economic strata, they are rendered ineffective.

To summarize, we see no evidence that government's involvement of the poor will generate a force for social change by nurturing their political capabilities or by activating them with the promise of benefits. Rather, governmental programs for the poor are likely to diminish whatever collective political vitality the poor still exhibit.

Future prospects for social change will be increasingly shaped by the expansionist forces of the public bureaucracies. How low-income people fare through this expansion will depend on the extent and kinds of benefits distributed by the bureaucracies. These benefits have been formed chiefly in accommodation to the middle-class consensus on which the bureaucracies depend for support. At the same time, public benefits have been designed to placate unrest among the poor and to deflect any political articulation of this unrest.

Under these conditions, the best the poor can expect are programs such as those generated by the Office of Economic Opportunity programs, that impart to them the skills through which they may be integrated into occupational roles. At worst, they will get more programs such as public assistance which further isolate them while controlling them—from major social roles in the society. If future programs do successfully impart competitive skills, the bureaucracies, in pursuing their own enhancement, may thereby succeed in raising many low-income people into the middle class. In this way the clients of the bureaucracy can one by one join the middle-class political majority and public benefits can indeed be said to increase their political influence. It will have done so, however, at the price of diminishing the ranks and therefore the influence of those who are still in the lower class. Thus the social change accomplished by bureaucratic expansion will not challenge the middle-class consensus as to appropriate forms of political participation and will not enlarge the capacity of the dispossessed to influence their environment. In particular, it will not enlarge the capacity of the poor to influence the public bureaucracies upon which they depend. This is the path marked out by public benefit systems which act to reinforce the existing alignment of influence.

Milwaukee's National Media Riot

H. R. Wilde

ON SUNDAY, July 30th, 1967, Milwaukee, a city known for its peaceful small town atmosphere, its provincialism, and its Germanic heritage of honest government and good beer, suddenly erupted into violence. At about nine at night crowds of Negro youths gathered following some church dances in the city's Negro "core." All at once boys and young men began breaking store windows, throwing bottles at passing cars, and jeering at police who rushed into the area. Apparently with nothing but vandalism in mind, they set dozens of small fires, almost all of them in vacant buildings. They broke into stores, but seldom stopped to loot them. It was not at all clear whether or in what sense the outbreak was "racial," for the youths knocked out windows in the Urban League headquarters, the Black Muslim Temple, and twelve storefront Negro churches.

Police Chief Harold Brier at first assured Mayor Henry W. Maier that his men could handle the disturbance. At 2 a.m., when he got word that several of his men had been shot by a "sniper," he changed his mind; on the chief's advice the mayor at once declared a state of emergency and asked the governor to send in the national guard. By this time it had begun to rain and the rampage by youths was over. The guard arrived, however, 4800 strong, and the next day the mayor put the whole city under a strict curfew. The suburbs followed his lead and for 24 hours not a store, factory, or office was open anywhere in the metropolitan area. For three days there were isolated incidents—a few fires, some looting, and some sniping—on the third day (Wednesday) the police shot and killed an 18-year-old college student who was alleged to be looting. After that the incidents soon ceased. The mayor tapered the curfew off over a period of a week and nine days after its arrival the guard was withdrawn.

Superficially, it looked as if Milwaukee was "another Detroit." That, certainly, was the theory of the mayor, who behaved as if he expected the whole metropolitan area to go up in flames; of the newspapers, the headlines of which screamed "RIOT;" and of Father James Groppi, the militant civil rights leader, who announced "this is not a riot—it's a revolt." As it turned out the facts did not really justify such language.

682

Fewer than 300 persons participated in the disorders Sunday night, the police chief reported, and it was then that the action was heaviest. In the course of nine days 1,740 persons were arrested, but most of them were charged with nothing worse than violation of the curfew. Three people were killed and a dozen injured, but two of the deaths were caused by the police (the looter was one; the other was an old woman hit in her room by a stray bullet) and the third death (that of a policeman) and most of the serious injuries (also of policemen) were inflicted by one man, probably deranged, who fired a blast from his house with a shot-gun. One hundred and twenty-nine fires were set, the fire chief said, but the total damage from the fires was estimated at only $116,262. The main money cost of the riot was in extra pay for police and firemen and, especially, in lost retail sales and lowered factory production and employment. These costs resulted from the protracted curfew rather than from the riot itself.

It is hard to doubt that the mayor did the right thing in promptly calling out the guard. It was his duty to protect the city from violence, whether that of teenagers or others. (Former Mayor Frank Zeidler, a vigorous critic of the mayor, said that he too would have called out the guard.) What *is* surprising, however, is that the mayor, the newspapers, Father Groppi, and everyone else of importance in the city perceived the affair not as a youth rampage or even a riot but as a RIOT. Milwaukee seemed to mistake itself for Detroit, Newark, or Watts. In fact, its Negro district was small (Negroes constituted about 12 percent of the city's population) and conservative (about 40 percent of the families owned their own homes). Anyone who knew anything about the "core" knew that the people who lived there—even the few militants among them—were more likely to sing "We Shall Overcome" along with the Reverend Martin Luther King, Jr., than to burn the city down. But the mayor and indeed the city as a whole talked and acted as if this was a real possibility. This general mis-perception of the situation requires explanation.

If one asks why everyone in Milwaukee from the mayor to the man on the street perceived a youth rampage as a RIOT the obvious answer is that real riots in other cities had dominated the news for many weeks causing Milwaukee to wonder if what had happened in the other cities might not happen there, too. (Indeed, the very day Milwaukee's riot broke out the *Journal* carried a front-page article comparing conditions in Detroit, where there had just been a riot, to those in Milwaukee.) If one pushes the question farther back, asking why the city was so suggestible, the answer is to be found in changes of a fundamental sort that have been going on for some time. A decade or so ago Milwaukeeans were, so to speak, face to face with local reality; at that time they would have seen a rampage of youths as just that, not as a riot and still less as a RIOT. Now they see the city and its life not directly but through a glass darkly—the glass being a television tube and the images that it projects being supplied by a few people whose perceptions, insofar as they are of reality at all, are of the reality of the largest cities, above all New York. In short, Milwaukee's political system has in recent years become oriented to the national media and has come to take its cues from them rather than from the facts of life in the city. The city's perception of the rampage as a RIOT is an example of this general phenomenon.

The change in the city's political style first became apparent with the election of Mayor Maier. In 1960 he became the city's first "national media mayor"—the first mayor, that is, to see the city in terms of concepts supplied by the national media, to communicate with it via the national media, and to employ the rhetoric of the national media. His 36 predecessors had all been locals; for two generations Milwaukee had been governed by homespun German Socialists who seemed to hardly know that the rest of the country existed. In those days, a mayor's staff reflected the city's ethnic and neighborhood composition; they had to be locals because their job was to deal with the locals who constituted the interest groups and the electorate. In the old days a mayor knew every block of the city and he depended on face-to-face relations to solve problems and win elections. City Hall was where the buck stopped; there was no use looking to Washington for a way out or an excuse. The result, of course, was conservative government. Projects were not launched unless it was clear that the local people wanted them—wanted them enough to pay for them.

Maier brought a new style to City Hall. He had a master's degree from the University of Wisconsin and he not only read books but wrote them (his *Challenge to the Cities* was published by Random House in 1966). To his predecessors the city was a patchwork of neighborhoods and interest groups that knew what they wanted—namely, honest and economical administration. To him it was three-quarters of a million people beset by the nationally advertised complex of problems known to the media as "the urban crisis" and accordingly requiring the services of experts like himself. As he explained in his book (sub-titled *An Approach to a Theory of Urban Leadership*):

> A key figure in the new world of urbanism is the mayor or chief executive of the large city. He occupies the only position that can provide overall leadership to cope with the demands of the modern urban policy. But his position is not a simple one. He faces multiple pressures and problems as complex as our society. His life is complicated by the fact that he must be one part institutional leader, one part political leader, one part educator, one part scapegoat, and some other part for whatever purpose his community wishes to use him. Of his various roles, however, that of institutional leader stands out as basic and crucial.

Mayor Maier was in close touch with the national centers of opinion and action in urban affairs. He had been a member of the President's Committee on Youth Employment, chairman of the advisory committee of the United States Conference of Mayors, and president of the National League of Cities, and when his book appeared the Under Secretary of HUD took him to the White House to present a copy to President Johnson. Because of all this national reputation and professionalism, Milwaukee stood somewhat in awe of its mayor. The press, the civic leaders, and even the aldermen were all oriented—more at least than their predecessors had been—to the national media and therefore took such signs of national repute very seriously.

The mayor's style was apparent in the way he handled the riot. He began preparing for it fifteen months before it occurred by working out elaborate contingency plans. Among other things, he installed a "hot line" to the Governor's office, worked out the legal and other preliminaries to imposing a curfew, and established a procedure for calling out the National Guard on very short notice. These contingency plans were a source of great pride to him and his associates, and during the second day of the riot he released them to the press to show how well the city government had prepared for what happened. A week before the riot, planning had gone forward feverishly. The mayor had cancelled plans to go east to a convention, ostensibly because he wanted to work on a "tax crusade" project, but actually because he expected a riot at any time. The police and fire departments went on the alert and the hospitals made ready extra emergency facilities. While he waited for the riot to occur he drafted a long statement for use after it was over. The statement said, among other things, that the American metropolis could have no future until the walls separating the central city from the suburbs were torn down and it called on Congress to help tear them down. Both the tone and the substance of the statement were what one would expect of a national expert on urban affairs rather than of a mayor addressing his fellow citizens in an emergency,

> This time of concern should be a time of commitment to the fight for the central city . . . a time for the long overdue massive infusion of federal and state funds needed to translate that concern into action which will treat and cure the hard core economic and social ills which blight not only the life of the central city but also the fabric of American society.

Although the mayor used portions of his statement in a message addressed to the city the morning after the rampage, it was written mainly for use as an advertisement in the *New York Times*, where it appeared on March 3. Asked why it was placed in the *Times*, the mayor's principal assistant answered,

precedented 90 percent of the vote, although he had rested on his laurels as a metropolitan statesman without campaigning at all.

Mayor Maier's theory of urban leadership has been thoroughly vindicated in Milwaukee. Those who before the riot were only groping for a national media strategy have learned from the mayor's example and are becoming adept at his style of leadership. Father Groppi, the militant civil rights leader, for example, has led daily demonstration-marches and has organized boycotts that have attracted national attention. Negro teenagers are, of course, looking forward to putting Milwaukee on the map again and to the television coverage that they may expect. Even conservative Negroes are solemnly telling whites that "there's another one coming, and it's going to be a REAL RIOT." In the future, obviously, there will be at least two sides playing the RIOT game. It is safe to say that Milwaukee will never settle back to the old style of politics which involved discussion and bargaining about concrete local issues. From now on matters will be decided by confrontations of sides, all getting their cues from Washington, New York, Los Angeles and all addressing the others via the national media. In this new style of politics there will probably be less room for facts, reason, or compromise and none at all for behind-the-scenes negotiation. Milwaukee, it seems, has ceased to be the city of good beer and honest government and has become "Any Big City, U.S.A."

Glossary

Annexation (See Metropolitan Organization)

Australian Ballot (See Ballot)

Ballot

A ballot is a list of candidates for office, on which the voter makes his choices, either by marking a piece of paper or by pulling the levers of a voting machine. In the early years of the United States, officials were generally elected by a voice vote, a show of hands, or by the deposit of small objects such as beads in urns. This system was gradually replaced by the use of printed ballots, which were prepared and distributed to voters by individual candidates or political parties. Secrecy was virtually impossible, for party ballots were readily distinguishable by their color, size, or symbols. Intimidation, bribery, and fraud were relatively easy. These abuses occurred particularly in cities, where the vote of large immigrant groups could easily be manipulated by party leaders.

The Australian ballot was designed to end these abuses. Originated in Australia in 1858 and introduced in the United States in 1888, the Australian ballot was printed at government expense, distributed at polling places by officials of the government, and marked in secret by voters. Candidates of both parties were listed on it. All states use it today, although Georgia makes its use optional with the counties.

The Australian ballot reduced fraud but did not eliminate it. Though preparation and distribution of the ballots was placed under public control, the "public" officials who administer elections have usually been the choices of political parties, for which electoral jobs constitute a form of petty patronage. Party organizations that obtain control of election machinery can find ways of manipulating the vote, even a secret vote. Spoilage of ballots is one possible technique. Deliberately inaccurate reporting of returns is another.

The length of the ballot has been an issue in municipal politics. Voters are often asked to decide on a long list of candidates and propositions, especially under the weak mayor form. Critics of the long ("bedsheet") ballot have claimed that if voters made fewer choices, their choices would be better informed. Specifically, short-ballot advocates have argued (1) that only policy-making officials should be elected, and (2) that few offices should be filled at any one time.

Partly as a by-product of the short-ballot movement, which flourished in the early 1900's, many city councils were reduced in size, and city elections were timed not to coincide with national and state elections.

Borough

A borough is a type of municipal corporation larger than a village but smaller than a city. Only four states—Connecticut, New Jersey, Pennsylvania, and Minnesota—include boroughs.

Boss

A boss is the leader of a political machine. From the Civil War until the Second World War, the boss system flourished in most large and many small United States cities. In its classic form, boss rule concentrated control over city government in a hierarchical organization of professional politicians —the machine—which placed its candidates in public office, filled city departments with its appointees, and controlled the actions of the council, and municipal courts and departments, including the police department.

Bosses were criticized for exercising power not legally theirs and for being corrupt and indifferent to the public interest. But even if these criticisms were justified (as in many cases they undoubtedly were), they do not adequately describe the distinguishing characteristics of the machine. The boss system was also significant as (1) a vehicle for the centralization of power in city government, (2) a means of providing social services to lower-class, mostly immigrant groups, and (3) an organization for the material maintenance of its members. *(See the introduction and readings in Section III.)*

Budget

A city budget is an annual statement of planned revenues and expenditures. In most cities it is prepared by a finance department under supervision of the mayor or city manager. In some it is prepared by an independently elected controller. In a few it is prepared by a committee of the council.

Early in this century, before widespread adoption of the strong-mayor form of government, the budget was generally prepared by the city council or by an independent board of estimate. But as strong municipal executives developed, they acquired additional powers of budget control. The role of the council is now typically confined to holding public hearings on the budget, perhaps amending it, and adopting it through an appropriation ordinance. The extent of the council's power to amend the budget varies from city to city; some charters permit the council to reduce items in the mayor's budget but not to increase them or add new items.

(See also Finance, City.)

Caucus

A caucus is an informal meeting at which candidates for public or party office are nominated. In the early history of the United States, caucuses were the most common nominating procedure. With the growth of urban populations, however, the caucus gave way to the convention, a more formal gathering better suited to making nominations for large, populous jurisdictions. By the end of the nineteenth century, party candidates for city office were generally nominated in city-wide conventions, and those for state office in state-wide conventions. Delegates to the city conventions were chosen in meetings at the precinct or ward level. Sometimes called caucuses, these meetings were also termed primaries. All party members were entitled to attend, but in practice the meetings were controlled by party leaders—the "machine."

During the early 1900's the convention system of nomination was replaced by a system of "direct" primaries, under which party members could vote directly on contestants for nomination rather than indirectly through convention delegates. But although the direct primary is now predominant in the United States, not all candidates for city office are nominated in party primaries. In nonpartisan cities, candidates obtain nomination by filing petitions signed by some specified number of voters. Ordinarily a nonpartisan primary is held, to pick two candidates for each office to oppose each other in the general election. But party committees continue to exist at the ward and district levels in many cities, and, even where elections are formally nonpartisan, these may "caucus" to endorse candidates or pick convention delegates in those states that still hold party conventions as well as direct primaries.

Charter, City

The charter of a city is its fundamental law, given by the state. The charter fixes the form of city government, defines the city's powers and the area of its jurisdiction, and describes the manner in which its powers may be exercised. Often the charter is not a single document, but includes all constitutional provisions, legislative acts, and judicial opinions that affect the structure and powers of the city.

City

"A comprehensive definition of a city," William B. Munro wrote in 1930, "must indicate that it is a social, political, legal and economic unit all rolled into one. It is a concentrated body of population possessing some significant social characteristics, chartered as a municipal corporation, having its own system of local government, carrying on multifarious economic enterprises and pursuing an elaborate program of social adjustment and amelioration." (*Encyclopaedia of the Social Sciences*)

City Manager (See Forms of City Government)

Civil Service (See Merit System)

Commission Plan (See Forms of City Government)

Consolidation, City and County (See Metropolitan Organization)

Corporation, Municipal

In law the city is a municipal corporation created by the state for the purpose of local government. Like any other corporation, public or private, it is invested with an artificial personality, may own property, make contracts, sue and be sued, and normally exists in perpetuity. But unlike a private corporation, the municipal corporation may exercise only such powers as are authorized under state law, and it may act only for a public purpose. Furthermore, its powers may be altered or revoked at will by the state legislature within limits imposed by state constitutions. The village and borough are also municipal corporations.

(*See also* Charter, City, *and* Dillon's Rule.)

Council, City

The council is the legislative organ of city government. Generally, it possesses all powers granted to the city that are not specifically vested elsewhere. This means that the council enacts municipal codes (ordinances) on crime, sanitation, traffic and streets, building and housing standards, zoning, taxation and appropriations, regulation of public utilities, organization of city departments, and other matters of local concern. The council also has some administrative duties, which vary greatly depending on the form of government. Under the council-manager form the council has sole responsibility for supervising administration, which is in the hands of the manager; under the weak-mayor form, the council has extensive responsibility for the performance of administration; under the strong-mayor form, its interest in administration is largely confined to occasional inquiry into the functioning of city departments.

In the early years of the United States the council was the most important organ of municipal government, but its power and prestige have steadily declined and it is now greatly overshadowed in cities where there is a strong mayor. The council has also decreased in size. Many councils were bicameral throughout much of the nineteenth century; today, all but a few are unicameral. They range in size from three to Chicago's fifty, but the most common size is nine, even in cities with a population of over 500,000.

Accompanying the decrease of the council's size has been a trend toward election at-large rather than on the basis of wards. In 1958 a sizable majority of cities under 500,000 elected councilmen at large on a non-partisan ballot.

The small at-large council, a favorite of reformers, is said to serve better the interests of the whole city, to attract better-quality candidates, and to be immune to pressures of a ward-based machine. Critics point out that it discriminates against minorities, increases the cost of councilmanic campaigns (thereby restricting candidates to high-status groups), lengthens the ballot, and increases the influence of wealthy city-wide pressure groups such as retail merchants and newspapers. The usual term of office under either the ward-based or at-large council system is two or four years.

The office of councilman rarely constitutes a full-time job, except in the largest cities, and the pay is low. Frequency of meetings varies greatly with the size of the city, ranging from perhaps once a month in small cities to once a day in large cities with full-time councilmen. Much council work is performed through committees, the chairmen of which are sometimes significantly influential.

(*See also* Forms of City Government.)

County

The county, like the city, is a creature of the state, deriving its powers from the state constitution or a grant of the state legislature. But while cities exist primarily for purposes of local government, counties function primarily as agents of the state. There are county governments in every state except Rhode Island, though in Lousiana the unit comparable to a county is called a "parish."

Courts, Municipal

The administration of justice is primarily a state function, but state legislatures have authorized the establishment of municipal courts with limited jurisdiction. In practice, the function of local courts is to relieve state courts of the burden of many minor cases, both civil and criminal. In large cities there are often many courts—for example, recorders courts, small claims courts, traffic courts (which handle a large volume of cases), domestic relations courts, and juvenile courts. Judges are either appointed or popularly eleted. The salaries of most municipal judges are so low and their jurisdiction so limited and routine that competent men often are not interested in serving. Municipal benches have frequently provided patronage for party organizations. The quality of municipal justice is generally considered to be low.

Departmental Organization, of City

The functions of city government are commonly administered by departments, which typically include, police, fire, health and welfare, parks and recreation, public works, buildings, elections, libraries, personnel, and planning. Departments that perform direct public services, such as police and fire, are usually called "line" agencies, while those that advise and service the city government, such as finance or personnel, are called "staff" agencies.

In the early days of municipal government, when the council was the dominant city agency, administrative functions were performed by council committees. Following the Civil War, the use of bipartisan or nonpartisan boards and commissions became widespread, reflecting a reformist desire to take government "out of politics." City departments are still often supervised by boards and commissions, especially in the case of transportation, libraries, planning, parks, and welfare. But the trend is toward placing each department under one man, an appointee of the mayor or, in the case of council-manager governments, the manager. This concentrates authority over city administration and maximizes the opportunity for coordination of functions. Under the weak-mayor form, major department heads are popularly elected.

Dillon's Rule

This is a rule, widely accepted by courts, that the powers of a municipal corporation shall be narrowly construed. As set forth in John F. Dillon's *Commentaries on the Law of Municipal Corporations* (1911), the rule states:

> It is a general and undisputed proposition of law that a municipal corporation possesses and can exercise the following powers, and no others: First, those granted in express words; second, those necessarily or fairly implied in or incident to the powers expressly granted; third, those essential to the declared objects and purposes of the corporation— not simply convenient, but indispensable. Any fair, reasonable, substantial doubt concerning the existence of the power is resolved by the courts against the corporation, and the power is denied.

District

Electoral units within cities include not only wards and precincts but also state legislative districts, which sometimes constitute an element in party organization. Large cities also usually encompass one or more congressional districts, which also provide a basis for party organization.

Electorate (See Voter, Qualifications of)

Elections, Municipal

Some municipal elections coincide with state and national elections, whereas others occur in "off-years"—that is, when there are no major national or state contests. When local elections occur apart from state or national elections, voter turnout is often extremely low. When they occur together with state or national elections, turnout is higher but the number of votes cast for municipal offices is lower than those cast for state or national offices.

The low turnout in municipal elections probably has made it easier for a party organization—the "machine"—to manage the outcome. Party organizations have found it easy to control the outcome of municipal primaries, in which (apart from some one-party states) participation is even lower than in general elections.

All elections—national, state and local—are administered by local officials, usually a bipartisan board or commission of the city or county or a city or county clerk of elections. Subject to state law, the board or clerk issue regulations for the conduct of elections and is responsible for selection of polling places; selection, instruction and supervision of precinct officials to conduct the election; preparation and distribution of booths, ballots, voting machines and other supplies; identification of voters; and tabulation of ballots. In practice, precinct election officials are chosen by party organizations (usually by the precinct captain), though in theory they are named by the central election agency.

The number and kind of choices put to the municipal voter vary greatly from city to city and state to state. He may be called to vote on many candidates (in the case of a weak-mayor form) or few (in the case of a strong-mayor or council-manager form). If he lives in a city with a council elected at large he will have to vote for more candidates than if he lives in a city that elects councilmen as ward representatives. But even under an at-large system, he is not likely to have to vote on a whole council at once, since councilmanic terms are usually staggered. In a few cities that use proportional representation, he may have to indicate a ranked preference for council candidates. He may be asked to vote on bond issues for major construction projects, although in some cities, for example Detroit, he may not be allowed to vote on these questions if he does not own property. If he lives in a home-rule city, he may be asked to approve amendments to the city charter. Or he may be asked to approve a tax increase. A great variety of questions are submitted in referenda.

Federal System

A federal system divides sovereignty between a central authority and regional authorities—in the case of the United States, between the national government and the fifty state governments. This arrangement is prescribed in the United States Constitution. Municipal corporations and other local governments are often popularly considered a third element in the federal system, but strictly speaking they are subdivisions of the states. Local government is not mentioned in the Constitution.

Federation, Metropolitan (See Metropolitan Organization)

Finance, City

The major source of city revenue has long been the tax on real property —land and buildings. In 1958 property taxes, including also some taxes on personal property such as automobiles and home appliances, accounted for three-fourths of city tax revenue. Taxes on sales, gross receipts, and payrolls accounted for most of the rest. All municipal taxes together accounted for nearly two-thirds of general revenue. Other major revenue sources were: (1) federal and state grants-in-aid and taxes shared by the states, and (2) fees collected for water, electric power, gas, transportation, licenses, and other services.

The major problem in administering the property tax is assessment, the process of determining property values. This is ordinarily the job of a city assessor, who is often an elected official and therefore sometimes vulnerable to pressures from property-owners seeking low valuations. Even impartial assessors are not necessarily good assessors, however, since the job requires a high degree of technical competence and judgment. And even for the competent, the job of keeping assessments current is sometimes nearly impossible.

Assessment abuses and inequities are varied and widespread. Undervaluation is quite common. One result of this is to limit the borrowing and tax capacities of the city, since these capacities are often fixed by state legislatures at some percentage of assessed valuation. On the other hand, some cities also have artificially inflated assessments. Some steps have been taken in recent years to end assessment abuses. Especially in large cities there is a trend toward appointment of assessors and creation of trained assessment staffs. In some places, county and state equalization boards have been set up to standardize assessment practices.

Though much criticized, the real property tax is likely to remain the mainstay of city revenues, since there are few other tax sources that have not been preempted by federal and state governments.

The lack of adequate tax revenue and a need for capital projects have led cities to increase their borrowing through issuance of municipal bonds. These are of three types: general-obligation, revenue, and mortgage. General obligation bonds are supported by the full faith and credit of the municipality. Payments on interest and principal are met out of tax revenues, and are protected by a statutory requirement that the annual tax levy must be sufficient to cover the debt service. Municipalities that have reached their statutory debt limit, however, cannot issue general obligation bonds. Revenue bonds are used to finance revenue-producing properties, such as toll bridges, tunnels, or gas and water supply systems, the returns from which are pledged to debt service. Municipalities agree to set rates high enough to meet debt payments. Mortgage bonds are often used for the purchase or construction of utilities, and they offer as security a mortgage on the utility. Because they bear a higher rate of interest than general obligation or revenue bonds, mortgage bonds are less widely used. In general, municipalities meet current operating expenses out of revenue and borrow for permanent improvements. The issuance of bonds is frequently submitted to the electorate in referenda, but in many cases councils possess the authority to issue them without voter approval.

Forms of City Government

Four forms of city government are usually distinguished:

1. The *weak-mayor-council* form, reflecting the American practice of separation of functions, assigns legislative powers to a council and executive powers to a mayor. However, the mayor has limited power to supervise administration. Administrative officers and department heads, such as the city attorney, city engineer, assessor, and controller, are either popularly elected or appointed by the council. The mayor may recommend legislation, preside over the council, and even exercise a veto, but he does not prepare the budget or possess full authority to administer ordinances. The weak-mayor system was the first to develop in the United States and remains in widespread use, particularly in small cities.

2. The *strong-mayor-council* form vests broader administrative powers in the mayor. He appoints and removes department heads and prepares and administers the budget. Since he receives much publicity, he often overshadows the council altogether.

In practice the distinction between weak and strong mayors is often hard to make. Gradations of mayoral authority are so subtle that they resist arbitrary classification. The trend is toward stronger mayors. According to the 1960 *Municipal Yearbook*, 1,238 cities used mayor-council forms. The *Yearbook* did not classify these as strong-mayor or weak-mayor.

3. The *council-manager* form vests in a small council (five to nine members, commonly elected at large on a nonpartisan ballot) the authority to legislate for the city and to hire, supervise and dismiss a full-time professional manager, who is charged with city administration. Ultimate responsibility for both legislative and executive functions is concentrated in the council. The council chooses a mayor from its own members, but he has only ceremonial functions. Promoted by reformers, this form was introduced in 1908 and spread rapidly. According to the *Municipal Yearbook* of 1960, it was used by 931 cities. Only one of these cities, however, (Cincinnati) had a population of more than 500,000. On the other hand, 48 per cent of cities in the 25,000-to-100,000 population range used it.

4. The *commissioner* form vests executive and legislative powers in elected commissioners (usually five), each of whom serves as head of a city department. Together they form a policy-making body. Like the council-manager plan, the commission plan was promoted by reformers, but it has not enjoyed comparable popularity. Introduced in Galveston, Texas, in 1900, it spread rapidly and by World War I was used in at least 500 cities. However, the number had dropped to 309 by 1960 and is still declining.

Gerrymander

This term refers to the practice of fixing legislative district boundaries in such a way as to gain partisan advantage. This may be accomplished in at least two ways. The dominant party in the legislature my create a peculiarly shaped district in which its voters will constitute a majority. Or it may attempt to concentrate the voters of the opposite party in as few districts as possible. Gerrymandering is done mostly by the state legislatures, which fix congressional as well as state legislative districts. Although it has usually benefited rural Republicans at the expense of urban Democrats, it also occurs within cities, where councils sometimes draw wards so as to minimize the voting strength of Negroes or other ethnic groups.

The word was derived in 1812 from the name of Governor Elbridge Gerry of Massachusetts, who allowed the state to be apportioned into fantastic shapes.

"Good Government" (See the introduction to Section IV)

Governmental and Proprietary Functions

These terms describe the legal status of city functions. "Governmental" functions are those done involuntarily as an agent of the state, in pursuance of such state purposes as protection of public health and safety. Fire and police protection are examples of governmental functions. "Proprietary" functions are those performed as a convenience to the municipal community —for example, public transportation. The distinction is significant because, as a general rule, a municipality is not liable for torts resulting from the performance of its governmental functions. The city cannot be sued, for example, by a pedestrian who suffers injury from a police cruiser pursuing a speeding car. But a pedestrian injured by a city transit bus may sue the city. In practice, distinctions between the two categories are hard to draw, and legislatures and courts have drawn them in different ways in different states.

Home Rule

Home rule is the power of municipalities to conduct their affairs without interference from the state.

Ever since the late nineteenth century, reformers have argued for home rule. As a result, more than half of the states have adopted home-rule constitutions or statutes, which grant their cities powers "relating to municipal affairs" or "[the city's] own government." Interpretation of these powers is left to courts, which have construed them narrowly. Acts of the state legislature normally take precedence over the charter provisions or ordinances of home-rule cities. As a result, a large majority of cities remain subject to extensive state control with respect to matters in which the state has a substantial interest such as law enforcement, welfare, education, utilities, and finance.

Initiative, Referendum, and Recall

These are three procedures for providing popular access to political power. Initiative is the proposal of legislation by the electorate. A referendum is the submission of a proposal of the legislature to the electorate for approval. Recall is the removal of public officials before expiration of their terms.

Initiative and recall begin with circulation of a petition. An initiative petition proposes language changing the city's charter or ordinances. If it receives the required number of signatures (usually 5 to 10 per cent of the vote cast at the preceding election), the proposal is considered by the council, which in some cases may adopt it outright. If the council does not adopt it, the measure is placed on the ballot at a special or general election. Usually recall petitions must bear a higher percentage of voter signatures than initiative petitions. If the prescribed number of signatures is secured, a recall election must be held. Voters may be asked simply whether they wish the officer to be removed, or they may be given an opportunity to vote on other candidates for the office.

Referenda, too, may originate with petitions, but often city councils are required by law to submit certain proposals—especially bond issues—for popular approval. Sometimes city councils may voluntarily seek popular advice in "straw votes." Such referenda require no action by the city government; they merely give evidence of popular opinion. San Francisco and Houston both use this procedure. Referenda are far more frequent than the initiative and recall, which are used very little.

These procedures have been most widely used in states and municipalities west of the Mississippi, where the Progressive movement was strongest. All three procedures have been criticized on the grounds that they lengthen the ballot, place excessive demands on the capacities of the electorate, and subject government officials to harassment by organized interest groups.

Legal Status of Cities (See Corporation, Municipal)

Machine, Political (See Party, Political)

Manager, City (See Forms of City Government)

Mayor (See Forms of City Government)

Merit System

Under a merit system government employees are selected on the basis of technical or professional competence, usually as determined by an examination. They are protected from removal for political reasons.

The first municipal merit systems were introduced in the 1880's at the same time as the merit system in the federal government. But the merit principle did not become widely accepted in municipalities until the 1930's when it was stimulated by the federal government, which frequently required state and local governments to adopt merit systems as a condition of grants-in-aid. Merit systems spread fastest among large cities.

While they have contributed to the decline of the machine, merit systems have not eliminated patronage altogether. In many cities some important positions, such as department heads or the mayor's staff, are exempt. Temporary jobs, particularly in the administration of elections, also provide patronage. One way of circumventing merit system regulations has been to classify a large number of jobs "provisional."

Civil service systems were at first administered by bipartisan commissions independent of the city administration. There is a trend, however, toward creation of a personnel department under a director who is responsible to the mayor or manager. This form of personnel administration, like the merit system itself, is most commonly found in council-manager governments.

Metropolitan Area

This term refers to the aggregate of a large central city and its surrounding communities—smaller cities, villages, and townships. In 1960 the U.S. Census Bureau reported data for units called "standard metropolitan statistical areas." According to a publication of the Census Bureau, these areas:

> are integrated economic and social units with a large volume of daily travel and communication between the central city (50,000 or more population) and outlying parts of the area. Each area (except in New England) consists of one or more whole counties. An area may contain not only highly industrialized counties but also adjoining counties which, though primarily residential in character, contribute significantly to the industrial counties' labor force.

As of Dec. 31, 1965 there were 224 SMSA's. The 1960 population of these places was 116,968,692.

Metropolitan Organization

No city has boundaries coinciding with the limits of the metropolitan area. There are no metropolitan governments; in every metropolitan area there are several governments (cities, villages, school districts, special districts, counties), each serving some part of the whole metropolitan area.

Major complaints against this division of authority in metropolitan areas are: (1) that functions that must be conducted on an area-wide basis, such as planning and transportation, are neglected; (2) that it is wasteful; (3) that it is inequitable because the quality of services varies throughout the metropolitan area; and (4) that it places a disproportionate burden of taxation and services on the central city. The suburbs, critics point out, have drawn high-income residents, retail and wholesale services, and industry from the central city, thereby reducing its tax base; at the same time, suburban residents use city services—transportation, hospitals, libraries, parks, and so forth—without paying city taxes.

Proposals for metropolitan integration have taken several forms:

Annexation of Adjacent Territory by City Governments. Several hundred annexations take place each year, but most are small. Legislatures in most states—Virginia, Texas, California, and Missouri are exceptions—have placed almost insuperable barriers in the way of annexation. There is in most places no practical prospect that metropolitan integration can be achieved by this method.

Consolidation of Counties and Cities. New Orleans, Boston, Philadelphia, and New York resulted from the consolidation of cities and counties. There have been no successful mergers in recent years except for Baton Rouge, Louisiana, which was consolidated with East Baton Rouge Parish in 1947. A variant of the consolidation scheme calls for transferring some municipal functions to county governments. Under a charter adopted in 1957, Dade County, Florida, which includes Miami, performs many functions of local government under the administration of a manager. Los Angeles County also provides some municipal-type services. An obvious shortcoming of this plan is that counties themselves are not necessarily contiguous with the metropolitan area. Furthermore, like annexation, county-city consolidation has failed to win support from state legislatures.

Federation of Local Governments. Under this plan, which has had no successful application in the United States, there would be two levels of government in the metropolitan area, one area-wide to perform services appropriate to area administration, the other local to handle functions of more narrow concern.

Voluntary Cooperation among Governmental Units. Agreements, formal or informal, between city and county governments or between city and suburban governments are an increasingly common means of metropolitan integration. Cities and counties often cooperate, for example, in the administration of hospitals, maintenance of a city-county building, traffic control, or other functions that they have in common. Central cities may make contracts with suburban governments or directly with suburban residents for the provision of water and gas or the disposal of sewage, garbage and rubbish. Some cooperation on fire and police protection is also fairly common. Though such agreements are politically more feasible than other forms of integration, they are not generally considered adequate to solve the problem.

The chief reason for the failure of proposals for metropolitan integration is that the suburbs and the central cities are divided by class, race, and party. Apart from these cleavages, there are also inevitable conflicts of interest between cities and suburbs with respect to transportation, taxes, and other problems of local government. These differences between central city and suburb are reflected in the state legislature, which in almost every case must approve proposals for metropolitan integration.

Municipality

This term is synonymous with "municipal corporation." Cities, villages, and boroughs are municipalities. As of 1957 there were 17,183 municipalities in the United States.

Nonpartisan System of Elections

According to the formal definition, a nonpartisan system of election exists where candidates are not identified by party affiliation on the ballot. More realistically, a nonpartisan system is one in which candidates receive no support from either the Republican or the Democratic party. Purely local parties may exist in such a case.

The nonpartisan ballot was introduced early in the twentieth century by "good-government" reformers, who hoped to divorce municipal government from state and national politics. According to the *Municipal Yearbook* of

1960, it is used by 61 per cent of cities over 5,000 population. Sixty-five per cent of the 17 cities of over 500,000 population use it.

The nonpartisan ballot has weakened party organizations, though strong parties manage to exist in a few cities where it is used. It gives an advantage to candidates who receive much publicity, who have names that appeal to large ethnic groups, or who are incumbent office-holders.

Ordinance

An ordinance is a rule or regulation issued by a municipal corporation. It must be made under authority granted in the corporation's charter and in conformity with state and national laws. Its application is limited to the area over which the corporation has jurisdiction. Technically, an ordinance is not a "law," since laws can be enacted only by sovereign bodies.

Party, Political

Political parties are groups that nominate and support candidates for public office. In theory, they compete for the control of the machinery of government by placing alternative programs and candidates before the electorate. Party organizations have often controlled municipal nominations and elections, but they have rarely been concerned with programs of governmental action.

Party organization in cities was strongest in the era of the machine, between the Civil War and World War II. An outstanding characteristic of the machine was the preoccupation of its members with personal gain and their indifference to political principle. One consequence of the pragmatic character of machines was that they did not compete against each other. Where more than one machine existed in the same city, they often cooperated in protecting each other from destruction by reformers.

In comparison to the machine era, municipal parties are now weakly organized. In many places party organizations continue to function, conducting campaign activity, handling federal, state, and city patronage, and putting forth candidates for public office. But nowhere, except possibly in Chicago, does this organization control municipal government as it once did. The amount of patronage available is often slim; blocs of "deliverable" votes are rare; and many municipal candidates are independent of party organization. The party organization is likely to be a loose congeries of factions and minor personal followings rather than a unified group consisting of a leader and loyal subordinates as in the days of the boss. To the extent that party organizations exist in large cities, they are likely to be Democratic, since a large majority of big-city voters favors the Democratic party in state and national elections.

Patronage (See Spoils System)

Planning

According to one of the standard works on city planning, Robert A. Walker's *The Planning Function in Urban Government* (1941), "The local planning process is an aspect of the process of local government. It is government looking to the future, determining desirable objectives and seeking the best and most economical means for achieving them." Walker also says:

> The over-all planning agency is designed to assist officials in formulating a public policy which treats the problems of the community as a closely knit whole. . . . The several operating departments can and should plan for their respective spheres of activity. The contribution of

the planning agency is not found in a duplication of this work but rather in supplying the element of "comprehensiveness" and hence integration, to planning the future development of the city. This calls for a systematic program of assembling information about the city (research), discovering what it means (analysis), and indicating what action it seems to call for (planning and specific recommendations). . . . the theoretical goal of a planning agency's work [is] the preparation of a plan for the future of an area—a plan which portrays the development conceived to make that area the best possible for human habitation.

According to the 1960 *Municipal Yearbook*, 914 of 1,002 cities with a population over 10,000 had official planning agencies. Only 303 of these had a full-time planning director.

Precinct

A precinct is a unit for the casting and counting of votes in elections and for police administration in a city. Precincts typically contain several hundred residents. Ten to thirty precincts usually constitute a ward. The party leader in the precinct is the "precinct captain."

Pressure Groups

These are organizations that attempt to influence the actions of government. They are active at all levels of government—local, state, and national. At the local level such organizations usually include: chambers of commerce, retail trade boards, real estate boards, and taxpayers' associations, which represent the interests of business; neighborhood improvement associations, which represent homeowners; citizens leagues, municipal research bureaus, and the League of Women Voters, which promote "good government"; AFL-CIO locals and units of COPE, labor's Committee on Political Education; municipal employee unions; and chapters of the National Association for the Advancement of Colored People and the Urban League, which represent Negroes.

Pressure groups seek to influence the actions of city government in various ways. Their representatives may speak at sessions of the city council or meet with the mayor and his administrative subordinates. They often use propaganda—posters, pamphlets, newspaper releases, and radio and TV appearances. Some exercise influence through campaign contributions or campaign activity in support of candidates or propositions. Municipal employees may exercise influence through strikes.

Groups with an interest in local affairs often concentrate much of their activity on the state level, where many decisions affecting local government are made.

Primary Elections

These are elections in which candidates for office are nominated. Most are "closed" primaries, in which a voter may participate only in balloting for nominees of the party to which he belongs. An "open" primary allows the voter to participate without regard to his party affiliation.

Primary elections are usually held even in cities that use a nonpartisan electoral system. All candidates appear on the primary ballot, having qualified by obtaining petition signatures and/or paying a fee. The two candidates receiving the highest vote for an office compete in the final election. In some cases a candidate who receives a majority in the primary is declared elected.

Property Tax (See Finance, City)

Proportional Representation

This is an election system under which voters indicate their preferences among the candidates in a ranked order—1, 2, 3, etc. These votes are weighted in determining the outcome. The purpose of proportional representation (PR) is to provide representation for elements of the electorate exactly in proportion to their numerical strength.

In the United States, PR was used first in Ashtabula, Ohio, in 1915. Since then it has been adopted by 24 other cities, but few have retained it. The experience of New York, Cincinnati, and other cities suggests that PR succeeds in providing minority representation, but arouses opposition from the disadvantaged majority. It is little used today.

Proprietary Functions (See Governmental and Proprietary Functions)

Recall (See Initiative, Referendum, and Recall)

Referendum (See Initiative, Referendum, and Recall)

Registration

Registration is the procedure whereby a list of qualified voters is compiled for use at elections. Such a system is required in urban areas in order to prevent fraud. Registration laws were adopted therefore in response to growth of the cities in the late nineteenth century.

Registration may be periodic or permanent. Under a periodic system the voter is required to register at regular intervals and is dropped from the rolls if he fails to register. Under a permanent system the voter registers only once, and remains on the rolls unless he moves or dies. About three-fourths of the states provide for permanent registration.

Representation of Cities in Legislatures

Historically, cities have not been represented in state legislatures in proportion to their population. This situation encouraged state action that was disadvantageous to urban areas. The recent decline of population in the central cities means that underrepresentation of these areas has been alleviated or ended.

Short Ballot (See Ballot)

School Districts

In all but four states, according to the *Municipal Yearbook* of 1960, school districts constitute a unit of local government independent of other units (counties, cities, villages, towns). In those four states, schools are administered by the state or by general-purpose local governments. Some states use both systems.

Special Districts

These are units of local government that perform one or a few specific functions, in contrast to municipalities, which are general-purpose governments. According to the *Municipal Yearbook* of 1960, there were 14,405 special districts in the United States in 1957, nearly half of them for fire protection, soil conservation, or drainage. Other special districts provided irrigation and water conservation, highways, sanitation, hospitals, libraries, and many other services.

Special districts often overlap other units of local government, and thus provide a partial solution to the problem of metropolitan organization. They are also a way to avoid placing additional service burdens on other local governments, many of which have reached statutory debt and taxing limits. Finally, special districts have been promoted as a device for taking some activities "out of politics." Usually they are directed by boards appointed by state or local officials. They are relatively immune to popular pressures.

The powers of special districts are fixed by state laws and vary greatly. In general these governments possess some corporate powers such as perpetual succession, the right to sue and be sued, to make contracts, and to acquire and dispose of property. Some have the power to tax and borrow. Most are limited to one function, but the best known, such as the Port of New York Authority and the Metropolitan District Commission of Massachusetts, perform many services. The number of special districts has increased substantially since World War II.

Special Legislation

Acts that apply to specific cities are called "special legislation." Between the Civil War and 1900 many state legislatures regulated the affairs of individual cities in detail. Virtually usurping the functions of city councils, they passed laws governing police departments, utility franchises, street paving, and even construction of municipal buildings. The home rule movement was a response to this practice. (See Home Rule)

Many states have adopted constitutional prohibitions against special legislation, but it continues to be used, especially in New England and the South. Legislatures sometimes circumvent the prohibition with acts that apply to certain categories of cities. For example, a legislature may pass a law applying to "all cities of over 500,000 population" when there is only one such city in the state.

Spoils System

This term refers to the practice of placing party workers in public jobs. The spoils system prevailed at all levels of government throughout much of the nineteenth century. In the cities, the promise of public employment—perhaps a municipal judgeship or a desk job at city hall—constituted the major incentive for machine workers at the precinct and ward level. Their ability in turn to dispense petty jobs to precinct residents was a means of building a following among the electorate. Jobs (usually called "patronage") were allotted through the machine hierarchy. Not only did patronage provide an incentive for machine workers, but it also helped finance campaigns. Men who owed their jobs to the organization were commonly expected to contribute a share of their salary to it at election time. The spoils system has been largely replaced in most cities by a comprehensive merit system.

Staff Services

Staff services assist the mayor with city administration. The principal staff services are planning, personnel, legal advice, and finance.

Standard Metropolitan Statistical Area (SMSA) (See Metropolitan Area)

State Control over Cities (See Corporation, Municipal, and Representation of Cities in Legislatures)

Taxes (See Finance, City)

Town

In a few states the "town" constitutes one class of municipality, like the city, village, and borough, but more generally it is an unincorporated unit of local government. In New England states the town is irregular in size and shape and often includes one or two villages as well as some rural area. New England town governments are authorized to perform certain functions of local government such as police, fire, welfare, streets, and water supply. Throughout the Midwest these are "townships," which are subdivisions of county government. Located in predominantly rural areas, they are regular in size and shape, usually five or six miles square. As of 1957 there were 17,198 towns or townships in the United States, roughly equivalent to the number of municipalities.

Urban Area

In 1960 the Census Bureau defined urban areas as: (1) places of 2,500 inhabitants or more that are incorporated as cities, boroughs, villages, and towns (except towns in New England, New York, and Wisconsin); (2) the densely settled urban fringe, whether incorporated or unincorporated, around cities of 50,000 or more; (3) towns in New England and townships in New Jersey and Pennsylvania which contain no incorporated municipalities as subdivisions and have either 25,000 inhabitants or more or a population of 2,500 to 25,000 and a density of 1,500 persons or more per square mile; (4) counties in states other than the New England states, New Jersey, and Pennsylvania that have no incorporated municipalities within their boundaries and have a density of 1,500 persons or more per square mile; and (5) unincorporated places of 2,500 inhabitants or more. All other territory is classified as rural.

Urban Renewal

Urban renewal is the process of restoring city slums. Renewal may be accomplished by redevelopment—the replacement of old buildings—or by rehabilitation of such buildings. Major governmental programs for urban renewal began with the Housing Act of 1949, which authorized federal grants to finance two-thirds of the net cost of acquiring, clearing, and preparing slum land for new construction. Housing Acts in 1954 and 1956 broadened the 1949 Act and placed new emphasis on rehabilitation and conservation as alternatives to redevelopment. Almost all of the states have authorized participation in the urban renewal program and have provided for financing the local share of the costs. The objective of urban renewal, according to the Housing Act of 1949, is "the realization as soon as feasible of the goal of a decent home and suitable living environment for every American family, thus contributing to the development and redevelopment of communities and to the advancement of the growth, wealth, and security of the Nation . . . and to an economy of maximum employment, production, and purchasing power."

Village

The village is a common type of municipality, usually (though not invariably) smaller than the city.

Voter, Qualifications of

Almost everywhere, anyone who qualifies as a voter under state laws is entitled to vote in municipal elections. The usual requirements are U.S. citizenship, a minimum age (eighteen in Georgia, twenty-one in all other states), a minimum period of residence in the electoral jurisdiction, and registration (though not all rural residents are required to register). In a few states, only property owners are permitted to vote on bond issues.

Ward

A ward is an electoral subdivision of a municipality, larger than a precinct and smaller than state legislative districts (though wards and districts are sometimes coterminous). Except where councilmen are elected at large, wards are the units from which councilmen are elected.

Zoning

Zoning is the control of land use and the size of buildings and lots. Virtually all large cities have adopted zoning ordinances, which divide the city into areas for commercial, industrial, and residential use. If a property owner wishes to deviate from the prescribed use, he must obtain approval of the city council.

Bibliography

NOTE: Books and articles from which materials have been reprinted are not included in this listing.

Bibliographical

The American Political Science Review, a quarterly journal, contains a current list of publications in the field of state and local government.

Daland, R. T. "Political Science and the Study of Urbanism," *American Political Science Review*, LI (June 1957), 491–509. An essay describing the literature of urban politics.

Government Affairs Foundation, Inc., *Metropolitan Communities: A Bibliography*. Chicago: Public Administration Service, 1956. A comprehensive annotated list of publications on the government and politics of metropolitan communities. A supplement issued in 1960 brings the list through 1957.

Graves, W. Brooke (comp.). *Intergovernmental Relations in the United States: A Selected Bibliography on Interlevel and Interjurisdictional Relations*. Commission on Intergovernmental Relations, mimeo., June 1955. An extensive compilation of publications on intergovernmental relations. There is a section on metropolitan regionalism.

Urban History Group Newsletter. Charles Glaab, ed. Department of History, University of Wisconsin, Milwaukee, Wisconsin.

Serials and Periodicals

Journal of the American Institute of Planners. A quarterly publication with many articles on urban planning and redevelopment.

Municipal Yearbook. A publication of the International City Managers' Association which summarizes municipal activities each year and provides basic statistical data on U.S. cities. A source of bibliography.

National Civic Review. Monthly publication of the National Municipal League. Until 1959 it was entitled *The National Municipal Review*.

Public Administration Review. A quarterly journal of the American Society for Public Administration. Contains frequent articles on municipal administration.

The Public Interest. Published quarterly by National Affairs, Inc. Contains articles on a wide range of urban policy problems.

Public Management. Monthly journal of the International City Managers' Association.

Books

Adrian, C. R. *Governing Urban America.* New York: McGraw-Hill Book Co., 1961. A text on municipal government and politics.

Banfield, Edward C. *Big City Politics.* New York: Random House, 1965. Brief accounts of politics in nine major American cities.

Bean, Walton. *Boss Ruef's San Francisco.* Berkeley: University of California Press, 1952. An account of a well-known boss.

Bollens, John C. *Appointed Executive Local Government: The California Experience.* Los Angeles: Haynes Foundation, 1952. Discusses executive management in California cities.

————, and H. J. Schmidt (eds.). *Exploring the Metropolitan Community.* Berkeley: University of California Press, 1961. A study of metropolitan social and governmental structure. Emphasis on St. Louis, city and county.

Bordua, David J. (ed.). *The Police: Six Sociological Essays.* New York: John Wiley & Sons, Inc., 1967. Essays dealing with diverse problems of the police in meeting the demands of modern society.

Buckley, William F., Jr. *The Unmaking of a Mayor.* New York: The Viking Press, 1966. A witty conservative reflects upon the campaign in which he was defeated by Mayor Lindsay.

Callow, Alexander B., Jr. *The Tweed Ring.* New York: Oxford University Press, 1966. An account of the most notorious municipal machine.

Childs, Richard S. *Civic Victories: The Story of an Unfinished Revolution.* New York: Harper & Row, 1952. The history of municipal reform by one of its foremost leaders.

Curley, James M. *I'd Do It Again.* Englewood Cliffs, N.J.: Prentice-Hall, 1957. The autobiography of one of the last and most popular of the big city bosses.

Dillon, John F. *Commentaries on the Law of Municipal Corporations.* 5 vols. 5th ed., Boston: Little, Brown & Co., 1911. A standard source of municipal law.

Duncan, Otis D., and others. *Metropolis and Region.* Baltimore: Johns Hopkins University Press, for Resources for the Future, 1960. An analysis of the economics of metropolitan regions, with emphasis on the relation between economics and geography.

————, and A. J. Reiss, Jr. *Social Characteristics of Urban and Rural Communities, 1950.* New York: John Wiley & Sons, 1956. Elaboration and interpretation of data from the 1950 census.

Eldredge, H. Wentworth (ed.). *Taming Megalopolis,* Vols. I and II. Garden City, N.Y.: Doubleday & Company, Inc., 1967. Readings on problems and prospects in urban planning.

Forthal, Sonya. *Cogwheels of Democracy: A Study of the Precinct Captain.* New York: William-Frederick Press, 1946. A brief description, derived from interviews in Chicago, of the machine's hardest workers.

Gilbert, Charles E. *Governing the Suburbs.* Bloomington: Indiana University Press, 1967. A scrutiny of the complex government and politics of three suburban counties of Philadelphia.

Greer, Scott. *The Emerging City: Myth and Reality.* New York: The Free Press, 1962. Urban politics as a factor in twentieth-century American society.

Hawley, Amos H. *The Changing Shape of Metropolitan America: Deconcen-*

tration Since 1920. New York: The Free Press, 1956. A report on patterns of population change in U.S. metropolitan areas.

Kammerer, Gladys, *et al. City Managers in Politics: An Analysis of Manager Tenure and Termination.* Gainesville: University of Florida Monographs: Social Sciences, No. 13 (Winter 1962). A study of the turnover problem in the city manager system.

Kaplan, Harold. *Urban Renewal Politics: Slum Clearance in Newark.* New York: Columbia University Press, 1963.

————. *Urban Political Systems: A Functional Analysis of Metro Toronto.* New York: Columbia University Press, 1967. History and evaluation of Metro Toronto.

Kurtzman, D. H. *Methods of Controlling Votes in Philadelphia.* Privately printed, 1935. A detailed study, based on field investigation, of the techniques for influencing votes in a major city.

Lee, Eugene C. *The Politics of Nonpartisanship: A Study of California City Elections.* Berkeley: University of California Press, 1960. Although based largely upon data gathered in six California cities, this is the most comprehensive account of the subject in print. Good bibliography.

Martin, Roscoe C. *Government and the Suburban School.* Syracuse: Syracuse University Press, 1962. Suburban public education.

————, and Frank Munger (eds.). *Decisions in Syracuse.* Bloomington: Indiana University Press, 1961.

McBain, Howard L. *The Law and Practice of Municipal Home Rule.* New York: Columbia University Press, 1916. Though dated, this and the following volume, by McGoldrick, remain the standard works on home rule.

McGoldrick, J. D. *Law and Practice of Municipal Home Rule, 1916–1930.* New York: Columbia University Press, 1933. A sequel to an earlier volume, by McBain, listed above.

McKean, Dayton D. *The Boss: The Hague Machine in Action.* Boston: Houghton Mifflin, 1940. A thorough study by a political scientist of one of the last machines.

McQuillin, Eugene. *The Law of Municipal Corporations.* 3rd ed.; Chicago: Callaghan & Co., 1949. A leading commentary on municipal law.

Moses, Robert. *La Guardia: A Salute and a Memoir.* New York: Simon & Schuster, 1957. A personal recollection of the flamboyant mayor.

Mosher, Frederick C., and others. *City Manager Government in Seven Cities.* Chicago: Public Administration Service, 1940. A collection of case studies on the development, politics, and administration of the city manager plan.

Myers, Gustavus. *History of Tammany Hall.* New York: Boni & Liveright, 1917. The basic source of information on Tammany.

New York Metropolitan Regional Study. Cambridge, Mass.: Regional Planning Association and Harvard University Press, 1959–1960. A series of reports on the economics and demography of the New York metropolitan region, prepared for the Regional Planning Commission by the Graduate School of Public Administration at Harvard. For specific works in the series see separate listing under authors. (The authors are: Hoover, Edgar M., and Raymond Vernon; Helfgott, Roy B., and James M. Hund; Handlin, Oscar; Segal, Martin; Robbins, Sidney M., and Nestor E. Terleckyj; Wood, Robert C.; Lichtenberg, Robert M.; and Vernon, Raymond.)

Ostrogorski, M. *Democracy and the Party System,* New York: The Macmillan

Co., 1910. An analysis of the machine by a contemporary European observer.

Peel, Roy V. *The Political Clubs of New York City.* New York: G. P. Putnam's Sons, 1935. An outstanding study of urban political activity.

Perloff, Harvey S. (ed.). *Planning and the Urban Community.* Pittsburgh: University of Pittsburgh Press, 1961. A collection of short essays representing the orthodoxy of the city planning movement on a dozen matters.

Polsby, N. W. *Community Power and Political Theory.* New Haven: Yale University Press, 1963. An exposition of the pluralist approach to the study of political power structures.

Ridley, Clarence E., and Orin F. Nolting. *The City Manager Profession.* Chicago: University of Chicago Press, 1934. Two city managers describe briefly the development and functions of the manager.

Rossi, Peter, and R. A. Dentler. *The Politics of Urban Renewal.* New York: The Free Press, 1961. A study of public and private enterprise in Chicago's urban renewal program.

Salter, J. T. *Boss Rule: Portraits in City Politics.* New York: McGraw-Hill Book Co., 1935. A study of ward politicians, chiefly in Philadelphia.

Schlesinger, Arthur M. *The Rise of the City.* New York: The Macmillan Co., 1933. A study of U.S. history from 1878 to 1898, years of rapid urbanization.

Segoe, Ladislas. *Local Planning Administration.* 3rd ed.: Chicago: International City Managers' Association, 1959. A handbook designed for planning officials.

Sofen, Edward. *The Miami Metropolitan Experiment.* Bloomington: Indiana University Press, 1963. A scrutiny of reform activity and government in the Miami metropolitan area.

Steffens, Lincoln. *Shame of the Cities.* New York: Sagamore Press, Inc., 1957. First published in 1904, this is a collection of articles on corruption in seven major cities.

Stewart, Frank M. *A Half Century of Municipal Reform: The History of the Municipal League.* Berkeley: University of California Press, 1950. A sympathetic account of the League.

Stone, Harold A., D. K. Price, and Kathryn H. Stone. *City Manager Government in Nine Cities.* Chicago: Public Administration Service, 1940. Case studies on the city manager plan.

Straetz, Ralph A. *PR Politics in Cincinnati.* New York: New York University Press, 1958. An analysis of politics in Cincinnati during the 32-year period of proportional representation (1926–1957).

U.S. Congress, Senate Subcommittee on Intergovernmental Relations of the Committee on Government Operations, *The Effectiveness of Metropolitan Planning,* Committee Print, June 30, 1964.

U.S. Department of Commerce, Bureau of the Census. *Governments in the United States in 1957.* Washington, D.C.: Government Printing Office, 1957. Basic data on all governmental units in the U.S.

Vernon, Raymond. *The Myth and Reality of Our Urban Problems.* Cambridge: Harvard University Press, 1962. Interpretation and recommendations by the director of the New York Metropolitan Regional Study.

Vidich, Arthur J., and Joseph Bensman. *Small Town in Mass Society.* Princeton: Princeton University Press, 1958. This study of a small community in upper New York State includes detailed treatment of local politics.

Walker, Robert. *The Planning Function in Urban Government.* Chicago:

University of Chicago Press, 1950. Describes the functions of city planning agencies.

Willbern, York. *The Withering Away of the City*. University, Ala.: University of Alabama Press, 1963. An essay on metropolitan affairs.

Wilson, James Q. *The Amateur Democrat*. Chicago: University of Chicago Press, 1962. An examination of nonprofessional party politics in three major American cities.

——. *City Politics and Public Policy*. New York: John Wiley & Sons, Inc., 1968. A collection of empirical studies that explain in political terms why cities adopt one policy rather than another.

—— (ed.). *Urban Renewal: The Record and the Controversy*. Cambridge: Harvard University Press, 1966. A collection of readings intended to present all sides.

Zink, Harold *City Bosses in the United States*. Durham: Duke University Press, 1930. Analyses of the biographies of twenty bosses.

Articles and Pamphlets

Adrian, Charles R. "A Typology for Nonpartisan Elections," *Western Political Quarterly*, XII (June 1959), 449–458. Nonpartisan elections are classified in four categories, differentiated by the degree of party support for candidates.

Anderson, William. "The Units of Government in the United States." Chicago: Public Administration Service, 1949. An analysis based on census data and private research. Enumerates and describes units of government in this country.

Bebout, John E. "Management for Large Cities." *Public Administration Review*, XV (Summer 1955), 188–195. An argument for adoption of the council-manager plan in large cities by the then assistant director of the National Municipal League.

Bosworth, Karl A. "The Manager Is a Politician," *Public Administration Review*, XVIII (Summer 1958), 216–222. A discussion of the various roles of the city manager. The author concludes that the city manager, whatever role he may choose, is and always has been involved in politics.

Dye, T. R. "Local-Cosmopolitan Dimension and the Study of Urban Politics," *Social Forces*, 41 (March 1963), 233–269. Observations of suburban political direction.

Freeman, J. L. "Local Party Systems: Theoretical Considerations and a Case Analysis," *American Journal of Sociology*, 64 (November 1958), 282–289.

Harder, Melvin A. "Nonpartisan Election: A Political Illusion" (Case Studies in Practical Politics.) New York: Holt, Rinehart & Winston, 1958. An account of the Wichita municipal election of 1957.

Harvard Law Review, 73 (January 1960), 526–582. "The Urban County: A Study of New Approaches to Local Government in Metropolitan Areas." A legal discussion of proposals for metropolitan integration.

Holden, Matthew, Jr. "The Governance of the Metropolis as a Problem in Diplomacy," *Journal of Politics*, 26 (August 1964), 627–647. An application of international rules to intrametropolitan politics.

Jones, Victor, and Herbert Kaufman. "The Mystery of Power," *Public Administration Review*, XIV (Summer 1954), 205–212. A critical review of Floyd Hunter's *Community Power Structure*.

Lockard, W. D. "City Manager, Administrative Theory and Political Power," *Political Science Quarterly*, 77 (June 1962), 224–236. A political and administrative appraisal of city manager government.

Mott, Rodney L. "Home Rule for America's Cities." Chicago: American Municipal Association, Urban Action Series Publication 101, 1949. A study of the operation of home rule. Useful as a recent supplement to the book by McGoldrick.

Nolting, Orin F. "City Manager of Tomorrow," *Public Management*, XL (October, 1958), 234–237. A prediction of new responsibilities for the city manager by the executive director of the International City Managers' Association.

Patton, Clifford W. "The Battle for Municipal Reform: Mobilization and Attack, 1875–1900." Washington, D.C.: American Council on Public Affairs, 1940. A brief account of the municipal reform movement.

Sayre, Wallace S. "The General Manager Idea for Large Cities," *Public Administration Review*, XIV (Autumn, 1954), 253–258. A discussion of the idea that management of large cities can best be handled by a general manager responsible to the mayor.

White, J. P., and N. C. Thomas. "Urban and Rural Representation and State Legislative Apportionment," *Western Political Quarterly*, 17 (December 1964), 724–742.

Williams, Oliver P., and Charles R. Adrian. "The Insulation of Local Politics under the Nonpartisan Ballot," *American Political Science Review*, LIII (December 1959), 1052–1063.

Wilson, James Q. "The Economy of Patronage," *Journal of Political Economy*, 69 (August 1961), 369–380. Analysis of the means by which political bosses retain control of their machines.

———. "Two Negro Politicians: An Interpretation," *Midwest Journal of Political Science*, IV (November 1960), 346–369. The contrasting behavior of Congressmen Adam Clayton Powell and William L. Dawson is related to the maintenance needs of their local organizations.

Wirt, F. M. "The Political Sociology of American Suburbia: A Reinterpretation," *Journal of Politics*, 27 (August 1965), 647–666. A socioeconomic view of suburban political behavior.

Wolfinger, R. E. "Influence of Precinct Worker on Voting Behavior," *Public Opinion Quarterly*, 27 (Fall 1963), 387–398. How precinct workers affect voters and elections.

Index